Monument

Words of Four Presidents

Who Sculpted America

❧

Monument

Words of Four Presidents Who Sculpted America

❋

George Washington
Thomas Jefferson
Abraham Lincoln
Theodore Roosevelt

Foreword by Robert Dallek
Introductions by Ken Mondschein, PhD

Canterbury Classics
San Diego

Canterbury Classics
An imprint of Printers Row Publishing Group
9717 Pacific Heights Blvd, San Diego, CA 92121
www.canterburyclassicsbooks.com • mail@canterburyclassicsbooks.com

Correspondence concerning the content of this book should be sent to Canterbury Classics, Editorial Department, at the above address.

Publisher: Peter Norton
Associate Publisher: Ana Parker
Publishing/Editorial Team: April Farr, Kathryn C. Dalby, Traci Douglas
Production Team: Jonathan Lopes, Rusty von Dyl
Cover and endpaper design: Ray Caramanna

Library of Congress Control Number: 2019950790

ISBN: 978-1-68412-907-2

Printed in China
25 24 23 22 21   2 3 4 5 6

Editor's Note: This book has been published in its original form to preserve the authors' intent and style. All grammar, spelling, punctuation, and capitalization in historic documents has been preserved. Some works were chosen from the authors' working documents and may not reflect the final version. "Applied Idealism" by Theodore Roosevelt has been abridged by the publisher.

Contents

FOREWORD

Of the forty-four people who have been president of the United States, only four have had their faces carved into Mount Rushmore—George Washington, Thomas Jefferson, Theodore Roosevelt, and Abraham Lincoln. The project began in 1927 and took fourteen years to complete at a cost slightly less than one million dollars. Gutzon Borglum, the principal architect, saw the four as representing the birth, growth, development, and preservation of the nation. The project came to an end in 1941; after Borglum's death that year, his son Lincoln continued the work until funds ran out. While James Madison and James Monroe might have been included as founders of the republic, it is easy to understand why other pre-1941 presidents were not included. They simply lacked the accomplishments or stature of the chosen four. Similarly, Franklin Roosevelt's inclusion in the ranks of great presidents awaited his victorious leadership in World War II. As important, despite having won an unprecedented third term, it would have been too politically contentious to include a sitting president with the four predecessors who had in various ways become iconic figures and served the nation's need to have heroic figures.

Each of these men, however controversial during their administrations, had achievements that transcended their shortcomings.

Washington was famous not just for leading the thirteen colonies to victory in the seven-year revolutionary war against the British, but also for putting in place democratic traditions that guided the country's political future. After the unhappy experience of being governed by a royal sovereign, Washington understood the need to create an executive authority with limited powers. He resisted suggestions that he make the Congress an extension of his control and was mindful of the importance of having an independent judiciary administering the rule of law. When he refused to run for a third term, he made it clear that no president, however popular, should have more than two terms. Though it would take more than 150 years before this tradition was enshrined in the 22nd amendment to the Constitution, after Franklin Roosevelt had responded to World War II by winning third and fourth terms, it has become a statement of how determined the country is to preserve democracy by limiting all presidents to two terms.

When Article II was written into the Constitution, it not only enumerated presidential powers but also made clear that the chief executive was only one of the three governing authorities. Even Richard Nixon, the only president to resign from the office, understood that arbitrary use of presidential power was legally and popularly unacceptable, as he demonstrated when he tried to cover up the wrongdoing that forced his resignation.

Jefferson won his enshrinement on Mount Rushmore by putting in place the peaceful transition of one political party to another. He declared in his first 1801 inaugural, "We are all Federalists. We are all Republicans. We are all Americans." In addition, he demonstrated how essential pragmatism was in providing effective leadership. Though he preached the virtues of limited government, he seized the opportunity to exceed what he thought was presidential authority when he made the Louisiana Purchase from France in 1803. He saw his first duty as serving the national well-being rather than any preconceived ideas of political behavior.

Despite serving less than five years as president, Abraham Lincoln is generally recognized by historians as America's greatest president. It was not just that he was assassinated in April 1865, though his death as the Union was winning the Civil War left an indelible scar on the nation's psyche. The tragedy of a war that cost the nation almost 700,000 lives—the costliest conflict in US history—and came close to ending the United States as we know it, will be remembered with sadness for as long as America lasts. But it was also that Lincoln ended the national shame of slavery and opened the way to fulfilling the Declaration of Independence's assertion that all men are created equal. Though it would be another hundred years before African Americans and women would enjoy the full benefits of the Declaration and Lincoln's Emancipation Proclamation, his 1863 announcement remains a landmark in the nation's history. If preserving the Union, his advances toward national equality, and his assassination were not enough to make him an unforgettable national icon, his brilliance as an orator, as demonstrated by documents in this book, make him a towering figure of American history. He holds an enduring place in our history with the majestic Lincoln memorial in Washington, D.C., and his sad but inspiring visage carved into Mount Rushmore.

In 1927, when work on the Mount Rushmore sculptures began, Theodore Roosevelt had been dead for only eight years. But alongside Lincoln's unimpressive successors, Roosevelt had become a towering figure who restored the standing of the presidency. He thought a president could not achieve greatness without a victorious war, but he was mistaken. His administration turned the federal government into a successful arbiter in the contemporary domestic conflicts between workers and owners. In particular, his arbitration of the coal miners' strike in the winter of 1904 made the federal government into a decisive force in managing and advancing the national economy and a defender of all citizens with the creation of a Food and Drug Administration (FDA) that protected consumers from the sale of spoiled food and harmful drugs. It was an expression of the Fair Deal that Roosevelt declared a hallmark of his presidency. At a time when the world's powers—Britain, France, Germany, and Russia in Europe, and Japan in Asia—were asserting their global influence, Roosevelt skillfully made the United States into a world power in the Western hemisphere, Europe, and Asia. His acquisition of the Panama Canal route and construction of a canal across the isthmus of Panama, facilitating travel between the Atlantic and Pacific oceans, not only advanced international commerce but also established the United States as a two-ocean power. Roosevelt's achievements in domestic and foreign affairs demonstrated Woodrow Wilson's subsequent observation that the president could be as big a man as he chooses to be.

The documents in this book are an illustration of what made these four presidents exceptional occupants of the White House in creating and sustaining the country's democracy and made America a great nation.

Robert Dallek
September 2019

INTRODUCTION

MT. RUSHMORE

Mount Rushmore National Memorial is America. The sixty-foot busts of George Washington, Thomas Jefferson, Abraham Lincoln, and Theodore Roosevelt carved by Gutzon Borglum into the granite of the Black Hills of South Dakota are a historical document, a testimony to our nation's past writ in stone. Borglum's great work, with its likenesses of four figures who inscribed their will not only over what was considered a wild and untamed land, but also over the unruly realm of human politics, memorializes the conquering of what Jefferson once called "an empire for liberty." As a monument, it is on par with the pyramids of Egypt or Mayan temples of the Yucatan Peninsula. As a pilgrimage site, it matches the great cathedrals of Europe, attracting over two million visitors annually. It will endure for centuries—possibly millennia—to come.

Borglum had a particular view of American history and the destiny of its people. In this, he embodied many of the paradoxes and conflicts implicit in American history itself. In his drive for self-promotion and his tireless ambition—the two traits that led to his choosing such a grandiose plan for Mt. Rushmore—Borglum was quintessentially American. Similarly, by its very nature, Mt. Rushmore is an endorsement of the "great man" school of history. This is the idea that it is powerful, visionary personalities who move humanity forward. Its philosophy is individualistic, emphasizing the power of a single person to change the course of civilizations, and it is very suited to a heroic history that makes myths—and monumental sculptures—out of great leaders. However, more recent work in history, including that developed in Borglum's own lifetime, tends to highlight the role of mass social movements and the contributions of women and people of color. (A 1936 attempt to have Borglum include Susan B. Anthony in the sculptural grouping died in the House Appropriations Committee, and in any case the sculptor himself rejected the idea out of hand.)

To be sure, Washington, Jefferson, Lincoln, and Roosevelt did indeed have profound effects on American history. Without their leadership, this country would be a very different place. However, modern historians have explored their legacies with a more critical eye: While Lincoln is best known for freeing enslaved African Americans, two of the presidents depicted—Washington and Jefferson—were slaveholders. Meanwhile, Roosevelt, whom Borglum had met and campaigned for, was an active participant in America's military expansion as an imperial power. Similarly, Mt. Rushmore was built on land that was, and still is, sacred to the Lakota people.

Mt. Rushmore today embodies all of these things: It is a "shrine of democracy" that memorializes four great American leaders, even as it is an implicit testimony to those often left out of the history books. Not only is Gutzon Borglum remembered for his work, so, too, are the everyday men and women who labored to create it. The mountain is a place that is still sacred to the Lakota, even as Gutzon Borglum sought to make a site that would be sacred to all Americans. It is the responsibility of the historian to tell all of these stories, and the National Parks Service does not shy away from telling the bad with the good in their visitors' center.

This book is much the same. It is a collection of historical documents intended to accompany and bear witness to the accomplishments of the four figures memorialized on the mountain. This introduction will give the history of the monument, while the introductions to the sections on Washington, Jefferson, Lincoln, and Roosevelt will explore their biographies in the context of the times in which they lived. In so doing, we hope to show that while the arc of American history has had its flaws, tragedies, and injustices, it does, as Martin Luther King Jr., said about the arc of the moral universe, in the end "bend toward justice."

JOHN GUTZON DE LA MOTHE BORGLUM

The sculptor who planned and executed Mt. Rushmore, John Gutzon de la Mothe Borglum, himself came from a background that was at the same time both unorthodox and quintessentially American. Though he later downplayed the unusual circumstances of his birth, Borglum was born in 1867 near Bear Lake, Idaho, to Danish immigrant parents who were in a Mormon polygamous relationship. Both his mother, Christina Mikkelsen Borglum and her sister Ida were married to Jens Moller Haugaard Borglum, a woodcarver who later became a homeopathic doctor. Jens eventually left the Mormon church, divorced Christina (though he continued to care for their children), and moved away from the Mormon community. During Gutzon Borglum's formative years, the family lived in places as varied as Nebraska, Kansas, and California. After their last move to California, the young Borglum, having received some art training in Kansas, apprenticed to a lithographer. Choosing to remain in California when his family returned to Nebraska, Borglum soon struck out on his own as an independent artist.

It was soon thereafter that Borglum met Elizabeth "Lisa" Jaynes Putnam, a divorced painter almost two decades his senior who would become his entrée into the art world. It was also in this period that his monumental ambition, and desire to make the social connections that could help him realize that ambition, first became manifest: His portrait of John C. Frémont, the famous Union general, explorer, abolitionist, and senator who had been the first Republican candidate for president, was completed in 1888 and did much to establish his reputation. Even though Frémont died shortly after the portrait was completed, his well-connected widow Jesse Benton Frémont was able to provide him with introductions to powerful men such as Leland Stanford and Theodore Roosevelt.

Painting was not a medium that could contain Gutzon Borglum's ego: it was too private, too small, too vulnerable to the ravages of time and accident. For him, it had to be sculpture—large public works that would survive the ages. Borglum's younger brother, Solon, had already become a successful sculptor; the shared family name and his connection to Frémont's widow helped advance the young artist's career. To truly become a great artist, however, would require study, and so Borglum made plans to travel to Paris, marrying Lisa Putnam shortly before his departure. He spent the years from 1890 to 1893 studying at the Julien Academy and the Ecole des Beaux-Arts, successfully exhibiting his work and also meeting the great sculptor Auguste Rodin. Borglum's Paris sojourn was followed by a visit to England from 1896 to 1901. Unfortunately, the travel put too much of a strain on his relationship with his wife, who had accompanied him on his journeys, and they grew estranged. However, on the return voyage in 1901, Borglum met Mary Montgomery, an American woman seven years his junior who had just earned her doctorate in Babylonian history at the University of Berlin. Mary's intelligence would have been remarkable in any time, but the degree of education she achieved was highly unusual for the late Victorian era: Her parents had been missionaries in Turkey, and she had an incredible talent for languages, mastering Turkish, Arabic, Greek, Egyptian, Hebrew, and Sanskrit. It was not until 1909 that Lisa granted Borglum a divorce and he was free to marry Mary. In the intervening years, the two lived in the burgeoning artistic center of New York, where he worked on sculptures for the Cathedral of St. John the Divine and other commissions. Two notable pieces he created in this period included the Mares of Diomedes, a sculpture group that was (and still is) shown at the Metropolitan Museum of Art, and a colossal bust of Abraham Lincoln exhibited at the White House, which gave Borglum the opportunity to meet Theodore Roosevelt. Today, the sculpture, carved from a six-ton block of marble, is in the Capitol Crypt. In 1910, the newly married Gutzon and Mary moved to Connecticut, and he continued to sculpt and show his work. Their son Lincoln, who would complete Mt. Rushmore, would be born three years later. They also had another son and a daughter.

One of Borglum's artistic goals was to develop a uniquely American style of sculpture. The art of the new land, he thought, should reflect its character and its meaning. He was particularly interested in using the mass of the stone to convey the "emotional impact of volume." Many of the aspects that would later be seen on Mt. Rushmore, especially the idea of size and the sense of impressiveness and weight rooted in the natural materials he was using, can be seen in his art from this period. Rodin's influence can be seen in Borglum's style—the French sculptor also emphasized the natural texture of his material—but the American took this further, giving his work an energy and sense of restlessness that reflected the recent closing of the American frontier. What's more, in a quintessentially American way, Borglum's work was larger than anything that was being attempted in Europe. Size, to him, was everything. "There isn't a monument in this country as big as a snuff box," he would complain.

BORGLUM AND MONUMENTAL SCULPTURE

Borglum soon had the chance to execute a work on the scale he had hoped for. In 1914, the octogenarian president of the United Daughters of the Confederacy, C. Helen Plane, contacted him: Would he like to carve a bust of Robert E. Lee into Stone Mountain in Georgia? Stone Mountain was to be a shrine to the defeated Confederacy and, implicitly, an endorsement of the "Lost Cause."

Borglum leapt at the opportunity. He had no special love for Southern revisionist history—he was an unabashed fan of Abraham Lincoln, the "great liberator" who had defeated the South and after whom he had named his eldest child—but like most men of his era, he accepted racial hierarchies unquestioningly. The most important factor seems to have been that the giant-sized commission, which was larger than any ever attempted and required that he develop entirely new techniques for sculpting, appealed to his immense ambition and ego. Indeed, Borglum's plans for Stone Mountain ultimately went beyond what was originally envisioned. "Ladies, the head of Lee on the side of that mountain would look like a postage stamp on a barn door!" he exclaimed, and instead proposed to carve Lee, Stonewall Jackson, and Jefferson Davis on horseback followed by a line of soldiers on foot, all executed as a high relief frieze.

Work on Stone Mountain began in June of 1923, and the frieze of Lee's head was ready to display on the anniversary of the Confederate general's birthday in January of the following year. The project fell into disarray, however, in the late winter and spring of 1925 when the disorganized Stone Mountain Confederate Monumental Association couldn't raise enough money. In 1924, Doane Robinson, an attorney and the state historian of South Dakota, approached Borglum about the Mt. Rushmore project. Borglum made a trip to see the site of the proposed monument that summer, accompanied by his then 12-year-old son Lincoln. The Stone Mountain project continued to implode, and the organizers fired Borglum in early 1925. A warrant was even issued for his arrest for breach of contract. In response, Borglum destroyed his models for the Confederate memorial and skipped town. The work he had already completed was blasted off the mountain, and a new sculptor, Henry Augustus Lukeman, was hired to begin anew.

As troublesome as it is for Stone Mountain to be part of the history of Mt. Rushmore, Borglum could not have executed the later monument without the experience of the first. For instance, it was in Georgia that Borglum learned how to project plans onto a mountainside and, from a visiting Belgian engineer, to do precision blasting with dynamite.

Mt. Rushmore was different from Stone Mountain in another important way: The first could only have ever been a project of regional interest. Doane Robinson, however, envisioned something of national importance, with historical figures of "unusual character" from the history of the West—Anglo-Americans, such as Lewis and Clark and Buffalo Bill Cody, as well as Native Americans, such as Red Cloud and Sacagawea. Borglum returned with a bigger idea: Washington, "the founder," and Lincoln, "the savior," to whom were soon added Jefferson and Roosevelt. These figures, too, had a connection to the history of the West: Jefferson, "the first expansionist," had made the Louisiana Purchase and sent Lewis and Clark out to explore the new land all the way to the sea. Roosevelt had fought in the Spanish-American War, which added former Spanish colonies to the United States, and had acquired the land used to build the Panama Canal. In short, Mt. Rushmore was to be a monument to Manifest Destiny, the special role of the United States in human history, the moral rectitude of its imperialistic ends, and the inevitability of its expansion to become a world power. American democracy, wrote historian Frederick Jackson Turner, was made by its frontier; the nation's character was shaped by its constant expansion. Mt. Rushmore would be "the shrine of democracy," a monument to the men that made that expansion possible.

THE BLACK HILLS

The natural setting where Robinson envisioned a shrine to democracy deserves its own biography no less than does its creator. In this case, the medium—the raw stone into which the images of the Presidents were jackhammered and dynamite-blasted—is the message, and Borglum's ideas of volume called for a suitably impressive starting material. The Black Hills (a translation from the Lakota *He Sápa*) are a small mountain range rising out of the Great Plains. They were formed by volcanic activity 1.8 billion years ago and formed like a bull's-eye, with a granite core, ringed by metamorphic rock and a sedimentary border. The creeks are filled with trout, while deer, bighorn sheep, bison, and mountain lions travel the conifer and spruce forests. These forests also lend the Black Hills their name, as the tree cover makes them seem dark when seen from far away.

The Black Hills passed from one Native American people to another, until the Lakota came to protect them after defeating the Cheyenne in 1776. The Lakota were one of the three tribes of the Sioux people, and the Black Hills would soon become a sacred place central to their culture. In the 1800s, however, the Sioux opposed American expansion into the West, which led to a number of conflicts such as Red Cloud's War (1866–68). The Fort Laramie Treaty that ended Red Cloud's War in 1868 promised that the Black Hills would remain Lakota property forever. But the promise only lasted about 20 years: George Armstrong Custer's 1874 expedition discovered gold in the Black Hills, and in 1889, the US Government moved the Lakota to five smaller reservations and sold off over nine million acres of land. The Lakota nation still claims sovereignty over the Black Hills, and has refused financial compensation awarded by the US Supreme Court.

The Lakota knew Mt. Rushmore as "The Six Grandfathers" (*Tunkasila Sakpe*) or "Cougar Mountain" (*Igmu Tanka Paha*), while white settlers called it by various other names. The wealthy Eastern investor Charles Rushmore, who visited the area on hunting and prospecting trips in the 1880s, joked that it should be named after him. The name Mt. Rushmore was recognized by the United States Board of Geographic Names in 1930, the year before Rushmore's death.

BUILDING OF MT. RUSHMORE

On August 10, 1927, President Calvin Coolidge, who was spending the summer in South Dakota, traveled at Borglum's behest to the Black Hills to formally dedicate the Mt. Rushmore site. (There had already been a dedication ceremony in 1925, but Gutzon Borglum relished the idea of one with a sitting president.) Coolidge rode a horse up through the newly blazed path through the woods, mounted a podium, and spoke:

> We have come here to dedicate a cornerstone laid by the hand of the Almighty. The union of these four presidents carved on the face of the everlasting Black Hills of South Dakota will be distinctly American in its conception, in its magnitude, in its meaning. No one can look upon it without realizing it is a picture of hope fulfilled. Its location will be significant. Here in the heart of the continent, on the side of a mountain which probably no white man had ever beheld in the days of Washington, in territory acquired by the action of Jefferson, which remained an unbroken wilderness beyond the days of Lincoln, which was especially loved by Roosevelt.

Coolidge symbolically presented Borglum with six steel drill bits with which the artist would start carving the mountain. In return, Borglum asked Coolidge to write the explanatory inscription Borglum envisioned as part of the sculpture.

Speaking fine words was the easy part. Funding still had to be secured, and the Mount Rushmore Commission had to be appointed to oversee the project. Borglum's personality did not make this any easier: A meeting with President Herbert Hoover was canceled after the sculptor got into an argument with the president's secretary. South Dakota Congressman William Williamson and John Boland, the secretary of the executive committee of the Commission, managed to smooth things over. Doane Robinson, however, was not nominated for a leadership role, and gradually drifted away from the project.

The project was, of course, immensely expensive, eventually totaling $989,999.32—around 18 million dollars in today's money. About 84 percent was paid by the federal government, despite Borglum's earlier belief that he would be able to find matching funds from private donors. Much of the rest came from private individuals. Charles Rushmore himself gave $5,000, the largest single donation. The sculptor was unfazed by the expense: "Call up Cheops and ask him how much his pyramid cost, and what he paid the creator—an inferior work to Mt. Rushmore," Borglum said in 1940, even as the country was gearing up for World War II.

Once funding was secured, almost 400 men and women worked on Mt. Rushmore for fourteen years, season after season, in the heat and the cold. Most were working-class miners. "I must have men who know how to carve mountains," Borglum said. Washington emerged from the stone first (dedicated in 1930), then Jefferson (dedicated in 1936 in a ceremony attended by President Franklin D. Roosevelt), Lincoln (1937), and Roosevelt (1939). Miraculously, none of the workers was killed on the job, though rock dust inhaled while working may have contributed to later premature deaths from silicosis. As at Stone Mountain, Borglum proved a difficult man to work for. He was a short-tempered, domineering perfectionist. He would fire a worker one day, then demand to know why he wasn't on the job the next. During the Depression, he feuded with Franklin D. Roosevelt's Parks Commission and the engineer, Julian Spotts, who was appointed as overseer. To him, anything less than complete control was unacceptable.

As always, his wife, the brilliant, highly educated Mary Borglum was an incredible helpmate—running the ranch in the near-wilderness to which her husband's ambition had dragged her, raising the children, and, of course, putting up with the irascible Gutzon's rages and moods. Borglum's son Lincoln also became an object of his ambition: He decided his son would also be his protégé and employed him as a "pointer." Though many of the workers saw Lincoln as the boss's privileged son, the humble, hard-working young man soon won their trust and affection. One of the longtime workers remarked, "The Old Man was always trying to push Lincoln along—to make him important. Lincoln never let it go to his head. He didn't know much about what he was doing at first, but he was such a nice kid that all the other pointers helped him out until he learned to do it by himself, so it all worked out okay. Lincoln was a good guy to work with."

Gutzon Borglum died on March 6, 1941, shortly before his 74th birthday, and the completion of Mt. Rushmore fell to his son Lincoln, who by that time was the general supervisor. Due to the lack of funding, the sculptor's plans to include the presidents' torsos and the entablature were never realized, and Lincoln Borglum's final drilling in October of 1941 left the sculpture as his father had finished it. Lincoln then became the park's first superintendent from 1941 to 1944. He went on to a distinguished career as a photographer and a sculptor in his own right, and died in 1986 at the age of 74; his grave is in San Antonio, Texas.

THE FUTURE OF MT. RUSHMORE

Gutzon Borglum's take on his creation's future place in history is nowhere more explicit than in his plans for "the Entablature." This was to have been the story of the United States in 500 words, carved in three-foot-high letters, fit into the shape of the Louisiana Purchase and positioned to one side of Washington's head. Future generations would have no doubt as to who created the monument, why, or what their beliefs were. Coolidge's first attempt at the text was quietly withdrawn after Borglum's edits led to public mockery, and the sculptor instead ran a contest in conjunction with Hearst newspapers. None of the reportedly

100,000 entries met with Borglum's approval, either, and none were publicly displayed until the one composed by a Nebraska college student named William Andrew Burkett was inscribed on a bronze tablet and erected in 1971. In it, we can see something of the intent behind Mt. Rushmore. Like Coolidge's dedicatory speech, Burkett's Entablature is an explicitly religious and Christian endorsement of Manifest Destiny, beginning with the words: "Almighty God, from this pulpit of stone the American people render thanksgiving and praise for the new era of civilization brought forth upon this continent." It goes on to express the founding creed of America: That the nation was founded on the principle that "life, liberty, equality, and pursuit of happiness were the birthrights of all mankind," and that the "sacred Constitution" "embodies our faith in God and in mankind by giving equal participation in government to all citizens." It then goes year-by-year through ways in which "far-sighted American statesmanship acquired by treaties, vast wilderness territories, where progressive, adventurous Americans spread civilization and Christianity": The Louisiana Purchase, the acquisition of Florida, Texas, California, Oregon, Alaska, and the Panama Canal Zone.

While the inscription on the side of the mountain never came to be, Borglum's idea of history can also be seen in a small door behind Lincoln's head. The Hall of Records was intended to be a time capsule to future civilizations containing the busts of great Americans (such as Susan B. Anthony), as well as documents, such as the Declaration of Independence and the Constitution. The Hall of Records was left unfinished as a 75-foot-long tunnel, until Borglum's ambition was realized, in part, in 1998, when four porcelain tablets telling the monument's history were installed there, sealed away behind a half-ton slab of rock.

The stories of the Entablature and the Hall of Records say something profound about Mt. Rushmore: No matter what meaning Gutzon Borglum and his contemporaries ascribed to the monument, each generation will reinterpret it in its own right. While future generations may bemoan the lack of women or people of color on the mountain, this is not the final word. Rather, the principles of liberty laid down by Washington and Jefferson, the justice brought by Lincoln, and the universalizing and globalizing tendencies of Roosevelt are alive and being expanded upon even today. The stone of Mt. Rushmore is a living document.

Ken Mondschein, PhD
October 2019

George Washington

❧

INTRODUCTION

Perhaps no other historical figure in the history of the United States, or even the modern world, has been as subject to myth-making and secular hagiography as George Washington. Indeed, the writings praising his character, foresight, and judgment approach those of a religious figure such as Jesus, Mohammad, or Buddha. In many ways, this was a deliberate attempt to create a national myth out of the granddaddy of all the Founding Fathers, the first president who led the budding nation through the American Revolution.

To cite one example, the "cherry tree" myth first appeared in 1806 in Mason Locke Weems' heavily fictionalized *Life of Washington* in which he tried to show that the future president's "unparalleled rise and elevation were due to his Great Virtues." Chief Justice John Marshall and the writer Washington Irving tried to pen rather more factually grounded biographies, but they were hardly critical in the modern sense. Modern "revisionist" historians, who critique him as a man whose fortune was built on slavery, often point out that his final will and testament—while radical for the time in that it provided for the welfare of all the people he owned—did not free his slaves until after Martha's death. However, to strip off the layers of varnish and find a true portrait of the man is no small task.

What do we know for certain about the man himself? George Washington was tall for his time—six feet, two inches—and his athletic ability was renowned, as were his endurance and strength. However, stories such as his throwing a silver dollar across the Potomac River are exaggerated—silver dollars weren't widely produced until five years after Washington's death. According to his step-grandson George Washington Parke Custis, he did, however, throw a piece of slate across Virginia's Rappahannock River. He also never had wooden teeth, as Weems asserted. Despite his good oral hygiene, his teeth, like those of many of his contemporaries, were bad; the fact that he was fond of sugar, a luxury good grown by enslaved labor in Barbados, could not have helped. Washington lost his first tooth at twenty-four. By the time of his inauguration, he had but one tooth left, which was soon extracted, and he wore dentures for the rest of his life. These were made of materials such as ivory, metal, and human teeth, including those of African Americans.

But what about his famed character? This is harder to know, since it deals with intangibles and opinions. The historian's task is to use verifiable facts, not to repeat the myths that have only grown in the retelling. Rather than sifting through the much-exaggerated accounts of those who knew and lionized him, we need to look at Washington's actions.

LIFE OF GEORGE WASHINGTON

Washington was born on February 22, 1732—which was actually a Tuesday, despite the fact that we celebrate his birthday on the third Monday in February. He was the eldest of the six children of Augustine and Mary Ball Washington; he also had three elder half-siblings from his father's first marriage. The future president came from a privileged background; his grandfather John Washington had immigrated in 1656 from Sulgrave, England, and acquired 5,000 acres along the Potomac River.

His older half-brother Lawrence's influential father-in-law William Fairfax, who owned the Mount Vernon plantation, acted as a parental figure and patron to the young Washington after his own father died when he was eleven. It was from Fairfax that Washington acquired his taste for the gracious, elegant lifestyle of the Southern gentry. His "Rules of Civility," copied into his schoolbook at the age of sixteen, reflect this desire to be accepted in polite society.

Despite his emphasis on manners and gentle living, Washington was also a tireless frontiersman. He worked surveying Fairfax's property as well as on the frontier and acquired 1,500 acres in Virginia's Shenandoah Valley in 1750. The following year he made his only trip abroad, accompanying Lawrence on a trip to Barbados in a vain attempt to cure the latter's tuberculosis. Washington contracted smallpox on the same trip; the disease likely left him sterile and he would never have children. Lawrence died in 1752, and his widow gained control of Mount Vernon. Washington would acquire the plantation outright in 1761.

Military Career

Serving in the colonial militia was expected of the colonial plantation class, and Washington received a commission as a major in 1752. The militia was a necessity at the time since westward expansion provoked the hostility of Native Americans, and the rivalry between the French and English played itself out in North America in the building of forts and forging of alliances with the indigenous peoples. The frontier was a dangerous place.

Washington's military career began inauspiciously. After completing a sensitive diplomatic mission in 1753, he was appointed a lieutenant colonel by Virginia Governor Robert Dinwiddie and, in early 1754, assigned to lead an expedition of about 150 men to the Ohio territory where the French were building Fort Duquesne. On May 28, he attacked and massacred a smaller French force in the Battle of Jumonville Glen. As no formal hostilities existed, this act began the French and Indian War; Washington later blamed his translator for the mistake, but Dinwiddie's instructions seemed to be an implicit order to stop the French by violence. Washington retreated to Fort Necessity, where he was attacked by the French and, outnumbered, forced to surrender and admit that the killing of the French commander, Joseph Coulon de Villiers de Jumonville, had been an assassination. In the aftermath, Washington resigned his commission rather than accept a demotion to captain.

He was somewhat redeemed the following year by his courageous conduct in July, 1755, when, ill from dysentery, he rallied the survivors of Edward Braddock's disastrous expedition to expel the French from Ohio and kept a defeat from becoming a rout. Washington had two horses shot out from under him and bullets pierced both his hat and coat; yet, he himself was untouched. This was Washington's last notable engagement of the French and Indian War. Impatient to take the strategically vital Fort Duquesne, he clashed with both his superiors and those of ostensibly equal rank who held superior royal commissions. The end of the French and Indian War in the Ohio Valley was almost anticlimatic. After a string of British victories, and with their indigenous allies abandoning their cause, the French blew up Fort Duquesne themselves. Washington's greatest success during this period was in organizing the Virginia militia into a large, well-trained body of 1,000 men and successfully defending the frontier against attack.

Marriage and Rise to Prominence

With the war winding down (though it would not formally end until the Treaty of Paris in 1763), the now-twenty-six-year-old Washington began thinking about marriage. He soon set his sights on the twenty-eight-year-old Martha Dandridge Custis, whom he married in 1759. As the widow of Daniel Parke Custis, a prosperous plantation owner, she brought considerable wealth to the marriage. Since Custis had died without a will, one-third of his estate went to his widow and two-thirds to their children, John Parke Custis and Martha Parke Custis (who died of uncontrolled epilepsy in 1773). As Martha's husband, Washington had control over the entirety. He was now one of the wealthiest men in Virginia and expanded his fortune by planting tobacco and wheat, speculating on land (including duping veterans of the French and Indian War out of their land bounties), and winning public office by plying voters with alcohol. But no one who reads Washington's letters to Martha can doubt his love for her. While she destroyed most of the letters after his death in order to preserve their marital privacy, we reproduce the two surviving letters here (see pages 91–93).

The Revolution

By the 1760s, Washington had become a critic of British mercantilist policies, which forced the colonists to export raw agricultural products such as cotton, tobacco, and indigo, and to import manufactured goods at high prices. His growing opposition to British rule may have been related to his own financial troubles. Low tobacco prices and his taste for imported luxuries had left him heavily in debt and prompted him to experiment with a more domestically based economy. When the British Parliament began interfering with colonial self-rule and passed onerous legislation in the 1760s and 1770s, such as the Stamp Act, he added these new grievances to the embarrassments of his military career and his financial difficulties. He and George Mason, a wealthy Virginia planter and lawmaker, authored the Fairfax Resolves calling for a Continental Congress. Washington became a delegate to the Congress, trained the Virginia militia, and helped enforce the boycott of British goods.

At the outbreak of hostilities in 1775, Washington was quickly nominated, and unanimously appointed, commander-in-chief of the Continental Army. He successfully captured Boston but made crucial errors that led to a forced retreat from Long Island and New York City in 1776. His famous surprise attack in Trenton in late 1776 provided the poorly equipped Americans with a much-needed morale boost, though the campaign season of 1777 was disastrous with defeats at Philadelphia, Germantown, and Brandywine, leading some (known as the Conway Cabal) to petition to have him removed as commander. The one bright spot was Horatio Gates's victory at Saratoga, which turned the tide of the revolution in the colonists' favor.

The winter of 1777, spent at Valley Forge in Pennsylvania, was brutal; some 2,000–3,000 of the 11,000-man army died of cold, hunger, and exposure. Washington fruitlessly sought money and supplies from the Continental Congress. In spite of the harsh winter, the Prussian General Friedrich Wilhelm von Steuben was able to transform the ragtag militia into a formidable fighting force, and additional aid arrived from the French. The years from 1777 to 1781 were marked by no major actions in the north, save for the inconclusive Battle of Monmouth Courthouse. However, there were notable American successes in the southern colonies, culminating in the British surrender at Yorktown. After overseeing the British evacuation, settling the business of the Continental Army, and suppressing a plotted coup known as the Newburgh Conspiracy, he resigned his commission in 1783, returning to Mount Vernon on Christmas Eve. His Letter of Farewell to the Army, which was sent out as a public circular, shows the same concerns that he emphasized throughout his public life. Namely, Washington was concerned that the new nation should be governed peaceably and justly under a strong federal government.

If we are to consider Washington's military career objectively, we see a man who often ignored sound advice, made mistakes, and acted overconfidently. Yet, he commanded the unquestioning loyalty of those around him and knew how to deploy his subordinates to their best advantage. He tried to emulate the discipline and coordination of professional European armies, but he was a tactical amateur, and many times his commanders were unable to execute his plans. Thus, at times, Washington found himself outmaneuvered on the battlefield, but he learned from his mistakes, kept the army together through trying conditions, and was astute at negotiating the political aspects of the conflict. His final strategic plan—to control the land, deny aid and comfort to the British, conserve his strength, and avoid battle unless it was a sure victory over an outnumbered foe—ultimately resulted in victory.

A MORE PERFECT UNION AND PRESIDENCY

While Washington had been away fighting, the business of his Mount Vernon plantation had suffered. Upon returning to civilian life, he undertook the huge task of repairing his finances and renovating Mount Vernon, but his interest in the nascent nation remained keen. He had long advocated a strong central government for the newly independent colonies. The Articles of Confederation, he wrote, were no more than a "rope of sand." It was little surprise that he was chosen—against his own wishes—as a delegate to the Constitutional Convention of 1787. He was unanimously chosen to serve as President of the Convention and lent his prestige to the Federalist project of creating a "more perfect union." Although it was considered radical for its time, the new constitution was nothing like what we would recognize as true democracy. In keeping with the prevailing attitudes of the time, it was accepted that the "natural aristocracy" of wealth, land, and power would rule. Unsurprisingly, the Electoral College appointed by the state legislatures elected the hero of the American Revolution the first President of the newly formed United States of America.

Washington did much to define the new office of the chief executive, from his style—the humble "Mr. President" rather than "His Excellency, the President"—to limiting himself to two terms and overseeing a smooth transition of power. (He had originally wished to serve only one term.) Working with Congress, he created cabinet posts and executive offices, established a national bank, and worked to pay off the war debt. Also, of no small importance, he established a permanent home for the federal government, which had been resident in New York and Philadelphia. Washington, D.C., was created and expanded with the Residence Act and his two Proclamations of 1791. In short, it is thanks to Washington's administration that the first large-scale republican government since the ancient world truly functioned and worked as a national government. The documents from his presidency—the inaugural addresses, Residence Act, and proclamations—reflect these concerns, while his annual addresses began the tradition of the presidential State of the Union address.

Those close to him soon formed the first political parties, which we will explore more in the introduction to Thomas Jefferson's documents. Rather than being a partisan, however, Washington sought to achieve consensus and delegate power to allies. His "Farewell Address" warns of the dangers of "factions" and expresses his fear that, like ancient Rome, the United States might degenerate into civil war. His fears were realized 65 years later, when the southern states seceded from the Union and formed the Confederacy. At stake was something Washington himself had been concerned with—the issue of states' rights versus the power of the federal government, which the question of slavery made painfully clear.

WASHINGTON AND SLAVERY

George Washington inherited the first ten African Americans he owned from his father at the age of eleven in 1743. Before he married Martha in 1759, he purchased at least a dozen more people. Marriage with Martha brought another eighty-four human beings under his control; to them, he added about forty additional slaves that he purchased before the Revolution.

Due mostly to the natural increase in population, slavery was on the rise in the South in Washington's lifetime. When he took control of Mount Vernon in 1754, 28 percent of the 6,500 people living in Fairfax County, Virginia, were slaves; by the end of the Revolution, the figure was 40 percent. The same held true for Washington's estate. By the beginning of the Revolutionary War there were 100 people held in bondage at Mount Vernon, and by the time he died in 1799, there were 317 enslaved people at his plantation, of whom 123 were his direct property. Forty were rented from other plantations; the remainder belonged to the estate of his wife's first husband.

How did George Washington treat his slaves? Sources differ: Richard Parkinson, a visiting Englishman who bore no love for Washington, claimed that he treated them "with more severity than any other man," fed and clothed them poorly, and spoke to them harshly. Then again, he also claimed that Washington put the horse that had borne him faithfully through the war up for sale. The Polish poet and statesman Julian Ursyn Niemcewicz, on the other hand, stated that Washington "treats his slaves far more humanely than do his fellow citizens of Virginia. Most of these gentlemen give to their blacks only bread, water, and blows."

No matter the conditions, slavery is still an inhumane institution, and enslaved African Americans resisted in whatever small ways they could. Theft was one means of resistance, and Washington's letters are rife with accounts of small items stolen by slaves. Slaves also might shirk work, though they risked being beaten for it, as an overseer named Anthony Whitting did with a hickory switch to a woman named Charlotte in 1793 for the crime of being "impudent." (Charlotte protested that she had not been whipped for fourteen years, which suggests such actions were not common, but Washington deemed the punishment "very proper.") A number also escaped—and not just field hands. Seventeen Mount Vernon slaves fled in 1781 when a British warship anchored in the river by the plantation. Christopher, Washington's personal servant, made plans to escape but was found out, and the cook, Hercules, ran away in the winter of 1796–97. Most famous of the escapees was Oney Judge, Martha Washington's mixed-race maidservant and a skilled seamstress, who simply walked out of the family home in Philadelphia in 1796; her motivation was learning that she would be given to Elizabeth Parke Custis upon Martha Washington's death. The Washingtons tried, unsuccessfully, to have her recaptured or induce her to return. In newspaper interviews given as late as 1845, Judge defended her choice and was proud that she had learned to read and write and had learned the basics of Christianity.

Washington's view of slavery changed radically during his lifetime. Not only did the cause of liberty conflict with the reality of enslavement, but he saw free African Americans fight the British with the Continental Army. (Though he initially opposed their enlistment, he relented when the British began allowing free blacks to enlist and they eventually comprised 10 percent of the army.) Lafayette, the French military hero who fought with the colonists, was decidedly against slavery, and he may have had an influence. Furthermore, Washington had grave doubts as to the economic viability of slavery both in his own operations and in the broader economy. Though he would never become a radical abolitionist—the mere question would have been political suicide in the fragile early republic—his sentiments over time turned decidedly against the institution.

During the American Revolution, Washington confided in a letter to his cousin that he wished to "to get quit of" slavery. In 1794, he wrote to his friend and neighbor Alexander Spotswood of his repugnance toward the idea of "selling

Negroes, as you would Cattle in the market." Yet, he was careful to rotate the slaves he brought with him to Philadelphia, so they would not be freed after six months' residency under Pennsylvania law, and he did not cease trying to recapture Oney Judge. "However well disposed I might be to a gradual emancipation, or even to an entire emancipation of that description of People (if the latter was in itself practicable at this moment)," he wrote, "it would neither be politic or just to reward unfaithfulness with a premature preference."

It was Washington's wish to free the human beings he owned after his death, in addition to—as was required by law—providing for the support of those too old to work. To do so, he sold his Ohio Valley lands and attempted to come up with complicated schemes. But when it came time to write his will, his hands were tied. Since Martha's first husband Daniel Parke Custis had died without a will, 153 of the enslaved African Americans at Mt. Vernon had to, by law, go to his heirs upon her death—that is, Martha's four surviving grandchildren by her son, John. Both George and Martha Washington were legally powerless to free them. Therefore, wishing to avoid the "most painful sensations, if not disagreeable consequences" of splitting up the families, Washington chose to delay manumission until after Martha's death. (She, however, executed the will early, on January 1, 1801.) The one exception was Washington's longtime manservant, William Lee, who upon Washington's death was given immediate freedom and a pension for his faithful wartime service.

Washington also provided for the basic education of enslaved people up to the age of twenty-five—something rare indeed in those times. Also, in contrast to the prevailing abolitionist idea of transporting freed slaves to Africa, he stated his wish to "expressly forbid the Sale, or transportation out of the said Commonwealth, of any Slave I may die possessed of, under any pretence whatsoever." Craig Bruce Smith of William Woods University suggests that by doing this, "Washington boldly suggested that America had the potential to become their home as well."

WASHINGTON AND NATIVE AMERICANS

George Washington had many dealings with Native Americans, from fighting beside them as well as against them during the French and Indian War and the Revolutionary War to negotiating treaties as part of his official duties as president. He could be quite cruel when he felt it necessary. In 1779, he had ordered General John Sullivan to inflict "total destruction and devastation" on Iroquois villages as retribution for raids on American civilians. However, at the beginning of his first term, Washington declared that a policy driven by the "great principles of Justice and humanity" was a priority. The fact that some tribes had supported the British in the Revolution was used as an excuse to dispossess every indigenous claim to land east of the Mississippi. Washington took the then-novel approach of treating them as if they were foreign powers. At the same time, he dispatched "Mad Anthony" Wayne to end the Northwest Indian War and negotiated the Treaty of New York to end the conflict between the Creek and the state of Georgia.

Recognizing that the westward expansion of white settlement was unstoppable, Washington and Secretary of War Henry Knox agonized over the distinct possibility of Native American extermination. Their solution was a combination of territorial protections—what would become the reservation system—and missionary activity. It was Washington's belief that Native American civilizations should assimilate to European norms, adopting agriculture and animal husbandry. His view of indigenous peoples as noble savages living in a state of nature was very much in keeping with what educated Europeans believed about Native Americans. Interestingly, recent research shows that before the arrival of the Europeans, Native Americans already lived in sophisticated societies that were devastated by the diseases and disorder introduced by European settlement.

The notion of the "noble savage" was also deployed in a bit of George Washington propaganda after his death. As Washington's personal physician James Craik later recalled, in 1770, a Native American chief who had fought against the British in the French and Indian War, and whom Washington later encountered during a trip to the Ohio Country, prophesied that the general would become the leader of a great nation. Martha's son and George's stepson George Washington Parke Custis repeated the story and even wrote a play in 1827 entitled *The Indian Prophecy*. In this way, the founding of America, and the idea of Manifest Destiny, were legitimized with the supposed assent of Native Americans.

WASHINGTON'S LEGACY

George Washington was no demigod, but rather a man like any other, with his flaws, ambitions, and imperfections. Yet, he was also a man of rare talents and uncommon vision. Even as he made many errors, he was in large part responsible for American victory in the Revolution. Likewise, the new Republic was, as we shall see, not without its flaws. In no small part, Washington's leadership was what made the government workable. In the coming generations, however, the very problems he had wrestled with—the question of slavery, the rise of political parties, and the rights of states and individuals over the necessity of a strong central government—would build towards the crisis of the Civil War.

RULES OF CIVILITY

Traced to their Sources and Restored

BY
MONCURE D. CONWAY

1890

Inscribed

TO MY SON
EUSTACE CONWAY.

THE RULES OF CIVILITY.

Among the manuscript books of George Washington, preserved in the State Archives at Washington City, the earliest bears the date, written in it by himself, 1745. Washington was born February 11, 1731 O.S., so that while writing in this book he was either near the close of his fourteenth, or in his fifteenth, year. It is entitled "Forms of Writing," has thirty folio pages, and the contents, all in his boyish handwriting, are sufficiently curious. Amid copied forms of exchange, bonds, receipts, sales, and similar exercises, occasionally, in ornate penmanship, there are poetic selections, among them lines of a religious tone on "True Happiness." But the great interest of the book centres in the pages headed: "Rules of Civility and Decent Behaviour in Company and Conversation." The book had been gnawed at the bottom by Mount Vernon mice, before it reached the State Archives, and nine of the 110 Rules have thus suffered, the sense of several being lost.

The Rules possess so much historic interest that it seems surprising that none of Washington's biographers or editors should have given them to the world. Washington Irving, in his "Life of Washington," excites interest in them by a tribute, but does not quote even one. Sparks quotes 57, but inexactly, and with his usual literary manipulation; these were reprinted (1886, 16°) by W.O. Stoddard, at Denver, Colorado; and in Hale's "Washington" (1888). I suspect that the old biographers, more eulogistic than critical, feared it would be an ill service to Washington's fame to print all of the Rules. There might be a scandal in the discovery that the military and political deity of America had, even in boyhood, written so gravely of the hat-in-hand deference due to lords, and other "Persons of Quality," or had concerned himself with things so trivial as the proper use of the fork, napkin, and toothpick. Something is said too about "inferiours," before whom one must not "Act ag'tt y'e Rules Moral." But in 1888 the Rules were subjected to careful and literal treatment by Dr. J.M. Toner, of Washington City, in the course of his magnanimous task of preserving, in the Library of Congress, by exact copies, the early and perishing note-books and journals of Washington. This able literary antiquarian has printed his transcript of the Rules (W.H. Morrison: Washington, D.C. 1888), and the pamphlet, though little known to the general public, is much valued by students of American history. With the exception of one word, to which he called my attention, Dr. Toner has given as exact a reproduction of the Rules, in their present damaged condition, as can be made in print. The illegible parts are precisely indicated, without any conjectural insertions, and young Washington's spelling and punctuation subjected to no literary tampering.

Concerning the source of these remarkable Rules there have been several guesses. Washington Irving suggests that it was probably his intercourse with the Fairfax family, and his ambition to acquit himself well in their society, that set him upon "compiling a code of morals and manners." (Knickerbocker Ed. i. p. 30.) Sparks, more cautiously, says: "The most remarkable part of the book is that in which is compiled a system of maxims and regulations of conduct, drawn from miscellaneous sources." (i. p. 7.) Dr. Toner says: "Having searched in vain to find these rules in print, I feel justified, considering all the circumstances, in assuming that they were compiled by George Washington himself when a schoolboy. But while making this claim it is proper to state, that nearly all the principles incorporated and injunctions given in these 110 maxims had been enunciated over and over again in the various works on good behaviour and manners prior to this compilation and for centuries observed in polite society. It will be noticed that, while the spirit of these maxims is drawn chiefly from the social life of Europe, yet, as formulated here, they are as broad as civilization itself, though a few of them are especially applicable to Society as it then existed in America, and, also, that but few refer to women."

Except for the word "parents," which occurs twice, Dr. Toner might have said that the Rules contain no allusion whatever to the female sex. This alone proved, to my own mind, that Washington was in nowise responsible for these Rules. In the school he was attending when they were written there were girls; and, as he was rather precocious in his admirations, a compilation of his own could hardly omit all consideration of conduct towards ladies, or in their presence. There were other reasons also which led me to dissent from my friend Dr. Toner, in this instance, and to institute a search, which has proved successful, for the source of the Rules of Civility.

While gathering materials for a personal and domestic biography of Washington,* I discovered that in 1745 he was attending school in Fredericksburg, Virginia. The first church (St. George's) of the infant town was just then finished, and the clergyman was the Rev. James Marye, a native of France. It is also stated in the municipal records of the town that its first school was taught by French people, and it is tolerably certain that Mr. Marye founded the school soon after his settlement there as Rector, which was in 1735, eight years after the foundation of Fredericksburg. I was thus led to suspect a French origin of the Rules of Civility. This conjecture I mentioned to my friend Dr. Garnett, of the British Museum, and, on his suggestion, explored an old work in French and Latin in which ninety-two of the Rules were found. This interesting discovery, and others to which it led, enable me to restore the damaged manuscript to completeness.

The various intrinsic interest of these Rules is much enhanced by the curious story of their migration from an old Jesuit College in France to the copy-book of George Washington. In Backer's Jesuit Bibliography it is related that the "pensionnaires" of the College of La Flèche sent to those of the College at Pont-à-Mousson, in 1595, a treatise entitled: "Bienseance de la Conversation entre les Hommes." The great Mussipontane father at that time was Léonard Périn (b. at Stenai 1567, d. at Besançon 1658), who had been a Professor of the Humanities at Paris. By order of Nicolas François, Bishop of Toul, Father Périn translated the La Flèche treatise into Latin, adding a chapter of his own on behaviour at table. The book, dedicated to the Bishop of Toul, was first printed (16°) at Pont-à-Mousson in 1617, (by Car. Marchand). It was printed at Paris in 1638, and at Rouen in 1631; it was translated into Spanish, German, and Bohemian. In 1629 one Nitzmann printed the Latin, German, and Bohemian translations in parallel columns, the German title being "Wolstand taglicher Gemainschafft mit dem Menschen." A comparison of this with the French edition of 1663 in the British Museum, on which I have had to depend, shows that there had been no alteration in Father Périn's Latin, though it is newly translated. This copy in the library of the British Museum was printed in Paris for the College of Clermont, and issued by Pierre de Bresche, "auec privilege du Roy." It is entitled: "Les Maximes de la

* George Washington and Mount Vernon. A collection of Washington's unpublished agricultural and personal letters. Edited, with historical and genealogical Introduction, by Moncure Daniel Conway. Published by the L.I. Historical Society: Brooklyn, New York, 1889.

Gentillesse et de l'Honnesteté en la Conversation entre les Hommes. Communis Vitæ inter homines scita urbanitas. Par un Père de la Compagnie de Jesus."

In dedicating this new translation (1663) to the youth of Clermont, Pierre de Bresche is severe on the French of the La Flèche pensionnaires. "It is a novelty surprising enough to find a very unpolished French book translated into the most elegant Latin ever met with." M. de Bresche declares that he was no longer able to leave so beautiful a work in such "abjection," and had added a translation which preserves the purity of the French tongue, and is proportioned to the merit of the exquisite Latin expressions. We can hardly suppose that Pierre de Bresche was eulogising his own work, but there is no other name in the book. Possibly his criticism on the French of the original edition was only that of an *editeur* desiring to supplant it. At any rate, as Father Périn wrote the elegant Latin we cannot doubt that the chapter he added to the book was in scholarly French.

The old book of the Jesuit "pensionnaires"—which, had they not ignored woman, might be called the mother of all works on Civility—is charming as well as curious. It duly opens with a chapter of religious proprieties, at mass, sacrament, sermon, and grace at meat. The Maxims of secular civility open with the second chapter, and it will be seen that they are for the gentry. They are mainly for youths whose environments are portrayed in the interesting frontispiece of the work, where they are seen in compartments—at church, in college, in conversation, at the fireside, in promenade, and at table. We have already seen, from Backer's Jesuit bibliography, that Father Léonard Périn added a chapter on "bienséance" at table; but after this there is another chapter—a wonderful chapter—and it would be interesting to learn whether we owe this also to Périn. This last chapter is exquisitely epicurean, dealing with table-setting, table-service, and the proper order of entrees, roasts, salads, and dessert. It closes—and the book closes—with a sort of sugarplum pæan, the sweets and spices being in the end gracefully spiritualised. But this concluding passage of Chapter XI. ("Des Services & honneurs de la Table") must be quoted:

> "Sugar-plums complete the pleasantness and enjoyment of the dessert, and serve, as it were, to satisfy pleasure. They are brought, while the table is still laid, in a handsome box on a salver, like those given by the ancients to be carried home.* Sometimes, also, they are handed round after the hands have been washed in rose water, and the table covered with a Turkey cloth.

* This is not unknown at some of the civic banquets in London.

> "These are riches which we possess in abundance, and your feasts cannot terminate more agreeably in your quarters than with our Verdun sugar-plums. Besides the exquisite delicacy of their sugar, cinnamon and aniseed, they possess a sweet, fragrant odour like the breeze of the Canaries—that is to say, like our sincerest attachment for you, of which you will also receive proof. Thus you see, then, the courteous advice we have undertaken to give you to serve for a profitable entertainment. If you please, then, we will bring it to a close, in order to devote ourselves more zealously to other duties which will contribute to your satisfaction, and prove agreeable to all those who truly esteem good-breeding and decent general conversation, as we ardently hope.
>
> "Praise be to God and to the glorious Virgin!"*

The earlier editions of the book do not appear to have been published for the outer world, but were printed in the various colleges where they were used. Another French work on the same subject, but including much about ladies, published about the year 1773, plagiarises largely from the Jesuit manual, but does not mention it. It is probable therefore that the Périn volume was not then known to the general public. The anonymous book just mentioned was translated into English.† Some of the phraseology of the Périn book, and many of its ideas,

* "Les dragées acheuent la douceur de la resjoüissance du dessert & font comme l'assouuissement du plaisir. Elles sont portées dans vne belle boëtte posées sur vn plat, les tables restans encore dressées à la façon de celles que les Anciens donnoient à emporter en la maison. Quelquefois aussi les mains estants desia lauées auec l'eau-rose, & la table couuerte de son tapis de Turquie, elle sont presentées.

"Ce sont des richesses que nous possedons en abondance & vos festins ne se peuuent pas termíner plus agreablement que par nos dragées de Verdun en vos quartiers. Elles ont parmy les charmantes delicatesses de leur succre, de leur canelle, & de leur anis, vne douce & suaue odeur qui égale celles de l'air de nos Canaries, c'est à dire de nos plus sinceres inclinations en vostre endroit dont vous receuerez de mesme les tesmoignages. Vous voyez donc icy les advis de la ciuilité que nous auons entrepris de vous donner, pour vous servir d'vn fructueux divertissement. Nous les finissons donc si vous le trouuiez agreable, pour nous porter auec plus de zele aux autres deuoirs qui contribuëront à vostre satisfaction, & qui seront agreables à touts les veritables estimateurs de la bien-seance & de l'honnesteté de la conuersation commune, comme nous le soutraittons auec passion.

"Loüange à Dieu & à la glorieuse Vierge."

† "The Rules of Civility, or Certain Ways of Deportment observed amongst all persons of Quality upon seueral Occasions." The earliest edition I have found is that of 1678 (in the British Museum Library), which is said to be "Newly revised and much Enlarged." The work is assigned a French origin on internal evidence—e.g., other nations than France are referred to as "foreign," and "Monsieur" is used in examples of conversation. The date is approximately fixed as 1673, because it is said that while it was in press there had appeared "The Education of a Young Prince." The latter work was a translation of "De l'education d'un Prince. Par le Sieur de Chanteresne" [P. Nicole], by Pierre du Moulin, the Younger, and published in London, 1673.

appear in a work of Obadiah Walker, Master of University College, Oxford, on Education, but it is not mentioned.* Eighteen of the Washington Rules, and an important addition to another, are not among the French Maxims. Two of these Rules, 24 and 42, are more damaged than any others in the Washington MS., and I had despaired of discovering their meaning. But after my translations were in press I learned from Dr. W.C. Minor that an early English version of the Maxims existed, and in this I have found additions to the French work which substantially include those of the Washington MS. Through this fortunate discovery the Rules of Civility are now completely restored.

The version just alluded to purports to be by a child in his eighth year. It was first printed in 1640 (London), but the earliest edition in the British Museum, where alone I have been able to find a copy, is that of 1646, which is described as the fourth edition.† The cover is stamped in gilt, "Gift of G. III." The translations are indeed rude, and sometimes inaccurate as to the sense, but that they were the unaided work of a child under eight is one of the "things hard to be believed" which a Maxim admonishes us not to tell. In the edition of 1651 there is a portrait of Master Hawkins at the age of eight, and the same picture appears in 1672 as the same person at ten. Moreover, in an edition of 1663 the "Bookseller," in an address "to the reader," seems rather vague in several statements. "A counsellor of the Middle Temple, in 1652, added twenty-five new Precepts marked thus (*) at which time a Gentleman of *Lincoln's*-Inn turned the Book into Latine." There are, however, in this edition thirty-one Precepts not in the French work, and of these twenty-six are in the edition of 1646. The Latin version appended (signed H.B.) is exactly that of Father Périn, with the exception of a few words, considerable

* Of Education. Especially of Young Gentlemen. In two Parts. The Fifth Impression. Oxford: Published at the Theatre for Amos Custeyne. 1887. [It was anonymous, but is known to be by Obadiah Walker, Master of University College, Oxford.]

† "Youth's Behaviour, or Decency in Conversation amongst men. Composed in French by grave persons for the Use and benefit of their youth. Now newly translated into English by Francis Hawkins. The fourth edition, with the addition of twenty-sixe new Precepts (which are marked thus *) London. Printed by W. Wilson for W. Lee, and are to be sold at the *Turks-head* neere the *Miter Taverne* in *Fleetstreet*. 1646." There are some lines "In laudem Authoris" by J.S., and the following: "Gentle Reader—Thinke it not amisse to peruse this Peece, yet connive at the Style: for it hath neede thereof, since wrought by an uncouth and rough File of one greene in yeares; as being aged under eight. Hence, worthy Reader, shew not thy self too-too-rigid a Censurer. This his version is little dignified, and therefore likely will it appeare to thee much imperfect. It ought to be his own, or why under the Title is his name written? Peradventure thou wilt say, what is it to me? yet heare: Such is it really, as that I presume the Author may therein be rendred faithfully: with this courteously be then satisfied.—This small Treatise in its use, will evidently appear to redound to the singular benefit of many a young spirit, to whom solely and purposely it is addressed. Passe it therefore without mistake and candidly."

omissions, and the additional Precepts. The additions are all evidently by a mature hand.

With the Hawkins volume of 1663 is bound, in the British Museum Library, a companion work, entitled, "The second Part of Youth's Behaviour, or Decency in Conversation amongst Women. 1664." This little book is apparently by Robert Codrington, whose name is signed to its remarkable dedicatory letter: "To the Mirrour of her Sex Mrs. Ellinor Pargiter, and the most accomplished with all reall Perfections Mrs. Elizabeth Washington, her only Daughter, and Heiress to the truly Honourable Laurence Washington Esquire, lately deceased."

This was Laurence Washington of Garsden, Wilts., who married Elianor, second daughter of Wm. Gyse; their only child, a daughter, having married Robert Shirley, Earl Ferrars. Laurence Washington died Jan. 17, 1662, and his widow married Sir William Pargiter.*

In a letter to the New York *Nation* (5th June 1890), I said: "Though my theory, that the Rev. James Marye taught Washington these 'Rules,' has done good service in leading to the discovery of their origin, it cannot be verified, unless the clergyman's descendants have preserved papers in which they can be traced." I have since learned from the family that no such papers exist. The discovery just mentioned, that a Part Second of Youth's Behaviour was published in 1664, and dedicated to two ladies of the Washington family in England, lends force to Dr. Minor's suggestion that Washington might have worked out his Rules from the Hawkins version. It would be natural that Part II. so dedicated should be preserved in the Virginia family, and should be bound up with Part I., published the year before, as it is bound in the British Museum. It is certain that one of the later editions of the Hawkins version was used in the preparation of Washington's "Rules," for the eighteen Rules not in the French book are all from "Youth's Behaviour" (1663). Moreover, the phraseology is sometimes the same, and one or two errors of translation follow the Hawkins version. *E.g.*, Maxim ii. 16 begins: "Prenez garde de vous échauffer trop au jeu, & aux emportements qui s'y eleuet." The second clause, a warning against being too much carried away by excitements of play, is rendered by Hawkins, "Contend not, nor speake louder than thou maist with moderation;" and in the Washington MS., "affect not to Speak Louder than ordenary."

A careful comparison, however, of Washington's Rules with the Hawkins version renders it doubtful whether the Virginia boy used the work of the London boy. The differences are more than the resemblances. If in some cases the faults of the Washington version appear gratuitous, the printed copy being before him,

* See "An Examination of the English Ancestry of George Washington. By Henry F. Waters, A.M., Boston. New England Historic Genealogical Society, 1889."

on the other hand it often suggests a closer approach to the French—of which language Washington is known to have been totally ignorant. As to the faults, where Hawkins says ceremonies "are too troublesome," Washington says they "is troublesome;" where the former translates correctly that one must not approach where "another readeth a letter," Washington has "is writing a letter;" where he writes "infirmityes" Washington has "Infirmaties;" the printed "manful" becomes "manfull," and "courtesy" "curtesie." Among the variations which suggest a more intimate knowledge of French idioms than that of Hawkins the following may be mentioned. The first Maxim with which both versions open is: "Que toutes actions qui se font publiquement fassent voir son sentiment respectueux à toute la compagnie." Hawkins: "Every action done in view of the world ought to be accompanied with some signe of reverence which one beareth to all who are present." Washington: "Every action done in company ought to be with some sign of respect to those that are present." Here the restoration of "respectueux," and the limitation of "publiquement" by "compagnie," make the latter rendering much neater. In Maxim viii. 47, which admonishes one not to be angry at table, it is said, "bien si vous vous fâchez," you are not to show it. Hawkins translates "if so bee thou bee vexed;" but Washington more finely, "if you have reason to be so, Shew it not." Or compare the following versions of "Si vous vous reposez chez vous, ayãt quelque siege, faites en sorte de traiter chacun selõ son merite." Hawkins: "if there be anything for one to sit on, be it a chair, be it a stool, give to each one his due." Washington: "when you present seats let it be to every one according to his degree." Rule 45, for "moderation et douceur" has "Sweetness and Mildness," Hawkins only "sweetness." Again: "si vous rencontrez ioliment, si vous donnez quelque bon-mot, en faisant rire les autres, empeschez-vous-en, le plus qu'il vous sera possible." Hawkins: "When so it falleth out that thou deliver some happy lively an jolly conceit abstaine thou, and let others laugh." Washington: "if you Deliver anything witty and Pleasent abtain from laughing thereat yourself."

Yet how curt is the version last quoted, and how blundering the sentence! Washington's spelling was always faulty, but it is not characteristic of him to write "abtain" for "abstain." This is one of many signs of haste, suggesting that his pen was following oral instruction. The absence of punctuation is normal; in some cases words have dropped out: such clerical mistakes occur as "eys," "but" for "put," "top" for "of," "whth" for "without," and "affection" for "affectation"—the needed letters being in the last case interlined. Except as regards punctuation, no similar errors occur in any manuscript from Washington's hand, either in youth or age. Another reason for supposing that he may have been following an instructor is the excessive abbreviation. It was by no means characteristic of Washington to suppress details, but here his condensation sometimes deprives maxims of something of their force, if not of their sense. *E.g.*, Rule 59: "Never express anything unbecoming, nor Act against the Rules Moral before your inferiours." *Cf.* Hawkins: "Never expresse anything unbeseeming, nor act against the Rules morall, before thy inferiours, for in these things, thy own guilt will multiply Crimes by example, and as it were, confirme Ill by authority." And "Shift not yourself in the sight of others" hardly does duty for the precept, "It is insufferable impoliteness to stretch the body, extend the arms, and assume different postures." There are, however, but few instances in which the sense of the original has been lost; indeed, the rendering of the Washington MS. is generally an improvement on the original, which is too diffuse, and even more an improvement on the Hawkins version.

Indeed, although Washington was precocious—a surveyor at seventeen—it would argue qualities not hitherto ascribed to him were we to suppose that, along with his faulty grammar and spelling, he was competent at fourteen for such artistic selection and prudent omission as are shown by a comparison of his 110 Rules with the 170 much longer ones of the English version. The omission of religious passages, save the very general ones with which the Rules close, and of all scriptural ones, is equally curious whether we refer the Rules to young Washington or to the Rector who taught him. But it would be of some significance if we suppose the boy to have omitted the precept to live "peeceably in that vocation unto which providence hath called thee;" and still more that he should have derived nothing from the following: "Do not think thou canst be a friend to the King whilst thou art an enemy to God: if thy crying iniquity should invite God's judgments to the Court, it would cost thy Soveraigne dear, to give them entertainment." If Washington was acquainted with Part II. of "Youth's Behaviour," relating to women and dedicated to ladies of the Washington race, it is remarkable that no word relating to that sex is found among his Rules.*

* In the edition of Hawkins (1663) bound up with Part II. in the British Museum (bearing on the cover the name and arms of the "Hon'ble Thos. Greville") there is just one precept concerning women: "If thou art yet unmarried, but intendest to get thee a wife modest, rather than beautiful, meddle not with those Ladies of the Game, who make pageants of their Cheeks, and Shops of their Shoulders, and (contrary to all other Trades) keep open their Windows on the Sabbath-day, impudently exposing their nakedness to the view of a whole Congregation," &c. There are, in an appendix, pictures of a puritanically shrouded "Virtue," and a "Vice" who, apart from the patches on her face, singularly resembles a portrait of pretty Lady Ferrars in Codrington's book (ante, p. 21) ed. 1672.

On the whole, though it is very uncertain, the balance of probabilities seems to favour the theory that the Rules of Civility, found in a copy-book among school exercises, exceedingly abbreviated, and marked by clerical errors unusual with Washington, were derived from the oral teachings of his preceptor; that this Frenchman utilised (and was once or twice misled by) the English version along with the original, which had been used as a manual in his Rouen College.

The Marie family of Rouen—from which came the Maryes of Virginia—is distinguished both in Catholic and Huguenot annals. Among the eminent Jesuit authors was Pierre Marie, who was born at Rouen, 1589, and died at Bourges, 1645. He was author of "La Sainte Solitude; ou les Entretiens solitaires de l'ame," and of "La Science du Crucifix: en forme de méditations." The family was divided by the Huguenot movement, and a Protestant branch took root in England. Concerning the latter, Agnew (*French Protestant Exiles*, i. p. 100) gives the following information:

> "Jean Marie, pasteur of Lion-sur-mer, was a refugee in England from the St. Bartholomew massacre. He is supposed to have belonged to the same family as the Huguenot martyr, Marin Marie, a native of St. George in the diocese of Lisieux. It was in the year 1559 that that valiant man, who had become a settler in Geneva, was arrested at Sens when on a missionary journey to France, laden with a bale of Bibles and New Testaments, and publications for the promotion of the Protestant Reformation; he was burnt at Paris, in the place Maubert, on the 3d of August of that year. Our pasteur was well received in England, and was sent to Norwich, of which city he appears to have been the first French minister. He was lent to the reformed churches of France when liberty of preaching revived, and so returned to Normandy, where we find him in 1583. The first National Synod of Vitré held its meetings in that year, between the 15th and 27th of May. Quick's 'Synodicon' (vol. i. p. 153) quotes the following minute: 'Our brother, Monsieur Marie, minister of the church of Norwich in England, but living at present in Normandy, shall be obliged to return unto his church upon its first summons; yet, because of the great success of his ministry in these parts, his church may be entreated to continue for some longer time his absence from it.' He certainly did return to Norwich, because on 29th April 1589 the manuscript Book of Discipline was submitted to the consistory for signature; and Jan Marie signed first, and his colleague M. Basnage, second. One of his sons, Nathaniel Marie, became one of the pasteurs

> of the London French Church, and married 1st, Ester, daughter of the pasteur Guillaume De Laune, and 2dly (in 1637), Ester le Hure, widow of André Joye. The Norwich pasteur had probably another son named after himself, a commercial residenter in his native city; for two sons of a Jan Marie were baptized in Norwich French Church: (1) Jan on 3d February 1600, and (2) Pierre, on 6th July 1602. Madame Marie, probably the pasteur's widow, was a witness at the first baptism."

James Marye, with whom we are particularly concerned, sprang from the Catholic family, and was born at Rouen near the close of the seventeenth century. He was educated for the priesthood, no doubt at the Jesuit College in Rouen—where, as we have seen, Father Périn's book on manners was printed in 1651. However, James Marye abjured the Catholic religion in 1726. This caused a breach between himself and the family, which consisted of a widowed mother and her two other sons—Peter and William (the latter an officer), both of whose names, however, reappeared in their protestant brother's family. In consequence of this alienation James migrated to England, where he pursued his studies, and was ordained by the Bishop of London. In 1728 he married Letitia Maria Anne Staige. She was a sister of the Rev. Theodosius Staige, who was already in Virginia. For that colony the Rev. James Marye also embarked, in 1729, with his bride. Their first child (Lucy) was born during the voyage.

It would appear that the purpose of this emigration was to minister to a settlement of French Huguenots at Monacan (or Manakintown, as it was called) on James River. The first band of these refugees had gone over in 1690, under the leadership of Olivier de la Muce, and 600 others had followed in 1699, with their clergyman, Phillipe de Richebourg. The Assembly of Virginia gave them a large tract of land in Henrico County—not far from where Richmond now stands—exempting them from taxation. The name of James Marye first appears in Virginia (1730) as christening a child in King William Parish, as it was called—after the King who had favoured this Huguenot colony.

In 1727 the town of Fredericksburg was founded. In 1732 Col. Byrd visited the place, and wrote: "Besides Col. Willis, who is the top man of the place, there are only one merchant, a tailor, a smith, an ordinary keeper, and a lady who acts both as a doctress and coffeewoman." This "Col. Willis" had married Washington's aunt (and godmother), and there were other families of the neighbourhood connected with the Washingtons. It was not until 1739 that Captain Augustine Washington (the General's father) went to reside near Fredericksburg. Soon after the birth of George (Feb. 11, 1731 Old Style) the family left their homestead in

Westmoreland county, Virginia, and resided on their farm, now known as "Mount Vernon." (It was so named by Washington's elder half-brother, Lawrence, who built the mansion, in 1743-5, in honour of the English Admiral Vernon, with whom he served as an officer at Carthagena.) Although he nowhere alludes to the fact, George Washington's earliest memories, as I have elsewhere shown*, were associated with the estate on which he lavished so much devotion, and which the Ladies' Mount Vernon Association has made his most characteristic monument. The Rev. Jonathan Boucher, teacher of Mrs. George Washington's son John Custis, says that Washington was "taught by a convict servant whom his father had bought for a schoolmaster." This was probably one of a shipload of convicts brought by Captain Augustine Washington from England in 1737. When the family removed to the neighbourhood of Fredericksburg (from which, however, they were separated by the Rappahannock river), the children went to school (probably) at Falmouth—a village fifty years older than Fredericksburg, and about two miles above, on the opposite side of the river. A church had been erected in Falmouth (Brunswick parish), but that in Fredericksburg was not completed until some years later. After the death of his father (April 12, 1743) George was sent to reside with his half-brother Augustine, at "Wakefield," the old homestead in Westmoreland where he was born. He returned to live with his mother, near Fredericksburg, in 1715. That he then went to school in Fredericksburg appears by a manuscript left by Col. Byrd Willis, grandson of Col. Harry Willis, founder of the town, in which he states that his father, Lewis Willis, was Washington's schoolmate. The teacher's name is not given, but there can be little doubt that it was James Marye.

The Rev. James Marye's brother-in-law, Rev. Theodosius Staige, had for a time preached in the temporary structure in which the congregation of St. George's, Fredericksburg, met before the church was completed. It was probably during a visit to Mr. Staige that Mr. Marye made an impression on the people of that place. At any rate the early Vestry-book shows that, in 1735, the churchwardens, after the colonial custom, asked leave of the Governor of Virginia to call James Marye to their pulpit, and it was granted. He is described as "Mr. Marie of St. James," being then officiating at St. James Church, Northam Parish (Goochland county, Virginia). At what time and why he left Manakintown is not clear. He fixed his first abode eight miles out of Fredericksburg, in a place which he called "Fayetteville;" and it is not improbable that some of his Huguenot congregation had come with him, and attempted to found there a village. Several infant churches in the county

* George Washington and Mount Vernon. Introduction, p. xxvii.

(Spottsylvania), besides that of Fredericksburg, were under supervision of the Rector of St. George's Parish.

The Rev. James Marye remained in active and successful ministry at Fredericksburg from 1735 until his death, in 1767. He founded the large Virginia family which bears his name, and which has always had eminent representatives. On his death he was succeeded in St. George's Church, Fredericksburg, by his son of the same name, whose honourable tradition was maintained. His great-grandson, John L. Marye—whose mansion, "Brompton," stood on "Marye's Heights," so famous in the Civil War—was an eminent lawyer; as also is a son of the latter, John L. Marye Jr., former Lieutenant-Governor of Virginia.*

The founder of the Virginia Maryes, who should be ranked among American worthies, was an eloquent clergyman, and built up a noble congregation in Fredericksburg. He was also an accomplished gentleman and a scholar. That he founded and taught the school is tolerably certain. The Municipal Records, as we have seen, ascribe the school a French origin. The name and condition of every respectable resident of Fredericksburg, at the time of his settling there, when it was little more than a "paper town" (in colonial phrase), is known. There was in the place no one—certainly no "Frenchman"—except Marye who could have taught a school of such importance as that at Fredericksburg. For it presently became known throughout Virginia as the chief Academy, especially for classical education, and its reputation continued for more than a hundred years.†

Some of the Rules may strike the modern reader as snobbish, even for the observance of youth. But the originals are in that respect toned down in Washington's MS. Rule 9 takes no cognizance of the principle of the original, that to approach nearer the fire than others, and to turn one's back to it are privileges of persons of rank. The 17th Maxim of chapter iii., which directed certain kissings of the hands of superiors, or of the robe, and other abasements, is entirely omitted. Where the original commands that we should never dispute in any fashion with our superiors in rank, Rule 34 says we ought not to "begin" with them. The only thing clear about which is that the instructor did not wish to admit authority so absolutely into the realm of argument. Rule 46 omits so much of the original as

* For valuable information concerning the Marye family and its descendants, see Brock's "Huguenot Emigration to Virginia." (Virginia Hist. Soc., Richmond, 1886.)

† In a note I have from John L. Marye (sometime Lieutenant-Governor of Virginia), he says: "As to the habit of the Parish Minister to conduct or overlook the schools, it would appear most probable that this was the case in 1745, when we remember how destitute at that era colonial society was of well-organized public or private schools (save the Tutors in families). When I entered Mr. Hanson's school in 1834, it was the custom of Parson McGuire and some of the Vestry to attend the annual Examinations."

counsels grateful acceptance of reproof from another "the more if you depend on his authority." Other instances of this more liberal tendency will be noticed by those who make a careful comparison of the Rules and the French Maxims.

Here then are rules of conduct, taught, if my theory be correct, by a French protestant pilgrim, unknown to fame, in the New World. They were taught to a small school of girls and boys, in a town of hardly a hundred inhabitants. They are maxims partly ethical, but mainly relate to manners and civility; they are wise, gentle, and true. A character built on them would be virtuous, and probably great. The publisher of the English version (1663) says that "Mr. Pinchester, a learned scholar of Oxford," bought 250 copies for a great school he was about to open in London. Probably the school founded by James Marye was the first in the New World in which good manners were seriously taught.* Nay, where is there any such school to day?

Just this one colonial school, by the good fortune of having for its master or superintendent an ex-jesuit French scholar, we may suppose instructed in civility; and out of that school, in what was little more than a village, came an exceptionally large number of eminent men. In that school three American Presidents received their early education—Washington, Madison, and Monroe.

It may be pretty confidently stated that both Madison and Monroe owed their success and eminence more to their engaging manners than to great intellectual powers. They were even notably deficient in that oratorical ability which counted for so much in the political era with which they were connected. They rarely spoke in Congress. When speaking, Madison was hesitating, and was heard with difficulty; but his quietness and modesty, his consideration for others, made the eloquent speak for him. Whether these two statesmen were personally taught by James Marye is doubtful, for he was getting old when they were at school in Fredericksburg; but we may feel sure that civility was still taught there in their time, as, indeed it was within the memory of many now living.

George Washington, though even less able than the two others to speak in public, had naturally a strong intellect. But in boyhood he had much more against

* It is probable that Mr. Marye's fine precedent was followed, to some extent, in the Fredericksburg Academy. The present writer, who entered it just a hundred years after George Washington recorded the "Rules," recalls, as his first clear remembrance of the school, some words of the worthy Principal, Thomas Hanson, on gentlemanly behaviour. Alluding to some former pupil, who had become distinguished, he said, "I remember, on one occasion, in a room where all were gathered around the fire—the weather being very cold—that some one entered, and this boy promptly arose and gave the new-comer his seat at the fire. It made an impression on me which I have never forgotten." And how long have lasted in the memory of the writer hereof the very words of our teacher's homage to the considerate boy who obeyed Washington's eighth Rule!

him than most of his young comrades—obstructions that could be surmounted only by character. His father had much land but little money; at his death (1743,) the lands were left chiefly to his sons by the first wife. His widow was left poor, and her eldest son, George, had not the fair prospect of most of his schoolmates. Instead of being prepared for William and Mary College, he was prepared only for going into some business as soon as possible, so as to earn support for his mother and her four younger children. In his old book of school-exercises, the "Rules of Civility" are found in proximity to business forms that bear pathetic testimony to the severe outlook of this boy of fourteen. In the MS. of Col. Byrd Willis, already referred to (loaned me by his granddaughter, Mrs. Tayloe, of Fredericksburg), he says: "My father, Lewis Willis, was a schoolmate of General Washington, his cousin, who was two years his senior. He spoke of the General's industry and assiduity at school as very remarkable. Whilst his brother and other boys at playtime were at bandy and other games, he was behind the door ciphering. But one youthful ebullition is handed down while at that school, and that was romping with one of the largest girls; this was so unusual that it excited no little comment among the other lads." It is also handed down that in boyhood this great soldier, though never a prig, had no fights, and was often summoned to the playground as a peacemaker, his arbitration in disputes being always accepted.

Once more it may be well enough to remind the reader that it may yet be found that Washington, in his mother's humble home on the Rappahannock, read and pondered "Youth's Behaviour," wrote out what it held for him, and himself became an instructor of his schoolmates in rules of civility. It would be wonderful, but not incredible.

Although Washington became a fine-looking man, he was not of prepossessing appearance in early life; he was lank and hollow-chested. He was by no means a favourite with the beauties for which Fredericksburg was always famous, and had a cruel disappointment of his early love for Betsy Fauntleroy. In his youth he became pitted by smallpox while attending his invalid half-brother, Lawrence, on a visit to the Barbadoes.

But the experienced eye of Lord Fairfax, and of other members of the Fairfax family, had discovered beneath the unattractive appearance of George Washington a sterling character. Their neighbourhood, on the upper Potomac, was much less civilised and refined than Fredericksburg, and this young gentleman, so well instructed in right rules of behaviour and conduct, won their hearts and their confidence. It had been necessary that he should leave school at the age of sixteen to earn a living. At seventeen he was appointed by Lord Fairfax surveyor of his vast estates in Virginia, and for a time he resided with his lordship at Greenway

Court. There can be little doubt that it was partly through the training in manners which Washington gained from the old French maxims that he thus made headway against circumstances, and gained the friendship of the highly-educated and powerful Fairfax family.

It should be mentioned, however, that young Washington's head was not in the least turned by this intimacy with the aristocracy. He wrote letters to his former playmates in which no snobbish line is discoverable. He writes to his "Dear friend Robin": "My place of residence is at present at his lordship's where I might, was my heart disengaged, pass my time very pleasantly, as there's a very agreeable young lady lives in the same house (Col. George Fairfax's wife's sister). But as that's only adding fuel to fire, it makes me the more uneasy, for by often and unavoidably being in company with her revives my former passion for your Lowland beauty; whereas, was I to live more retired from young women, I might eleviate in some measure my sorrows by burying that chaste and troublesome passion in the grave of oblivion or etearnall forgetfulness, for as I am very well assured, that's the only antidote or remedy that I ever shall be relieved by or only recess that can administer any cure or help to me, as I am well convinced, was I ever to attempt anything, I should only get a denial which would be only adding grief to uneasiness."

The young lady at Greenway Court was Mary Cary, and the Lowland beauty was Betsy Fauntleroy, whose hand Washington twice sought, but who became the wife of the Hon. Thomas Adams. While travelling on his surveys, often among the red men, the youth sometimes gives vent to his feelings in verse.

"Oh Ye Gods why should my Poor resistless Heart
  Stand to oppose thy might and Power
At last surrender to Cupid's feather'd Dart
  And now lays bleeding every Hour
For her that's Pityless of my grief and Woes,
  And will not on me Pity take.
I'll sleep among my most inveterate Foes
  And with gladness never wish to wake,
In deluding sleepings let my Eyelids close
  That in an enraptured dream I may
In a rapt lulling sleep and gentle repose
  Possess those joys denied by Day."

And it must also be recorded that if he had learned how to conduct himself in the presence of persons superior to himself in position, age, and culture—and it will be remembered that Lord Fairfax was an able contributor to the "Spectator" (which Washington was careful to study while at Greenway,)—this youth no less followed the instruction of his 108th rule: "Honour your natural parents though they be poor." His widowed mother was poor, and she was ignorant, but he was devoted to her; being reverential and gracious to her even when with advancing age she became somewhat morose and exacting, while he was loaded with public cares.

I am no worshipper of Washington. But in the hand of that man of strong brain and powerful passions once lay the destiny of the New World—in a sense, human destiny. But for his possession of the humility and self-discipline underlying his Rules of Civility, the ambitious politicians of the United States might to-day be popularly held to a much lower standard. The tone of his character was so entirely that of modesty, he was so fundamentally patriotic, that even his faults are transformed to virtues, and the very failures of his declining years are popularly accounted successes. He alone was conscious of his mental decline, and gave this as a reason for not accepting a third nomination for the Presidency. This humility has established an unwritten law of limitation on vaulting presidential ambitions. Indeed, intrigue and corruption in America must ever struggle with the idealised phantom of this grand personality.

These Rules of Civility go forth with the hope that they will do more than amuse the reader by their quaintness, and that their story will produce an impression beyond that of its picturesqueness. The strong probabilities that they largely moulded the character of Washington, and so influenced the human race, may raise the question, whether the old French Jesuits, and the pilgrim, James Marye, did not possess more truly than our contemporary educators, the art and mystery of moral education. In these days, when ethical is replacing theological instruction, in the home and in the school, there appears danger that it may repeat some of the mistakes of its predecessor. The failure of what was called Religion to promote moral culture is now explicable: its scheme of terror and hope appealed to and powerfully stimulated selfishness, and was also fundamentally anti-social, cultivating alienation of all who did not hold certain dogmas. The terrors and hopes having faded away, the selfishness they developed remains, and is only unchained by the decay of superstition. On the other hand, the social sentiment has thrown off sectarian restrictions, and an enthusiasm of humanity has succeeded. It is now certain that the social instinct is the only one which can be depended on to influence conduct to an extent comparable with the sway once exercised by superstitious terrors and expectations of celestial reward. The child is spiritually a creation of the commune; there can be no other motive so early responsive as that which desires the approval and admiration of those by whom it is surrounded.

To attempt the training of human character by means of ethical philosophy or moral science—as it used to be called—appears to be somewhat of a theological "survival." When the sanctions of authority were removed from the pagan deities they were found to have been long reduced in the nursery to the dimensions of fairies. The tremendous conceptions of Christian theology may some day be revealed as similarly diminished in the catechised mind of childhood. And the abstract principles of ethical philosophy cannot hope for any better fate. The child's mind cannot receive the metaphysics of virtue. It is impossible to explain to a child, for instance, the reasons for truthfulness, which, indeed, have grown out of the experience of the human race as matured by many ages. And so of humanity to animals, which is mainly a Darwinian revival of Buddhist sentiment based on a doctrine of transmigration. And the same may be said of other virtues. We must not suppose that a child has no scepticism because he cannot express or explain it in words; it will appear in the sweetness to him of stolen apples, in the fact that to label a thing "naughty" may only render it more tempting to a healthy boy. A philosopher said, "A fence is the temptation to a jump."

Our ethical teaching is vitiated by an inheritance from theology of a superstition which subordinates conduct to its motives. Really, if conduct be good, the motive (generally too complex for even consciousness to analyse) is of least importance. Motives are important as causing conduct, but the Law is just in assuming good or bad motives for the corresponding actions. The world does not depend on a man's inner but on his outer life. Emerson once scandalised some of his admirers by saying that he preferred a person who did not respect the truth to an unpresentable person. But, no doubt, he would regard the presentable person as possessing virtues of equal importance. The nurture of "civility and decent behaviour in company and conversation," is not of secondary, but primary, importance.

For what does it imply? If the Rules about to be submitted are examined, it will be found that their practice draws on the whole moral world, as in walking every step draws on the universal gravitation. Scarcely one Rule is there that does not involve self-restraint, modesty, habitual consideration of others, and, to a large extent, living for others. Yet other Rules draw on the profounder deeps of wisdom and virtue, under a subtle guise of handsome behaviour. If youth can be won to excellence by love of beauty, who shall gainsay?

It may occur to the polished reader that well-bred youths know and practise these rules of civility by instinct. But the best bred man's ancestors had to learn them, and the rude progenitors of future gentlemen have to learn them. Can it be said, however, that those deemed well-bred do really know and practise these rules of civility instinctively? Do they practise them when out of the region of the persons or the community in whose eyes they wish to find approval? How do they act with Indians, Negroes, or when travelling amongst those to whose good opinion they are indifferent? In a Kentucky court a witness who had spoken of a certain man as "a gentleman," was pressed for his reasons, and answered, "If any man goes to his house he sets out the whisky, then goes and looks out of the window." It is doubtful if what commonly passes for politeness in more refined regions is equally humanised with that of the Kentuckian so described. Indeed the only difficulty in the way of such teaching as is here suggested, is the degree to which the words "lady" and "gentleman" have been lowered from their original dignity.

The utilization of the social sentiment as a motive of conduct in the young need not, however, depend on such terms, though these are by no means beyond new moralization in any home or school. An eminent Englishman told me that he once found his little son pointing an old pistol at his sister. The ancient pistol was not dangerous, but the action was. "Had I told him it was dangerous," he said, "it might only have added spice to the thing, but I said, 'I am surprised. I thought you were a little gentleman, but that is the most ungentlemanly thing you could do.' The boy quickly laid aside the pistol, with deep shame. I have found nothing so restraining for my children as to suggest that any conduct is ungentlemanly or unladylike." And let my reader note well the great moral principles in these rules of civility and decent behaviour. The antithesis of "sinfull" is "manfull." Washington was taught that all good conduct was gentlemanly, all bad conduct ill-bred.

It is to be hoped that the time is not far distant when in every school right rules of civility will be taught as a main part of the curriculum. Something of the kind was done by the late Bronson Alcott, in the school he founded in Boston, Massachusetts, near fifty years ago, for children gathered from the street. The school was opened every morning with a "conduct lesson," as it was called. It will be seen by Miss Elizabeth Peabody's "Records of a School" that the children crowded to the door before it was opened in their anxiety not to lose a word of this lesson. And, rude as most of the children were, this instruction, consisting of questions and answers, gradually did away with all necessity for corporal punishments.

It were a noble task for any competent hand to adapt the Rules given in this volume, and those of the later French work, and still more those of Master Obadiah Walker's book on "Education," to the conditions and ideas of our time, for the use of schools. From the last-named work, that of a Master of University College, Oxford, I will take for my conclusion a pregnant passage.

> "The greatest *Magnetismes* in the World are *Civility*, Conforming to the innocent humours, and infirmities, sometimes, of others, readiness to do courtesies for all, Speaking well of all behind their backs. And 2ly *Affability*, which is not only to be used in common and unconcerning speech, but upon all occasions. A man may deny a request, chide, reprehend, command &c. *affably*, with good words, nor is there anything so harsh which may not be inoffensively represented."

NOTE.

There has been no alteration of the original French and English documents in the pages following. The spelling, punctuation, use of small or capital letters, italics, etc., whether faults or archaisms, are strictly preserved.

The word "Maxim" refers to the early French work (of the Jesuit Fathers). "Rule" refers to Washington's MS.

"Hawkins" indicates the English version of the Maxims, chiefly the anonymous additions thereto. See p. 17.

"Walker" refers to Obadiah Walker's work on Education, spoken of on p. 16.

"The later French book" refers to the anonymous work of 1673, translated into English, mentioned on p. 16.

1st. Every Action done in Company ought to be with Some Sign of Respect, to those that are Present.

MAXIMES, Chap. II.

Chapter ii. 1. Que toutes actions qui se font publiquement fassent voir son sentiment respectueux à toute la compagnie.

All actions done before others should be with some sign of respectful feeling to the entire company.

2D. WHEN IN COMPANY, PUT NOT YOUR HANDS TO ANY PART OF THE BODY NOT USUALLY DISCOVERED.

Chapter ii. 3. Gardez-vous bien de toucher de la main aucune partie de vostre corps, de celles qui ne sont point en veuë, en la presence d'aucune autre personne. Pour les mains, & le visage, cela leur est ordinaire. Et afin de vous y accoustumer pratiquez ce poinct de ciuilité mesme en vostre particulier.

In the presence of any one, never put your hand to any part of the person not usually uncovered. As for the hands and face they are usually visible. In order to form a habit in this point of decency, practise it even when with your intimate friend.

3D. SHEW NOTHING TO YOUR FRIEND THAT MAY AFFRIGHT HIM.

Chapter ii. 4. Ne faites pas voir a vostre compagnon, ce qui luy pourroit faire mal au coeur.

Show nothing to your companion that may grieve him.

4TH. IN THE PRESENCE OF OTHERS SING NOT TO YOURSELF WITH A HUMMING NOISE, NOR DRUM, WITH YOUR FINGERS OR FEET.

Chapter ii. 5. Ne vous amusez pas à chanter en vous mesme, si vous ne vous rencontrez si fort à l'écart qu'aucun autre ne vous puisse entendre, non plus qu'à contre-faire le son du tambour par l'agitation des pieds ou des mains.

Do not seek amusement in singing to yourself, unless beyond the hearing of others, nor drum with your hands or feet.

5TH. IF YOU COUGH, SNEEZE, SIGH, OR YAWN, DO IT NOT LOUD, BUT PRIVATELY; AND SPEAK NOT IN YOUR YAWNING, BUT PUT YOUR HANDKERCHIEF OR HAND BEFORE YOUR FACE AND TURN ASIDE.

Chapter ii. 8. Quand vous toussez ou quand vous esternuez, si vous pouuez estre le maistre de ces efforts de nature, n'éclatez pas si hautement & si fort. Ne poussez soûpirs si aigres que les autres les puissent entendre.

9. Ne soufflez pas si asprement, faisant des hurlements en baaillant. Et s'il vous est possible, empeschez vous absolumet de baailler; mais ayez en un bien plus soin, quand vous entretenez avec quelqu'vn, ou dans quelque conuersation. Car c'est un signe manifest d'un certain dégoust de ceux avec qui vous vivez. Si vous

ne pouvez pas empescher de baailler, du moins gardez vous bien de parler en cet instant mesme, & d'ouurir extraordinairemet la bouche; mais pressez la sagement, ou en détournant tant soi peu la face de la cõpagnie.

[Sidenote: The later French book advises one, in sneezing, not to shake the foundations of the house.]

Whenever you cough or sneeze, if you can control these efforts of nature, do not let the sound be high or strong. Do not heave sighs so piercing as to attract attention. Do not breathe heavily, or make noises in yawning. If you can, abstain from yawning, especially while with any one, or in conversation. For it is a plain sign of a certain dislike of those with whom you dwell. If you cannot keep from yawning, at least be careful not to speak while doing so, and not to gape excessively; press your mouth adroitly or n turning a little from the company.

6TH. SLEEP NOT WHEN OTHERS SPEAK, SIT NOT WHEN OTHERS STAND, SPEAK NOT WHEN YOU SHOULD HOLD YOUR PEACE, WALK NOT WHEN OTHERS STOP

Chapter ii. 11. C'est vne inciuilité & vne impertinence de dormir, pendant que la cõpagnie s'entretient de discours; de se tenir assis lors que tout le monde est debout, de se promener lors que personne ne branle, & de parler, quãd il est temps de se taire ou d'écouter. Pour celuy toutesfois qui a l'authorité, il y a des temps & des lieux où il luy est permis de se promener seul, comme à un Precepteur qui est dans la classe.

It is an incivility and an impertinence to doze while the company is conversing, to be seated while the rest stand, to walk on when others pause, and to speak when you should be silent, or listen. For those in authority, as a Master in school, there are times and places when it is admissible to walk alone.

7TH. PUT NOT OFF YOUR CLOTHS IN THE PRESENCE OF OTHERS, NOR GO OUT OF YOUR CHAMBER HALF DREST.

Chapter ii. 12. Il n'est pas seant d'auoir son liet en mauuais ordre dans sa chambre, non plus que de s'habiller en la presence des autres, ou de s'y dépoüiller, ou de sortir de sa mesme chambre à demy habillé, couuert de sa coiffe, ou bonnet-de-nuiet, de rester debout en sa chãbre ou estre attaché à son pulpitre auec sa robe ouverté. Et quoy que vous ne manquiez pas de serviteur qui prenne le soin de faire vostre liet; toutesfois en sortant, prenez garde de le laisser découvert.

It is not seemly to leave your bed disarranged, to dress or undress before others, or to leave your chamber half-dressed, covered with a hood, or night-cap, or to remain standing in your room or at your desk with open gown. And although you have a servant to make your bed, nevertheless, take care when you go out to leave it uncovered.

8TH. AT PLAY AND AT FIRE ITS GOOD MANNERS TO GIVE PLACE TO THE LAST COMMER, AND AFFECT NOT TO SPEAK LOUDER THAN ORDENARY.

Chapter ii. 15. Il est mal-seant, dans le jeu, ou aupres du feu de faire attendre trop long-temps ceux qui viennent à s'y presenter.

It is impolite at play, or at the fireside, to make the new-comers wait for places too long.

(In the second clause, "affect not" &c., the Washington MS. follows Hawkins in misunderstanding a phrase of the next Maxim: "Prenez garde de vous échauffer trop au jeu, & aux emportements qui s'y eleuet,"—a warning against being overheated at play, and "carried away by its excitements.")

9TH. SPIT NOT IN THE FIRE, NOR STOOP LOW BEFORE IT NEITHER PUT YOUR HANDS INTO THE FLAMES TO WARM THEM, NOR SET YOUR FEET UPON THE FIRE ESPECIALLY IF THERE BE MEAT BEFORE IT.

Chapter ii. 17. C'est une action peu hõneste de cracher dans la cheminée , d'approcher ses mains trop prés de la flâme pour les échauffer, & de les mettre même dedans, de se baisser deuãt le feu, comme si l'on estoit assis à terre& s'y tenir courbé. S'il arriue qu'il y ait quelque chose deuantle feu, a cuire, prenez bien garde d'estendre le pied pardessus le feu. Dans une honneste compagnie n'y tournez iamais le dos, & ne vous en approchez point plus prés que les autres: car ce sont des priuileges de personnes qualifiées. Quand il n'en est point besoin , de remuer le feu, y pousser le bois, l'y fourrer plus auant ou l'en leuer, il n'appartient qu'à celuy qui doit auoir le soin de tout ce qui est à faire.

It is not a handsome action to spit in the fireplace, or, in warming the hands, to hold them nearly in the flame, or as if resting on the ground and crouching beside it. If anything is cooked before the fire, do not extend your foot over it. In polite society do not turn your back to the fire, and do not approach it closer than others; these are privileges of persons of rank. When there is need of stirring the fire, putting wood on it, pulling or lifting it, this belongs to the person who has the general superintendence of those things.

[Sidenote: The use of the negative in the French original (n'en est point) seems erroneous, and is disregarded in this translation.]

10TH. WHEN YOU SIT DOWN, KEEP YOUR FEET FIRM AND EVEN, WITHOUT PUTTING ONE ON THE OTHER OR CROSSING THEM

Chapter ii. 18. Pour l'ordre que l'on doit tenir étant assis, c'est de placer bien ses pieds à terre en égale distance que les cuisses, non pas de croiser vne cuisse ou vn pied sur l'autre.

When seated, the feet should be placed well on the ground, in even distance with the legs, and neither a leg or a foot should be crossed on the other.

11TH. SHIFT NOT YOURSELF IN THE SIGHT OF OTHERS NOR GNAW YOUR NAILS.

Chapter ii. 7. C'est vne inciuilité insupportable d'allonger son corps en estendant les bras, ou de faire differents postures.

Chapter iii. 19. Il ne faut iamais rogner ses ongles dans le public, & bien moins les prendre à beiles dents.

It is insufferably impolite to stretch the body, extend the arms, or to assume different postures.

Do not pare your nails in public, much less gnaw them.

12TH. SHAKE NOT THE HEAD, FEET, OR LEGS ROWL NOT THE EYS, LIFT NOT ONE EYEBROW HIGHER THAN THE OTHER WRY NOT THE MOUTH, AND BEDEW NO MANS FACE WITH YOUR SPITTLE, BY APPR[OACHING TOO NEA]R [WHEN] YOU SPEAK.

Chapter ii. 21. Vous ne hocherez la teste, vous ne remuerez point les jambes, ny ne roüillerez les yeux, ne froncerez point les sourcils, ou tordrez la bouche. Vous vous garderez de laisser aller auec vos paroles de la saliue, ou du crachat aux visages de ceux, auec qui vous conversez. Pour obvier à cét accident, vous ne vous en approcherez point si prés; mais vous les entretiendrez dans vne distãce raisonnable.

Shake not the head, nor fidget the legs, nor roll the eyes, nor frown, nor make mouths. Be careful not to let saliva escape with your words, nor any spittle fly into the faces of those with whom you converse. To avoid such accident do not approach them too near, but keep at a reasonable distance.

13th. Kill no Vermin as Fleas, lice ticks &c in the Sight of Others, if you See any filth or thick Spittle put your foot Dexteriously upon it if it be upon the Cloths of your Companions, Put it off privately, and if it be upon your own Cloths return Thanks to him who puts it off

Chapter ii. 22. Gardez vous bié de vous arrester à tuër vne puce, ou quelque sale bestiole de cette espece, en presence de qui que a puisse estre. Que si quelque chose d'immõde vient à vous offenser la veuë, en regardant à terre, comme quelque crachat infect, ou quelque autre chose semblable, mettez le pied dessus. S'il en attache quelque'vne aux habits de celuy à qui vous parlez, ou voltige dessus, gardez vouz bien de la luy monstrer, ou à quelqu'autre personne; mais trauaillez autant que vous pourrez à l'oster adroitement. Et s'il arriue que quelqu'vn vous oblige tant que de vous défaire de quelque chose de semblable, faites luy paroistre vostre reconnoissance.

Do not stop to kill a flea, or other disgusting insect of the kind, in the presence of any one. If anything disgusting offends the sight on the ground, as phlegm, etc., put your foot on it. If it be on any garment of one to whom you are talking, do not show it to him or another, but do your best to remove it unobserved. If any one oblige you in a thing of that kind make him your acknowledgments.

14th. Turn not your Back to others especially in Speaking, Jog not the Table or Desk on which Another reads or writes lean not upon any one.

Chapter ii. 24. En la rencontre que l'on fait des personnes, quand on les entretient, c'est une chose malseante de leur tourner le dos & les épaules. C'est vne action impertinente de heurter la table ou d'ébranler le pupitre, dont vn autre se sert pour lire, ou pour écrire. C'est vne inciuilité de s'appuyer sur quelqu'vn, de tirer sa robbe, lors que l'on luy parle ou que l'on le peut entretenir.

When one meets people, it is very unbecoming in speaking to them to turn one's back and shoulders to them. It is an impertinent action to knock against the table, or to shake the desk, which another person is using for reading or writing. It is uncivil to lean against any one, or to pluck his dress when speaking to him, or while entertaining him in conversation.

15th. Keep your Nails clean and Short, also your Hands and Teeth Clean, yet without Shewing any great Concern for them

Chapter ii. 25. Gardez vous bien de vous arrester en toute sorte de conuersation, à rajuster vostre rabat, ou à rehausser vos chausses pour les faire ioindre & en paroitre plus galaud. Que vos ongles ne soient point replis d'ordures, ny trop longs. Ayez grand soin de la netteté de vos mains; mais n'y recherchez point la volupté.

[Sidenote: Hawkins: "without overmuch attendance thereon or curiosity."]

Take good care not to stop, in any sort of conversation, to adjust your bands, or to pull up your stockings to make them join so as to look more gallant. Do not let your nails be full of dirt or too long. Have a great regard for the cleanliness of your hands, but do not be finikin about it.

16th. Do not puff up the Cheeks, Loll not out the tongue rub the Hands, or beard, thrust out the lips, or bite them or keep the lips too open or too close.

Chapter ii. 26. C'est une vilainie de s'enfler les joües, de tirer la langue, de se manier la barbe, se frotter les mains, d'estendre ses levres ou les mordre, de les tenir trop serrées ou trop entrouuertes.

It is very low to puff out the cheeks, to put out the tongue, to pull one's beard, rub one's hands, poke out or bite the lips, or to keep them too tightly closed or too open.

17th. Be no Flatterer, neither Play with any that delights not to be Play'd Withal.

Chapter ii. 27. Ne flattez & n'amadoüez personne par belles paroles, car celui qui pretend d'en gagner un autre par les discours emmiellez, fait voir qu'il n'en a pas grande estime, & qu'il le tient pour peu sensé & adroit, dés qu'il le prend pour vn hõme que l'on peut ioüer en cette maniere: n'usez point de gausseries auprés d'vne personne qui s'en offense.

Do not flatter or wheedle any one with fair words, for he who aspires to gain another person by his honied words shows that he does not hold him in high esteem and that he deems him far from sensible or clever, in taking him for a man who may be tricked in this manner: do not play practical jokes on those who do not like it.

18th. Read no Letters, Books, or Papers in Company but when there is a Necessity for the doing of it you must ask leave: come not near the Books or Writings of Another so as to read them unless desired or give your opinion of them unask'd also look not nigh when another is writing a Letter

Chapter ii. 28. C'est vne action directement opposée à la bien-séance, de lire quelque livre, quelques lettres ou autres choses semblables dans vne conversation ordinaire, si ce n'est en vne affaire pressante, ou pour quelque peu de moments; & mesme encore en ce cas, est-il à propos d'en demãder la permission, si vous n'estes, possible, le Superieur de la compagnie. C'est encore pis de manier les ouvrages des autres, leurs livres, & d'autres choses de cette nature, de s'y attacher, d'en approcher la veuë de plus prés, sans la permission de celuy à qui la chose appartient, aussi bien que de leur donner des loüanges, ou les censurer, auant que l'on vous en demande vostre sentiment; de s'approcher trop prés, & d'incommoder celuy de qui ou est voisin, lors qu'il prend la lecture de ses lettres ou de quelqu'-autre chose.

It is an act directly opposed to politeness to read a book, letters or anything else during ordinary conversation, if it be not a pressing matter, or only for a few moments, and even in that case it is proper to ask leave unless you are, possibly, the highest in rank of the company. It is even worse to handle other people's work, their books or other things of that nature, to go close to them, to look at them closely without the permission of the owner, and also to praise or find fault with them before your opinion has been asked; to come too close to any one near by, when he is reading his letters or anything else.

19th. let your Countenance be pleasant but in Serious Matters Somewhat grave

Chapter ii. 29. Que le visage ne paroisse point fantastique, changeant, égaré, rauy en admiration, couuert de tristesse, divers & volage, & ne fasse paroître aucun signe d'vn esprit inquiet: Au contraire, qu'il soil ouuert & tranquille, mais qu'il ne soit pas trop épanoüy de joye dans les affaires serieuses, ny trop retiré par vne grauité affectée dans la conversation ordinaire & familiere de la vie humaine.

The face should not look fantastic, changeable, absent, rapt in admiration, covered with sadness, various and volatile, and it should not show any signs of an unquiet mind. On the contrary, it should be open and tranquil, but not too expansive with joy in serious affairs, nor too self-contained by an affected gravity in the ordinary and familiar conversation of human life.

20TH. THE GESTURES OF THE BODY MUST BE SUITED TO THE DISCOURSE YOU ARE UPON

Hawkins i. 30. Let the gestures of thy body, be agreeable to the matter of thy discourse. For it hath been ever held a solaesime in oratory, to poynt to the Earth, when thou talkest of Heaven.

(The nearest Maxim to this is one directed against excessive and awkward gesticulation in speaking, in which it is said: "Parmy les discours regardez à mettre vostre corps en belle posture" (While speaking be careful to assume an elegant posture).

21ST. REPROACH NONE FOR THE INFIRMATIES OF NATURE, NOR DELIGHT TO PUT THEM THAT HAVE IN MIND THEREOF.)

Chapter iv. 6. Ne reprochez les défauts à personne, non pas mesme de la nature, & ne prenez plaisir à faire confusion à qui que ce soit, par vos paroles.

[Sidenote: Hawkins adds: "which by no Art can be amended."]

Reproach none for their Infirmities—avoid it equally when they are natural ones—and do not take pleasure in uttering words that cause any one shame, whoever it may be.

22D. SHEW NOT YOURSELF GLAD AT THE MISFORTUNE OF ANOTHER THOUGH HE WERE YOUR ENEMY

Hawkins i. 32. When thou shalt heare the misfortunes of another, shew not thy selfe gladed for it, though it happ to thy enemy, for that will argue a mind mischievous, and will convict thee of a desire to have executed it thy selfe, had either power or opertunity seconded thy will.

(Nothing corresponding to Rule 22 is found among the Maxims of the Jesuit fathers; but the later French book has the following: "Shew not your self joyful and pleased at the misfortunes that have befallen another, though you hated him, it argues a mischievous mind, and that you had a desire to have done it your self, if you had had the power or opportunity to your will.")

23D. WHEN YOU SEE A CRIME PUNISHED, YOU MAY BE INWARDLY PLEASED; BUT ALWAYS SHEW PITY TO THE SUFFERING OFFENDER.

Hawkins i. 33. When thou seest justice executed on any, thou maist inwardly take delight in his vigilancy, to punish offenders, because it tends to publique quiet, yet shew pity to the offender, and ever Constitute the defect of his morality, thy precaution.

[24TH. DO NOT LAUGH TOO LOUD OR] TOO MUCH AT ANY PUBLICK [SPECTACLE, LEST YOU CAUSE YOURSELF TO BE LAUGHED AT.]

[Sidenote: This Rule has been nearly destroyed by mice.]

Hawkins i. 34. Laugh not too much or too Loud, in any publique spectacle least for thy so doing, thou present thy selfe, the only thing worthy to be laughed at.

25TH. SUPERFLUOUS COMPLEMENTS AND ALL AFFECTATION OF CEREMONY ARE TO BE AVOIDED, YET WHERE DUE THEY ARE NOT TO BE NEGLECTED

Chapter iii. 1. Quoy qu'il soit bon de s'épargner vn trop grand soing de pratiquer vne ciuilité affectée, il faut pourtant estre exact à en obseruer ce qui est necessaire & auantageux pour faire paroistre une belle éducation, & ce qui ne se peut obmettre sans choquer ceux auec qui l'on converse.

Though it is right to avoid too great care in practising an affected civility, yet one must be exact in observing what is necessary and advantageous in order to show a good education, and all that cannot be omitted without shocking those with whom one is conversing.

26TH. IN PULLING OFF YOUR HAT TO PERSONS OF DISTINCTION, AS NOBLEMEN, JUSTICES, CHURCHMEN, &C MAKE A REVERENCE, BOWING MORE OR LESS ACCORDING TO THE CUSTOM OF THE BETTER BRED, AND QUALITY OF THE PERSONS. AMONGST YOUR EQUALS EXPECT NOT ALWAYS THAT THEY SHOULD BEGIN WITH YOU FIRST, BUT TO PULL OFF THE HAT WHEN THERE IS NO NEED IS AFFECTATION, IN THE MANNER OF SALUTING AND RESALUTING IN WORDS KEEP TO THE MOST USUAL CUSTOM.

Chapter iii. 2. Témoignez vos respects aux hommes illustres & honorables, le chappeau en la main, comme aux Ecclesiastiques, ou aux Magistrats, ou à quelques autres personnes qualifiées; en tenant vers vous le dedans du chappeau que vous aurez osté: Faites leur aussi la reverence par quelque inclination de corps, autant que la dignité de chacun d'eux, & la belle coûtume des enfants bien nourris, le semble exiger. Et comme c'est vne chose fort inciuile de ne se pas découurir devant ceux à qui l'on doit ce respect, pour les saluër, ou d'attendre que vostre égal vous rend le premier ce deuoir; aussi de le faire, quand il n'est pas à propos, ressent sa ciuilité affectée: mais c'est vne honteuse impertinence de prendre garde si l'on vous rend vostre salutation. Au reste pour saluër quelqu'vn de parole, ce compliment semble le plus propre, qui est vsité par personnes le plus polies.

Show your respect for illustrious and honourable men—such as Ecclesiastics, Magistrates, or other persons of quality—hat in hand, holding the inside of the removed hat towards you; make your reverence to them by inclining your body as much as the dignity of each and the custom of well-bred youth seems to demand. And, as it is very rude not to uncover the head before those to whom one owes such respect, in order to salute them, or to wait till your equal should perform this duty towards you first, so also, to do it when it is not fitting savours of affected politeness: but it is shameful impertinence to be anxious for the return of one's salute. Finally, it seems most fitting to salute any one in words, a compliment which the politest persons are in the habit of using.

27TH. TIS ILL MANNERS TO BID ONE MORE EMINENT THAN YOURSELF BE COVERED AS WELL AS NOT TO DO IT TO WHOM IT'S DUE. LIKEWISE HE THAT MAKES TOO MUCH HASTE TO PUT ON HIS HAT DOES NOT WELL, YET HE OUGHT TO PUT IT ON AT THE FIRST, OR AT MOST THE SECOND TIME OF BEING ASK'D; NOW WHAT IS HEREIN SPOKEN, OF QUALIFICATION IN BEHAVIOUR IN SALUTING, OUGHT ALSO TO BE OBSERVED IN TAKING OF PLACE, AND SITTING DOWN FOR CEREMONIES WITHOUT BOUNDS IS TROUBLESOME.

Chapter iii. 3. C'est une grande inciuilité d'entreprendre de prier vn superieur de se couurir, aussi bien que de n'en pas supplier celuy à qui cela se peut faire. Et celuy qui se haste trop de se couurir, particulierement en parlant à quelque personne qualifiée, ou qui pressé par plusieurs fois de ce faire, le refuse, choque la bienscéance; c'est pour cela qu'à la 1. ou 2. fois il est permis de se couurir, si l'vsage ne se trouue contraire en quelque Prouince ou Royaume. Et en effet entre les égaux, ou auec de plus âgez, soit Religieux, ou domestiques, il est permis d'accorder cette requeste à vn égal ou à vn plus ieune, dés la 1. fois. Toutefois ceux qui sõt égaux, ou fort peu differents les vns des autres, ont coustume de se faire cette priere, & de se couurir tout ensemble. Toutes les remarques doc qui se sont faites icy de la bonne conduite, doiuent estre aussi entenduës de l'ordre qu'il faut tenir à prendre place, & à s'asseoir: car le plaisir que l'on prend aux ciuilitez & aux complimens, est tout à fait importun.

It is very impolite to ask a superior to be covered, as it is not to do so in the case of one with regard to whom it is proper. And the man who is in haste to put his hat on, especially in talking to a person of quality, or who, having been urged several times to do so, refuses, shocks good manners; for this reason, after the first or second request, it is allowable to put the hat on, unless in some province or kingdom where the usage is otherwise. In fact, amongst equals, or with those who are older, or who belong to religious orders, or domestics, it is allowable to grant that request to one's equal or to a younger man, at the very first time. However, those of equal rank, or between whom there is little difference of rank, usually make the request and put on their hats at the same time. All the remarks here made on polite conduct, must also be extended to the order to be observed in taking places, and in sitting down; for the pleasure taken in ceremonies and compliments is really irksome.

28TH. IF ANY ONE COME TO SPEAK TO YOU WHILE YOU ARE SITTING STAND UP THO HE BE YOUR INFERIOUR, AND WHEN YOU PRESENT SEATS LET IT BE TO EVERY ONE ACCORDING TO HIS DEGREE.

Chapter iii. 5. Si vous estes assis, lors que quelq'vn vous vient rendre visite, leuez-vous dés qu'il approche; si la dignité de la personne demande cette deference, comme s'il a quelque aduantage sur vous, s'il vous est égal, ou inferieur; mais non pas fort familier. Si vous vous reposez chez vous, ayant quelque siege, faites en soite de traiter chacun selõ son merite.

If you are sitting down when any one pays you a call rise as soon as he comes near; whether his position demands that deference, as having precedence over you, or if he be your equal, or inferior; but not if he is on very intimate terms with you. If you are in your own house, having any seat to offer, manage to treat each guest according to his station.

29TH. WHEN YOU MEET WITH ONE OF GREATER QUALITY THAN YOURSELF, STOP, AND RETIRE ESPECIALLY IF IT BE AT A DOOR OR ANY STRAIGHT PLACE TO GIVE WAY FOR HIM TO PASS

Chapter iii. 6. Quand vous rencontrez des personnes à qui vous deuez du respect, outre les devoirs d'vne salutation ordinaire, vous estes obligé de vous arrester quelque peu de temps, ou de rebrousser chemin jusqu'à l'entrée des portes, ou aux coins des ruës, pour leur donner passage.

[Sidenote: Walker says, "If you meet a superior in a narrow way, stop, and press to make him more room."]

In meeting those to whom you should shew respect beyond the salutations which are their due, you should stop a little, or retreat to a threshold, or to the corner of the street, so as to make way for them.

30TH. IN WALKING THE HIGHEST PLACE IN MOST COUNTRYS SEEMS TO BE ON THE RIGHT HAND THEREFORE PLACE YOURSELF ON THE LEFT OF HIM WHOM YOU DESIRE TO HONOUR: BUT IF THREE WALK TOGETHER THE MIDDLE PLACE IS THE MOST HONOURABLE THE WALL IS USUALLY GIVEN TO THE MOST WORTHY IF TWO WALK TOGETHER.

Chapter iii. 7. S'il arriue que vous faciez la promenade auec eux, vous leur laisserez tousiours la place hõnorable, qui est celle qui sera marquée par l'vsage. A parler generalemet, il semble que plusieurs Nations ont passé en coustume que la droite soit tenuë pour vne marque de reuerence, de telle soit, que quand quelq'vn veut deferer à un autre, il le mette à sa droicte, en prenant sa gauche. Lors que trois hommes se promenent ensemble, le plus qualifié a tousiours le milieu: Celuy qui tient la droite, a le second lieu, & l'autre qui reste à la gauche, n'a que le troisiéme. Mais en France, quand l'on se promene au long d'vn mur; par ce que ce lieu est presque toûjours plus eleué & plus net à cause de sa pente, la coûtume porte presque par tout qu'elle soit laissée au plus qualifié, & particulieremet quand deux personnes marchet ensemble.

If you happen to take a walk with them, always give them the place of honour, which is that pointed out by usage. To speak generally, it appears that several nations have made it a custom that the right should always be held as a mark of esteem, so that, when any one wishes to honour another, he will put him on his right, himself taking the left. When three are walking together, he of the highest quality always has the middle: he who takes the right has the second place, and the other who remains on the left has the third. But in France, when walking by the side of a wall, that place being almost always higher and cleaner because of the slope, the custom almost always is that it be yielded to the man of the highest quality, and particularly when two are walking together.

31ST. IF ANY ONE FAR SURPASSES OTHERS, EITHER IN AGE ESTATE, OR MERIT [YET, IN ANY PARTICULAR INSTANCE,] WOULD GIVE PLACE TO A MEANER THAN HIMSELF [IN HIS OWN HOUSE OR ELSEWHERE] THE ONE OUGHT NOT TO EXCEPT IT, SO [THE OTHER, FOR FEAR OF MAKING HIM APPEAR UNCIVIL, OUGHT NOT TO PRESS] IT ABOVE ONCE OR TWICE.

Chapter iii. 9. Si celuy qui se trouuera beaucoup plus avancé en âge, ou auantagé en dignité, soit en sa maison ou en quelqu'autre lieu, veut honorer son inferieur, comme il n'est pas à propos que cet inferieur s'en estime digne, de mesme aussi ne faut-il pas que celuy qui est superieur, l'en presse auec trop de soin, ou luy témoigne sa deference plus d'vne ou deux fois, de crainte que l'assiduité de sa supplication reïterée ne rabatte quelque chose de la boñe opinion que celuy qui le refuse, avoit cõceu de son addresse & de sa courtoisie, ou qu'il luy fasse commettre enfin une inciuilité.

If he who is much the older, or has the advantage of rank, wishes, in his house or elsewhere, to honour his inferior, as it is not fitting that such inferior should think himself worthy, so also the superior must not press him too much or show such deference more than once or twice, lest the assiduity of his reiterated requests lower somewhat the good opinion which he who refuses, had conceived of his tact and courtesy, or lest, at last, it cause him to be guilty of some incivility.

32D. TO ONE THAT IS YOUR EQUAL, OR NOT MUCH INFERIOR YOU ARE TO GIVE THE CHIEF PLACE IN YOUR LODGING AND HE TO WHO, 'TIS OFFERED OUGHT AT THE FIRST TO REFUSE IT BUT AT THE SECOND TO ACCEPT THOUGH NOT WITHOUT ACKNOWLEDGING HIS OWN UNWORTHINESS.

Chapter iii. 10. Mais entre les égaux, il est bien à propos en receuant quelqu'vn dans sa maison, de luy donner la place la plus honnorable. Et celuy à qui l'on fait un si bon accueil, en doit faire quelque refus d'abord, mais à la seconde instance de son amy, il luy doit obeyr.

[Sidenote: Maxim iii. 8, which says that acceptance of a first place should be accompanied by an acknowledgement of unworthiness, is represented in the last words of Rule 32.]

But amongst equals, it is quite right, in receiving any one into one's house, to give him the most honourable place; and the person to whom one accords such a good reception ought at first rather to refuse it, but, when his friend insists a second time, he ought to obey him.

33D. THEY THAT ARE IN DIGNITY OR IN OFFICE HAVE IN ALL PLACES PRECEEDENCY BUT WHILST THEY ARE YOUNG THEY OUGHT TO RESPECT THOSE THAT ARE THEIR EQUALS IN BIRTH OR OTHER QUALITYS, THOUGH THEY HAVE NO PUBLICK CHARGE.

Chapter iii. 12. A ceux qui ont le cõmandement, & qui sont dans le pouuoir, ou qui exercent les Charges de Judicature, l'on donne tousiours les premieres places en toute sorte de compagnie. Mais qu'ils sçachent eux-mesmes que s'ils sont jeunes, ils sont obligez de respecter ceux qui sont d'aussi noble maison qu'eux, on qui les deuancent de beaucoup en âge, & sont honorez du degré de Doctorat; quoy qu'ils n'exercent aucune charge publique; Et bien plus, ils leur doiuent d'abord remettre la premiere place qu'il leur auoient deferé, & en suitte auec modestie, receuoir cest honneur comme une grace.

In every company the first place is always given to those in command, or in power, or who exercise judicial charges. But these, if young, should realise that they ought to respect those who belong to houses as noble as their own, or who are much older, and those honoured with the degree of Doctor, though not exercising any public function; and moreover they ought, at first, to return an offer of the highest place, and afterwards receive that honour modestly, as a favour.

34TH. IT IS GOOD MANNERS TO PREFER THEM TO WHOM WE SPEAK BEFORE OURSELVES ESPECIALLY IF THEY BE ABOVE US WITH WHOM IN NO SORT WE OUGHT TO BEGIN.

[Sidenote: The second clause is not in the French Maxims.]

Chapter iii. 13. Il est de la derniere ciuilité de parler tousiours mieux de ceux auec qui nous avons à conuerser, que de vous mesmes: Et particulieremet quãd ce sont des personnes éleuées audessus de nous, auec qui il ne faut iamais contester en aucune maniere.

It is the height of politeness always to speak better of those with whom we have to converse than of ourselves. And particularly when they are persons of a superior rank to ourselves, with whom we ought never to dispute in any fashion.

[Sidenote: Compare the last clause of this Maxim with Rule 40.]

35TH. LET YOUR DISCOURSE WITH MEN OF BUSINESS BE SHORT AND COMPREHENSIVE.

Chapter iii. 15. Le temps & le lieu, l'âge & la difference des personnes doivent regler tout cét vsage de compliments qui se fait parmy les plus polis, & particulierement ceux qui consistent dans les paroles. Mais l'on doit trancher court auec les personnes affairées & ne leur presenter plus aux nez toutes ses agreables fleurettes: il les faut épargner, & se faire entendre plustost par mines, qu'auec des paroles.

Time and place, age and the difference between persons, ought to regulate the whole custom of compliments as is done amongst the most polite, especially compliments that consist in words. But one should cut matters short with men of business, and not put one's fine flowerets under their nose; one should spare them, and make himself understood rather by looks than words.

36TH. ARTIFICERS & PERSONS OF LOW DEGREE OUGHT NOT TO USE MANY CEREMONIES TO LORDS, OR OTHERS OF HIGH DEGREE BUT RESPECT AND HIGHLY HONOUR THEM, AND THOSE OF HIGH DEGREE OUGHT TO TREAT THEM WITH AFFIBILITY & COURTESIE, WITHOUT ARROGANCY

Chapter iii. 16. Comme le soin de la ciuilité la plus raffinée ne doit pas beaucoup trauailler les esprits des Artisants & de la lie du peuple enuers les Grands & les Magistrats; aussi est-il raisonnable qu'ils ayent soin de leur rendre de l'honneur: de mesme il est à propos que la Noblesse les traitte [*sic*] doucement & les épargne, & qu'elle éuite toute sorte de superbe.

As the care for the most refined politeness ought not to trouble much the minds of artizans and of the dregs of the people, as regards Nobles and Magistrates, while it is reasonable that they should take care to honour such, so it is also right that the nobility should treat them gently, spare them, and avoid all manner of arrogance.

37TH. IN SPEAKING TO MEN OF QUALITY DO NOT LEAN NOR LOOK THEM FULL IN THE FACE, NOR APPROACH TOO NEAR THEM AT LEST KEEP A FULL PACE FROM THEM.

Chapter iii. 18. En parlant aux personnes qualifiées, ne vous appuyez point le corps; ne leuez point vos yeux iusques sur leur visage; ne vous en approchez pas trop prés, & faites en sorte que ce ne soit iamais qu'à vn grãd pas de distance.

In speaking to persons of quality, do not lean your body on any thing; do not raise your eyes to their face; do not go too near, and manage to keep a full step from them.

38TH. IN VISITING THE SICK, DO NOT PRESENTLY PLAY THE PHYSICION IF YOU BE NOT KNOWING THEREIN.

Chapter iii. 19. Quãd vous visiterez quelque malade, ne faites pas aussi-tost le Medicin, si vous n'estes point experimenté en cette science.

When you go to see any sick person do not immediately act the physician if you are not experienced in that science.

39TH. IN WRITING OR SPEAKING, GIVE TO EVERY PERSON HIS DUE TITLE ACCORDING TO HIS DEGREE & THE CUSTOM OF THE PLACE.

Chapter iii. 20. Lors que vous addresserez des lettres à des personnes qui seront dans l'estime publique; vous vous gouuernerez aupres d'eux, selon la coustume du pays & le degré de leur dignité. Quand vous aurez acheué vos lettres, relisez-les, pour en oster les fautes; mettez de la poudre sur l'escriture, lors qu'il en sera besoin & ne pliez iamais vostre papier que les characteres ne soient bien desechez, de crainte qu'ils ne s'effacent.

In addressing letters to persons held in public esteem, you will be regulated by the customs of the country and the degree of their dignity. When you have finished your letters, read them over again so as to correct mistakes; sand the writing, when necessary, and never fold your paper until the letters are quite dry, lest they be effaced.

40TH. STRIVE NOT WITH YOUR SUPERIERS IN ARGUMENT, BUT ALWAYS SUBMIT YOUR JUDGMENT TO OTHERS WITH MODESTY

Hawkins ii. 20. Strive not with thy Superiours, in argument or discourse, but alwayes submit thy opinion to their riper judgment, with modesty; since the possibility of Erring, doth rather accompany greene than gray hairs.

41ST. UNDERTAKE NOT TO TEACH YOUR EQUAL IN THE ART HIMSELF PROFESSES; IT FLAVOURS OF ARROGANCY.

Hawkins ii. 21. Doe not undertake to teach thy equal, in the Art himself professeth, for that will savour of Arrogancy, and serve for little other than to brand thy judgment with Rashnesse.

(Nothing has been found in the French Maxims resembling Rule 41. Walker has the following: "Cautious also must be he who discourseth even of that he understands amongst persons of that profession: an affectation that more Scholars than wise men are guilty of; I mean to discourse with every man in his own faculty; except it be by asking questions and seeming to learn" (p. 266)).

[42D. LET YOUR CEREMONIES IN] CURTESIE BE PROPER TO THE DIGNITY OF HIS PLACE [WITH WHOM YOU CONVERSE; IT IS ABSURD TO AC]T YE SAME WITH A CLOWN AND A PRINCE.

Hawkins ii. 22. Let thy Seremonyes in Courtesy be proper to the dignity and place, of him with whom thou conversest. For it is absurd to honour a Clown with words courtly and of magnificence.

43D. DO NOT EXPRESS JOY BEFORE ONE SICK OR IN PAIN FOR THAT CONTRARY PASSION WILL AGGRAVATE HIS MISERY

Hawkins ii. 23. Do not thou expresse joy before one sick, or in paine; for that contrary passion, will aggravate his misery. But do thou rather sympathize his infirmityes, for that will afford a gratefull easement, by a seeming participation.

44TH. WHEN A MAN DOES ALL HE CAN THOUGH IT SUCCEEDS NOT WELL BLAME NOT HIM THAT DID IT.

Chapter iv. 3. Celui qui fait tout ce qui luy est possible, pour auancer vostre affaire, quoy qu'il ne la meine pas, & n'en puisse auoir le succez cõme vous l'esperez, ne doit point entendre de reprimãde; puis qu'il est plus digne de loüange que de blâme.

The man who does all he can to advance your business, even though he should not bring it about, and may not be able to obtain the success you hoped for, ought not to hear reproaches, since he is more worthy of praise than of blame.

45TH. BEING TO ADVISE OR REPREHEND ANY ONE, CONSIDER WHETHER IT OUGHT TO BE IN PUBLICK OR IN PRIVATE; PRESENTLY, OR AT SOME

OTHER TIME IN WHAT TERMS TO DO IT & IN REPROVING SHEW NO SIGNS OF CHOLAR BUT DO IT WITH ALL SWEETNESS AND MILDNESS

[Sidenote: Hawkins has only "sweetness," Washington being here closer to the French.]

Chapter iv. 4. Si vous auez à exhorter ou reprendre quelqu'vn, prenez bien garde, s'il est plus à propos de le faire en particulier ou en public, en ce temps ou en vn autre, bien plus, quelles paroles vous y deuez employer: Et particulierement lors que quelqu'vn ayãt esté desia reprimãdé d'autres fois, ne se corrige point des fautes passées, & ne promet point d'amandement. Et soit que vous donniez quelques auis, ou que vous fassiez quelque reprimande, donnez-vous de garde de vous mettre en cholere, au contraire pratiquez ces actions auec moderation & douceur.

If you have to exhort or to reproach any one, consider whether it be better to do so in private or in public; at this time or another and, above all, what words you should use: and particularly when some one having been already reprimanded at other times does not correct himself of his past faults, and does not promise any amendment. And if you give any advice, or impart any reprimand, carefully avoid anger; on the contrary, do such acts with moderation and sweetness.

46TH. TAKE ALL ADMONITIONS THANKFULLY IN WHAT TIME OR PLACE SOEVER GIVEN BUT AFTERWARDS NOT BEING CULPABLE TAKE A TIME OR PLACE CONVENIENT TO LET HIM KNOW IT THAT GAVE THEM.

Chapter iv. 5. Aussi quiconque se donnera la peine de vous remonstrer de quelque façõ, en quelque lieu, & en quelque temps qu'il le fasse, qu'il soit écouté de vostre part auec beaucoup de ressentiment de bienueillance & de reconnoissance. Et apres cela, si vous vous sentez innocent, & qu'il vous semble à propos de vous prouuer tel, il vous sera bien permis de le faire; mais auec ce soin de predre bien vostre temps, & plustost pour luy en faire voir la verité, & le tirer de peine, & plus si vous estes en sa charge, ou si vous releuez de son pouuoir, que pour vous appuyer de quelque excuse.

Also when any one takes the trouble to rebuke you, no matter how, where, or when he does it, hear him for your part with much feeling of goodwill and acknowledgment. And after that, if innocent, and it seems right to prove yourself so, you will be quite at liberty to do so; being careful, however, to choose a proper time, and rather to make him see the truth, and relieve him from anxiety—the more if you are in his charge or depend on his authority—than to defend yourself with some excuse.

[4]7TH. MOCK NOT NOR JEST AT ANYTHING OF IMPORTANCE BREAK NO JEST THAT ARE SHARP BITING, AND IF YOU DELIVER ANYTHING WITTY AND PLEASENT ABTAIN FROM LAUGHING THEREAT YOURSELF.

Chapter iv. 7. Ne vous amusez point aux equiuoques ny en matiere importante, ny en choses honteuses. Si vous trouuez bon de railler, gardez vous bien de mordre, & bien plus de déchirer comme un chien. Que les bons-mots & les rencontres soient tirées du suiet, que les vns & les autres ayent leur gentillesse & leur pointe, sans attirer l'indignation de personne. Que les plaisãteries ne soient point comme celles des bouffons, qui font rire par des representations extrauagãtes, & des actions deshonnestes: si vous rencontrez ioliment, si vous donnez quelque bon-mot, en faisant rire les autres, empeschez-vous-en, le plus qu'il vous sera possible.

Do not divert yourself with *equivoques*, either in important or in mean matters. If you find good occasion for a joke, be careful not to bite, still less to tear, like a dog. Witticisms and repartee should be to the point, and should have elegance and appropriateness without exciting the indignation of any. Do not let your pleasantries degenerate into those of buffoons, who raise laughter by extravagant representations and indecent action. If you are clever in repartee, if you say a good thing, manage if possible, in making others laugh, to abstain from it yourself.

48TH. WHEREIN YOU REPROVE ANOTHER BE UNBLAMEABLE YOURSELF; FOR EXAMPLE IS IS MORE PREVALENT THAN PRECEPTS

Hawkins iii. 8. Be sure thy conversation be in that poynt vertuous, wherein thou art desirous to retaine another, least thy Actions render thy advice unprofitable. Since the ratification of any advice is the serious prosecution of that vertue. For example hath ever been more prevalent than precept.

49TH. USE NO REPROACHFULL LANGUAGE AGAINST ANY ONE NEITHER CURSE NOR REVILE

Hawkins iii. 11. Use no reproachfull language against any man, nor Curse, or Revile. For improperations and imprecations will rather betray thy affections than in any manner, hurt him against whom thou utters them.

[5]0th. Be not hasty to believe flying Reports to the Disparagement of any

Hawkins iii. 10. Thou oughtest not too suddenly to believe a flying Rumour of a friend, or any other. But let charity guid thy judgment, untill more certainty: for by this meanes thou securest his Reputation, and frees thy self of rashness.

51st. Wear not your Cloths, foul, unript or Dusty but See they be Brush'd once every day at least and take heed that you approach not to any Uncleanness

Chapter v. 4. Que vos habits ne demeurent point sales, déchirez, couuerts de poussiere, ou pelez. Qu'ils soient tous les iours du moins vne fois nettoyez auec les époussettes. Et prenez bien garde aussi en quel lieu vous vous assoirez, où vous vous mettrez à genoux, où vous vous accouderez, que le lieu ne soit point malpropre, ny reply d'immondices. Ne portez point le manteau sur le bras, à l'imitation des Fanfarons. Et mettant bas ou vostre robbe, ou vôtre mãteau, pliez les bien proprement & adroitement, & prenez bien garde où vous les posez.

Do not let your clothes be dirty, torn, covered with dust or threadbare. Have them brushed at least once a day. And take care also in what place you sit down, or kneel, or rest your elbows, that it be not unfit or filthy. Do not carry your cloak over your arm after the manner of swaggerers. And when you take off your coat or cloak, fold them neatly and carefully, and take care where you put them.

52nd. In your Apparel be Modest and endeavour to accomodate Nature, rather than to procure Admiration keep to the Fashion of your equals Such as are Civil and orderly with respect to Times and Places

[Sidenote: "Accomodate nature" is a phrase from a precept in Hawkins concerning apparel.]

Chapter v. 5. Choisissez tousiours des habits semblables à ceux de vos compagnons qui passent pour les plus honnestes & moderez, en considerant les lieux & les temps auec discretion: & outre cela, faites qu'en ce poinct vous paroissiez souhaitter d'estre vestu le plus simplement & modestement de tous vos égaux, bien plustost que d'affecter les plus beaux vestements.

Always choose clothes like those of your companions who pass for the most genteel and moderate, in discreet consideration of time and place: and more, make it a point to be the most simply and modestly dressed of all your equals, rather than to affect the finest raiment.

53d. Run not in the Streets, neither go too slowly nor with Mouth open go not Shaking y'r Arms [stamping, or shuffling; nor pull up your stockings in the street. Walk] not upon the toes, nor in a Dancing [or skipping manner, nor yet with measured steps. Strike not the heels together, nor stoop when there is no occasion]

Chapter vi. 1. Faites en sorte quand vous marchez, de ne pas faire des démarches precipitées, d'auoir la bouche ouuerte & comme beante, & de ne vous trop demener le corps, ou le pancher, ou laisser vos mains pendantes, ou remuer & secoüer les bras; sans frapper trop rudement la terre, ou letter à vos pieds de part & d'autre. Cette sorte d'action demande encore ces conditions, que l'on ne s'arreste pas à retirer ses chausses en haut, dans le chemin, que l'on ne marche sur les extremitez des pieds, ny en sautillant ou s'eleuant, comme il se pratique en la dance, que l'on ne courbe point le corps, que l'on ne baisse point la teste, qne l'on n'auance point à pas cõptez, que l'on ne se choque point les talons l'un contre l'autre en entrant dans l'Eglise, que l'on ne reste point teste nuë a la sortie. Si la deuotion n'y oblige, comme lors qu'il est question d'accompagner le Tres-sainct Sacrement.

In walking guard against hurried steps, or having your mouth open and gaping; and do not move your body too much, or stoop, or let your hands hang down, or move and shake your arms; walk without striking the ground too hard or throwing your feet this way and that. That sort of action also demands these conditions—not to stop to pull up one's stockings in the street, not to walk on the toes, or in a skipping rising as in dancing; do not stoop, nor bend the head; do not advance with measured steps; do not strike the heels against each other on entering church, nor leave it bareheaded, unless devotion requires it, as in accompanying the Holy Sacrament.

54th. Play not the Peacock, looking everywhere about you, to See if you be well Deck't, if your Shoes fit well if your Stockings Sit neatly, and Cloths handsomely.

Chapter vi. 2. Ne vous amusez pas à vous quarer comme vn Paon, & regarder superbement autour de vous, si vous estes bien mis, & bien chaussé, si vos hautsdechausses & vos autres habits vous sont bienfaits. Ne sortez point de vostre chãbre, portant vostre plume à vostre bouche, ou sur vostre aureille. Ne vous amusez pas à mettre des fleurs à vos aureilles, à vostre bonnet, ou à vostre chappeau. Ne tenez point vostre mouchoir à la main, ou pendu à vostre bouche, ny à vostre ceinture, ny sous vostre aiselle, ny sur vostre espaule, ou caché sous vostre robbe. Mettez-le en lieu d'où il ne puisse être veu, & il puisse estre toutesfois cõmodément tiré, dez qu'il en sera besoin. Ne le presentez iamais à personne, s'il n'est tout blanc, ou presque pas deployé.

Do not delight in strutting like a peacock, or look proudly around to see if you are well decked, if your breeches and other clothes fit well. Do not leave your room carrying your pen in your mouth or behind your ear. Do not indulge yourself by putting flowers in your ears, cap, or hat. Do not hold your pocket-handkerchief in your hand, hanging from your mouth, at your girdle, under your armpit, on your shoulder, or stuffed under your coat. Put it in some place where it cannot be seen, but from whence you may easily draw it when you want it. Never offer it to anybody unless it be quite clean, or hardly unfolded.

55TH. EAT NOT IN THE STREETS, NOR IN YE HOUSE, OUT OF SEASON.

Chapter vi. 3. Ne marchez jamais par les chemins, en mangeant, soit seul ou en compagnie, & particulierement parmy la foule de la ville. Ne vous mettez pas mesme à manger en la maison hors de temps du repas, & du moins abstenez vous en, quand il s'y rencontrera quelqu'vn.

Never walk on the roads eating, whether alone or in company, especially amid the crowd in a town. Do not set to eating even in the house out of meal-times; at least abstain from it in the presence of others.

56TH. ASSOCIATE YOURSELF WITH MEN OF GOOD QUALITY IF YOU ESTEEM YOUR OWN REPUTATION; FOR 'TIS BETTER TO BE ALONE THAN IN BAD COMPANY.

Chapter vi. 5. Et si vous voulez passer pour honneste, accostez vous tousiours des Gents-de-bien, si vous n'en trouuez pas la commodité, ou par ce que vous n'en connoissez point, ou pour quelqu'autre raison, il vaut tousiours mieux que vous alliez seul, qu'en mauuaise compagnie.

If you wish to pass as genteel, always go with well-bred people; if you cannot get the chance—from not knowing any, or any other reason—it is always better to go alone than in bad company.

57TH. IN WALKING UP AND DOWN IN A HOUSE, ONLY WITH ONE IN COMPANY IF HE BE GREATER THAN YOURSELF, AT THE FIRST GIVE HIM THE RIGHT HAND AND STOP NOT TILL HE DOES AND BE NOT THE FIRST THAT TURNS, AND WHEN YOU DO TURN LET IT BE WITH YOUR FACE TOWARDS HIM, IF HE BE A MAN OF GREAT QUALITY, WALK NOT WITH HIM CHEEK BY JOWL BUT SOMEWHAT BEHIND HIM; BUT YET IN SUCH A MANNER THAT HE MAY EASILY SPEAK TO YOU.

Chapter vi. 7. Si vous promenez auec vne personne seule dans la maison, & qu'il soit d'vne conditiõ qui luy fasse meriter quelque deference, dés le premier pas de la promenade, ne manquez pas de luy donner la droite: Ne cessez point de marcher, s'il ne vient à s'arrester: Ne changez pas le premier le diuertissement, & en vous tournant, ne luy montrez iamais les épaules; mais tousiours le visage. Si elle est dans vne charge releuée, gardez bien de marcher d'vn pas tout à fait égal; mais suiuez tant soit peu derriere, auec tant de iustesse pourtant & de moderatiõ, qu'elle vous puisse bien parler sans s'incõmoder. Si elle vous est égale allez d'un mesme pas tout le long de la promenade, & ne tournez pas tovsiours le premier, à chaque bout de champ; ne faites pas si souuent des pauses au milieu du chemin sans suiet. Car cette liberté ressent sa grandeur & donne du mécontentement. Celuy qui tient le milieu dans vne compagnie dont il est enuironné, si ceux qui la composent, sont égaux, ou presque égaux, il se doit tourner vne fois à droit dans la promenade, & s'ils se rencontrent notablement inegaux, il se doit plus souuent tourner vers le plus qualifié. Enfin que ceux qui l'enuironnent, viennent tousiours à se détourner de son costé & en mesme temps que luy, non point deuant ny apres; puis qu'il est comme le but de la promenade.

[Sidenote: The repetition of the feminine "Elle" refers to 'vne personne,' in the first line, although the masculine ('qu'il' and 's'il') has twice followed it. There is no allusion to the female sex in the French Maxims.]

If you are walking about the house alone with a person whose rank demands some deference, at the very first step be sure and give him the right hand: Do not stop walking if he does not wish to stop: Be not the first to change the diversion, and, in turning, never show him your shoulder but always your face. If he has a high public appointment take care not to walk quite side by side with him but a very little behind him with so much exactness and moderation that he may be able to speak to you without inconvenience. If he is your equal in rank, keep step with him during the whole walk, and do not always turn first at every end of the walk. Do not stop often midway without reason, such liberty touches his dignity and gives dissatisfaction. He who is the centre of the company by whom he is surrounded ought, if those of whom it consists are equal or nearly equal in rank, always to turn to the right once during the walk, and if they are manifestly unequal, he should oftenest turn towards the most distinguished. Lastly those who are about him should always turn round towards his side and at the same time as he, neither before nor after, as he is, so to say, the object of the walk.

58TH. LET YOUR CONVERSATION BE WITHOUT MALICE OR ENVY, FOR 'TIS A SIGN OF A TRACTABLE AND COMMENDABLE NATURE: & IN ALL CAUSES OF PASSION ADMIT REASON TO GOVERN

Hawkins v. 9. Let thy conversation be without malice or envye, for that is a signe of a tractable and commendable nature. And in all causes of passion, admit reason for thy governesse. So shall thy Reputation be either altogether inviolable, or at the least not stayned with common Tinctures.

59TH. NEVER EXPRESS ANYTHING UNBECOMING, NOR ACT AGAINST THE RULES MORAL BEFORE YOUR INFERIOURS

Hawkins v. 10. Never expresse any thing unbeseeming, nor act against the Rules morall, before thy inferiours, For in these things, thy own guilt will multiply Crimes by example, and as it were, confirme Ill by authority.

[Sidenote: Walker: "A man should not divertise himself with his Inferiors, nor make his Servants privy to his infirmities and failures."]

60TH. BE NOT IMMODEST IN URGING YOUR FRIENDS TO DISCOVER A SECRET

Hawkins v. 11. Be not immodest in urging thy friend to discover his secrets; lest an accidentall discovery of them work a breach in your amitye.

61ST. UTTER NOT BASE AND FRIVILOUS THINGS AMONGST GRAVE AND LEARN'D MEN NOR VERY DIFFICULT QUESTIONS OR SUBJECTS, AMONG THE IGNORANT OR THINGS HARD TO BE BELIEVED, STUFF NOT YOUR DISCOURSE WITH SENTENCES AMONGST YOUR BETTERS NOR EQUALS

[Sidenote: Hawkins uses the word "Farce" instead of "Stuff."]

Chapter vii. 1. Dans la conuersation de Gents doctes & habiles ne debitez pas des bagatelles, & n'auancez pas des discours trop releuez parmy les ignorants, qu'ils ne soient point capables d'entendre, ou qu'ils ne puissent pas croire fort facilement. Ne debutez pas toûjours par des prouerbes, particulierement parmy vos égaux, & bien moins auec vos superieurs. Ne parlez point de choses à cõtreteps, ou qui puissent choquer les esprits de vos auditeurs. Parmy les banquets, & dans les iours de resioüissance ne mettez point sur le tapis de tristes nouuelles, point de recits de rudes calamitez, point d'ordures, point de deshõnestetez, point d'afflictions. Bien au cõtraire si tels discours se trouuent entamez par quelqu'autre, faites vostre possible pour en détourner adroictement la suitte. Ne contez iamais vos songes qu'à de vos confidents, & encore que ce soit pour profiter de leur interpretation; vous gardant bien d'y donner aucune croyance.

When talking with learned and clever men, do not introduce trifles, and do not bring forward too advanced conversation before ignorant people which they cannot understand nor easily believe. Do not always begin with proverbs, especially among your equals, and still less with your superiors. Do not speak of things out of place, or of such as may shock your hearers. At banquets and on days of rejoicing do not bring up sorrowful news or accounts of sad calamities, no filth, nothing improper, nothing afflicting. On the contrary, if such conversation is begun by any one else, do your best adroitly to turn the subject. Never relate your dreams except to your confidants, and then only to profit by their interpretation, taking care not to put the least belief in it.

[Sidenote: Walker says—"nor tell your dreams when perhaps your best waking actions are not worth the reciting."]

62D. Speak not of doleful Things in a Time of Mirth or at the Table; Speak not of Melancholy Things as Death and Wounds, and if others Mention them Change if you can the Discourse tell not your Dreams, but to your intimate Friend

(The substance of Rule 62 is in the French Maxim quoted under the previous Rule (61), beginning with the third sentence, "Ne parlez point, etc.")

63D. A Man ought not to value himself of his Atchievements or rare Qua[lities, his Riches, Tit]les Virtue or Kindred[; but he need not speak meanly of himself.]

Chapter vii. 2. Vne personne bien nourrie ne s'amuse iamais à faire parade de ses belles actions, de son esprit, de sa vertu, & de ses autres bonnes & loüables qualitez, au cõtraire il ne faut iamais s'entretenir auec les autres de sa haute naissance, ou de la Noblesse de ses parents, de ses richesses, ny de ses grandeurs, si l'on n'y est contrainct. Il ne faut pas aussi se raualler entierement.

A well-bred person never makes parade of his good actions, wit, virtue, and other good and praiseworthy qualities; on the contrary, one ought never to speak with another about his high birth, the nobility of his parents, his wealth or dignities, unless obliged to do so. But one need not efface himself altogether.

64TH. BREAK NOT A JEST WHERE NONE TAKE PLEASURE IN MIRTH LAUGH NOT ALOUD, NOR AT ALL WITHOUT OCCASION, DERIDE NO MAN'S MISFORTUNE, THO' THERE SEEM TO BE SOME CAUSE

Chapter vii. 3. Il ne faut pas se mettre sur la raillerie, quãd il n'est point temps de solastrer. Gardez-vous bien d'éclater en risées, d'y passer les bornes de la bienseance, & de le faire sans un suiet raisonnable, pour suiure l'inclinatiõ qui vous porte à rire. Ne prenez iamais suiet de rire du malheur d'autruy, quoy qu'il semble en quelque façon digne de risée.

Jesting must be avoided when it is out of season. Beware of bursting out into laughter, beyond the limits of decorum, and of doing so without reasonable cause, merely from an inclination to laugh. Never laugh at the misfortunes of others, although they seem in some sort laughable.

65TH. SPEAK NOT INJURIOUS WORDS NEITHER IN JEST NOR EARNEST SCOFF AT NONE ALTHOUGH THEY GIVE OCCASION

Chapter vii. 4. Ne donnez iamais de sobriquet, soit dans le jeu, ou bien hors du jeu. Gardez vous bien de picquer qui que ce puisse estre; ne vous mocquez d'aucune personne, particulierement d'entre celles qui sont qualifiées, quoy qu'auec occasion.

Never give nicknames, whether in fun or not. Take care not to hurt anybody, whoever it may be; do not mock any one, especially persons of distinction, although there be occasion.

66th. Be not forward but friendly and Courteous; the first to Salute hear and answer & be not Pensive when it's a time to converse.

Chapter vii. 5. Ne vous rendez point morne & de fâcheux abord; mais affable & prompt à rendre de bons offices, & soyez toûjours le premier à saluër. Entendez bien ce que l'on vous dit & y respondez; Ne vous retirez point à l'écart, quand le deuoir vous engage à la conversation.

Do not be glum and unfriendly of approach; but affable, prompt in rendering kind offices, and always the first to salute. Listen carefully to what is said and respond; do not keep aloof when duty requires you to take a share in the conversation.

67th. Detract not from others neither be excessive in Commending.

Chapter vii. 6. Gardez vous bien de medire d'aucune personne ou de vous entretenir des affaires d'autruy. Et mesme souuenez vous de garder la moderation dans vos loüanges.

Take care not to speak ill of any one or to gossip of other people's affairs. At the same time do not forget moderation in your praises.

[Sidenote: Walker says: "Carry even between adulation and soureness."]

(Dr. Toner thinks the last word of Rule 67 is written "Commanding." Sparks has "commending.")

68th. Go not thither, where you know not, whether you Shall be Welcome or not. Give not Advice whth being Ask'd & when desired do it briefly

Chapter vii. 7. Ne vous ingerez pas dans les entretiens & les consultations, où vous ne serez pas asseuré d'estre le bien venu. Ne dites iamais vostre aduis des affaires que l'on ne vous l'ait demandé, si toutesfois vous n'estes le premier en authorité, & que ce ne soit point à contre-temps, ou sans apparence de quelque auantage. Quand vous en estes prié, abregez vostre discours, & prenez de bonne heure le noeud de l'affaire à demesler.

Do not force yourself into interviews or consultations at which you are not sure of being welcome. Never give your advice on matters when it has not been asked, unless you happen to be the highest in authority; and do not let it be done out of place or without prospect of any benefit. When your opinion is requested, be brief, and reach quickly the knot of the matter under discussion.

69TH. IF TWO CONTEND TOGETHER TAKE NOT THE PART OF EITHER UNCONSTRAINED, AND BE NOT OBSTINATE IN YOUR OPINION, IN THINGS INDIFERENT BE OF THE MAJOR SIDE.

Chapter vii. 8. Si deux personnes out quelque chose à decider ensemble, ne prenez le party ny de l'vn, ny de l'autre, si quelque grãde raison ne vous y oblige. Ne soustenez pas vos sentiments auec vne trop grande obstination. Dans les matieres où les opiniõs sont libres, prenez tousiours le party qui est le plus appuyé.

If two persons have anything to decide between themselves, do not take the part of either unless some pressing reason obliges you to do so. Do not maintain your ideas too obstinately. In matters in which opinions are free, always take the side which has the most support.

[Sidenote: Walker says: "Thrust not your self to be Moderator or Umpire in Controversies, till required"]

70TH. REPREHEND NOT THE IMPERFECTIONS OF OTHERS FOR THAT BELONGS TO PARENTS MASTERS AND SUPERIORS.

Chapter vii. 9. Ne faites pas le censeur & le juge des fautes d'autruy, car cela n'appartient qu'aux maistres, aux peres, & à ceux qui out quelque superiorité. Il vous est toutesfois permis de faire paroistre l'auersion que vous en cõceuez. Et vous pouuez bien quelquesfois dõner aduis avantageux au defaillants.

Do not be the censor and judge of other peoples' faults, for that only belongs to masters, fathers, and those who have some superiority. But it is nevertheless allowable for you to show an aversion you have conceived. And at times you may give advantageous advice to those who are in the wrong.

71ST. GAZE NOT AT THE MARKS OR BLEMISHES OF OTHERS AND ASK NOT HOW THEY CAME. WHAT YOU MAY SPEAK IN SECRET TO YOUR FRIEND DELIVER NOT BEFORE OTHERS

Chapter vii. 10. Ne vous amusez pas à considerer curieusement les defauts ou les taches, quoy que naturelles, particulierement si elles se rencontrent au visage, & ne vous enquerez pas d'où elles ont precedé. Ce que vous diriez bien volontiers en l'oreille à vn amy, doit estre conserué sous la clef du silece, lors que vous vous trouuez en cempagnie

Take no pleasure in examining curiously defects or blemishes, although natural, especially if they be in the face, nor enquire what they proceed from. What you would readily say in the ear of a friend ought to be preserved under the key of silence when you are in society.

72D. SPEAK NOT IN AN UNKNOWN TONGUE IN COMPANY BUT IN YOUR OWN LANGUAGE AND THAT AS THOSE OF QUALITY DO AND NOT AS Y'E VULGAR; SUBLIME MATTERS TREAT SERIOUSLY.

Chapter vii. 11. Ne vous seruez iamais en vos discours & n'employez vne langue qui ne vous est pas bien cognuë & familiere, si ce n'est en vne occasiõ bien pressante, pour donner plus clairement à connoistre vostre pensée. Parlez tousiours en la vostre maternelle & natale, non pas grossierement, comme la lie du peuple, ou les pauures chambrieres; mais comme les plus delicats & les plus gros Bourgeois, auec erudition & auec elegance. Et prenez à tâche d'obseruer en vos discours les regles de l'honnesteté & de la modestie; & vous gardez bien de ces contes vn peu trop libres; ne les faites ny en l'oreille d'vn autre, ny ne les poussez par jeu auec profusiõ. N'employez point de termes bas & raualez ou populaires en des matieres hautes & reluées.

In your conversation never use a language with which you are not thoroughly acquainted and familiar, unless in some very urgent case to render your idea more clearly. Always speak in your native and mother tongue, not coarsely like the dregs of the people, or poor chamber-maids, but like the most refined and well-to-do citizens, with erudition and elegance. And in your discourse take care to observe the rules of decorum and modesty, and be sure to avoid rather risky tales; do not whisper such to another, and do not indulge them too frequently in sport. Do not use low, base or vulgar expressions when treating of serious and sublime subjects.

73'D. THINK BEFORE YOU SPEAK PRONOUNCE NOT IMPERFECTLY NOR BRING OUT YOUR WORDS TOO HASTILY BUT ORDERLY AND DISTINCTLY

Chapter vii. 12. Ne vous mettez point à discourir, que vous ne vous y soyez bien preparé, & que vous n'ayez bien estudié vostre suiet. Dans l'entretien ordinaire, n'allez point chercher de periphrases, point de subtilitez, ny de figures. Ne confondez point vos paroles dans les coutumes d'vne langue trop brusque &

begayante; mais aussi, ne parlez pas si lentement, & à tant de reprises, que vous donniez de l'ennuy.

Do not begin speaking unless you are quite prepared, and have well studied your subject. In ordinary conversation do not seek periphrases, subtleties, or figures of speech. Do not let your words become confused by too abrupt or hesitating a delivery, and do not let your speech be so slow and broken as to become tedious.

74TH. WHEN ANOTHER SPEAKS BE ATTENTIVE YOUR SELF AND DISTURB NOT THE AUDIENCE IF ANY HESITATE IN HIS WORDS HELP HIM NOT NOR PROMPT HIM WITHOUT DESIRED, INTERRUPT HIM NOT, NOR ANSWER HIM TILL HIS SPEECH BE ENDED

[Sidenote: Hawkins: "If any drawl forth his words, help him not"]

Chapter vii. 13. Quand quelque autre parle, prenez garde de donner suiet à ses Auditeurs de s'en detourner; & pour vous, écoutez-le fauorablement & auec attention, sans destourner les yeux d'vn autre costé, ou vous arrester à quelqu'autre pensée. Si quelqu'vn a de la peine à tirer ses mots comme par force, ne vous amusez pas á luy en suggerer, pour faire paroistre quelque desir d'aider celuy qui parle, si'l ne vient à vous en prier, ou que le tout se passe dãs le particulier, & qu'encore cette persõne soit de vos plus intimes & familiers amis; & apres tout ne l'interrompez point, & ne luy repliquez en aucune maniere, iusques à ce que luy-mesme ait acheué.

When another person is speaking, beware of drawing off the attention of his hearers; and as for yourself, listen to him favourably and attentively, without turning your eyes aside or directing your thoughts elsewhere. If any one finds difficulty in expressing himself, do not amuse yourself by suggesting words to him, so as to show a desire to assist the speaker, unless he so requests, or you are quite in private, and the person is also one of your most intimate and familiar friends. Above all, do not interrupt him, and in nowise reply to him until he has finished.

[Sidenote: The later French book has: "It is not Civil when a Person of Quality hesitates or stops in his discourse for you to strike in, though with pretence of helping his memory."]

75TH. IN THE MIDST OF DISCOURSE ASK [NOT WHAT IT IS ABOUT], BUT IF YOU PERCEIVE ANY STOP BECAUSE OF [YOUR ARRIVAL, RATHER REQUEST THE

SPEAKER] TO PROCEED: IF A PERSON OF QUALITY COMES IN WHILE YOUR CONVERSING ITS HANDSOME TO REPEAT WHAT WAS SAID BEFORE

Chapter vii. 14. Quand vous arriuez sur la moitié de quelque discours, ne vous enquerez pas du suiet de l'entretien; car cela est trop hardy & ressent l'hõme d'authorité. Suppliez plûtost honnestement & courtoisement que l'on le poursuiue, si vous voyez qu'il se soit interrõpu à vostre arriuée, parquel que sorte de deference. Au contraire s'il suruient quelqu'vn, lors que vous parlerez, & particulierement si c'est vne personne qualifiée & de merite, il est de la bienseance de faire vne petite recapitulation de ce qui a esté auancé, & de poursuiure la deduction de tout le reste de la matiere.

[Sidenote: Hawkins: "It is seemely to make a little Epilogue and briefe collection of what thou deliveredst."]

If you arrive in the middle of any discussion, do not ask what it is about; for that is too bold and savours of one in authority. Rather ask, genteelly and courteously, that it may be continued, if you see that the speaker has paused on your arrival, out of civility. On the other hand, if any one comes whilst you are speaking, and particularly if it be a person of quality or of merit, it is in accordance with good manners to give a slight recapitulation of what has been advanced, and then carry out the deduction of all the rest of the matter.

76TH. WHILE YOU ARE TALKING, POINT NOT WITH YOUR FINGER AT HIM OF WHOM YOU DISCOURSE NOR APPROACH TOO NEAR HIM TO WHOM YOU TALK ESPECIALLY TO HIS FACE

Chapter vi. 17. Ne mõtrez point au doigt la personne dont vous parlez, & ne vous approchez point trop prés de celuy que vous entretenez, non plus que de son visage, à qui il faut toûjours porter quelque reuerence.

Do not point your finger at the person of whom you are speaking, and do not go too near any one with whom you are conversing, especially not near his face, which should always be held in some reverence.

77TH. TREAT WITH MEN AT FIT TIMES ABOUT BUSINESS & WHISPER NOT IN THE COMPANY OF OTHERS

Chapter vi. 18. Si vous auez vne affaire particuliere à communiquer a l'vne de deux personnes ou de plusieurs qui s'entretiennent ensemble, expediez en trois mots, & ne luy dites pas en l'oreille ce que vous auez à proposer; mais si la chose est secrette, tirez-la tant soit peu à l'écart, s'il vous est possible, & que rien ne vous en empesche; parlez luy en la langue que les assistants entendent.

If you have any particular matter to communicate to one of two persons or of several, who are talking together, finish it off in three words, and do not whisper in his ear what you have to say; if the matter be secret, take him aside a little, if possible, and nothing prevents; speak to him in the language which those present understand.

78TH. MAKE NO COMPARISONS AND IF ANY OF THE COMPANY BE COMMENDED FOR ANY BRAVE ACT OF VIRTUE, COMMEND NOT ANOTHER FOR THE SAME

Chapter vii. 21. Abstenez vous de faire des comparaisons des personnes l'vne auec l'autre; Et partant si l'on donne des loüanges à quelqu'vn pour vne bonne action, ou pour sa vertu, gardez vous bien de loüer la mesme vertu en quelque autre. Car toute comparaison se trouue odieuse.

Abstain from drawing comparisons between different persons; and if any one is praised for a good action, or for his virtue, do not praise another for the same. For all comparisons are odious.

79TH. BE NOT APT TO RELATE NEWS IF YOU KNOW NOT THE TRUTH THEREOF. IN DISCOURSING OF THINGS YOU HAVE HEARD NAME NOT YOUR AUTHOR ALWAYS A SECRET DISCOVER NOT

Chapter vii. 22. Ne faites pas aisément dessein de redire aux autres les nouuelles & les rapports qui aurõt couru touchant les rencontres des affaires, si vous n'auez vn garant de leur verité. Et ne vous amusez pas en racontant ces vau-de-villes, d'en citer l'Autheur, que vous ne soyez bien asseuré qu'il ne le trouuera pas mauuais. Gardez tousiours bien le secret qui vous a esté confié & ne le ditez à personne, de crainte qu'il ne soit diuulgué.

Be not apt to relate rumours of events, if you know not their truth. And in repeating such things do not mention your authority, unless you are sure he will like it. Always keep the secret confided to you; tell it to no one, lest it be divulged.

[Sidenote: The later French book says: "Discover not the secret of a friend, it argues a shallow understanding and a weakness."]

80TH. BE NOT TEDIOUS IN DISCOURSE OR IN READING UNLESS YOU FIND THE COMPANY PLEASED THEREWITH

Chapter vii. 23. Si vous racontez, ou lisez, ou entreprenez d'en prouuer par raisonnements quoy que ce soit, tranchez-le-court, & particulieremet quãd le suiet en est peu importãt, ou quand vous recõnoissez les dégousts qu'en ont les Auditeurs.

If you are relating or reading anything, or arguing any point, be brief—particularly when the subject is of small importance, or if you detect weariness in the listeners.

81ST. BE NOT CURIOUS TO KNOW THE AFFAIRS OF OTHERS NEITHER APPROACH TO THOSE THAT SPEAK IN PRIVATE

Chapter vii. 24. Ne témoignez pas de curiosité dans les affaires d'autruy, & ne vous approchez dè là où l'on parle en secret.

Do not show any curiosity about other people's affairs, and do not go near the place where persons are talking in private.

82D. UNDERTAKE NOT WHAT YOU CANNOT PERFORM BUT BE CAREFULL TO KEEP YOUR PROMISE

Chapter vii. 25. Ne vous chargez point d'vne chose dont vous ne vous pouuez acquiter; maintenez ce que vous auez promis.

Do not undertake anything that you cannot perform; keep your promise.

83D. WHEN YOU DELIVER A MATTER DO IT WITHOUT PASSION & WITH DISCRETION, HOWEVER MEAN Y'E PERSON BE YOU DO IT TOO

Chapter vii. 27. Quand vous faites vne ambassade, vn rapport, ou donnez l'ouuerture de quelque affaire, taschez de le faire sans passion & auec discretion, soit que vous ayez à traitter auec personnes de peu, ou personnes de qualité.

When you fulfil a mission, deliver a report, or undertake the opening of any matter, try to do it dispassionately and discreetly, whether those with whom you have to treat be of humble or high position.

84TH. WHEN YOUR SUPERIOURS TALK TO ANY BODY HEARKEN NOT NEITHER SPEAK NOR LAUGH

Chapter vii. 27. Quand ceux qui ont sur vous commandement, parlent à quelqu'vn, gardez vous bien de parler, de rire, ou de les escouter.

When your Superiors talk to any one, do not speak, laugh, or listen.

85TH. IN COMPANY OF THESE OF HIGHER QUALITY THAN YOURSELF SPEAK NOT TILL YOU ARE ASK'D A QUESTION THEN STAND UPRIGHT PUT OFF YOUR HAT & ANSWER IN FEW WORDS

Chapter vii. 30. Estant auec de plus grands que vous, principalement s'ils ont du pouuoir sur vous, ne parlez pas deuant que d'estre interrogé, & alors leuez-vous debout, découurez-vous, & répondez en peu de mots, si toutesfois l'on ne vous donne congé de vous asseoir, ou de vous tenir couuert.

Being with persons of higher position than yourself, and especially if they have authority over you, do not speak until you are interrogated; then rise, remove your hat, and answer in few words—unless indeed you are invited to remain seated, or to keep your hat on.

86TH. IN DISPUTES, BE NOT SO DESIROUS TO OVERCOME AS NOT TO GIVE LIBERTY TO EACH ONE TO DELIVER HIS OPINION AND SUBMIT TO Y'E JUDGMENT OF Y'E MAJOR PART ESPECIALLY IF THEY ARE JUDGES OF THE DISPUTE.

Chapter vii. 31. Dans les disputes qui arriuent, principalement en conuersation, ne soyez pas si desireux de gagner, que vous ne laissiez dire a chacun son aduis, & soit que vous ayez tort, ou raison, vous deuez acquiescer au jugement du plus grand nombre, ou mesme des plus fascheux, & beaucoup plus de ceux de qui vous dépendez, ou qui sont juges de la dispute.

In disputes that arise, especially in conversation, be not so desirous to overcome as not to leave each one liberty to deliver his opinion; and whether you be wrong or right you should acquiesce in the judgment of the majority, or even of the most persistent, all the more if they are your masters or patrons, or judges of the discussion.

87TH. [LET YOUR BEARING BE SUCH] AS BECOMES A MAN GRAVE SETTLED AND ATTENTIVE [TO WHAT IS SAID, WITHOUT BEING TOO SERIOUS. CONTRA]DICT NOT AT EVERY TURN WHAT OTHERS SAY

Chapter vii. 35. Vostre maintien soit d'homme moderément graue, posé, & attentif a ce qui se dit, afin de n'auoir pas à dire à tout propos: *Comment ditez-vous? comment se passe cela? je ne vous ay pas entendu*, & d'autres semblables niaiseries.

33. Ne contredictes pas a tout bout de champ, à ce que disent les autres, en contestant & disant: Il n'est pas ainsi, la chose est comme je la dy; mais rapportez-vous en à l'opinion des autres principalement dans les choses, qui sont de peu de consequence.

35. Let your bearing be that of a moderately grave, serious man, and attentive to what is said so as to avoid having to say every moment: *"How did that happen? I did not understand you,"*—and other similar foolish remarks.

33. Do not continually contradict what others say, by disputing and saying: "That is not the case, it is as I say;" but defer to the opinion of others, especially in matters of small consequence.

88TH. BE NOT TEDIOUS IN DISCOURSE, MAKE NOT MANY DIGRESSIONS, NOR REPEAT OFTEN THE SAME MANNER OF DISCOURSE

Chapter vii. 39. N'employez pas vn an à vostre preface, & en certaines longues excuses ou ceremonies, en disant, *Monsieur: excusez-moy! si ie ne sçay pas si bien dire*, &c., *toutesfois pour vous obeyr*, &c., & autres semblables ennuyeuses and sottes trainées de paroles; mais entrez promptement en matiere tant que faire se pourra auec vne hardiesse moderée: Et puis poursuiuez, sans vous troubler, iusques à la fin. Ne soyez pas long; sans beaucoup de digressions, ne reïterez pas souuent vne mesme façon de dire.

Do not take a year in your preface, or in certain long apologies or ceremonies, such as: "*Pardon me Sir if I do not know how to express myself sufficiently well,*" &.c.; "*nevertheless in order to obey you,*" &c., and other similarly tedious and stupid circumlocutions; but enter promptly on the subject, as far as possible, with moderate boldness; then continue to the end without hesitation. Do not be prolix; avoid digressions; do not often reiterate the same expression.

89TH. SPEAK NOT EVIL OF THE ABSENT FOR IT IS UNJUST

Hawkins vi. 40. Speak not evill of one absent, for it is unjust to detract from the worth of any, or besmeare a good name by condemning, where the party is not present, to clear himselfe, or undergo a rationall conviction.

90TH. BEING SET AT MEAT SCRATCH NOT NEITHER SPIT COUGH OR BLOW YOUR NOSE EXCEPT THERE'S A NECESSITY FOR IT

Chapter viii. 2. Estant assis à table, ne vous grattez point, & vous gardez tant que vous pourrez, de cracher, de tousser, de vous moucher: que s'il y a necessité, faites-le adroitement, sans beaucoup de bruit, en tournant le visage de costé.

Being seated at the table, do not scratch yourself, and if you can help it, do not spit, cough, or blow your nose; should either be necessary do it adroitly, with least noise, turning the face aside.

(In the Washington MS. there is a notable omission of all that is said in the French and English books concerning grace before meat. At Washington's table grace was never said.)

91ST. MAKE NO SHEW OF TAKING GREAT DELIGHT IN YOUR VICTUALS, FEED NOT WITH GREEDINESS; CUT YOUR BREAD WITH A KNIFE, LEAN NOT ON THE TABLE NEITHER FIND FAULT WITH WHAT YOU EAT.

Chapter viii. 3. Ne prenez pas vostre repas en gourmand.

4. Ne rompez point le pain auec les mains, mais auec le cousteau, si ce n'estoit vn pain fort petil & tout frais, & que tous les autres fissent de mesme, ou la pluspart.

5. Ne vous iettez pas sur table, à bras estendus iusques aux coudes, & ne vous accostez pas indecemment les épaules ou les bras sur vostre siege.

8. Ne monstrez nullement d'avoir pris plaisir à la viande, ou au vin; mais si celuy que vous traittez, vous en demande vostre goust, vous pourrez luy respondre avec modestie & prudence: beaucoup moins faut il blasmer les viandes, ou en demander d'autres, ny dauantage.

3. Eat not like a glutton. (4.) Do not break the bread with your hands, but with a knife; unless, indeed, it is a small and quite fresh roll, and where the others present, or most of them, use their hands. (5.) Do not throw yourself on the table, as far as the elbows, nor unbecomingly rest shoulders or arms on your chair. (8.) Do not make a show of taking delight in your food, or in the wine; but if your host inquires your preference you should answer with modesty and tact: whatever you do, do not complain of the dishes, ask for others, or anything of that sort.

(At Washington's table it was a custom to invite each guest to call for the wine he preferred.)

92D. TAKE NO SALT OR CUT BREAD WITH YOUR KNIFE GREASY.

Chapter viii. 9. Prenant du sel, gardez que le cousteau ne soit gras: quand il le faut nettoyer, ou la fourchette on le peut faire honnestement auec vn peu de pain, ou comme il se pratique en certains lieux, auec la serviette, mais iamais sur le pain entier.

In taking salt be careful that the knife is not greasy: when necessary your knife or fork may with propriety be cleaned on a piece of bread—or, as is done in some places, with the napkin—but it must never be wiped on the whole loaf.

93D. ENTERTAINING ANY ONE AT TABLE IT IS DECENT TO PRESENT HIM W'T MEAT, UNDERTAKE NOT TO HELP OTHERS UNDESIRED BY Y'E MASTER

Chapter viii. 10. Traittant quelqu'vn, il est de la bien-seance de le seruir en table, & luy presenter des viandes, voire mesme de celles qui sont proches de luy. Que si l'on estoit invité chez autruy, il est plus à propos d'attendre que le Maistre ou vn autre serue, que de prendre des viandes soy-mesme, si ce n'estoit que le Maistre priast les conuiez de prendre librement, ou que l'on fust en maison familiere. L'on se doit aussi peu ingerer à seruir les autres hors de sa maison, où l'on avoir peu de pouuoir, n'étoit que le nombre des conuiez fust grand, & que le Maistre de la maison ne peust pas avoir l'oeil sur tout; Et pour lors l'on peut seruir ceux qui sont proches de soy.

When entertaining any one it is polite to serve him at table and to present the dishes to him, even such as are near him. When invited by another it is more seemly to wait to be served by the host, or some one else, than to take the dishes oneself, unless the host begs the guests to help themselves freely, or one is at home in the house. One ought also not to be officious in helping others when out of one's own house, where one has but little authority, unless the guests are very numerous and the host cannot attend to everything; in that case we may help those nearest us.

[9]4TH. IF YOU SOAK BREAD IN THE SAUCE LET IT BE NO MORE THAN WHAT YOU PUT IN YOUR MOUTH AT A TIME AND BLOW NOT YOUR BROTH AT TABLE BUT STAY TILL COOLS OF IT SELF

Chapter viii. 14. Si vous trempez en la saulce le pain ou la chair, ne les trempez pas derechef, apres y auoir mordu, trempez-y à chaque fois vn morceau mediocre, qui se puisse manger tout d'vne bouchée.

11. Ne soufflez point sur les viandes; mais si elles sont chaudes, attendez qu'elles se refroidissent: le potage se pourra refroidir, le remuant modestement auec la cuilliere, mais il ne sied pas bien de humer son potage en table, il le faut prendre auec la cuilliere.

If you dip bread or meat into the gravy, do not do so immediately after biting a piece off, but dip each time a moderately-sized morsel which can be eaten at one mouthful. (II.) Do not blow on the viands, but if they are hot, wait till they cool. Soup may be cooled by stirring it gently with a spoon, but it is not becoming to drink up the soup at table. It should be taken with a spoon.

95TH. PUT NOT YOUR MEAT TO YOUR MOUTH WITH YOUR KNIFE IN YOUR HAND NEITHER SPIT FORTH THE STONES OF ANY FRUIT PYE UPON A DISH NOR CAST ANYTHING UNDER THE TABLE

Chapter viii. 17. Ne portez pas le morceau à la bouche, tenant le cousteau en la main, à la mode des villageois.

16. Aussi ne semble-il bien seant de cracher les noyaux de prunes, cerises, ou autre chose semblable sur le plat; mais premierement on doit les recueiller decemment, comme il a esté dit, en la main gauche, l'approchant à la bouche, & puis les mettre sur le bord de l'assiette.

15. L'on ne doit point jetter sous la table, ou par terre, les os, les écorces, le vin ou autre chose semblable.

[Sidenote: Maxim 15 is much longer]

Do not carry a morsel to your mouth, knife in hand, like the rustics. (16.) Moreover, it does not seem well bred to spit out the kernels of prunes, cherries, or anything of the kind, on your plate, but, as already said, they should be decently collected in the left hand (raised to the mouth), and placed on the edge of the plate. (15.) Bones, peel, wine, and the like, should not be thrown under the table.

96TH. ITS UNBECOMING TO STOOP MUCH TO ONE'S MEAT KEEP YOUR FINGERS CLEAN & WHEN FOUL WIPE THEM ON A CORNER OF YOUR TABLE NAPKIN.

Chapter viii. 21. Il est messeant de se baisser beaucoup sur son escuelle ou sur la viande, c'est assez de s'encliner vn peu lors que l'on porte le morceau trempé à la bouche, de crainte de se salir, & puis redresser la teste.

25. Ne vous nettoyez pas les mains à vostre pain, s'il est entier; toutesfois les ayant fort grasses, il semble que vous les puissiez nettoyer premierement à vn morceau de pain que vous ayez à manger tout à l'heure & puis à la seruiette, afin de ne la point tant salir: ce qui vous arriuera rarement, si vous sçauez vous seruir de la cuilliere, & de la fourchette, selon le style des plus honnestes. Beaucoup moins deuez vous lêcher les doigts, principalement les succçant auec grand bruit.

It is ill-bred to stoop too close to one's porringer or the meat. It suffices to bend a little when conveying a soaked morsel to one's mouth, in order to avoid soiling oneself, then straighten up again. (25.) Do not clean your hands on a loaf; if very greasy you might, it would seem, partly clean them on a bit of bread you are about to eat, then on your napkin, so as not to soil the latter too much: this will rarely happen if you know how to use spoon and fork in the most approved manner. Much less should you lick your fingers, especially not suck them noisily.

[9]7TH. PUT NOT ANOTHER BIT INTO YOUR MOUTH TILL THE FORMER BE SWALLOWED LET NOT YOUR MORSELS BE TOO BIG FOR THE JOWLS

Chapter viii. 30. Ne portez pas le morceau à la bouche que l'autre ne soit aualIé, & que tous soient tels qu'ils ne fassent pas enfler les jouës hors de mesure; ne vous seruez pas des deux mains pour vous mettre le morceau à la bouche, mais seruez vous d'ordinaire de la droite.

Carry not another morsel to the mouth till the other be swallowed, and let each be such as will not stretch the jaws beyond measure; do not take both hands to raise a morsel to the mouth, but, usually, serve yourself with the right hand.

98TH. DRINK NOT NOR TALK WITH YOUR MOUTH FULL NEITHER GAZE ABOUT YOU WHILE YOU ARE A DRINKING

Chapter viii. 32. Ne boiuez ayant le morceau en la bouche, ne demandez point à boire, ne parlez, ne vous versez point à boire, & ne boiuez cependant que vostre voisin boit, ou celuy qui est au haut bout.

33. En boiuant, ne regardez point çà & là.

Do not drink with your mouth full of food; do not ask anything while drinking, nor talk, nor turn round; and do not drink because your neighbour does, or the head of the table. (33.) While drinking, gaze not here and there.

[Sidenote: The later French book recommends keeping the eyes "fixed at the bottom of the glass" while drinking.]

99TH. DRINK NOT TOO LEISURELY NOR YET TOO HASTILY. BEFORE AND AFTER DRINKING WIPE YOUR LIPS BREATH NOT THEN OR EVER WITH TOO GREAT A NOISE, FOR ITS UNCIVIL

Chapter viii. 34. Ne boiuez point trop lentement ny trop à la haste, ny cõme en maschant le vin, ny trop souuent ny sans eau, car c'est à faire aux yvrognes. Deuant & apres que vous aurez beu, effuyez-vous les lévres, & ne respirez pas auec trop grand bruit, ny alors, ny iamais, car c'est vne chose bien inciuile.

Drink neither too slowly nor too hastily, nor as if gulping the wine, nor too frequently, nor without water—as drunkards do. Wipe your lips before and after drinking, and do not breathe too loudly then or at any other time, for that is very inelegant.

100TH. CLEANSE NOT YOUR TEETH WITH THE TABLE CLOTH NAPKIN FORK OR KNIFE BUT IF OTHERS DO IT LET IT BE DONE W'T A PICK TOOTH

Chapter viii. 36. Ne vous nettoyez pas les dents auec la nappe, ou la seruiette, ny auec le doigt, la fourchette, ou le cousteau. Ce seroit faire pis de le faire auec les ongles, mais faites-le auec le curedent. Aussi ne semble-il estre bien-seant de se les nettoyer en table, si ce n'estoit que les autres le fissent, & que ce fust la coustume des mieux ciuilisez.

Do not clean your teeth with the tablecloth, napkin, finger, fork, or knife. It were still more objectionable to do so with the nails. Use a toothpick. It also does not appear well-bred to pick them at table, unless others do so, and where such is a custom of the more gentlemanly.

101ST. RINCE NOT YOUR MOUTH IN THE PRESENCE OF OTHERS

Chapter viii. 37. Ne vous rincez point la bouche auec du vin, pour le reietter en presence des autres; mais sorty que vous serez de table, accoustumez vous à lauer les mains auec les autres. Quant à la bouche, il semble n'estre pas à propos de la lauer en presence des gens, & partant quand l'on donne à lauer, mesme en table, l'on doit seulement lauer les mains.

Do not rinse your mouth with wine, to be rejected in the presence of others; but, having left the table, accustom yourself to wash your hands with the rest. As to the mouth, it does not appear proper to wash it in company at all, and consequently when an opportunity of washing is offered, even at the table, the hands only should be washed.

102D. IT IS OUT OF USE TO CALL UPON THE COMPANY OFTEN TO EAT NOR NEED YOU DRINK TO OTHERS EVERY TIME YOU DRINK

Chapter viii. 38. C'est chose peu loüable & presque aujourd'huy hors d'vsage, d'inuiter la compagnie à manger, principalement trop souuent & auec importunité, car il semble qu'on luy osté la liberté. Beaucoup moins deuez-vous boire à autruy toutes les fois que vous boiuez: que si l'on boit à vous, vous pouuez le refuser modestement, remerciant de bonne grace, & confessant de vous rendre; ou bien essayez vn peu le vin par courtoisie, principalement auec gens qui sont accoustumez à cela, & prennent le refus à iniure.

It is not commendable, and now almost out of fashion, to call on the company to eat, especially to invite them too often and urgently, for it appears to take away their freedom. Much less should you drink to others every time you drink: if one drinks to you, it is permissible to decline modestly, thanking him gracefully, and acknowledging your response; or you may well sip a little wine for courtesy, especially with people who are accustomed to it, and who are offended by refusal.

103D. IN COMPANY OF YOUR BETTERS BE NOT [LONGER IN EATING] THAN THEY ARE LAY NOT YOUR ARM BUT AR[ISE WITH ONLY A TOUCH ON THE EDGE OF THE TABLE.]

Chapter viii. 42. Quand les autres ont acheué de manger, despechez vous aussi, & ne tenez pas les bras sur la table, mais posez les mains seulement sur le bout.

When the rest have finished eating, you should do the same quickly; do not hold your arms on the table, but only place your hands on the edge of it.

104TH. IT BELONGS TO Y'E CHIEFEST IN COMPANY TO UNFOLD HIS NAPKIN AND FALL TO MEAT FIRST, BUT HE OUGHT TO BEGIN IN TIME & TO DISPATCH WITH DEXTERITY THAT Y'E SLOWEST MAY HAVE TIME ALLOWED HIM

Chapter viii. 45. C'est à faire au plus honnorable de la compagnie de déplier le premier sa seruiette, & toucher aux viandes: & partant les autres doiuent attendre paisiblement sans mettre la main à chose aucune deuant lui.

46. Et au contraire il doit estre soigneux de commencer en son temps, de pouruoir à tout, d'entretenir les conuiez, & finir le tout auec telle addresse; qu'il donne temps aux plus tardifs de manger à leur aise, s'entretenant, s'il est de besoin, à gouster legerement des viandes, ou quand il est loisible de discourir à table;

entremesler auec le manger quelque petit discours, afin que les autres puissent auec loisir d'acheuer.

It is for the most distinguished member of the company to unfold first his napkin and touch the food, and the rest should wait quietly, without laying hand on anything before he does. (46.) On the other hand, he ought in due time to commence, to consider everything, entertaining the guests, and managing all so adroitly as to give time to the more dilatory to eat at their leisure; if necessary for this, slowly tasting the viands, or, when table-talk is permissible, introducing a little chat during the meal, so that the others can finish at their ease.

105TH. BE NOT ANGRY AT TABLE WHATEVER HAPPENS & IF YOU HAVE REASON TO BE SO, SHEW IT NOT PUT ON A CHEARFULL COUNTENANCE ESPECIALLY IF THERE BE STRANGERS FOR GOOD HUMOUR MAKES ONE DISH OF MEAT A FEAST

[Sidenote: Toner has "but" instead of "put" in this Rule.]

Chapter viii. 47. Ne vous fâchez iamais en table, quoy qu'il aduienne, ou bien si vous vous fâchez, n'ent faites point de semblant, principalement y ayant des estrangers à table.

Never be angry at table, no matter what may happen, or even if you have cause for anger, do not show it, especially if strangers are present.

[Sidenote: Hawkins vii. 40. "A cheerefull countenance makes one dish a Feast."]

106TH. SET NOT YOURSELF AT Y'E UPPER [END] OF Y'E TABLE BUT IF IT BE YOUR DUE OR THAT Y'E MASTER OF Y'E HOUSE WILL HAVE IT SO, CONTEND NOT LEAST YOU SHOULD TROUBLE Y'E COMPANY.

[Sidenote: There is a blank in the MS. after upper.]

Chapter viii. 48. Ne vous asséez point de vous mesme au haut-bout; mais s'il vous appartient, ou si le maistre du logis le veut ainsi, ne faites pas tant de resistance pour n'y point aller, que vous fachiez toute la compagnie.

Seat not yourself voluntarily at the top; but if the place properly belongs to you, or the master of the house so wills, do not offer so much resistance to its acceptance as to annoy the company.

[Sidenote: Walker: "Desire not the highest place, nor be troublesome with impertinent debasing yourself by refusing," etc.]

107TH. IF OTHERS TALK AT TABLE BE ATTENTIVE BUT TALK NOT WITH MEAT IN YOUR MOUTH

Chapter viii. 49. Si on lit ou deuise en table, soyez attentif, & s'il faut parler, ne parlez point auec le morceau en la bouche.

If there be reading or chat at table, be attentive, and if you have to speak, do not speak with your mouth full.

108TH. WHEN YOU SPEAK OF GOD OR HIS ATTRIBUTES, LET IT BE SERIOUSLY & [WITH WORDS OF] REVERENCE. HONOUR & OBEY YOUR NATURAL PARENTS ALTHO THEY BE POOR

Hawkins vii. 43. Let thy speeches be seriously reverent when thou speakest of God or his Attributes, for to jest or utter thy selfe lightly in matters divine, is an unhappy impiety, provoking heaven to justice, and urging all men to suspect thy beliefe.—vii. *(unnumbered)* Honour and obey thy natural parents although they be poor; for if thy earthly Parents cannot give thee riches and honour, yet thy heavenly Father hath promised thee length of days.

(There is nothing in the French Maxims corresponding to the second sentence of Rule 108. *The Maxim nearest to the first sentence is the 9th of Chapter i.: "Il se faut bien garder de prononcer aucuns noueaux mots, quand l'on parle de Dieu ou des Saincts, & d'en faire de sots contes, soit tout bon, ou par raillerie." "Avoid irreverent words in speaking of God, or of the Saints, and of telling foolish stories about them, either in jest or earnest." Compare also the last sentence of Maxim vii,* II, ante, *under Rule* 72.*)*

109TH. LET YOUR RECREATIONS BE MANFULL NOT SINFULL.

Hawkins vii. *(unnumbered)*. Let thy recreations be manful not sinful; there is a great vanity in the baiting of Beasts, the Bears and Bulls lived quietly enough before the fall; it was our sin that set them together by the ears, rejoyce not therefore to see them fight, for that would be to glory in thy shame.

110TH. LABOUR TO KEEP ALIVE IN YOUR BREAST THAT LITTLE SPARK OF CELESTIAL FIRE CALLED CONSCIENCE.

Hawkins vii. *(unnumbered)*. Labour to keep alive in thy breast, that little sparke of Celestial fire called Conscience, for Conscience to an evil man is a never dying worm, but unto a good man its a perpetual feast.

THE JOURNAL OF MAJOR GEORGE WASHINGTON SENT BY THE HON. ROBERT DINWIDDIE, ESQ. ... TO THE COMMANDANT OF THE FRENCH FORCES ON OHIO

Printed in Williamsburg, 1754

As it was thought adviseable by his Honour the Governor to have the following Account of my Proceedings to and from the French on Ohio, committed to Print; I think I can do no less than apologize, in some Measure, for the numberless Imperfections of it.

There intervened but one Day between my Arrival in Williamsburg, and the Time for the Council's Meeting, for me to prepare and transcribe, from the rough Minutes I had taken in my Travels, this Journal; the writing of which only was sufficient to employ me closely the whole Time, consequently admitted of no Leisure to consult of a new and proper Form to offer it in, or to correct or amend the Diction of the old; neither was I apprised, nor did in the least conceive, when I wrote this for his Honour's Perusal, that it ever would be published, or even have more than a cursory Reading; 'til I was informed, at the Meeting of the present General Assembly, that it was already in the Press.

There is nothing can recommend it to the Public, but this. Those Things which came under the Notice of my own Observation, I have been explicit and just in a Recital of:——Those which I have gathered from Report, I have been particularly cautious not to augment, but collected the Opinions of the several Intelligencers, and selected from the whole, the most probable and consistent Account.

G. Washington.

Wednesday, October 31, 1753.

I was commissioned and appointed by the Honourable Robert Dinwiddie, Esq; Governor, &c., of Virginia, to visit and deliver a Letter to the Commandant of the French Forces on the Ohio, and set out on the intended Journey the same Day; the next, I arrived at Fredericksburg, and engaged Mr. Jacob Vanbraam, to be my French Interpreter; and proceeded with him to Alexandria, where we provided Necessaries; from thence we went to Winchester, and got Baggage, Horses, &c.

and from thence we pursued the new Road to Wills-Creek, where we arrived the 14th of November.

Here I engaged Mr. Gist to pilot us out, and also hired four others as Servitors, Barnaby Currin and John MacQuire, Indian Traders, Henry Steward, and William Jenkins; and in Company with those Persons, left the Inhabitants the Day following.

The excessive Rains and vast Quantity of Snow that had fallen, prevented our reaching Mr. Frazier's an Indian Trader, at the Mouth of Turtle-Creek, on Monongahela, 'til Thursday, the 22d. We were informed here, that Expresses were sent a few Days ago to the Traders down the River, to acquaint them with the French General's Death, and the Return of the major Part of the French Army into Winter Quarters.

The Waters were quite impassable, without swimming our Horses; which obliged us to get the Loan of a Canoe from Frazier, and to send Barnaby Currin and Henry Steward, down Monongahela, with our Baggage, to meet us at the Forks of Ohio, about 10 Miles, to cross Aligany.

As I got down before the Canoe, I spent some Time in viewing the Rivers, and the Land in the Fork, which I think extremely well situated for a Fort, as it has the absolute Command of both Rivers. The Land at the Point is 20 or 25 Feet above the common Surface of the Water, and a considerable Bottom of flat, well-timbered Land all around it, very convenient for Building: The Rivers are each a Quarter of a Mile, or more, across, and run here very near at right Angles: Aligany bearing N. E. and Monongahela S. E. the former of these two is a very rapid and swift running Water, the other deep and still, without any perceptible Fall.

About two Miles from this, on the South East Side of the River, at the Place where the Ohio Company intended to erect a Fort, lives Shingiss, king of the Delawares, we call'd upon him, to invite him to Council at the Loggs-Town.

As I had taken a good deal of Notice Yesterday of the Situation at the Forks, my Curiosity led me to examine this more particularly, and I think it greatly inferior, either for Defence or Advantages; especially the latter, for a Fort at the Forks would be equally well situated on Ohio, and have the entire Command of the Monongahela, which runs up to our Settlements and is extremely well design'd for Water Carriage, as it is of a deep still Nature, besides, a Fort at the Fork might be built at a much less Expence, than at the other Place.

Nature has well contrived this lower Place, for Water Defence; but the Hill whereon it must stand being about a Quarter of a Mile in Length, and then descending gradually on the Land Side, will render it difficult and very expensive, making a sufficient Fortification there. The whole Flat upon the Hill must be taken in, or the Side next the Descent made extremely high; or else the Hill itself cut away: Otherwise, the Enemy may raise Batteries within that Distance without being expos'd to a single Shot from the Fort.

Shingiss attended us to the Loggs-Town, where we arrived between Sun-setting and Dark, the 25th Day after I left Williamsburg: We travelled over some extreme good, and bad Land, to get to this Place.

As soon as I came into Town, I went to Monacatoocha (as the Half-King was out at his hunting-Cabbin on little Beaver Creek, about 15 Miles off) and inform'd him by John Davison, my Indian Interpreter, that I was sent a Messenger to the French General; and was ordered to call upon the Sachems of the Six Nations, to acquaint them with it. I gave him a String of Wampum, and a Twist of Tobacco, and desired him to send for the Half-King; which he promised to do by a Runner in the Morning, and for other Sachems. I invited him and the other great Men present to my Tent, where they stay'd about an Hour and return'd.

According to the best Observations I could make, Mr. Gist's new Settlement (which we pass'd by) bears about W. N. W. 70 Miles from Wills-Creek; Shanapins, or the Forks N. by W. or N. N. W. about 50 Miles from that; and from thence to the Loggs-Town, the Course is nearly West about 18 or 20 Miles; so that the whole Distance, as we went and computed it, is at least 135 or 140 Miles from our back Inhabitants.

25TH.

Came to Town four or ten Frenchmen who had deserted from a Company at the Cuscuscas,1which lies at the Mouth of this River; I got the following Account from them. They were sent from New-Orleans with 100 Men, and 8 Canoe Loads of Provisions to this Place; where they expected to have met the same Number of Men, from the Forts this Side Lake Erie, to convey them and the Stores up, who were not arrived when they ran off.

I enquired into the Situation of the French, on the Mississippi, their Number, and what Forts they had built: They inform'd me, That there were four small Forts between New-Orleans and the Black-Islands, garrison'd with about 30 or 40 Men, and a few small Pieces, in each: That at New-Orleans, which is near the Mouth of the Mississippi, there are 35 Companies, of 40 Men each, with a pretty strong Fort mounting 8 Carriage Guns; and at the Black-Islands there are several Companies, and a Fort with 6 Guns. The Black-Islands are about 130 Leagues above the Mouth of the Ohio, which is about 350 above New-Orleans: They also acquainted me, that there was a small pallisado'd Fort on the Ohio, at the Mouth of the Obaish about 60 Leagues from the Mississippi: The Obaish heads near the West End of Lake Erie, and affords the Communication between the French on Mississippi and those on the Lakes. These Deserters came up from the lower Shanoah Town with one Brown, an Indian Trader, and were going to Philadelphia.

About 3 o'Clock this Evening the Half-King came to Town; I went up and invited him and Davison, privately, to my Tent, and desir'd him to relate some of the Particulars of his Journey to the French Commandant, and Reception there; and to give me an Account of the Ways and Distance. He told me, that the nearest and levellest Way was now impassable, by Reason of many large miry Savannas; that we must be obliged to go by Venango, and should not get to the near Fort under 5 or 6 Night's Sleep, good Travelling. When he went to the Fort, he said he was received in a very stern Manner by the late Commander; Who ask'd him very abruptly, what he had come about, and to declare his Business, which he said he did in the following Speech.

Fathers, I am come to tell you your own Speeches; what your own Mouths have declared. Fathers, You, in former Days, set a Silver Bason before us, wherein there was the Leg of a Beaver, and desir'd of all Nations to come and eat of it; to eat in Peace and Plenty, and not to be churlish to one another; and that if any such Person should be found to be a Disturber, I here lay down by the Edge of the Dish a Rod, which you must scourge them with; and if I your Father, should get foolish, in my old Days, I desire you may use it upon me as well as others.

Now Fathers, it is you who are the Disturbers in this Land, by coming and building your Towns, and taking it away unknown to us, and by Force.

Fathers, We kindled a fire a long Time ago, at a Place called Montreal, where we desired you to stay, and not to come and intrude upon our Land. I now desire you may dispatch to that Place; for be it known to you, Fathers, that this is our Land, and not yours.

Fathers, I desire you may hear me in Civilness; if not, we must handle that Rod which was laid down for the Use of the abstreperous. If you had come in a peaceable Manner, like our Brothers the English, we should not have been against your trading with us, as they do; but to come, Fathers, and build Houses upon our Land, and to take it by Force, is what we cannot submit to.

Fathers, Both you and the English are white, we live in a Country between; therefore the Land belongs to neither one nor t'other: But the Great Being above allow'd it to be a Place of Residence for us; so Fathers, I desire you to withdraw, as I have done our Brothers the English; for I will keep you at Arms length: I lay this down as a Trial for both, to see which will have the greatest Regard to it, and that Side we will stand by, and make equal Shares with us. Our Brothers, the English, have heard this, and I come now to tell it to you, for I am not afraid to discharge you off this Land.

This he said was the Substance of what he said to the General, who made this Reply.

Now my Child, I have heard your Speech, you spoke first, but it is my Time to speak now. Where is my Wampum that you took away, with the Marks of Towns in it? This Wampum I do not know, which you have discharged me off the Land with; but you need not put yourself to the Trouble of speaking, for I will not hear you: I am not afraid of Flies, or Musquitos, for Indians are such as those; I tell you, down that River I will go, and will build upon it, according to my Command: If the River was block'd up, I have Forces sufficient to burst it open, and tread under my Feet all that stand in Opposition, together with their Alliances; for my Force is as the Sand upon the Sea Shore: Therefore, here is your Wampum, I fling it at you. Child, you talk foolish; you say this Land belongs to you, but there is not the Black of my Nail yours: I saw that Land sooner than you did, before the Shannoahs and you were at War: Lead was the Man who went down, and took Possession of that River: It is my Land, and I will have it, let who will stand up for, or say against it. I'll buy and sell with the English, (mockingly). If People will be rul'd by me, they may expect kindness, but not else.

The Half-King told me he enquired of the General after two Englishmen that were made Prisoners, and received this Answer.

Child, You think it is a very great Hardship that I made Prisoners of those two People at Venango, don't you concern yourself with it, we took and carried them to Canada, to get Intelligence of what the English were doing in Virginia.

He informed me that they had built two Forts, one on Lake Erie, and another on French-Creek near a small Lake about 15 Miles asunder, and a large Waggon

Road between; they are both built after the same Model, but different in the Size; that on the Lake the largest; he gave me a Plan of them, of his own drawing.

The Indians enquired very particularly after their Brothers in Carolina Goal.

They also asked what sort of a Boy it was that was taken from the South-Branch; for they had, by some Indians, heard that a Party of French Indians had carried a white Boy by the Cuscusca Town, towards the Lakes.

26TH.

We met in Council at the Long-House, about 9 o'clock, where I spoke to them as follows:

Brothers, I have called you together in Council, by Order of your Brother the Governor of Virginia, to acquaint you that I am sent, with all possible Dispatch, to visit, and deliver a Letter to the French Commandant, of very great Importance to your Brothers the English; and I dare say, to you their Friends and Allies.

I was desired, Brothers, by your Brother the Governor, to call upon you, the Sachems of the Nations, to inform you of it, and to ask your Advice and Assistance to proceed the nearest and best Road to the French. You see, Brothers, I have gotten thus far on my Journey.

His Honour likewise desired me to apply to you for some of your young Men, to conduct and provide Provisions for us on our Way, and be a Safeguard against those French Indians who have taken up the Hatchet against us. I have spoke this particularly to you, Brothers, because his Honour our Governor treats you as good Friends and Allies, and holds you in great Esteem. To confirm what I have said, I give you this String of Wampum.

After they had considered for some Time on the above, the Half-King got up and spoke.

Now, my Brothers, in Regard to what my Brother the Governor has desired of me, I return you this Answer.

I rely upon you as a Brother ought to do, as you say we are Brothers and one People: We shall put Heart in Hand, and speak to our Fathers the French concerning the Speech they made to me, and you may depend that we will endeavour to be your Guard.

Brother, as you have asked my Advice, I hope you will be ruled by it, and stay 'til I can provide a Company to go with you: The French Speech-Belt is not here, I have it to go for to my hunting Cabbin; likewise the People which I have ordered in, are not yet come, nor cannot 'til the third Night from this, till which Time, Brother, I must beg you to stay.

I intend to send a Guard of Mingo's, Shannoah's, and Delawares, that our Brothers may see the Love and Loyalty we bear them.

As I had Orders to make all possible Dispatch, and waiting here was very contrary to my Inclination, I thanked him in the most suitable Manner I could, and told him that my Business required the greatest Expedition, and would not admit of that Delay: He was not well pleased that I should offer to go before the Time he had appointed, and told me that he could not consent to our going without a Guard, for Fear some Accident should befal us, and draw a Reflection upon him; besides, says he, this is a Matter of no small Moment, and must not be entered into without due Consideration; for now I intend to deliver up the French-Speech-Belt, and make the Shanoahs and Delawares do the same; and accordingly he gave Orders to King Shingiss, who was present, to attend on Wednesday Night with the Wampum, and two Men of their Nation to be in Readiness to set out with us next Morning. As I found it was impossible to get off without affronting them in the most egregious Manner, I consented to stay.

I gave them back a String of Wampum that I met with at Mr. Frazier's, which they had sent with a Speech to his Honour the Governor, to inform him, that three Nations of French Indians, viz: Chippoways, Ottoways, and Orundacks, had taken up the Hatchet against the English, and desired them to repeat it over again, which they postponed doing 'til they met in full Council with the Shannoahs and Delaware Chiefs.

27TH.

Runners were dispatched very early for the Shannoah Chiefs, the Half-King set out himself to fetch the French-Speech-Belt from his hunting Cabbin.

28TH.

He returned this Evening, and came with Monocatoocha, and two other Sachems to my Tent; and begged, (as they had complied with his Honour the Governor's Request, in providing Men, &c.) to know on what Business we were going to the French? this was a Question I all along expected, and had provided as satisfactory Answers to, as I could, and which allayed their Curiosity a little.

Monocatoocha informed me, that an Indian from Venango brought News, a few Days ago, that the French had called all the Mingos, Delawares, &c. together at that Place, and told them that they intended to have been down the River this Fall, but the Waters were growing cold, and the Winter advancing, which obliged them to go into Quarters: But that they might assuredly expect them in the Spring, with a far greater Number; and desired that they might be quite passive, and not to intermeddle, unless they had a Mind to draw all their Force upon them, for that they expected to fight the English three Years, (as they supposed there would be some Attempts made to stop them), in which Time they should conquer: But if they should prove equally Strong, that they and the English would join to cut them all off, and divide the Land between them; that though they had lost their General, and some few of their Soldiers, yet there were Men enough to reinforce them, and make them masters of the Ohio.

This Speech, he said, was delivered to them by one Captain Joncaire, their Interpreter in Chief, living at Venango, and a Man of Note in the Army.

29TH.

The Half-King and Monocatoocha came very early, and begged me to stay one Day more; for notwithstanding they had used all the Diligence in their Power, the Shanoah Chiefs had not brought the Wampum they ordered, but would certainly be in To-night; if not, they would delay me no longer, but would send it after us as soon as they arrived. When I found them so pressing in their Request, and knew that returning of Wampum was the abolishing of Agreements; and giving this up, was shaking of all Dependence upon the French, I consented to stay, as I believed an Offence offered at this Crisis, might be attended with greater ill Consequence, than another Day's Delay. They also informed me, that Shingiss could not get in his Men, and was prevented from coming himself by his Wife's Sickness (I believe, by Fear of the French); but that the Wampum of that Nation was lodged with Custaloga one of their Chiefs at Venango.

In the Evening late they came again and acquainted me that the Shannoahs were not yet come, but it should not retard the Prosecution of our Journey. He delivered in my Hearing, the Speeches that were to be made to the French by Jeskakake, one of their old Chiefs, which was giving up the Belt the late Commandant had asked for, and repeating near the same Speech he himself had done before.

He also delivered a String of Wampum to this Chief, which was sent by King Shingiss, to be given to Custaloga, with orders to repair to the French, and deliver up the Wampum.

He likewise gave a very large String of black and white Wampum, which was to be sent up immediately to the Six Nations, if the French refused to quit the Land at this Warning; which was the third and last Time, and was the Right of this Jeskakake to deliver.

30TH.

Last Night the great Men assembled to their Council-House, to consult further about this Journey, and who were to go; the Result of which was, that only three of their Chiefs, with one of their best Hunters, should be our Convoy. The Reason which they gave for not sending more, after what had been proposed at Council the 26th, was, that a greater Number might give the French Suspicions of some bad Design, and cause them to be treated rudely: But I rather think they could not get their Hunters in.

We set out about 9 o'Clock with the Half-King Jeskakake, White Thunder, and the Hunter, and travelled on the Road to Venango, where we arrived the 4th of December, without any Thing remarkable happening but a continued Series of bad Weather.

This is an old Indian Town, situated at the Mouth of French Creek on Ohio, and lies near N. about 60 Miles from the Loggs-Town, but more than 70 the Way we were obliged to go.

We found the French Colours hoisted at a House which they drove Mr. John Frazier, an English Subject, from; I immediately repaired to it, to know where the Commander resided. There were three Officers, one of whom, Capt. Joncaire, informed me, that he had the Command of the Ohio, but that there was a General Officer at the near Fort, which he advised me to apply for an Answer. He invited us to sup with them, and treated us with the greatest Complaisance.

The Wine, as they dosed themselves pretty plentifully with it, soon banished the Restraint which at first appeared in their Conversation, and gave a Licence to their Tongues to reveal their Sentiments more freely.

They told me, That it was their absolute Design to take Possession of the Ohio, and by G— they would do it, for that altho' they were sensible the English could raise two Men for their one; yet they knew their Motions were too slow and dilatory to prevent any Undertaking of theirs. They pretend to have an undoubted Right to the River, from a Discovery made by one La Sol 60 Years ago; and the Rise of this Expedition is, to prevent our settling on the River or Waters of it, as they had heard of some Families moving out in Order thereto. From the best Intelligence I could get, there have been 1500 Men on their Side Ontario Lake, but upon the Death of the General all were recalled to about 6 or 700, who were left to garrison four Forts, 150 or there abouts in each. The first of them is on French Creek near a small Lake, about 60 Miles from Venango, near N.N.W. the next lies on Lake Erie, where the greater Part of their Stores are kept, about 15 Miles from the other. From that it is 120 Miles to the carrying Place, at the Falls of Lake Erie, where there is a small Fort; which they lodge their Goods at, in bringing them from Montreal, the Place that all their Stores come from. The next Fort lies about 20 Miles from this, on Ontario Lake. Between this Fort and Montreal there are three others, the first of which is near opposite to the English Fort Oswego. From the Fort on Lake Erie to Montreal is about 600 Miles, which they say requires no more, if good Weather, than four Weeks Voyage, if they go in Barks or large Vessels, so that they may cross the Lake, but if they come in Canoes it will require 5 or 6 Weeks, for they are obliged to keep under the Shore.

5TH.

Rain'd excessively all Day, which prevented our Travelling. Capt. Joncaire sent for the Half-King, as he had but just heard that he came with me: He affected to be much concerned that I did not make free to bring them in before. I excused it in the best Manner I was capable, and told him I did not think their company agreeable, as I had heard him say a good deal in Dispraise of Indians in general, but another Motive prevented me from bringing them into his Company: I knew he was Interpreter, and a Person of very great Influence among the Indians, and had lately used all possible Means to draw them over to their Interest; therefore I was desirous of giving no Opportunity that could be avoided.

When they came in, there was great Pleasure expressed at seeing them. He wondered how they could be so near without coming to visit him, made several trifling Presents, and applied Liquor so fast, that they were soon rendered incapable of the Business they came about, notwithstanding the Caution which was given.

6TH.

The Half-King came to my Tent, quite sober, and insisted very much that I should stay and hear what he had to say to the French. I fain would have prevented his speaking any Thing 'til he came to the Commandant, but could not prevail. He told me that at this Place a Council Fire was kindled, where all their Business with these People was to be transacted; and that the Management of the Indian affairs was left solely to Monsieur Joncaire. As I was desirous of knowing the Issue of this, I agreed to stay, but sent our Horses a little way up French Creek to raft over and encamp; which I knew would make it near Night.

About 10 o'Clock they met in Council. The King spoke much the same as he had before done to the General, and offered the French Speech-Belt which had before been demanded, with the Marks of four Towns on it, which Monsieur Joncaire refused to receive; but desired him to carry it to the Fort to the Commander.

7TH.

Monsieur La Force, Commissary of the French Stores, and three other Soldiers came over to accompany us up. We found it extremely difficult to get the Indians off To-day, as every Stratagem had been used to prevent their going up with me: I had last Night left John Davison (the Indian Interpreter that I brought from the Loggs-Town with me) strictly charg'd not to be out of their Company, as I could not get them over to my Tent (they having some Business with Custaloga to know the Reason why he did not deliver up the French Belt which he had in Keeping) but was obliged to send Mr. Gist over To-day to fetch them, which he did with great Persuasion.

At 11 o'Clock we set out for the Fort; and were prevented from arriving there 'til the 11th by excessive Rains, Snows, and bad Travelling, through many Mires and Swamps, which we were obliged to pass, to avoid crossing the Creek, which was impossible, either by fording or rafting, the Water was so high and rapid.

We passed over much good Land since we left Venango, and through several extensive and very rich Meadows; one of which I believe was near four Miles in Length, and considerably wide in some Places.

12TH.

I prepared early to wait upon the Commander, and was received and conducted to him by the second Officer in Command; I acquainted him with my Business, and offer'd my Commission and Letter, both of which he desired me to keep 'til the Arrival of Monsieur Riparti, Captain, at the next Fort, who was sent for and expected every Hour.

This Commander is a Knight of the military Order of St. Lewis, and named *Legardeur de St. Piere*. He is an elderly Gentleman, and has much the Air of a Soldier; he was sent over to take the Command, immediately upon the Death of the late General, and arrived here about seven Days before me.

At 2 o'Clock the Gentleman who was sent for arrived, when I offer'd the Letter, &c., again; which they receiv'd, and adjourn'd into a private Apartment for the Captain to translate, who understood a little English; after he had done it, the Commander desired I would walk in, and bring my Interpreter to peruse and correct it, which I did.

13TH.

The chief Officers retired, to hold a Council of War, which gave me an Opportunity of taking the Dimensions of the Fort, and making what Observations I could.

It is situated on the South, or West Fork of French Creek, near the Water, and is almost surrounded by the Creek, and a small Branch of it which forms a Kind of Island; four Houses compose the Sides; the Bastions are made of Piles driven into the Ground, and about 12 Feet above, and sharp at Top, with Port-Holes cut for Cannon and Loop-Holes for the small Arms to fire through; there are eight 6 lb. Pieces mounted, two in each Bastion, and one Piece of four Pound before the Gate; in the Bastions are a Guard-House, Chapel, Doctor's Lodging, and the Commander's private Store, round which are laid Plat-Forms for the Cannon and Men to stand on: There are several Barracks without the Fort, for the Soldiers Dwelling, covered, some with Bark, and some with Boards, made chiefly of Loggs: There are also several other Houses, such as Stables, Smiths Shops, &c.

I could get no certain Account of the Number of Men here; but according to the best Judgment I could form, there are an Hundred exclusive of Officers, of which there are many. I also gave Orders to the People that were with me, to take an exact Account of the Canoes that were haled up to convey their Forces down in the Spring, which they did, and told 50 of Birch Bark, and 170 of Pine, besides many others which were block'd out, in Readiness to make.

14TH.

As the Snow encreased very fast, and our Horses daily became weaker, I sent them off unloaded, under the Care of Barnaby Currin and two others, to make all convenient Dispatch to Venango, and there wait our Arrival if there was a Prospect of the Rivers freezing, if not, then to continue down to Shanapin's Town, at the Forks of Ohio, and there to wait 'til we came to cross Aligany, intending myself to go down by Water, as I had the Offer of a Canoe or Two.

As I found many Plots concerted to retard the Indians Business, and prevent their returning with me; I endeavor'd all that lay in my Power to frustrate their Schemes, and hurry them on to execute their intended Design; they accordingly pressed for Admittance this Evening, which at Length was granted them, privately, with the Commander and one or two other officers: The Half-King told me, that he offer'd the Wampum to the Commander, who evaded taking it, and made many fair Promises of Love and Friendship; said he wanted to live in Peace, and trade amicably with them, as a Proof of which he would send some Goods immediately down to the Loggs-Town for them; but I rather think the Design of that is, to bring away all our straggling Traders they meet with, as I privately understood they intended to carry an Officer, &c. with them; and what rather confirms this Opinion, I was enquiring of the Commander, by what Authority he had made Prisoners of several of our English Subjects; he told me that the Country belong'd to them, that no Englishman had a Right to trade upon those Waters; and that he had Orders to make every Person Prisoner that attempted it on the Ohio, or the Waters of it.

I enquir'd of Capt. Riparti about the Boy that was carried by, as it was done while the Command devolved on him, between the Death of the late General, and the Arrival of the present; he acknowledged, that a Boy had been carried past, and that the Indians had two or three white Men's Scalps (I was told by some of the Indians at Venango Eight) but pretended to have forgot the Name of the Place that the Boy came from, and all the Particulars, though he question'd him for some Hours, as they were carrying him past: I likewise enquired what they had done with John Trotter and James MacClocklan, two Pensylvania Traders, whom they had taken, with all their Goods: They told me, that they had been sent to Canada, but were now returned Home.

This Evening I received an Answer to his Honour the Governor's Letter from the Commandant.

15th.

The Commandant ordered a plentiful Store of Liquor, Provision, &c., to be put on Board our Canoe, and appeared to be extremely complaisant, though he was exerting every Artifice that he could invent to set our own Indians at Variance with us, to prevent their going 'til after our Departure: Presents, Rewards, and every Thing which could be suggested by him or his Officers.—I can't say that ever in my Life I suffered so much Anxiety as I did in this Affair; I saw that every Stratagem that the most fruitful Brain could invent, was practised, to win the Half-King to their Interest, and that leaving him here was giving them the Opportunity they aimed at.—I went to the Half-King and press'd him in the strongest Terms to go: He told me the Commandant would not discharge him 'til the Morning. I then went to the Commandant, and desired him to do their Business; and complain'd of ill Treatment: For keeping them, as they were Part of my Company, was detaining me; which he promised not to do, but to forward my Journey as much as he could: He protested he did not keep them, but was ignorant of the Cause of their Stay; though I soon found it out: He had promised them a present of Guns, &c., if they would wait 'til the Morning.

As I was very much press'd, by the Indians, to wait this Day for them, I consented, on a Promise, That nothing should hinder them in the Morning.

16TH.

The French were not slack in their Inventions to keep the Indians this Day also; but as they were obligated, according to Promise, to give the Present, they then endeavoured to try the Power of Liquor; which I doubt not would have prevailed at any other Time than this, but I urged and insisted with the King so closely upon his Word, that he refrained, and set off with us as he had engaged.

We had a tedious and very fatiguing Passage down the Creek, several Times we had like to have been staved against Rocks, and many Times were obliged all Hands to get out and remain in the Water Half an Hour or more, getting over the Shoals; at one Place the Ice had lodged and made it impassable by Water; therefore we were obliged to carry our Canoe across a Neck of Land, a quarter of a Mile over. We did not reach Venango, till the 22d, where we met with our Horses.

This Creek is extremely crooked, I dare say the Distance between the Fort and Venango can't be less than 130 Miles, to follow the Meanders.

23D.

When I got Things ready to set off, I sent for the Half-King, to know whether he intended to go with us, or by Water, he told me that White-Thunder had hurt himself much, and was sick and unable to walk; therefore he was obliged to carry him down in a Canoe: As I found he intended to stay here a Day or two, and knew that Monsieur Joncaire would employ every Scheme to set him against the English as he had before done; I told him I hoped he would guard against his Flattery, and let no fine Speeches influence him in their Favour: He desired I might not be concerned, for he knew the French too well, for any Thing to engage him in their Behalf, and though he could not go down with us, he would endeavour to meet at the Forks with Joseph Campbell, to deliver a Speech for me to carry to his Honour the Governor. He told me he would order the young Hunter to attend us, and get Provision, &c. if wanted.

Our Horses were now so weak and feeble, and the Baggage so heavy as we here obliged to provide all the Necessaries that the Journey would require; that we doubted much their performing it: therefore myself and others (except the Drivers, who were obliged to ride) gave up our Horses for Packs, to assist along with the Baggage; I put myself in an Indian walking Dress, and continued with them three Days, till I found there was no Probability of their getting in, in any reasonable Time; the Horses grew less able to travel every Day; the Cold increased very fast, and the Roads were becoming much worse by a deep Snow, continually freezing; and as I was uneasy to get back, to make Report of my Proceedings to his Honour the Governor, I determined to prosecute my Journey the nearest Way through the Woods, on Foot.

Accordingly I left Mr. Vanbraam in Charge of our Baggage, with Money and Directions, to Provide Necessaries from Place to Place for themselves and Horses, and to make the most convenient Dispatch in.

I took my necessary Papers, pulled off my Cloaths; tied myself up in a Match Coat; and with my Pack at my Back with my Papers and Provisions in it, and a Gun, set out with Mr. Gist, fitted in the same Manner, on Wednesday the 26th. The Day following, just after we had passed a Place called the Murdering-Town, where we intended to quit the Path, and steer across the Country for Shannapins Town, we fell in with a Party of French Indians, who had lain in Wait for us; one of them fired at Mr. Gist or me, not 15 steps, but fortunately missed. We took this Fellow into Custody, and kept him till about 9 o'clock at Night, and then let him go, and walked all the remaining Part of the Night without making any Stop, that we might get the Start, so far, as to be out of the Reach of their Pursuit the next Day, as we were well assured they would follow our Tract as soon as it was light: The next Day we continued travelling till quite dark, and got to the River about two Miles above Shannapins; we expected to have found the River frozen, but it was not, only about 50 Yards from each Shore; the Ice I suppose had broke up above, for it was driving in vast Quantities.

There was no Way for getting over but on a Raft, which we set about, with but one poor Hatchet, and finished just after Sun-setting, after a whole Day's Work; we got it launched, and on Board of it, and set off; but before we were Half Way over, we were jammed in the Ice in such a Manner that we expected every Moment our Raft to sink, and ourselves to perish; I put out my setting Pole to try to stop the Raft, that the Ice might pass by, when the Rapidity of the Stream threw it with so much Violence against the Pole, that it jirked me out into ten Feet Water, but I fortunately saved myself by catching hold of one of the Raft Logs; notwithstanding all our Efforts we could not get the Raft to either Shore, but were obliged, as we were near an Island, to quit our Raft and make to it.

The Cold was so extremely severe, that Mr. Gist, had all his Fingers, and some of his Toes frozen, and the water was shut up so hard, that we found no Difficulty in getting off the Island, on the Ice, in the Morning, and went to Mr. Frazier's. We met here with 20 Warriors who were going to the Southward to War, but coming to a Place upon the Head of the great Cunnaway, where they found seven People killed and scalped, all but one Woman with very light Hair, they turned about and ran back, for fear the Inhabitants should rise and take them as the Authors of the Murder: They report that the People were lying about the House, and some of them much torn and eaten by Hogs: By the Marks that were left, they say they were French Indians of the Ottaway Nation, &c. that did it.

As we intended to take Horses here, and it required some Time to find them, I went up about three Miles to the Mouth of Yaughyaughgane to visit Queen Alliquippa, who had expressed great Concern that we passed her in going to the Fort. I made her a Present of a Matchcoat and a Bottle of Rum, which latter was thought much the best Present of the Two.

Tuesday the 1st Day of January, we left Mr. Frazier's House, and arrived at Mr. Gist's at Monongahela the 2d, where I bought a Horse, Saddle, &c. the 6th we met 17 Horses loaded with Materials and Stores for a Fort at the Forks of Ohio, and the Day after some Families going out to settle: This Day we arrived at Wills-Creek, after as fatiguing a Journey as it is possible to conceive, rendered so by excessive bad Weather: From the first Day of December to the 15th, there was but one Day but it rained or snowed incessantly; and throughout the whole Journey we met with nothing but one continued Series of cold wet Weather, which occasioned very uncomfortable Lodgings, especially after we had left our Tent, which was some Screen from the Inclemency of it.

On the 11th I got to Belvoir where I stopped one Day to take necessary Rest, and then set out, and arrived in Williamsburg the 16th, and waited upon his Honour the Governor with the Letter I had brought from the French Commandant, and to give an Account of the Proceedings of my Journey, which I beg leave to do by offering the foregoing, as it contains the most remarkable Occurrences that happened to me.

I hope it will be sufficient to satisfy your Honour with my Proceedings; for that was my Aim in undertaking the Journey, and chief Study throughout the Prosecution of it.

With the hope of doing it, I, with infinite Pleasure, subscribe myself,

Your Honour's most Obedient,

And very humble Servant,

G. Washington

LETTER TO MARTHA WASHINGTON

Martha Washington destroyed all of her correspondence with George shortly before her death in 1802, save for these two letters that were found in a small writing desk inherited by one of her granddaughters.

Philadelphia June 18th 1775

My Dearest,

I am now set down to write to you on a subject which fills me with inexpressable concern—and this concern is greatly aggravated and Increased, when I reflect on the uneasiness I know it will give you—It has been determined in Congress, that the whole Army raised for the defence of the American Cause shall be put under my care, and that it is necessary for me to proceed immediately to Boston to take upon me the Command of it. You may beleive me my dear Patcy, when I assure you, in the most solemn manner, that, so far from seeking this appointment I have used every endeavour in my power to avoid it, not only from my unwillingness to part with you and the Family, but from a consciousness of its being a trust too great for my Capacity and that I should enjoy more real happiness and felicity in one month with you, at home, than I have the most distant prospect of reaping abroad, if my stay was to be Seven times Seven years. But, as it has been a kind of destiny that has thrown me upon this Service, I shall hope that my undertaking of it, is designd to answer some good purpose—You might, and I suppose did perceive, from the Tenor of my letters, that I was apprehensive I could not avoid this appointment, as I did not even pretend to intimate when I should return—that was the case—it was utterly out of my power to refuse this appointment without exposing my Character to such censures as would have reflected dishonour upon myself, and given pain to my friends—this I am sure could not, and ought not to be pleasing to you, & must have lessend me considerably in my own esteem. I shall rely therefore, confidently, on that Providence which has heretofore preservd, & been bountiful to me, not doubting but that I shall return safe to you in the fall—I shall feel no pain from the Toil, or the danger of the Campaign—My unhappiness will flow, from the uneasiness I know you will feel at being left alone—I therefore beg of you to summon your whole fortitude & Resolution, and pass your time as agreeably as possible—nothing will give me so much sincere satisfaction as to hear this, and to hear it from your own Pen.

If it should be your desire to remove into Alexandria (as you once mentioned upon an occasion of this sort) I am quite pleased that you should put it in practice, & Lund Washington may be directed, by you, to build a Kitchen and other Houses there proper for your reception—if on the other hand you should rather Incline to spend good part of your time among your Friends below, I wish you to do so—In short, my earnest, & ardent desire is, that you would pursue any Plan that is most likely to produce content, and a tolerable degree of Tranquility as it must add greatly to my uneasy feelings to hear that you are dissatisfied, and complaining at what I really could not avoid.

As Life is always uncertain, and common prudence dictates to every Man the necessity of settling his temporal Concerns whilst it is in his power—and whilst the Mind is calm and undisturbed, I have, since I came to this place (for I had not time to do it before I left home) got Colo. Pendleton to Draft a Will for me by the directions which I gave him, which Will I now Inclose—The Provision made for you, in case of my death, will, I hope, be agreeable; I have Included the Money for which I sold my own Land (to Doctr Mercer) in the Sum given you, as also all other Debts. What I owe myself is very trifling—Cary's Debt excepted, and that would not have been much if the Bank stock had been applied without such difficulties as he made in the Transference.

I shall add nothing more at present as I have several Letters to write, but to desire you will remember me to Milly & all Friends, and to assure you that I am with most unfeigned regard,

My dear
Patcy Yr Affecte
Go: Washington

P.S. Since writing the above I have receivd your Letter of the 15th and have got two suits of what I was told was the prettiest Muslin. I wish it may please you—it cost 50/. a suit that is 20/. a yard.

LETTER TO MARTHA WASHINGTON

Phila. June 23d 1775

My dearest,

As I am within a few Minutes of leaving this City, I could not think of departing from it without dropping you a line; especially as I do not know whether it may be in my power to write again till I get to the Camp at Boston—I go fully trusting in that Providence, which has been more bountiful to me than I deserve, & in full confidence of a happy meeting with you sometime in the Fall—I have not time to add more, as I am surrounded with Company to take leave of me—I retain an unalterable affection for you, which neither time or distance can change, my best love to Jack & Nelly, & regard for the rest of the Family concludes me with the utmost truth & sincerity,

Yr entire
Go: Washington

LETTER OF FAREWELL TO THE ARMY

Head Quarters Newburgh
8th June 1783

Sir,

The great object for which I had the honor to hold an appointment in the Service of my Country, being accomplished, I am now preparing to resign it into the hands of Congress, and to return to that domestic retirement, which, it is well known, I left with the greatest reluctance, a Retirement, for which I have never ceased to sigh through a long and painfull absence, and in which (remote from the noise and trouble of the World) I meditate to pass the remainder of life in a state of undisturbed repose; But before I carry this resolution into effect, I think it a duty incumbent on me, to make this my last official communication, to congratulate you on the glorious events which Heaven has been pleased to produce in our favor, to offer my sentiments respecting some important subjects, which appear to me, to be intimately connected with the tranquility of the United States, to take my leave of your Excellency as a public Character, and to give my final blessing to that Country, in whose service I have spent the prime of my life, for whose sake I have consumed so many anxious days and watchfull nights, and whose happiness being extremely dear to me, will always constitute no inconsiderable part of my own.

Impressed with the liveliest sensibility on this pleasing occasion, I will claim the indulgence of dilating the more copiously on the subjects of our mutual felicitation. When we consider the magnitude of the prize we contended for, the doubtfull nature of the contest, and the favorable manner in which it has terminated, we shall find the greatest possible reason for gratitude and rejoicing; this is a theme that will afford infinite delight to every benevolent & liberal mind, whether the event in contemplation, be considered as the source of present enjoyment, or the parent of future happiness, and we shall have equal occasion to felicitate ourselves on the lot which Providence has assigned us, whether we view it in a natural, a political or moral point of light.

The Citizens of America, placed in the most enviable condition, as the sole Lords and Proprietors of a vast Tract of Continent, comprehending all the various soils and climates of the World, and abounding with all the necessaries & conveniencies of life, are now by the late satisfactory pacification, acknowledged to be possessed of absolute freedom and Independency; They are, from this period, to be considered as the Actors on a most conspicuous Theatre, which seems to be peculiarly designated by Providence, for the display of human greatness & felicity; Here, they are not only surrounded with every thing which can contribute to the completion of private and domestic enjoyment, but Heaven has crowned all its other blessings, by giving a fairer oppertunity for political happiness, than any other Nation has ever been favored with. Nothing can illustrate these observations more forcibly, than a recollection of the happy conjuncture of times & circumstances, under which our Republic assumed its rank among the Nations; The foundation of our Empire was not laid in the gloomy age of Ignorance and Superstition, but at an Epocha when the rights of mankind were better understood and more clearly defined, than at any former period, the researches of the human mind, after social happiness, have been carried to a great extent, the Treasures of knowledge, acquired by the labours of Philosophers, Sages & Legislatures, through a long succession of years, are laid open for our use, and their collected wisdom may be happily applied in the Establishment of our forms of Government; the free cultivation of Letters, the unbounded extension of Commerce, the progressive refinement of Manners, the growing liberality of sentiment, and above all, the pure and benign light of Revelation, have had ameliorating influences on mankind and increased the blessings of Society. At this auspicious period, the United States came into existence as a Nation, and if their Citizens should not be completely free and happy, the fault will be entirely their own.

Such is our situation, and such are our prospects: but notwithstanding the cup of blessing is thus reached out to us, notwithstanding happiness is ours, if we have a disposition to seize the occasion & make it our own; yet, it appears to me there is an option still left to the United States of America, that it is in their choice, and depends upon their conduct, whether they will be respectable and prosperous, or contemptable and miserable as a Nation; This is the time of their political probation, this is the moment when the eyes of the whole World are turned upon them, this is the moment to establish or ruin their national Character forever, this is the favorable moment to give such a tone to our Federal Government, as will enable it to answer the ends of its institution, or this may be the ill-fated moment for relaxing the powers of the Union, annihilating the cement of the Confederation, and exposing us to become the sport of European politics, which may play one State against another to prevent their growing importance, and to serve their own interested purposes. For, according to the system of Policy the States shall adopt at this moment, they will stand or fall, and by their confirmation or lapse, it is yet to be decided, whether the Revolution must ultimately be considered as a blessing or a curse: a blessing or a curse, not to the present age alone, for with our fate will the destiny of unborn Millions be involved.

With this conviction of the importance of the present Crisis, silence in me would be a crime; I will therefore speak to your Excellency, the language of freedom and of sincerity, without disguise; I am aware, however, that those who differ from me in political sentiment, may perhaps remark, I am stepping out of the proper line of my duty, and they may possibly ascribe to arrogance or ostentation, what I know is alone the result of the purest intention, but the rectitude of my own heart, which disdains such unworthy motives, the part I have hitherto acted in life, the determination I have formed, of not taking any share in public business hereafter, the ardent desire I feel, and shall continue to manifest, of quietly enjoying in private life, after all the toils of War, the benefits of a wise and liberal Government, will, I flatter myself, sooner or later convince my Countrymen, that I could have no sinister views in delivering with so little reserve, the opinions contained in this Address.

There are four things, which I humbly conceive, are essential to the well being, I may even venture to say, to the existence of the United States as an Independent Power—

1st. An indissoluble Union of the States under one Federal Head.

2dly. A Sacred regard to Public Justice.

3dly. The adoption of a proper Peace Establishment and

4thly. The prevalence of that pacific and friendly Disposition, among the People of the United States, which will induce them to forget their local prejudices and policies, to make those mutual concessions which are requisite to the general prosperity, and in some instances, to sacrifice their individual advantages to the interest of the Community.

These are the pillars on which the glorious Fabrick of our Independency and National Character must be supported; Liberty is the Basis, and whoever would dare to sap the foundation, or overturn the Structure, under whatever specious pretexts he may attempt it, will merit the bitterest execration, & the severest punishment which can be inflicted by his injured Country.

On the three first Articles I will make a few observations, leaving the last to the good sense & serious consideration of those immediately concerned.

Under the first head, altho' it may not be necessary or proper for me in this place to enter into a particular disquisition of the principles of the Union, and to take up the great question which has been frequently agitated, whether it be expedient & requisite for the States to delegate a larger proportion of Power to Congress, or not, Yet it will be a part of my duty, and that of every true Patriot, to assert without reserve, and to insist upon the following positions, That unless the States will suffer Congress to exercise those prerogatives, they are undoubtedly invested with by the Constitution, every thing must very rapidly tend to Anarchy and confusion, That it is indispensable to the happiness of the individual States, that there should be lodged somewhere, a Supreme Power to regulate & govern the general concerns of the Confederated Republic, without which the Union cannot be of long duration. That there must be a faithfull & pointed compliance on the part of every State, with the late proposals and demands of Congress, or the most fatal consequences will ensue, That whatever measures have a tendency to dissolve the Union, or contribute to violate or lessen the Sovereign Authority, ought to be considered as hostile to the Liberty and Independency of America, and the Authors of them treated accordingly, and lastly, that unless we can be enabled by the concurrence of the States, to participate of the fruits of the Revolution, and enjoy the essential benefits of Civil Society, under a form of Government so free & uncorrupted, so happily guarded against the danger of oppression, as has been devised & adopted by the Articles of Confederation, it will be a subject of regret, that so much blood & treasure have been lavished for no purpose, that so many sufferings have been encountered without a compensation, and that so many sacrifices have been made in vain. Many other considerations might here be adduced to prove, that without an entire conformity to the Spirit of the Union, we cannot exist as an Independent Power; it will be sufficient for my purpose to mention but one or two which seem to me of the greatest importance. It is only in our united Character as an Empire, that our Independence is acknowledged, that our power can be regarded, or our Credit supported among Foreign Nations. The Treaties of the European Powers with the United States of America, will have no validity on a dissolution of the Union. We shall be left nearly in a state of Nature, or we may find by our own unhappy experience, that there is a natural and necessary progression, from the extreme of anarchy to the extreme of Tyranny; and that arbitrary power is most easily established on the ruins of Liberty abused to licentiousness.

As to file second Article, which respects the performance of Public Justice, Congress have, in their late Address to the United States, almost exhausted the subject, they have explained their Ideas so fully, and have enforced the obligations the States are under, to render compleat justice to all the Public Creditors, with so much dignity and energy, that in my opinion, no real friend to the honor and Independency of America, can hesitate a single moment respecting the propriety of complying with the just and honorable measures proposed; if their Arguments do not produce conviction, I know of nothing that will have greater influence; especially when we recollect that the System referred to, being the result of the collect'd Wisdom of the Continent, must be esteemed, if not perfect, certainly the least objectionable of any that could be devised; and that if it shall not be carried into immediate execution, a National Bankruptcy, with all its deplorable consequences will take place, before any different Plan can possibly be proposed and adopted; So pressing are the present circumstances! and such is the alternative now offered to the States!

The ability of the Country to discharge the debts which have been incurred in its defence, is not to be doubted, an inclination, I flatter myself, will not be wanting, the path of our duty is plain before us, honesty will be found on every experiment, to be the best and only true policy, let us then as a Nation be just, let us fulfil the public Contracts, which Congress had undoubtedly a right to make for the purpose of carrying on the War, with the same good faith we suppose ourselves bound to perform our private engagements; in the mean time, let an attention to the chearfull performance of their proper business, as Individuals, and as members of Society, be earnestly inculcated on the Citizens of America, that will they strengthen the hands of Government, and be happy under its protection: every one will reap the fruit of his labours, every one will enjoy his own acquisitions without molestation and without danger.

In this state of absolute freedom and perfect security, who will grudge to yield a very little of his property to support the common interest of Society, and insure the protection of Government? Who does not remember, the frequent declarations, at the commencement of the War, that we should be compleatly satisfied, if at the expence of one half, we could defend the remainder of our possessions? Where is the Man to be found, who wishes to remain indebted, for the defence of his own person and property, to the exertions, the bravery, and the blood of others, without making one generous effort to repay the debt of honor and of gratitude? In what part of the Continent shall we find any Man, or body of Men, who would not blush to stand up & propose measures, purposely calculated to rob the Soldier of his Stipend, and the Public Creditor of his due? and were it possible that such a flagrant instance of Injustice could ever happen, would it not excite the general indignation, and tend to bring down, upon the Authors of such measures, the aggravated vengeance of Heaven? If after all, a spirit of disunion or a temper of obstinacy and perverseness, should manifest itself in any of the States, if such an ungracious disposition should attempt to frustrate all the happy effects that might be expected to flow from the Union, if there should be a refusal to comply with the requisitions for Funds to discharge the annual interest of the public debts, and if that refusal should revive again all those jealousies & produce all those evils, which are now happily removed, Congress, who have in all their Transaction shewn a great degree of magnanimity and justice, will stand justified in the sight of God & Man, and the State alone which puts itself in opposition to the aggregate Wisdom of the Continent, and follows such mistaken and pernicious Councils, will be responsible for all the consequences.

For my own part, conscious of having acted while a Servant of the Public, in the manner I conceived best suited to promote the real interests of my Country; having in consequence of my fixed belief in some measure pledged myself to the Army, that their Country would finally do them compleat and ample Justice, and not wishing to conceal any instance of my official conduct from the eyes of the World, I have thought proper to transmit to your Excellency the enclosed collection of Papers, relative to the half pay & commutation granted by Congress to the Officers of the Army; From these communications, my decided sentiment will be clearly comprehended, together with the conclusive reasons which induced me, at an early period, to recommend the adoption of the measure, in the most earnest and serious manner. As the proceedings of Congress, the Army, and myself are open to all, and contain in my opinion, sufficient information to remove the prejudices and errors which may have been entertained by any; I think it unnecessary to say any thing more, than just to observe, that the Resolutions of Congress, now alluded to, are undoubtedly as absolutely binding upon the United States, as the most solemn Acts of Confederation or Legislation. As to the Idea, which I am informed has in some instances prevailed, that the half pay & commutation are to be regarded merely in the odious light of a Pension, it ought to be exploded forever; that Provision, should be viewed as it really was, a reasonable compensation offered by Congress, at a time when they had nothing else to give, to the Officers of the Army, for services then to be performed. It was the only means to prevent a total dereliction of the Service, It was a part of their hire, I may be allowed to say, it was the price of their blood & of your Independency, it is therefore more than a common debt, it is a debt of honour, it can never be considered as a Pension or gratuity, nor be cancelled until it is fairly discharged.

With regard to a distinction between Officers and Soldiers, it is sufficient that the uniform experience of every Nation of the World, combined with our own, proves the utility and propriety of the discrimination. Rewards in proportion to the aids the public derives from them, are unquestionably due to all its Servants; In some Lines, the Soldiers have perhaps generally had as ample a compensation for their Services, by the large Bounties which have been paid to them, as their Officers will receive in the proposed Commutation, in others, if besides the donation of Lands, the payment of Arrearages of Cloathing & Wages (in which Articles all the component parts of the Army must be put upon the same footing) we take into the estimate, the Bounties many of the Soldiers have received and the gratuity of one Year's full pay, which is promised to all, possibly their situation (every circumstance being duly considered) will not be deemed less eligible than that of the Officers. Should a farther reward, however, be judged equitable, I will venture to assert, no one will enjoy greater satisfaction than myself, on seeing an exemption from Taxes for a limited time, (which has been petitioned for in some instances) or any other adequate immunity or compensation, granted to the brave defenders of their Country's Cause; but neither the adoption or rejection of this proposition will in any manner affect, much less militate against, the Act of Congress, by which they have offered five years full pay, in lieu of the half pay for life, which had been before promised to the Officers of the Army.

Before I conclude the subject of public justice, I cannot omit to mention the obligations this Country is under, to that meritorious Class of veteran Non-commissioned Officers & Privates, who have been discharged for inability, in consequence of the Resolution of Congress of the 23d of April 1782, on an annual pension for life, their peculiar sufferings, their singular merits and claims to that provision need only be known, to interest all the feelings of humanity in their behalf: nothing but a punctual payment of their annual allowance can rescue them from the most complicated misery, and nothing could be a more melancholy and distressing sight, than to behold those who have shed their blood or lost their limbs in the service of their Country, without a shelter, without a friend, and without the means of obtaining any of the necessaries or comforts of Life; compelled to beg their daily bread from door to door! suffer me to recommend those of this discription, belonging to your State, to the warmest patronage of your Excellency and your Legislature.

It is necessary to say but a few words on the third topic which was proposed, and which regards particularly the defence of the Republic, As there can be little doubt but Congress will recommend a proper Peace Establishment for the United States, in which a due attention will be paid to the importance of placing the Militia of the Union upon a regular & respectable footing; If this should be the case, I would beg leave to urge the great advantage of it in the strongest terms. The Militia of this Country must be considered as the Palladium of our security, and the first effectual resort in case of hostility; It is essential therefore, that the same system should pervade the whole; that the formation & discipline of the Militia of the Continent should be absolutely uniform, and that the same species of Arms, Accoutrements & Military Apparatus, should be introduced in every part of the United States; No one, who has not learned it from experience, can conceive the difficulty, expence, and confusion which result from a contrary system, or the vague Arrangements which have hitherto prevailed.

If in treating of political points, a greater latitude than usual has been taken in the course of this Address, the importance of the Crisis, and the magnitude of the objects in discussion, must be my apology: It is, however, neither my wish or expectation, that the preceding observations should claim any regard, except so far as they shall appear to be dictated by a good intention, consonant to the immutable rules of Justice; calculated to produce a liberal system of policy, and founded on whatever experience may have been acquired by a long and close attention to public business. Here I might speak with the more confidence from my actual observations, and, if it would not swell this Letter (already too prolix) beyond the bounds I had prescribed myself: I could demonstrate to every mind open to conviction, that in less time & with much less expence than has been incurred, the War might have been brought to the same happy conclusion, if the resourses of the Continent could have been properly drawn forth, that the distresses & disappointments which have very often occurred, have in too many instances, resulted more from a want of energy in the Continental Government, than a deficiency of means in the particular States. That the inefficiency of measures, arising from the want of an adequate authority in the Supreme Power, from a partial compliance with the Requisitions of Congress in some of the States, and from a failure of punctuality in others, while it tended to damp the zeal of those which were more willing to exert themselves; served also to accumulate the expences of the War, and to frustrate the best concerted Plans, and that the discouragement occasioned by the complicated difficulties & embarrassments, in which our affairs were, by this means involved, would have long ago produced the dissolution of any Army, less patient, less virtuous and less persevering, than that which I have had the honor to command. But while I mention these things, which are notorious facts, as the defects of our Federal Constitution, particularly in the prosecution of a War, I beg it may be understood, that as I have ever taken a pleasure in gratefully acknowledging the assistance and support I have derived from every Class of Citizens, so shall I always be happy to do justice to the unparalleled exertion of the individual States, on many interesting occasions.

I have thus freely disclosed what I wished to make known, before I surrendered up my Public trust to those who committed it to me, the task is now accomplished, I now bid adieu to your Excellency as the Chief Magistrate of your State, at the same time I bid a last farewell to the cares of Office, and all the imployments of public life.

It remains then to be my final and only request, that your Excellency will communicate these sentiments to your Legislature at their next meeting, and that they may be considered as the Legacy of One, who has ardently wished, on all occasions, to be useful to his Country, and who, even in the shade of Retirement, will not fail to implore the divine benediction upon it.

I now make it my earnest prayer, that God would have you, and the State over which you preside, in his holy protection, that he would incline the hearts of the Citizens to cultivate a spirit of subordination & obedience to Government, to entertain a brotherly affection & love for one another, for their fellow Citizens of the United States at large, and particularly for their brethren who have served in the Field, and finally, that he would most graciously be pleased to dispose us all, to do Justice, to love mercy, and to demean ourselves with that Charity, humility & pacific temper of mind, which were the Characteristicks of the Divine Author of our blessed Religion, & without an humble imitation of whose example in these things, we can never hope to be a happy Nation.

FIRST INAUGURAL ADDRESS

April 30, 1789

Fellow Citizens of the Senate and of the House of Representatives:

Among the vicissitudes incident to life, no event could have filled me with greater anxieties than that of which the notification was transmitted by your order, and received on the 14th day of the present month. On the one hand, I was summoned by my Country, whose voice I can never hear but with veneration and love, from a retreat which I had chosen with the fondest predilection, and, in my flattering hopes, with an immutable decision, as the asylum of my declining years: a retreat which was rendered every day more necessary as well as more dear to me, by the addition of habit to inclination, and of frequent interruptions in my health to the gradual waste committed on it by time. On the other hand, the magnitude and difficulty of the trust to which the voice of my Country called me, being sufficient to awaken in the wisest and most experienced of her citizens a distrustful scrutiny into his qualifications, could not but overwhelm with despondence one who, (inheriting inferior endowments from nature and unpracticed in the duties of civil administration), ought to be peculiarly conscious of his own deficiencies. In this conflict of emotions, all I dare aver is that it has been my faithful study to collect my duty from a just appreciation of every circumstance by which it might be affected. All I dare hope is that if, in executing this task, I have been too much swayed by a grateful remembrance of former instances, or by an affectionate sensibility to this transcendent proof of the confidence of my fellow citizens, and have thence too little consulted my incapacity as well as disinclination for the weighty and untried cares before me, my error will be palliated by the motives which mislead me, and its consequences be judged by my Country with some share of the partiality in which they originated.

Such being the impressions under which I have, in obedience to the public summons, repaired to the present station, it would be peculiarly improper to omit in this first official act my fervent supplications to that Almighty Being who rules over the Universe, who presides in the Councils of Nations, and whose providential aids can supply every human defect, that his benediction may consecrate to the liberties and happiness of the People of the United States, a Government instituted by themselves for these essential purposes, and may enable every instrument employed in its administration to execute with success the functions allotted to his charge. In tendering this homage to the Great Author of every public and private good, I assure myself that it expresses your sentiments not less than my own, nor those of my fellow citizens at large less than either.

No People can be bound to acknowledge and adore the Invisible Hand which conducts the affairs of men more than those of the United States. Every step by which they have advanced to the character of an independent nation seems to have been distinguished by some token of providential agency; and in the important revolution just accomplished in the system of their United Government, the tranquil deliberations and voluntary consent of so many distinct communities, from which the event has resulted, can not be compared with the means by which most Governments have been established, without some return of pious gratitude, along with an humble anticipation of the future blessings which the past seem to presage. These reflections, arising out of the present crisis, have forced themselves too strongly on my mind to be suppressed. You will join with me, I trust, in thinking that there are none under the influence of which the proceedings of a new and free Government can more auspiciously commence.

By the article establishing the Executive Department, it is made the duty of the President "to recommend to your consideration such measures as he shall judge necessary and expedient." The circumstances under which I now meet you will acquit me from entering into that subject further than to refer to the Great Constitutional Charter under which you are assembled, and which, in defining your powers, designates the objects to which your attention is to be given. It will be more consistent with those circumstances, and far more congenial with the feelings which actuate me, to substitute, in place of a recommendation of particular measures, the tribute that is due to the talents, the rectitude, and the patriotism which adorn the characters selected to devise and adopt them. In these honorable qualifications I behold the surest pledges, that as on one side, no local prejudices, or attachments; no separate views, nor party animosities, will misdirect the comprehensive and equal eye which ought to watch over this great assemblage of communities and interests: so, on another, that the foundations of our National policy will be laid in the pure and immutable principles of private morality; and the preeminence of free Government be exemplified by all the attributes which can win the affections of its Citizens, and command the respect of the world.

I dwell on this prospect with every satisfaction which an ardent love for my Country can inspire: since there is no truth more thoroughly established than that there exists in the economy and course of nature an indissoluble union between virtue and happiness, between duty and advantage, between the genuine maxims of an honest and magnanimous policy and the solid rewards of public prosperity and felicity: Since we ought to be no less persuaded that the propitious smiles of Heaven can never be expected on a nation that disregards the eternal rules of order and right, which Heaven itself has ordained: And since the preservation of the sacred fire of liberty, and the destiny of the Republican model of Government, are justly considered, perhaps, as deeply, as finally staked on the experiment entrusted to the hands of the American people.

Besides the ordinary objects submitted to your care, it will remain with your judgment to decide how far an exercise of the occasional power delegated by the Fifth article of the Constitution is rendered expedient at the present juncture by the nature of objections which have been urged against the system, or by the degree of inquietude which has given birth to them. Instead of undertaking particular recommendations on this subject, in which I could be guided by no lights derived from official opportunities, I shall again give way to my entire confidence in your discernment and pursuit of the public good; for I assure myself that whilst you carefully avoid every alteration which might endanger the benefits of an united and effective Government, or which ought to await the future lessons of experience; a reverence for the characteristic rights of freemen, and a regard for the public harmony, will sufficiently influence your deliberations on the question how far the former can be impregnably fortified, or the latter be safely and advantageously promoted.

To the proceeding observations I have one to add, which will be most properly addressed to the House of Representatives. It concerns myself, and will therefore be as brief as possible. When I was first honored with a call into the Service of my Country, then on the eve of an arduous struggle for its liberties, the light in which I contemplated my duty required that I should renounce every pecuniary compensation. From this resolution I have in no instance departed; and being still under the impressions which produced it, I must decline as inapplicable to myself, any share in the personal emoluments which may be indispensably included in a permanent provision for the Executive Department, and must accordingly pray that the pecuniary estimates for the Station in which I am placed, may, during my continuance in it, be limited to such actual expenditures as the public good may be thought to require.

Having thus imparted to you my sentiments, as they have been awakened by the occasion which brings us together, I shall take my present leave; but not without resorting once more to the benign Parent of the Human Race in humble supplication that, since He has been pleased to favor the American people with opportunities for deliberating in perfect tranquillity, and dispositions for deciding with unparalleled unanimity on a form of Government, for the security of their Union, and the advancement of their happiness, so His divine blessing may be equally *conspicuous* in the enlarged views, the temperate consultations, and the wise measures on which the success of this Government must depend.

SECOND INAUGURAL ADDRESS

March 4, 1793

Fellow Citizens,

I am again called upon by the voice of my Country to execute the functions of its Chief Magistrate. When the occasion proper for it shall arrive, I shall endeavor to express the high sense I entertain of this distinguished honor, and of the confidence which has been reposed in me by the people of United America.

Previous to the execution of any official act of the President, the Constitution requires an oath of office. This oath I am now about to take, and in your presence, that if it shall be found during my administration of the Government, I have in any instance violated, willingly or knowingly, the injunctions thereof, I may (besides incurring Constitutional punishment) be subject to the upbraidings of all who are now witnesses of the present solemn Ceremony.

RESIDENCE ACT OF 1790

July 16, 1790

Congress of the United States:

AT THE SECOND SESSION,

Begun and held at the City of New-York on Monday the fourth day of January, one thousand seven hundred and ninety.

An Act for establishing the Temporary and Permanent Seat of the Government of the United States.

Be it enacted by the Senate and House of Representatives of the United States of America in Congress assembled, That a district of territory, not exceeding ten miles square, to be located as hereafter directed on the river Potomack, at some place between the mouths of the Eastern-Branch and Connogochegue be, and the same is hereby accepted for the permanent seat of the government of the United States: *Provided nevertheless*, That the operation of the laws of the state within such district shall not be affected by this acceptance, until the time fixed for the removal of the government thereto, and until Congress shall otherwise by law provide.

And be it further enacted, That the President of the United States be authorized to appoint, and by supplying vacancies happening from refusals to act, or other causes, to keep in appointment, as long as may be necessary, three commissioners, who, or any two of whom, shall under the direction of the President, survey, and by proper metes and bounds, define and limit a district of territory, under the limitations above-mentioned; and the district so defined, limited and located, shall be deemed the district accepted by this act, for the permanent seat of the government of the United States.

And be it enacted, That the said commissioners, or any two of them shall have power to purchase or accept such quantity of land on the eastern side of the said river within the said district, as the President shall deem proper for the use of the United States, and according to such plans as the President shall approve, the said commissioners, or any two of them shall, prior to the first Monday in December, in the year one thousand eight hundred, provide suitable buildings for the accommodation of Congress, and of the President, and for the public offices of the government of the United States.

And be it enacted, That for defraying the expence of such purchases and buildings, the President of the United States be authorized and requested to accept grants of money.

And be it enacted, That prior to the first Monday in December next, all offices attached to the seat of the government of the United States, shall be removed to, and until the said first Monday in December, in the year one thousand eight hundred, shall remain at the city of Philadelphia, in the state of Pennsylvania; at which place the session of Congress next ensuing the present, shall be held.

And be it enacted, That on the said first Monday in December, in the year one thousand eight hundred, the seat of the government of the United States, shall, by virtue of this act, be transferred to the district and place aforesaid: And all offices attached to the said seat of government, shall accordingly be removed thereto by their respective holders, and shall, after the said day, cease to be exercised elsewhere; and that the necessary expence of such removal shall be defrayed out of the duties on imposts and tonnage, of which a sufficient sum is hereby appropriated.

Frederick Augustus Muhlenberg,
Speaker of the House of Representatives.
John Adams, *Vice-President of the United States,*
and President of the Senate.

Approved, July the sixteenth, 1790.

George Washington, President of the United States.

PROCLAMATION OF JANUARY 24, 1791

BY THE PRESIDENT OF THE U.S. OF AMERICA.
A PROCLAMATION.

Whereas the general assembly of the State of Maryland, by an act passed on the 23d day of December, A.D. 1788, intituled "an act to cede to Congress a district of 10 miles square in this state for the seat of the government of the U.S." did enact that the representatives of the said state, in the house of representatives of the Congress of the U.S. appointed to assemble at New York on the first Wednesday of March then next ensuing, should be, and they were thereby, authorized and required, on the behalf of the said state to cede to the Congress of the U.S. any district in the said State not exceeding 10 miles square which the Congress might fix upon and accept for the seat of government of the U.S.

And the General assembly of the commonwealth of Virginia, by an act passed on the 3d day of December 1789, and intituled "an Act for the cession of 10 miles square, or any lesser quantity of territory within this state, to the U.S. in Congress assembled, for the permanent seat of the General government," did enact that a tract of country not exceeding 10 miles square, or any lesser quantity, to be located within the limits of the said state, and in any part thereof as Congress might by law direct, should be, and the same was thereby forever ceded and relinquished to the Congress and government of the U.S. in full and absolute right and exclusive jurisdiction, as well of soil as of persons residing or to reside thereon, pursuant to the tenor and effect of the 8th section of the first article of the constitution of government of the U.S.

And the Congress of the U.S. by their act passed the 16th day of July 1790 and intituled "an act for establishing the temporary and permanent seat of the government of the U.S." authorized the President of the U.S. to appoint three commissioners to survey under his direction and by proper metes and bounds to limit a district of territory, not exceeding 10 miles square, on the river Potomac, at some place between the mouths of the Eastern branch and Connogocheque, which district so to be located and limited, was accepted by the said act of Congress, as the district for the permanent seat of the government of the U.S.

Now, therefore, in pursuance of the powers to me confided, and after duly examining and weighing the advantages and disadvantages of the several situations within the limits aforesaid, I do hereby declare and make known that the location of one part of the said district of 10 miles square shall be found by running four lines of experiment in the following manner, that is to say, running from the Courthouse of Alexandria in Virginia due South West half a mile, and thence a due South East course till it shall strike Hunting creek, to fix the Beginning of the said four lines of experiment:

Then beginning the first of the said four lines of experiment at the point on Hunting creek where the said South East course shall have struck the same, and running the said first line due North West 10 miles: thence the second line into Maryland due North East 10 miles: thence the third line due South East 10 miles: and thence the fourth line due South West 10 miles to the beginning on Hunting creek.

And the said four lines of experiment being so run, I do hereby declare and make known that all that part within the said four lines of experiment which shall be within the state of Maryland and above the Eastern branch, and all that part within the same four lines of experiment which shall be within the commonwealth of Virginia and above a line to be run from the point of land forming the upper cape of the mouth of the Eastern branch due South West and no more, is now fixed upon and directed to be surveyed, defined, limited, and located for a part of the said district accepted by the said act of Congress for the permanent seat of the government of the U.S. (Hereby expressly reserving the direction of the survey and location of the remaining part of the said district to be made hereafter contiguous to such part or parts of the present location as is, or shall be agreeable to law.)

And I do accordingly direct the said Commissioners, appointed agreeably to the tenor of the said act, to proceed forthwith to run the said lines of experiment, and the same being run, to survey and by proper metes and bounds to define and limit the part within the same which is hereinbefore directed for immediate location and acceptance, and thereof to make due report to me under their hands and seals.

In testimony whereof I have caused the seal of the U.S. to be affixed to these presents and signed the same with my hand. Done at the city of Philadelphia the 24th day of January in the year of our Lord 1791, and of the Independence of the United States the fifteenth.

George Washington.
By the President
Th: Jefferson

PROCLAMATION OF FEDERAL DISTRICT MARCH 31, 1791

BY THE PRESIDENT OF THE U.S. OF AMERICA.

A PROCLAMATION.

Whereas by a proclamation bearing date the 24th day of January of this present year, and in pursuance of certain acts of the states of Maryland and Virginia, and of the Congress of the U.S. therein mentioned, certain lines of experiment were directed to be run in the neighborhood of Georgetown in Maryland for the purpose of determining the location of a part of the territory of 10 miles square for the permanent seat of the government of the U.S. and a certain part was directed to be located within the said lines of experiment on both sides of the Potomac and above the limit of the Eastern branch prescribed by the said act of Congress:

And Congress by an amendatory act passed on the 3d day of this present month of March have given further authority to the President of the U.S. "to make any part of the territory below the said limit and above the mouth of Hunting creek a part of the said district, so as to include a convenient part of the Eastern branch, and of the lands lying on the lower side thereof, and also the town of Alexandria."

Now therefore for the purpose of amending and completing the location of the whole of the said territory of ten miles square in conformity with the said amendatory act of Congress, I do hereby declare and make known that the whole of the said territory shall be located and included within the four lines following, that is to say:

Beginning at Jones's Point, being the upper cape of Hunting creek in Virginia, and at an angle, in the outset, of 45 degrees West of the North; and running in a direct line ten miles for the first line: then beginning again at the same Jones's Point, and running another direct line, at a right angle with the first, across the Potomac, ten miles for the second line: then from the termination of the said first and second lines, running two other direct lines of ten miles each, the one crossing the Eastern branch aforesaid and the other the Potomac, and meeting each other in a point.

And I do accordingly direct the Commissioners named under the authority of the said first mentioned act of Congress to proceed forthwith to have the said four lines run, and by proper metes and bounds defined and limited, and thereof to make due report under their hands and seals: and the territory so to be located, defined, and limited shall be the whole territory accepted by the said acts of Congress as the district for the permanent seat of the government of the U.S.

And whereas the said first mentioned act of Congress did further enact that the said Commissioners should, under the direction of the President of the U.S. provide suitable buildings for the accomodation of Congress and of the President and for the public offices of the government of the United States.

I do hereby further declare and make known that [the highest summit of lands in the town heretofore called Hamburg, within the said territory, with a convenient extent of grounds circumjacent, shall be appropriated for a Capitol for the accomodation of Congress and such other lands between Georgetown and the stream heretofore called the Tyber, as shall on due examination be found convenient and sufficient, shall be appropriated for the accomodation of the President of the United States for the time being, and for the public offices of the government of the U.S.]* And I do hereby direct the said Commissioners accordingly."

In testimony whereof I have caused the seal of the U.S. to be affixed to these presents and sighed the same with my hand. Done at Georgetown aforesaid the ___ day of March, in the year of our Lord 1791, and of the Independence of the U.S. the fifteenth.

* The part within [ ] being conjectural, will be to be rendered conformable to the ground when more accurately examined.

FIRST ANNUAL ADDRESS TO CONGRESS

Speech of the President of the United States to both Houses of Congress

January 8, 1790

Fellow Citizens of the Senate, and House of Representatives,

I embrace with great satisfaction the opportunity, which now presents itself, of congratulating you upon the present favourable prospects of our public affairs. The recent acscession of the important State of North Carolina to the Constitution of the United States (of which official information has been received)—the rising credit and respectability of our country—the general and increasing good will towards the Government of the Union, and the concord, peace and plenty, with which we are blessed, are circumstances auspicious, in an eminent degree, to our national prosperity.

In resuming your consultations for the general good, you can not but derive encouragement from the reflection, that the measures of the last session have been as satisfactory to your Constituents as the novelty and difficulty of the work allowed you to hope. Still further to realize their expectations and to secure the blessings which a Gracious Providence has placed within our reach, will in the course of the present important session, call for the cool and deliberate exertion of your patriotism, firmness and wisdom.

Among the many interesting objects which will engage your attention, that of providing for the common defence will merit particular regard. To be prepared for War is one of the most effectual means of preserving peace.

A free people ought not only to be armed but disciplined; to which end a uniform and well digested plan is requisite: And their safety and interest require that they should promote such manufactories, as tend to render them independent on others for essential, particularly for military supplies.

The proper establishment of the Troops, which may be deemed indispensable, will be entitled to mature deliberation. In the arrangements, which may be made respecting it, it will be of importance to conciliate the comfortable support of the Officers and Soldiers with a due regard to economy.

There was reason to hope that the pacific measures adopted with regard to certain hostile tribes of Indians would have relieved the inhabitants of our Southern and Western frontiers from their depredations. But you will perceive, from the information contained in the papers, which I shall direct to be laid before you (comprehending a communication from the Commonwealth of Virginia) that we ought ot be prepared to afford protection to those parts of the Union; and if necessary, to punish aggressors.

The interests of the United States require that our intercourse with other nations should be facilitated, by such provisions as will enable me to fulfill my duty in that respect, in the manner which circumstances may render most conducive to the public good: And to this end that the compensations to be made to the persons who may be employed, should according to the nature of their appointments be defined by law; and a competent fund designated for defraying the expences incident to the conduct of our foreign affairs.

Various considerations also render it expedient, that the terms on which foreigners may be admitted to the rights of Citizens, should be speedily ascertained by a uniform rule of naturalization.

Uniformity in the Currency, Weights and Measures of the United States is an object of great importance, and will I am persuaded be duly attended to.

The advancement of Agriculture, Commerce and Manufactures, by all proper means, will not I trust need recommendation. But I can not forbear intimating to you the expediency of giving effectual encouragement as well to the introduction of new and useful inventions from abroad, as to the exertions of skill and genius in producing them at home; and of facilitating the intercourse between the distant parts of our Country by a due attention to the Post Office and Post Roads.

Nor am I less persuaded that you will agree with me in opinion, that there is nothing which can better deserve your patronage than the promotion of Science and Literature. Knowledge is in every country the surest basis of public happiness. In one in which the measures of Government receive their impression so immediately from the sense of the Community as in ours it is proportionably essential. To the security of a free Constitution it contributes in various ways: By convincing those who are entrusted with the public administration, that every valuable end of Government is best answered by the enlightened confidence of the people: And by teaching the people themselves to know and to value their own rights; to discern and provide against invasions of them; to distinguish between oppression and the necessary exercise of lawful authority; between burthens proceeding from a disregard to their convenience, and those resulting from the inevitable exigencies of Society; to discriminate the spirit of liberty from that of licentiousness, cherishing the first, avoiding the last, and uniting a speedy but temperate vigilance against encroachments, with an inviolable respect to the Laws.

Whether this desirable object will be best promoted by affording aids to seminaries of learning already established, by the institution of a national

University, or by any other expedients, will be well worthy of a place in the deliberations of the Legislature.

Gentlemen of the House of Representatives

I saw with peculiar pleasure at the close of the last session the resolution entered into by you, expressive of your opinion, that an adequate provision for the support of the public credit is a matter of high importance to the national honour and prosperity. In this sentiment I entirely concur. And to a perfect confidence in your best endeavors to devise such a provision as will be truly consistent with the end, I add an equal reliance on the chearful cooperation of the other branch of the Legislature. It would be superfluous to specify inducements to a measure in which the Character and permanent interests of the United States are so obviously and so deeply concerned; and which has received so explicit a sanction from your declaration.

Gentlemen of the Senate, and House of Representatives.

I have directed the proper Officers to lay before you respectively such papers and estimates as regard the affairs particularly recommended to your consideration and necessary to convey to you that information of the state of the Union, which it is my duty to afford.

The welfare of our Country is the great object to which our Cares and efforts ought to be directed. And I shall derive great satisfaction from a cooperation with you, in the pleasing tho' arduous task of ensuring to our fellow citizens the blessings which they have a right to expect from a free, efficient and equal Government.

United States
January 8th 1790

signed) G.Washington

SECOND ADDRESS TO CONGRESS

December 8, 1790

Fellow Citizens of the Senate and the House of Representatives:

In meeting you again I feel much satisfaction in being able to repeat my congratulations on the favorable prospects which continue to distinguish our public affairs. The abundant fruits of another year have blessed our country with plenty and with the means of a flourishing commerce.

The progress of public credit is witnessed by a considerable rise of American stock abroad as well as at home, and the revenues allotted for this and other national purposes have been productive beyond the calculations by which they were regulated. This latter circumstance is the more pleasing, as it is not only a proof of the fertility of our resources, but as it assures us of a further increase of the national respectability and credit, and, let me add, as it bears an honorable testimony to the patriotism and integrity of the mercantile and marine part of our citizens. The punctuality of the former in discharging their engagements has been exemplary.

In conformity to the powers vested in me by acts of the last session, a loan of 3,000,000 florins, toward which some provisional measures had previously taken place, has been completed in Holland. As well the celerity with which it has been filled as the nature of the terms (considering the more than ordinary demand for borrowing created by the situation of Europe) give a reasonable hope that the further execution of those powers may proceed with advantage and success. The Secretary of the Treasury has my directions to communicate such further particulars as may be requisite for more precise information.

Since your last sessions I have received communications by which it appears that the district of Kentucky, at present a part of Virginia, has concurred in certain propositions contained in a law of that State, in consequence of which the district is to become a distinct member of the Union, in case the requisite sanction of Congress be added. For this sanction application is now made. I shall cause the papers on this very transaction to be laid before you.

The liberality and harmony with which it has been conducted will be found to do great honor to both the parties, and the sentiments of warm attachment to the Union and its present Government expressed by our fellow citizens of Kentucky can not fail to add an affectionate concern for their particular welfare to the great national impressions under which you will decide on the case submitted to you.

It has been heretofore known to Congress that frequent incursion have been made on our frontier settlements by certain banditti of Indians from the northwest side of the Ohio. These, with some of the tribes dwelling on and near the Wabash, have of late been particularly active in their depredations, and being emboldened by the impunity of their crimes and aided by such parts of the neighboring tribes as could be seduced to join in their hostilities or afford them a retreat for their prisoners and plunder, they have, instead of listening to the humane invitations and overtures made on the part of the United States, renewed their violences with fresh alacrity and greater effect. The lives of a number of valuable citizens have thus been sacrificed, and some of them under circumstances peculiarly shocking, whilst others have been carried into a deplorable captivity.

These aggravated provocations rendered it essential to the safety of the Western settlements that the aggressors should be made sensible that the Government of the Union is not less capable of punishing their crimes than it is disposed to respect their rights and reward their attachments. As this object could not be effected by defensive measures, it became necessary to put in force the act which empowers the President to call out the militia for the protection of the frontiers, and I have accordingly authorized an expedition in which the regular troops in that quarter are combined with such drafts of militia as were deemed sufficient. The event of the measure is yet unknown to me. The Secretary of War is directed to lay before you a statement of the information on which it is founded, as well as an estimate of the expense with which it will be attended.

The disturbed situation of Europe, and particularly the critical posture of the great maritime powers, whilst it ought to make us the more thankful for the general peace and security enjoyed by the United States, reminds us at the same time of the circumspection with which it becomes us to preserve these blessings. It requires also that we should not overlook the tendency of a war, and even of preparations for a war, among the nations most concerned in active commerce with this country to abridge the means, and thereby at least enhance the price, of transporting its valuable productions to their markets. I recommend it to your serious reflections how far and in what mode it may be expedient to guard against embarrassments from these contingencies by such encouragements to our own navigation as will render our commerce and agriculture less dependent on foreign bottoms, which may fail us in the very moments most interesting to both of these great objects. Our fisheries and the transportation of our own produce offer us abundant means for guarding ourselves against this evil.

Your attention seems to be not less due to that particular branch of our trade which belongs to the Mediterranean. So many circumstances unite in rendering the present state of it distressful to us that you will not think any deliberations misemployed which may lead to its relief and protection.

The laws you have already passed for the establishment of a judiciary system have opened the doors of justice to all descriptions of persons. You will consider in your wisdom whether improvements in that system may yet be made, and particularly whether an uniform process of execution on sentences issuing from the Federal courts be not desirable through all the States.

The patronage of our commerce, of our merchants and sea men, has called for the appointment of consuls in foreign countries. It seems expedient to regulate by law the exercise of that jurisdiction and those functions which are permitted them, either by express convention or by a friendly indulgence, in the places of their residence. The consular convention, too, with His Most Christian Majesty has stipulated in certain cases the aid of the national authority to his consuls established here. Some legislative provision is requisite to carry these stipulations into full effect.

The establishment of the militia, of a mint, of standards of weights and measures, of the post office and post roads are subjects which I presume you will resume of course, and which are abundantly urged by their own importance.

GENTLEMEN OF THE HOUSE OF REPRESENTATIVES:

The sufficiency of the revenues you have established for the objects to which they are appropriated leaves no doubt that the residuary provisions will be commensurate to the other objects for which the public faith stands now pledged. Allow me, moreover, to hope that it will be a favorite policy with you, not merely to secure a payment of the interest of the debt funded, but as far and as fast as the growing resources of the country will permit to exonerate it of the principal itself. The appropriation you have made of the Western land explains your dispositions on this subject, and I am persuaded that the sooner that valuable fund can be made to contribute, along with the other means, to the actual reduction of the public debt the more salutary will the measure be to every public interest, as well as the more satisfactory to our constituents.

GENTLEMEN OF THE SENATE AND HOUSE OF REPRESENTATIVES:

In pursuing the various and weighty business of the present session I indulge the fullest persuasion that your consultation will be equally marked with wisdom and animated by the love of your country. In whatever belongs to my duty you shall have all the cooperation which an undiminished zeal for its welfare can inspire. It will be happy for us both, and our best reward, if, by a successful administration of our respective trusts, we can make the established Government more and more instrumental in promoting the good of our fellow citizens, and more and more the object of their attachment and confidence.

THIRD ADDRESS TO CONGRESS

October 25, 1791

Fellow Citizens of the Senate and the House of Representatives:

I meet you upon the present occasion with the feelings which are naturally inspired by a strong impression of the prosperous situations of our common country, and by a persuasion equally strong that the labors of the session which has just commenced will, under the guidance of a spirit no less prudent than patriotic, issue in measures conducive to the stability and increase of national prosperity.

Numerous as are the providential blessings which demand our grateful acknowledgments, the abundance with which another year has again rewarded the industry of the husbandman is too important to escape recollection.

Your own observations in your respective situations will have satisfied you of the progressive state of agriculture, manufactures, commerce, and navigation. In tracing their causes you will have remarked with particular pleasure the happy effects of that revival of confidence, public as well as private, to which the Constitution and laws of the United States have so eminently contributed; and you will have observed with no less interest new and decisive proofs of the increasing reputation and credit of the nation. But you nevertheless can not fail to derive satisfaction from the confirmation of these circumstances which will be disclosed in the several official communications that will be made to you in the course of your deliberations.

The rapid subscriptions to the Bank of the United States, which completed the sum allowed to be subscribed in a single day, is among the striking and pleasing evidences which present themselves, not only of confidence in the Government, but of resource in the community.

In the interval of your recess due attention has been paid to the execution of the different objects which were specially provided for by the laws and resolutions of the last session.

Among the most important of these is the defense and security of the western frontiers. To accomplish it on the most humane principles was a primary wish.

Accordingly, at the same time the treaties have been provisionally concluded and other proper means used to attach the wavering and to confirm in their friendship the well-disposed tribes of Indians, effectual measures have been adopted to make those of a hostile description sensible that a pacification was desired upon terms of moderation and justice.

Those measures having proved unsuccessful, it became necessary to convince the refractory of the power of the United States to punish their depredations. Offensive operations have therefore been directed, to be conducted, however, as consistently as possible with the dictates of humanity.

Some of these have been crowned with full success and others are yet depending. The expeditions which have been completed were carried on under the authority and at the expense of the United States by the militia of Kentucky, whose enterprise, intrepidity, and good conduct are entitled of peculiar commendation.

Overtures of peace are still continued to the deluded tribes, and considerable numbers of individuals belonging to them have lately renounced all further opposition, removed from their former situations, and placed themselves under the immediate protection of the United States.

It is sincerely to be desired that all need of coercion in future may cease and that an intimate intercourse may succeed, calculated to advance the happiness of the Indians and to attach them firmly to the United States.

In order to this it seems necessary—

That they should experience the benefits of an impartial dispensation of justice.

That the mode of alienating their lands, the main source of discontent and war, should be so defined and regulated as to obviate imposition and as far as may be practicable controversy concerning the reality and extent of the alienations which are made.

That commerce with them should be promoted under regulations tending to secure an equitable deportment toward them, and that such rational experiments should be made for imparting to them the blessings of civilization as may from time to time suit their condition.

That the Executive of the United States should be enabled to employ the means to which the Indians have been long accustomed for uniting their immediate interests with the preservation of peace.

And that efficacious provision should be made for inflicting adequate penalties upon all those who, by violating their rights, shall infringe the treaties and endanger the peace of the Union.

A system corresponding with the mild principles of religion and philanthropy toward an unenlightened race of men, whose happiness materially depends on the conduct of the United States, would be as honorable to the national character as conformable to the dictates of sound policy.

The powers specially vested in me by the act laying certain duties on distilled spirits, which respect the subdivisions of the districts into surveys, the appointment of officers, and the assignment of compensations, have likewise carried into effect.

In a manner in which both materials and experience were wanting to guide the calculation it will be readily conceived that there must have been difficulty in such an adjustment of the rates of compensation as would conciliate a reasonable competency with a proper regard to the limits prescribed by the law. It is hoped that the circumspection which has been used will be found in the result to have secured that last two objects; but it is probable that with a view to the first in some instances a revision of the provision will be found advisable.

The impressions with which this law has been received by the community have been upon the whole such as were to be expected among enlightened and well-disposed citizens from the propriety and necessity of the measure. The novelty, however, of the tax in a considerable part of the United States and a misconception of some of its provisions have given occasion in particular places to some degree of discontent; but it is satisfactory to know that this disposition yields to proper explanations and more just apprehensions of the true nature of the law, and I entertain a full confidence that it will in all give way to motives which arise out of a just sense of duty and a virtuous regard to the public welfare.

If there are any circumstances in the law which consistently with its main design may be so varied as to remove any well-intentioned objections that may happen to exist, it will consist with a wise moderation to make the proper variations. It is desirable on all occasions to unite with a steady and firm adherence to constitutional and necessary acts of Government the fullest evidence of a disposition as far as may be practicable to consult the wishes of every part of the community and to lay the foundations of the public administration in the affections of the people.

Pursuant to the authority contained in the several acts on that subject, a district of 10 miles square for the permanent seat of the Government of the United State has been fixed and announced by proclamation, which district will comprehend lands on both sides of the river Potomac and the towns of Alexandria and Georgetown. A city has also been laid out agreeably to a plan which will be placed before Congress, and as there is a prospect, favored by the rate of sales which have already taken place, of ample funds for carrying on the necessary public buildings, there is every expectation of their due progress.

The completion of the census of the inhabitants, for which provision was made by law, has been duly notified (excepting one instance in which the return has been informal, and another in which it has been omitted or miscarried), and the returns of the officers who were charged with this duty, which will be laid before you, will give you the pleasing assurance that the present population of the United States borders on 4,000,000 persons.

It is proper also to inform you that a further loan of 2,500,000 florins has been completed in Holland, the terms of which are similar to those of the one last announced, except as to a small reduction of charges. Another, on like terms, for 6,000,000 florins, had been set on foot under circumstances that assured an immediate completion.

GENTLEMEN OF THE SENATE:

Two treaties which have been provisionally concluded with the Cherokees and Six Nations of Indians will be laid before you for your consideration and ratification.

GENTLEMEN OF THE HOUSE OF REPRESENTATIVES:

In entering upon the discharge of your legislative trust you must anticipate with pleasure that many of the difficulties necessarily incident to the first arrangements of a new government for an extensive country have been happily surmounted by the zealous and judicious exertions of your predecessors in cooperation with the other branch of the Legislature. The important objects which remain to be accomplished will, I am persuaded, be conducted upon principles equally comprehensive and equally well calculated of the advancement of the general weal.

The time limited for receiving subscriptions to the loans proposed by the act making provision for the debt of the United States having expired, statements from the proper department will as soon as possible apprise you of the exact result. Enough, however, is known already to afford an assurance that the views of that act have been substantially fulfilled. The subscription in the domestic debt of the United States has embraced by far the greatest proportion of that debt, affording at the same time proof of the general satisfaction of the public creditors with the system which has been proposed to their acceptance and of the spirit of accommodation to the convenience of the Government with which they are actuated. The subscriptions in the debts of the respective States as far as the provisions of the law have permitted may be said to be yet more general. The part of the debt of the United States which remains unsubscribed will naturally engage your further deliberations.

It is particularly pleasing to me to be able to announce to you that the revenues which have been established promise to be adequate to their objects, and may be permitted, if no unforeseen exigency occurs, to supersede for the present the necessity of any new burthens upon our constituents.

An object which will claim your early attention is a provision for the current service of the ensuing year, together with such ascertained demands upon the Treasury as require to be immediately discharged, and such casualties as may have arisen in the execution of the public business, for which no specific appropriation may have yet been made; of all which a proper estimate will be laid before you.

GENTLEMEN OF THE SENATE AND OF THE HOUSE OF REPRESENTATIVES:

I shall content myself with a general reference to former communications for several objects upon which the urgency of other affairs has hitherto postponed any definitive resolution. Their importance will recall them to your attention, and I trust that the progress already made in the most arduous arrangements of the Government will afford you leisure to resume them to advantage.

These are, however, some of them of which I can not forbear a more particular mention. These are the militia, the post office and post roads, the mint, weights and measures, a provision for the sale of the vacant lands of the United States.

The first is certainly an object of primary importance whether viewed in reference to the national security to the satisfaction of the community or to the preservation of order. In connection with this the establishment of competent magazines and arsenals and the fortification of such places as are peculiarly important and vulnerable naturally present themselves to consideration. The safety of the United States under divine protection ought to rest on the basis of systematic and solid arrangements, exposed as little as possible to the hazards of fortuitous circumstances.

The importance of the post office and post roads on a plan sufficiently liberal and comprehensive, as they respect the expedition, safety, and facility of communication, is increased by their instrumentality in diffusing a knowledge of the laws and proceedings of the Government, which, while it contributes to the security of the people, serves also to guard them against the effects of misrepresentation and misconception. The establishment of additional cross posts, especially to some of the important points in the Western and Northern parts of the Union, can not fail to be of material utility.

The disorders in the existing currency, and especially the scarcity of small change, a scarcity so peculiarly distressing to the poorer classes, strongly recommend the carrying into immediate effect the resolution already entered into concerning the establishment of a mint. Measures have been taken pursuant to that resolution for procuring some of the most necessary artists, together with the requisite apparatus.

An uniformity in the weights and measures of the country is among the important objects submitted to you by the Constitution, and if it can be derived from a standard at once invariable and universal, must be no less honorable to the public councils than conducive to the public convenience.

A provision for the sale of the vacant lands of the United States is particularly urged, among other reasons, by the important considerations that they are pledged as a fund for reimbursing the public debt; that if timely and judiciously applied they may save the necessity of burthening our citizens with new taxes for the extinguishment of the principal; and that being free to discharge the principal but in a limited proportion, no opportunity ought to be lost for availing the public of its right.

FOURTH ADDRESS TO CONGRESS

November 6, 1792

Fellow Citizens of the Senate and of the House of Representatives:

It is some abatement of the satisfaction with which I meet you on the present occasion that, in felicitating you on a continuance of the national prosperity generally, I am not able to add to it information that the Indian hostilities which have for some time past distressed our Northwestern frontier have terminated.

You will, I am persuaded, learn with no less concern than I communicate it that reiterated endeavors toward effecting a pacification have hitherto issued only in new and outrageous proofs of persevering hostility on the part of the tribes with whom we are in contest. An earnest desire to procure tranquillity to the frontier, to stop the further effusion of blood, to arrest the progress of expense, to forward the prevalent wish of the nation for peace has led to strenuous efforts through various channels to accomplish these desirable purposes; in making which efforts I consulted less my own anticipations of the event, or the scruples which some considerations were calculated to inspire, than the wish to find the object attainable, or if not attainable, to ascertain unequivocally that such is the case.

A detail of the measures which have been pursued and of their consequences, which will be laid before you, while it will confirm to you the want of success thus far, will, I trust, evince that means as proper and as efficacious as could have been devised have been employed. The issue of some of them, indeed, is still depending, but a favorable one, though not to be despaired of, is not promised by anything that has yet happened.

In the course of the attempts which have been made some valuable citizens have fallen victims to their zeal for the public service. A sanction commonly respected even among savages has been found in this instance insufficient to protect from massacre the emissaries of peace. It will, I presume, be duly considered whether the occasion does not call for an exercise of liberality toward the families of the deceased.

It must add to your concern to be informed that, besides the continuation of hostile appearances among the tribes north of the Ohio, some threatening symptoms have of late been revived among some of those south of it.

A part of the Cherokees, known by the name of Chickamaugas, inhabiting five villages on the Tennessee River, have long been in the practice of committing depredations on the neighboring settlements.

It was hoped that the Treaty of Holston, made with the Cherokee Nation in July, 1791, would have prevented a repetition of such depredations; but the event has not answered this hope. The Chickamaugas, aided by some banditti of another tribe in their vicinity, have recently perpetrated wanton and unprovoked hostilities upon the citizens of the United States in that quarter. The information which has been received on this subject will be laid before you. Hitherto defensive precautions only have been strictly enjoined and observed.

It is not understood that any breach of treaty or aggression whatsoever on the part of the United States or their citizens is even alleged as a pretext for the spirit of hostility in this quarter.

I have reason to believe that every practicable exertion has been made (pursuant to the provision by law for that purpose) to be prepared for the alternative of a prosecution of the war in the event of a failure of pacific overtures. A large proportion of the troops authorized to be raised have been recruited, though the number is still incomplete, and pains have been taken to discipline and put them in condition for the particular kind of service to be performed. A delay of operations (besides being dictated by the measures which were pursuing toward a pacific termination of the war) has been in itself deemed preferable to immature efforts. A statement from the proper department with regard to the number of troops raised, and some other points which have been suggested, will afford more precise information as a guide to the legislative consultations, and among other things will enable Congress to judge whether some additional stimulus to the recruiting service may not be advisable.

In looking forward to the future expense of the operations which may be found inevitable I derive consolation from the information I receive that the product of the revenues for the present year is likely to supersede the necessity of additional burthens on the community for the service of the ensuing year. This, however, will be better ascertained in the course of the session, and it is proper to add that the information alluded to proceeds upon the supposition of no material extension of the spirit of hostility.

I can not dismiss the subject of Indian affairs without again recommending to your consideration the expediency of more adequate provision for giving energy to the laws throughout our interior frontier and for restraining the commission of outrages upon the Indians, without which all pacific plans must prove nugatory. To enable, by competent rewards, the employment of qualified and trusty persons to reside among them as agents would also contribute to the preservation of peace and good neighborhood. If in addition to these expedients an eligible plan could be devised for promoting civilization among the friendly tribes and for carrying on trade with them upon a scale equal to their wants and under regulations calculated to protect them from imposition and extortion, its influence in cementing their interest with ours could not but be considerable.

The prosperous state of our revenue has been intimated. This would be still more the case were it not for the impediments which in some places continue to embarrass the collection of the duties on spirits distilled within the United States. These impediments have lessened and are lessening in local extent, and, as applied to the community at large, the contentment with the law appears to be progressive.

But symptoms of increased opposition having lately manifested themselves in certain quarters, I judged a special interposition on my part proper and advisable, and under this impression have issued a proclamation warning against all unlawful combinations and proceedings having for their object or tending to obstruct the operation of the law in question, and announcing that all lawful ways and means would be strictly put in execution for bringing to justice the infractors thereof and securing obedience thereto.

Measures have also been taken for the prosecution of offenders, and Congress may be assured that nothing within constitutional and legal limits which may depend upon me shall be wanting to assert and maintain the just authority of the laws. In fulfilling this trust I shall count entirely upon the full cooperation of the other departments of the Government and upon the zealous support of all good citizens.

I can not forbear to bring again into the view of the Legislature the subject of a revision of the judiciary system. A representation from the judges of the Supreme Court, which will be laid before you, points out some of the inconveniences that are experienced. In the course of the execution of the laws considerations arise out of the structure of the system which in some cases tend to relax their efficacy. As connected with this subject, provisions to facilitate the taking of bail upon processes out of the courts of the United States and a supplementary definition of offenses against the Constitution and laws of the Union and of the punishment for such offenses will, it is presumed, be found worthy of particular attention.

Observations on the value of peace with other nations are unnecessary. It would be wise, however, by timely provisions to guard against those acts of our own citizens which might tend to disturb it, and to put ourselves in a condition to give that satisfaction to foreign nations which we may sometimes have occasion to require from them. I particularly recommend to your consideration the means of preventing those aggressions by our citizens on the territory of other nations, and other infractions of the law of nations, which, furnishing just subject of complaint, might endanger our peace with them; and, in general, the maintenance of a friendly intercourse with foreign powers will be presented to your attention by the expiration of the law for that purpose, which takes place, if not renewed, at the close of the present session.

In execution of the authority given by the Legislature measures have been taken for engaging some artists from abroad to aid in the establishment of our mint. Others have been employed at home. Provision has been made of the requisite buildings, and these are now putting into proper condition for the purposes of the establishment. There has also been a small beginning in the coinage of half dimes, the want of small coins in circulation calling the first attention to them.

The regulation of foreign coins in correspondency with the principles of our national coinage, as being essential to their due operation and to order in our money concerns, will, I doubt not, be resumed and completed.

It is represented that some provisions in the law which establishes the post office operate, in experiment, against the transmission of news papers to distant parts of the country. Should this, upon due inquiry, be found to be the fact, a full conviction of the importance of facilitating the circulation of political intelligence and information will, I doubt not, lead to the application of a remedy.

The adoption of a constitution for the State of Kentucky has been notified to me. The Legislature will share with me in the satisfaction which arises from an event interesting to the happiness of the part of the nation to which it relates and conducive to the general order.

It is proper likewise to inform you that since my last communication on the subject, and in further execution of the acts severally making provision for the public debt and for the reduction thereof, three new loans have been effected, each for 3,000,000 florins—one at Antwerp, at the annual interest of 4.5%, with an allowance of 4% in lieu of all charges, in the other 2 at Amsterdam, at the annual interest of 4%, with an allowance of 5.5% in one case and of 5% in the other in lieu of all charges. The rates of these loans and the circumstances under which they have been made are confirmations of the high state of our credit abroad.

Among the objects to which these funds have been directed to be applied, the payment of the debts due to certain foreign officers, according to the provision made during the last session, has been embraced.

Gentlemen of the House of Representatives:

I entertain a strong hope that the state of the national finances is now sufficiently matured to enable you to enter upon a systematic and effectual arrangement for the regular redemption and discharge of the public debt, according to the right which has been reserved to the Government. No measure can be more desirable, whether viewed with an eye to its intrinsic importance or to the general sentiment and wish of the nation.

Provision is likewise requisite for the reimbursement of the loan which has been made of the Bank of the United States, pursuant to the eleventh section of the act by which it is incorporated. In fulfilling the public stipulations in this particular it is expected a valuable saving will be made.

Appropriations for the current service of the ensuing year and for such extraordinaries as may require provision will demand, and I doubt not will engage, your early attention.

Gentlemen of the Senate and of the House of Representatives:

I content myself with recalling your attention generally to such objects, not particularized in my present, as have been suggested in my former communications to you.

Various temporary laws will expire during the present session. Among these, that which regulates trade and intercourse with the Indian tribes will merit particular notice.

The results of your common deliberations hitherto will, I trust, be productive of solid and durable advantages to our constituents, such as, by conciliating more and more their ultimate suffrage, will tend to strengthen and confirm their attachment to that Constitution of Government upon which, under Divine Providence, materially depend their union, their safety, and their happiness.

Still further to promote and secure these inestimable ends there is nothing which can have a more powerful tendency than the careful cultivation of harmony, combined with a due regard to stability, in the public councils.

FIFTH ADDRESS TO CONGRESS

December 3, 1793

Fellow Citizens of the Senate and of the House of Representatives:

Since the commencement of the term for which I have been again called into office no fit occasion has arisen for expressing to me fellow citizens at large the deep and respectful sense which I feel of the renewed testimony of public approbation. While on the one hand it awakened my gratitude for all those instances of affectionate partiality with which I have been honored by my country, on the other it could not prevent an earnest wish for that retirement from which no private consideration should ever have torn me. But influenced by the belief that my conduct would be estimated according to its real motives, and that the people, and the authorities derived from them, would support exertions having nothing personal for their object, I have obeyed the suffrage which commanded me to resume the Executive power; and I humbly implore that Being on whose will the fate of nations depends to crown with success our mutual endeavors for the general happiness.

As soon as the war in Europe had embraced those powers with whom the United States have the most extensive relations there was reason to apprehend that our intercourse with them might be interrupted and our disposition for peace drawn into question by the suspicions too often entertained by belligerent nations. It seemed, therefore, to be my duty to admonish our citizens of the consequences of a contraband trade and of hostile acts to any of the parties, and to obtain by a declaration of the existing legal state of things an easier admission of our right to the immunities belonging to our situation. Under these impressions the proclamation which will be laid before you was issued.

In this posture of affairs, both new and delicate, I resolved to adopt general rules which should conform to the treaties and assert the privileges of the United States. These were reduced into a system, which will be communicated to you. Although I have not thought of myself at liberty to forbid the sale of the prizes permitted by our treaty of commerce with France to be brought into our ports, I have not refused to cause them to be restored when they were taken within the protection of our territory, or by vessels commissioned or equipped in a warlike form within the limits of the United States.

It rests with the wisdom of Congress to correct, improve, or enforce this plan of procedure; and it will probably be found expedient to extend the legal code and the jurisdiction of the courts of the United States to many cases which, though dependent on principles already recognized, demand some further provisions.

Where individuals shall, within the United States, array themselves in hostility against any of the powers at war, or enter upon military expeditions or enterprises within the jurisdiction of the United States, or usurp and exercise judicial authority within the United States, or where the penalties on violations of the law of nations may have been indistinctly marked, or are inadequate—these offenses can not receive too early and close an attention, and require prompt and decisive remedies.

Whatsoever those remedies may be, they will be well administered by the judiciary, who possess a long-established course of investigation, effectual process, and officers in the habit of executing it.

In like manner, as several of the courts have doubted, under particular circumstances, their power to liberate the vessels of a nation at peace, and even of a citizen of the United States, although seized under a false color of being hostile property, and have denied their power to liberate certain captures within the protection of our territory, it would seem proper to regulate their jurisdiction in these points. But if the Executive is to be the resort in either of the two last-mentioned cases, it is hoped that he will be authorized by law to have facts ascertained by the courts when for his own information he shall request it.

I can not recommend to your notice measures for the fulfillment of our duties to the rest of the world without again pressing upon you the necessity of placing ourselves in a condition of complete defense and of exacting from them the fulfillment of their duties toward us. The United States ought not to indulge a persuasion that, contrary to the order of human events, they will forever keep at a distance those painful appeals to arms with which the history of every other nation abounds. There is a rank due to the United States among nations which will be withheld, if not absolutely lost, by the reputation of weakness. If we desire to avoid insult, we must be able to repel it; if we desire to secure peace, one of the most powerful instruments of our rising prosperity, it must be known that we are at all times ready for war. The documents which will be presented to you will shew the amount and kinds of arms and military stores now in our magazines and arsenals; and yet an addition even to these supplies can not with prudence be neglected, as it would leave nothing to the uncertainty of procuring warlike apparatus in the moment of public danger.

Nor can such arrangements, with such objects, be exposed to the censure or jealousy of the warmest friends of republican government. They are incapable of abuse in the hands of the militia, who ought to possess a pride in being the depository of the force of the Republic, and may be trained to a degree of energy equal to every military exigency of the United States. But it is an inquiry which can not be too solemnly pursued, whether the act "more effectually to provide for the national defense by establishing an uniform militia throughout the United States" has organized them so as to produce their full effect; whether your own experience in the several States has not detected some imperfections in the scheme, and whether a material feature in an improvement of it ought not to be to afford an opportunity for the study of those branches of the military art which can scarcely ever be attained by practice alone.

The connection of the United States with Europe has become extremely interesting. The occurrences which relate to it and have passed under the knowledge of the Executive will be exhibited to Congress in a subsequent communication.

When we contemplate the war on our frontiers, it may be truly affirmed that every reasonable effort has been made to adjust the causes of dissension with the Indians north of the Ohio. The instructions given to the commissioners evince a moderation and equity proceeding from a sincere love of peace, and a liberality having no restriction but the essential interests and dignity of the United States. The attempt, however, of an amicable negotiation having been frustrated, the troops have marched to act offensively. Although the proposed treaty did not arrest the progress of military preparation, it is doubtful how far the advance of the season, before good faith justified active movements, may retard them during the remainder of the year. From the papers and intelligence which relate to this important subject you will determine whether the deficiency in the number of troops granted by law shall be compensated by succors of militia, or additional encouragements shall be proposed to recruits.

An anxiety has been also demonstrated by the Executive for peace with the Creeks and the Cherokees. The former have been relieved with corn and with clothing, and offensive measures against them prohibited during the recess of Congress. To satisfy the complaints of the latter, prosecutions have been instituted for the violences committed upon them. But the papers which will be delivered to you disclose the critical footing on which we stand in regard to both those tribes, and it is with Congress to pronounce what shall be done.

After they shall have provided for the present emergency, it will merit their most serious labors to render tranquillity with the savages permanent by creating ties of interest. Next to a rigorous execution of justice on the violators of peace, the establishment of commerce with the Indian nations in behalf of the United States is most likely to conciliate their attachment. But it ought to be conducted without fraud, without extortion, with constant and plentiful supplies, with a ready market for the commodities of the Indians and a stated price for what they give in payment and receive in exchange. Individuals will not pursue such a traffic unless they be allured by the hope of profit; but it will be enough for the United States to be reimbursed only. Should this recommendation accord with the opinion of Congress, they will recollect that it can not be accomplished by any means yet in the hands of the Executive.

Gentlemen of the House of Representatives:

The commissioners charged with the settlement of accounts between the United States and individual States concluded their important function within the time limited by law, and the balances struck in their report, which will be laid before Congress, have been placed on the books of the Treasury.

On the first day of June last an installment of 1,000,000 florins became payable on the loans of the United States in Holland. This was adjusted by a prolongation of the period of reimbursement in nature of a new loan at an interest of 5% for the term of ten years, and the expenses of this operation were a commission of 3%.

The first installment of the loan of $2,000,000 from the Bank of the United States has been paid, as was directed by law. For the second it is necessary that provision be made.

No pecuniary consideration is more urgent than the regular redemption and discharge of the public debt. On none can delay be more injurious or an economy of time more valuable.

The productiveness of the public revenues hitherto has continued to equal the anticipations which were formed of it, but it is not expected to prove commensurate with all the objects which have been suggested. Some auxiliary provisions will therefore, it is presumed, be requisite, and it is hoped that these may be made consistently with a due regard to the convenience of our citizens, who can not but be sensible of the true wisdom of encountering a small present addition to their contributions to obviate a future accumulation of burthens.

But here I can not forbear to recommend a repeal of the tax on the transportation of public prints. There is no resource so firm for the Government of the United States as the affections of the people, guided by an enlightened policy; and to this primary good nothing can conduce more than a faithful representation of public proceedings, diffused without restraint throughout the United States.

An estimate of the appropriations necessary for the current service of the ensuing year and a statement of a purchase of arms and military stores made during the recess will be presented to Congress.

GENTLEMEN OF THE SENATE AND OF THE HOUSE OF REPRESENTATIVES:

The several subjects to which I have now referred open a wide range to your deliberations and involve some of the choicest interests of our common country. Permit me to bring to your remembrance the magnitude of your task. Without an unprejudiced coolness the welfare of the Government may be hazarded; without harmony as far as consists with freedom of sentiment its dignity may be lost. But as the legislative proceedings of the United States will never, I trust, be reproached for the want of temper or of candor, so shall not the public happiness languish from the want of my strenuous and warmest cooperation.

SIXTH ADDRESS TO CONGRESS

November 19, 1794

Fellow Citizens of the Senate and of the House of Representatives:

When we call to mind the gracious indulgence of Heaven by which the American people became a nation; when we survey the general prosperity of our country, and look forward to the riches, power, and happiness to which it seems destined, with the deepest regret do I announce to you that during your recess some of the citizens of the United States have been found capable of insurrection. It is due, however, to the character of our Government and to its stability, which can not be shaken by the enemies of order, freely to unfold the course of this event.

During the session of the year 1790 it was expedient to exercise the legislative power granted by the Constitution of the United States "to lay and collect excises". In a majority of the States scarcely an objection was heard to this mode of taxation. In some, indeed, alarms were at first conceived, until they were banished by reason and patriotism. In the four western counties of Pennsylvania a prejudice, fostered and imbittered by the artifice of men who labored for an ascendency over the will of others by the guidance of their passions, produced symptoms of riot and violence.

It is well known that Congress did not hesitate to examine the complaints which were presented, and to relieve them as far as justice dictated or general convenience would permit. But the impression which this moderation made on the discontented did not correspond with what it deserved. The arts of delusion were no longer confined to the efforts of designing individuals. The very forbearance to press prosecutions was misinterpreted into a fear of urging the execution of the laws, and associations of men began to denounce threats against the officers employed. From a belief that by a more formal concert their operation might be defeated, certain self-created societies assumed the tone of condemnation. Hence, while the greater part of Pennsylvania itself were conforming themselves to the acts of excise, a few counties were resolved to frustrate them. It is now perceived that every expectation from the tenderness which had been hitherto pursued was unavailing, and that further delay could only create an opinion of impotency or irresolution in the Government. Legal process was therefore delivered to the marshal against the rioters and delinquent distillers.

No sooner was he understood to be engaged in this duty than the vengeance of armed men was aimed at his person and the person and property of the inspector of the revenue. They fired upon the marshal, arrested him, and detained him for some time as a prisoner. He was obliged, by the jeopardy of his life, to renounce the service of other process on the west side of the Allegheny Mountain, and a deputation was afterwards sent to him to demand a surrender of that which he had served. A numerous body repeatedly attacked the house of the inspector, seized his papers of office, and finally destroyed by fire his buildings and whatsoever they contained. Both of these officers, from a just regard to their safety, fled to the seat of Government, it being avowed that the motives to such outrages were to compel the resignation of the inspector, to withstand by force of arms the authority of the United States, and thereby to extort a repeal of the laws of excise and an alteration in the conduct of Government.

Upon testimony of these facts an associate justice of the Supreme Court of the United States notified to me that "in the counties of Washington and Allegheny, in Pennsylvania, laws of the United States were opposed, and the execution thereof obstructed, by combinations too powerful to be suppressed by the ordinary course of judicial proceedings or by the powers vested in the marshal of that district".

On this call, momentous in the extreme, I sought and weighted what might best subdue the crisis. On the one hand the judiciary was pronounced to be stripped of its capacity to enforce the laws; crimes which reached the very existence of social order were perpetrated without control; the friends of Government were insulted, abused, and overawed into silence or an apparent acquiescence; and to yield to the treasonable fury of so small a portion of the United States would be to violate the fundamental principle of our Constitution, which enjoins that the will of the majority shall prevail. On the other, to array citizen against citizen, to publish the dishonor of such excesses, to encounter the expense and other embarrassments of so distant an expedition, were steps too delicate, too closely interwoven with many affecting considerations, to be lightly adopted.

I postponed, therefore, the summoning of the militia immediately into the field, but I required them to be held in readiness, that if my anxious endeavors to reclaim the deluded and to convince the malignant of their danger should be fruitless, military force might be prepared to act before the season should be too far advanced.

My proclamation of the 7th of August last was accordingly issued, and accompanied by the appointment of commissioners, who were charged to repair to the scene of insurrection. They were authorized to confer with any bodies of men or individuals. They were instructed to be candid and explicit in stating the sensations which had been excited in the Executive, and his earnest wish to avoid a resort to coercion; to represent, however, that, without submission, coercion must be the resort; but to invite them, at the same time, to return to the demeanor of faithful citizens, by such accommodations as lay within the sphere of Executive power. Pardon, too, was tendered to them by the Government of the United States and that of Pennsylvania, upon no other condition than a satisfactory assurance of obedience to the laws.

Although the report of the commissioners marks their firmness and abilities, and must unite all virtuous men, by shewing that the means of conciliation have been exhausted, all of those who had committed or abetted the tumults did not subscribe the mild form which was proposed as the atonement, and the indications of a peaceable temper were neither sufficiently general nor conclusive to recommend or warrant the further suspension of the march of the militia.

Thus the painful alternative could not be discarded. I ordered the militia to march, after once more admonishing the insurgents in my proclamation of the 25th of September last.

It was a task too difficult to ascertain with precision the lowest degree of force competent to the quelling of the insurrection. From a respect, indeed, to economy and the ease of my fellow citizens belonging to the militia, it would have gratified me to accomplish such an estimate. My very reluctance to ascribe too much importance to the opposition, had its extent been accurately seen, would have been a decided inducement to the smallest efficient numbers. In this uncertainty, therefore, I put into motion 15K men, as being an army which, according to all human calculation, would be prompt and adequate in every view, and might, perhaps, by rendering resistance desperate, prevent the effusion of blood. Quotas had been assigned to the States of New Jersey, Pennsylvania, Maryland, and Virginia, the governor of Pennsylvania having declared on this occasion an opinion which justified a requisition to the other States.

As commander in chief of the militia when called into the actual service of the United States, I have visited the places of general rendezvous to obtain more exact information and to direct a plan for ulterior movements. Had there been room for a persuasion that the laws were secure from obstruction; that the civil magistrate was able to bring to justice such of the most culpable as have not embraced the proffered terms of amnesty, and may be deemed fit objects of example; that the friends to peace and good government were not in need of that aid and countenance which they ought always to receive, and, I trust, ever will receive, against the vicious and turbulent, I should have caught with avidity the opportunity of restoring the militia to their families and homes. But succeeding intelligence has tended to manifest the necessity of what has been done, it being now confessed by those who were not inclined to exaggerate the ill conduct of the insurgents that their malevolence was not pointed merely to a particular law, but that a spirit inimical to all order has actuated many of the offenders. If the state of things had afforded reason for the continuance of my presence with the army, it would not have been withholden. But every appearance assuring such an issue as will redound to the reputation and strength of the United States, I have judged it most proper to resume my duties at the seat of Government, leaving the chief command with the governor of Virginia.

Still, however, as it is probable that in a commotion like the present, whatsoever may be the pretense, the purposes of mischief and revenge may not be laid aside, the stationing of a small force for a certain period in the four western counties of Pennsylvania will be indispensable, whether we contemplate the situation of those who are connected with the execution of the laws or of others who may have exposed themselves by an honorable attachment to them. Thirty days from the commencement of this session being the legal limitation of the employment of the militia, Congress can not be too early occupied with this subject.

Among the discussions which may arise from this aspect of our affairs, and from the documents which will be submitted to Congress, it will not escape their observation that not only the inspector of the revenue, but other officers of the United States in Pennsylvania have, from their fidelity in the discharge of their functions, sustained material injuries to their property. The obligation and policy of indemnifying them are strong and obvious. It may also merit attention whether policy will not enlarge this provision to the retribution of other citizens who, though not under the ties of office, may have suffered damage by their generous exertions for upholding the Constitution and the laws. The amount, even if all the injured were included, would not be great, and on future emergencies the Government would be amply repaid by the influence of an example that he who incurs a loss in its defense shall find a recompense in its liberality.

While there is cause to lament that occurrences of this nature should have disgraced the name or interrupted the tranquillity of any part of our community, or should have diverted to a new application any portion of the public resources, there are not wanting real and substantial consolations for the misfortune. It has demonstrated that our prosperity rests on solid foundations, by furnishing an additional that my fellow citizens understand the true principles of government and liberty; that they feel their inseparable union; that notwithstanding all the devices which have been used to sway them from their interest and duty, they are not as ready to maintain the authority of the laws against licentious invasions as they were to defend their rights against usurpation. It has been a spectacle displaying to the highest advantage of republican government to behold the most and the least wealthy of our citizens standing in the same ranks as private soldiers, preeminently distinguished by being the army of the Constitution—undeterred by a march of 300 miles over rugged mountains, by approach of an inclement season, or by any other discouragement. Nor ought I to omit to acknowledge the efficacious and patriotic cooperation which I have experienced from the chief magistrates of the States to which my requisitions have been addressed.

To every description of citizens, let praise be given, but let them persevere in their affectionate vigilance over that precious depository of American happiness, the Constitution of the United States. Let them cherish it, too, for the sake of those who, from every clime, are daily seeking a dwelling in our land. And when in the calm moments of reflection they shall have retraced the origin and progress of the insurrection, let them determine whether it has not been fomented by combinations of men who, careless of consequences and disregarding the unerring truth that those who rouse can not always appease a civil convulsion, have disseminated, from an ignorance or perversion of facts, suspicions, jealousies, and accusations of the whole Government.

Having thus fulfilled the engagement which I took when I entered into office, "to the best of my ability to preserve, protect, and defend the Constitution of the United States", on you, gentlemen, and the people by whom you are deputed, I rely for support.

In the arrangement to which the possibility of a similar contingency will naturally draw your attention it ought not to be forgotten that the militia laws have exhibited such striking defects as could not have been supplied by the zeal of our citizens. Besides the extraordinary expense and waste, which are not the least of the defects, every appeal to those laws is attended with a doubt on its success.

The devising and establishing of a well regulated militia would be a genuine source of legislative honor and a perfect title to public gratitude. I therefore entertain a hope that the present session will not pass without carrying to its full energy the power of organizing, arming, and disciplining the militia, and thus providing, in the language of the Constitution, for calling them forth to execute the laws of the Union, suppress insurrections, and repel invasions.

As auxiliary to the state of our defense, to which Congress can never too frequently recur, they will not omit to inquire whether the fortifications which have been already licensed by law be commensurate with our exigencies.

The intelligence from the army under the command of General Wayne is a happy presage to our military operations against the hostile Indians north of the Ohio. From the advices which have been forwarded, the advance which he has made must have damped the ardor of the savages and weakened their obstinacy in waging war against the United States. And yet, even at this late hour, when our power to punish them can not be questioned, we shall not be unwilling to cement a lasting peace upon terms of candor, equity, and good neighborhood.

Toward none of the Indian tribes have overtures of friendship been spared. The Creeks in particular are covered from encroachment by the imposition of the General Government and that of Georgia. From a desire also to remove the discontents of the Six Nations, a settlement mediated at Presque Isle, on Lake Erie, has been suspended, and an agent is now endeavoring to rectify any misconception into which they may have fallen. But I can not refrain from again pressing upon your deliberations the plan which I recommended at the last session for the improvement of harmony with all the Indians within our limits by the fixing and conducting of trading houses upon the principles then expressed.

GENTLEMEN OF THE HOUSE OF REPRESENTATIVES:

The time which has elapsed since the commencement of our fiscal measures has developed our pecuniary resources so as to open the way for a definite plan for the redemption of the public debt. It is believed that the result is such as to encourage Congress to consummate this work without delay. Nothing can more promote the permanent welfare of the nation and nothing would be more grateful to our constituents. Indeed, whatsoever is unfinished of our system of public credit can not be benefited by procrastination; and as far as may be practicable we ought to place that credit on grounds which can not be disturbed, and to prevent that progressive accumulation of debt which must ultimately endanger all governments.

An estimate of the necessary appropriations, including the expenditures into which we have been driven by the insurrection, will be submitted to Congress.

GENTLEMEN OF THE SENATE AND OF THE HOUSE OF REPRESENTATIVES:

The Mint of the United States has entered upon the coinage of the precious metals, and considerable sums of defective coins and bullion have been lodged with the Director by individuals. There is a pleasing prospect that the institution will at no remote day realize the expectation which was originally formed of its utility.

In subsequent communications certain circumstances of our intercourse with foreign nations will be transmitted to Congress. However, it may not be unseasonable to announce that my policy in our foreign transactions has been to cultivate peace with all the world; to observe the treaties with pure and absolute faith; to check every deviation from the line of impartiality; to explain what may have been misapprehended and correct what may have been injurious to any nation, and having thus acquired the right, to lose no time in acquiring the ability to insist upon justice being done to ourselves.

Let us unite, therefore, in imploring the Supreme Ruler of Nations to spread his holy protection over these United States; to turn the machinations of the wicked to the confirming of our Constitution; to enable us at all times to root out internal sedition and put invasion to flight; to perpetuate to our country that prosperity which his goodness has already conferred, and to verify the anticipations of this Government being a safeguard of human rights.

SEVENTH ADDRESS TO CONGRESS

December 8, 1795

Fellow Citizens of the Senate and of the House of Representatives:

I trust I do not deceive myself when I indulge the persuasion that I have never met you at any period when more than at the present the situation of our public affairs has afforded just cause for mutual congratulations, and for inviting you to join with me in profound gratitude to the Author of all Good for the numerous and extraordinary blessings we enjoy.

The termination of the long, expensive, and distressing war in which we have been engaged with certain Indians northwest of the Ohio is placed in the option of the United States by a treaty which the commander of our army has concluded provisionally with the hostile tribes in that region.

In the adjustment of the terms the satisfaction of the Indians was deemed worthy no less of the policy than of the liberality of the United States as the necessary basis of durable tranquillity. The object, it is believed, has been fully attained. The articles agreed upon will immediately be laid before the Senate for their consideration.

The Creek and Cherokee Indians, who alone of the Southern tribes had annoyed our frontiers, have lately confirmed their preexisting treaties with us, and were giving evidence of a sincere disposition to carry them into effect by the surrender of the prisoners and property they had taken. But we have to lament that the fair prospect in this quarter has been once more clouded by wanton murders, which some citizens of Georgia are represented to have recently perpetrated on hunting parties of the Creeks, which have again subjected that frontier to disquietude and danger, which will be productive of further expense, and may occasion more effusion of blood. Measures are pursuing to prevent or mitigate the usual consequences of such outrages, and with the hope of their succeeding at least to avert general hostility.

A letter from the Emperor of Morocco announces to me his recognition of our treaty made with his father, the late Emperor, and consequently the continuance of peace with that power. With peculiar satisfaction I add that information has been received from an agent deputed on our part to Algiers importing that the terms of the treaty with the Day and Regency of that country had been adjusted in such a manner as to authorize the expectation of a speedy peace and the resolution of our unfortunate fellow citizens from a grievous captivity.

The latest advices from our envoy at the Court of Madrid give, moreover, the pleasing information that he had assurances of a speedy and satisfactory conclusion of his negotiation. While the event depending upon unadjusted particulars can not be regarded as ascertained, it is agreeable to cherish the expectation of an issue which, securing amicably very essential interests of the United States, will at the same time lay the foundation of lasting harmony with a power whose friendship we have uniformly and sincerely desired to cultivate.

Though not before officially disclosed to the House of Representatives, you, gentlemen, are all apprised that a treaty of amity, commerce, and navigation has been negotiated with Great Britain, and that the Senate have advised and consented to its ratification upon a condition which excepts part of one article. Agreeably thereto, and to the best judgment I was able to form of the public interest after full and mature deliberation, I have added my sanction. The result on the part of His Britannic Majesty is unknown. When received, the subject will without delay be placed before Congress.

This interesting summary of our affairs with regard to the foreign powers between whom and the United States controversies have subsisted, and with regard also to those of our Indian neighbors with whom we have been in a state of enmity or misunderstanding, opens a wide field for consoling and gratifying reflections. If by prudence and moderation on every side the extinguishment of all the causes of external discord which have heretofore menaced our tranquillity, on terms compatible with our national rights and honor, shall be the happy result, how firm and how precious a foundation will have been laid for accelerating, maturing, and establishing the prosperity of our country.

Contemplating the internal situation as well as the external relations of the United States, we discover equal cause for contentment and satisfaction. While many of the nations of Europe, with their American dependencies, have been involved in a contest unusually bloody, exhausting, and calamitous, in which the evils of foreign war have been aggravated by domestic convulsion and insurrection; in which many of the arts most useful to society have been exposed to discouragement and decay; in which scarcity of subsistence has imbittered other sufferings; while even the anticipations of a return of the blessings of peace and repose are alloyed by the sense of heavy and accumulating burthens, which press upon all the departments of industry and threaten to clog the future springs of government, our favored country, happy in a striking contrast, has enjoyed tranquillity—a tranquillity the more satisfactory because maintained at the expense of no duty. Faithful to ourselves, we have violated no obligation to others.

Our agriculture, commerce, and manufactures prosper beyond former example, the molestations of our trade (to prevent a continuance of which, however, very pointed remonstrances have been made) being overbalanced by the aggregate benefits which it derives from a neutral position. Our population advances with a celerity which, exceeding the most sanguine calculations, proportionally augments our strength and resources, and guarantees our future security.

Every part of the Union displays indications of rapid and various improvement; and with burthens so light as scarcely to be perceived, with resources fully adequate to our present exigencies, with governments founded on the genuine principles of rational liberty, and with mild and wholesome laws, is it too much to say that our country exhibits a spectacle of national happiness never surpassed, if ever before equaled?

Placed in a situation every way so auspicious, motives of commanding force impel us, with sincere acknowledgment to Heaven and pure love to our country, to unite our efforts to preserve, prolong, and improve our immense advantages. To cooperate with you in this desirable work is a fervent and favorite wish of my heart.

It is a valuable ingredient in the general estimate of our welfare that the part of our country which was lately the scene of disorder and insurrection now enjoys the blessings of quiet and order. The misled have abandoned their errors, and pay the respect to our Constitution and laws which is due from good citizens to the public authorities of the society. These circumstances have induced me to pardon generally the offenders here referred to, and to extend forgiveness to those who had been adjudged to capital punishment. For though I shall always think it a sacred duty to exercise with firmness and energy the constitutional powers with which I am vested, yet it appears to me no less consistent with the public good than it is with my personal feelings to mingle in the operations of Government every degree of moderation and tenderness which the national justice, dignity, and safety may permit.

Gentlemen: Among the objects which will claim your attention in the course of the session, a review of our military establishment is not the least important. It is called for by the events which have changed, and may be expected still further to change, the relative situation of our frontiers. In this review you will doubtless allow due weight to the considerations that the questions between us and certain foreign powers are not yet finally adjusted, that the war in Europe is not yet terminated, and that our Western posts, when recovered, will demand provision for garrisoning and securing them. A statement of our present military force will be laid before you by the Department of War.

With the review of our Army establishment is naturally connected that of the militia. It will merit inquiry what imperfections in the existing plan further experience may have unfolded. The subject is of so much moment in my estimation as to excite a constant solicitude that the consideration of it may be renewed until the greatest attainable perfection shall be accomplished. Time is wearing away some advantages for forwarding the object, while none better deserves the persevering attention of the public councils.

While we indulge the satisfaction which the actual condition of our Western borders so well authorizes, it is necessary that we should not lose sight of an important truth which continually receives new confirmations, namely, that the provisions heretofore made with a view to the protection of the Indians from the violences of the lawless part of our frontier inhabitants are insufficient. It is demonstrated that these violences can now be perpetrated with impunity, and it can need no argument to prove that unless the murdering of Indians can be restrained by bringing the murderers to condign punishment, all the exertions of the Government to prevent destructive retaliations by the Indians will prove fruitless and all our present agreeable prospects illusory. The frequent destruction of innocent women and children, who are chiefly the victims of retaliation, must continue to shock humanity, and an enormous expense to drain the Treasury of the Union.

To enforce upon the Indians the observance of justice it is indispensable that there shall be competent means of rendering justice to them. If these means can be devised by the wisdom of Congress, and especially if there can be added an adequate provision for supplying the necessities of the Indians on reasonable terms (a measure the mention of which I the more readily repeat, as in all the conferences with them they urge it with solicitude), I should not hesitate to entertain a strong hope of rendering our tranquillity permanent. I add with pleasure that the probability even of their civilization is not diminished by the experiments which have been thus far made under the auspices of Government. The accomplishment of this work, if practicable, will reflect undecaying luster on our national character and administer the most grateful consolations that virtuous minds can know.

Gentlemen of the House of Representatives:

The state of our revenue, with the sums which have been borrowed and reimbursed pursuant to different acts of Congress, will be submitted from the proper Department, together with an estimate of the appropriations necessary to be made for the service of the ensuing year.

Whether measures may not be advisable to reinforce the provision of the redemption of the public debt will naturally engage your examination. Congress have demonstrated their sense to be, and it were superfluous to repeat mine, that whatsoever will tend to accelerate the honorable extinction of our public debt accords as much with the true interest of our country as with the general sense of our constituents.

GENTLEMEN OF THE SENATE AND OF THE HOUSE OF REPRESENTATIVES:

The statements which will be laid before you relative to the Mint will shew the situation of that institution and the necessity of some further legislative provisions for carrying the business of it more completely into effect, and for checking abuses which appear to be arising in particular quarters.

The progress in providing materials for the frigates and in building them, the state of the fortifications of our harbors, the measures which have been pursued for obtaining proper sites for arsenals and for replenishing our magazines with military stores, and the steps which have been taken toward the execution of the law for opening a trade with the Indians will likewise be presented for the information of Congress.

Temperate discussion of the important subjects which may arise in the course of the session and mutual forbearance where there is a difference of opinion are too obvious and necessary for the peace, happiness, and welfare of our country to need any recommendation of mine.

EIGHTH ADDRESS TO CONGRESS

December 7, 1796

Fellow Citizens of the Senate and of the House of Representatives:

In recurring to the internal situation of our country since I had last the pleasure to address you, I find ample reason for a renewed expression of that gratitude to the Ruler of the Universe which a continued series of prosperity has so often and so justly called forth.

The acts of the last session which required special arrangements have been as far as circumstances would admit carried into operation.

Measures calculated to insure a continuance of the friendship of the Indians and to preserve peace along the extent of our interior frontier have been digested and adopted. In the framing of these care has been taken to guard on the one hand our advanced settlements from the predatory incursions of those unruly individuals who can not be restrained by their tribes, and on the other hand to protect the rights secured to the Indians by treaty—to draw them nearer to the civilized state and inspire them with correct conceptions of the power as well as justice of the Government.

The meeting of the deputies from the Creek Nation at Colerain, in the State of Georgia, which had for a principal object the purchase of a parcel of their land by that State, broke up without its being accomplished, the nation having previous to their departure instructed them against making any sale. The occasion, however, has been improved to confirm by a new treaty with the Creeks their preexisting engagements with the United States, and to obtain their consent to the establishment of trading houses and military posts within their boundary, by means of which their friendship and the general peace may be more effectually secured.

The period during the late session at which the appropriation was passed for carrying into effect the treaty of amity, commerce, and navigation between the United States and His Brittanic Majesty necessarily procrastinated the reception of the posts stipulated to be delivered beyond the date assigned for that event. As soon, however, as the Governor-General of Canada could be addressed with propriety on the subject, arrangements were cordially and promptly concluded for their evacuation, and the United States took possession of the principal of them, comprehending Oswego, Niagara, Detroit, Michilimackinac, and Fort Miami, where such repairs and additions have been ordered to be made as appeared indispensable.

The commissioners appointed on the part of the United States and of Great Britain to determine which is the river St. Croix mentioned in the treaty of peace of 1783, agreed in the choice of Egbert Benson, esq., of New York, for the 3rd commissioner. The whole met at St. Andrew's, in Passamaquoddy Bay, in the beginning of October, and directed surveys to be made of the rivers in dispute; but deeming it impracticable to have these surveys completed before the next year, they adjourned to meet at Boston in August, 1797, for the final decision of the question.

Other commissioners appointed on the part of the United States, agreeably to the 7th article of the treaty with Great Britain, relative to captures and condemnation of vessels and other property, met the commissioners of His Britannic Majesty in London in August last, when John Trumbull, esq., was chosen by lot for the 5th commissioner. In October following the board were to proceed to business. As yet there has been no communication of commissioners on the part of Great Britain to unite with those who have been appointed on the part of the United States for carrying into effect the 6th article of the treaty.

The treaty with Spain required that the commissioners for running the boundary line between the territory of the United States and His Catholic Majesty's provinces of East and West Florida should meet at the Natchez before the expiration of 6 months after the exchange of the ratifications, which was effected at Aranjuez on the 25th day of April; and the troops of His Catholic Majesty occupying any posts within the limits of the United States were within the same time period to be withdrawn. The commissioner of the United States therefore commenced his journey for the Natchez in September, and troops were ordered to occupy the posts from which the Spanish garrisons should be withdrawn. Information has been recently received of the appointment of a commissioner on the part of His Catholic Majesty for running the boundary line, but none of any appointment for the adjustment of the claims of our citizens whose vessels were captured by the armed vessels of Spain.

In pursuance of the act of Congress passed in the last session for the protection and relief of American sea-men, agents were appointed, one to reside in Great Britain and the other in the West Indies. The effects of the agency in the West Indies are not yet fully ascertained, but those which have been communicated afford grounds to believe the measure will be beneficial. The agent destined to reside in Great Britain declining to accept the appointment, the business has consequently devolved on the minister of the United States in London, and will command his attention until a new agent shall be appointed.

After many delays and disappointments arising out of the European war, the final arrangements for fulfilling the engagements made to the Dey and Regency of Algiers will in all present appearance be crowned with success, but under great, though inevitable, disadvantages in the pecuniary transactions occasioned by that war, which will render further provision necessary. The actual liberation of all our citizens who were prisoners in Algiers, while it gratifies every feeling of heart, is itself an earnest of a satisfactory termination of the whole negotiation. Measures are in operation for effecting treaties with the Regencies of Tunis and Tripoli.

To an active external commerce the protection of a naval force is indispensable. This is manifest with regard to wars in which a State is itself a party. But besides this, it is in our own experience that the most sincere neutrality is not a sufficient guard against the depredations of nations at war. To secure respect to a neutral flag requires a naval force organized and ready to vindicate it from insult or aggression. This may even prevent the necessity of going to war by discouraging belligerent powers from committing such violations of the rights of the neutral party as may, first or last, leave no other option. From the best information I have been able to obtain it would seem as if our trade to the Mediterranean without a protecting force will always be insecure and our citizens exposed to the calamities from which numbers of them have but just been relieved.

These considerations invite the United States to look to the means, and to set about the gradual creation of a navy. The increasing progress of their navigation promises them at no distant period the requisite supply of sea-men, and their means in other respects favor the undertaking. It is an encouragement, likewise, that their particular situation will give weight and influence to a moderate naval force in their hands. Will it not, then, be advisable to begin without delay to provide and lay up the materials for the building and equipping of ships of war, and to proceed in the work by degrees, in proportion as our resources shall render it practicable without inconvenience, so that a future war of Europe may not find our commerce in the same unprotected state in which it was found by the present?

Congress have repeatedly, and not without success, directed their attention to the encouragement of manufactures. The object is of too much consequence not to insure a continuance of their efforts in every way which shall appear eligible. As a general rule, manufactures on public account are inexpedient; but where the state of things in a country leaves little hope that certain branches of manufacture will for a great length of time obtain, when these are of a nature essential to the furnishing and equipping of the public force in time of war, are not establishments for procuring them on public account to the extent of the ordinary demand for the public service recommended by strong considerations of national policy as an exception to the general rule?

Ought our country to remain in such cases dependent on foreign supply, precarious because liable to be interrupted? If the necessary article should in this mode cost more in time of peace, will not the security and independence thence arising form an ample compensation?

Establishments of this sort, commensurate only with the calls of the public service in time of peace, will in time of war easily be extended in proportion to the exigencies of the Government, and may even perhaps be made to yield a surplus for the supply of our citizens at large, so as to mitigate the privations from the interruption of their trade. If adopted, the plan ought to exclude all those branches which are already, or likely soon to be, established in the country, in order that they may be no danger of interference with pursuits of individual industry.

It will not be doubted that with reference either to individual or national welfare agriculture is of primary importance. In proportion as nations advance in population and other circumstances of maturity this truth becomes more apparent, and renders the cultivation of the soil more and more an object of public patronage. Institutions for promoting it grow up, supported by the public purse; and to what object can it be dedicated with greater propriety?

Among the means which have been employed to this end none have been attended with greater success than the establishment of boards (composed of proper characters) charged with collecting and diffusing information, and enabled by premiums and small pecuniary aids to encourage and assist a spirit of discovery and improvement. This species of establishment contributes doubly to the increase of improvement by stimulating to enterprise and experiment, and by drawing to a common center the results everywhere of individual skill and observation, and spreading them thence over the whole nation. Experience accordingly has shewn that they are very cheap instruments of immense national benefits.

I have heretofore proposed to the consideration of Congress the expediency of establishing a national university and also a military academy. the desirableness of both these institutions has so constantly increased with every new view I have taken of the subject that I can not omit the opportunity of once for all recalling your attention to them.

The assembly to which I address myself is too enlightened not to be fully sensible how much a flourishing state of the arts and sciences contributes to national prosperity and reputation.

True it is that our country, much to its honor, contains many seminaries of learning highly repeatable and useful; but the funds upon which they rest are too narrow to command the ablest professors in the different departments of liberal knowledge for the institution contemplated, though they would be excellent auxiliaries.

Amongst the motives to such an institution, the assimilation of the principles, opinions, and manners of our country-men by the common education of a portion of our youth from every quarter well deserves attention. The more homogenous our citizens can be made in these particulars the greater will be our prospect of permanent union; and a primary object of such a national institution should be the education of our youth in the science of government. In a republic what species of knowledge can be equally important and what duty more pressing on its legislature than to patronize a plan for communicating it to those who are to be the future guardians of the liberties of the country?

The institution of a military academy is also recommended by cogent reasons. However pacific the general policy of a nation may be, it ought never to be without an adequate stock of military knowledge for emergencies. The 1st would impair the energy of its character, and both would hazard its safety or expose it to greater evils when war could not be avoided; besides that, war might often not depend upon its own choice. In proportion as the observance of pacific maxims might exempt a nation from the necessity of practicing the rules of the military art ought to be its care in preserving and transmitting, by proper establishments, the knowledge of that art.

Whatever argument may be drawn from particular examples superficially viewed, a thorough examination of the subject will evince that the art of war is at once comprehensive and complicated, that it demands much previous study, and that the possession of it in its most improved and perfect state is always of great moment to the security of a nation. This, therefore, ought to be a serious care of every government, and for this purpose an academy where a regular course of instruction is given is an obvious expedient which different nations have successfully employed.

The compensation to the officers of the United States in various instances, and in none more than in respect to the most important stations, appear to call for legislative revision. The consequences of a defective provision are of serious import to the Government. If private wealth is to supply the defect of public retribution, it will greatly contract the sphere within which the selection of character for office is to be made, and will proportionally diminish the probability of a choice of men able as well as upright. Besides that, it should be repugnant to the vital principles of our Government virtually to exclude from public trusts talents and virtue unless accompanied by wealth.

While in our external relations some serious inconveniences and embarrassments have been overcome and others lessened, it is with much pain and deep regret I mention that circumstances of a very unwelcome nature have lately occurred. Our trade has suffered and is suffering extensive injuries in the West Indies from the cruisers and agents of the French Republic, and communications have been received from its minister here which indicate the danger of a further disturbance of our commerce by its authority, and which are in other respects far from agreeable.

It has been my constant, sincere, and earnest wish, in conformity with that of our nation, to maintain cordial harmony and a perfectly friendly understanding with that Republic. This wish remains unabated, and I shall persevere in the endeavor to fulfill it to the utmost extent of what shall be consistent with a just and indispensable regard to the rights and honor of our country; nor will I easily cease to cherish the expectation that a spirit of justice, candor, and friendship on the part of the Republic will eventually insure success.

In pursuing this course, however, I can not forget what is due to the character of our Government and nation, or to a full and entire confidence in the good sense, patriotism, self-respect, and fortitude of my country-men.

I reserve for a special message a more particular communication on this interesting subject.

Gentlemen of the House of Representatives:

I have directed an estimate of the appropriations necessary for the service of the ensuing year to be submitted from the proper Department, with a view of the public receipts and expenditures to the latest period to which an account can be prepared.

It is with satisfaction I am able to inform you that the revenues of the United States continue in a state of progressive improvement.

A reenforcement of the existing provisions for discharging our public debt was mentioned in my address at the opening of the last session. Some preliminary steps were taken toward it, the maturing of which will no doubt engage your zealous attention during the present. I will only add that it will afford me a heart-felt satisfaction to concur in such further measures as will ascertain to our country the prospect of a speedy extinguishment of the debt. Posterity may have cause to regret if from any motive intervals of tranquillity are left unimproved for accelerating this valuable end.

Gentlemen of the Senate and of the House of Representatives:

My solicitude to see the militia of the United States placed on an efficient establishment has been so often and so ardently expressed that I shall but barely recall the subject to your view on the present occasion, at the same time that I shall submit to your inquiry whether our harbors are yet sufficiently secured.

The situation in which I now stand for the last time, in the midst of the representatives of the people of the United States, naturally recalls the period when the administration of the present form of government commenced, and I can not omit the occasion to congratulate you and my country on the success of the experiment, nor to repeat my fervent supplications to the Supreme Ruler of the Universe and Sovereign Arbiter of Nations that His providential care may still be extended to the United States, that the virtue and happiness of the people may be preserved, and that the Government which they have instituted for the protection of their liberties may be perpetual.

FAREWELL ADDRESS

To the People of the United States

Friends and Fellow-Citizens:

The period for a new election of a Citizen to Administer the Executive government of the United States, being not far distant, and the time actually arrived, when your thoughts must be employed in designating the person, who is to be cloathed with that important trust, it appears to me proper, especially as it may conduce to a more distinct expression of the public voice, that I should now apprise you of the resolution I have formed, to decline being considered among the number of those, out of whom a choice is to be made.

I beg you, at the same time, to do me the justice to be assured, that this resolution has not been taken, without a strict regard to all the considerations appertaining to the relation, which binds a dutiful citizen to his Country; and that, in withdrawing the tender of service which silence in my situation might imply, I am influenced by no diminution of zeal for your future interest; no deficiency of grateful respect for your past kindness, but am supported by a full conviction that the step is compatible with both.

The acceptance of, and continuance hitherto in the office to which your suffrages have twice called me, have been a uniform sacrifice of inclination to the opinion of duty and to a deference for what appeared to be your desire. I constantly hoped, that it would have been much earlier in my power, consistently with motives, which I was not at liberty to disregard, to return to that retirement from which I had been reluctantly drawn. The strength of my inclination to do this, previous to the last election, had even led to the preparation of an address to declare it to you; but mature reflection on the then perplexed and critical posture of our affairs with foreign nations, and the unanimous advice of persons entitled to my confidence, impelled me to abandon the idea.

I rejoice that the state of your concerns, external as well as internal, no longer renders the pursuit of inclination incompatible with the sentiment of duty or propriety; and am persuaded, whatever partiality may be retained for my services, that, in the present circumstances of our Country, you will not disapprove my determination to retire.

The impressions with which I first undertook the arduous trust were explained on the proper occasion. In the discharge of this trust, I will only say, that I have with good intentions, contributed towards the organization and administration of the government, the best exertions of which a very fallible judgment was capable. Not unconscious in the outset, of the inferiority of my qualifications, experience in my own eyes, perhaps still more in the eyes of others, has strengthened the motives to diffidence of myself; and every day the encreasing weight of years admonishes me more and more, that the shade of retirement is as necessary to me as it will be welcome. Satisfied that if any circumstances have given peculiar value to my services, they were temporary. I have the consolation to believe, that while choice and prudence invite me to quit the political scene, patriotism does not forbid it.

In looking forward to the moment, which is intended to terminate the career of my public life, my feelings do not permit me to suspend the deep acknowledgment of that debt of gratitude which I owe to my beloved Country, for the many honours it has conferred upon me; still more for the steadfast confidence with which it has supported me; and for the opportunities I have thence enjoyed of manifesting my inviolable attachment, by services faithful and persevering, though in usefulness unequal to my zeal. If benefits have resulted to our Country from these services, let it always be remembered to your praise, and as an instructive example in our annals, that under circumstances in which the passions, agitated in every direction, were liable to mislead, amidst appearances sometimes dubious—vicissitudes of fortune often discouraging—in situations in which not unfrequently want of success has countenanced the spirit of criticism, the constancy of your support was the essential prop of the efforts, and a guarantee of the plans by which they were effected—Profoundly penetrated with this idea, I shall carry it with me to my grave, as a strong incitement to unceasing vows that Heaven may continue to you the choicest tokens of its beneficence—that your union and brotherly affection may be perpetual—that the free Constitution, which is the work of your hands, may be sacredly maintained—that its administration in every department may be stamped with wisdom and virtue—that, in fine, the happiness of the people of these states, under the auspices of Liberty, may be made complete by so careful a preservation and so prudent a use of this blessing as will acquire to them the glory of recommending it to the applause, the affection, and adoption of every nation which is yet a stranger to it.

Here, perhaps, I ought to stop. But a solicitude for your welfare, which cannot end but with my life, and the apprehension of danger, natural to that solicitude, urge me, on an occasion like the present, to offer to your solemn contemplation, and to recommend to your frequent review some sentiments which are the result of much reflection, of no inconsiderable observation, and which appear to me all-important to the permanency of your felicity as a people. These will be offered to you with the more freedom, as you can only see in them the disinterested warnings of a parting friend, who can possibly have no personal motive to bias his Council. Nor can I forget, as an encouragement to it, your indulgent reception of my sentiments on a former and not dissimilar occasion.

Interwoven as is the love of Liberty with every ligament of your hearts, no recommendation of mine is necessary to fortify or confirm the attachment.

The unity of Government which constitutes you one people is also now dear to you. It is justly so; for it is a main pillar in the edifice of your real independence, the support of your tranquility at home, your peace abroad; of your safety; of your prosperity; of that very Liberty which you so highly prize. But as it is easy to foresee that, from different causes and from different quarters, much pains will be taken, many artifices employed to weaken in your minds the conviction of this truth; as this is the point in your political fortress against which the batteries of internal and external enemies will be most constantly and actively (though often covertly and insidiously) directed, it is of infinite moment that you should properly estimate the immense value of your national Union to your collective and individual happiness; that you should cherish a cordial, habitual, and immovable attachment to it; accustoming yourselves to think and speak of it as of the Palladium of your political safety and prosperity; watching for its preservation with jealous anxiety; discountenancing whatever may suggest even a suspicion that it can in any event be abandoned; and indignantly frowning upon the first dawning of every attempt to alienate any portion of our Country from the rest, or to enfeeble the sacred ties which now link together the various parts.

For this you have every inducement of sympathy and interest. Citizens, by birth or choice, of a common Country, that Country has a right to concentrate your affections. The name of American, which belongs to you in your national capacity, must always exalt the just pride of Patriotism more than any appellation derived from local discriminations. With slight shades of difference, you have the same religion, manners, habits, and political principles. You have in a common cause fought and triumphed together; the Independence and Liberty you possess are the work of joint councils, and joint efforts of common dangers, sufferings, and successes.

But these considerations, however powerfully they address themselves to your sensibility, are greatly outweighed by those which apply more immediately to your interest. Here every portion of our Country finds the most commanding motives for carefully guarding and preserving the Union of the whole.

The North, in an unrestrained intercourse with the South, protected by the equal laws of a common Government, finds in the productions of the latter great additional resources of maritime and commercial enterprise and precious materials of manufacturing industry. The South in the same intercourse benefiting by the agency of the North sees its agriculture grow and its commerce expand. Turning partly into its own channels the seamen of the North, it finds its particular navigation invigorated; and, while it contributes, in different ways, to nourish and increase the General mass of the national navigation, it looks forward to the protection of a maritime strength, to which itself is unequally adapted. The East, in a like intercourse with the West, already finds, and in the progressive improvement of interior communications by land and water, will more and more find a valuable vent for the commodities which it brings from abroad, or manufactures at home. The West derives from the East supplies requisite to its growth and comfort, and, what is perhaps of still greater consequence, it must of necessity owe the secure enjoyment of indispensable outlets for its own productions to the weight, influence, and the future maritime strength of the Atlantic side of the Union, directed by an indissoluble community of interest as one nation. Any other tenure by which the West can hold this essential advantage, whether derived from its own separate strength, or from an apostate and unnatural connection with any foreign power, must be intrinsically precarious.

While, then, every part of our country thus feels an immediate and particular interest in Union, all the parts combined cannot fail to find in the united mass of means and efforts greater strength, greater resource, proportionably greater security from external danger, a less frequent interruption of their peace by foreign nations; and, what is of inestimable value! They must derive from Union an exemption from those broils and wars between themselves, which so frequently afflict neighbouring countries not tied together by the same Governments; which their own rival ships alone would be sufficient to produce, but which opposite foreign alliances, attachments, and intrigues would stimulate and imbitter. Hence, likewise, they will avoid the necessity of those overgrown military establishments which, under any form of Government are inauspicious to Liberty, and which are to be regarded as particularly hostile to Republican Liberty. In this sense it is that your Union ought to be considered as a main prop of your liberty, and that the love of the one ought to endear to you the preservation of the other.

These considerations speak a persuasive language to every reflecting and virtuous mind, and exhibit the continuance of the Union as a primary object of patriotic desire. Is there a doubt whether a common government can embrace so large a sphere? Let experience solve it. To listen to mere speculation in such a case were criminal. We are authorised to hope that a proper organization of the whole, with the auxiliary agency of governments for the respective subdivisions, will afford a happy issue to the experiment. 'Tis well worth a fair and full experiment. With such powerful and obvious motives to Union, affecting all parts of our country, while experience shall not have demonstrated its impracticability, there will always be reason to distrust the patriotism of those who in any quarter may endeavor to weaken its bands.

In contemplating the causes which may disturb our Union, it occurs as matter of serious concern that any ground should have been furnished for characterising parties by Geographical discriminations—Northern and Southern—Atlantic and Western; whence designing men may endeavour to excite a belief that there is a real difference of local Interests and views. One of the expedients of party to acquire influence within particular districts is to misrepresent the opinions and aims of other districts. You cannot shield yourselves too much against the jealousies and heart burnings which spring from these misrepresentations: they tend to render alien to each other those who ought to be bound together by fraternal affection. The inhabitants of our Western country have lately had a useful lesson on this head: they have seen, in the negotiation by the Executive, and in the unanimous ratification by the Senate, of the Treaty with Spain, and in the universal satisfaction at that event throughout the United States, a decisive proof how unfounded were the suspicions propagated among them of a policy in the General Government and in the Atlantic States unfriendly to their interests in regard to the Mississippi: they have been witnesses to the formation of two treaties, that with great Britain, and that with Spain, which secure to them everything they could desire, in respect to our foreign relations, towards confirming their prosperity. Will it not be their wisdom to rely for the preservation of these advantages on the Union by which they were procured ? Will they not henceforth be deaf to those advisers, if such there are, who would sever them from their Brethren and connect them with aliens?

To the efficacy and permanency of your union a Government for the whole is indispensable. No alliances, however strict, between the parts can be an adequate substitute; they must inevitably experience the infractions and interruptions which all alliances in all times have experienced. Sensible of this momentous truth you have improved upon your first essay, by the adoption of a Constitution of Government better calculated than your former for an intimate union, and for the efficacious management of your common concerns. This Government, the offspring of our own choice, uninfluenced and unawed, adopted upon full investigation and mature deliberation, completely free in its principles, in the distribution of its powers, uniting security with energy, and containing within itself a provision for its own amendment, has a just claim to your confidence and your support. Respect for its authority, compliance with its laws, acquiescence in its measures, are duties enjoined by the fundamental maxims of true Liberty. The basis of our political systems is the right of the people to make and to alter their Constitutions of Government. But the Constitution which at any time exists, till changed by an explicit and authentic act of the whole people, is sacredly obligatory upon all. The very idea of the power and the right of the people to establish Government presupposes the duty of every individual to obey the established Government.

All obstructions to the execution of the Laws, all combinations and associations, under whatever plausible character, with the real design to direct, control, counteract, or awe the regular deliberation and action of the constituted authorities, are destructive of this fundamental principle, and of fatal tendency. They serve to organize faction, to give it an artificial and extraordinary force—to put, in the place of the delegated will of the nation the will of a party, often a small but artful and enterprising minority of the community; and, according to the alternate triumphs of different parties, to make the public administration the mirror of the ill-concerted and incongruous projects of faction, rather than the organ of consistent and wholesome plans digested by common councils and modified by mutual interests.

However combinations or associations of the above description may now and then answer popular ends, they are likely, in the course of time and things, to become potent engines, by which cunning, ambitious, and unprincipled men will be enabled to subvert the power of the people and to usurp for themselves the reins of Government; destroying afterwards the very engines which have lifted them to unjust dominion.

Towards the preservation of your Government, and the permanency of your present happy state, it is requisite, not only that you steadily discountenance irregular oppositions to its acknowledged authority, but also that you resist with care the spirit of innovation upon its principles, however specious the pretexts. One method of assault may be to effect, in the forms of the Constitution, alterations which will impair the energy of the system, and thus to undermine what cannot be directly overthrown. In all the changes to which you may be invited, remember that time and habit are at least as necessary to fix the true character of Governments as of other human institutions—that experience is the surest standard by which to test the real tendency of the existing constitution of a country—that facility in changes, upon the credit of mere hypothesis and opinion, exposes to perpetual change, from the endless variety of hypothesis and opinion; and remember, especially, that for the efficient management of your common interests, in a country so extensive as ours, a Government of as much vigor as is consistent with the perfect security of liberty is indispensable. Liberty itself will find in such a Government, with powers properly distributed and adjusted, its surest guardian. It is, indeed, little else than a name, where the government is too feeble to withstand the enterprises of faction, to confine each member of the Society within the limits prescribed by the laws, and to maintain all in the secure and tranquil enjoyment of the rights of person and property.

I have already intimated to you the danger of parties in the state, with particular reference to the founding of them on geographical discriminations. Let me now take a more comprehensive view, and warn you in the most solemn manner against the baneful effects of the spirit of party generally.

This spirit, unfortunately, is inseparable from our nature, having its root in the strongest passions of the human mind. It exists under different shapes in all governments, more or less stifled, controlled, or repressed; but, in those of the popular form, it is seen in its greatest rankness, and is truly their worst enemy.

The alternate domination of one faction over another, sharpened by the spirit of revenge, natural to party dissension, which in different ages and countries has perpetrated the most horrid enormities, is itself a frightful despotism. But this leads at length to a more formal and permanent despotism. The disorders and miseries which result, gradually incline the minds of men to seek security and repose in the absolute power of an individual: and sooner or later the chief of some prevailing faction, more able or more fortunate than his competitors, turns this disposition to the purposes of his own elevation, on the ruins of Public Liberty.

Without looking forward to an extremity of this kind (which nevertheless ought not to be entirely ought of sight), the common and continual mischiefs of the spirit of party are sufficient to make it the interest and duty of a wise People to discourage and restrain it.

It serves always to distract the public councils and enfeeble the Public Administration. It agitates the Community with ill-founded jealousies and false alarms, kindles the animosity of one part against another, foments occasionally riot and insurrection. It opens the door to foreign influence and corruption, which finds a facilitated access to the Government itself through the channels of party passions. Thus the policy and the will of one country are subjected to the policy and will of another.

There is an opinion that parties in free countries are useful checks upon the administration of the Government and serve to keep alive the spirit of Liberty. This within certain limits is probably true; and in Governments of a monarchical cast, Patriotism may look with indulgence, if not with favour, upon the spirit of party. But in those of the popular character, in Governments purely elective, it is a spirit not to be encouraged. From their natural tendency, it is certain there will always be enough of that spirit for every salutary purpose. And there being constant danger of excess, the effort ought to be by force of public opinion, to mitigate and assuage it. A fire not to be quenched, it demands a uniform vigilance to prevent its bursting into a flame, lest, instead of warming it should consume.

It is important, likewise, that the habits of thinking in a free country should inspire caution in those entrusted with its administration, to confine themselves within their respective constitutional spheres, avoiding in the exercise of the powers of one department to encroach upon another. The spirit of encroachment tends to consolidate the powers of all the departments in one, and thus to create, whatever the form of Government, a real despotism. A just estimate of that love of power, and proneness to abuse it, which predominates in the human heart, is sufficient to satisfy us of the truth of this position. The necessity of reciprocal checks in the exercise of political power, by dividing and distributing it into different depositaries, and constituting each the guardian of the public weal against invasions by the others, has been evinced by experiments ancient and modern: some of them in our country and under our own eyes. To preserve them must be as necessary as to institute them. If, in the opinion of the People, the distribution or modification of the constitutional powers be in any particular wrong, let it be corrected by an amendment in the way which the Constitution designates. But let there be no change by usurpation; for tho' this, in one instance, may be the instrument of good, it is the customary weapon by which free Governments are destroyed. The precedent must always greatly overbalance in permanent evil any partial or transient benefit, which the use can at any time yield.

Of all the dispositions and habits which lead to political prosperity, Religion and Morality are indispensable supports. In vain would that man claim the tribute of Patriotism, who should labour to subvert these great pillars of human happiness, these firmest props of the duties of Men and Citizens. The mere Politician, equally with the pious man, ought to respect and to cherish them—A volume could not trace all their connections with private and public felicity. Let it simply be asked: Where is the security for property, for reputation, for Life, if the sense of religious obligation desert the oaths which are the instruments of investigation in Courts of Justice? And let us with caution indulge the supposition that morality can be maintained without religion. Whatever may be conceded to the influence of refined education on minds of peculiar structure, reason and experience both forbid us to expect that national morality can prevail in exclusion of religious principle.

'Tis substantially true that virtue or morality is a necessary spring of popular government. The rule, indeed, extends with more or less force to every species of free government. Who that is a sincere friend to it can look with indifference upon attempts to shake the foundation of the fabric?

Promote then, as an object of primary importance, institutions for the general diffusion of knowledge—In proportion as the structure of a Government gives force to public opinion, it is essential that public opinion should be enlightened.

As a very important source of strength and security, cherish public credit. One method of preserving it is to use it as sparingly as possible, avoiding occasions of expense by cultivating peace, but remembering also that timely disbursements to prepare for danger frequently prevent much greater disbursements to repel it, avoiding likewise the accumulation of debt, not only by shunning occasions of expense, but by vigorous exertion in time of peace to discharge the debts which unavoidable wars may have occasioned, not ungenerously throwing upon posterity the burthen which we ourselves ought to bear. The execution of these maxims belongs to your representatives, but it is necessary that public opinion should cooperate. To facilitate to them the performance of their duty, it is essential that you should practically bear in mind that towards the payment of debts there must be Revenue; that to have Revenue there must be taxes; that no taxes can be devised which are not more or less inconvenient and unpleasant; that the intrinsic embarrassment, inseparable from the selection of the proper objects (which is always a choice of difficulties) ought to be a decisive motive for a candid construction of the conduct of the government in making it, and for a spirit of acquiescence in the measures for obtaining Revenue, which the public exigencies may at any time dictate.

Observe good faith and justice towards all Nations; cultivate peace and harmony with all. Religion and Morality enjoin this conduct; and can it be, that good policy does not equally enjoin it? It will be worthy of a free, enlightened, and at no distant period, a great nation, to give to mankind the magnanimous and too novel example of a people always guided by an exalted justice and benevolence. Who can doubt that, in the course of time and things, the fruits of such a plan would richly repay any temporary advantages which might be lost by a steady adherence to it? Can it be that Providence has not connected the permanent felicity of a nation with its virtue? The experiment, at least, is recommended by every sentiment which ennobles human nature. Alas! is it rendered impossible by its vices?

In the execution of such a plan, nothing is more essential than that permanent, inveterate antipathies against particular Nations, and passionate attachments for others, should be excluded; and that, in place of them, just and amicable feelings towards all should be cultivated. The Nation, which indulges towards another an habitual hatred, or an habitual fondness, is in some degree a slave. It is a slave to its animosity or to its affection, either of which is sufficient to lead it astray from its duty and its interest. Antipathy in one nation against another disposes each more readily to offer insult and injury, to lay hold of slight causes of umbrage, and to be haughty and intractable, when accidental or trifling occasions of dispute occur. Hence, frequent collisions, obstinate, envenomed, and bloody contests. The Nation, prompted by ill will and resentment, sometimes impels to war the Government, contrary to the best calculations of policy. The Government sometimes participates in the national propensity, and adopts through passion what reason would reject; at other times it makes the animosity of the nation subservient to projects of hostility instigated by pride, ambition, and other sinister and pernicious motives. The peace often, sometimes perhaps the liberty, of nations, has been the victim.

So likewise, a passionate attachment of one Nation for another produces a variety of evils. Sympathy for the favorite Nation, facilitating the illusion of an imaginary common interest in cases where no real common interest exists, and infusing into one the enmities of the other, betrays the former into a participation in the quarrels and wars of the latter without adequate inducement or justification. It leads also to concessions to the favorite nation of privileges denied to others which is apt doubly to injure the nation making the concessions; by unnecessarily parting with what ought to have been retained, and by exciting jealousy, ill will, and a disposition to retaliate, in the parties from whom equal privileges are withheld. And it gives to ambitious, corrupted, or deluded Citizens (who devote themselves to the favorite nation), facility to betray or sacrifice the interests of their own Country, without odium, sometimes even with popularity; gilding, with the appearances of a virtuous sense of obligation, a commendable deference for public opinion, or a laudable zeal for public good, the base or foolish compliances of ambition, corruption, or infatuation.

As avenues to foreign influence in innumerable ways, such attachments are particularly alarming to the truly enlightened and independent Patriot. How many opportunities do they afford to tamper with domestic factions, to practice the arts of seduction, to mislead public opinion, to influence or awe the public councils. Such an attachment of a small or weak towards a great and powerful nation dooms the former to be the satellite of the latter.

Against the insidious wiles of foreign influence (I conjure you to believe me, fellow Citizens) the jealousy of a free people ought to be constantly awake, since history and experience prove that foreign influence is one of the most baneful foes of Republican Government. But that jealousy to be useful must be impartial;

else it becomes the instrument of the very influence to be avoided, instead of a defense against it. Excessive partiality for one foreign nation and excessive dislike of another cause those whom they actuate to see danger only on one side, and serve to veil and even second the arts of influence on the other. Real patriots who may resist the intrigues of the favourite are liable to become suspected and odious, while its tools and dupes usurp the applause and confidence of the people, to surrender their interests.

The great rule of conduct for us in regard to foreign nations is in extending our commercial relations, to have with them as little political connection as possible. So far as we have already formed engagements, let them be fulfilled with perfect good faith. Here let us stop.

Europe has a set of primary interests which to us have none, or a very remote relation. Hence she must be engaged in frequent controversies, the causes of which are essentially foreign to our concerns. Hence, therefore, it must be unwise in us to implicate ourselves by artificial ties in the ordinary vicissitudes of her politics, or the ordinary combinations and collisions of her friendships or enmities.

Our detached and distant situation invites and enables us to pursue a different course. If we remain one people under an efficient government, the period is not far off when we may defy material injury from external annoyance; when we may take such an attitude as will cause the neutrality we may at any time resolve upon to be scrupulously respected; when belligerent nations, under the impossibility of making acquisitions upon us, will not lightly hazard the giving us provocation; when we may choose peace or war, as our interest, guided by justice, shall counsel.

Why forego the advantages of so peculiar a situation? Why quit our own to stand upon foreign ground? Why, by interweaving our destiny with that of any part of Europe, entangle our peace and prosperity in the toils of European ambition, rivalship, interest, humour or caprice?

'Tis our true policy to steer clear of permanent alliances with any portion of the foreign world; so far, I mean, as we are now at liberty to do it; for let me not be understood as capable of patronising infidelity to existing engagements. I hold the maxim no less applicable to public than to private affairs, that honesty is always the best policy. I repeat it, therefore, let those engagements be observed in their genuine sense. But, in my opinion, it is unnecessary and would be unwise to extend them.

Taking care always to keep ourselves by suitable establishments on a respectable defensive posture, we may safely trust to temporary alliances for extraordinary emergencies.

Harmony, liberal intercourse with all nations, are recommended by policy, humanity, and interest. But even our commercial policy should hold an equal and impartial hand; neither seeking nor granting exclusive favours or preferences; consulting the natural course of things*; establishing with powers so disposed, in order to give trade a stable course, to define the rights of our Merchants, and to enable the government to support them; conventional rules of intercourse, the best that present circumstances and mutual opinion will permit, but temporary, and liable to be from time to time abandoned or varied, as experience and circumstances shall dictate; constantly keeping in view that 'tis folly in one nation to look for disinterested favours from another; that it must pay with a portion of its independence for whatever it may accept under that character; that, by such acceptance, it may place itself in the condition of having given equivalents for nominal favors, and yet of being reproached with ingratitude for not giving more. There can be no greater error than to expect or calculate upon real favors from nation to nation. 'Tis an illusion, which experience must cure, which a just pride ought to discard.

In offering to you, my Countrymen, these counsels of an old and affectionate friend, I dare not hope they will make the strong and lasting impression I could wish; that they will controul the usual current of the passions, or prevent our nation from running the course which has hitherto marked the destiny of nations: But, if I may even flatter myself, that they may be productive of some partial benefit, some occasional good; that they may now and then recur to moderate the fury of party spirit, to warn against the mischiefs of foreign intrigue, to guard against the impostures of pretended patriotism; this hope will be a full recompense for the solicitude for your welfare, by which they have been dictated.

How far in the discharge of my official duties I have been guided by the principles which have been delineated, the public records and other evidences of my conduct must witness to you and to the world. To myself, the assurance of my own conscience is, that I have at least believed myself to be guided by them.

In relation to the still subsisting War in Europe, my proclamation of the 22d of April 1793 is the index to my plan. Sanctioned by your approving voice, and by that of your Representatives in both Houses of Congress, the spirit of that measure has continually governed me, uninfluenced by any attempts to deter or divert me from it.

After deliberate examination, with the aid of the best lights I could obtain, I was well satisfied that our country, under all the circumstances of the case, had a right to take, and was bound in duty and interest to take, a neutral position. Having taken it, I determined, as far as should depend upon me, to maintain it, with moderation, perseverance and firmness.

* Diffusing and diversifying by by gentle means the streams of commerce, but forcing nothing;

The considerations which respect the right to hold this conduct, it is not necessary on this occasion to detail. I will only observe that, according to my understanding of the matter, that right, so far from being denied by any of the Belligerent powers, has been virtually admitted by all.

The duty of holding a neutral conduct may be inferred, without anything more, from the obligation which justice and humanity impose on every nation, in cases in which it is free to act, to maintain inviolate the relations of peace and amity towards other nations.

The inducements of interest for observing that conduct will best be referred to your own reflections and experience. With me a predominant motive has been to endeavour to gain time to our country to settle and mature its yet recent institutions, and to progress without interruption to that degree of strength and consistency which is necessary to give it, humanly speaking, the command of its own fortunes.

Though, in reviewing the incidents of my administration, I am unconscious of intentional error, I am nevertheless too sensible of my defects not to think it probable that I may have committed many errors. Whatever they may be, I fervently beseech the Almighty to avert or mitigate the evils to which they may tend. I shall also carry with me the hope that my Country will never cease to view them with indulgence; and that, after forty five years of my life dedicated to its service with an upright zeal, the faults of incompetent abilities will be consigned to oblivion, as myself must soon be to the mansions of rest.

Relying on its kindness in this as in other things, and actuated by that fervent love towards it, which is so natural to a man who views in it the native soil of himself and his progenitors for several generations, I anticipate with pleasing expectation that retreat in which I promise myself to realize, without alloy, the sweet enjoyment of partaking, in the midst of my fellow Citizens, the benign influence of good laws under a free Government—the ever favourite object of my heart, and the happy reward, as I trust, of our mutual cares, labours, and dangers.

United States,}
17th September, 1796}

G. Washington.

THOMAS JEFFERSON

INTRODUCTION

Like George Washington, Thomas Jefferson played an active role in the expansion of the western frontier. Gutzon Borglum considered the first president's fellow Virginian to have earned his place on Mt. Rushmore through the Louisiana Purchase—the act that, more than any other, made the idea of Manifest Destiny into a practical reality and served to further Jefferson's vision of an "empire of liberty." Related to this vision was Jefferson's notion of how the country should be governed—a democratic nation of small farmers where all people (or at least all free white men) could vote and where decisions were made at a local level. Rather than wealth and influence concentrating in the hands of rich southern plantation-owners and well-established northern bankers and merchants, Jefferson believed power should reside with the people—and to do this in an agricultural society with a rapidly expanding population would require land and preserving the rights of the states.

This idea of a "Jeffersonian democracy" (actually, a constellation of related causes) was opposed by the Federalists, led by Alexander Hamilton, who believed in the necessity of a stronger central government. While in the end, the result was a compromise, and the demands of the presidency would force him to make hard choices that betrayed his principles, Jefferson did much to shape the course of American history.

We thus need to consider the legacy of the third president not just through his role in expanding the nation's physical borders, but also through the effects of his political ideals and his actions as a public servant. These ideals would not only greatly shape the young nation; in many ways, they would set it on course to the Civil War, which would ultimately make the federal government supreme over the states. They would also have a grave impact on Native Americans and African Americans, both enslaved and free.

EARLY LIFE

Thomas Jefferson was born in 1743, the third child of a wealthy planter, Peter Jefferson. He inherited 5,000 acres, including what would become his famed estate at Monticello, upon his father's death in 1757. The young Jefferson received an excellent education with tutelage in Greek, Latin, and French. He attended the College of William & Mary, and later trained as a lawyer. He remained a great reader and advocate for education throughout his life, amassing several libraries, founding the University of Virginia, beginning the Library of Congress, and learning several languages. Part of this devotion to learning was aspirational:

the young Jefferson moved in some of the most elite political and intellectual circles in Virginia, and his home at Monticello, which he began constructing in 1768, was designed as a model of gracious living. However, his erudition would also serve him well in life: Jefferson's familiarity with Greek and Roman history, as well as with thinkers of the French Enlightenment such as Montesquieu, are evident in his later political writings. Most especially, Jefferson was a devotee of natural philosophy—what we would today call "science"—and empiricism, the philosophy that we can only know truth through the experience of our senses. Like many empiricists, Jefferson tended to look to "scientific" explanations to defend his political ideas. In later years, however, his youthful ideals would often give way to practical necessity.

Jefferson was elected to the Virginia House of Burgesses in 1769 and served until 1775 when, at the age of 33, he became one of the youngest representatives to the Continental Congress. During the time of increased tension with Great Britain, Jefferson took an active role in affairs, authoring numerous pieces arguing the colonies' right to self-government. Though he was a militia officer, his greatest role was as a propagandist and legislator. He was, of course, the author of the Declaration of Independence, and as a member of the Virginia House of Delegates, he helped to draft a state government for the future state. Many of his proposed ideas, such as not allowing an established religion, providing for public education, and dismantling large landowners' attempts to turn themselves into a sort of aristocracy by means of inheritance laws, would be profoundly influential. Jefferson's thoughts on the matter were strongly conveyed in his *Notes on the State of Virginia*, written in response to an inquiry from the French diplomat François Barbé-Marbois and published in 1785. The *Notes*, though not reproduced here for reasons of space, is well worth reading as a compendium of the physical, social, legal, and other aspects of the society Jefferson helped to shape.

Jefferson's personal life was considerably more tragic than his public career. In 1772, at the age of twenty-eight, he married his distant cousin, the twenty-three-year-old widow Martha Wayles Skelton. Martha was a gracious hostess and entertainer, and the two frequently held social gatherings at Monticello. The couple had six children, only two of whom lived past infancy—a daughter, also named Martha, who was born in 1772 and survived until 1836; and another daughter named Mary, who was born in 1778 and lived until 1804. Jefferson's wife suffered many complications from her pregnancies, however, and died after giving birth to her last child in 1782. Grief-stricken, Jefferson promised never to marry again; something of his feelings may be seen in his "Letter to Marquis de Chastellux." This promise may cast some light on his relationship with an enslaved woman, Sally Hemings, which will be further explored below.

It is also in this period that he developed a close friendship—and perhaps had a brief affair with—Maria Cosway, a married Italian-English musician, artist, and educator, who is the addressee of the "Dialogue Between My Heart and My Head." The two would maintain a lifelong correspondence.

FRANCE, PRESIDENCY, AND THE LOUISIANA PURCHASE

Following the American Revolution, Jefferson briefly served as a member of the dysfunctional Congress under the Articles of Confederation before being sent to join Benjamin Franklin and John Adams in Paris, where they were negotiating with the powers of Europe. The duties were a welcome distraction for the grieving Jefferson. He would succeed Franklin as the official American ambassador, remaining in France for five years and becoming an ardent Francophile. Jefferson became close friends with the Marquis de Lafayette and was a strong supporter of the French Revolution—among other things, he consulted on the writing of the Declaration of the Rights of Man and Citizen.

Jefferson returned to America in 1789, where George Washington appointed him the first secretary of state. He quickly found himself in opposition to the secretary of the treasury, Alexander Hamilton. While their disagreement was ostensibly about the war debt and whether there should be national credit and a national bank, at its core, it was about how much power the federal government should have compared to the states. Hamilton and the supporters of his position became known as "Federalists," whereas Jefferson's states-rights ideas formed the basis for the "Democratic-Republican" party. The dispute spilled over into the press where both men anonymously and venomously attacked one another in newspaper articles and pamphlets (of which Jefferson's "Opinion on the Constitutionality of a National Bank" is but the most polite echo). The ugly feud led to a rupture between Jefferson and Hamilton, and also a falling out between Jefferson and Washington. Jefferson was also a continual partisan for the French Revolution even as events in France degenerated into the Reign of Terror; to betray the Revolution, he felt, would betray the principles of American democracy. This would lead to his final rupture with Washington, who wanted the new nation to remain neutral as Great Britain waged war against France, and led to Jefferson quitting Washington's cabinet.

Jefferson ran for President on Democratic-Republican party lines in the first contested election in 1796, and though defeated by Federalist John Adams, became vice president due to the way the Electoral College vote was managed: Before the 12th Amendment in 1804, each elector cast two votes; the winner became president and the runner-up vice president. Thus, for the only time in

American history, the president and vice president were from opposing parties. While Jefferson did not take an active role in the Senate as vice president, he used his position to undermine Adams with French diplomats (the infamous XYZ Affair) and to fiercely oppose the Alien and Sedition Acts, which he feared would be used to prosecute the Democratic-Republicans. The Kentucky Resolution and Virginia Resolution he and James Madison anonymously authored, which argued that the states could nullify unconstitutional actions by the federal government such as the Alien and Sedition Acts, were deeply damaging and formed part of the basis for the South's later secession.

Adams' presidency only lasted one term, and Jefferson became the third president in the hotly contested election of 1800. Chief among the challenges he faced were reconciling the Federalist/Democratic-Republican divide and the national debt. While the first problem was never really settled—in fact, it gave rise to the American two-party political system—he could certainly do something about the second. Jefferson accordingly set about trying to shrink the national government as much as possible and was able to decrease the debt from $83 million to $57 million in his two terms. However, an opportunity soon arose that simultaneously ensured Jefferson's place in history and forced him to betray his most deeply held principles: the opportunity to expand the new nation's territory beyond what had been thought possible.

THE LOUISIANA PURCHASE

From 1699 to 1762, and again after 1800, France claimed a vast inland empire in North America. The French Revolution had ruined the country's economy, however, and the slave revolt in Haiti and war with Britain had diminished the desire of the new ruler of France, Napoleon Bonaparte, to remain entangled in the New World. When Jefferson sent James Monroe and Robert Livingston in 1803 to purchase the strategically and economically critical port of New Orleans from Napoleon, they were astounded when he offered the entirety of the Louisiana Territory. The sum was $15 million dollars, or around $600 billion in today's money. The offer was too good to refuse. In one stroke, Jefferson had not only secured the vital Mississippi River, but also almost doubled the size of the United States. Much remained to be determined, however, such as what lay in the interior, how to settle and govern this land, whether the new territory should be slave or free, and whether the government even had the right to make this purchase. To make this enormous purchase was something quite against Jefferson's principles of a small, limited federal government, but the opportunity was too good to pass up. For a time, he even felt a Constitutional amendment would be necessary.

The Senate quickly ratified the purchase, and Jefferson dispatched Meriwether Lewis and William Clark to explore the new land and claim unexplored territories all the way to the Pacific. Jefferson himself taught Lewis the natural sciences he would need to know and gave him unlimited access to the library at Monticello. From May 1804 to September of 1806, the Corps of Discovery made unprecedented findings, eventually reaching the Pacific Ocean and returning with information on the land, natural resources, and Native American peoples of the interior, including the Lakota. Their achievements bolstered the United States' claim to the disputed Pacific Northwest.

JEFFERSON'S NATIVE AMERICAN POLICY

Like George Washington, Jefferson had to contend with the question of what should be done with the aboriginal peoples living in the lands claimed by the young United States. For instance, he wrote of Native Americans as equals of the descendants of Europeans. During the American Revolution and as president, he worked to keep peace with tribes that the British were trying to turn against the settlers.

Jefferson's plan for Native Americans, like that of many of his educated and liberal countrymen, was one that could best be described as assimilationist. The best result would be for them to adopt agriculture and European civilization. The second best option would be for them to move, or be forcibly removed, west of the Mississippi. The fact was that the young, land-hungry nation was more than eager to seize land from Native American peoples, and Jefferson was forced to acquiesce to the prevailing desires. For instance, he offered the state of Georgia military aid in expelling the Cherokee in exchange for lands the state claimed west of the Appalachians. Thus, he was complicit in the disinheritance of entire peoples.

JEFFERSON AND SLAVERY

Thomas Jefferson had a complex relationship with the institution of slavery. On the one hand, he himself was a slaveholder, owning approximately 600 people through his lifetime. On the other, from the time of his earliest career, he pursued reforms to slavery, including legislation that would allow slaveholders to emancipate the people they owned. He also represented African Americans seeking freedom in court, and probably helped at least one enslaved man escape. These efforts rarely met with success. Likewise, as one of the authors of the Land Ordinance of 1784, which provided that the lands west of the Ohio River should become states in their own rights, he tried to ban slavery in the new territory.

This "Jefferson Proviso," though defeated, was incorporated into the Northwest Ordinance of 1787.

In no way was Jefferson ignorant of the problems inherent in slavery: Aside from being undemocratic and establishing the thing he wished to most avoid in America—a landed gentry—he believed that African Americans and European-Americans could not live together in freedom because those oppressed would always be justifiably resentful.

What was to be done about this troublesome institution and those it affected? Jefferson recognized the complexity of the question and favored gradual emancipation. To suddenly free the African American population, he held, would be disastrous. The best option—albeit an impractical one—would be to move freed African Americans elsewhere, such as to the west coast of Africa. (This sentiment gave rise to the modern nation of Liberia, which has itself a troubled imperialist history.) Best of all, he thought, was if it had never existed, but such regrets did nothing to change the impossible and hypocritical situation of a nation that at once espoused liberty and slavery. Modern America is still struggling with the legacy of these questions.

In the end, Jefferson's position on slavery may be one of despair and even cynicism. As he prepared for his 1794 presidential bid, he recognized that slaveholders possessed considerable political power and he often appeased southern states in order to keep the new nation together. The rest of the time, he maintained a studied silence on the matter. His fears of states seceding over the matter, or even a race-war, trumped any moral feelings he might have had. Unlike Washington, Jefferson did not free his slaves—save for his four surviving children by Sally Hemings—after his death. He could not: He was deeply in debt, and his goods, including his human chattels, were auctioned off after his death. Historians remain divided over Jefferson's true feelings about slavery, and how to judge him on the matter.

One thing, however, is an established fact, and that is Jefferson's troubling relationship with Sally Hemings. The two first became involved in 1787. Jefferson had brought the sixteen-year-old Sally and her brother James along to France (Jefferson was forty-four at the time). Considering their ages and Jefferson's position of power over Sally Hemings, we can in no way consider their relationship to be fully consensual in the modern sense—but to what degree it was coerced, or even a calculated decision made by Hemings out of necessity or a desire for certain advantages, we can never know. Claims that Jefferson and Hemings had a relationship were made as early as 1802, when a vengeful political rival made a public accusation; in the 1870s, Madison Hemings, one of their children, reiterated the charge in an Ohio newspaper. Modern genetic testing comparing the paternal

DNA of Sally Hemings' male-line descendants and those of male descendants of Jefferson's uncle have established the connection as a historical fact.

POLITICAL LEGACY

Thomas Jefferson's legacy to the new nation was not only the physical expansion of territory, but also an ideology that went along with it. Two of the most important concepts he framed, the "empire of liberty" and the concept of Jeffersonian democracy, would have a deep and abiding effect on America.

THE "EMPIRE OF LIBERTY"

One of Jefferson's key phrases was the "empire of liberty," a theme that would be expanded upon by future presidents—notably, for our purposes, Theodore Roosevelt. Jefferson first articulated this idea during the Revolution, envisioning a land united in spirit if not in politics, devoted to freedom, and able to check the worst tendencies of the British Empire. As president, Jefferson's foreign policy made these ideals more concrete: He sent US naval ships to the Mediterranean to fight pirates (the First Barbary War) and ensure freedom of navigation; he made the Louisiana Purchase; and his foreign policy presaged the Monroe Doctrine, in which James Monroe, following advice given by Jefferson himself, declared the Western hemisphere off-limits to European colonization. He also advocated freeing Canada from British rule. Jefferson was thus (ironically, considering his belief in a small central government) one of the first political leaders to explicitly stress that an interventionist mandate was an integral part of the United States' democratic mission.

THE LEGACY OF JEFFERSONIAN DEMOCRACY

The concept of "Jeffersonian democracy" perhaps did more than any other political concept to shape the early republic and move the young nation down the path to the Civil War. Its principles were simple: Expansion of the electorate; taking power away from the wealthy; impartial, participatory, and transparent government; individual rights; and limited central government. These principles, Jefferson and his allies held, were the best insurance against tyranny. It was a mixed success. While at the beginning of Jefferson's presidency, only Kentucky and Vermont had universal male suffrage, by the end of his second term, it was the rule in the majority of states. On the other hand, as president, Jefferson was forced to strengthen the central government, which ran counter to his deeply held belief in decentralized power. The Louisiana Purchase is one example of an expanded federal reach; another is how in 1807 he was forced to issue the Embargo Act, which claimed broad federal powers, during a period of increased tensions with Great Britain. The paradox of the great populist moving in such an autocratic direction has not been lost on historians.

Jefferson's dream of a decentralized nation made up of small farmers, perhaps resembling that of ancient Athens or the Roman Republic, was perhaps never achievable even in his own day. The exigencies of navigating a functional country's course needed a guiding hand on the tiller. Furthermore, the struggle between local government and states' rights against those of the federal government helped to intensify the debate over slavery in the early and mid-nineteenth century. In fact, it was the unsolved question of states' rights on the one crucial question that defeated Jefferson's own political and moral genius—that of slavery—that would be magnified in the decades after his death and lead to the cataclysmic conflict of the Civil War.

LETTER TO CHEVALIER DE CHASTELLUX

Dear Sir Ampthill Nov. 26. 1782

I received your friendly letters of _____* and June 30 but the latter not till the 17th. of Oct. It found me a little emerging from that stupor of mind which had rendered me as dead to the world as she† was whose loss occasioned it. Your letter recalled to my memory, that there were persons still living of much value to me. If you should have thought me remiss in not testifying to you sooner how deeply I had been impressed with your worth in the little time I had the happiness of being with you you will I am sure ascribe it to it's true cause the state of dreadful suspence in which I had been kept all the summer and the catastrophe which closed it. Before that event my scheme of life had been determined. I had folded myself in the arms of retirement, and rested all prospects of future happiness on domestic and literary objects. A single event wiped away all my plans and left me a blank which I had not the spirits to fill up. In this state of mind an appointment from Congress found me, requiring me to cross the Atlantic, and that temptation might be added to duty I was informed at the same time from his Excy. the Chevalier de la Luzerne that a vessel of force would be sailing about the middle of Dec. in which you would be passing to France. I accepted the appointment and my only object now is so to hasten over those obstacles which would retard my departure as to be ready to join you in your voiage, fondly measuring your affections by my own and presuming your consent. It is not certain that by any exertions I can be in Philadelphia by the middle of December. The contrary is most probable. But hoping it will not be much later and counting on those procrastinations which usually attend the departure of vessels of size I have hopes of being with you in time. This will give me full Leisure to learn the result of your observations on the Natural bridge, to communicate to you my answers to the queries of Monsr. de Marbois, to receive edification from you on these and on other subjects of science, considering chess too as a matter of science. Should I be able to set out in tolerable time and any extraordinary delays attend the sailing of the vessel I shall certainly do myself the honour of waiting on his Excy. Count Rochambeau at his Headquarters and of assuring him in person of my high respect and esteem for him—an object of which I have never lost sight. To yourself I am unable to express the warmth of those sentiments of friendship and attachment with which I have the honour to be, Dr Sir, Your most obedt. & mo. hble. servt.

---

* May have referred to a letter dated June 10, 1782, but it was left blank in the manuscript. -Ed.

† In the draft, the word was deleted, but it may have read, "...rendered me as dead to the world, as was she..." -Ed.

"DIALOGUE BETWEEN MY HEAD AND MY HEART" LETTER TO MARIA COSWAY

To Maria Cosway
Paris Octob. 12. 1786.

[My dear] Madam,

Having performed the last sad office of handing you into your carriage at the Pavillon de St. Denis, and seen the wheels get actually into motion, I turned on my heel and walked, more dead than alive, to the opposite door, where my own was awaiting me. Mr. Danquerville was missing. He was sought for, found, and dragged down stairs. [We] were crammed into the carriage, like recruits for the Bastille, and not having [sou]l enough to give orders to the coachman, he presumed Paris our destination, [and] drove off. After a considerable interval, silence was broke with a "*je suis vraiment affligé du depart de ces bons gens.*" This was the signal for a mutual confession [of dist]ress. We began immediately to talk of Mr. and Mrs. Cosway, of their goodness, their [talents], their amability, and tho we spoke of nothing else, we seemed hardly to have entered into matter when the coachman announced the rue St. Denis, and that we were opposite Mr. Danquerville's. He insisted on descending there and traversing a short passage to his lodgings. I was carried home. Seated by my fire side, solitary and sad, the following dialogue took place between my Head and my Heart.

Head. Well, friend, you seem to be in a pretty trim.

Heart. I am indeed the most wretched of all earthly beings. Overwhelmed with grief, every fibre of my frame distended beyond it's natural powers to bear, I would willingly meet whatever catastrophe should leave me no more to feel or to fear.

Head. These are the eternal consequences of your warmth and precipitation. This is one of the scrapes into which you are ever leading us. You confess your follies indeed: but still you hug and cherish them, and no reformation can be hoped, where there is no repentance.

Heart. Oh my friend! This is no moment to upbraid my foibles. I am rent into fragments by the force of my grief! If you have any balm, pour it into my wounds: if none, do not harrow them by new torments. Spare me in this awful moment! At any other I will attend with patience to your admonitions.

Head. On the contrary I never found that the moment of triumph with you was the moment of attention to my admonitions. While suffering under your follies you may perhaps be made sensible of them, but, the paroxysm over, you fancy it can never return. Harsh therefore as the medecine may be, it is my office to administer it. You will be pleased to remember that when our friend Trumbull used to be telling us of the merits and talents of these good people, I never ceased whispering to you that we had no occasion for new acquaintance; that the greater their merit and talents, the more dangerous their friendship to our tranquillity, because the regret at parting would be greater.

Heart. Accordingly, Sir, this acquaintance was not the consequence of my doings. It was one of your projects which threw us in the way of it. It was you, remember, and not I, who desired the meeting, at Legrand & Molinos. I never trouble myself with domes nor arches. The Halle aux bleds might have rotted down before I should have gone to see it. But you, forsooth, who are eternally getting us to sleep with your diagrams and crotchets, must go and examine this wonderful piece of architecture. And when you had seen it, oh! it was the most superb thing on earth! What you had seen there was worth all you had yet seen in Paris! I thought so too. But I meant it of the lady and gentleman to whom we had been presented, and not of a parcel of sticks and chips put together in pens. You then, Sir, and not I, have been the cause of the present distress.

Head. It would have been happy for you if my diagrams and crotchets had gotten you to sleep on that day, as you are pleased to say they eternally do. My visit to Legrand & Molinos had publick utility for it's object. A market is to be built in Richmond. What a commodious plan is that of Legrand & Molinos: especially if we put on it the noble dome of the Halle aux bleds. If such a bridge as they shewed us can be thrown across the Schuylkill at Philadelphia, the floating bridges taken up, and the navigation of that river opened, what a copious resource will be added, of wood and provisions, to warm and feed the poor of that city. While I was occupied with these objects, you were dilating with your new acquaintances, and contriving how to prevent a separation from them. Every soul of you had an engagement for the day. Yet all these were to be sacrificed, that you might dine together. Lying messengers were to be dispatched into every quarter of the city with apologies for your breach of engagement. You particularly had the effrontery [to] send word to the Dutchess Danville that, in the moment we were setting out to d[ine] with her, dispatches came to hand which required immediate attention. You [wanted] me to invent a more ingenious excuse; but I knew you were getting into a scrape, and I would have nothing to do with it. Well, after dinner to St. Cloud, from St. Cloud to Ruggieri's, from Ruggieri to Krumfoltz, and if the day had been as long as a Lapland summer day, you would still have contrived means, among you, to have filled it.

Heart. Oh! my dear friend, how you have revived me by recalling to my mind the transactions of that day! How well I remember them all, and that when I came home at night and looked back to the morning, it seemed to have been a month agone. Go on then, like a kind comforter, and paint to me the day we went to St. Germains. How beautiful was every object! the Port de Neuilly, the hills along the Seine, the rainbows of the machine of Marly, the terras of St. Germains, the chateaux, the gardens, the [statues] of Marly, the pavillon of Lucienne. Recollect too Madrid, Bagatelle, the King's garden, the Dessert. How grand the idea excited by the remains of such a column! The spiral staircase too was beautiful. Every moment was filled with something agreeable. The wheels of time moved on with a rapidity of which those of our carriage gave but a faint idea, and yet in the evening, when one took a retrospect of the day, what a mass of happiness had we travelled over! Retrace all those scenes to me, my good companion, and I will forgive the unkindness with which you were chiding me. The day we went to St. Germains was a little too warm, I think, was not it?

Head. Thou art the most incorrigible of all the beings that ever sinned! I reminded you of the follies of the first day, intending to deduce from thence some useful lessons for you, but instead of listening to these, you kindle at the recollection, you retrace the whole series with a fondness which shews you want nothing but the opportunity to act it over again. I often told you during it's course that you were imprudently engaging your affections under circumstances that must cost you a great deal of pain: that the persons indeed were of the greatest merit, possessing good sense, good humour, honest hearts, honest manners, and eminence in a lovely art: that the lady had moreover qualities and accomplishments, belonging to her sex, which might form a chapter apart for her: such as music, modesty, beauty, and that softness of disposition which is the ornament of her sex and charm of ours. But that all these considerations would increase the pang of separation: that their stay here was to be short: that you rack our whole system when you are parted from those you love, complaining that such a separation is worse than death, inasmuch as this ends our sufferings, whereas that only begins them: and that the separation would in this instance be the more severe as you would probably never see them again.

Heart. But they told me they would come back again the next year.

Head. But in the mean time see what you suffer: and their return too depends on so many circumstances that if you had a grain of prudence you would not count upon it. Upon the whole it is improbable and therefore you should abandon the idea of ever seeing them again.

Heart. May heaven abandon me if I do!

HEAD. Very well. Suppose then they come back. They are to stay here two months, and when these are expired, what is to follow? Perhaps you flatter yourself they may come to America?

HEART. God only knows what is to happen. I see nothing impossible in that supposition, and I see things wonderfully contrived sometimes to make us happy. Where could they find such objects as in America for the exercise of their enchanting art? Especially the lady, who paints landscape so inimitably. She wants only subjects worthy of immortality to render her pencil immortal. The Falling spring, the Cascade of Niagara, the Passage of the Potowmac thro the Blue mountains, the Natural bridge. It is worth a voiage across the Atlantic to see these objects; much more to paint, and make them, and thereby ourselves, known to all ages. And our own dear Monticello, where has nature spread so rich a mantle under the eye? Mountains, forests, rocks, rivers. With what majesty do we there ride above the storms! How sublime to look down into the workhouse of nature, to see her clouds, hail, snow, rain, thunder, all fabricated at our feet! And the glorious Sun, when rising as if out of a distant water, just gilding the tops of the mountains, and giving life to all nature!—I hope in god no circumstance may ever make either seek an asylum from grief! With what sincere sympathy I would open every cell of my composition to receive the effusion of their woes! I would pour my tears into their wounds: and if a drop of balm could be found at the top of the Cordilleras, or at the remotest sources of the Missouri, I would go thither myself to seek and to bring it. Deeply practised in the school of affliction, the human heart knows no joy which I have not lost, no sorrow of which I have not drank! Fortune can present no grief of unknown form to me! Who then can so softly bind up the wound of another as he who has felt the same wound himself? But Heaven forbid they should ever know a sorrow!—Let us turn over another leaf, for this has distracted me.

HEAD. Well. Let us put this possibility to trial then on another point. When you consider the character which is given of our country by the lying newspapers of London, and their credulous copyers in other countries; when you reflect that all Europe is made to believe we are a lawless banditti, in a state of absolute anarchy, cutting one another's throats, and plundering without distinction, how can you expect that any reasonable creature would venture among us?

HEART. But you and I know that all this is false: that there is not a country on earth where there is greater tranquillity, where the laws are milder, or better obeyed: where every one is more attentive to his own business, or meddles less with that of others: where strangers are better received, more hospitably treated, and with a more sacred respect.

HEAD. True, you and I know this, but your friends do not know it.

Heart. But they are sensible people who think for themselves. They will ask of impartial foreigners who have been among us, whether they saw or heard on the spot any instances of anarchy. They will judge too that a people occupied as we are in opening rivers, digging navigable canals, making roads, building public schools, establishing academies, erecting busts and statues to our great men, protecting religious freedom, abolishing sanguinary punishments, reforming and improving our laws in general, they will judge I say for themselves whether these are not the occupations of a people at their ease, whether this is not better evidence of our true state than a London newspaper, hired to lie, and from which no truth can ever be extracted but by reversing everything it says.

Head. I did not begin this lecture my friend with a view to learn from you what America is doing. Let us return then to our point. I wished to make you sensible how imprudent it is to place your affections, without reserve, on objects you must so soon lose, and whose loss when it comes must cost you such severe pangs. Remember the last night. You knew your friends were to leave Paris to-day. This was enough to throw you into agonies. All night you tossed us from one side of the bed to the other. No sleep, no rest. The poor crippled wrist too, never left one moment in the same position, now up, now down, now here, now there; was it to be wondered at if all it's pains returned? The Surgeon then was to be called, and to be rated as an ignoramus because he could not devine the cause of this extraordinary change.—In fine, my friend, you must mend your manners. This is not a world to live at random in as you do. To avoid these eternal distresses, to which you are for ever exposing us, you must learn to look forward before you take a step which may interest our peace. Everything in this world is matter of calculation. Advance then with caution, the balance in your hand. Put into one scale the pleasures which any object may offer; but put fairly into the other the pains which are to follow, and see which preponderates. The making an acquaintance is not a matter of indifference. When a new one is proposed to you, view it all round. Consider what advantages it presents, and to what inconveniencies it may expose you. Do not bite at the bait of pleasure till you know there is no hook beneath it. The art of life is the art of avoiding pain: and he is the best pilot who steers clearest of the rocks and shoals with which it is beset. Pleasure is always before us; but misfortune is at our side: while running after that, this arrests us. The most effectual means of being secure against pain is to retire within ourselves, and to suffice for our own happiness. Those, which depend on ourselves, are the only pleasures a wise man will count on: for nothing is ours which another may deprive us of. Hence the inestimable value of intellectual pleasures. Ever in our power, always leading us to something new, never cloying, we ride, serene and sublime, above the concerns of this mortal world, contemplating truth and nature, matter and motion, the laws which bind up their existence, and that eternal being who made and bound them up by these laws. Let this be our employ. Leave the bustle and tumult of society to those who have not talents to occupy themselves without them. Friendship is but another name for an alliance with the follies and the misfortunes of others. Our own share of miseries is sufficient: why enter then as volunteers into those of another? Is there so little gall poured into our own cup that we must needs help to drink that of our neighbor? A friend dies or leaves us: we feel as if a limb was cut off. He is sick: we must watch over him, and participate of his pains. His fortune is shipwrecked: ours must be laid under contribution. He loses a child, a parent or a partner: we must mourn the loss as if it was our own.

HEART. And what more sublime delight than to mingle tears with one whom the hand of heaven hath smitten! To watch over the bed of sickness, and to beguile it's tedious and it's painful moments! To share our bread with one to whom misfortune has left none! This world abounds indeed with misery: to lighten it's burthen we must divide it with one another. But let us now try the virtues of your mathematical balance, and as you have put into one scale the burthens of friendship, let me put it's comforts into the other. When languishing then under disease, how grateful is the solace of our friends! How are we penetrated with their assiduities and attentions! How much are we supported by their encouragements and kind offices! When Heaven has taken from us some object of our love, how sweet is it to have a bosom whereon to recline our heads, and into which we may pour the torrent of our tears! Grief, with such a comfort, is almost a luxury! In a life where we are perpetually exposed to want and accident, yours is a wonderful proposition, to insulate ourselves, to retire from all aid, and to wrap ourselves in the mantle of self-sufficiency! For assuredly nobody will care for him who cares for nobody. But friendship is precious not only in the shade but in the sunshine of life: and thanks to a benevolent arrangement of things, the greater part of life is sunshine. I will recur for proof to the days we have lately passed. On these indeed the sun shone brightly! How gay did the face of nature appear! Hills, vallies, chateaux, gardens, rivers, every object wore it's liveliest hue! Whence did they borrow it? From the presence of our charming companion. They were pleasing, because she seemed pleased. Alone, the scene would have been dull and insipid: the participation of it with her gave it relish. Let the gloomy Monk, sequestered from the world, seek unsocial pleasures in the bottom of his cell! Let the sublimated philosopher grasp visionary happiness while pursuing phantoms dressed in the garb of truth! Their supreme wisdom is supreme folly: and they mistake for happiness the mere absence of pain. Had they ever felt the solid pleasure of one generous spasm of the heart, they would exchange for it all the frigid speculations of their lives, which you have been vaunting in such elevated terms. Believe me then, my friend, that that is a miserable arithmetic which would estimate friendship at nothing, or at less than nothing. Respect for you has induced me to enter into this discussion, and to hear principles uttered which I detest and abjure. Respect for myself now obliges me to recall you into the proper limits of your office. When nature assigned us the same habitation, she gave us over it a divided empire. To you she allotted the field of science, to me that of morals. When the circle is to be squared, or the orbit of a comet to be traced; when the arch of greatest strength, or the solid of least resistance is to be investigated, take you the problem: it is yours: nature has given me no cognisance of it. In like manner in denying to you the feelings of sympathy, of benevolence, of gratitude, of justice, of love, of friendship, she has excluded you from their controul. To these she has adapted the mechanism of the heart. Morals were too essential to the happiness of man to be risked on the incertain combinations of the head. She laid their foundation therefore in sentiment, not in science. That she gave to all, as necessary to all: this to a few only, as sufficing with a few. I know indeed that you pretend authority to the sovereign controul of our conduct in all it's parts: and a respect for your grave saws and maxims, a desire to do what is right, has sometimes induced me to conform to your counsels. A few facts however which I can readily recall to your memory, will suffice to prove to you that nature has not organised you for our moral direction. When the poor wearied souldier, whom we overtook at Chickahominy with his pack on his back, begged us to let him get up behind our chariot, you began to calculate that the road was full of souldiers, and that if all should be taken up our horses would fail in their journey. We drove on therefore. But soon becoming sensible you had made me do wrong, that tho we cannot relieve all the distressed we should relieve as many as we can, I turned about to take up the souldier; but he had entered a bye path, and was no more to be found: and from that moment to this I could never find him out to ask his forgiveness. Again, when the poor woman came to ask a charity in Philadelphia, you whispered that she looked like a drunkard, and that half a dollar was enough to give her for the ale-house. Those who want the dispositions to give, easily find reasons why they ought not to give. When I sought her out afterwards, and did what I should have done at first, you know that she employed the money immediately towards placing her child at school. If our country, when pressed with wrongs at the point of the bayonet, had been governed by it's heads instead of it's hearts, where should we have been now? Hanging on a gallows as high as Haman's. You began to calculate and to compare wealth and numbers: we threw up a few pulsations of our warmest blood: we supplied enthusiasm against wealth and numbers: we put our existence to the hazard, when the hazard seemed against us, and we saved our country: justifying at the same time the ways of Providence, whose precept is to do always what is right, and leave the issue to him. In short, my friend, as far as my recollection serves me, I do not know that I ever did a good thing on your suggestion, or a dirty one without it. I do for ever then disclaim your interference in my province. Fill paper as you please with triangles and squares: try how many ways you can hang and combine them together. I shall never envy nor controul your sublime delights. But leave me to decide when and where friendships are to be contracted. You say I contract them at random, so you said the woman at Philadelphia was a drunkard. I receive no one into my esteem till I know they are worthy of it. Wealth, title, office, are no recommendations to my friendship. On the contrary great good qualities are requisite to make amends for their having wealth, title and office. You confess that in the present case I could not have made a worthier choice. You only object that I was so soon to lose them. We are not immortal ourselves, my friend; how can we expect our enjoiments to be so? We have no rose without it's thorn; no pleasure without alloy. It is the law of our existence; and we must acquiesce. It is the condition annexed to all our pleasures, not by us who receive, but by him who gives them. True, this condition is pressing cruelly on me at this moment. I feel more fit for death than life. But when I look back on the pleasures of which it is the consequence, I am conscious they were worth the price I am paying. Notwithstanding your endeavors too to damp my hopes, I comfort myself with expectations of their promised return. Hope is sweeter than despair, and they were too good to mean to deceive me. In the summer, said the gentleman; but in the spring, said the lady: and I should love her forever, were it only for that! Know then, my friend, that I have taken these good people into my bosom: that I have lodged them in the warmest cell I could find: that I love them, and will continue to love them thro life: that if fortune should dispose them on one side the globe, and me on the other, my affections shall pervade it's whole mass to reach them. Knowing then my determination, attempt not to disturb it. If you can at any time furnish matter for their amusement, it will be the office of a good neighbor to do it. I will in like manner seize any occasion which may offer to do the like good turn for you with Condorcet, Rittenhouse, Madison, La Cretelle, or any other of those worthy sons of science whom you so justly prize.'

I thought this a favorable proposition whereon to rest the issue of the dialogue. So I put an end to it by calling for my nightcap. Methinks I hear you wish to heaven I had called a little sooner, and so spared you the ennui of such a tedious sermon. I did not interrupt them sooner because I was in a mood for hearing sermons. You too were the subject; and on such a thesis I never think the theme long; not even if I am to write it, and that slowly and awkwardly, as now, with the left hand. But that you may not be discoraged from a correspondence which begins so formidably, I will promise you on my honour that my future letters shall be of a reasonable length. I will even agree to express but half my esteem for you, for fear of cloying you with too full a dose. But, on your part, no curtailing. If your letters are as long as the bible, they will appear short to me. Only let them be brim full of affection. I shall read them with the dispositions with which Arlequin in les deux billets spelt the words 'je t'aime' and wished that the whole alphabet had entered into their composition.

We have had incessant rains since your departure. These make me fear for your health, as well as that you have had an uncomfortable journey. The same cause has prevented me from being able to give you any account of your friends here. This voiage to Fontainbleau will probably send the Count de Moutier and the Marquise de Brehan to America. Danquerville promised to visit me, but has not done it as yet. De latude comes sometimes to take family soupe with me, and entertains me with anecdotes of his five and thirty years imprisonment. How fertile is the mind of man which can make the Bastille and Dungeon of Vincennes yeild interesting anecdotes. You know this was for making four verses on Mme. de Pompadour. But I think you told me you did not know the verses. They were these. 'Sans esprit, sans sentiment, Sans etre belle, ni neuve, En France on peut avoir le premier amant: Pompadour en est l'epreuve.' I have read the memoir of his three escapes. As to myself my health is good, except my wrist which mends slowly, and my mind which mends not at all, but broods constantly over your departure. The lateness of the season obliges me to decline my journey into the South of France. Present me in the most friendly terms to Mr. Cosway, and receive me into your own recollection with a partiality and a warmth, proportioned, not to my own poor merit, but to the sentiments of sincere affection and esteem with which I have the honour to be, my dear Madam, your most obedient humble servant,

Th: Jefferson

AUTOBIOGRAPHY

January 6, 1821

At the age of 77, I begin to make some memoranda and state some recollections of dates & facts concerning myself, for my own more ready reference & for the information of my family.

The tradition in my father's family was that their ancestor came to this country from Wales, and from near the mountain of Snowdon, the highest in Gr. Br. I noted once a case from Wales in the law reports where a person of our name was either pl. or def. and one of the same name was Secretary to the Virginia company. These are the only instances in which I have met with the name in that country. I have found it in our early records, but the first particular information I have of any ancestor was my grandfather who lived at the place in Chesterfield called Ozborne's and ownd. the lands afterwards the glebe of the parish. He had three sons, Thomas who died young, Field who settled on the waters of Roanoke and left numerous descendants, and Peter my father, who settled on the lands I still own called Shadwell adjoining my present residence. He was born Feb. 29, 1707/8, and intermarried 1739. with Jane Randolph, of the age of 19. daur of Isham Randolph one of the seven sons of that name & family settled at Dungeoness in Goochld. They trace their pedigree far back in England & Scotland, to which let every one ascribe the faith & merit he chooses.

My father's education had been quite neglected; but being of a strong mind, sound judgment and eager after information, he read much and improved himself insomuch that he was chosen with Joshua Fry, professor of Mathem. in W. & M. college to continue the boundary line between Virginia & N. Caroline which had been begun by Colo Byrd, and was afterwards employed with the same Mr. Fry to make the 1st map of Virginia which had ever been made, that of Capt Smith being merely a conjectural sketch. They possessed excellent materials for so much of the country as is below the blue ridge; little being then known beyond that ridge. He was the 3d or 4th settler of the part of the country in which I live, which was about 1737. He died Aug. 17. 1757, leaving my mother a widow who lived till 1776, with 6 daurs & 2. sons, myself the elder. To my younger brother he left his estate on James river called Snowden after the supposed birth-place of the family. To myself the lands on which I was born & live. He placed me at the English school at 5. years of age and at the Latin at 9. where I continued until his death. My teacher Mr. Douglas a clergyman from Scotland was but a superficial Latinist, less instructed in Greek, but with the rudiments of these languages he taught me French, and on the death of my father I went to the revd Mr. Maury a correct classical scholar, with whom I continued two years, and then went to Wm. and

Mary college, to wit in the spring of 1760, where I continued 2. years. It was my great good fortune, and what probably fixed the destinies of my life that Dr. Wm. Small of Scotland was then professor of Mathematics, a man profound in most of the useful branches of science, with a happy talent of communication, correct and gentlemanly manners, & an enlarged & liberal mind. He, most happily for me, became soon attached to me & made me his daily companion when not engaged in the school; and from his conversation I got my first views of the expansion of science & of the system of things in which we are placed. Fortunately the Philosophical chair became vacant soon after my arrival at college, and he was appointed to fill it per interim: and he was the first who ever gave in that college regular lectures in Ethics, Rhetoric & Belles lettres. He returned to Europe in 1762, having previously filled up the measure of his goodness to me, by procuring for me, from his most intimate friend G. Wythe, a reception as a student of law, under his direction, and introduced me to the acquaintance and familiar table of Governor Fauquier, the ablest man who had ever filled that office. With him, and at his table, Dr. Small & Mr. Wythe, his amici omnium horarum, & myself, formed a partie quarree, & to the habitual conversations on these occasions I owed much instruction. Mr. Wythe continued to be my faithful and beloved Mentor in youth, and my most affectionate friend through life. In 1767, he led me into the practice of the law at the bar of the General court, at which I continued until the revolution shut up the courts of justice. [For a sketch of the life & character of Mr. Wythe see my letter of Aug. 31. 20. to Mr. John Saunderson]

In 1769, I became a member of the legislature by the choice of the county in which I live, & continued in that until it was closed by the revolution. I made one effort in that body for the permission of the emancipation of slaves, which was rejected: and indeed, during the regal government, nothing liberal could expect success. Our minds were circumscribed within narrow limits by an habitual belief that it was our duty to be subordinate to the mother country in all matters of government, to direct all our labors in subservience to her interests, and even to observe a bigoted intolerance for all religions but hers. The difficulties with our representatives were of habit and despair, not of reflection & conviction. Experience soon proved that they could bring their minds to rights on the first summons of their attention. But the king's council, which acted as another house of legislature, held their places at will & were in most humble obedience to that will: the Governor too, who had a negative on our laws held by the same tenure, & with still greater devotedness to it: and last of all the Royal negative closed the last door to every hope of amelioration.

On the 1st of January, 1772 I was married to Martha Skelton widow of Bathurst Skelton, & daughter of John Wayles, then 23. years old. Mr. Wayles was a lawyer of much practice, to which he was introduced more by his great industry, punctuality & practical readiness, than to eminence in the science of his profession. He was a most agreeable companion, full of pleasantry & good humor, and welcomed in every society. He acquired a handsome fortune, died in May, 1773, leaving three daughters, and the portion which came on that event to Mrs. Jefferson, after the debts should be paid, which were very considerable, was about equal to my own patrimony, and consequently doubled the ease of our circumstances.

When the famous Resolutions of 1765, against the Stamp-act, were proposed, I was yet a student of law in Wmsbg. I attended the debate however at the door of the lobby of the H. of Burgesses, & heard the splendid display of Mr. Henry's talents as a popular orator. They were great indeed; such as I have never heard from any other man. He appeared to me to speak as Homer wrote. Mr. Johnson, a lawyer & member from the Northern Neck, seconded the resolns, & by him the learning & the logic of the case were chiefly maintained. My recollections of these transactions may be seen pa. 60, Wirt's life of P. H., to whom I furnished them.

In May, 1769, a meeting of the General Assembly was called by the Govr., Ld. Botetourt. I had then become a member; and to that meeting became known the joint resolutions & address of the Lords & Commons of 1768—9, on the proceedings in Massachusetts. Counter-resolutions, & an address to the King, by the H. of Burgesses were agreed to with little opposition, & a spirit manifestly displayed of considering the cause of Massachusetts as a common one. The Governor dissolved us: but we met the next day in the Apollo of the Raleigh tavern, formed ourselves into a voluntary convention, drew up articles of association against the use of any merchandise imported from Gr. Britain, signed and recommended them to the people, repaired to our several counties, & were re-elected without any other exception than of the very few who had declined assent to our proceedings.

Nothing of particular excitement occurring for a considerable time our countrymen seemed to fall into a state of insensibility to our situation. The duty on tea not yet repealed & the Declaratory act of a right in the British parl to bind us by their laws in all cases whatsoever, still suspended over us. But a court of inquiry held in R. Island in 1762,* with a power to send persons to England to be tried for offences committed here was considered at our session of the spring of 1773. as demanding attention. Not thinking our old & leading members up to the point of forwardness & zeal which the times required, Mr. Henry, R. H. Lee, Francis L. Lee, Mr. Carr & myself agreed to meet in the evening in a private room of the Raleigh to consult on the state of things. There may have been a

* This date should actually be 1772. –Ed.

member or two more whom I do not recollect. We were all sensible that the most urgent of all measures was that of coming to an understanding with all the other colonies to consider the British claims as a common cause to all, & to produce an unity of action: and for this purpose that a commee of correspondce in each colony would be the best instrument for intercommunication: and that their first measure would probably be to propose a meeting of deputies from every colony at some central place, who should be charged with the direction of the measures which should be taken by all. We therefore drew up the resolutions which may be seen in Wirt pa 87. The consulting members proposed to me to move them, but I urged that it should be done by Mr. Carr, my friend & brother in law, then a new member to whom I wished an opportunity should be given of making known to the house his great worth & talents. It was so agreed; he moved them, they were agreed to nem. con. and a commee of correspondence appointed of whom Peyton Randolph, the Speaker, was chairman. The Govr. (then Ld. Dunmore) dissolved us, but the commee met the next day, prepared a circular letter to the Speakers of the other colonies, inclosing to each a copy of the resolns and left it in charge with their chairman to forward them by expresses.

The origination of these commees of correspondence between the colonies has been since claimed for Massachusetts, and Marshall II. 151, has given into this error, altho' the very note of his appendix to which he refers, shows that their establmt was confined to their own towns. This matter will be seen clearly stated in a letter of Samuel Adams Wells to me of Apr. 2., 1819, and my answer of May 12. I was corrected by the letter of Mr. Wells in the information I had given Mr. Wirt, as stated in his note, pa. 87, that the messengers of Massach. & Virga crossed each other on the way bearing similar propositions, for Mr. Wells shows that Mass. did not adopt the measure but on the receipt of our proposn delivered at their next session. Their message therefore which passed ours, must have related to something else, for I well remember P. Randolph's informing me of the crossing of our messengers.

The next event which excited our sympathies for Massachusets was the Boston port bill, by which that port was to be shut up on the 1st of June, 1774. This arrived while we were in session in the spring of that year. The lead in the house on these subjects being no longer left to the old members, Mr. Henry, R. H. Lee, Fr. L. Lee, 3. or 4. other members, whom I do not recollect, and myself, agreeing that we must boldly take an unequivocal stand in the line with Massachusetts, determined to meet and consult on the proper measures in the council chamber, for the benefit of the library in that room. We were under conviction of the necessity of arousing our people from the lethargy into which they had fallen as to passing events; and thought that the appointment of a day of general fasting & prayer would be most likely to call up & alarm their attention. No example of such a solemnity had existed since the days of our distresses in the war of 55. since which a new generation had grown up. With the help therefore of Rushworth, whom we rummaged over for the revolutionary precedents & forms of the Puritans of that day, preserved by him, we cooked up a resolution, somewhat modernizing their phrases, for appointing the 1st day of June, on which the Port bill was to commence, for a day of fasting, humiliation & prayer, to implore heaven to avert from us the evils of civil war, to inspire us with firmness in support of our rights, and to turn the hearts of the King & parliament to moderation & justice. To give greater emphasis to our proposition, we agreed to wait the next morning on Mr. Nicholas, whose grave & religious character was more in unison with the tone of our resolution and to solicit him to move it. We accordingly went to him in the morning. He moved it the same day; the 1st of June was proposed and it passed without opposition. The Governor dissolved us as usual. We retired to the Apollo as before, agreed to an association, and instructed the commee of correspdce to propose to the corresponding commees of the other colonies to appoint deputies to meet in Congress at such place, *annually*, as should be convenient to direct, from time to time, the measures required by the general interest: and we declared that an attack on any one colony should be considered as an attack on the whole. This was in May. We further recommended to the several counties to elect deputies to meet at Wmsbg the 1st of Aug ensuing, to consider the state of the colony, & particularly to appoint delegates to a general Congress, should that measure be acceded to by the commees of correspdce generally. It was acceded to, Philadelphia was appointed for the place, and the 5th of Sep. for the time of meeting. We returned home, and in our several counties invited the clergy to meet assemblies of the people on the 1st of June, to perform the ceremonies of the day, & to address to them discourses suited to the occasion. The people met generally, with anxiety & alarm in their countenances, and the effect of the day thro' the whole colony was like a shock of electricity, arousing every man & placing him erect & solidly on his centre. They chose universally delegates for the convention. Being elected one for my own county I prepared a draught of instructions to be given to the delegates whom we should send to the Congress, and which I meant to propose at our meeting. In this I took the ground which, from the beginning I had thought the only one orthodox or tenable, which was that the relation between Gr. Br. and these colonies was exactly the same as that of England & Scotland after the accession of James & until the Union, and the same as her present relations with Hanover, having the same Executive chief but no other necessary political connection; and that our emigration from England to this country gave her no more rights over us, than the emigrations of the Danes and Saxons gave to the present authorities of the mother country over England. In this doctrine however I had never been able to get any one to agree with me but Mr. Wythe. He concurred in it from the first dawn of the question What was the political relation between us & England? Our other patriots Randolph, the Lees, Nicholas, Pendleton stopped at the half-way house of John Dickinson who admitted that England had a right to regulate our commerce, and to lay duties on it for the purposes of regulation, but not of raising revenue. But for this ground there was no foundation in compact, in any acknowledged principles of colonization, nor in reason: expatriation being a natural right, and acted on as such, by all nations, in all ages. I set out for Wmsbg some days before that appointed for our meeting, but was taken ill of a dysentery on the road, & unable to proceed. I sent on therefore to Wmsbg two copies of my draught, the one under cover to Peyton Randolph, who I knew would be in the chair of the convention, the other to Patrick Henry. Whether Mr. Henry disapproved the ground taken, or was too lazy to read it (for he was the laziest man in reading I ever knew) I never learned: but he communicated it to nobody. Peyton Randolph informed the convention he had received such a paper from a member prevented by sickness from offering it in his place, and he laid it on the table for perusal. It was read generally by the members, approved by many, but thought too bold for the present state of things; but they printed it in pamphlet form under the title of *A Summary view of the rights of British America*. It found its way to England, was taken up by the opposition, interpolated a little by Mr. Burke so as to make it answer opposition purposes, and in that form ran rapidly thro' several editions. This information I had from Parson Hurt, who happened at the time to be in London, whether he had gone to receive clerical orders. And I was informed afterwards by Peyton Randolph that it had procured me the honor of having my name inserted in a long list of proscriptions enrolled in a bill of attainder commenced in one of the houses of parliament, but suppressed in embryo by the hasty step of events which warned them to be a little cautious. Montague, agent of the H. of Burgesses in England made extracts from the bill, copied the names, and sent them to Peyton Randolph. The names I think were about 20 which he repeated to me, but I recollect those only of Hancock, the two Adamses, Peyton Randolph himself, Patrick Henry, & myself. The convention met on the 1st of Aug, renewed their association, appointed delegates to the Congress, gave them instructions very temperately & properly expressed, both as to style & matter; and they repaired to Philadelphia at the time appointed. The splendid proceedings of that Congress at their 1st session belong to general history, are known to every one, and need not therefore be noted here. They terminated their session on the 26th of Octob, to meet again on the 10th May ensuing. The convention at their ensuing session of

Mar, '75, approved of the proceedings of Congress, thanked their delegates and reappointed the same persons to represent the colony at the meeting to be held in May: and foreseeing the probability that Peyton Randolph their president and Speaker also of the H. of B. might be called off, they added me, in that event to the delegation.

Mr. Randolph was according to expectation obliged to leave the chair of Congress to attend the Gen. Assembly summoned by Ld. Dunmore to meet on the 1st day of June 1775. Ld. North's conciliatory propositions, as they were called, had been received by the Governor and furnished the subject for which this assembly was convened. Mr. Randolph accordingly attended, and the tenor of these propositions being generally known, as having been addressed to all the governors, he was anxious that the answer of our assembly, likely to be the first, should harmonize with what he knew to be the sentiments and wishes of the body he had recently left. He feared that Mr. Nicholas, whose mind was not yet up to the mark of the times, would undertake the answer, & therefore pressed me to prepare an answer. I did so, and with his aid carried it through the house with long and doubtful scruples from Mr. Nicholas and James Mercer, and a dash of cold water on it here & there, enfeebling it somewhat, but finally with unanimity or a vote approaching it. This being passed, I repaired immediately to Philadelphia, and conveyed to Congress the first notice they had of it. It was entirely approved there. I took my seat with them on the 21st of June. On the 24th, a commee which had been appointed to prepare a declaration of the causes of taking up arms, brought in their report (drawn I believe by J. Rutledge) which not being liked they recommitted it on the 26th, and added Mr. Dickinson and myself to the committee. On the rising of the house, the commee having not yet met, I happened to find myself near Govr W. Livingston, and proposed to him to draw the paper. He excused himself and proposed that I should draw it. On my pressing him with urgency, "we are as yet but new acquaintances, sir, said he, why are you so earnest for my doing it?" "Because, said I, I have been informed that you drew the Address to the people of Gr. Britain, a production certainly of the finest pen in America." "On that, says he, perhaps sir you may not have been correctly informed." I had received the information in Virginia from Colo Harrison on his return from that Congress. Lee, Livingston & Jay had been the commee for that draught. The first, prepared by Lee, had been disapproved & recommitted. The second was drawn by Jay, but being presented by Govr Livingston, had led Colo Harrison into the error. The next morning, walking in the hall of Congress, many members being assembled but the house not yet formed, I observed Mr. Jay, speaking to R. H. Lee, and leading him by the button of his coat, to me. "I understand, sir, said he to me, that this gentleman informed you that Govr Livingston drew the Address to the people of Gr Britain." I assured him at once that I had not received that information from Mr. Lee & that not a word had ever passed on the subject between Mr. Lee & myself; and after some explanations the subject was dropt. These gentlemen had had some sparrings in debate before, and continued ever very hostile to each other.

I prepared a draught of the Declaration committed to us. It was too strong for Mr. Dickinson. He still retained the hope of reconciliation with the mother country, and was unwilling it should be lessened by offensive statements. He was so honest a man, & so able a one that he was greatly indulged even by those who could not feel his scruples. We therefore requested him to take the paper, and put it into a form he could approve. He did so, preparing an entire new statement, and preserving of the former only the last 4. paragraphs & half of the preceding one. We approved & reported it to Congress, who accepted it. Congress gave a signal proof of their indulgence to Mr. Dickinson, and of their great desire not to go too fast for any respectable part of our body, in permitting him to draw their second petition to the King according to his own ideas, and passing it with scarcely any amendment. The disgust against this humility was general; and Mr. Dickinson's delight at its passage was the only circumstance which reconciled them to it. The vote being passed, altho' further observn on it was out of order, he could not refrain from rising and expressing his satisfaction and concluded by saying "there is but one word, Mr. President, in the paper which I disapprove, & that is the word *Congress*," on which Ben Harrison rose and said "there is but on word in the paper, Mr. President, of which I approve, and that is the word *Congress*."

On the 22d of July Dr. Franklin, Mr. Adams, R. H. Lee, & myself, were appointed a commee to consider and report on Ld. North's conciliatory resolution. The answer of the Virginia assembly on that subject having been approved I was requested by the commee to prepare this report, which will account for the similarity of feature in the two instruments.

On the 15th of May, 1776, the convention of Virginia instructed their delegates in Congress to propose to that body to declare the colonies independent of G. Britain, and appointed a commee to prepare a declaration of rights and plan of government.

In Congress, Friday June 7. 1776. The delegates from Virginia moved in obedience to instructions from their constituents that the Congress should declare that these United colonies are & of right ought to be free & independent states, that they are absolved from all allegiance to the British crown, and that all political connection between them & the state of Great Britain is & ought to be, totally dissolved; that measures should be immediately taken for procuring the assistance of foreign powers, and a Confederation be formed to bind the colonies more closely together.

The house being obliged to attend at that time to some other business, the proposition was referred to the next day, when the members were ordered to attend punctually at ten o'clock.

Saturday June 8. They proceeded to take it into consideration and referred it to a committee of the whole, into which they immediately resolved themselves, and passed that day & Monday the 10th in debating on the subject.

It was argued by Wilson, Robert R. Livingston, E. Rutledge, Dickinson and others

That tho' they were friends to the measures themselves, and saw the impossibility that we should ever again be united with Gr. Britain, yet they were against adopting them at this time:

That the conduct we had formerly observed was wise & proper now, of deferring to take any capital step till the voice of the people drove us into it:

That they were our power, & without them our declarations could not be carried into effect;

That the people of the middle colonies (Maryland, Delaware, Pennsylva, the Jerseys & N. York) were not yet ripe for bidding adieu to British connection, but that they were fast ripening & in a short time would join in the general voice of America:

That the resolution entered into by this house on the 15th of May for suppressing the exercise of all powers derived from the crown, had shown, by the ferment into which it had thrown these middle colonies, that they had not yet accommodated their minds to a separation from the mother country:

That some of them had expressly forbidden their delegates to consent to such a declaration, and others had given no instructions, & consequently no powers to give such consent:

That if the delegates of any particular colony had no power to declare such colony independant, certain they were the others could not declare it for them; the colonies being as yet perfectly independant of each other:

That the assembly of Pennsylvania was now sitting above stairs, their convention would sit within a few days, the convention of New York was now sitting, & those of the Jerseys & Delaware counties would meet on the Monday following, & it was probable these bodies would take up the question of Independance & would declare to their delegates the voice of their state:

That if such a declaration should now be agreed to, these delegates must retire & possibly their colonies might secede from the Union:

That such a secession would weaken us more than could be compensated by any foreign alliance:

That in the event of such a division, foreign powers would either refuse to join themselves to our fortunes, or, having us so much in their power as that desperate declaration would place us, they would insist on terms proportionably more hard and prejudicial:

That we had little reason to expect an alliance with those to whom alone as yet we had cast our eyes:

That France & Spain had reason to be jealous of that rising power which would one day certainly strip them of all their American possessions:

That it was more likely they should form a connection with the British court, who, if they should find themselves unable otherwise to extricate themselves from their difficulties, would agree to a partition of our territories, restoring Canada to France, & the Floridas to Spain, to accomplish for themselves a recovery of these colonies:

That it would not be long before we should receive certain information of the disposition of the French court, from the agent whom we had sent to Paris for that purpose:

That if this disposition should be favorable, by waiting the event of the present campaign, which we all hoped would be successful, we should have reason to expect an alliance on better terms:

That this would in fact work no delay of any effectual aid from such ally, as, from the advance of the season & distance of our situation, it was impossible we could receive any assistance during this campaign:

That it was prudent to fix among ourselves the terms on which we should form alliance, before we declared we would form one at all events:

And that if these were agreed on, & our Declaration of Independance ready by the time our Ambassador should be prepared to sail, it would be as well as to go into that Declaration at this day.

On the other side it was urged by J. Adams, Lee, Wythe, and others

That no gentleman had argued against the policy or the right of separation from Britain, nor had supposed it possible we should ever renew our connection; that they had only opposed its being now declared:

That the question was not whether, by a declaration of independance, we should make ourselves what we are not; but whether we should declare a fact which already exists:

That as to the people or parliament of England, we had alwais been independent of them, their restraints on our trade deriving efficacy from our acquiescence only, & not from any rights they possessed of imposing them, & that so far our connection had been federal only & was now dissolved by the commencement of hostilities:

That as to the King, we had been bound to him by allegiance, but that this bond was now dissolved by his assent to the late act of parliament, by which he declares us out of his protection, and by his levying war on us, a fact which had long ago proved us out of his protection; it being a certain position in law that allegiance & protection are reciprocal, the one ceasing when the other is withdrawn:

That James the IId. never declared the people of England out of his protection yet his actions proved it & the parliament declared it:

No delegates then can be denied, or ever want, a power of declaring an existing truth:

That the delegates from the Delaware counties having declared their constituents ready to join, there are only two colonies Pennsylvania & Maryland whose delegates are absolutely tied up, and that these had by their instructions only reserved a right of confirming or rejecting the measure:

That the instructions from Pennsylvania might be accounted for from the times in which they were drawn, near a twelvemonth ago, since which the face of affairs has totally changed:

That within that time it had become apparent that Britain was determined to accept nothing less than a carte-blanche, and that the King's answer to the Lord Mayor Aldermen & common council of London, which had come to hand four days ago, must have satisfied every one of this point:

That the people wait for us to lead the way:

That *they* are in favour of the measure, tho' the instructions given by some of their *representatives* are not:

That the voice of the representatives is not always consonant with the voice of the people, and that this is remarkably the case in these middle colonies:

That the effect of the resolution of the 15th of May has proved this, which, raising the murmurs of some in the colonies of Pennsylvania & Maryland, called forth the opposing voice of the freer part of the people, & proved them to be the majority, even in these colonies:

That the backwardness of these two colonies might be ascribed partly to the influence of proprietary power & connections, & partly to their having not yet been attacked by the enemy:

That these causes were not likely to be soon removed, as there seemed no probability that the enemy would make either of these the seat of this summer's war:

That it would be vain to wait either weeks or months for perfect unanimity, since it was impossible that all men should ever become of one sentiment on any question:

That the conduct of some colonies from the beginning of this contest, had given reason to suspect it was their settled policy to keep in the rear of the confederacy, that their particular prospect might be better, even in the worst event:

That therefore it was necessary for those colonies who had thrown themselves forward & hazarded all from the beginning, to come forward now also, and put all again to their own hazard:

That the history of the Dutch revolution, of whom three states only confederated at first proved that a secession of some colonies would not be so dangerous as some apprehended:

That a declaration of Independence alone could render it consistent with European delicacy for European powers to treat with us, or even to receive an Ambassador from us:

That till this they would not receive our vessels into their ports, nor acknowledge the adjudications of our courts of admiralty to be legitimate, in cases of capture of British vessels:

That though France & Spain may be jealous of our rising power, they must think it will be much more formidable with the addition of Great Britain; and will therefore see it their interest to prevent a coalition; but should they refuse, we shall be but where we are; whereas without trying we shall never know whether they will aid us or not:

That the present campaign may be unsuccessful, & therefore we had better propose an alliance while our affairs wear a hopeful aspect:

That to await the event of this campaign will certainly work delay, because during this summer France may assist us effectually by cutting off those supplies of provisions from England & Ireland on which the enemy's armies here are to depend; or by setting in motion the great power they have collected in the West Indies, & calling our enemy to the defence of the possessions they have there:

That it would be idle to lose time in settling the terms of alliance, till we had first determined we would enter into alliance:

That it is necessary to lose no time in opening a trade for our people, who will want clothes, and will want money too for the paiment of taxes:

And that the only misfortune is that we did not enter into alliance with France six months sooner, as besides opening their ports for the vent of our last year's produce, they might have marched an army into Germany and prevented the petty princes there from selling their unhappy subjects to subdue us.

It appearing in the course of these debates that the colonies of N. York, New Jersey, Pennsylvania, Delaware, Maryland, and South Carolina were not yet matured for falling from the parent stem, but that they were fast advancing to that state, it was thought most prudent to wait a while for them, and to postpone the final decision to July 1. but that this might occasion as little delay as possible a committee was appointed to prepare a declaration of independence. The commee were J. Adams, Dr. Franklin, Roger Sherman, Robert R. Livingston & myself. Committees were also appointed at the same time to prepare a plan of confederation for the colonies, and to state the terms proper to be proposed for foreign alliance. The committee for drawing the declaration of Independence desired me to do it. It was accordingly done, and being approved by them, I reported it to the house on Friday the 28th of June when it was read and ordered to lie on the table. On Monday, the 1st of July the house resolved itself into a commee of the whole & resumed the consideration of the original motion made by the delegates of Virginia, which being again debated through the day, was carried in the affirmative by the votes of N. Hampshire, Connecticut, Massachusetts, Rhode Island, N. Jersey, Maryland, Virginia, N. Carolina, & Georgia. S. Carolina and Pennsylvania voted against it. Delaware having but two members present, they were divided. The delegates for New York declared they were for it themselves & were assured their constituents were for it, but that their instructions having been drawn near a twelvemonth before, when reconciliation was still the general object, they were enjoined by them to do nothing which should impede that object. They therefore thought themselves not justifiable in voting on either side, and asked leave to withdraw from the question, which was given them. The commee rose & reported their resolution to the house. Mr. Edward Rutledge of S. Carolina then requested the determination might be put off to the next day, as he believed his colleagues, tho' they disapproved of the resolution, would then join in it for the sake of unanimity. The ultimate question whether the house would agree to the resolution of the committee was accordingly postponed to the next day, when it was again moved and S. Carolina concurred in voting for it. In the meantime a third member had come post from the Delaware counties and turned the vote of that colony in favour of the resolution. Members of a different sentiment attending that morning from Pennsylvania also, their vote was changed, so that the whole 12 colonies who were authorized to vote at all, gave their voices for it; and within a few days, the convention of N. York approved of it and thus supplied the void occasioned by the withdrawing of her delegates from the vote.

Congress proceeded the same day to consider the declaration of Independance which had been reported & lain on the table the Friday preceding, and on Monday referred to a commee of the whole. The pusillanimous idea that we had friends in England worth keeping terms with, still haunted the minds of many. For this reason those passages which conveyed censures on the people of England were struck out, lest they should give them offence. The clause too, reprobating the enslaving the inhabitants of Africa, was struck out in complaisance to South

Carolina and Georgia, who had never attempted to restrain the importation of slaves, and who on the contrary still wished to continue it. Our northern brethren also I believe felt a little tender under those censures; for tho' their people have very few slaves themselves yet they had been pretty considerable carriers of them to others. The debates having taken up the greater parts of the 2d 3d & 4th days of July were, in the evening of the last, closed the declaration was reported by the commee, agreed to by the house and signed by every member present except Mr. Dickinson. As the sentiments of men are known not only by what they receive, but what they reject also, I will state the form of the declaration as originally reported. The parts struck out by Congress shall be distinguished by a black line drawn under them; & those inserted by them shall be placed in the margin or in a concurrent column.

A DECLARATION BY THE REPRESENTATIVES OF THE UNITED STATES OF AMERICA, IN GENERAL CONGRESS ASSEMBLED

When in the course of human events it becomes necessary for one people to dissolve the political bands which have connected them with another, and to assume among the powers of the earth the separate & equal station to which the laws of nature and of nature's God entitle them, a decent respect to the opinions of mankind requires that they should declare the causes which impel them to the separation.

We hold these truths to be self-evident: that all men are created equal; that they are endowed by their creator with *inherent and* [certain] inalienable rights; that among these are life, liberty, & the pursuit of happiness: that to secure these rights, governments are instituted among men, deriving their just powers from the consent of the governed; that whenever any form of government becomes destructive of these ends, it is the right of the people to alter or abolish it, & to institute new government, laying it's foundation on such principles, & organizing it's powers in such form, as to them shall seem most likely to effect their safety & happiness. Prudence indeed will dictate that governments long established should not be changed for light & transient causes; and accordingly all experience hath shown that mankind are more disposed to suffer while evils are sufferable, than to right themselves by abolishing the forms to which they are accustomed. But when a long train of abuses & usurpations *begun at a distinguished period and* pursuing invariably the same object, evinces a design to reduce them under absolute despotism, it is their right, it is their duty to throw off such government, & to provide new guards for their future security. Such has been the patient sufferance of these colonies; & such is now the necessity which constrains them to *expunge* [alter] their former systems of government. The history of the present king of Great Britain is a history of *unremitting* [repeated] injuries & usurpations, *among which appears no solitary fact to contradict the uniform tenor of the rest but all have* [all having] in direct object the establishment of an absolute tyranny over these states. To prove this let facts be submitted to a candid world *for the truth of which we pledge a faith yet unsullied by falsehood.*

He has refused his assent to laws the most wholesome & necessary for the public good.

He has forbidden his governors to pass laws of immediate & pressing importance, unless suspended in their operation till his assent should be obtained; & when so suspended, he has utterly neglected to attend to them.

He has refused to pass other laws for the accommodation of large districts of people, unless those people would relinquish the right of representation in the legislature, a right inestimable to them, & formidable to tyrants only.

He has called together legislative bodies at places unusual, uncomfortable, and distant from the depository of their public records, for the sole purpose of fatiguing them into compliance with his measures.

He has dissolved representative houses repeatedly *& continually* for opposing with manly firmness his invasions on the rights of the people.

He has refused for a long time after such dissolutions to cause others to be elected, whereby the legislative powers, incapable of annihilation, have returned to the people at large for their exercise, the state remaining in the meantime exposed to all the dangers of invasion from without & convulsions within.

He has endeavored to prevent the population of these states; for that purpose obstructing the laws for naturalization of foreigners, refusing to pass others to encourage their migrations hither, & raising the conditions of new appropriations of lands.

He has *suffered* [obstructed] the administration of justice *totally to cease in some of these states* [by] refusing his assent to laws for establishing judiciary powers.

He has made *our* judges dependant on his will alone, for the tenure of their offices, & the amount & paiment of their salaries.

He has erected a multitude of new offices *by a self assumed power* and sent hither swarms of new officers to harass our people and eat out their substance.

He has kept among us in times of peace standing armies *and ships of war* without the consent of our legislatures.

He has affected to render the military independant of, & superior to the civil power.

He has combined with others to subject us to a jurisdiction foreign to our constitutions & unacknowledged by our laws, giving his assent to their acts of pretended legislation for quartering large bodies of armed troops among us; for protecting them by a mock-trial from punishment for any murders which they should commit on the inhabitants of these states; for cutting off our trade with all parts of the world; for imposing taxes on us without our consent; for depriving us [in many cases] of the benefits of trial by jury; for transporting us beyond seas to be tried for pretended offences; for abolishing the free system of English laws in a neighboring province, establishing therein an arbitrary government, and enlarging it's boundaries, so as to render it at once an example and fit instrument for introducing the same absolute rule into these *states* [colonies]; for taking away our charters, abolishing our most valuable laws, and altering fundamentally the forms of our governments; for suspending our own legislatures, & declaring themselves invested with power to legislate for us in all cases whatsoever.

He has abdicated government here *withdrawing his governors, and declaring us out of his allegiance & protection.* [by declaring us out of his protection, and waging war against us.]

He has plundered our seas, ravaged our coasts, burnt our towns, & destroyed the lives of our people.

He is at this time transporting large armies of foreign mercenaries to compleat the works of death, desolation & tyranny already begun with circumstances of cruelty and perfidy [scarcely paralleled in the most barbarous ages, & totally] unworthy the head of a civilized nation.

He has constrained our fellow citizens taken captive on the high seas to bear arms against their country, to become the executioners of their friends & brethren, or to fall themselves by their hands.

He has [excited domestic insurrection among us, & has] endeavored to bring on the inhabitants of our frontiers the merciless Indian savages, whose known rule of warfare is an undistinguished destruction of all ages, sexes, & conditions *of existence.*

He has incited treasonable insurrections of our fellow citizens, with the allurements of forfeiture & confiscation of our property.

He has waged cruel war against human nature itself, violating it's most sacred rights of life and liberty in the persons of a distant people who never offended him, captivating & carrying them into slavery in another hemisphere, or to incur miserable death in their transportation thither. This piratical warfare, the opprobium of INFIDEL powers, is the warfare of the CHRISTIAN king of Great Britain. Determined to keep open a market where MEN should be bought & sold, he has prostituted his negative for suppressing every legislative attempt to prohibit or to restrain this execrable commerce. And that this assemblage of horrors might want no fact of distinguished die, he is now exciting those very people to rise in arms among us, and to purchase that liberty of which he has deprived them, by murdering the people on whom he also obtruded them: thus paying off former crimes committed against the LIBERTIES *of one people, with crimes which he urges them to commit against the* LIVES *of another.*

In every stage of these oppressions we have petitioned for redress in the most humble terms: our repeated petitions have been answered only by repeated injuries.

A prince whose character is thus marked by every act which may define a tyrant is unfit to be the ruler of a [free] people *who mean to be free. Future ages will scarcely believe that the hardiness of one man adventured, within the short compass of twelve years only, to lay a foundation so broad & so undisguised for tyranny over a people fostered & fixed in principles of freedom.*

Nor have we been wanting in attentions to our British brethren. We have warned them from time to time of attempts by their legislature to extend *a* [an unwarrantable] jurisdiction over *these our states* [us]. We have reminded them of the circumstances of our emigration & settlement here, *no one of which could warrant so strange a pretension: that these were effected at the expense of our own blood & treasure, unassisted by the wealth or the strength of Great Britain: that in constituting indeed our several forms of government, we had adopted one common king, thereby laying a foundation for perpetual league & amity with them: but that submission to their parliament was no part of our constitution, nor ever in idea, if history may be credited: and*, we [have] appealed to their native justice and magnanimity *as well as to* [and we have conjured them by] the ties of our common kindred to disavow these usurpations which *were likely to* [would inevitably] interrupt our connection and correspondence. They too have been deaf to the voice of justice & of consanguinity, *and when occasions have been given them, by the regular course of their laws, of removing from their councils the disturbers of our harmony, they have, by their free election, re-established them in power. At this very time too they are permitting their chief magistrate to send over not only soldiers of our common blood, but Scotch & foreign mercenaries to invade & destroy us. These facts have given the last stab to agonizing affection, and manly spirit bids us to renounce forever these unfeeling brethren. We must [We must therefore] endeavor to forget our former love for them, and hold them as we hold the rest of mankind, enemies in war, in peace friends. We might have been a free and a great people together; but a communication of grandeur & of freedom it seems is below their dignity. Be it so, since they will have it. The road to happiness & to glory is open to us too. We will tread it apart from them, and* acquiesce in the necessity which denounces our *eternal* separation [and hold them as we hold the rest of mankind, enemies in war, in peace friends]!

We therefore the representatives of the United States of America in General Congress assembled do in the name & by authority of the good people of these *states reject & renounce all allegiance & subjection to the kings of Great Britain & all others who may hereafter claim by, through or under them: we utterly dissolve all political connection which may heretofore have subsisted between us & the people or parliament of Great Britain: & finally we do assert & declare these colonies to be free & independent states,* & that as free and independent states, they have full power to levy war, conclude peace contract alliances, establish commerce, & to do all other acts & things which independent states may of right do.

And for the support of this declaration we mutually pledge to each other our lives, our fortunes, & our sacred honor.

We therefore the representatives of the United States of America in General Congress assembled, appealing to the supreme judge of the world for the rectitude of our intentions, do in the name, & by authority of the good people of these colonies, solemnly publish & declare that these united colonies are & of right ought to be free & independent states; that they are absolved from all allegiance to the British crown, and that all political connection between them & the state of Great Britain is, & ought to be, totally dissolved; & that as free & independent states they have full power to levy war, conclude peace, contract alliances, establish commerce & to do all other acts & things which independent states may of right do.

And for the support of this declaration, with a firm reliance on the protection of divine providence we mutually pledge to each other our lives, our fortunes, & our sacred honor.*

The Declaration thus signed on the 4th, on paper was engrossed on parchment, & signed again on the 2d. of August.†

On Friday July 12. the Committee appointed to draw the articles of confederation reported them, and on the 22d. the house resolved themselves into a committee to take them into consideration. On the 30th. & 31st. of that month & 1st. of the ensuing, those articles were debated which determined the proportion or quota of money which each state should furnish to the common treasury, and the manner of voting in Congress. The first of these articles was expressed in the

* Jefferson prepared this for the press in the same manner in which this is printed. –Ed.

† Some erroneous statements of the proceedings on the declaration of independence having got before the public in latter times, Mr. Samuel A. Wells asked explanations of me, which are given in my letter to him of May 12. 19. before and now again referred to. I took notes in my place while these things were going on, and at their close wrote them out in form and with correctness and from 1 to 7 of the two preceding sheets are the originals then written; as the two following are of the earlier debates on the Confederation, which I took in like manner.

original draught in these words. "Art. XI. All charges of war & all other expenses that shall be incurred for the common defence, or general welfare, and allowed by the United States assembled, shall be defrayed out of a common treasury, which shall be supplied by the several colonies in proportion to the number of inhabitants of every age, sex & quality, except Indians not paying taxes, in each colony, a true account of which, distinguishing the white inhabitants, shall be triennially taken & transmitted to the Assembly of the United States."

Mr. [Samuel] Chase moved that the quotas should be fixed, not by the number of inhabitants of every condition, but by that of the "white inhabitants." He admitted that taxation should be alwais in proportion to property, that this was in theory the true rule, but that from a variety of difficulties, it was a rule which could never be adopted in practice. The value of the property in every State could never be estimated justly & equally. Some other measure for the wealth of the State must therefore be devised, some standard referred to which would be more simple. He considered the number of inhabitants as a tolerably good criterion of property, and that this might alwais be obtained. He therefore thought it the best mode which we could adopt, with one exception only. He observed that negroes are property, and as such cannot be distinguished from the lands or personalities held in those States where there are few slaves, that the surplus of profit which a Northern farmer is able to lay by, he invests in cattle, horses, &c. whereas a Southern farmer lays out that same surplus in slaves. There is no more reason therefore for taxing the Southern states on the farmer's head, & on his slave's head, than the Northern ones on their farmer's heads & the heads of their cattle, that the method proposed would therefore tax the Southern states according to their numbers & their wealth conjunctly, while the Northern would be taxed on numbers only: that negroes in fact should not be considered as members of the state more than cattle & that they have no more interest in it.

Mr. John Adams observed that the numbers of people were taken by this article as an index of the wealth of the state, & not as subjects of taxation, that as to this matter it was of no consequence by what name you called your people, whether by that of freemen or of slaves. That in some countries the labouring poor were called freemen, in others they were called slaves; but that the difference as to the state was imaginary only. What matters it whether a landlord employing ten labourers in his farm, gives them annually as much money as will buy them the necessaries of life, or gives them those necessaries at short hand. The ten labourers add as much wealth annually to the state, increase it's exports as much in the one case as the other. Certainly 500 freemen produce no more profits, no greater surplus for the paiment of taxes than 500 slaves. Therefore the state in which are the labourers called freemen should be taxed no more than that in which are those called slaves. Suppose by any extraordinary operation of nature or of law one half the labourers of a state could in the course of one night be transformed into slaves: would the state be made the poorer or the less able to pay taxes? That the condition of the laboring poor in most countries, that of the fishermen particularly of the Northern states, is as abject as that of slaves. It is the number of labourers which produce the surplus for taxation, and numbers therefore indiscriminately, are the fair index of wealth. That it is the use of the word "property" here, & it's application to some of the people of the state, which produces the fallacy. How does the Southern farmer procure slaves? Either by importation or by purchase from his neighbor. If he imports a slave, he adds one to the number of labourers in his country, and proportionably to it's profits & abilities to pay taxes. If he buys from his neighbor it is only a transfer of a labourer from one farm to another, which does not change the annual produce of the state, & therefore should not change it's tax. That if a Northern farmer works ten labourers on his farm, he can, it is true, invest the surplus of ten men's labour in cattle: but so may the Southern farmer working ten slaves. That a state of one hundred thousand freemen can maintain no more cattle than one of one hundred thousand slaves. Therefore they have no more of that kind of property. That a slave may indeed from the custom of speech be more properly called the wealth of his master, than the free labourer might be called the wealth of his employer: but as to the state, both were equally it's wealth, and should therefore equally add to the quota of it's tax.

Mr. [Benjamin] Harrison proposed as a compromise, that two slaves should be counted as one freeman. He affirmed that slaves did not do so much work as freemen, and doubted if two effected more than one. That this was proved by the price of labor. The hire of a labourer in the Southern colonies being from 8 to £12. while in the Northern it was generally £24.

Mr. [James] Wilson said that if this amendment should take place the Southern colonies would have all the benefit of slaves, whilst the Northern ones would bear the burthen. That slaves increase the profits of a state, which the Southern states mean to take to themselves; that they also increase the burthen of defence, which would of course fall so much the heavier on the Northern. That slaves occupy the places of freemen and eat their food. Dismiss your slaves & freemen will take their places. It is our duty to lay every discouragement on the importation of slaves; but this amendment would give the jus trium liberorum to him who would import slaves. That other kinds of property were pretty equally distributed thro' all the colonies: there were as many cattle, horses, & sheep, in the North as the South, & South as the North; but not so as to slaves. That experience has shown that those colonies have been alwais able to pay most which have the most inhabitants, whether they be black or white, and the practice of the Southern colonies has alwais been to make every farmer pay poll taxes upon all his labourers whether they be black or white. He acknowledges indeed that freemen work the most; but they consume the most also. They do not produce a greater surplus for taxation. The slave is neither fed nor clothed so expensively as a freeman. Again white women are exempted from labor generally, but negro women are not. In this then the Southern states have an advantage as the article now stands. It has sometimes been said that slavery is necessary because the commodities they raise would be too dear for market if cultivated by freemen; but now it is said that the labor of the slave is the dearest.

Mr. Payne urged the original resolution of Congress, to proportion the quotas of the states to the number of souls.

Dr. [John] Witherspoon was of opinion that the value of lands & houses was the best estimate of the wealth of a nation, and that it was practicable to obtain such a valuation. This is the true barometer of wealth. The one now proposed is imperfect in itself, and unequal between the States. It has been objected that negroes eat the food of freemen & therefore should be taxed. Horses also eat the food of freemen; therefore they also should be taxed. It has been said too that in carrying slaves into the estimate of the taxes the state is to pay, we do no more than those states themselves do, who alwais take slaves into the estimate of the taxes the individual is to pay. But the cases are not parallel. In the Southern colonies slaves pervade the whole colony; but they do not pervade the whole continent. That as to the original resolution of Congress to proportion the quotas according to the souls, it was temporary only, & related to the monies heretofore emitted: whereas we are now entering into a new compact, and therefore stand on original ground.

Aug 1. The question being put the amendment proposed was rejected by the votes of N. Hampshire, Massachusetts, Rhode island, Connecticut, N. York, N. Jersey, & Pennsylvania, against those of Delaware, Maryland, Virginia, North & South Carolina. Georgia was divided.

The other article was in these words. "Art. XVII. In determining questions each colony shall have one vote."

July 30. 31. Aug 1. Present 41. members. Mr. Chase observed that this article was the most likely to divide us of any one proposed in the draught then under consideration. That the larger colonies had threatened they would not confederate at all if their weight in congress should not be equal to the numbers of people they added to the confederacy; while the smaller ones declared against a union if they did not retain an equal vote for the protection of their rights. That it was of the utmost consequence to bring the parties together, as should we sever from each other, either no foreign power will ally with us at all, or the different states will form different alliances, and thus increase the horrors of those scenes of civil war and bloodshed which in such a state of separation & independance would render us a miserable people. That our importance, our interests, our peace required that we should confederate, and that mutual sacrifices should be made to effect a compromise of this difficult question. He was of opinion the smaller colonies would lose their rights, if they were not in some instances allowed an equal vote; and therefore that a discrimination should take place among the questions which would come before Congress. That the smaller states should be secured in all questions concerning life or liberty & the greater ones in all respecting property. He therefore proposed that in votes relating to money, the voice of each colony should be proportioned to the number of its inhabitants.

Dr. Franklin thought that the votes should be so proportioned in all cases. He took notice that the Delaware counties had bound up their Delegates to disagree to this article. He thought it a very extraordinary language to be held by any state, that they would not confederate with us unless we would let them dispose of our money. Certainly if we vote equally we ought to pay equally; but the smaller states will hardly purchase the privilege at this price. That had he lived in a state where the representation, originally equal, had become unequal by time & accident he might have submitted rather than disturb government; but that we should be very wrong to set out in this practice when it is in our power to establish what is right. That at the time of the Union between England and Scotland the latter had made the objection which the smaller states now do. But experience had proved that no unfairness had ever been shown them. That their advocates had prognosticated that it would again happen as in times of old, that the whale would swallow Jonas, but he thought the prediction reversed in event and that Jonas had swallowed the whale, for the Scotch had in fact got possession of the government and gave laws to the English. He reprobated the original agreement of Congress to vote by colonies and therefore was for their voting in all cases according to the number of taxables.

Dr. Witherspoon opposed every alteration of the article. All men admit that a confederacy is necessary. Should the idea get abroad that there is likely to be no union among us, it will damp the minds of the people, diminish the glory of our struggle, & lessen it's importance; because it will open to our view future prospects of war & dissension among ourselves. If an equal vote be refused, the smaller states will become vassals to the larger; & all experience has shown that the vassals & subjects of free states are the most enslaved. He instanced the Helots of Sparta & the provinces of Rome. He observed that foreign powers discovering this blemish would make it a handle for disengaging the smaller states from so unequal a confederacy. That the colonies should in fact be considered as individuals; and that as such, in all disputes they should have an equal vote;

that they are now collected as individuals making a bargain with each other, & of course had a right to vote as individuals. That in the East India company they voted by persons, & not by their proportion of stock. That the Belgic confederacy voted by provinces. That in questions of war the smaller states were as much interested as the larger, & therefore should vote equally; and indeed that the larger states were more likely to bring war on the confederacy in proportion as their frontier was more extensive. He admitted that equality of representation was an excellent principle, but then it must be of things which are coordinate; that is, of things similar & of the same nature: that nothing relating to individuals could ever come before Congress; nothing but what would respect colonies. He distinguished between an incorporating & a federal union. The union of England was an incorporating one; yet Scotland had suffered by that union: for that it's inhabitants were drawn from it by the hopes of places & employments. Nor was it an instance of equality of representation; because while Scotland was allowed nearly a thirteenth of representation they were to pay only one fortieth of the land tax. He expressed his hopes that in the present enlightened state of men's minds we might expect a lasting confederacy, if it was founded on fair principles.

John Adams advocated the voting in proportion to numbers. He said that we stand here as the representatives of the people. That in some states the people are many, in others they are few; that therefore their vote here should be proportioned to the numbers from whom it comes. Reason, justice, & equity never had weight enough on the face of the earth to govern the councils of men. It is interest alone which does it, and it is interest alone which can be trusted. That therefore the interests within doors should be the mathematical representatives of the interests without doors. That the individuality of the colonies is a mere sound. Does the individuality of a colony increase it's wealth or numbers. If it does, pay equally. If it does not add weight in the scale of the confederacy, it cannot add to their rights, nor weigh in argument. A. has £50. B. £500. C. £1000. in partnership. Is it just they should equally dispose of the monies of the partnership? It has been said we are independent individuals making a bargain together. The question is not what we are now, but what we ought to be when our bargain shall be made. The confederacy is to make us one individual only; it is to form us, like separate parcels of metal, into one common mass. We shall no longer retain our separate individuality, but become a single individual as to all questions submitted to the confederacy. Therefore all those reasons which prove the justice & expediency of equal representation in other assemblies, hold good here. It has been objected that a proportional vote will endanger the smaller states. We answer that an equal vote will endanger the larger. Virginia, Pennsylvania, & Massachusetts are the three greater colonies. Consider their distance, their difference of produce, of interests

& of manners, & it is apparent they can never have an interest or inclination to combine for the oppression of the smaller. That the smaller will naturally divide on all questions with the larger. Rhode isld, from it's relation, similarity & intercourse will generally pursue the same objects with Massachusetts; Jersey, Delaware & Maryland, with Pennsylvania.

Dr. [Benjamin] Rush took notice that the decay of the liberties of the Dutch republic proceeded from three causes. 1. The perfect unanimity requisite on all occasions. 2. Their obligation to consult their constituents. 3. Their voting by provinces. This last destroyed the equality of representation, and the liberties of great Britain also are sinking from the same defect. That a part of our rights is deposited in the hands of our legislatures. There it was admitted there should be an equality of representation. Another part of our rights is deposited in the hands of Congress: why is it not equally necessary there should be an equal representation there? Were it possible to collect the whole body of the people together, they would determine the questions submitted to them by their majority. Why should not the same majority decide when voting here by their representatives? The larger colonies are so providentially divided in situation as to render every fear of their combining visionary. Their interests are different, & their circumstances dissimilar. It is more probable they will become rivals & leave it in the power of the smaller states to give preponderance to any scale they please. The voting by the number of free inhabitants will have one excellent effect, that of inducing the colonies to discourage slavery & to encourage the increase of their free inhabitants.

Mr. [Stephen] Hopkins observed there were 4 larger, 4 smaller, & 4 middle-sized colonies. That the 4 largest would contain more than half the inhabitants of the confederated states, & therefore would govern the others as they should please. That history affords no instance of such a thing as equal representation. The Germanic body votes by states. The Helvetic body does the same; & so does the Belgic confederacy. That too little is known of the ancient confederations to say what was their practice.

Mr. Wilson thought that taxation should be in proportion to wealth, but that representation should accord with the number of freemen. That government is a collection or result of the wills of all. That if any government could speak the will of all, it would be perfect; and that so far as it departs from this it becomes imperfect. It has been said that Congress is a representation of states; not of individuals. I say that the objects of its care are all the individuals of the states. It is strange that annexing the name of "State" to ten thousand men, should give them an equal right with forty thousand. This must be the effect of magic, not of reason. As to those matters which are referred to Congress, we are not so many states, we are one large state. We lay aside our individuality, whenever we come here. The Germanic body is a burlesque on government; and their practice on any point is a sufficient authority & proof that it is wrong. The greatest imperfection in the constitution of the Belgic confederacy is their voting by provinces. The interest of the whole is constantly sacrificed to that of the small states. The history of the war in the reign of Q. Anne sufficiently proves this. It is asked shall nine colonies put it into the power of four to govern them as they please? I invert the question, and ask shall two millions of people put it in the power of one million to govern them as they please? It is pretended too that the smaller colonies will be in danger from the greater. Speak in honest language & say the minority will be in danger from the majority. And is there an assembly on earth where this danger may not be equally pretended? The truth is that our proceedings will then be consentaneous with the interests of the majority, and so they ought to be. The probability is much greater that the larger states will disagree than that they will combine. I defy the wit of man to invent a possible case or to suggest any one thing on earth which shall be for the interests of Virginia, Pennsylvania & Massachusetts, and which will not also be for the interest of the other states.

* * *

These articles reported July 12. 76 were debated from day to day, & time to time for two years, were ratified July 9, '78, by 10 states, by N. Jersey on the 26th. of Nov. of the same year, and by Delaware on the 23d. of Feb. following. Maryland alone held off 2 years more, acceding to them Mar 1, 81. and thus closing the obligation.

Our delegation had been renewed for the ensuing year commencing Aug. 11. but the new government was now organized, a meeting of the legislature was to be held in Oct. and I had been elected a member by my county. I knew that our legislation under the regal government had many very vicious points which urgently required reformation, and I thought I could be of more use in forwarding that work. I therefore retired from my seat in Congress on the 2d. of Sep. resigned it, and took my place in the legislature of my state, on the 7th. of October.

On the 11th. I moved for leave to bring in a bill for the establishment of courts of justice, the organization of which was of importance; I drew the bill it was approved by the commee, reported and passed after going thro' it's due course.

On the 12th. I obtained leave to bring in a bill declaring tenants in tail to hold their lands in fee simple. In the earlier times of the colony when lands were to be obtained for little or nothing, some provident individuals procured large grants, and, desirous of founding great families for themselves, settled them on their descendants in fee-tail. The transmission of this property from generation to generation in the same name raised up a distinct set of families who, being privileged by law in the perpetuation of their wealth were thus formed into a Patrician order, distinguished by the splendor and luxury of their establishments. From this order too the king habitually selected his Counsellors of State, the hope of which distinction devoted the whole corps to the interests & will of the crown. To annul this privilege, and instead of an aristocracy of wealth, of more harm and danger, than benefit, to society, to make an opening for the aristocracy of virtue and talent, which nature has wisely provided for the direction of the interests of society, & scattered with equal hand through all it's conditions, was deemed essential to a well ordered republic. To effect it no violence was necessary, no deprivation of natural right, but rather an enlargement of it by a repeal of the law. For this would authorize the present holder to divide the property among his children equally, as his affections were divided; and would place them, by natural generation on the level of their fellow citizens. But this repeal was strongly opposed by Mr. Pendleton, who was zealously attached to ancient establishments; and who, taken all in all, was the ablest man in debate I have ever met with. He had not indeed the poetical fancy of Mr. Henry, his sublime imagination, his lofty and overwhelming diction; but he was cool, smooth and persuasive; his language flowing, chaste & embellished, his conceptions quick, acute and full of resource; never vanquished; for if he lost the main battle, he returned upon you, and regained so much of it as to make it a drawn one, by dexterous manœuvres, skirmishes in detail, and the recovery of small advantages which, little singly, were important altogether. You never knew when you were clear of him, but were harassed by his perseverance until the patience was worn down of all who had less of it than himself. Add to this that he was one of the most virtuous & benevolent of men, the kindest friend, the most amiable & pleasant of companions, which ensured a favorable reception to whatever came from him. Finding that the general principle of entails could not be maintained, he took his stand on an amendment which he proposed, instead of an absolute abolition, to permit the tenant in tail to convey in fee simple, if he chose it: and he was within a few votes of saving so much of the old law. But the bill passed finally for entire abolition.

In that one of the bills for organizing our judiciary system which proposed a court of chancery, I had provided for a trial by jury of all matters of fact in that as well as in the courts of law. He defeated it by the introduction of 4. words only, "*if either party chuse.*" The consequence has been that as no suitor will say to his judge, "Sir, I distrust you, give me a jury" juries are rarely, I might say perhaps never seen in that court, but when called for by the Chancellor of his own accord.

The first establishment in Virginia which became permanent was made in 1607. I have found no mention of negroes in the colony until about 1650. The first brought here as slaves were by a Dutch ship; after which the English commenced the trade and continued it until the revolutionary war. That suspended, ipso facto, their further importation for the present, and the business of the war pressing constantly on the legislature, this subject was not acted on finally until the year 78. when I brought in a bill to prevent their further importation. This passed without opposition, and stopped the increase of the evil by importation, leaving to future efforts its final eradication.

The first settlers of this colony were Englishmen, loyal subjects to their king and church, and the grant to Sr. Walter Raleigh contained an express Proviso that their laws "should not be against the true Christian faith, now professed in the church of England." As soon as the state of the colony admitted, it was divided into parishes, in each of which was established a minister of the Anglican church, endowed with a fixed salary, in tobacco, a glebe house and land with the other necessary appendages. To meet these expenses all the inhabitants of the parishes were assessed, whether they were or not, members of the established church. Towards Quakers who came here they were most cruelly intolerant, driving them from the colony by the severest penalties. In process of time however, other sectarisms were introduced, chiefly of the Presbyterian family; and the established clergy, secure for life in their glebes and salaries, adding to these generally the emoluments of a classical school, found employment enough, in their farms and schoolrooms for the rest of the week, and devoted Sunday only to the edification of their flock, by service, and a sermon at their parish church. Their other pastoral functions were little attended to. Against this inactivity the zeal and industry of sectarian preachers had an open and undisputed field; and by the time of the revolution, a majority of the inhabitants had become dissenters from the established church, but were still obliged to pay contributions to support the Pastors of the minority. This unrighteous compulsion to maintain teachers of what they deemed religious errors was grievously felt during the regal government, and without a hope of relief. But the first republican legislature which met in 76. was crowded with petitions to abolish this spiritual tyranny. These brought on the severest contests in which I have ever been engaged. Our great opponents were Mr. Pendleton & Robert Carter Nicholas, honest men, but zealous churchmen. The petitions were referred to the commee of the whole house on the state of the country; and after desperate contests in that committee, almost daily from the 11th of Octob. to the 5th of December, we prevailed so far only as to repeal the laws which rendered criminal the maintenance of any religious opinions, the forbearance of repairing to church, or the exercise of any mode of worship: and further, to exempt dissenters from contributions to the support of the established church; and to suspend, only until the next session levies on the members of that church for the salaries of their own incumbents. For although the majority of our citizens were dissenters, as has been observed, a majority of the legislature were churchmen. Among these however were some reasonable and liberal men, who enabled us, on some points, to obtain feeble majorities. But our opponents carried in the general resolutions of the commee of Nov. 19. a declaration that religious assemblies ought to be regulated, and that provision ought to be made for continuing the succession of the clergy, and superintending their conduct. And in the bill now passed was inserted an express reservation of the question Whether a general assessment should not be established by law, on every one, to the support of the pastor of his choice; or whether all should be left to voluntary contributions; and on this question, debated at every session from 76 to 79 (some of our dissenting allies, having now secured their particular object, going over to the advocates of a general assessment) we could only obtain a suspension from session to session until 79. when the question against a general assessment was finally carried, and the establishment of the Anglican church entirely put down. In justice to the two honest but zealous opponents, who have been named I must add that altho', from their natural temperaments, they were more disposed generally to acquiesce in things as they are, than to risk innovations, yet whenever the public will had once decided, none were more faithful or exact in their obedience to it.

The seat of our government had been originally fixed in the peninsula of Jamestown, the first settlement of the colonists; and had been afterwards removed a few miles inland to Williamsburg. But this was at a time when our settlements had not extended beyond the tide water. Now they had crossed the Alleghany; and the center of population was very far removed from what it had been. Yet Williamsburg was still the depository of our archives, the habitual residence of the Governor & many other of the public functionaries, the established place for the sessions of the legislature, and the magazine of our military stores: and it's situation was so exposed that it might be taken at any time in war, and, at this time particularly, an enemy might in the night run up either of the rivers between which it lies, land a force above, and take possession of the place, without the possibility of saving either persons or things. I had proposed it's removal so early as Octob. 76. but it did not prevail until the session of May. '79.

Early in the session of May 79. I prepared, and obtained leave to bring in a bill declaring who should be deemed citizens, asserting the natural right of expatriation, and prescribing the mode of exercising it. This, when I withdrew from the house on the 1st of June following, I left in the hands of George Mason and it was passed on the 26th of that month.

In giving this account of the laws of which I was myself the mover & draughtsman, I by no means mean to claim to myself the merit of obtaining their passage. I had many occasional and strenuous coadjutors in debate, and one most steadfast, able, and zealous; who was himself a host. This was George Mason, a man of the first order of wisdom among those who acted on the theatre of the revolution, of expansive mind, profound judgment, cogent in argument, learned in the lore of our former constitution, and earnest for the republican change on democratic principles. His elocution was neither flowing nor smooth, but his language was strong, his manner most impressive, and strengthened by a dash of biting cynicism when provocation made it seasonable.

Mr. Wythe, while speaker in the two sessions of 1777. between his return from Congress and his appointment to the Chancery, was an able and constant associate in whatever was before a committee of the whole. His pure integrity, judgment and reasoning powers gave him great weight. Of him see more in some notes inclosed in my letter of August 31. 1821, to Mr. John Saunderson.

Mr. Madison came into the House in 1776. a new member and young; which circumstances, concurring with his extreme modesty, prevented his venturing himself in debate before his removal to the Council of State in Nov. 77. From thence he went to Congress, then consisting of few members. Trained in these successive schools, he acquired a habit of self-possession which placed at ready command the rich resources of his luminous and discriminating mind, & of his extensive information, and rendered him the first of every assembly afterwards of which he became a member. Never wandering from his subject into vain declamation, but pursuing it closely in language pure, classical, and copious, soothing always the feelings of his adversaries by civilities and softness of expression, he rose to the eminent station which he held in the great National convention of 1787. and in that of Virginia which followed, he sustained the new constitution in all its parts, bearing off the palm against the logic of George Mason, and the fervid declamation of Mr. Henry. With these consummate powers were united a pure and spotless virtue which no calumny has ever attempted to sully. Of the powers and polish of his pen, and of the wisdom of his administration in the highest office of the nation, I need say nothing. They have spoken, and will forever speak for themselves.

So far we were proceeding in the details of reformation only; selecting points of legislation prominent in character & principle, urgent, and indicative of the strength of the general pulse of reformation. When I left Congress, in 76. it was in the persuasion that our whole code must be reviewed, adapted to our republican form of government, and, now that we had no negatives of Councils, Governors & Kings to restrain us from doing right, that it should be corrected, in all it's parts, with a single eye to reason, & the good of those for whose government it was framed. Early therefore in the session of 76. to which

I returned, I moved and presented a bill for the revision of the laws; which was passed on the 24th. of October, and on the 5th. of November Mr. Pendleton, Mr. Wythe, George Mason, Thomas L. Lee and myself were appointed a committee to execute the work. We agreed to meet at Fredericksburg to settle the plan of operation and to distribute the work. We met there accordingly, on the 13th. of January 1777. The first question was whether we should propose to abolish the whole existing system of laws, and prepare a new and complete Institute, or preserve the general system, and only modify it to the present state of things. Mr. Pendleton, contrary to his usual disposition in favor of antient things, was for the former proposition, in which he was joined by Mr. Lee. To this it was objected that to abrogate our whole system would be a bold measure, and probably far beyond the views of the legislature; that they had been in the practice of revising from time to time the laws of the colony, omitting the expired, the repealed and the obsolete, amending only those retained, and probably meant we should now do the same, only including the British statutes as well as our own: that to compose a new Institute like those of Justinian and Bracton, or that of Blackstone, which was the model proposed by Mr. Pendleton, would be an arduous undertaking, of vast research, of great consideration & judgment; and when reduced to a text, every word of that text, from the imperfection of human language, and it's incompetence to express distinctly every shade of idea, would become a subject of question & chicanery until settled by repeated adjudications; that this would involve us for ages in litigation, and render property uncertain until, like the statutes of old, every word had been tried, and settled by numerous decisions, and by new volumes of reports & commentaries; and that no one of us probably would undertake such a work, which, to be systematical, must be the work of one hand. This last was the opinion of Mr. Wythe, Mr. Mason & myself. When we proceeded to the distribution of the work, Mr. Mason excused himself as, being no lawyer, he felt himself unqualified for the work, and he resigned soon after. Mr. Lee excused himself on the same ground, and died indeed in a short time. The other two gentlemen therefore and myself divided the work among us. The common law and statutes to the 4. James I. (when our separate legislature was established) were assigned to me; the British statutes from that period to the present day to Mr. Wythe, and the Virginia laws to Mr. Pendleton. As the law of Descents, & the criminal law fell of course within my portion, I wished the commee to settle the leading principles of these, as a guide for me in framing them. And with respect to the first, I proposed to abolish the law of primogeniture, and to make real estate descendible in parcenary to the next of kin, as personal property is by the statute of distribution. Mr. Pendleton wished to preserve the right of primogeniture, but seeing at once that that could not prevail, he proposed we should adopt the Hebrew principle, and give a double portion to the elder son. I observed that if the eldest son could eat twice as much, or do double work, it might be a natural evidence of his right to a double portion; but being on a par in his powers & wants, with his brothers and sisters, he should be on a par also in the partition of the patrimony, and such was the decision of the other members.

On the subject of the Criminal law, all were agreed that the punishment of death should be abolished, except for treason and murder; and that, for other felonies should be substituted hard labor in the public works, and in some cases, the Lex talionis. How this last revolting principle came to obtain our approbation, I do not remember. There remained indeed in our laws a vestige of it in a single case of a slave. It was the English law in the time of the Anglo-Saxons, copied probably from the Hebrew law of "an eye for an eye, a tooth for a tooth," and it was the law of several antient people. But the modern mind had left it far in the rear of it's advances. These points however being settled, we repaired to our respective homes for the preparation of the work.

Feb. 6. In the execution of my part I thought it material not to vary the diction of the antient statutes by modernizing it, nor to give rise to new questions by new expressions. The text of these statutes had been so fully explained and defined by numerous adjudications, as scarcely ever now to produce a question in our courts. I thought it would be useful also, in all new draughts, to reform the style of the later British statutes, and of our own acts of assembly, which from their verbosity, their endless tautologies, their involutions of case within case, and parenthesis within parenthesis, and their multiplied efforts at certainty by *saids* and *aforesaids*, by *ors* and by *ands*, to make them more plain, do really render them more perplexed and incomprehensible, not only to common readers, but to the lawyers themselves. We were employed in this work from that time to Feb. 1779, when we met at Williamsburg, that is to say, Mr. Pendleton, Mr. Wythe & myself, and meeting day by day, we examined critically our several parts, sentence by sentence, scrutinizing and amending until we had agreed on the whole. We then returned home, had fair copies made of our several parts, which were reported to the General Assembly June 18. 1779. by Mr. Wythe and myself, Mr. Pendleton's residence being distant, and he having authorized us by letter to declare his approbation. We had in this work brought so much of the Common law as it was thought necessary to alter, all the British statutes from Magna Charta to the present day, and all the laws of Virginia, from the establishment of our legislature, in the 4th. Jac. 1. to the present time, which we thought should be retained, within the compass of 126 bills, making a printed folio of 90 pages only. Some bills were taken out occasionally, from time to time, and passed; but the main body of the work was not entered on by the legislature until after the general peace, in 1785.

when by the unwearied exertions of Mr. Madison, in opposition to the endless quibbles, chicaneries, perversions, vexations and delays of lawyers and demi-lawyers, most of the bills were passed by the legislature, with little alteration.

The bill for establishing religious freedom, the principles of which had, to a certain degree, been enacted before, I had drawn in all the latitude of reason & right. It still met with opposition; but, with some mutilations in the preamble, it was finally passed; and a singular proposition proved that it's protection of opinion was meant to be universal. Where the preamble declares that coercion is a departure from the plan of the holy author of our religion, an amendment was proposed, by inserting the word "Jesus Christ," so that it should read "a departure from the plan of Jesus Christ, the holy author of our religion." The insertion was rejected by a great majority, in proof that they meant to comprehend, within the mantle of it's protection, the Jew and the Gentile, the Christian and Mahometan, the Hindoo, and infidel of every denomination.

Beccaria and other writers on crimes and punishments had satisfied the reasonable world of the unrightfulness and inefficacy of the punishment of crimes by death; and hard labor on roads, canals and other public works, had been suggested as a proper substitute. The Revisors had adopted these opinions; but the general idea of our country had not yet advanced to that point. The bill therefore for proportioning crimes and punishments was lost in the House of Delegates by a majority of a single vote. I learnt afterwards that the substitute of hard labor in public was tried (I believe it was in Pennsylvania) without success. Exhibited as a public spectacle, with shaved heads and mean clothing, working on the high roads produced in the criminals such a prostration of character, such an abandonment of self-respect, as, instead of reforming, plunged them into the most desperate & hardened depravity of morals and character.—To pursue the subject of this law.—I was written to in 1785 (being then in Paris) by Directors appointed to superintend the building of a Capitol in Richmond, to advise them as to a plan, and to add to it one of a prison. Thinking it a favorable opportunity of introducing into the state an example of architecture in the classic style of antiquity, and the Maison quarrée of Nismes, an antient Roman temple, being considered as the most perfect model existing of what may be called Cubic architecture, I applied to M. Clerissault, who had published drawings of the Antiquities of Nismes, to have me a model of the building made in stucco, only changing the order from Corinthian to Ionic, on account of the difficulty of the Corinthian capitals. I yielded with reluctance to the taste of Clerissault, in his preference of the modern capital of Scamozzi to the more noble capital of antiquity. This was executed by the artist whom Choiseul Gouffier had carried with him to Constantinople, and employed while Ambassador there, in making those beautiful models of the remains of Grecian architecture which are to be seen at Paris. To adapt the exterior to our use, I drew a plan for the interior, with the apartments necessary for legislative, executive & judiciary purposes, and accommodated in their size and distribution to the form and dimensions of the building. These were forwarded to the Directors in 1786. and were carried into execution, with some variations not for the better, the most important to which however admit of future correction. With respect of the plan of a Prison, requested at the same time, I had heard of a benevolent society in England which had been indulged by the government in an experiment of the effect of labor in *solitary confinement* on some of their criminals, which experiment had succeeded beyond expectation. The same idea had been suggested in France, and an Architect of Lyons had proposed a plan of a well contrived edifice on the principle of solitary confinement. I procured a copy, and as it was too large for our purposes, I drew one on a scale, less extensive, but susceptible of additions as they should be wanting. This I sent to the Directors instead of a plan of a common prison, in the hope that it would suggest the idea of labor in solitary confinement instead of that on the public works, which we had adopted in our Revised Code. It's principle accordingly, but not it's exact form, was adopted by Latrobe in carrying the plan into execution, by the erection of what is now called the Penitentiary, built under his direction. In the meanwhile the public opinion was ripening by time, by reflection, and by the example of Pensylva, where labor on the highways had been tried without approbation from 1786 to 89. & had been followed by their Penitentiary system on the principle of confinement and labor, which was proceeding auspiciously. In 1796. our legislature resumed the subject and passed the law for amending the Penal laws of the commonwealth. They adopted solitary, instead of public labor, established a gradation in the duration of the confinement, approximated the style of the law more to the modern usage, and instead of the settled distinctions of murder & manslaughter, preserved in my bill, they introduced the new terms of murder in the 1st & 2d degree. Whether these have produced more or fewer questions of definition I am not sufficiently informed of our judiciary transactions to say. I will here however insert the text of my bill, with the notes I made in the course of my researches into the subject.

Feb. 7. The acts of assembly concerning the College of Wm. & Mary, were properly within Mr. Pendleton's portion of our work. But these related chiefly to it's revenue, while it's constitution, organization and scope of science were derived from it's charter. We thought, that on this subject a systematical plan of general education should be proposed, and I was requested to undertake it. I accordingly prepared three bills for the Revisal, proposing three distinct grades of education, reaching all classes. 1. Elementary schools for all children generally, rich and poor. 2. Colleges for a middle degree of instruction, calculated for the common purposes of life, and such as would be desirable for all who were in easy circumstances. And 3d. an ultimate grade for teaching the sciences generally, & in their highest degree. The first bill proposed to lay off every county into Hundreds or Wards, of a proper size and population for a school, in which reading, writing, and common arithmetic should be taught; and that the whole state should be divided into 24 districts, in each of which should be a school for classical learning, grammar, geography, and the higher branches of numerical arithmetic. The second bill proposed to amend the constitution of Wm. & Mary College, to enlarge it's sphere of science, and to make it in fact an University. The third was for the establishment of a library. These bills were not acted on until the same year '96. and then only so much of the first as provided for elementary schools. The College of Wm. & Mary was an establishment purely of the Church of England, the Visitors were required to be all of that Church; the Professors to subscribe it's 39 Articles, it's Students to learn it's Catechism, and one of its fundamental objects was declared to be to raise up Ministers for that church. The religious jealousies therefore of all the dissenters took alarm lest this might give an ascendancy to the Anglican sect and refused acting on that bill. Its local eccentricity too and unhealthy autumnal climate lessened the general inclination towards it. And in the Elementary bill they inserted a provision which completely defeated it, for they left it to the court of each county to determine for itself when this act should be carried into execution, within their county. One provision of the bill was that the expenses of these schools should be borne by the inhabitants of the county, every one in proportion to his general tax-rate. This would throw on wealth the education of the poor; and the justices, being generally of the more wealthy class, were unwilling to incur that burthen, and I believe it was not suffered to commence in a single county. I shall recur again to this subject towards the close of my story, if I should have life and resolution enough to reach that term; for I am already tired of talking about myself.

The bill on the subject of slaves was a mere digest of the existing laws respecting them, without any intimation of a plan for a future & general emancipation. It was thought better that this should be kept back, and attempted only by way of amendment whenever the bill should be brought on. The principles of the amendment however were agreed on, that is to say, the freedom of all born after a certain day, and deportation at a proper age. But it was found that the public mind would not yet bear the proposition, nor will it bear it even at this day. Yet the day is not distant when it must bear and adopt it, or worse will follow. Nothing is more certainly written in the book of fate than that these people are to be free. Nor is it less certain that the two races, equally free, cannot live in the same government. Nature, habit, opinion has drawn indelible lines of distinction between them. It is still in our power to direct the process of emancipation and deportation peaceably and in such slow degree as that the evil will wear off insensibly, and their place be pari passu filled up by free white laborers. If on the contrary it is left to force itself on, human nature must shudder at the prospect held up. We should in vain look for an example in the Spanish deportation or deletion of the Moors. This precedent would fall far short of our case.

I considered 4 of these bills, passed or reported, as forming a system by which every fibre would be eradicated of antient or future aristocracy; and a foundation laid for a government truly republican. The repeal of the laws of entail would prevent the accumulation and perpetuation of wealth in select families, and preserve the soil of the country from being daily more & more absorbed in Mortmain. The abolition of primogeniture, and equal partition of inheritances removed the feudal and unnatural distinctions which made one member of every family rich, and all the rest poor, substituting equal partition, the best of all Agrarian laws. The restoration of the rights of conscience relieved the people from taxation for the support of a religion not theirs; for the establishment was truly of the religion of the rich, the dissenting sects being entirely composed of the less wealthy people; and these, by the bill for a general education, would be qualified to understand their rights, to maintain them, and to exercise with intelligence their parts in self-government: and all this would be effected without the violation of a single natural right of any one individual citizen. To these too might be added, as a further security, the introduction of the trial by jury, into the Chancery courts, which have already ingulfed and continue to ingulf, so great a proportion of the jurisdiction over our property.

On the 1st of June 1779. I was appointed Governor of the Commonwealth and retired from the legislature. Being elected also one of the Visitors of Wm. & Mary college, a self-electing body, I effected, during my residence in Williamsburg that year, a change in the organization of that institution by abolishing the Grammar school, and the two professorships of Divinity & Oriental languages, and substituting a professorship of Law & Police, one of Anatomy Medicine and Chemistry, and one of Modern languages; and the charter confining us to six professorships, we added the law of Nature & Nations, & the Fine Arts to the duties of the Moral professor, and Natural history to those of the professor of Mathematics and Natural philosophy.

Being now, as it were, identified with the Commonwealth itself, to write my own history during the two years of my administration, would be to write the public history of that portion of the revolution within this state. This has been done by others, and particularly by Mr. Girardin, who wrote his Continuation of Burke's history of Virginia while at Milton, in this neighborhood, had free access to all my papers while composing it, and has given as faithful an account as I could myself. For this portion therefore of my own life, I refer altogether to his history. From a belief that under the pressure of the invasion under which we were then laboring the public would have more confidence in a Military chief, and that the Military commander, being invested with the Civil power also, both might be wielded with more energy promptitude and effect for the defence of the state, I resigned the administration at the end of my 2d. year, and General Nelson was appointed to succeed me.

Soon after my leaving Congress in Sep. '76, to wit on the last day of that month, I had been appointed, with Dr. Franklin, to go to France, as a Commissioner to negotiate treaties of alliance and commerce with that government. Silas Deane, then in France, acting as agent for procuring military stores, was joined with us in commission. But such was the state of my family that I could not leave it, nor could I expose it to the dangers of the sea, and of capture by the British ships, then covering the ocean. I saw too that the laboring oar was really at home, where much was to be done of the most permanent interest in new modelling our governments, and much to defend our fanes and fire-sides from the desolations of an invading enemy pressing on our country in every point. I declined therefore and Dr. Lee was appointed in my place. On the 15th. of June 1781. I had been appointed with Mr. Adams, Dr. Franklin, Mr. Jay, and Mr. Laurens a Minister plenipotentiary for negotiating peace, then expected to be effected thro' the mediation of the Empress of Russia. The same reasons obliged me still to decline; and the negotiation was in fact never entered on. But, in the autumn of the next year 1782 Congress receiving assurances that a general peace would be concluded in the winter and spring, they renewed my appointment on the 13th. of Nov. of that year. I had two months before that lost the cherished companion of my life, in whose affections, unabated on both sides, I had lived the last ten years in unchequered happiness. With the public interests, the state of my mind concurred in recommending the change of scene proposed; and I accepted the appointment, and left Monticello on the 19th. of Dec. 1782. for Philadelphia, where I arrived on the 27th. The Minister of France, Luzerne, offered me a passage in the *Romulus* frigate, which I accepting. But she was then lying a few miles below Baltimore blocked up in the ice. I remained therefore a month in Philadelphia, looking over the papers in the office of State in order to possess myself of the general state of our foreign relations, and then went to Baltimore to await the liberation of the frigate from the ice. After waiting there nearly a month, we received information that a Provisional treaty of peace had been signed by our Commissioners on the 3d. of Sept. 1782. to become absolute on the conclusion of peace between France and Great Britain. Considering my proceeding to Europe as now of no utility to the public, I returned immediately to Philadelphia to take the orders of Congress, and was excused by them from further proceeding. I therefore returned home, where I arrived on the 15th. of May, 1783.

On the 6th. of the following month I was appointed by the legislature a delegate to Congress, the appointment to take place on the 1st. of Nov. ensuing, when that of the existing delegation would expire. I accordingly left home on the 16th. of Oct. arrived at Trenton, where Congress was sitting, on the 3d. of Nov. and took my seat on the 4th., on which day Congress adjourned to meet at Annapolis on the 26th.

Congress had now become a very small body, and the members very remiss in their attendance on it's duties insomuch that a majority of the states, necessary by the Confederation to constitute a house even for minor business did not assemble until the 13th. of December.

They as early as Jan. 7. 1782. had turned their attention to the monies current in the several states, and had directed the Financier, Robert Morris, to report to them a table of rates at which the foreign coins should be received at the treasury. That officer, or rather his assistant, Gouverneur Morris, answered them on the 15th in an able and elaborate statement of the denominations of money current in the several states, and of the comparative value of the foreign coins chiefly in circulation with us. He went into the consideration of the necessity of establishing a standard of value with us, and of the adoption of a money-Unit. He proposed for the Unit such a fraction of pure silver as would be a common measure of the penny of every state, without leaving a fraction. This common divisor he found to be 1–1440 of a dollar, or 1–1600 of the crown sterling. The value of a dollar was therefore to be expressed by 1440 units, and of a crown by 1600. Each Unit containing a quarter of a grain of fine silver. Congress turning again their attention to this subject the following year, the financier, by a letter of Apr. 30, 1783. further explained and urged the Unit he had proposed; but nothing more was done on it until the ensuing year, when it was again taken up, and referred to a commee of which I was a member. The general views of the financier were sound, and the principle was ingenious on which he proposed to found his Unit. But it was too minute for ordinary use, too laborious for computation either by the head or in figures. The price of a loaf of bread 1–20 of a dollar would be 72. units.

A pound of butter 1–5 of a dollar 288. units.

A horse or bullock of 80. D value would require a notation of 6. figures, to wit 115,200, and the public debt, suppose of 80. millions, would require 12. figures, to wit 115,200,000,000 units. Such a system of money-arithmetic would be entirely unmanageable for the common purposes of society. I proposed therefore, instead of this, to adopt the Dollar as our Unit of account and payment, and that it's divisions and sub-divisions should be in the decimal ratio. I wrote some Notes on the subject, which I submitted to the consideration of the financier. I received his answer and adherence to his general system, only agreeing to take for his Unit 100. of those he first proposed, so that a Dollar should be 14 40—100 and a crown 16. units. I replied to this and printed my notes and reply on a flying sheet, which I put into the hands of the members of Congress for consideration, and the Committee agreed to report on my principle. This was adopted the ensuing year and is the system which now prevails. I insert here the Notes and Reply, as shewing the different views on which the adoption of our money system hung. The division into dimes, cents & mills is now so well understood, that it would be easy of introduction into the kindred branches of weights & measures. I use, when I travel, an Odometer of Clarke's invention which divides the mile into cents, and I find every one comprehend a distance readily when stated to them in miles & cents; so they would in feet and cents, pounds & cents, &c.

The remissness of Congress, and their permanent session, began to be a subject of uneasiness and even some of the legislatures had recommended to them intermissions, and periodical sessions. As the Confederation had made no provision for a visible head of the government during vacations of Congress, and such a one was necessary to superintend the executive business, to receive and communicate with foreign ministers & nations, and to assemble Congress on sudden and extraordinary emergencies, I proposed early in April the appointment of a commee to be called the Committee of the states, to consist of a member from each state, who should remain in session during the recess of Congress: that the functions of Congress should be divided into Executive and Legislative, the latter to be reserved, and the former, by a general resolution to be delegated to that Committee. This proposition was afterwards agreed to; a Committee appointed, who entered on duty on the subsequent adjourn-ment of Congress, quarrelled very soon, split into two parties, abandoned their post, and left the government without any visible head until the next meeting in Congress. We have since seen the same thing take place in the Directory of France; and I believe it will forever take place in any Executive consisting of a plurality. Our plan, best I believe, combines wisdom and practicability, by providing a plurality of Counsellors, but a single Arbiter for ultimate decision. I was in France when we heard of this schism, and separation of our Committee, and, speaking with Dr. Franklin of this singular disposition of men to quarrel and divide into parties, he gave his sentiments as usual by way of Apologue. He mentioned the Eddystone lighthouse in the British channel as being built on a rock in the mid-channel, totally inaccessible in winter, from the boisterous character of that sea, in that season. That therefore, for the two keepers employed to keep up the lights, all provisions for the winter were necessarily carried to them in autumn, as they could never be visited again till the return of the milder season. That on the first practicable day in the spring a boat put off to them with fresh supplies. The boatmen met at the door one of the keepers and accosted him with a How goes it friend? Very well. How is your companion? I do not know. Don't know? Is not he here? I can't tell. Have not you seen him to-day? No. When did you see him? Not since last fall. You have killed him? Not I, indeed. They were about to lay hold of him, as having certainly murdered his companion; but he desired them to go up stairs & examine for themselves. They went up, and there found the other keeper. They had quarrelled it seems soon after being left there, had divided into two parties, assigned the cares below to one, and those above to the other, and had never spoken to or seen one another since.

But to return to our Congress at Annapolis, the definitive treaty of peace which had been signed at Paris on the 3d. of Sep. 1783. and received here, could not be ratified without a House of 9. states. On the 23d. of Dec. therefore we addressed letters to the several governors, stating the receipt of the definitive treaty, that 7 states only were in attendance, while 9. were necessary to its ratification, and urging them to press on their delegates the necessity of their immediate attendance. And on the 26th. to save time I moved that the Agent of Marine (Robert Morris) should be instructed to have ready a vessel at this place, at N. York, & at some Eastern port, to carry over the ratification of the treaty when agreed to. It met the general sense of the house, but was opposed by Dr. Lee on the ground of expense which it would authorize the agent to incur for us; and he said it would be better to ratify at once & send on the ratification. Some members had before suggested that 7 states were competent to the ratification. My motion was therefore postponed and another brought forward by Mr. Read of S. C. for an immediate ratification. This was debated the 26th. and 27th. Reed, Lee, [Hugh] Williamson & Jeremiah Chace urged that ratification was a mere matter of form, that the treaty was conclusive from the moment it was signed by the ministers; that although the Confederation requires the assent of 9. *states* to *enter into* a treaty, yet that it's conclusion could not be called *entrance into it*; that supposing 9. states requisite, it would be in the power of 5. states to keep us always at war; that 9. states had virtually authorized the ratifion having ratified the provisional treaty, and instructed their ministers to agree to a definitive one in the same terms, and the present one was in fact substantially and almost verbatim the same; that there now remain but 67. days for the ratification, for it's passage across the Atlantic, and it's exchange; that there was no hope of our soon having 9. states present; in fact that this was the ultimate point of time to which we could venture to wait; that if the ratification was not in Paris by the time stipulated, the treaty would become void; that if ratified by

7 states, it would go under our seal without it's being known to Gr. Britain that only 7. had concurred; that it was a question of which they had no right to take cognizance, and we were only answerable for it to our constituents; that it was like the ratification which Gr. Britain had received from the Dutch by the negotiations of Sr. Wm. Temple.

On the contrary, it was argued by Monroe, Gerry, Howel, Ellery & myself that by the modern usage of Europe the ratification was considered as the act which gave validity to a treaty, until which it was not obligatory. That the commission to the ministers reserved the ratification to Congress; that the treaty itself stipulated that it should be ratified; that it became a 2d. question who were competent to the ratification? That the Confederation expressly required 9 states to enter into any treaty; that, by this, that instrument must have intended that the assent of 9. states should be necessary as well to the *completion* as to the *commencement* of the treaty, it's object having been to guard the rights of the Union in all those important cases where 9. states are called for; that, by the contrary construction, 7 states, containing less than one third of our whole citizens, might rivet on us a treaty, commenced indeed under commission and instructions from 9. states, but formed by the minister in express contradiction to such instructions, and in direct sacrifice of the interests of so great a majority; that the definitive treaty was admitted not to be a verbal copy of the provisional one, and whether the departures from it were of substance or not, was a question on which 9. states alone were competent to decide; that the circumstances of the ratification of the provisional articles by 9. states, the instructions to our ministers to form a definitive one by them, and their actual agreement in substance, do not render us competent to ratify in the present instance; if these circumstances are in themselves a ratification, nothing further is requisite than to give attested copies of them, in exchange for the British ratification; if they are not, we remain where we were, without a ratification by 9. states, and incompetent ourselves to ratify; that it was but 4. days since the seven states now present unanimously concurred in a resolution to be forwarded to the governors of the absent states, in which they stated as a cause for urging on their delegates, that 9. states were necessary to ratify the treaty; that in the case of the Dutch ratification, Gr. Britain had courted it, and therefore was glad to accept it as it was; that they knew our constitution, and would object to a ratification by 7. that if that circumstance was kept back, it would be known hereafter, & would give them ground to deny the validity of a ratification into which they should have been surprised and cheated, and it would be a dishonorable prostitution of our seal; that there is a hope of 9. states; that if the treaty would become null if not ratified in time, it would not be saved by an imperfect ratification; but that in fact it would not be null, and would be placed on better ground, going in unexceptionable form, tho' a few days too late, and rested on the small importance of this circumstance, and the physical impossibilities which had prevented a punctual compliance in point of time; that this would be approved by all nations, & by Great Britain herself, if not determined to renew the war, and if determined, she would never want excuses, were this out of the way. Mr. Reade gave notice he should call for the yeas & nays; whereon those in opposition prepared a resolution expressing pointedly the reasons of the dissent from his motion. It appearing however that his proposition could not be carried, it was thought better to make no entry at all. Massachusetts alone would have been for it; Rhode Island, Pennsylvania and Virginia against it, Delaware, Maryland & N. Carolina, would have been divided.

Our body was little numerous, but very contentious. Day after day was wasted on the most unimportant questions. My colleague Mercer was one of those afflicted with the morbid rage of debate, of an ardent mind, prompt imagination, and copious flow of words, he heard with impatience any logic which was not his own. Sitting near me on some occasion of a trifling but wordy debate, he asked how I could sit in silence hearing so much false reasoning which a word should refute? I observed to him that to refute indeed was easy, but to silence impossible. That in measures brought forward by myself, I took the laboring oar, as was incumbent on me; but that in general I was willing to listen. If every sound argument or objection was used by some one or other of the numerous debaters, it was enough: if not, I thought it sufficient to suggest the omission, without going into a repetition of what had been already said by others. That this was a waste and abuse of the time and patience of the house which could not be justified. And I believe that if the members of deliberative bodies were to observe this course generally, they would do in a day what takes them a week, and it is really more questionable, than may at first be thought, whether Bonaparte's dumb legislature which said nothing and did much, may not be preferable to one which talks much and does nothing. I served with General Washington in the legislature of Virginia before the revolution, and, during it, with Dr. Franklin in Congress. I never heard either of them speak ten minutes at a time, nor to any but the main point which was to decide the question. They laid their shoulders to the great points, knowing that the little ones would follow of themselves. If the present Congress errs in too much talking, how can it be otherwise in a body to which the people send 150. lawyers, whose trade it is to question everything, yield nothing, & talk by the hour? That 150. lawyers should do business together ought not to be expected. But to return again to our subject.

Those who thought 7. states competent to the ratification being very restless under the loss of their motion, I proposed, on the 3d. of January to meet them on middle ground, and therefore moved a resolution which premising that there were but 7. states present, who were unanimous for the ratification, but, that they differed in opinion on the question of competency. That those however in the negative were unwilling that any powers which it might be supposed they possessed should remain unexercised for the restoration of peace, provided it could be done saving their good faith, and without importing any opinion of Congress that 7. states were competent, and resolving that treaty be ratified so far as they had power; that it should be transmitted to our ministers with instructions to keep it uncommunicated; to endeavor to obtain 3. months longer for exchange of ratifications; that they should be informed that so soon as 9. states shall be present a ratification by 9. shall be sent them; if this should get to them before the ultimate point of time for exchange, they were to use it, and not the other; if not, they were to offer the act of the 7. states in exchange, informing them the treaty had come to hand while Congress was not in session, that but 7. states were as yet assembled, and these had unanimously concurred in the ratification. This was debated on the 3d. and 4th. and on the 5th. a vessel being to sail for England from this port (Annapolis) the House directed the President to write to our ministers accordingly.

Jan. 14. Delegates from Connecticut having attended yesterday, and another from S. Carolina coming in this day, the treaty was ratified without a dissenting voice, and three instruments of ratification were ordered to be made out, one of which was sent by Colo. Harmer, another by Colo. Franks, and the 3d. transmitted to the agent of Marine to be forwarded by any good opportunity.

Congress soon took up the consideration of their foreign relations. They deemed it necessary to get their commerce placed with every nation on a footing as favorable as that of other nations; and for this purpose to propose to each a distinct treaty of commerce. This act too would amount to an acknowledgment by each of our independance and of our reception into the fraternity of nations; which altho', as possessing our station of right and in fact, we would not condescend to ask, we were not unwilling to furnish opportunities for receiving their friendly salutations & welcome. With France the United Netherlands and Sweden we had already treaties of commerce, but commissions were given for those countries also, should any amendments be thought necessary. The other states to which treaties were to be proposed were England, Hamburg, Saxony, Prussia, Denmark, Russia, Austria, Venice, Rome, Naples, Tuscany, Sardinia, Genoa, Spain, Portugal, the Porte, Algiers, Tripoli, Tunis & Morocco.

Mar. 16. On the 7th. of May Congress resolved that a Minister Plenipotentiary should be appointed in addition to Mr. Adams & Dr. Franklin for negotiating treaties of commerce with foreign nations, and I was elected to that duty. I accordingly left Annapolis on the 11th. Took with me my elder daughter then at Philadelphia (the two others being too young for the voyage) & proceeded to Boston in quest of a passage. While passing thro' the different states, I made a point of informing myself of the state of the commerce of each, went on to New Hampshire with the same view and returned to Boston. From thence I sailed on the 5th. of July in the *Ceres* a merchant ship of Mr. Nathaniel Tracey, bound to Cowes. He was himself a passenger, and, after a pleasant voyage of 19. days from land to land, we arrived at Cowes on the 26th. I was detained there a few days by the indisposition of my daughter. On the 30th. we embarked for Havre, arrived there on the 31st. left it on the 3d. of August, and arrived at Paris on the 6th. I called immediately on Doctr. Franklin at Passy, communicated to him our charge, and we wrote to Mr. Adams, then at the Hague to join us at Paris.

Before I had left America, that is to say in the year 1781. I had received a letter from M. de Marbois, of the French legation in Philadelphia, informing me he had been instructed by his government to obtain such statistical accounts of the different states of our Union, as might be useful for their information; and addressing to me a number of queries relative to the state of Virginia. I had always made it a practice whenever an opportunity occurred of obtaining any information of our country, which might be of use to me in any station public or private, to commit it to writing. These memoranda were on loose papers, bundled up without order, and difficult of recurrence when I had occasion for a particular one. I thought this a good occasion to embody their substance, which I did in the order of Mr. Marbois' queries, so as to answer his wish and to arrange them for my own use. Some friends to whom they were occasionally communicated wished for copies; but their volume rendering this too laborious by hand, I proposed to get a few printed for their gratification. I was asked such a price however as exceeded the importance of the object. On my arrival at Paris I found it could be done for a fourth of what I had been asked here. I therefore corrected and enlarged them, and had 200. copies printed, under the title of *Notes on Virginia.* I gave a very few copies to some particular persons in Europe, and sent the rest to my friends in America. An European copy, by the death of the owner, got into the hands of a bookseller, who engaged it's translation, & when ready for the press, communicated his intentions & manuscript to me, without any other permission than that of suggesting corrections. I never had seen so wretched an attempt at translation. Interverted, abridged, mutilated, and often reversing the sense of the original, I found it a blotch of errors from beginning to end. I corrected some of the most material, and in that form it was printed in French. A London bookseller, on seeing the translation, requested me to permit him to print the English original. I thought it best to do so to let the world see that it was not really so bad as the French translation had made it appear. And this is the true history of that publication.

Mr. Adams soon joined us at Paris, & our first employment was to prepare a general form to be proposed to such nations as were disposed to treat with us. During the negotiations for peace with the British Commissioner David Hartley, our Commissioners had proposed, on the suggestion of Doctr. Franklin, to insert an article exempting from capture by the public or private armed ships of either belligerent, when at war, all merchant vessels and their cargoes, employed merely in carrying on the commerce between nations. It was refused by England, and unwisely, in my opinion. For in the case of a war with us, their superior commerce places infinitely more at hazard on the ocean than ours; and as hawks abound in proportion to game, so our privateers would swarm in proportion to the wealth exposed to their prize, while theirs would be few for want of subjects of capture. We inserted this article in our form, with a provision against the molestation of fishermen, husbandmen, citizens unarmed and following their occupations in unfortified places, for the humane treatment of prisoners of war, the abolition of contraband of war, which exposes merchant vessels to such vexatious & ruinous detentions and abuses; and for the principle of free bottoms, free goods.

In a conference with the Count de Vergennes, it was thought better to leave to legislative regulation on both sides such modifications of our commercial intercourse as would voluntarily flow from amicable dispositions. Without urging, we sounded the ministers of the several European nations at the court of Versailles, on their dispositions towards mutual commerce, and the expediency of encouraging it by the protection of a treaty. Old Frederic of Prussia met us cordially and without hesitation, and appointing the Baron de Thulemeyer, his minister at the Hague, to negotiate with us, we communicated to him our Project, which with little alteration by the King, was soon concluded. Denmark and Tuscany entered also into negotiations with us. Other powers appearing indifferent we did not think it proper to press them. They seemed in fact to know little about us, but as rebels who had been successful in throwing off the yoke of the mother country. They were ignorant of our commerce, which had been always monopolized by England, and of the exchange of articles it might offer advantageously to both parties. They were inclined therefore to stand aloof until they could see better what relations might be usefully instituted with us. The negotiations therefore begun with Denmark & Tuscany we protracted designedly until our powers had expired; and abstained from making new propositions to others having no colonies; because our commerce being an exchange of raw for wrought materials, is a competent price for admission into the colonies of those possessing them: but were we to give it, without price, to others, all would claim it without price on the ordinary ground of gentis amicissimae.

Mr. Adams being appointed Min. Pleny. of the U S. to London, left us in June, and in July 1785. Dr. Franklin returned to America, and I was appointed his successor at Paris. In Feb. 1786. Mr. Adams wrote to me pressingly to join him in London immediately, as he thought he discovered there some symptoms of better disposition towards us. Colo. Smith, his Secretary of legation, was the bearer of his urgencies for my immediate attendance. I accordingly left Paris on the 1st. of March, and on my arrival in London we agreed on a very summary form of treaty, proposing an exchange of citizenship for our citizens, our ships, and our productions generally, except as to office. On my presentation as usual to the King and Queen at their levées, it was impossible for anything to be more ungracious than their notice of Mr. Adams & myself. I saw at once that the ulcerations in the narrow mind of that mulish being left nothing to be expected on the subject of my attendance; and on the first conference with the Marquis of Caermarthen, his Minister of foreign affairs, the distance and disinclination which he betrayed in his conversation, the vagueness & evasions of his answers to us, confirmed me in the belief of their aversion to have anything to do with us. We delivered him however our Projét, Mr. Adams not despairing as much as I did of it's effect. We afterwards, by one or more notes, requested his appointment of an interview and conference, which, without directly declining, he evaded by pretences of other pressing occupations for the moment. After staying there seven weeks, till within a few days of the expiration of our commission, I informed the minister by note that my duties at Paris required my return to that place, and that I should with pleasure be the bearer of any commands to his Ambassador there. He answered that he had none, and wishing me a pleasant journey, I left London the 26th. arrived at Paris on the 30th. of April.

While in London we entered into negotiations with the Chevalier Pinto, Ambassador of Portugal at that place. The only article of difficulty between us was a stipulation that our bread stuff should be received in Portugal in the form of flour as well as of grain. He approved of it himself, but observed that several Nobles, of great influence at their court, were the owners of wind mills in the neighborhood of Lisbon which depended much for their profits on manufacturing our wheat, and that this stipulation would endanger the whole treaty. He signed it however, & it's fate was what he had candidly portended.

My duties at Paris were confined to a few objects; the receipt of our whale-oils, salted fish, and salted meats on favorable terms, the admission of our rice on equal terms with that of Piedmont, Egypt & the Levant, a mitigation of the monopolies of our tobacco by the Farmers-general, and a free admission of our productions into their islands; were the principal commercial objects which required attention; and on these occasions I was powerfully aided by all the influence and the energies of the Marquis de La Fayette, who proved himself equally zealous for the friendship and welfare of both nations; and in justice I must also say that I found the government entirely disposed to befriend us on all occasions, and to yield us every indulgence not absolutely injurious to themselves. The Count de Vergennes had the reputation with the diplomatic corps of being wary & slippery in his diplomatic intercourse; and so he might be with those whom he knew to be slippery and double-faced themselves. As he saw that I had no indirect views, practised no subtleties, meddled in no intrigues, pursued no concealed object, I found him as frank, as honorable, as easy of access to reason as any man with whom I had ever done business; and I must say the same for his successor Montmorin, one of the most honest and worthy of human beings.

Our commerce in the Mediterranean was placed under early alarm by the capture of two of our vessels and crews by the Barbary cruisers. I was very unwilling that we should acquiesce in the European humiliation of paying a tribute to those lawless pirates, and endeavored to form an association of the powers subject to habitual depredations from them. I accordingly prepared and proposed to their ministers at Paris, for consultation with their governments, articles of a special confederation in the following form.

* * *

"Proposals for concerted operation among the powers at war with the Piratical States of Barbary.

"1. It is proposed that the several powers at war with the Piratical States of Barbary, or any two or more of them who shall be willing, shall enter into a convention to carry on their operations against those states, in concert, beginning with the Algerines.

"2. This convention shall remain open to any other power who shall at any future time wish to accede to it; the parties reserving a right to prescribe the conditions of such accession, according to the circumstances existing at the time it shall be proposed.

"3. The object of the convention shall be to compel the piratical states to perpetual peace, without price, & to guarantee that peace to each other.

"4. The operations for obtaining this peace shall be constant cruises on their coast with a naval force now to be agreed on. It is not proposed that this force shall be so considerable as to be inconvenient to any party. It is believed that half a dozen frigates, with as many Tenders or Xebecs, one half of which shall be in cruise, while the other half is at rest, will suffice.

"5. The force agreed to be necessary shall be furnished by the parties in certain quotas now to be fixed; it being expected that each will be willing to contribute in such proportion as circumstance may render reasonable.

"6. As miscarriages often proceed from the want of harmony among officers of different nations, the parties shall now consider & decide whether it will not be better to contribute their quotas in money to be employed in fitting out, and keeping on duty, a single fleet of the force agreed on.

"7. The difficulties and delays too which will attend the management of these operations, if conducted by the parties themselves separately, distant as their courts may be from one another, and incapable of meeting in consultation, suggest a question whether it will not be better for them to give full powers for that purpose to their Ambassadors or other ministers resident at some one court of Europe, who shall form a Committee or Council for carrying this convention into effect; wherein the vote of each member shall be computed in proportion to the quota of his sovereign, and the majority so computed shall prevail in all questions within the view of this convention. The court of Versailles is proposed, on account of it's neighborhood to the Mediterranean, and because all those powers are represented there, who are likely to become parties to this convention.

"8. To save to that council the embarrassment of personal solicitations for office, and to assure the parties that their contributions will be applied solely to the object for which they are destined, there shall be no establishment of officers for the said Council, such as Commis, Secretaries, or any other kind, with either salaries or perquisites, nor any other lucrative appointments but such whose functions are to be exercised on board the sd vessels.

"9. Should war arise between any two of the parties to this convention it shall not extend to this enterprise, nor interrupt it; but as to this they shall be reputed at peace.

"10. When Algiers shall be reduced to peace, the other pyratical states, if they refuse to discontinue their pyracies shall become the objects of this convention, either successively or together as shall seem best.

"11. Where this convention would interfere with treaties actually existing between any of the parties and the sd states of Barbary, the treaty shall prevail, and such party shall be allowed to withdraw from the operations against that state."

* * *

Spain had just concluded a treaty with Algiers at the expense of 3. millions of dollars, and did not like to relinquish the benefit of that until the other party should fail in their observance of it. Portugal, Naples, the two Sicilies, Venice, Malta, Denmark and Sweden were favorably disposed to such an association; but their representatives at Paris expressed apprehensions that France would interfere, and, either openly or secretly support the Barbary powers; and they required that I should ascertain the dispositions of the Count de Vergennes on the subject. I had before taken occasion to inform him of what we were proposing, and therefore did not think it proper to insinuate any doubt of the fair conduct of his government; but stating our propositions, I mentioned the apprehensions entertained by us that England would interfere in behalf of those piratical governments. "She dares not do it," said he. I pressed it no further. The other agents were satisfied with this indication of his sentiments, and nothing was now wanting to bring it into direct and formal consideration, but the assent of our government, and their authority to make the formal proposition. I communicated to them the favorable prospect of protecting our commerce from the Barbary depredations, and for such a continuance of time as, by an exclusion of them from the sea, to change their habits & characters from a predatory to an agricultural people: towards which however it was expected they would contribute a frigate, and it's expenses to be in constant cruise. But they were in no condition to make any such engagement. Their recommendatory powers for obtaining contributions were so openly neglected by the several states that they declined an engagement which they were conscious they could not fulfill with punctuality; and so it fell through.

May 17. In 1786. while at Paris I became acquainted with John Ledyard of Connecticut, a man of genius, of some science, and of fearless courage, & enterprise. He had accompanied Capt Cook in his voyage to the Pacific, had distinguished himself on several occasions by an unrivalled intrepidity, and published an account of that voyage with details unfavorable to Cook's deportment towards the savages, and lessening our regrets at his fate. Ledyard had come to Paris in the hope of forming a company to engage in the fur trade of the Western coast of America. He was disappointed in this, and being out of business, and of a roaming, restless character, I suggested to him the enterprise of exploring the Western part of our continent, by passing thro St. Petersburg to Kamschatka, and procuring a passage thence in some of the Russian vessels to Nootka Sound, whence he might make his way across the continent to America; and I undertook to have the permission of the Empress of Russia solicited. He eagerly embraced the proposition, and M. de Semoulin, the Russian Ambassador, and more particularly Baron Grimm the special correspondent of the Empress, solicited her permission for him to pass thro' her dominions to the Western coast of America. And here I must correct a material error which I have committed in another place to the prejudice of the Empress. In writing some Notes of the life of Capt Lewis, prefixed to his expedition to the Pacific, I stated that the Empress gave the permission asked, & afterwards retracted it. This idea, after a lapse of 26 years, had so insinuated itself into my mind, that I committed it to paper without the least suspicion of error. Yet I find, on recurring to my letters of that date that the Empress refused permission at once, considering the enterprise as entirely chimerical. But Ledyard would not relinquish it, persuading himself that by proceeding to St. Petersburg he could satisfy the Empress of it's practicability and obtain her permission. He went accordingly, but she was absent on a visit to some distant part of her dominions, and he pursued his course to within 200. miles of Kamschatka, where he was overtaken by an arrest from the Empress, brought back to Poland, and there dismissed. I must therefore in justice, acquit the Empress of ever having for a moment countenanced, even by the indulgence of an innocent passage thro' her territories this interesting enterprise.

May 18. The pecuniary distresses of France produced this year a measure of which there had been no example for near two centuries, & the consequences of which, good and evil, are not yet calculable. For it's remote causes we must go a little back.

Celebrated writers of France and England had already sketched good principles on the subject of government. Yet the American Revolution seems first to have awakened the thinking part of the French nation in general from the sleep of despotism in which they were sunk. The officers too who had been to America, were mostly young men, less shackled by habit and prejudice, and more ready to assent to the suggestions of common sense, and feeling of common rights. They came back with new ideas & impressions. The press, notwithstanding it's shackles, began to disseminate them. Conversation assumed new freedoms. Politics became the theme of all societies, male and female, and a very extensive & zealous party was formed which acquired the appellation of the Patriotic party, who, sensible of the abusive government under which they lived, sighed for occasions of reforming it. This party comprehended all the honesty of the kingdom sufficiently at it's leisure to think, the men of letters, the easy Bourgeois, the young nobility partly from reflection, partly from mode, for these sentiments became matter of mode, and as such united most of the young women to the party. Happily for the nation, it happened at the same moment that the dissipations of the Queen and court, the abuses of the pension-list, and dilapidations in the administration of every branch of the finances, had exhausted the treasures and credit of the nation, insomuch that it's most necessary functions were paralyzed. To reform these abuses would have overset the minister; to impose new taxes by the authority of the King was known to be impossible from the determined opposition of the parliament to their enregistry. No resource remained then but to appeal to the nation. He advised therefore the call of an assembly of the most distinguished characters of the nation, in the hope that by promises of various and valuable improvements in the organization and regimen of the government, they would be induced to authorize new taxes, to controul the opposition of the parliament, and to raise the annual revenue to the level of expenditures. An Assembly of Notables therefore, about 150. in number named by the King, convened on the 22d. of Feb. The Minister (Calonne) stated to them that the annual excess of expenses beyond the revenue, when Louis XVI. came to the throne, was 37. millions of livres; that 440. millns. had been borrowed to reestablish the navy; that the American war had cost them 1440. millns. (256. mils. of Dollars) and that the interest of these sums, with other increased expenses had added 40 millns. more to the annual deficit. (But a subseqt. and more candid estimate made it 56. millns.) He proffered them an universal redress of grievances, laid open those grievances fully, pointed out sound remedies, and covering his canvas with objects of this magnitude, the deficit dwindled to a little accessory, scarcely attracting attention. The persons chosen were the most able & independent characters in the kingdom, and their support, if it could be obtained, would be enough for him. They improved the occasion for redressing their grievances, and agreed that the public wants should be relieved; but went into an examination of the causes of them. It was supposed that Calonne was conscious that his accounts could not bear examination; and it was said and believed that he asked of the King to send 4. members to the Bastile, of whom the M. de la Fayette was one, to banish 20. others, & 2. of his Ministers. The King found it shorter to banish him. His successor went on in full concert with the Assembly. The result was an augmentation of the revenue, a promise of economies in it's expenditure, of an annual settlement of the public accounts before a council, which the Comptroller, having been heretofore obliged to settle only with the King in person, of course never settled at all; an acknowledgment that the King could not lay a new tax, a reformation of the criminal laws, abolition of torture, suppression of Corvées, reformation of the gabelles, removal of the interior custom houses, free commerce of grain internal & external, and the establishment of Provincial assemblies; which alltogether constituted a great mass of improvement in the condition of the nation. The establishment of the Provincial assemblies was in itself a fundamental improvement. They would be of the choice of the people, one third renewed every year, in those provinces where there are no States, that is to say over about three fourths of the kingdom. They would be partly an Executive themselves, & partly an Executive council to the Intendant, to whom the Executive power, in his province had been heretofore entirely delegated. Chosen by the people, they would soften the execution of hard laws, & having a right of representation to the King, they would censure bad laws, suggest good ones, expose abuses, and their representations, when united, would command respect. To the other advantages might be added the precedent itself of calling the Assemblée des Notables, which would perhaps grow into habit. The hope was that the improvements thus promised would be carried into effect, that they would be maintained during the present reign, & that that would be long enough for them to take some root in the constitution, so that they might come to be considered as a part of that, and be protected by time, and the attachment of the nation.

The Count de Vergennes had died a few days before the meeting of the Assembly, & the Count de Montmorin had been named Minister of foreign affairs in his place. Villedeuil succeeded Calonnes as Comptroller general, & Lomenie de Bryenne, Archbishop of Thoulouse, afterwards of Sens, & ultimately Cardinal Lomenie, was named Minister principal, with whom the other ministers were to transact the business of their departments, heretofore done with the King in person, and the Duke de Nivernois, and M. de Malesherbes were called to the Council. On the nomination of the Minister principal the Marshals de Segur & de Castries retired from the departments of War & Marine, unwilling to act subordinately, or to share the blame of proceedings taken out of their direction. They were succeeded by the Count de Brienne, brother of the Prime minister, and the Marquis de la Luzerne, brother to him who had been Minister in the United States.

May 24. A dislocated wrist, unsuccessfully set, occasioned advice from my Surgeon to try the mineral waters of Aix in Provence as a corroborant. I left Paris for that place therefore on the 28th. of Feb. and proceeded up the Seine, thro' Champagne & Burgundy, and down the Rhone thro' the Beaujolais by Lyons, Avignon, Nismes to Aix, where finding on trial no benefit from the waters, I concluded to visit the rice country of Piedmont, to see if anything might be learned there to benefit the rivalship of our Carolina rice with that, and thence to make a tour of the seaport towns of France, along it's Southern and Western coast, to inform myself if anything could be done to favor our commerce with them. From Aix therefore I took my route by Marseilles, Toulon, Hieres, Nice, across the Col de Tende, by Coni, Turin, Vercelli, Novara, Milan, Pavia, Novi, Genoa. Thence returning along the coast by Savona, Noli, Albenga, Oneglia, Monaco, Nice, Antibes, Frejus, Aix, Marseilles, Avignon, Nismes, Montpellier, Frontignan, Cette, Agde, and along the canal of Languedoc, by Bezieres, Narbonne, Cascassonne, Castelnaudari, thro' the Souterrain of St. Feriol and back by Castelnaudari, to Toulouse, thence to Montauban & down the Garonne by Langon to Bordeaux. Thence to Rochefort, la Rochelle, Nantes, L'Orient, then back by Rennes to Nantes, and up the Loire by Angers, Tours, Amboise, Blois to New Orleans, thence direct to Paris where I arrived on the 10th. of June. Soon after my return from this journey to wit, about the latter part of July, I received my younger daughter Maria from Virginia by the way of London, the youngest having died some time before.

The treasonable perfidy of the Prince of Orange, Stadtholder & Captain General of the United Netherlands, in the war which England waged against them for entering into a treaty of commerce with the U. S. is known to all. As their Executive officer, charged with the conduct of the war, he contrived to baffle all the measures of the States General, to dislocate all their military plans, & played false into the hands of England and against his own country on every possible occasion, confident in her protection, and in that of the King of Prussia, brother to his Princess. The States General indignant at this patricidal conduct applied to France for aid, according to the stipulations of the treaty concluded with her in 85. It was assured to them readily, and in cordial terms, in a letter from the Ct. de Vergennes to the Marquis de Verac, Ambassador of France at the Hague, of which the following is an extract.

> "Extrait de la depeche de Monsr. le Comte de Vergennes à Monsr. le Marquis de Verac, Ambassadeur de France à la Haye, du 1er Mars 1786.
>
> "Le Roi concourrera, autant qu'il sera en son pouvoir, au succes de la chose, et vous inviterez de sa part les patriotes de lui communiquer leurs vues, leurs plans, et leurs envieux. Vous les assurerez que le roi prend un interêt veritable à leurs personnes comme à leur cause, et qu' ils peuvent compter sur sa protection. Ils doivent y compter d' autant plus, Monsieur, que nous ne dissimulons pas que si Monsr. le Stadhoulder reprend son ancienne influence, le systeme Anglois ne tardera pas de prevaloir, et que notre alliance deviendroit un être de raison. Les Patriotes sentiront facilement que cette position seroit incompatible avec la dignité, comme avec la consideration de sa majesté. Mais dans le cas, Monsieur, ou les chefs des Patriotes auroient à craindre une scission, ils auroient le temps suffisant pour ramener ceux de leurs amis que les Anglomanes ont egarés, et preparer les choses de maniere que la question de nouveau mise en deliberation soit decidé selon leurs desirs. Dans cette hypothese, le roi vous autorise à agir de concert avec eux, de suivre la direction qu' ils jugeront devoir vous donner, et d' employer tous les moyens pour augmenter le nombre des partisans de la bonne cause. Il me reste, Monsieur, il me reste, Monsieur, de vous parler de la sureté personelle des patriotes. Vous les assurerez que dans tout etat de cause, le roi les prend sous sa protection immediate, et vous ferez connoitre partout ou vous le jugerez necessaire, que sa Majesté regarderoit comme une offense personnelle tout ce qu'

> on entreprenderoit contre leur liberte. Il est à presumer que ce langage, tenu avec energie, en imposera à l'audace des Anglomanes et que Monsr. le Prince de Nassau croira courir quelque risque en provoquant le ressentiment de sa Majesté."

This letter was communicated by the Patriots to me when at Amsterdam in 1788. and a copy sent by me to Mr. Jay in my letter to him of Mar. 16. 1788.

The object of the Patriots was to establish a representative and republican government. The majority of the States general were with them, but the majority of the populace of the towns was with the Prince of Orange; and that populace was played off with great effect by the triumvirate of * * * Harris* the English Ambassador afterwards Ld. Malmesbury, the Prince of Orange a stupid man, and the Princess as much a man as either of her colleagues, in audaciousness, in enterprise, & in the thirst of domination. By these the mobs of the Hague were excited against the members of the States general, their persons were insulted & endangered in the streets, the sanctuary of their houses was violated, and the Prince whose function & duty it was to repress and punish these violations of order, took no steps for that purpose. The States General, for their own protection were therefore obliged to place their militia under the command of a Committee. The Prince filled the courts of London and Berlin with complaints at this usurpation of his prerogatives, and forgetting that he was but the first servant of a republic, marched his regular troops against the city of Utrecht, where the States were in session. They were repulsed by the militia. His interests now became marshalled with those of the public enemy & against his own country. The States therefore, exercising their rights of sovereignty, deprived him of all his powers. The great Frederic had died in August 86. He had never intended to break with France in support of the Prince of Orange. During the illness of which he died, he had thro' the Duke of Brunswick, declared to the Marquis de la Fayette, who was then at Berlin, that he meant not to support the English interest in Holland: that he might assure the government of France his only wish was that some honorable place in the Constitution should be reserved for the Stadtholder and his children, and that he would take no part in the quarrel unless an entire abolition of the Stadtholderate should be attempted. But his place was now occupied by Frederic William, his great nephew, a man of little understanding, much caprice, & very inconsiderate; and the Princess his sister, altho' her husband was in arms against the legitimate authorities of the country, attempting to go to Amsterdam for the purpose of exciting the mobs of that place and being refused permission to pass a military post on the way, he put the Duke of Brunswick at the head of 20,000 men, and made

* Sir James Harris –Ed.

demonstrations of marching on Holland. The King of France hereupon declared, by his Chargé des Affaires in Holland that if the Prussian troops continued to menace Holland with an invasion, his Majesty, in quality of Ally, was determined to succor that province. In answer to this Eden gave official information to Count Montmorin, that England must consider as at an end, it's convention with France relative to giving notice of it's naval armaments and that she was arming generally. War being now imminent, Eden questioned me on the effect of our treaty with France in the case of a war, & what might be our dispositions. I told him frankly and without hesitation that our dispositions would be neutral, and that I thought it would be the interest of both these powers that we should be so; because it would relieve both from all anxiety as to feeding their W. India islands. That England too, by suffering us to remain so, would avoid a heavy land-war on our continent, which might very much cripple her proceedings elsewhere; that our treaty indeed obliged us to receive into our ports the armed vessels of France, with their prizes, and to refuse admission to the prizes made on her by her enemies: that there was a clause also by which we guaranteed to France her American possessions, which might perhaps force us into the war, if these were attacked. "Then it will be war, said he, for they will assuredly be attacked." Liston, at Madrid, about the same time, made the same inquiries of Carmichael. The government of France then declared a determination to form a camp of observation at Givet, commenced arming her marine, and named the Bailli de Suffrein their Generalissimo on the Ocean. She secretly engaged also in negotiations with Russia, Austria, & Spain to form a quadruple alliance. The Duke of Brunswick having advanced to the confines of Holland, sent some of his officers to Givet to reconnoitre the state of things there, and report them to him. He said afterwards that "if there had been only a few tents at that place, he should not have advanced further, for that the King would not merely for the interest of his sister, engage in a war with France." But finding that there was not a single company there, he boldly entered the country, took their towns as fast as he presented himself before them, and advanced on Utrecht. The States had appointed the Rhingrave of Salm their Commander-in-chief, a Prince without talents, without courage, and without principle. He might have held out in Utrecht for a considerable time, but he surrendered the place without firing a gun, literally ran away & hid himself so that for months it was not known what had become of him. Amsterdam was then attacked and capitulated. In the meantime the negotiations for the quadruple alliance were proceeding favorably. But the secrecy with which they were attempted to be conducted, was penetrated by Fraser, Chargé des affaires of England at St. Petersburg, who instantly notified his court, and gave the alarm to Prussia. The King saw at once what would be his situation between the jaws of France, Austria, and Russia. In great dismay he besought the court of London not to abandon him, sent Alvensleben to Paris to explain and soothe, and England thro' the D. of Dorset and Eden, renewed her conferences for accommodation. The Archbishop, who shuddered at the idea of war, and preferred a peaceful surrender of right to an armed vindication of it, received them with open arms, entered into cordial conferences, and a declaration, and counter declaration were cooked up at Versailles and sent to London for approbation. They were approved there, reached Paris at 1 o'clock of the 27th. and were signed that night at Versailles. It was said and believed at Paris that M. de Montmorin, literally "pleuroit comme un enfant," when obliged to sign this counter declaration; so distressed was he by the dishonor of sacrificing the Patriots after assurances so solemn of protection, and absolute encouragement to proceed. The Prince of Orange was reinstated in all his powers, now become regal. A great emigration of the Patriots took place, all were deprived of office, many exiled, and their property confiscated. They were received in France, and subsisted for some time on her bounty. Thus fell Holland, by the treachery of her chief, from her honorable independence to become a province of England, and so also her Stadtholder from the high station of the first citizen of a free republic, to be the servile Viceroy of a foreign sovereign. And this was effected by a mere scene of bullying & demonstration, not one of the parties, France England or Prussia having ever really meant to encounter actual war for the interest of the Prince of Orange. But it had all the effect of a real and decisive war.

Our first essay in America to establish a federative government had fallen, on trial, very short of it's object. During the war of Independance, while the pressure of an external enemy hooped us together, and their enterprises kept us necessarily on the alert, the spirit of the people, excited by danger, was a supplement to the Confederation, and urged them to zealous exertions, whether claimed by that instrument, or not. But when peace and safety were restored, and every man became engaged in useful and profitable occupation, less attention was paid to the calls of Congress. The fundamental defect of the Confederation was that Congress was not authorized to act immediately on the people, & by it's own officers. Their power was only requisitory, and these requisitions were addressed to the several legislatures, to be by them carried into execution, without other coercion than the moral principle of duty. This allowed in fact a negative to every legislature, on every measure proposed by Congress; a negative so frequently exercised in practice as to benumb the action of the federal government, and to render it inefficient in it's general objects, & more especially in pecuniary and foreign concerns. The want too of a separation of the legislative, executive, & judiciary functions worked disadvantageously in practice. Yet this state of things afforded a happy augury of the future march of our confederacy, when it was seen that the good sense and good dispositions of the people, as soon as they perceived the incompetence of their first compact, instead of leaving it's correction to insurrection and civil war, agreed with one voice to elect deputies to a general convention, who should peaceably meet and agree on such a constitution as "would ensure peace, justice, liberty, the common defence & general welfare."

This Convention met at Philadelphia on the 25th. of May '87. It sate with closed doors and kept all it's proceedings secret, until it's dissolution on the 17th. of September, when the results of their labors were published all together. I received a copy early in November, and read and contemplated it's provisions with great satisfaction. As not a member of the Convention however, nor probably a single citizen of the Union, had approved it in all it's parts, so I too found articles which I thought objectionable. The absence of express declarations ensuring freedom of religion, freedom of the press, freedom of the person under the uninterrupted protection of the Habeas corpus, & trial by jury in civil as well as in criminal cases excited my jealousy; and the re-eligibility of the President for life, I quite disapproved. I expressed freely in letters to my friends, and most particularly to Mr. Madison & General Washington, my approbations and objections. How the good should be secured, and the ill brought to rights was the difficulty. To refer it back to a new Convention might endanger the loss of the whole. My first idea was that the 9. states first acting should accept it unconditionally, and thus secure what in it was good, and that the 4. last should accept on the previous condition that certain amendments should be agreed to, but a better course was devised of accepting the whole and trusting that the good sense & honest intentions of our citizens would make the alterations which should be deemed necessary. Accordingly all accepted, 6. without objection, and 7. with recommendations of specified amendments. Those respecting the press, religion, & juries, with several others, of great value, were accordingly made; but the Habeas corpus was left to the discretion of Congress, and the amendment against the reeligibility of the President was not proposed by that body. My fears of that feature were founded on the importance of the office, on the fierce contentions it might excite among ourselves, if continuable for life, and the dangers of interference either with money or arms, by foreign nations, to whom the choice of an American President might become interesting. Examples of this abounded in history; in the case of the Roman emperors for instance, of the Popes while of any significance, of the German emperors, the Kings of Poland, & the Deys of Barbary. I had observed too in the feudal History, and in the recent instance particularly of the Stadtholder of Holland, how easily offices or tenures for life slide into inheritances. My wish therefore was that the President should be elected for 7. years & be ineligible afterwards. This term I thought sufficient to enable him, with the concurrence of the legislature, to carry thro' & establish any system of improvement he should propose for the general good. But the practice adopted I think is better allowing his continuance for 8. years with a liability to be dropped at half way of the term, making that a period of probation. That his continuance should be restrained to 7. years was the opinion of the Convention at an early stage of it's session, when it voted that term by a majority of 8. against 2. and by a simple majority that he should be ineligible a second time. This opinion &c. was confirmed by the house so late as July 26. referred to the committee of detail, reported favorably by them, and changed to the present form by final vote on the last day but one only of their session. Of this change three states expressed their disapprobation, N. York by recommending an amendment that the President should not be eligible a third time, and Virginia and N. Carolina that he should not be capable of serving more than 8. in any term of 16. years. And altho' this amendment has not been made in form, yet practice seems to have established it. The example of 4 Presidents voluntarily retiring at the end of their 8th year, & the progress of public opinion that the principle is salutary, have given it in practice the force of precedent & usage; insomuch that should a President consent to be a candidate for a 3d. election, I trust he would be rejected on this demonstration of ambitious views.

But there was another amendment of which none of us thought at the time and in the omission of which lurks the germ that is to destroy this happy combination of National powers in the General government for matters of National concern, and independent powers in the states for what concerns the states severally. In England it was a great point gained at the Revolution, that the commissions of the judges, which had hitherto been during pleasure, should thenceforth be made during good behavior. A Judiciary dependent on the will of the King had proved itself the most oppressive of all tools in the hands of that Magistrate. Nothing then could be more salutary than a change there to the tenure of good behavior; and the question of good behavior left to the vote of a simple majority in the two houses of parliament. Before the revolution we were all good English Whigs, cordial in their free principles, and in their jealousies of their executive Magistrate. These jealousies are very apparent in all our state constitutions; and, in the general government in this instance, we have gone even beyond the English caution, by requiring a vote of two thirds in one of the Houses for removing a judge; a vote so impossible where* any defence is made, before men of ordinary prejudices & passions, that our judges are effectually independent of the nation. But this ought not to be. I would not indeed make them dependant on the Executive authority,

* In the impeachment of judge Pickering of New Hampshire, a habitual & maniac drunkard, no defence was made. Had there been, the party vote of more than one third of the Senate would have acquirted him.

as they formerly were in England; but I deem it indispensable to the continuance of this government that they should be submitted to some practical & impartial controul: and that this, to be imparted, must be compounded of a mixture of state and federal authorities. It is not enough that honest men are appointed judges. All know the influence of interest on the mind of man, and how unconsciously his judgment is warped by that influence. To this bias add that of the esprit de corps, of their peculiar maxim and creed that "it is the office of a good judge to enlarge his jurisdiction," and the absence of responsibility, and how can we expect impartial decision between the General government, of which they are themselves so eminent a part, and an individual state from which they have nothing to hope or fear. We have seen too that, contrary to all correct example, they are in the habit of going out of the question before them, to throw an anchor ahead and grapple further hold for future advances of power. They are then in fact the corps of sappers & miners, steadily working to undermine the independant rights of the States, & to consolidate all power in the hands of that government in which they have so important a freehold estate. But it is not by the consolidation, or concentration of powers, but by their distribution, that good government is effected. Were not this great country already divided into states, that division must be made, that each might do for itself what concerns itself directly, and what it can so much better do than a distant authority. Every state again is divided into counties, each to take care of what lies within it's local bounds; each county again into townships or wards, to manage minuter details; and every ward into farms, to be governed each by it's individual proprietor. Were we directed from Washington when to sow, & when to reap, we should soon want bread. It is by this partition of cares, descending in gradation from general to particular, that the mass of human affairs may be best managed for the good and prosperity of all. I repeat that I do not charge the judges with wilful and ill-intentioned error; but honest error must be arrested where it's toleration leads to public ruin. As, for the safety of society, we commit honest maniacs to Bedlam, so judges should be withdrawn from their bench, whose erroneous biases are leading us to dissolution. It may indeed injure them in fame or in fortune; but it saves the republic, which is the first and supreme law. In the impeachment of judge Pickering of New Hampshire, a habitual & maniac drunkard, no defence was made. Had there been, the party vote of more than one third of the Senate would have acquitted him.

Among the debilities of the government of the Confederation, no one was more distinguished or more distressing than the utter impossibility of obtaining, from the states, the monies necessary for the payment of debts, or even for the ordinary expenses of the government. Some contributed a little, some less, & some nothing, and the last furnished at length an excuse for the first to do nothing also. Mr. Adams, while residing at the Hague, had a general authority to borrow what sums might be requisite for ordinary & necessary expenses. Interest on the public debt, and the maintenance of the diplomatic establishment in Europe, had been habitually provided in this way. He was now elected Vice President of the U. S. was soon to return to America, and had referred our bankers to me for future councel on our affairs in their hands. But I had no powers, no instructions, no means, and no familiarity with the subject. It had always been exclusively under his management, except as to occasional and partial deposits in the hands of Mr. Grand, banker in Paris, for special and local purposes. These last had been exhausted for some time, and I had fervently pressed the Treasury board to replenish this particular deposit; as Mr. Grand now refused to make further advances. They answered candidly that no funds could be obtained until the new government should get into action, and have time to make it's arrangements. Mr. Adams had received his appointment to the court of London while engaged at Paris, with Dr. Franklin and myself, in the negotiations under our joint commissions. He had repaired thence to London, without returning to the Hague to take leave of that government. He thought it necessary however to do so now, before he should leave Europe, and accordingly went there. I learned his departure from London by a letter from Mrs. Adams received on the very day on which he would arrive at the Hague. A consultation with him, & some provision for the future was indispensable, while we could yet avail ourselves of his powers. For when they would be gone, we should be without resource. I was daily dunned by a company who had formerly made a small loan to the U S. the principal of which was now become due; and our bankers in Amsterdam had notified me that the interest on our general debt would be expected in June; that if we failed to pay it, it would be deemed an act of bankruptcy and would effectually destroy the credit of the U S. and all future prospect of obtaining money there; that the loan they had been authorized to open, of which a third only was filled, and now ceased to get forward, and rendered desperate that hope of resource. I saw that there was not a moment to lose, and set out for the Hague on the 2d. morning after receiving the information of Mr. Adams's journey. I went the direct road by Louvres, Senlis, Roye, Pont St. Maxence, Bois le duc, Gournay, Peronne, Cambray, Bouchain, Valenciennes, Mons, Bruxelles, Malines, Antwerp, Mordick, and Rotterdam, to the Hague, where I happily found Mr. Adams. He concurred with me at once in opinion that something must be done, and that we ought to risk ourselves on doing it without instructions, to save the credit of the U S. We foresaw that before the new government could be adopted, assembled, establish it's financial system, get the money into the treasury, and place it in Europe, considerable time would elapse; that therefore we had better provide at once for the years 88. 89. & 90. in order to place our government at it's ease, and our credit in security, during that trying interval. We set out therefore by the way of Leyden for Amsterdam, where we arrived on the 10th. I had prepared an estimate showing that

		Florins.
there would be necessary for the year		88–531,937–10
		89–538,540
		90–473,540
Total,		1,544,017–10
	Flor.	
to meet this the bankers had in hand	79,268–2–8	
& the unsold bonds would yield	542,800	622,068–2–8
leaving a deficit of		921,949–7–4
we proposed then to borrow a million yielding .		920,000
which would leave a small deficiency of .		1,949–7–4

Mr. Adams accordingly executed 1000. bonds, for 1000. florins each, and deposited them in the hands of our bankers, with instructions however not to issue them until Congress should ratify the measure. This done, he returned to London, and I set out for Paris; and as nothing urgent forbade it, I determined to return along the banks of the Rhine to Strasburg, and thence strike off to Paris. I accordingly left Amsterdam on the 30th of March, and proceeded by Utrecht, Nimeguen, Cleves, Duysberg, Dusseldorf, Cologne, Bonne, Coblentz, Nassau, Hocheim, Frankfort, & made an excursion to Hanau, thence to Mayence and another excursion to Rude-sheim, & Johansberg; then by Oppenheim, Worms, and Manheim, and an excursion to Heidelberg, then by Spire, Carlsruh, Rastadt & Kelh, to Strasburg, where I arrived Apr. 16th, and proceeded again on the 18th, by Phalsbourg, Fenestrange, Dieuze, Moyenvie, Nancy, Toul, Ligny, Barleduc, St. Diziers, Vitry, Chalons sur Marne, Epernay, Chateau Thierri, Meaux, to Paris where I arrived on the 23d. of April; and I had the satisfaction to reflect that by this journey our credit was secured, the new government was placed at ease for two years to come, and that as well as myself were relieved from the torment of incessant duns, whose just complaints could not be silenced by any means within our power.

A Consular Convention had been agreed on in 84. between Dr. Franklin and the French government containing several articles so entirely inconsistent with the laws of the several states, and the general spirit of our citizens, that Congress withheld their ratification, and sent it back to me with instructions to get those articles expunged or modified so as to render them compatible with our laws. The minister retired unwillingly from these concessions, which indeed authorized the exercise of powers very offensive in a free state. After much discussion it was reformed in a considerable degree, and the Convention was signed by the Count Montmorin and myself, on the 14th. of Nov. 88 not indeed such as I would have wished; but such as could be obtained with good humor & friendship.

On my return from Holland, I had found Paris still in high fermentation as I had left it. Had the Archbishop, on the close of the assembly of Notables, immediately carried into operation the measures contemplated, it was believed they would all have been registered by the parliament, but he was slow, presented his edicts, one after another, & at considerable intervals of time, which gave time for the feelings excited by the proceedings of the Notables to cool off, new claims to be advanced, and a pressure to arise for a fixed constitution, not subject to changes at the will of the King. Nor should we wonder at this pressure when we consider the monstrous abuses of power under which this people were ground to powder, when we pass in review the weight of their taxes, and inequality of their distribution; the oppressions of the tythes, of the tailles, the corvées, the gabelles, the farms & barriers; the shackles on Commerce by monopolies; on Industry by gilds & corporations; on the freedom of conscience, of thought, and of speech; on the Press by the Censure; and of person by lettres de Cachet; the cruelty of the criminal code generally, the atrocities of the Rack, the venality of judges, and their partialities to the rich; the Monopoly of Military honors by the Noblesse; the enormous expenses of the Queen, the princes & the Court; the prodigalities of pensions; & the riches, luxury, indolence & immorality of the clergy. Surely under such a mass of misrule and oppression, a people might justly press for a thoro' reformation, and might even dismount their rough-shod riders, & leave them to walk on their own legs. The edicts relative to the corvées & free circulation of grain, were first presented to the parliament and registered. But those for the impôt territorial, & stamp tax, offered some time after, were refused by the parliament, which proposed a call of the States General as alone competent to their authorization. Their refusal produced a Bed of justice, and their exile to Troyes. The advocates however refusing to attend them, a suspension in the administration of justice took place. The Parliament held out for awhile, but the ennui of their exile and absence from Paris begun at length to be felt, and some dispositions for compromise to appear. On their consent therefore to prolong some of the former taxes, they were recalled from exile, the King met them in session Nov. 19. 87. promised to call the States General in the year 92. and a majority expressed their assent to register an edict for successive and annual loans from 1788. to 92. But a protest being entered by the Duke of Orleans and this encouraging others in a disposition to retract, the King ordered peremptorily the registry of the edict, and left the assembly abruptly. The parliament immediately protested that the votes for the enregistry had not been legally taken, and that they gave no sanction to the loans proposed. This was enough to discredit and defeat them. Hereupon issued another edict for the establishment of a cour plenière, and the suspension of all the parliaments in the kingdom. This being opposed as might be expected by reclamations from all the parliaments & provinces, the King gave way and by an edict of July 5. 88 renounced his cour plenière, & promised the States General for the 1st. of May of the ensuing year: and the Archbishop finding the times beyond his faculties, accepted the promise of a Cardinal's hat, was removed [Sep. 88] from the ministry, and Mr. Necker was called to the department of finance. The innocent rejoicings of the people of Paris on this change provoked the interference of an officer of the city guards, whose order for their dispersion not being obeyed, he charged them with fixed bayonets, killed two or three, and wounded many. This dispersed them for the moment; but they collected the next day in great numbers, burnt 10. or 12. guard houses, killed two or three of the guards, & lost 6. or 8. more of their own number. The city was hereupon put under martial law, and after awhile the tumult subsided. The effect of this change of ministers, and the promise of the States General at an early day, tranquillized the nation. But two great questions now occurred. 1. What proportion shall the number of deputies of the tiers etat bear to those of the Nobles and Clergy? And 2. shall they sit in the same, or in distinct apartments? Mr. Necker, desirous of avoiding himself these knotty questions, proposed a second call of the same Notables, and that their advice should be asked on the subject. They met Nov. 9. 88. and, by five bureaux against one, they recommended the forms of the States General of 1614. wherein the houses were separate, and voted by orders, not by persons. But the whole nation declaring at once against this, and that the tiers etat should be, in numbers, equal to both the other orders, and the Parliament deciding for the same proportion, it was determined so to be, by a declaration of Dec. 27. 88. A Report of Mr. Necker to the King, of about the same date, contained other very important concessions. 1. That the King could neither lay a new tax, nor prolong an old one. 2. It expressed a readiness to agree on the periodical meeting of the States. 3. To consult on the necessary restriction on lettres de Cachet. And 4. how far the Press might be made free. 5. It admits that the States are to appropriate the public money; and 6. that Ministers shall be responsible for public expenditures. And these concessions came from the very heart of the King. He had not a wish but for the good of the nation, and for that object no personal sacrifice would ever have cost him a moment's regret. But his mind was weakness itself, his constitution timid, his judgment null, and without sufficient firmness even to stand by the faith of his word. His Queen too, haughty and bearing no contradiction, had an absolute ascendency over him; and around her were rallied the King's brother d'Artois, the court generally, and the aristocratic part of his ministers, particularly Breteuil, Broglio, Vauguyon, Foulon, Luzerne, men whose principles of government were those of the age of Louis XIV. Against this host the good counsels of Necker, Montmorin, St. Priest, altho' in unison with the wishes of the King himself, were of little avail. The resolutions of the morning formed under their advice, would be reversed in the evening by the influence of the Queen & court. But the hand of heaven weighed heavily indeed on the machinations of this junto; producing collateral incidents, not arising out of the case, yet powerfully co-exciting the nation to force a regeneration of it's government, and overwhelming with accumulated difficulties this liberticide resistance. For, while laboring under the want of money for even ordinary purposes, in a government which required a million of livres a day, and driven to the last ditch by the universal call for liberty, there came on a winter of such severe cold, as was without example in the memory of man, or in the written records of history. The Mercury was at times 50° below the freezing point of Fahrenheit and 22° below that of Reaumur. All out-door labor was suspended, and the poor, without the wages of labor, were of course without either bread or fuel. The government found it's necessities aggravated by that of procuring immense quantities of fire-wood, and of keeping great fires at all the cross-streets, around which the people gathered in crowds to avoid perishing with cold. Bread too was to be bought, and distributed daily gratis, until a relaxation of the season should enable the people to work: and the slender stock of bread-stuff had for some time threatened famine, and had raised that article to an enormous price. So great indeed was the scarcity of bread that from the highest to the lowest citizen, the bakers were permitted to deal but a scanty allowance per head, even to those who paid for it; and in cards of invitation to dine in the richest houses, the guest was notified to bring his own bread. To eke out the existence of the people, every person who had the means, was called on for a weekly subscription, which the Curés collected and employed in providing messes for the nourishment of the poor, and vied with each other in devising such economical compositions of food as would subsist the greatest number with the smallest means. This want of bread had been foreseen for some time past and M. de Montmorin had desired me to notify it in America, and that, in addition to the market price, a premium should be given on what should be brought from the U S. Notice was accordingly given and produced considerable supplies. Subsequent information made the importations from America, during the months of March, April & May, into the Atlantic ports of France, amount to about 21,000 barrels of flour, besides what went to other ports, and in other months, while our supplies to their West-Indian islands relieved them also from that drain. This distress for bread continued till July.

Hitherto no acts of popular violence had been produced by the struggle for political reformation. Little riots, on ordinary incidents, had taken place, as at other times, in different parts of the kingdom, in which some lives, perhaps a dozen or twenty, had been lost, but in the month of April a more serious one occurred in Paris, unconnected indeed with the revolutionary principle, but making part of the history of the day. The Fauxbourg St. Antoine is a quarter of the city inhabited entirely by the class of day-laborers and journeymen in every line. A rumor was spread among them that a great paper manufacturer, of the name of Reveillon, had proposed, on some occasion, that their wages should be lowered to 15 sous a day. Inflamed at once into rage, & without inquiring into it's truth, they flew to his house in vast numbers, destroyed everything in it, and in his magazines & work shops, without secreting however a pin's worth to themselves, and were continuing this work of devastation when the regular troops were called in. Admonitions being disregarded, they were of necessity fired on, and a regular action ensued, in which about 100. of them were killed, before the rest would disperse. There had rarely passed a year without such a riot in some part or other of the Kingdom; and this is distinguished only as cotemporary with the revolution, altho' not produced by it.

The States General were opened on the 5th. of May 89. by speeches from the King, the Garde des Sceaux Lamoignon, and Mr. Necker. The last was thought to trip too lightly over the constitutional reformations which were expected. His notices of them in this speech were not as full as in his previous "Rapport au Roi." This was observed to his disadvantage. But much allowance should have been made for the situation in which he was placed between his own counsels, and those of the ministers and party of the court. Overruled in his own opinions, compelled to deliver, and to gloss over those of his opponents, and even to keep their secrets, he could not come forward in his own attitude.

The composition of the assembly, altho' equivalent on the whole to what had been expected, was something different in it's elements. It has been supposed that a superior education would carry into the scale of the Commons a respectable portion of the Noblesse. It did so as to those of Paris, of it's vicinity and of the other considerable cities, whose greater intercourse with enlightened society had liberalized their minds, and prepared them to advance up to the measure of the times. But the Noblesse of the country, which constituted two thirds of that body, were far in their rear. Residing constantly on their patrimonial feuds, and familiarized by daily habit with Seigneurial powers and practices, they had not yet learned to suspect their inconsistence with reason and right. They were willing to submit to equality of taxation, but not to descend from their rank and prerogatives to be incorporated in session with the tiers etat. Among the clergy, on the other hand, it had been apprehended that the higher orders of the hierarchy, by their wealth and connections, would have carried the elections generally. But it proved that in most cases the lower clergy had obtained the popular majorities. These consisted of the Curés, sons of the peasantry who had been employed to do all the drudgery of parochial services for 10. 20. or 30 Louis a year; while their superiors were consuming their princely revenues in palaces of luxury & indolence.

The objects for which this body was convened being of the first order of importance, I felt it very interesting to understand the views of the parties of which it was composed, and especially the ideas prevalent as to the organization contemplated for their government. I went therefore daily from Paris to Versailles, and attended their debates, generally till the hour of adjournment. Those of the Noblesse were impassioned and tempestuous. They had some able men on both sides, and actuated by equal zeal. The debates of the Commons were temperate, rational and inflexibly firm. As preliminary to all other business, the awful questions came on, Shall the States sit in one, or in distinct apartments? And shall they vote by heads or houses? The opposition was soon found to consist of the Episcopal order among the clergy, and two thirds of the Noblesse; while the tiers etat were, to a man, united and determined. After various propositions of compromise had failed, the Commons undertook to cut the Gordian knot. The Abbe Sieyes, the most logical head of the nation, (author of the pamphlet *Qu'est ce que le tiers etat?* which had electrified that country, as Paine's *Common Sense* did us) after an impressive speech on the 10th of June, moved that a last invitation should be sent to the Nobles and Clergy, to attend in the Hall of the States, collectively or individually for the verification of powers, to which the commons would proceed immediately, either in their presence or absence. This verification being finished, a motion was made, on the 15th. that they should constitute themselves a National assembly; which was decided on the 17th. by a majority of four fifths. During the debates on this question, about twenty of the Curés had joined them, and a proposition was made in the chamber of the clergy that their whole body should join them. This was rejected at first by a small majority only; but, being afterwards somewhat modified, it was decided affirmatively, by a majority of eleven. While this was under debate and unknown to the court, to wit, on the 19th. a council was held in the afternoon at Marly, wherein it was proposed that the King should interpose by a declaration of his sentiments, in a *seance royale*. A form of declaration was proposed by Necker, which, while it censured in general the proceedings both of the Nobles and Commons, announced the King's views, such as substantially to coincide with the Commons. It was agreed to in council, the *seance* was fixed for the 22d. the meetings of the States were till then to be suspended, and everything, in the meantime, kept secret. The members the next morning (20th.) repairing to their house as usual, found the doors shut and guarded, a proclamation posted up for a seance royale on the 22d. and a suspension of their meetings in the meantime. Concluding that their dissolution was now to take place, they repaired to a building called the "Jeu de paume" (or Tennis court) and there bound themselves by oath to each other, never to separate of their own accord, till they had settled a constitution for the nation, on a solid basis, and if separated by force, that they would reassemble in some other place. The next day they met in the church of St. Louis, and were joined by a majority of the clergy. The heads of the Aristocracy saw that all was lost without some bold exertion. The King was still at Marly. Nobody was permitted to approach him but their friends. He was assailed by falsehoods in all shapes. He was made to believe that the Commons were about to absolve the army from their oath of fidelity to him, and to raise their pay. The court party were now all rage and desperate. They procured a committee to be held consisting of the King and his ministers, to which Monsieur & the Count d'Artois should be admitted. At this committee the latter attacked Mr. Necker personally, arraigned his declaration, and proposed one which some of his prompters had put into his hands. Mr. Necker was brow-beaten and intimidated, and the King shaken. He determined that the two plans should be deliberated on the next day and the seance royale put off a day longer. This encouraged a fiercer attack on Mr. Necker the next day. His draught of a declaration was entirely broken up, & that of the Count d'Artois inserted into it. Himself and Montmorin offered their resignation, which was refused, the Count d'Artois saying to Mr. Necker "No sir, you must be kept as the hostage; we hold you responsible for all the ill which shall happen." This change of plan was immediately whispered without doors. The Noblesse were in triumph; the people in consternation. I was quite alarmed at this state of things. The soldiery had not yet indicated which side they should take, and that which they should support would be sure to prevail. I considered a successful reformation of government in France, as ensuring a general reformation thro Europe, and the resurrection, to a new life, of their people, now ground to dust by the abuses of the governing powers. I was much acquainted with the leading patriots of the assembly. Being from a country which had successfully passed thro' a similar reformation, they were disposed to my acquaintance, and had some confidence in me. I urged most strenuously an immediate compromise; to secure what the government was now ready to yield, and trust to future occasions for what might still be wanting. It was well understood that the King would grant at this time 1. Freedom of the person by Habeas corpus. 2. Freedom of conscience. 3. Freedom of the press. 4. Trial by jury. 5. A representative legislature. 6. Annual meetings. 7. The origination of laws. 8. The exclusive right of taxation and appropriation. And 9. The responsibility of ministers; and with the exercise of these powers they would obtain in future whatever might be further necessary to improve and preserve their constitution. They thought otherwise however, and events have proved their lamentable error. For after 30. years of war, foreign and domestic, the loss of millions of lives, the prostration of private happiness, and foreign subjugation of their own country for a time, they have obtained no more, nor even that securely. They were unconscious of (for who could foresee?) the melancholy sequel of their well-meant perseverance; that their physical force would be usurped by a first tyrant to trample on the independance, and even the existence, of other nations: that this would afford fatal example for the atrocious conspiracy of Kings against their people; would generate their unholy and homicide alliance to make common cause among themselves, and to crush, by the power of the whole, the efforts of any part, to moderate their abuses and oppressions.

When the King passed, the next day, thro' the lane formed from the Chateau to the Hotel des etats, there was a dead silence. He was about an hour in the House delivering his speech & declaration. On his coming out a feeble cry of "Vive le Roy" was raised by some children, but the people remained silent & sullen. In the close of his speech he had ordered that the members should follow him, & resume their deliberations the next day. The Noblesse followed him, and so did the clergy, except about thirty, who, with the tiers, remained in the room, and entered into deliberation. They protested against what the King had done, adhered to all their former proceedings, and resolved the inviolability of their own persons. An officer came to order them out of the room in the King's name. "Tell those who sent you, said Mirabeau, that we shall not move hence but at our own will, or the point of the bayonet." In the afternoon the people, uneasy, began to assemble in great numbers in the courts, and vicinities of the palace. This produced alarm. The Queen sent for Mr. Necker. He was conducted amidst the shouts and acclamations of the multitude who filled all the apartments of the palace. He was a few minutes only with the queen, and what passed between them did not transpire. The King went out to ride. He passed thro' the crowd to his carriage and into it, without being in the least noticed. As Mr. Neckar followed him universal acclamations were raised of "vive Monsr. Neckar, vive le sauveur de la France opprimée." He was conducted back to his house with the same demonstrations of affection and anxiety. About 200. deputies of the Tiers, catching the enthusiasm of the moment, went to his house, and extorted from him a promise that he would not resign. On the 25th. 48. of the Nobles joined the tiers, & among them the D. of Orleans. There were then with them 164 members of the Clergy, altho' the minority of that body still sat apart & called themselves the chamber of the clergy. On the 26th. the Archbp. of Paris joined the tiers, as did some others of the clergy and of the Noblesse.

These proceedings had thrown the people into violent ferment. It gained the souldiery, first of the French guards, extended to those of every other denomination, except the Swiss, and even to the body guards of the King. They began to quit their barracks, to assemble in squads, to declare they would defend the life of the King, but would not be the murderers of their fellow citizens. They called themselves the souldiers *of the nation*, and left now no doubt on which side they would be, in case of rupture. Similar accounts came in from the troops in other parts of the kingdom, giving good reason to believe they would side with their fathers and brothers rather than with their officers. The operation of this medicine at Versailles was as sudden as it was powerful. The alarm there was so compleat that in the afternoon of the 27th. the King wrote with his own hand letters to the Presidents of the clergy and Nobles, engaging them immediately to join the Tiers. These two bodies were debating & hesitating when notes from the Ct. d'Artois decided their compliance. They went in a body and took their seats with the tiers, and thus rendered the union of the orders in one chamber compleat.

The Assembly now entered on the business of their mission, and first proceeded to arrange the order in which they would take up the heads of their constitution, as follows:

First, and as Preliminary to the whole a general Declaration of the Rights of Man. Then specifically the Principles of the Monarchy; rights of the Nation; rights of the King; rights of the citizens; organization & rights of the National assembly; forms necessary for the enactment of laws; organization & functions of the provincial & municipal assemblies; duties and limits of the Judiciary power; functions & duties of the military power.

A declaration of the rights of man, as the preliminary of their work, was accordingly prepared and proposed by the Marquis de la Fayette.

But the quiet of their march was soon disturbed by information that troops, and particularly the foreign troops, were advancing on Paris from various quarters. The King had been probably advised to this on the pretext of preserving peace in Paris. But his advisers were believed to have other things in contemplation. The Marshal de Broglio was appointed to their command, a high flying aristocrat, cool and capable of everything. Some of the French guards were soon arrested, under other pretexts, but really on account of their dispositions in favor of the National cause. The people of Paris forced their prison, liberated them, and sent a deputation to the Assembly to solicit a pardon. The Assembly recommended peace and order to the people of Paris, the prisoners to the king, and asked from him the removal of the troops. His answer was negative and dry, saying they might remove themselves, if they pleased, to Noyons or Soissons. In the meantime these troops, to the number of twenty or thirty thousand, had arrived and were posted in, and between Paris and Versailles. The bridges and passes were guarded. At three o'clock in the afternoon of the 11th July the Count de la Luzerne was sent to notify Mr. Neckar of his dismission, and to enjoin him to retire instantly without saying a word of it to anybody. He went home, dined, and proposed to his wife a visit to a friend, but went in fact to his country house at St. Ouen, and at midnight set out for Brussels. This was not known until the next day, 12th when the whole ministry was changed, except Villedeuil, of the Domestic department, and Barenton, Garde des sceaux. The changes were as follows.

The Baron de Breteuil, president of the council of finance; de la Galaisiere, Comptroller general in the room of Mr. Neckar; the Marshal de Broglio, minister of War, & Foulon under him in the room of Puy-Segur; the Duke de la Vauguyon, minister of foreign affairs instead of the Ct. de Montmorin; de La Porte, minister of Marine, in place of the Ct. de la Luzerne; St. Priest was also removed from the council. Luzerne and Puy-Segur had been strongly of the Aristocratic party in the Council, but they were not considered as equal to the work now to be done. The King was now compleatly in the hands of men, the principal among whom had been noted thro' their lives for the Turkish despotism of their characters, and who were associated around the King as proper instruments for what was to be executed. The news of this change began to be known at Paris about 1. or 2. o'clock. In the afternoon a body of about 100 German cavalry were advanced and drawn up in the Place Louis XV. and about 200. Swiss posted at a little distance in their rear. This drew people to the spot, who thus accidentally found themselves in front of the troops, merely at first as spectators; but as their numbers increased, their indignation rose. They retired a few steps, and posted themselves on and behind large piles of stones, large and small, collected in that Place for a bridge which was to be built adjacent to it. In this position, happening to be in my carriage on a visit, I passed thro' the lane they had formed, without interruption. But the moment after I had passed, the people attacked the cavalry with stones. They charged, but the advantageous position of the people, and the showers of stones obliged the horse to retire, and quit the field altogether, leaving one of their number on the ground, & the Swiss in their rear not moving to their aid. This was the signal for universal insurrection, and this body of cavalry, to avoid being massacred, retired towards Versailles. The people now armed themselves with such weapons as they could find in armorer's shops and private houses, and with bludgeons, and were roaming all night thro' all parts of the city, without any decided object. The next day (13th.) the assembly pressed on the king to send away the troops, to permit the Bourgeoisie of Paris to arm for the preservation of order in the city, and offer to send a deputation from their body to tranquillize them; but their propositions were refused. A committee of magistrates and electors of the city are appointed by those bodies to take upon them it's government. The people, now openly joined by the French guards, force the prison of St. Lazare, release all the prisoners, and take a great store of corn, which they carry to the Corn-market. Here they get some arms, and the French guards begin to form & train them. The City-committee determined to raise 48.000. Bourgeoise, or rather to restrain their numbers to 48.000. On the 14th. they send one of their members (Mons. de Corny) to the Hotel des Invalides, to ask arms for their Garde-Bourgeoise. He was followed by, and he found there a great collection of people. The Governor of the Invalids came out and represented the impossibility of his delivering arms without the orders of those from whom he received them. De Corny advised the people then to retire, and retired himself; but the people took possession of the arms. It was remarkable that not only the Invalids themselves made no opposition, but that a body of 5000. foreign troops, within 400. yards, never stirred. M. de Corny and five others were then sent to ask arms of M. de Launay, governor of the Bastile. They found a great collection of people already before the place, and they immediately planted a flag of truce, which was answered by a like flag hoisted on the Parapet. The deputation prevailed on the people to fall back a little, advanced themselves to make their demand of the Governor, and in that instant a discharge from the Bastile killed four persons, of those nearest to the deputies. The deputies retired. I happened to be at the house of M. de Corny when he returned to it, and received from him a narrative of these transactions. On the retirement of the deputies, the people rushed forward & almost in an instant were in possession of a fortification defended by 100. men, of infinite strength, which in other times had stood several regular sieges, and had never been taken. How they forced their entrance has never been explained. They took all the arms, discharged the prisoners, and such of the garrison as were not killed in the first moment of fury, carried the Governor and Lt. Governor to the Place de Grève (the place of public execution) cut off their heads, and sent them thro' the city in triumph to the Palais royal. About the same instant a treacherous correspondence having been discovered in M. de Flesselles, prevot des marchands, they seized him in the Hotel de Ville where he was in the execution of his office, and cut off his head. These events carried imperfectly to Versailles were the subject of two successive deputations from the assembly to the king, to both of which he gave dry and hard answers for nobody had as yet been permitted to inform him truly and fully of what had passed at Paris. But at night the Duke de Liancourt forced his way into the king's bed chamber, and obliged him to hear a full and animated detail of the disasters of the day in Paris. He went to bed fearfully impressed. The decapitation of de Launai worked powerfully thro' the night on the whole aristocratic party, insomuch that, in the morning, those of the greatest influence on the Count d'Artois represented to him the absolute necessity that the king should give up everything to the Assembly. This according with the dispositions of the king, he went about 11. o'clock, accompanied only by his brothers, to the Assembly, & there read to them a speech, in which he asked their interposition to re-establish order. Altho' couched in terms of some caution, yet the manner in which it was delivered made it evident that it was meant as a surrender at discretion. He returned to the Chateau afoot, accompanied by the assembly. They sent off a deputation to quiet Paris, at the head of which was the Marquis de la Fayette who had, the same morning, been named Commandant en chef of the Milice Bourgeoise, and Mons Bailly, former President of the States General, was called for as Prevot des marchands. The demolition of the Bastile was now ordered and begun. A body of the Swiss guards of the regiment of Ventimille, and the city horse guards joined the people. The alarm at Versailles increased. The foreign troops were ordered off instantly. Every minister resigned. The king confirmed Bailly as Prevot des Marchands, wrote to Mr. Neckar to recall him, sent his letter open to the assembly, to be forwarded by them, and invited them to go with him to Paris the next day, to satisfy the city of his dispositions; and that night, and the next morning the Count D'Artois and M. de Montesson a deputy connected with him, Madame de Polignac, Madame de Guiche, and the Count de Vaudreuil, favorites of the queen, the Abbe de Vermont her confessor, the Prince of Conde and Duke of Bourbon fled. The king came to Paris, leaving the queen in consternation for his return. Omitting the less important figures of the procession, the king's carriage was in the center, on each side of it the assembly, in two ranks afoot, at their head the M. de la Fayette, as Commander-in-chief, on horseback, and Bourgeois guards before and behind. About 60.000 citizens of all forms and conditions, armed with the muskets of the Bastile and Invalids, as far as they would go, the rest with pistols, swords, pikes, pruning hooks, scythes &c. lined all the streets thro' which the procession passed, and with the crowds of people in the streets, doors & windows, saluted them everywhere with cries of "vive la nation," but not a single "vive le roy" was heard. The King landed at the Hotel de Ville. There M. Bailly presented and put into his hat the popular cockade, and addressed him. The King being unprepared, and unable to answer, Bailly went to him, gathered from him some scraps of sentences, and made out an answer, which he delivered to the audience as from the king. On their return the popular cries were "vive le roy et la nation." He was conducted by a garde bourgeoise to his palace at Versailles, & thus concluded an amende honorable as no sovereign ever made, and no people ever received.

And here again was lost another precious occasion of sparing to France the crimes and cruelties thro' which she has since passed, and to Europe, & finally America the evils which flowed on them also from this mortal source. The king was now become a passive machine in the hands of the National assembly, and had he been left to himself, he would have willingly acquiesced in whatever they should devise as best for the nation. A wise constitution would have been formed, hereditary in his line, himself placed at it's head, with powers so large as to enable him to do all the good of his station, and so limited as to restrain him from it's abuse. This he would have faithfully administered, and more than this I do not believe he ever wished. But he had a Queen of absolute sway over his weak mind, and timid virtue; and of a character the reverse of his in all points. This angel, as gaudily painted in the rhapsodies of the Rhetor Burke, with some smartness of fancy, but no sound sense was proud, disdainful of restraint, indignant at all obstacles to her will, eager in the pursuit of pleasure, and firm enough to hold to her desires, or perish in their wreck. Her inordinate gambling and dissipations, with those of the Count d'Artois and others of her clique, had been a sensible item in the exhaustion of the treasury, which called into action the reforming hand of the nation; and her opposition to it her inflexible perverseness, and dauntless spirit, led herself to the Guillotine, & drew the king on with her, and plunged the world into crimes & calamities which will forever stain the pages of modern history. I have ever believed that had there been no queen, there would have been no revolution. No force would have been provoked nor exercised. The king would have gone hand in hand with the wisdom of his sounder counsellors, who, guided by the increased lights of the age, wished only, with the same pace, to advance the principles of their social institution. The deed which closed the mortal course of these sovereigns, I shall neither approve nor condemn. I am not prepared to say that the first magistrate of a nation cannot commit treason against his country, or is unamenable to it's punishment: nor yet that where there is no written law, no regulated tribunal, there is not a law in our hearts, and a power in our hands, given for righteous employment in maintaining right, and redressing wrong. Of those who judged the king, many thought him wilfully criminal, many that his existence would keep the nation in perpetual conflict with the horde of kings, who would war against a regeneration which might come home to themselves, and that it were better that one should die than all. I should not have voted with this portion of the legislature. I should have shut up the Queen in a Convent, putting harm out of her power, and placed the king in his station, investing him with limited powers, which I verily believe he would have honestly exercised, according to the measure of his understanding. In this way no void would have been created, courting the usurpation of a military adventurer, nor occasion given for those enormities which demoralized the nations of the world, and destroyed, and is yet to destroy millions and millions of it's inhabitants. There are three epochs in history signalized by the total extinction of national morality. The first was of the successors of Alexander, not omitting himself. The next the successors of the first Cæsar, the third our own age. This was begun by the partition of Poland, followed by that of the treaty of Pilnitz; next the conflagration of Copenhagen; then the enormities of Bonaparte partitioning the earth at his will, and devastating it with fire and sword; now the conspiracy of kings, the successors of Bonaparte, blasphemously calling themselves the Holy Alliance, and treading in the footsteps of their incarcerated leader, not yet indeed usurping the government of other nations avowedly and in detail, but controuling by their armies the forms in which they will permit them to be governed; and reserving in petto the order and extent of the usurpations further meditated. But I will return from a digression, anticipated too in time, into which I have been led by reflection on the criminal passions which refused to the world a favorable occasion of saving it from the afflictions it has since suffered.

M. Necker had reached Basle before he was overtaken by the letter of the king, inviting him back to resume the office he had recently left. He returned immediately, and all the other ministers having resigned, a new administration was named, to wit St. Priest & Montmorin were restored; the Archbishop of Bordeaux was appointed Garde des sceaux; La Tour du Pin Minister of War; La Luzerne Minister of Marine. This last was believed to have been effected by the friendship of Montmorin; for altho' differing in politics, they continued firm in friendship, & Luzerne, altho' not an able man was thought an honest one. And the Prince of Bauvau was taken into the Council.

Seven princes of the blood royal, six ex-ministers, and many of the high Noblesse having fled, and the present ministers, except Luzerne, being all of the popular party, all the functionaries of government moved for the present in perfect harmony.

In the evening of Aug. 4. and on the motion of the Viscount de Noailles brother in law of La Fayette, the assembly abolished all titles of rank, all the abusive privileges of feudalism, the tythes and casuals of the clergy, all provincial privileges, and, in fine, the Feudal regimen generally. To the suppression of tythes the Abbe Sieyes was vehemently opposed; but his learned and logical arguments were unheeded, and his estimation lessened by a contrast of his egoism (for he was beneficed on them) with the generous abandonment of rights by the other members of the assembly. Many days were employed in putting into the form of laws the numerous demolitions of ancient abuses; which done, they proceeded to the preliminary work of a Declaration of rights. There being much concord of sentiment on the elements of this instrument, it was liberally framed, and passed with a very general approbation. They then appointed a Committee for the reduction of a projet of a Constitution, at the head of which was the Archbishop of Bordeaux. I received from him, as Chairman of the Committee a letter of July 20. requesting me to attend and assist at their deliberations; but I excused myself on the obvious considerations that my mission was to the king as Chief Magistrate of the nation, that my duties were limited to the concerns of my own country, and forbade me to intermeddle with the internal transactions of that in which I had been received under a specific character only. Their plan of a constitution was discussed in sections, and so reported from time to time, as agreed to by the Committee. The first respected the general frame of the government; and that this should be formed into three departments, Executive, Legislative and Judiciary was generally agreed. But when they proceeded to subordinate developments, many and various shades of opinion came into conflict, and schism, strongly marked, broke the Patriots into fragments of very discordant principles. The first question Whether there should be a king, met with no open opposition, and it was readily agreed that the government of France should be monarchical & hereditary. Shall the king have a negative on the laws? shall that negative be absolute, or suspensive only? Shall there be two chambers of legislation? or one only? If two, shall one of them be hereditary? or for life? or for a fixed term? and named by the king? or elected by the people? These questions found strong differences of opinion, and produced repulsive combinations among the Patriots. The Aristocracy was cemented by a common principle of preserving the ancient regime, or whatever should be nearest to it. Making this their Polar star, they moved in phalanx, gave preponderance on every question to the minorities of the Patriots, and always to those who advocated the least change. The features of the new constitution were thus assuming a fearful aspect, and great alarm was produced among the honest patriots by these dissensions in their ranks. In this uneasy state of things, I received one day a note from the Marquis de la Fayette, informing me that he should bring a party of six or eight friends to ask a dinner of me the next day. I assured him of their welcome. When they arrived, they were La Fayette himself, Duport, Barnave, Alexander La Meth, Blacon, Mounier, Maubourg, and Dagout. These were leading patriots, of honest but differing opinions sensible of the necessity of effecting a coalition by mutual sacrifices, knowing each other, and not afraid therefore to unbosom themselves mutually. This last was a material principle in the selection. With this view the Marquis had invited the conference and had fixed the time & place inadvertently as to the embarrassment under which it might place me. The cloth being removed and wine set on the table, after the American manner, the Marquis introduced the objects of the conference by summarily reminding them of the state of things in the Assembly, the course which the principles of the constitution were taking, and the inevitable result, unless checked by more concord among the Patriots themselves. He observed that altho' he also had his opinion, he was ready to sacrifice it to that of his brethren of the same cause: but that a common opinion must now be formed, or the Aristocracy would carry everything, and that whatever they should now agree on, he, at the head of the National force, would maintain. The discussions began at the hour of four, and were continued till ten o'clock in the evening; during which time I was a silent witness to a coolness and candor of argument unusual in the conflicts of political opinion; to a logical reasoning, and chaste eloquence, disfigured by no gaudy tinsel of rhetoric or declamation, and truly worthy of being placed in parallel with the finest dialogues of antiquity, as handed to us by Xenophon, by Plato and Cicero. The result was an agreement that the king should have a suspensive veto on the laws, that the legislature should be composed of a single body only, & that to be chosen by the people. This Concordate decided the fate of the constitution. The Patriots all rallied to the principles thus settled, carried every question agreeably to them, and reduced the Aristocracy to insignificance and impotence. But duties of exculpation were now incumbent on me. I waited on Count Montmorin the next morning, and explained to him with truth and candor how it had happened that my house had been made the scene of conferences of such a character. He told me he already knew everything which had passed, that, so far from taking umbrage at the use made of my house on that occasion, he earnestly wished I would habitually assist at such conferences, being sure I should be useful in moderating the warmer spirits, and promoting a wholesome and practicable reformation only. I told him I knew too well the duties I owed to the king, to the nation, and to my own country to take any part in councils concerning their internal government, and that I should persevere with care in the character of a neutral and passive spectator, with wishes only and very sincere ones, that those measures might prevail which would be for the greatest good of the nation. I have no doubt indeed that this conference was previously known and approved by this honest minister, who was in confidence and communication with the patriots, and wished for a reasonable reform of the Constitution.

Here I discontinue my relation of the French revolution. The minuteness with which I have so far given it's details is disproportioned to the general scale of my narrative. But I have thought it justified by the interest which the whole world must take in this revolution. As yet we are but in the first chapter of it's history. The appeal to the rights of man, which had been made in the U S. was taken up by France, first of the European nations. From her the spirit has spread over those of the South. The tyrants of the North have allied indeed against it, but it is irresistible. Their opposition will only multiply it's millions of human victims; their own satellites will catch it, and the condition of man thro' the civilized world will be finally and greatly ameliorated. This is a wonderful instance of great events from small causes. So inscrutable is the arrangement of causes & consequences in this world that a two-penny duty on tea, unjustly imposed in a sequestered part of it, changes the condition of all it's inhabitants. I have been more minute in relating the early transactions of this regeneration because I was in circumstances peculiarly favorable for a knowledge of the truth. Possessing the confidence and intimacy of the leading patriots, & more than all of the Marquis Fayette, their head and Atlas, who had no secrets from me, I learnt with correctness the views & proceedings of that party; while my intercourse with the diplomatic missionaries of Europe at Paris, all of them with the court, and eager in prying into it's councils and proceedings, gave me a knolege of these also. My information was always and immediately committed to writing, in letters to Mr. Jay, and often to my friends, and a recurrence to these letters now insures me against errors of memory.

These opportunities of information ceased at this period, with my retirement from this interesting scene of action. I had been more than a year soliciting leave to go home with a view to place my daughters in the society & care of their friends, and to return for a short time to my station at Paris. But the metamorphosis thro' which our government was then passing from it's Chrysalid to it's Organic form suspended it's action in a great degree; and it was not till the last of August that I received the permission I had asked.—And here I cannot leave this great and good country without expressing my sense of it's preeminence of character among the nations of the earth. A more benevolent people, I have never known, nor greater warmth & devotedness in their select friendships. Their kindness and accommodation to strangers is unparalleled, and the hospitality of Paris is beyond anything I had conceived to be practicable in a large city. Their eminence too in science, the communicative dispositions of their scientific men, the politeness of the general manners, the ease and vivacity of their conversation, give a charm to their society to be found nowhere else. In a comparison of this with other countries we have the proof of primacy, which was given to Themistocles after the battle of Salamis. Every general voted to himself the first reward of valor, and the second to Themistocles. So ask the travelled inhabitant of any nation, In what country on earth would you rather live?—Certainly in my own, where are all my friends, my relations, and the earliest & sweetest affections and recollections of my life. Which would be your second choice? France.

On the 26th. of Sep. I left Paris for Havre, where I was detained by contrary winds until the 8th. of Oct. On that day, and the 9th. I crossed over to Cowes, where I had engaged the *Clermont*, Capt. Colley, to touch for me. She did so, but here again we were detained by contrary winds until the 22d. when we embarked and landed at Norfolk on the 23d. of November. On my way home I passed some days at Eppington in Chesterfield, the residence of my friend and connection, Mr. Eppes, and, while there, I received a letter from the President, Genl. Washington, by express, covering an appointment to be Secretary of State. I received it with real regret. My wish had been to return to Paris, where I had left my household establishment, as if there myself, and to see the end of the Revolution, which, I then thought would be certainly and happily closed in less than a year. I then meant to return home, to withdraw from Political life, into which I had been impressed by the circumstances of the times, to sink into the bosom of my family and friends, and devote myself to studies more congenial to my mind. In my answer of Dec. 15. I expressed these dispositions candidly to the President, and my preference of a return to Paris; but assured him that if it was believed I could be more useful in the administration of the government, I would sacrifice my own inclinations without hesitation, and repair to that destination; this I left to his decision. I arrived at Monticello on the 23d. of Dec. where I received a second letter from the President, expressing his continued wish that I should take my station there, but leaving me still at liberty to continue in my former office, if I could not reconcile myself to that now proposed. This silenced my reluctance, and I accepted the new appointment.

In the interval of my stay at home my eldest daughter had been happily married to the eldest son of the Tuckahoe branch of Randolphs, a young gentleman of genius, science and honorable mind, who afterwards filled a dignified station in the General Government, & the most dignified in his own State. I left Monticello on the 1st of March 1790. for New York. At Philadelphia I called on the venerable and beloved Franklin. He was then on the bed of sickness from which he never rose. My recent return from a country in which he had left so many friends, and the perilous convulsions to which they had been exposed, revived all his anxieties to know what part they had taken, what had been their course, and what their fate. He went over all in succession, with a rapidity and animation almost too much for his strength. When all his inquiries were satisfied, and a pause took place, I told him I had learnt with much pleasure that, since his return to America, he had been occupied in preparing for the world the history of his own life. I cannot say much of that, said he; but I will give you a sample of what I shall leave: and he directed his little grandson (William Bache) who was standing by the bedside, to hand him a paper from the table to which he pointed. He did so; and the Doctr. putting it into my hands, desired me to take it and read it at my leisure. It was about a quire of folio paper, written in a large and running hand very like his own. I looked into it slightly, then shut it and said I would accept his permission to read it and would carefully return it. He said, "no, keep it." Not certain of his meaning, I again looked into it, folded it for my pocket, and said again, I would certainly return it. "No," said he, "keep it." I put it into my pocket, and shortly after took leave of him. He died on the 17th. of the ensuing month of April; and as I understood that he had bequeathed all his papers to his grandson William Temple Franklin, I immediately wrote to Mr. Franklin to inform him I possessed this paper, which I should consider as his property, and would deliver to his order. He came on immediately to New York, called on me for it, and I delivered it to him. As he put it into his pocket, he said carelessly he had either the original, or another copy of it, I do not recollect which. This last expression struck my attention forcibly, and for the first time suggested to me the thought that Dr. Franklin had meant it as a confidential deposit in my hands, and that I had done wrong in parting from it. I have not yet seen the collection he published of Dr. Franklin's works, and therefore know not if this is among them. I have been told it is not. It contained a narrative of the negotiations between Dr. Franklin and the British Ministry, when he was endeavoring to prevent the contest of arms which followed. The negotiation was brought about by the intervention of Ld. Howe and his sister, who, I believe, was called Lady Howe, but I may misremember her title. Ld. Howe seems to have been friendly to America, and exceedingly anxious to prevent a rupture. His intimacy with Dr. Franklin, and his position with the Ministry induced him to undertake a mediation between them; in which his sister seemed to have been associated. They carried from one to the other, backwards and forwards, the several propositions and answers which past, and seconded with their own intercessions the importance of mutual sacrifices to preserve the peace & connection of the two countries. I remember that Ld. North's answers were dry, unyielding, in the spirit of unconditional submission, and betrayed an absolute indifference to the occurrence of a rupture; and he said to the mediators distinctly, at last that "a rebellion was not to be deprecated on the part of Great Britain; that the confiscations it would produce would provide for many of their friends." This expression was reported by the mediators to Dr. Franklin, and indicated so cool and calculated a purpose in the Ministry, as to render compromise hopeless, and the negotiation was discontinued. If this is not among the papers published, we ask what has become of it? I delivered it with my own hands into those of Temple Franklin. It certainly established views so atrocious in the British government that it's suppression would to them be worth a great price. But could the grandson of Dr. Franklin be in such degree an accomplice in the parricide of the memory of his immortal grandfather? The suspension for more than 20 years of the general publication bequeathed and confided to him, produced for awhile hard suspicions against him: and if at last all are not published, a part of these suspicions may remain with some.

I arrived at New York on the 21st. of Mar. where Congress was in session.

. So far July 29. 21.

A SUMMARY VIEW OF THE RIGHTS OF BRITISH AMERICA

Resolved, that it be an instruction to the said deputies, when assembled in general congress with the deputies from the other states of British America, to propose to the said congress that an humble and dutiful address be presented to his majesty, begging leave to lay before him, as chief magistrate of the British empire, the united complaints of his majesty's subjects in America; complaints which are excited by many unwarrantable encroachments and usurpations, attempted to be made by the legislature of one part of the empire, upon those rights which God and the laws have given equally and independently to all. To represent to his majesty that these his states have often individually made humble application to his imperial throne to obtain, through its intervention, some redress of their injured rights, to none of which was ever even an answer condescended; humbly to hope that this their joint address, penned in the language of truth, and divested of those expressions of servility which would persuade his majesty that we are asking favours, and not rights, shall obtain from his majesty a more respectful acceptance. And this his majesty will think we have reason to expect when he reflects that he is no more than the chief officer of the people, appointed by the laws, and circumscribed with definite powers, to assist in working the great machine of government, erected for their use, and consequently subject to their superintendance. And in order that these our rights, as well as the invasions of them, may be laid more fully before his majesty, to take a view of them from the origin and first settlement of these countries.

To remind him that our ancestors, before their emigration to America, were the free inhabitants of the British dominions in Europe, and possessed a right which nature has given to all men, of departing from the country in which chance, not choice, has placed them, of going in quest of new habitations, and of there establishing new societies, under such laws and regulations as to them shall seem most likely to promote public happiness. That their Saxon ancestors had, under this universal law, in like manner left their native wilds and woods in the north of Europe, had possessed themselves of the island of Britain, then less charged with inhabitants, and had established there that system of laws which has so long been the glory and protection of that country. Nor was ever any claim of superiority or dependence asserted over them by that mother country from which they had migrated; and were such a claim made, it is believed that his majesty's subjects in Great Britain have too firm a feeling of the rights derived to them from their ancestors, to bow down the sovereignty of their state before such visionary pretensions. And it is thought that no circumstance has occurred to distinguish materially the British from the Saxon emigration. America was conquered, and her settlements made, and firmly established, at the expence of individuals, and not of the British public. Their own blood was spilt in acquiring lands for their settlement, their own fortunes expended in making that settlement effectual; for themselves they fought, for themselves they conquered, and for themselves alone they have right to hold. No shilling was ever issued from the public treasures of his majesty, or his ancestors, for their assistance, till of very late times, after the colonies had become established on a firm and permanent footing. That then, indeed, having become valuable to Great Britain for her commercial purposes, his parliament was pleased to lend them assistance against an enemy, who would fain have drawn to herself the benefits of their commerce, to the great aggrandizement of herself, and danger of Great Britain. Such assistance, and in such circumstances, they had often before given to other allied states, with whom they carry on a commercial intercourse; yet these states never supposed, that by calling in her aid, they thereby submitted themselves to her sovereignty. Had such terms been proposed, they would have rejected them with disdain, and trusted for better to the moderation of their enemies, or to a vigorous exertion of their own force. We do not, however, mean to under-rate those aids, which to us were doubtless valuable, on whatever principles granted; but we would shew that they cannot give a title to that authority which the British parliament would arrogate over us, and that they may amply be repaid by our giving to the inhabitants of Great Britain such exclusive privileges in trade as may be advantageous to them, and at the same time not too restrictive to ourselves. That settlements having been thus effected in the wilds of America, the emigrants thought proper to adopt that system of laws under which they had hitherto lived in the mother country, and to continue their union with her by submitting themselves to the same common sovereign, who was thereby made the central link connecting the several parts of the empire thus newly multiplied.

But that not long were they permitted, however far they thought themselves removed from the hand of oppression, to hold undisturbed the rights thus acquired, at the hazard of their lives, and loss of their fortunes. A family of princes was then on the British throne, whose treasonable crimes against their people brought on them afterwards the exertion of those sacred and sovereign rights of punishment reserved in the hands of the people for cases of extreme necessity, and judged by the constitution unsafe to be delegated to any other judicature. While every day brought forth some new and unjustifiable exertion of power over their subjects on that side the water, it was not to be expected that those here, much less able at that time to oppose the designs of despotism, should be exempted from injury.

Accordingly that country, which had been acquired by the lives, the labours, and the fortunes, of individual adventurers, was by these princes, at several times, parcelled out and distributed among the favourites and followers of their fortunes*, and, by an assumed right of the crown alone, was erected into distinct and independent governments; a measure which it is believed his majesty's prudence and understanding would prevent him from imitating at this day, as no exercise of such a power, of dividing and dismembering a country, has ever occurred in his majesty's realm of England, though now of very antient standing; nor could it be justified or acquiesced under there, or in any other part of his majesty's empire.

That the exercise of a free trade with all parts of the world, possessed by the American colonists, as of natural right, and which no law of their own had taken away or abridged, was next the object of unjust encroachment. Some of the colonies having thought proper to continue the administration of their government in the name and under the authority of his majesty king Charles the first, whom, notwithstanding his late deposition by the commonwealth of England, they continued in the sovereignty of their state; the parliament for the commonwealth took the same in high offence, and assumed upon themselves the power of prohibiting their trade with all other parts of the world, except the island of Great Britain. This arbitrary act, however, they soon recalled, and by solemn treaty, entered into on the 12th day of March, 1651, between the said commonwealth by their commissioners, and the colony of Virginia by their house of burgesses, it was expressly stipulated, by the 8th article of the said treaty, that they should have "free trade as the people of England do enjoy to all places and with all nations, according to the laws of that commonwealth." But that, upon the restoration of his majesty king Charles the second, their rights of free commerce fell once more a victim to arbitrary power; and by several acts† of his reign, as well as of some of his successors, the trade of the colonies was laid under such restrictions, as shew what hopes they might form from the justice of a British parliament, were its uncontrouled power admitted over these states. History has informed us that bodies of men, as well as individuals, are susceptible of the spirit of tyranny. A view of these acts of parliament for regulation, as it has been

* In 1625. Nova Scotia was granted by James I. to Sir Wm. Alexander. In 1632. Maryland was granted by Charles I. to Lord Baltimore. In 1664. New York was granted by Charles II. to the D. of York: so also was New Jersey, which the D. of York conveied again to Lord Berkeley & Sir Geo. Cartinet. So also were the Delaware counties which the same Duke conveied again to Wm. Penn in 1665. the country including North & South Carolina, Georgia & the Floridas was granted by Charles II. to the E. of Clarendon, D. of Albemarle, E. of Craven, Lord Berkeley, Lord Ashley, Sir George Carteret, Sir John Coleton & Sir Wm. Berkeley. in 1681. Pennsylvania was granted by Charles II. to Wm. Penn.

† 12. c. 2. c. 18. 15. c. 2. c. II. 25. c. 2. c. 7. 7. 8. W. M. c. 22. II. W. 3. 4. Anne. 6. G. 2. c. 13.

affectedly called, of the American trade, if all other evidence were removed out of the case, would undeniably evince the truth of this observation. Besides the duties they impose on our articles of export and import, they prohibit our going to any markets northward of Cape Finesterre, in the kingdom of Spain, for the sale of commodities which Great Britain will not take from us, and for the purchase of others, with which she cannot supply us, and that for no other than the arbitrary purposes of purchasing for themselves, by a sacrifice of our rights and interests, certain privileges in their commerce with an allied state, who in confidence that their exclusive trade with America will be continued, while the principles and power of the British parliament be the same, have indulged themselves in every exorbitance which their avarice could dictate, or our necessities extort; have raised their commodities, called for in America, to the double and treble of what they sold for before such exclusive privileges were given them, and of what better commodities of the same kind would cost us elsewhere, and at the same time give us much less for what we carry thither than might be had at more convenient ports. That these acts prohibit us from carrying in quest of other purchasers the surplus of our tobaccoes remaining after the consumption of Great Britain is supplied; so that we must leave them with the British merchant for whatever he will please to allow us, to be by him reshipped to foreign markets, where he will reap the benefits of making sale of them for full value. That to heighten still the idea of parliamentary justice, and to shew with what moderation they are like to exercise power, where themselves are to feel no part of its weight, we take leave to mention to his majesty certain other acts of British parliament, by which they would prohibit us from manufacturing for our own use the articles we raise on our own lands with our own labour. By an act* passed in the 5th Year of the reign of his late majesty king George the second, an American subject is forbidden to make a hat for himself of the fur which he has taken perhaps on his own soil; an instance of despotism to which no parallel can be produced in the most arbitrary ages of British history. By one other act†, passed in the 23d year of the same reign, the iron which we make we are forbidden to manufacture, and heavy as that article is, and necessary in every branch of husbandry, besides commission and insurance, we are to pay freight for it to Great Britain, and freight for it back again, for the purpose of supporting not men, but machines, in the island of Great Britain. In the same spirit of equal and impartial legislation is to be viewed the act of parliament‡, passed in the 5th year of the same reign, by which American lands are made subject to the demands of British creditors, while their own lands were

* 5. G. 2.

† 23. G. 2. c. 29.

‡ 5. G. 270.

still continued unanswerable for their debts; from which one of these conclusions must necessarily follow, either that justice is not the same in America as in Britain, or else that the British parliament pay less regard to it here than there. But that we do not point out to his majesty the injustice of these acts, with intent to rest on that principle the cause of their nullity; but to shew that experience confirms the propriety of those political principles which exempt us from the jurisdiction of the British parliament. The true ground on which we declare these acts void is, that the British parliament has no right to exercise authority over us.

That these exercises of usurped power have not been confined to instances alone, in which themselves were interested, but they have also intermeddled with the regulation of the internal affairs of the colonies. The act of the 9th of Anne for establishing a post office in America seems to have had little connection with British convenience, except that of accommodating his majesty's ministers and favourites with the sale of a lucrative and easy office.

That thus have we hastened through the reigns which preceded his majesty's, during which the violations of our right were less alarming, because repeated at more distant intervals than that rapid and bold succession of injuries which is likely to distinguish the present from all other periods of American story. Scarcely have our minds been able to emerge from the astonishment into which one stroke of parliamentary thunder has involved us, before another more heavy, and more alarming, is fallen on us. Single acts of tyranny may be ascribed to the accidental opinion of a day; but a series of oppressions, begun at a distinguished period, and pursued unalterably through every change of ministers, too plainly prove a deliberate and systematical plan of reducing us to slavery.

That the act* passed in the 4th year of his majesty's reign, intitled "An act for granting certain duties in the British colonies and plantations in America, &c."

One other act†, passed in the 5th year of his reign, intitled "An act for granting and applying certain stamp duties and other duties in the British colonies and plantations in America, &c."

One other act‡, passed in the 6th year of his reign, intitled "An act for the better securing the dependency of his majesty's dominions in America upon the crown and parliament of Great Britain;" and one other act§, passed in the 7th year of his reign, intitled "An act for granting duties on paper, tea, &c." form that connected chain of parliamentary usurpation, which has already been the subject of frequent applications to his majesty, and the houses of lords and commons of

* 4. G. 3. c. 15.

† 5. G. 3. c. 12.

‡ 6. G. 3. c. 12.

§ 7. G. 3.

Great Britain; and no answers having yet been condescended to any of these, we shall not trouble his majesty with a repetition of the matters they contained.

But that one other act*, passed in the same 7th year of his reign, having been a peculiar attempt, must ever require peculiar mention; it is intitled "An act for suspending the legislature of New York." One free and independent legislature hereby takes upon itself to suspend the powers of another, free and independent as itself; thus exhibiting a phoenomenon unknown in nature, the creator and creature of its own power. Not only the principles of common sense, but the feelings of human nature, must be surrendered up before his majesty's subjects here can be persuaded to believe that they hold their political existence at the will of a British parliament. Shall these governments be dissolved, their property annihilated, and their people reduced to a state of nature, at the imperious breath of a body of men, whom they never saw, in whom they never confided, and over whom they have no powers of punishment or removal, let their crimes against the American public be ever so great? Can any one reason be assigned why 160,000 electors in the island of Great Britain should give law to four millions in the states of America, every individual of whom is equal to every individual of them, in virtue, in understanding, and in bodily strength? Were this to be admitted, instead of being a free people, as we have hitherto supposed, and mean to continue ourselves, we should suddenly be found the slaves, not of one, but of 160,000 tyrants, distinguished too from all others by this singular circumstance, that they are removed from the reach of fear, the only restraining motive which may withhold the hand of a tyrant.

That by "an act† to discontinue in such manner and for such time as are therein mentioned the landing and discharging, lading or shipping, of goods, wares, and merchandize, at the town and within the harbour of Boston, in the province of Massachusetts Bay, in North America," which was passed at the last session of British parliament; a large and populous town, whose trade was their sole subsistence, was deprived of that trade, and involved in utter ruin. Let us for a while suppose the question of right suspended, in order to examine this act on principles of justice: An act of parliament had been passed imposing duties on teas, to be paid in America, against which act the Americans had protested as inauthoritative. The East India company, who till that time had never sent a pound of tea to America on their own account, step forth on that occasion the assertors of parliamentary right, and send hither many ship loads of that obnoxious commodity. The masters of their several vessels, however, on their arrival in America, wisely attended to admonition, and returned with their cargoes. In the province of Massachusets

* 7. G. 3. c. 59.

† 14. G. 3.

alone the remonstrances of the people were disregarded, and a compliance, after being many days waited for, was flatly refused. Whether in this the master of the vessel was governed by his obstinancy, or his instructions, let those who know, say. There are extraordinary situations which require extraordinary interposition. An exasperated people, who feel that they possess power, are not easily restrained within limits strictly regular. A number of them assembled in the town of Boston, threw the tea into the ocean, and dispersed without doing any other act of violence. If in this they did wrong, they were known and were amenable to the laws of the land, against which it could not be objected that they had ever, in any instance, been obstructed or diverted from their regular course in favour of popular offenders. They should therefore not have been distrusted on this occasion. But that ill fated colony had formerly been bold in their enmities against the house of Stuart, and were now devoted to ruin by that unseen hand which governs the momentous affairs of this great empire. On the partial representations of a few worthless ministerial dependents, whose constant office it has been to keep that government embroiled, and who, by their treacheries, hope to obtain the dignity of the British knighthood*, without calling for a party accused, without asking a proof, without attempting a distinction between the guilty and the innocent, the whole of that antient and wealthy town is in a moment reduced from opulence to beggary. Men who had spent their lives in extending the British commerce, who had invested in that place the wealth their honest endeavours had merited, found themselves and their families thrown at once on the world for subsistence by its charities. Not the hundredth part of the inhabitants of that town had been concerned in the act complained of; many of them were in Great Britain and in other parts beyond sea; yet all were involved in one indiscriminate ruin, by a new executive power, unheard of till then, that of a British parliament. A property, of the value of many millions of money, was sacrificed to revenge, not repay, the loss of a few thousands. This is administering justice with a heavy hand indeed! and when is this tempest to be arrested in its course? Two wharfs are to be opened again when his majesty shall think proper. The residue which lined the extensive shores of the bay of Boston are forever interdicted the exercise of commerce. This little exception seems to have been thrown in for no other purpose than that of setting a precedent for investing his majesty with legislative powers. If the pulse of his people shall beat calmly under this experiment, another and another will be tried, till the measure of despotism be filled up. It would be an insult on common sense to pretend that this exception was made in order to restore its commerce to that great town. The trade which cannot be received at two wharfs alone must of necessity be transferred to some other place; to which it will soon

* Alluding to the knighting of Francis Barnard

be followed by that of the two wharfs. Considered in this light, it would be an insolent and cruel mockery at the annihilation of the town of Boston.

By the act* for the suppression of riots and tumults in the town of Boston, passed also in the last session of parliament, a murder committed there is, if the governor pleases, to be tried in the court of King's Bench, in the island of Great Britain, by a jury of Middlesex. The witnesses, too, on receipt of such a sum as the governor shall think it reasonable for them to expend, are to enter into recognizance to appear at the trial. This is, in other words, taxing them to the amount of their recognizance, and that amount may be whatever a governor pleases; for who does his majesty think can be prevailed on to cross the Atlantic for the sole purpose of bearing evidence to a fact? His expences are to be borne, indeed, as they shall be estimated by a governor; but who are to feed the wife and children whom he leaves behind, and who have had no other subsistence but his daily labour? Those epidemical disorders, too, so terrible in a foreign climate, is the cure of them to be estimated among the articles of expence, and their danger to be warded off by the almighty power of parliament? And the wretched criminal, if he happen to have offended on the American side, stripped of his privilege of trial by peers of his vicinage, removed from the place where alone full evidence could be obtained, without money, without counsel, without friends, without exculpatory proof, is tried before judges predetermined to condemn. The cowards who would suffer a countryman to be torn from the bowels of their society, in order to be thus offered a sacrifice to parliamentary tyranny, would merit that everlasting infamy now fixed on the authors of the act! A clause† for a similar purpose had been introduced into an act, passed in the 12th year of his majesty's reign, intitled "An act for the better securing and preserving his majesty's dockyards, magazines, ships, ammunition, and stores;" against which, as meriting the same censures, the several colonies have already protested.

That these are the acts of power, assumed by a body of men, foreign to our constitutions, and unacknowledged by our laws, against which we do, on behalf of the inhabitants of British America, enter this our solemn and determined protest; and we do earnestly entreat his majesty, as yet the only mediatory power between the several states of the British empire, to recommend to his parliament of Great Britain the total revocation of these acts, which, however nugatory they be, may yet prove the cause of further discontents and jealousies among us.

That we next proceed to consider the conduct of his majesty, as holding the executive powers of the laws of these states, and mark out his deviations from the line of duty: By the constitution of Great Britain, as well as of the several

* 14. G. 3.

† 12. G. 3. c. 24.

American states, his majesty possesses the power of refusing to pass into a law any bill which has already passed the other two branches of legislature. His majesty, however, and his ancestors, conscious of the impropriety of opposing their single opinion to the united wisdom of two houses of parliament, while their proceedings were unbiassed by interested principles, for several ages past have modestly declined the exercise of this power in that part of his empire called Great Britain. But by change of circumstances, other principles than those of justice simply have obtained an influence on their determinations; the addition of new states to the British empire has produced an addition of new, and sometimes opposite interests. It is now, therefore, the great office of his majesty, to resume the exercise of his negative power, and to prevent the passage of laws by any one legislature of the empire, which might bear injuriously on the rights and interests of another. Yet this will not excuse the wanton exercise of this power which we have seen his majesty practise on the laws of the American legislatures. For the most trifling reasons, and sometimes for no conceivable reason at all, his majesty has rejected laws of the most salutary tendency. The abolition of domestic slavery is the great object of desire in those colonies, where it was unhappily introduced in their infant state. But previous to the enfranchisement of the slaves we have, it is necessary to exclude all further importations from Africa; yet our repeated attempts to effect this by prohibitions, and by imposing duties which might amount to a prohibition, have been hitherto defeated by his majesty's negative: Thus preferring the immediate advantages of a few British corsairs to the lasting interests of the American states, and to the rights of human nature, deeply wounded by this infamous practice. Nay, the single interposition of an interested individual against a law was scarcely ever known to fail of success, though in the opposite scale were placed the interests of a whole country. That this is so shameful an abuse of a power trusted with his majesty for other purposes, as if not reformed, would call for some legal restrictions.

With equal inattention to the necessities of his people here has his majesty permitted our laws to lie neglected in England for years, neither confirming them by his assent, nor annulling them by his negative; so that such of them as have no suspending clause we hold on the most precarious of all tenures, his majesty's will, and such of them as suspend themselves till his majesty's assent be obtained, we have feared, might be called into existence at some future and distant period, when time, and change of circumstances, shall have rendered them destructive to his people here. And to render this grievance still more oppressive, his majesty by his instructions has laid his governors under such restrictions that they can pass no law of any moment unless it have such suspending clause; so that, however immediate may be the call for legislative interposition, the law cannot be executed till it has twice crossed the atlantic, by which time the evil may have spent its whole force.

But in what terms, reconcileable to majesty, and at the same time to truth, shall we speak of a late instruction to the governor of the colony of Virginia, by which he is forbidden to assent to any law for the division of a county, unless the new county will consent to have no representative in assembly? That colony has as yet fixed no boundary to the westward. Their western counties, therefore, are of indefinite extent; some of them are actually seated many hundred miles from their eastern limits. Is it possible, then, that his majesty can have bestowed a single thought on the situation of those people, who, in order to obtain justice for injuries, however great or small, must, by the laws of that colony, attend their county court, at such a distance, with all their witnesses, monthly, till their litigation be determined? Or does his majesty seriously wish, and publish it to the world, that his subjects should give up the glorious right of representation, with all the benefits derived from that, and submit themselves the absolute slaves of his sovereign will? Or is it rather meant to confine the legislative body to their present numbers, that they may be the cheaper bargain whenever they shall become worth a purchase.

One of the articles of impeachment against Tresilian, and the other judges of Westminister Hall, in the reign of Richard the second, for which they suffered death, as traitors to their country, was, that they had advised the king that he might dissolve his parliament at any time; and succeeding kings have adopted the opinion of these unjust judges. Since the reign of the Second William, however, under whom the British constitution was settled on its free and antient principles, neither his majesty, nor his ancestors, have exercised such a power of dissolution in the island of Great Britain; and when his majesty was petitioned, by the united voice of his people there, to dissolve the present parliament, who had become obnoxious to them, his ministers were heard to declare, in open parliament, that his majesty possessed no such power by the constitution.* But how different their language and his practice here! To declare, as their duty required, the known rights of their country, to oppose the usurpations of every foreign judicature, to disregard the imperious mandates of a minister or governor, have been the avowed causes of dissolving houses of representatives in America. But if such powers be really vested in his majesty, can he suppose they are there placed to awe the members from such purposes as these? When the representative body have lost the confidence of their constituents, when they have notoriously made sale of their most valuable rights, when they have assumed to themselves

* Since this period the king has several times dissolved the parliament a few weeks before its expiration, merely as an assertion of the right.

powers which the people never put into their hands, then indeed their continuing in office becomes dangerous to the state, and calls for an exercise of the power of dissolution. Such being the causes for which the representative body should, and should not, be dissolved, will it not appear strange to an unbiassed observer, that that of Great Britain was not dissolved, while those of the colonies have repeatedly incurred that sentence?

But your majesty, or your governors, have carried this power beyond every limit known, or provided for, by the laws: After dissolving one house of representatives, they have refused to call another, so that, for a great length of time, the legislature provided by the laws has been out of existence. From the nature of things, every society must at all times possess within itself the sovereign powers of legislation. The feelings of human nature revolt against the supposition of a state so situated as that it may not in any emergency provide against dangers which perhaps threaten immediate ruin. While those bodies are in existence to whom the people have delegated the powers of legislation, they alone possess and may exercise those powers; but when they are dissolved by the lopping off one or more of their branches, the power reverts to the people, who may exercise it to unlimited extent, either assembling together in person, sending deputies, or in any other way they may think proper*. We forbear to trace consequences further; the dangers are conspicuous with which this practice is replete.

That we shall at this time also take notice of an error in the nature of our land holdings, which crept in at a very early period of our settlement. The introduction of the feudal tenures into the kingdom of England, though antient, is well enough understood to set this matter in a proper light. In the earlier ages of the Saxon settlement feudal holdings were certainly altogether unknown; and very few, if any, had been introduced at the time of the Norman conquest. Our Saxon ancestors held their lands, as they did their personal property, in absolute dominion, disencumbered with any superior, answering nearly to the nature of those possessions which the feudalists term allodial. William, the Norman, first introduced that system generally. The lands which had belonged to those who fell in the battle of Hastings, and in the subsequent insurrections of his reign, formed a considerable proportion of the lands of the whole kingdom. These he granted out, subject to feudal duties, as did he also those of a great number of his new subjects, who, by persuasions or threats, were induced to surrender them for that purpose. But still much was left in the hands of his Saxon subjects; held of no superior, and not subject to feudal conditions. These, therefore, by express

* Insert: "and the frame of government thus dissolved, should the people take upon them to lay the throne of your majesty prostrate, or to discontinue their connection with the British empire, none will be so bold as to decide against the right or the efficacy of such avulsion."

laws, enacted to render uniform the system of military defence, were made liable to the same military duties as if they had been feuds; and the Norman lawyers soon found means to saddle them also with all the other feudal burthens. But still they had not been surrendered to the king, they were not derived from his grant, and therefore they were not holden of him. A general principle, indeed, was introduced, that "all lands in England were held either mediately or immediately of the crown," but this was borrowed from those holdings, which were truly feudal, and only applied to others for the purposes of illustration. Feudal holdings were therefore but exceptions out of the Saxon laws of possession, under which all lands were held in absolute right. These, therefore, still form the basis, or ground-work, of the common law, to prevail wheresoever the exceptions have not taken place. America was not conquered by William the Norman, nor its lands surrendered to him, or any of his successors. Possessions there are undoubtedly of the allodial nature. Our ancestors, however, who migrated hither, were laborers, not lawyers. The fictitious principle that all lands belong originally to the king, they were early persuaded to believe real; and accordingly took grants of their own lands from the crown. And while the crown continued to grant for small sums, and on reasonable rents; there was no inducement to arrest the error, and lay it open to public view. But his majesty has lately taken on him to advance the terms of purchase, and of holding to the double of what they were; by which means the acquisition of lands being rendered difficult, the population of our country is likely to be checked. It is time, therefore, for us to lay this matter before his majesty, and to declare that he has no right to grant lands of himself. From the nature and purpose of civil institutions, all the lands within the limits which any particular society has circumscribed around itself are assumed by that society, and subject to their allotment only. This may be done by themselves, assembled collectively, or by their legislature, to whom they may have delegated sovereign authority; and if they are alloted in neither of these ways, each individual of the society may appropriate to himself such lands as he finds vacant, and occupancy will give him title.

That in order to enforce the arbitrary measures before complained of, his majesty has from time to time sent among us large bodies of armed forces, not made up of the people here, nor raised by the authority of our laws: Did his majesty possess such a right as this, it might swallow up all our other rights whenever he should think proper. But his majesty has no right to land a single armed man on our shores, and those whom he sends here are liable to our laws made for the suppression and punishment of riots, routs, and unlawful assemblies; or are hostile bodies, invading us in defiance of law. When in the course of the late war it became expedient that a body of Hanoverian troops should be brought over for the defence of Great Britain, his majesty's grandfather, our late sovereign, did not pretend to introduce them under any authority he possessed. Such a measure would have given just alarm to his subjects in Great Britain, whose liberties would not be safe if armed men of another country, and of another spirit, might be brought into the realm at any time without the consent of their legislature. He therefore applied to parliament, who passed an act for that purpose, limiting the number to be brought in and the time they were to continue. In like manner is his majesty restrained in every part of the empire. He possesses, indeed, the executive power of the laws in every state; but they are the laws of the particular state which he is to administer within that state, and not those of any one within the limits of another. Every state must judge for itself the number of armed men which they may safely trust among them, of whom they are to consist, and under what restrictions they shall be laid.

To render these proceedings still more criminal against our laws, instead of subjecting the military to the civil powers, his majesty has expressly made the civil subordinate to the military. But can his majesty thus put down all law under his feet? Can he erect a power superior to that which erected himself? He has done it indeed by force; but let him remember that force cannot give right.

That these are our grievances which we have thus laid before his majesty, with that freedom of language and sentiment which becomes a free people claiming their rights, as derived from the laws of nature, and not as the gift of their chief magistrate: Let those flatter who fear; it is not an American art. To give praise which is not due might be well from the venal, but would ill beseem those who are asserting the rights of human nature. They know, and will therefore say, that kings are the servants, not the proprietors of the people. Open your breast, sire, to liberal and expanded thought. Let not the name of George the third be a blot in the page of history. You are surrounded by British counsellors, but remember that they are parties. You have no ministers for American affairs, because you have none taken from among us, nor amenable to the laws on which they are to give you advice. It behoves you, therefore, to think and to act for yourself and your people. The great principles of right and wrong are legible to every reader; to pursue them requires not the aid of many counsellors. The whole art of government consists in the art of being honest. Only aim to do your duty, and mankind will give you credit where you fail. No longer persevere in sacrificing the rights of one part of the empire to the inordinate desires of another; but deal out to all equal and impartial right. Let no act be passed by any one legislature which may infringe on the rights and liberties of another. This is the important post in which fortune has placed you, holding the balance of a great, if a well poised empire. This, sire, is the advice of your great American council, on the observance of which may perhaps depend your felicity and future fame, and the preservation of that harmony which alone can continue both to Great Britain and America the reciprocal advantages of their connection. It is neither our wish, nor our interest, to separate from her. We are willing, on our part, to sacrifice every thing which reason can ask to the restoration of that tranquillity for which all must wish. On their part, let them be ready to establish union on a generous plan. Let them name their terms, but let them be just. Accept of every commercial preference it is in our power to give for such things as we can raise for their use, or they make for ours. But let them not think to exclude us from going to other markets to dispose of those commodities which they cannot use, or to supply those wants which they cannot supply. Still less let it be proposed that our properties within our own territories shall be taxed or regulated by any power on earth but our own. The God who gave us life gave us liberty at the same time; the hand of force may destroy, but cannot disjoin them. This, sire, is our last, our determined resolution; and that you will be pleased to interpose with that efficacy which your earnest endeavours may ensure to procure redress of these our great grievances, to quiet the minds of your subjects in British America, against any apprehensions of future encroachment, to establish fraternal love and harmony through the whole empire, and that these may continue to the latest ages of time, is the fervent prayer of all British America!

THE DECLARATION OF INDEPENDENCE

IN CONGRESS, JULY 4, 1776.

THE UNANIMOUS DECLARATION OF THE THIRTEEN UNITED STATES OF AMERICA,

When in the Course of human events, it becomes necessary for one people to dissolve the political bands which have connected them with another, and to assume among the powers of the earth, the separate and equal station to which the Laws of Nature and of Nature's God entitle them, a decent respect to the opinions of mankind requires that they should declare the causes which impel them to the separation.

We hold these truths to be self-evident, that all men are created equal, that they are endowed by their Creator with certain unalienable Rights, that among these are Life, Liberty and the pursuit of Happiness. That to secure these rights, Governments are instituted among Men, deriving their just powers from the consent of the governed, That whenever any Form of Government becomes destructive of these ends, it is the Right of the People to alter or to abolish it, and to institute new Government, laying its foundation on such principles and organizing its powers in such form, as to them shall seem most likely to effect their Safety and Happiness. Prudence, indeed, will dictate that Governments long established should not be changed for light and transient causes; and accordingly all experience hath shewn, that mankind are more disposed to suffer, while evils are sufferable, than to right themselves by abolishing the forms to which they are accustomed. But when a long train of abuses and usurpations, pursuing invariably the same Object evinces a design to reduce them under absolute Despotism, it is their right, it is their duty, to throw off such Government, and to provide new Guards for their future security. Such has been the patient sufferance of these Colonies; and such is now the necessity which constrains them to alter their former Systems of Government. The history of the present King of Great Britain is a history of repeated injuries and usurpations, all having in direct object the establishment of an absolute Tyranny over these States. To prove this, let Facts be submitted to a candid world.

He has refused his Assent to Laws, the most wholesome and necessary for the public good.

He has forbidden his Governors to pass Laws of immediate and pressing importance, unless suspended in their operation till his Assent should be obtained; and when so suspended, he has utterly neglected to attend to them.

He has refused to pass other Laws for the accommodation of large districts of people, unless those people would relinquish the right of Representation in the Legislature, a right inestimable to them and formidable to tyrants only.

He has called together legislative bodies at places unusual, uncomfortable, and distant from the depository of their public Records, for the sole purpose of fatiguing them into compliance with his measures.

He has dissolved Representative Houses repeatedly, for opposing with manly firmness his invasions on the rights of the people.

He has refused for a long time, after such dissolutions, to cause others to be elected; whereby the Legislative powers, incapable of Annihilation, have returned to the People at large for their exercise; the State remaining in the mean time exposed to all the dangers of invasion from without, and convulsions within.

He has endeavoured to prevent the population of these States; for that purpose obstructing the Laws for Naturalization of Foreigners; refusing to pass others to encourage their migrations hither, and raising the conditions of new Appropriations of Lands.

He has obstructed the Administration of Justice, by refusing his Assent to Laws for establishing Judiciary powers.

He has made Judges dependent on his Will alone, for the tenure of their offices, and the amount and payment of their salaries.

He has erected a multitude of New Offices, and sent hither swarms of Officers to harrass our people, and eat out their substance.

He has kept among us, in times of peace, Standing Armies without the Consent of our legislatures.

He has affected to render the Military independent of and superior to the Civil power.

He has combined with others to subject us to a jurisdiction foreign to our constitution, and unacknowledged by our laws; giving his Assent to their Acts of pretended Legislation:

For Quartering large bodies of armed troops among us:

For protecting them, by a mock Trial, from punishment for any Murders which they should commit on the Inhabitants of these States:

For cutting off our Trade with all parts of the world:

For imposing Taxes on us without our Consent:

For depriving us in many cases, of the benefits of Trial by Jury:

For transporting us beyond Seas to be tried for pretended offences

For abolishing the free System of English Laws in a neighbouring Province, establishing therein an Arbitrary government, and enlarging its Boundaries so as to render it at once an example and fit instrument for introducing the same absolute rule into these Colonies:

For taking away our Charters, abolishing our most valuable Laws, and altering fundamentally the Forms of our Governments:

For suspending our own Legislatures, and declaring themselves invested with power to legislate for us in all cases whatsoever.

He has abdicated Government here, by declaring us out of his Protection and waging War against us.

He has plundered our seas, ravaged our Coasts, burnt our towns, and destroyed the lives of our people.

He is at this time transporting large Armies of foreign Mercenaries to compleat the works of death, desolation and tyranny, already begun with circumstances of Cruelty & perfidy scarcely paralleled in the most barbarous ages, and totally unworthy the Head of a civilized nation.

He has constrained our fellow Citizens taken Captive on the high Seas to bear Arms against their Country, to become the executioners of their friends and Brethren, or to fall themselves by their Hands.

He has excited domestic insurrections amongst us, and has endeavoured to bring on the inhabitants of our frontiers, the merciless Indian Savages, whose known rule of warfare, is an undistinguished destruction of all ages, sexes and conditions.

In every stage of these Oppressions We have Petitioned for Redress in the most humble terms: Our repeated Petitions have been answered only by repeated injury. A Prince whose character is thus marked by every act which may define a Tyrant, is unfit to be the ruler of a free people.

Nor have We been wanting in attentions to our Brittish brethren. We have warned them from time to time of attempts by their legislature to extend an unwarrantable jurisdiction over us. We have reminded them of the circumstances of our emigration and settlement here. We have appealed to their native justice and magnanimity, and we have conjured them by the ties of our common kindred to disavow these usurpations, which, would inevitably interrupt our connections and correspondence. They too have been deaf to the voice of justice and of consanguinity. We must, therefore, acquiesce in the necessity, which denounces our Separation, and hold them, as we hold the rest of mankind, Enemies in War, in Peace Friends.

We, therefore, the Representatives of the United States of America, in General Congress, Assembled, appealing to the Supreme Judge of the world for the rectitude of our intentions, do, in the Name, and by Authority of the good People of these Colonies, solemnly publish and declare, That these United Colonies are, and of Right ought to be Free and Independent States; that they are Absolved from all Allegiance to the British Crown, and that all political connection between them and the State of Great Britain, is and ought to be totally dissolved; and that as Free and Independent States, they have full Power to levy War, conclude Peace, contract Alliances, establish Commerce, and to do all other Acts and Things which Independent States may of right do. And for the support of this Declaration, with a firm reliance on the protection of divine Providence, we mutually pledge to each other our Lives, our Fortunes and our sacred Honor.

PLAN FOR ESTABLISHING UNIFORMITY IN THE COINAGE, WEIGHTS, AND MEASURES OF THE UNITED STATES

COMMUNICATED TO THE HOUSE OF REPRESENTATIVES

JULY 13, 1790

New York, July 4, 1790

Sir:—In obedience to the order of the House of Representatives of January 15th, I have now the honor to enclose you a report on the subject of measures, weights, and coins. The length of time which intervened between the date of the order and my arrival in this city, prevented my receiving it till the 15th of April; and an illness which followed soon after added, unavoidably, some weeks to the delay; so that it was not till about the 20th May that I was able to finish the report. A desire to lessen the number of its imperfections induced me still to withhold it awhile, till, on the 15th of June, came to my hands, from Paris, a printed copy of a proposition made by the Bishop of Autun, to the National Assembly of France, on the subject of weights and measures; and three days afterwards I received, through the channel of the public papers, the speech of Sir John Riggs Miller, of April 13th, in the British House of Commons, on the same subject. In the report which I had prepared, and was then about to give in, I had proposed the latitude of 38 degrees, as that which should fix our standard, because it was the medium latitude of the United States; but the proposition before the National Assembly of France, to take that of 45 degrees as being a middle term between the equator and both poles, and a term which consequently might unite the nations of both hemispheres, appeared to me so well chosen, and so just, that I did not hesitate a moment to prefer it to that of 38 degrees. It became necessary, of course, to conform all my calculations to that standard—an operation which has been retarded by my other occupations.

These circumstances will, I hope, apologize for the delay which has attended the execution of the order of the House; and, perhaps, a disposition on their part to have due regard for the proceedings of other nations, engaged on the same subject, may induce them still to defer deciding ultimately on it till their next session. Should this be the case, and should any new matter occur in the meantime, I shall think it my duty to communicate it to the House, as supplemental to the present report.

I have the honor to be, with sentiments of the most profound respect,

Sir, your most obedient and most humble servant.

FIRST FORM OF THE REPORT ON MEASURES, WEIGHTS & COINS

The Secretary of State, to whom was referred, by the House of Representatives, to prepare and report a proper plan or plans for establishing uniformity in the Currency, Weights, and Measures of the United States, in obedience thereto, makes the following report:

To obtain uniformity in Measures, Weights, and Coins, it is necessary to find some measure of invariable length, with which, as a standard, these subjects may be compared.

There exists not in Nature, as far as has been hitherto observed, any one body accessible to man, which presents a single invariable dimension.

The globe of the Earth itself, indeed, might be considered as invariable in all its dimensions, and that its circumference would furnish an invariable measure; but no one of its circles, great or small, is accessible to a measurement through all its parts, and the various trials to measure definite portions of them, have been of such various result as to show there is no dependence on that operation for certainty.

Matter, then, by its mere extension, furnishing nothing invariable, its motion is the only remaining resource.

The motion of the Earth round its axis is uniform and invariable. It is measured obviously, but unequally, by the departure of a given meridian from the sun, and its return to it, constituting a solar day. Throwing together the inequalities of solar days, a mean interval, or day, has been found, and divided, by very general consent, into 86,400 equal parts.

A pendulum, vibrating freely, in small and equal arcs, may be so adjusted in its length, as, by its vibrations, to make this division of the Earth's motion into 86,400 equal parts, called seconds of mean time.

Such a pendulum then becomes itself a measure of determinate length, to which all others may be referred to as to a Standard.

But even the pendulum is not without its uncertainties.

1. The difficulty of ascertaining its center of oscillation, as depending on the form of the bob, and its distance from the point of suspension; the effect of the weight of the suspending wire towards displacing the center of oscillation; that center being seated within the body of the bob, and therefore inaccessible to the measure, are sources of considerable uncertainty.

2. Both theory and experience prove that, to preserve its isochronism, it must be shorter towards the equator, and longer towards the poles.

3. Being made of metal, as is best, it varies its length with the variations in the temperature of the atmosphere.

---

1. In order to avoid the uncertainties which respect the center of oscillation, it has been proposed by a Mr. Leslie, an ingenious artist of Philadelphia, to substitute for the pendulum a rod of uniform diameter, without a bob.

   Any* diameter sufficient to render it inflexible in its vibrations may be taken because, be that great or small, the center of oscillation remains the same.

   This center being known to reside at one Third of the whole Length of the Rod, measured from the lower Extremity, might be easily and accurately ascertained in Practice. But the whole Rod is better for a Standard, then any portion of it because sensibly defined at both its Extremities.

2. The Uncertainty arising from the Difference of Length requisite for the second pendulum, or the second Rod, in different Latitudes, may be avoided by fixing on some one Latitude, to which our standard shall refer. The middle Latitude of the United States would seem the most convenient to give the Standard to the others; and the Completion of the 38th Degree may be taken as the Middle Latitude; neglecting, as to this purpose, the Parts beyond the completion of the 31st and 45th Degrees.

   The differences between a Rod so adjusted to 30° of Latitude, and those for the extremes of 38° and 45° are to be examined.

   The second pendulum for 38° of Latitude, according to Sir Isaac Newton's computation, must be of 39.1285 inches English measure; and a Rod, to vibrate in the same Time, must be of the same Length between the centers of Suspension and Oscillation; and, consequently, its whole Length 58.7 or, more exactly, 58.69275 inches. This is but† 1/18 of an inch too long for the

---

* A convenient one might perhaps be that which would make the whole rod of the weight of the bob of a common house clock.

† Sir Isaac Newton computed the second pendulum for 51° 31' (the Latitude of London) to be 36 Pouces 8.6426 Lignes French measure, which is 39.1682 Inches, English at 11 Pouces 3 Lignes to the English foot, at less than which this Foot cannot be estimated, according to the best authorities. Yet most English authors state Sir Isaac Newton's computation at 39.2 English Inches, which would suppose the English Foot to be only 11 Pouces 2.09 Lignes. Perhaps they adopt 39.2 Inches as the nearest simplification of the fraction. Some lateexperiments and calculations by Messieurs Whitehurst and Hutton make the Length of the second Pendulum 39.1196.

Doctor Halley's calculations made it 39.125.
Sir Isaac Newton's, according to the Equation of the English Foot = 11_.3.
French make it 39.1682.
And the same, according to the common statement of it, is 39.2.

Sir Isaac Newton's Computation

	Pouces	Lignes	Inches
31°	36_	7.978 =	39.0915
38°	36_	8.1962 =	39.1205
45°	36_	8.428 =	39.1491

Southern limit of 38°and 1/33 of an inch too short for the northern one of 45°. Differences so minute that they may be neglected as insensible for all the common purposes of Life. But in cases meriting perfect exactness, the second Rod, found by Trial of its Vibration in any part of the United States may be corrected by . . .* Computation . . . . for the Latitude of the Place, and so brought exactly to the Standard of 38°.

3. The expansion and contraction of the Rod with the Change of Temperature, is the Third Source of Uncertainty before mentioned. According to the High† Authority before quoted, an iron Rod, of given length, may vary, between Summer and Winter, in temperate Latitudes, and in the common exposure of House Clocks, from 1/1728 to 1/2592 of its whole length, which, in a Rod of 58.7 inches, will be from about two to three hundredths of an inch. This may be avoided by adjusting and preserving the Standard in a Cellar, or other Place, the Temperature of which never varies. Iron is named for this Purpose, because the least expansible of the Metals.

Let the Standard of Measure then be an iron Rod of uniform Diameter, and of such length as in Latitude 38°, and in a better or other Place, the temperature of which does not vary through the year, shall performs its Vibrations, in small and equal arcs, in one Second of Mean Time.

A Standard of invariable Length being thus obtained, we may proceed to identify by that the Measures, Weights, and Coins of the United States. But here a doubt presents itself, as to the Extent of the Reformation meditated by the House of Representatives. The Experiment made by Congress in the year 1786, by declaring that there should be one Money of account and Payment through the United States, and that its Parts and Multiples should be in a decimal Ratio, has obtained such general approbation both at Home and abroad, that nothing seems wanting but the actual Coinage to banish the discordant Pounds, Shillings, Pence and Farthings of the different States and to establish in their stead the new Denominations. Is it in Contemplation with

* Sir Isaac Newton's Computations for from 30° to 45° Latitude are as follows:

Lat.	Pieds_Lignes
30	.3_7.948
35	.3_8.099
40	.3_8.261
41	.3_8.294
42	.3_8.327
43	.3_8.361
44	.3_8.394
45	.3_8.428

† Princip. L. 3. prop.20. prob.4.

the House of Representatives to extend a like Improvement to our Measures and Weights, and to arrange them also in a decimal Ratio? The facility which this would introduce into the vulgar arithmetic, would unquestionably be soon and sensibly felt by the whole Mass of the People, who would thereby be enabled to compute for themselves whatever they should have occasion to buy, to sell, or to measure, which the present complicated and difficult Ratios place beyond their Computation for the most part. Or, is it the Opinion of the Representatives that the Difficulty of changing the established Habits of a whole Nation opposes an insuperable Bar to this improvement? Under this uncertainty the Secretary of State thinks it his Duty to submit alternative Plans that the House may at their Will adopt either the one or the other exclusively; or the one for the Present, and the other for a future Time, when the public Mind may be supposed to have become familiarised to it.

I.

And first on the supposition that the present Measures and Weights are to be retained, but to be rendered uniform and invariable by bringing them to the same invariable Standards.

The first settlers of these States having come chiefly from England, brought with them the Measures and Weights of that Country. These alone are generally established among us, either by Law or Usage, and these therefore are alone to be retained and fixed. We must resort to that Country for information of what they are or ought to be.

This rests principally on the Evidence of certain standard Measures and Weights, which have been preserved of long Time in different Deposits. But Differences among these having been known to exist, the House of Commons, in the years 1757 and 1758 appointed Committees to enquire into the original Standards of their Weights and Measures. These Committees, assisted by able Mathematicians and Artists, examined and compared with each other the several standard Measures and Weights, and made Reports on them in the years 1758 and 1759. The Circumstances under which these Reports were made entitle them to be considered as far as they go, as the best written testimony existing of the Standard Measures and Weights of England: and as such they will be relied on in the progress of this Report.

MEASURES OF LENGTH.

The measures of length in use among us are:

the League of 3 Miles, the Ell of a Yard and quarter,

the Mile of 8 Furlongs,
the Furlong of 40 Poles or Perches,
the Pole or Perch of 5 ½ Yards,
the Fathom of 2 Yards,
the Yard of 3 Feet,
the Foot of 12 Inches,
and
the Inch of 10 Lines.

On this branch of their subject, the committee of 1757.1758, says that the Standard Measures of Length at the Receipt of the Exchequer, are a Yard, supposed to be of the Time of H. 7.*, and a Yard and Ell supposed to have been made about the year 1601; that they are brass Rods, very coarsely made, their Divisions not exact, and the Rods bent; and that in the year 1742, some Members of the Royal Society had been at great Pains in taking an exact Measure of these Standards by very curious Instruments, prepared by the ingenious Mr Graham; that the Royal Society had had a brass Rod made pursuant to their Experiments, which was made so accurately, and by persons so skilful and exact, that it was thought not easy to obtain a more exact one; and the committee, in Fact, found it to agree with the Standards at the Exchequer, as near as it was possible. They furnish no Means, to Persons at a Distance, of knowing what this Standard is. This, however, is supplied by the Testimony of the learned of that Nation who agree very generally that the second Pendulum, as computed by Sir Isaac Newton for the Latitude of London is 39.2 Inches of their Measure, consequently, the second Rod for that Latitude would be 58.8; which is a Line, or 1⁄10 of an Inch longer than the Standard Rod of 38°, that is to say 1⁄588 of the whole Rod.

Let the standard rod of 38° then be divided into 587 equal Parts, let each of these parts be declared a Line.

10 Lines an Inch,
12 Inches a Foot,
3 Feet a Yard,
3 Feet 9 Inches an Ell,
6 Feet a Fathom,
5½ Yards a Perch or Pole,
40 Poles or Perches a Furlong,
8 Furlongs a Mile,
3 Miles a League.

SUPERFICIAL MEASURES.

Our measures of Surface are the acre of 4 Rood, and the Rood of 40 square Poles; so established by a Statute of 33 E. I.† Let them remain the same.

* Henry VII–Ed.

† Edward I–Ed.

MEASURES OF CAPACITY.

The Measures of Capacity in use among us are of the following Names and Proportions:

The Gill, 4 of which make a Pint,

2 Pints make a Quart,

2 Quarts a Pottle,

2 Pottles a Gallon,

2 Gallons a Peck, Dry measure,

8 Gallons make a measure called a Firkin, in liquid Substances, and a Bushel, dry,

2 Firkins, or Bushels, make a Measure called a Rundlet or Kilderkin, liquid, and a Strike, dry;

2 Kilderkins or Strikes make a Measure called a Barrel, liquid, and a Coomb, dry; this last Term being ancient and little used,

2 Barrels, or Coombs, make a Measure called a Hogshead, liquid, or a Quarter, dry; each being the Quarter of a Ton,

A Hogshead and a third make a Tierce, or third of a Ton,

2 Hogsheads make a Pipe, Butt, or Puncheon; and

2 Pipes make a Ton.

But no one of these Measures is of a determinate Capacity. The Report of the Committee of 1757–8, shews that the gallon is of very various content: and that being the Unit, all the others must vary with that.

The Gallon and Bushel contain

224 and 1792 cubic Inches, according to the Standard Wine Gallon preserved at Guildhall,

231 and 1848, according to the Statute of 5th Anne,

264.8 and 2118.4, according to the ancient Rumford Quart of 1228 examined by the Committee,

265.5 and 2124, according to three standard Bushels preserved in the Exchequer, to wit: one of H. 7., without a Rim; one dated 1091, supposed for 1591, or 1601, and one dated 1601,

266.25 and 2130, according to the ancient Rumford Gallon of 1228, examined by the Committee,

268.75 and 2150, according to the Winchester bushel, as declared by Stat. 13. 14. W. 3.*, which has been the Model for some of the grain States,

271, less 2 Spoonfuls, and 2168 less 16 Spoonfuls, according to a Standard Gallon of H. 7., and another dated 1601, marked E. E., both in the Exchequer,

* William III–Ed.

271 and 2168, according to a standard gallon in the Exchequer, dated 1601, marked E., and called the Corn Gallon,

272 and 2176, according to the three standard corn gallons last mentioned, as measured in 1688, by an artist for the Commissioners of the Excise, generally used in the seaport towns, and by mercantile people, and thence introduced into some of the grain States.

277.18 and 2217.44, as established for the measure of Coal by the Statute 12 Anne,

278 and 2224, according to a Standard Bushel of H. 7. with a copper Rim, in the Exchequer,

278.4 and 2227.2 according to two Standard Pints of 1601 and 1602, in the Exchequer,

280 and 2240, according to the Standard Quart of 1601, in the Exchequer,

282 and 2256, according to the Standard Gallon for beer and ale in the Treasury.

There are, moreover, varieties on these varieties, from the Barrel to the Ton inclusive; for, if the Barrel be of Herrings, it must contain 28 Gallons by the Stat. 13. El.* c. 11. If of Wine, it must contain 31½ gallons by the Stat. 2. H. 6. c. 11 & 1 R. III. c. 15. If of beer or ale, it must contain 34 Gallons by the Stat. 1 W & M.† c. 24, and the higher Measures in Proportion.

In those of the United States which have not adopted the Statutes of W and M, and of Anne before cited, nor their Substance, the Wine Gallon of 231 cubic Inches rests on the authority of very long usage, before the 5th of Anne, the origin and foundation of which are unknown; the bushel is the Winchester Bushel, by the 11 H. 7. undefined; and the Barrel of ale 32 Gallons, and of beer 36 Gallons, by the Stat. 23 H. 8.‡ c. 4.

The Secretary of State is not informed whether there have been any and what Alterations of these Measures by the Laws of the particular States.

It is proposed to retain this Series of Measures, but to fix the Gallon to one determinate capacity as the Unit of Measure, both wet and dry; for Convenience is in Favor of abolishing the Distinction even between wet and dry measures.

The wine gallon, whether of 224 or 231 cubic Inches, may be altogether disregarded, as concerning principally the mercantile and the wealthy, the least numerous Part of the Society, and the most capable of Reducing one Measure to another by Calculation. This Gallon is little used among the Mass of Farmers, whose chief Habits and Interests are in the Size of the Corn Bushel.

* Elizabeth I–Ed.

† William & Mary–Ed.

‡ Henry VIII–Ed.

Of the standard measures before stated, two are principally distinguished in Authority and Practice. The statute bushel of 2150 cubic Inches, which gives a Gallon of 268.75 cubic Inches, and the standard gallon of 1601, called the corn gallon of 271 or 272 cubic Inches, which has introduced the mercantile Bushel of 2176 Inches. The former of these is most used in some of the grain States, the latter in others. The middle term of 270 cubic Inches may be taken as a mutual compromise of Convenience, and as offering this general advantage: that the Bushel being of 2160 cubic Inches, is exactly a cubic Foot and a quarter, and so facilitates the Conversion of wet and dry Measures into solid Contents and Tonnage, and simplifies the Connection of Measures and Weights, as will be shown hereafter. It may be added, in Favor of this, as a medium Measure, that eight of the standard or Statute Measures before enumerated are below this Term, and nine above it.

The Measures to be made for use, being foursided, with rectangular Sides and Bottom.

the Pint will be 3 Inches square, and 3¾ I. deep;
the Quart 3 Inches square, and 7½ Inches deep;
the Pottle 3 Inches square, and 15 Inches deep, or 4½, 5, and 6 Inches.
the Gallon 6 Inches square, and 7½ Inches deep, or 5, 6, and 9 Inches;
the Peck 6, 9, and 10 Inches;
the Half bushel 12 Inches square, and 7½ Inches deep; and
the Bushel 12 Inches square, and 15 Inches deep, or 9, 15, and 16 Inches.

Cylindrical measures have the advantage of superior Strength, but square ones have the greater advantage of enabling every one who has a rule in his Pocket to verify their Contents by measuring them. Moreover, till the Circle can be squared, the Cylinder cannot be cubed, nor its Contents expressed in figures.

Let the Measures of Capacity, then, for the United States be,
a Gallon of 270 cubic Inches;
the Gallon to contain two Pottles;
the Pottle 2 Quarts;
the Quart 2 Pints;
the Pint 4 Gills.
2 Gallons to make a Peck,
8 Gallons a Bushel or Firkin,
2 Bushels or Firkin a Strike or Kilderkin,
2 Strikes or Kilderkins a Coomb or Barrel,
2 Coombs or Barrels a Quarter or Hogshead,
a Hogshead and a third one Tierce,

2 Hogsheads a Pipe, Butt, or Puncheon; and
2 Pipes a Ton.
And let all Measures of Capacity of dry subjects be stricken with a strait Strike.

WEIGHTS.

There are two Series of Weights in use among us; the one called Avoirdupois, the other Troy.

In the Avoirdupois Series,
the Pound is divided into 16 Ounces;
the Ounce into 16 Drams;
the Dram into 4 Quarters.

In the Troy series,
the Pound is divided into 12 Ounces;
the Ounce (according to the Subdivision of the Apothecaries) into 8 Drams;
the Dram into 3 Scruples;
the Scruple into 20 Grains.

According to the Subdivision for Gold and Silver, the Ounce is divided into 20 Pennyweights, and the Pennyweight into 24 Grains. So that the Pound Troy contains 5760 Grains, of which 7000 are requisite to make the Pound Avoirdupois. Of course the weight of the Pound Troy is to that of the pound Avoirdupois as 5760 to 7000, or as 144 to 175.

It is remarkable that this is exactly the Proportion of the ancient liquid Gallon of Guildhall of 224 cubic Inches, to the corn Gallon of 272; for 224 are to 272* as 144 to 175.

It is further remarkable still, that this is also the exact Proportion between the specific Weight of any Measure of Wheat, and of the same Measure of Water. For the statute Bushel is of 64 Pints and each Pint a Pound of Wheat. Now as 144 to 175, so are 64 Pounds to 77.7 Pounds; but 77.7 Pounds is known to be the Weight of 2150.4† cubic Inches of pure Water, which is exactly the Content of the Winchester Bushel, as declared by the Stat. 13. 14. W. 3. That Statute determined the Bushel to be a Cylinder of 18½ inches Diameter, and 8 Inches depth. Such a Cylinder, as nearly as it can be cubed and expressed in Figures, contains 2150.425 cubic Inches: a result which reflects Authority on the Declaration of Parliament, and induces a favorable opinion of the Care with which they investigated the

* or more exactly 144:175::224:272.2

† or more exactly 62.5:1728::77.7:2150.39

Contents of the ancient Bushel, and also a Belief that there might exist Evidence of it at that day unknown to the Committees of 1758 and 1759.

We find then in a continued Proportion 64 to 77.7 as 224 to 272, and as 144 to 175, that is to say, the specific Weight of a Measure of Wheat to that of the same Measure of Water as the cubic Contents of the wet Gallon to those of the dry; and as the Weight of a Pound Troy to that of a Pound Avoirdupois.

This seems to have been so combined as to render it indifferent whether a Thing were dealt out by Weight or Measure; for the dry Gallon of Wheat, and the liquid one of Wine, were of the same Weight; and the Avoirdupois pound of Wheat, and the Troy pound of Wine, were of the same Measure. Water and the vinous Liquors, which enter most into Commerce, are so nearly of a Weight, that the Difference, in moderate Quantities, would be neglected by both Buyer and Seller; some of the Wines being a little heavier, and some a little lighter, than Water.

Another remarkable Correspondence is that between Weights and solid Measures. For 1000 Ounces Avoirdupois of pure Water fill a cubic Foot with mathematical Exactness.

What Circumstances of the Times, or Purposes of Barter or Commerce called for this Combination of Weights and Measures with the subjects to be exchanged or purchased, are not now to be ascertained. But a triple Set of exact Proportionals representing Weights, Measures, and the Things to be weighed and measured, and a Relation so integral between Weights and solid Measures, must have been the Result of Design and scientific Calculation, and not a mere coincidence of Hazard. It proves that the dry and wet Measures, the heavy and light Weights, must have been original Parts of the System they compose: contrary to the Opinion of the Committee of 1757. 1758, who thought that the Avoirdupois Weight was not an ancient Weight of the Kingdom, nor ever even a legal Weight, but during a single Year of the Reign of H. 8. and, therefore, concluded otherwise than will be here Proposed, to suppress it altogether. Their opinion was founded chiefly on the silence of the Laws as to this Weight. But the harmony here developed in the system of Weights and Measures, of which the Avoirdupois makes an essential Member, corroborated by a general Use, from very high Antiquity, of that or of a nearly similar Weight under another name*, seem stronger Proofs that this is legal Weight, than the mere Silence of the written Laws is of the contrary.

Be this as it may, it is in such general use with us, that, on the Principle of popular Convenience, its higher Denominations, at least, must be preserved. It is by the Avoirdupois pound and ounce that our Citizens have been used to buy and sell. But the smaller subdivisions of Drams and Quarters are not in use with them. On the other Hand, they have been used to weigh their Money and Medicine with

* the Merchants Weight

the Pennyweights and Grains Troy Weight, and are not in the habit of using the Pounds and Ounces of that Series. It would be for their convenience, then, to suppress the Pound and Ounce Troy, and the Dram and Quarter Avoirdupois; and to form into one Series the Avoirdupois Pound and Ounce, and the Troy Pennyweight and Grain. The Avoirdupois ounce contains 18 Pennyweight 5½ Grains Troyweight. Divide it, then, into 18 Pennyweight, and the Pennyweight as heretofore, into 24 Grains, and the new Pennyweight will contain between a third and a Quarter of a Grain more than the present Troy pennyweight; or, more accurately, it will be to that as 875 to 864 a Difference not to be noticed, either in Money or Medicine, below the Denomination of an Ounce.

But it will be necessary to refer these Weights to a Determinate Mass of some Substance, the specific Gravity of which is invariable. Rain water is such a Substance, and may be referred to everywhere and through all Time. It has been found by accurate experiments that a cubic Foot of Rainwater weighs 1000 ounces Avoirdupois, Standard Weights of the Exchequer. It is true that among these Standard Weights the Committee reports small variations; but this Experiment must decide in Favor of those particular Weights between which and an integral mass of Water, so remarkable a Coincidence has been found.

Let it then be established that an Ounce is of the Weight of a cube of Rainwater, of one Tenth of a Foot, weighed in the standard Temperature; that the Series of Weights of the United States shall consist of Pounds, Ounces, Pennyweights, and Grains; whereof

24 Grains shall be one pennyweight,

18 Pennyweight one Ounce,

16 Ounces one Pound.

COINS.

Congress in 1786, established the money-unit at 375.64 Troy grains of pure Silver. It is proposed to make this less by about the quarter of a Grain, or Fifteenth of a cent, that is to say to establish it at 375.4 instead of 375.64 Grains because it will be shewn that this, as the Unit of Coin, will link in system with the Units of Length, Surface, Capacity, and Weight, whenever it shall be thought proper to extend the decimal Ratio through all these Branches. It is to preserve the Possibility of doing this, that this very minute alteration is proposed.

We have this proportion then 875 to 864 as 375.4 Grains Troy to 370.68; the Expression of the Unit in the new Grains.

Let it be declared therefore that the money unit, or dollar of the United States shall contain 370.68 American Grains of pure Silver.

If nothing more then is proposed than to render uniform and stable the System we already possess, this may be effected on the Plan herein detailed, the Sum of which is: 1. that the present Measures of Length be retained and fixed by an invariable Standard. 2. that the Measures of surface remain as they are and be invariable also as the Measures of Length to which they are to refer. 3. that the Unit of Capacity now so equivocal be settled at a Medium and convenient Term, and defined by the same invariable Measures of Length. 4. that the more known Terms in the two Kinds of Weights be retained, and reduced to one Series, and that they be referred to a definite Mass of some Substance, the specific Gravity of which never changes: and 5. that the quantity of pure Silver in the Money unit be expressed in Parts of the Weight so defined.

In the whole of this no Change is proposed, except an insensible one in the Troy Grain and pennyweight, and the very minute one in the Money unit.

II.

But if it be thought that, either now, or at any future Time, the Citizens of the United States may be induced to undertake a thorough Reformation of their whole System of Measures, Weights and Coins, reducing every Branch to the same decimal Ratio already established in their Coins, and thus bringing the Calculation of the principal Affairs of Life within the Arithmetic of every Man who can multiply and divide plain numbers, greater Changes will be necessary.

The Unit of Measure is still that which must give Law through the whole system; and from whatever unit we set out, the coincidences between the old and new Ratios will be rare. All that can be done, will be to choose such a Unit as will Produce the most of these. In this respect the second Rod has been found on Trial to be far preferable to the second Pendulum.

MEASURES OF LENGTH.

Let the Second Rod then, as before described, be the Standard of Measure, and let it be divided into five equal Parts, each of which shall be called a Foot; for, perhaps, it may be better generally to retain the Name of the nearest present Measure, where there is one tolerably near. It will be about one Quarter of an Inch shorter than the present Foot.

let the Foot be divided into 10 Inches;
the Inch into 10 lines;
the Line into 10 Points;
let 10 Feet make a Decad;
10 Decads a Rood;

10 Roods a Furlong;
10 Furlongs a Mile.

SUPERFICIAL MEASURES.

Superficial Measures have been estimated, and so may continue to be, in Squares of the Measures of Length, except in the Case of Lands, which have been estimated by Squares, called Roods and Acres. Let the Rood be equal to a Square, every Side of which is 100 Feet. This will be 4.355 English feet less than the English Rood every way, and 1328 square Feet less in its whole Contents; that is to say, about one Eighth, in which Proportion also 4 Rood will be less than the present acre.

MEASURES OF CAPACITY.

Let the Unit of Capacity be the cubic foot, to be called a Bushel. It will contain 1617½ cubic inches English; be about ¼ less than that before proposed to be adopted as a Medium; 1⁄10 less than the Bushel made from 8 of the Guildhall Gallons; and 1⁄14 less than the Bushel made from 8 Irish gallons of 217.6 Cubic inches.

Let the Bushel be divided into 10 Pottles;
each Pottle into 10 Demi-pints;
each Demi-pint into 10 Metres, which will be of a Cubic inch each,
Let 10 Bushels be a Quarter, and
10 Quarters a Last, or double ton.

The measures for use being foursided, and the Sides and Bottoms rectangular, the Bushel will be a Foot cube.

The Pottle 5 Inches square and 4 Inches deep;
the Demi-pint 2 Inches square, and 2½ Inches deep;
the metre, an Inch cube.

WEIGHTS.

Let the Weight of a cubic Inch of Rain water be called an Ounce, and let the Ounce be divided into 10 double Scruples; the double Scruple into 10 Carats; the Carat into 10 Minims or Demi-grains; the Minim into 10 Mites.

Let 10 Ounces make a Pound; 10 Pounds a Stone; 16 Stone a Kintal; 10 Kintal a Hogshead.

COINS.

Let the Money-unit, or Dollar, contain eleventh Twelfths of an ounce of pure Silver. This will be 375.4 Troy grains, (or more exactly, 375.39555 Troy grains,) which will be a quarter of a Grain (or more exactly .24445 of a Grain) less than the present Unit. This, with the Twelfth of Alloy, already established, will make the Dollar or Unit of the Weight of an Ounce, or of a cubic inch of Rain-water exactly. The series of Mills, Cents, Dimes, Dollars, and Eagles, to remain as already established.

The second Rod, or the second Pendulum, expressed in the Measures of other Countries, will give the Proportion between their Measures and those of the United States.

Measures, Weights and Coins, thus referred to Standards unchangeable in their Nature, (as is the Length of a Rod vibrating Seconds, and the weight of a definite Mass of Rainwater) will themselves be unchangeable. These Standards, too, are such as to be accessible to all Persons, in all Times and Places. The Measures and Weights derived from them fall in so nearly with some of those now in use, as to facilitate their Introduction; and being arranged in decimal Ratio, they are within the Calculation of every one who possesses the first Elements of Arithmetic, and of easy Comparison, both for Foreigners and Citizens, with the Measures, Weights, and Coins of other countries.

A gradual Introduction would lessen the Inconveniences which might attend too sudden a Substitution, even of an easier or a more difficult system. After a given term, for instance, it might begin in the Custom Houses, where the Merchants would become familiarised to it. After a further Term, it might be introduced into all legal Proceedings, and Merchants and Traders in foreign commodities might be required to use it in their Dealings with one another. After a still further Term, all other Descriptions of People might receive it into common Use. Too long a Postponement, on the other Hand, would increase the Difficulties of its Reception with the Increase of our Population.

The Measures, Weights, and Coins of the decimal system estimated in those of England, now used in the United States.

1. MEASURES OF LENGTH

	Feet	*Equivalent in English Measures*
the Point	.001	.011 Inch
Line	.01	.117
Inch	.1	1.173 about 1/7 more than the English Inch.
Foot	1	{11.738 I}
		{.978 feet} about 1/48 less than the English Foot.

	Feet	*Equivalent in English Measures*
Decad	10.	9.782 about 1/48 less than the 10 foot Rod of the Carpenters.
Rood	100.	97.821 about 1/16 less than the Side of an English square Rood.
Furlong	1000	978.212 about 1/3 more than the English Furlong.
Mile	10000.	9782.425 about 1 6/7 English mile, nearly the Scotch and Irish Mile, and 1/2 the German Mile.

2. SUPERFICIAL MEASURE.

	Rood	*Square feet*
the Rood	1.	9568.948 about 1/8 less than the English Rood.

3. MEASURE OF CAPACITY.

	Bushels	*cubic Inches*
the Metre	.001	1.617
Demi-pint	.01	16.174 about 1/24 less than the English Half-pint.
Pottle	.1	161.749 about 1/6 more the English Pottle.
Bushel	1.	{1617.496547987 l} {.936051243048 cub. f.} about 1/4 less than the middle sized English Bushel.
Quarter	10	9.3605 about 1/5 less than the English Quarter.
Last	100.	93.605 about 1/7 more than the English Last.

4. WEIGHTS.

	Pounds.	*Avoirdupois.*	*Troy.*	
the Mite	.00001		.0409	Grains, about 1/5 less than the English Mite.
Minim, or} Demi-grain}	.0001		.409	about 1/5 less than the English Half-grain Troy.
Carat	.001		4.095	almost exactly the Carat Troy.
Double scruple	.01		40.952	about 1/40 more than 2 scruples Troy.
Ounce	.1	.936051203	{409.522.410} {.853 1717 oz.}	about 1/10 less than the Ounce Avoirdupois.

	Pounds.	*Avoirdupois.*	*Troy.*	
Pound	1.	{9.3605} {.585032 lb.}	710 lb.	about ¼ less than the Pound Troy.
Stone	10.	{93.605 oz.} {5.8503 lb.}	7.409	about ¼ less than the English Stone of 8 lb. Avoirdupois.
Kental	100.	{936.051 oz.} {58.503 lb.}	71.097	about 4/10 less than the English Kental of 100 lb. Avoirdupois.
Hogshead	1000.	{9360.512 oz.} {585.032 lb.}	710.9764.	

5. COINS.

	Dollars
the Mill	.001
Cent	.01
Dime	.1
Dollar	1.
Eagle	10.

OPINION ON THE CONSTITUTIONALITY OF A NATIONAL BANK
1791

The bill for establishing a National Bank undertakes, among other things

1. to form the subscribers into a Corporation.

2. to enable them, in their corporate capacities to receive grants of land; and so far is against the laws of *Mortmain.**

3. to make alien subscribers capable of holding lands, and so far is against the laws of *Alienage*.

4. to transmit these lands, on the death of a proprietor, to a certain line of successors: and so far changes the course of *Descents*.

5. to put the lands out of the reach of forfeiture or escheat and so far is against the laws of *Forfeiture and Escheat*.

6. to transmit personal chattels to successors in a certain line: and so far is against the laws of *Distribution*.

7. to give them the sole and exclusive right of banking under the national authority: and so far is against the laws of *Monopoly*.

8. to communicate to them a power to make laws paramount to the laws of the states: for so they must be construed, to protect the institution from the controul of the state legislatures; and so, probably they will be construed.

I consider the foundation of the Constitution as laid on this ground that "all powers not delegated to the U.S. by the Constitution, not prohibited by it to the states, are reserved to the states or to the people" [XIIth. Amendmt.]. To take a single step beyond the boundaries thus specially drawn around the powers of Congress, is to take possession of a boundless feild of power, no longer susceptible of any definition.

The incorporation of a bank, and other powers assumed by this bill have not, in my opinion, been delegated to the U.S. by the Constitution.

I.

They are not among the powers specially enumerated, for these are

1. A power to *lay taxes* for the purpose of paying the debts of the U.S. But no debt is paid by this bill, nor any tax laid. Were it a bill to raise money, it's origination in the Senate would con demn it by the constitution.

---

* Though the constitution controuls the laws of Mortmain so far as to permit Congress itself to hold lands for certain purposes, yet not so far as to permit them to communicate a similar right to other corporate bodies.

2. "to borrow money." But this bill neither borrows money, nor ensures the borrowing it. The proprietors of the bank will be just as free as any other money holders, to lend or not to lend their money to the public. The operation proposed in the bill, first to lend them two millions, and then borrow them back again, cannot change the nature of the latter act, which will still be a payment, and not a loan, call it by what name you please.

3. "to regulate commerce with foreign nations, and among the states, and with the Indian tribes." To erect a bank, and to regulate commerce, are very different acts. He who erects a bank creates a subject of commerce in it's bills: so does he who makes a bushel of wheat, or digs a dollar out of the mines. Yet neither of these persons regulates commerce thereby. To erect a thing which may be bought and sold, is not to prescribe regulations for buying and selling. Besides; if this was an exercise of the power of regulating commerce, it would be void, as extending as much to the internal commerce of every state, as to it's external. For the power given to Congress by the Constitution, does not extend to the internal regulation of the commerce of a state (that is to say of the commerce between citizen and citizen) which remains exclusively with it's own legislature; but to it's external commerce only, that is to say, it's commerce with another state, or with foreign nations or with the Indian tribes. Accordingly the bill does not propose the measure as a "regulation of trade," but as "productive of considerable advantage to trade."

Still less are these powers covered by any other of the special enumerations.

II.

Nor are they within either of the general phrases, which are the two following.

1. "To lay taxes to provide for the general welfare of the U.S." that is to say "to lay taxes for the purpose of providing for the general welfare." For the laying of taxes is the power and the general welfare the purpose for which the power is to be exercised. They are not to lay taxes ad libitum for any purpose they please; *but only to pay the debts or provide for the welfare of the Union.* In like manner they are not to do anything they please to provide for the general welfare, but only to lay taxes for that purpose. To consider the latter phrase, not as describing the purpose of the first, but as giving a distinct and independent power to do any act they please, which might be for the good of the Union, would render all the preceding and subsequent enumerations of power completely useless. It would reduce the whole instrument to a single phrase, that of instituting a Congress with power to do whatever would be for the good of the U.S. and as they would be the sole judges of the good or evil, it would be also a power to do whatever evil they pleased. It is an established rule of construction, where a phrase will bear

either of two meanings, to give it that which will allow some meaning to the other parts of the instrument, and not that which would render all the others useless. Certainly no such universal power was meant to be given them. It was intended to lace them up straitly within the enumerated powers, and those without which, as means, these powers could not be be carried into effect. It is known that the very power now proposed as a means, was rejected as an end, by the Convention which formed the constitution. A proposition was made to them to authorize Congress to open canals, and an amendatory one to empower them to incorporate. But the whole was rejected, and one of the reasons of rejection urged in debate was that then they would have a power to erect a bank, which would render the great cities, where there were prejudices and jealousies on that subject adverse to the reception of the constitution.

2. The second general phrase is "to make all laws *necessary* and proper for carrying into execution the enumerated powers." But they can all be carried into execution without a bank. A bank therefore is not *necessary*, and consequently not authorised by this phrase.

It has been much urged that a bank will give great facility, or convenience in the collection of taxes. Suppose this were true: yet the constitution allows only the means which are "necessary" not those which are merely "convenient" for effecting the enumerated powers. If such a latitude of construction be allowed to this phrase as to give any non-enumerated power, it will go to every one, for these is no one which ingenuity may not torture into a *convenience, in some way or other*, to *some one* of so long a list of enumerated powers. It would swallow up all the delegated powers, and reduce the whole to one phrase as before observed. Therefore it was that the constitution restrained them to the necessary means, that is to say, to those means without which the grant of the power would be nugatory.

But let us examine this *convenience*, and see what it is. The report on this subject, page 3. states the only *general* convenience to be the preventing the transportation and re-transportation of money between the states and the treasury. (For I pass over the increase of circulating medium ascribed to it as a merit, and which, according to my ideas of paper money is clearly a demerit.) Every state will have to pay a sum of tax-money into the treasury: and the treasury will have to pay, in every state, a part of the interest on the public debt, and salaries to the officers of government resident in that state. In most of the states there will still be a surplus of tax-money to come up to the seat of government for the officers residing there. The payments of interest and salary in each state may be made by treasury-orders on the state collector. This will take up the greater part of the money he has collected in his state, and consequently prevent the great mass of it from being drawn out of the state. If there be a balance of commerce in favour of that state against the one in which the government resides, the surplus of taxes will be remitted by the bills of exchange drawn for that commercial balance. And so it must be if there was a bank. But if there be no balance of commerce, either direct or circuitous, all the banks in the world could not bring up the surplus of taxes but in the form of money. Treasury orders then and bills of exchange may prevent the displacement of the main mass of the money collected, without the aid of any bank: and where these fail, it cannot be prevented even with that aid.

Perhaps indeed bank bills may be a more *convenient* vehicle than treasury orders. But a little *difference* in the degree of *convenience*, cannot constitute the necessity which the constitution makes the ground for assuming any non-enumerated power.

Besides; the existing banks will without a doubt, enter into arrangements for lending their agency: and the more favourable, as there will be a competition among them for it: whereas the bill delivers us up bound to the national bank, who are free to refuse all arrangement, but on their own terms, and the public not free, on such refusal, to employ any other bank. That of Philadelphia, I believe, now does this business, by their post-notes, which by an arrangement with the treasury, are paid by any state collector to whom they are presented. This expedient alone suffices to prevent the existence of that necessity which may justify the assumption of a non-enumerated power as a means for carrying into effect an enumerated one. The thing may be done, and has been done, and well done without this assumption; therefore it does not stand on that degree of *necessity* which can honestly justify it.

It may be said that a bank, whose bills would have a currency all over the states, would be more convenient than one whose currency is limited to a single state. So it would be still more convenient that there should be a bank whose bills should have a currency all over the world. But it does not follow from this superior conveniency that there exists anywhere a power to establish such a bank; or that the world may not go on very well without it.

Can it be thought that the Constitution intended that for a shade or two of *convenience*, more or less, Congress should be authorised to break down the most antient and fundamental laws of the several states, such as those against Mortmain, the laws of alienage, the rules of descent, the acts of distribution, the laws of escheat and forfeiture, the laws of monopoly? Nothing but a necessity invincible by any other means, can justify such a prostration of laws which constitute the pillars of our whole system of jurisprudence. Will Congress be too strait-laced to carry the constitution into honest effect, unless they may pass over the foundation-laws of the state-governments for the slightest convenience to theirs?

The Negative of the President is the shield provided by the constitution to protect against the invasions of the legislature 1. the rights of the Executive 2. of the Judiciary 3. of the states and state legislatures. The present is the case of a right remaining exclusively with the states and is consequently one of those intended by the constitution to be placed under his protection.

It must be added however, that unless the President's mind on a view of every thing which is urged for and against this bill, is tolerably clear that it is unauthorised by the constitution, if the pro and the con hang so even as to balance his judgment, a just respect for the wisdom of the legislature would naturally decide the balance in favour of their opinion. It is chiefly for cases where they are clearly misled by error, ambition, or interest, that the constitution has placed a check in the negative of the President.

Th: Jefferson
Feb. 15. 1791.

FIRST INAUGURAL ADDRESS

March 4, 1801

Friends and Fellow Citizens:

Called upon to undertake the duties of the first Executive office of our country, I avail myself of the presence of that portion of my fellow-citizens which is here assembled to express my grateful thanks for the favor with which they have been pleased to look toward me, to declare a sincere consciousness that the task is above my talents, and that I approach it with those anxious and awful presentiments which the greatness of the charge and the weakness of my powers so justly inspire. A rising nation, spread over a wide and fruitful land, traversing all the seas with the rich productions of their industry, engaged in commerce with nations who feel power and forget right, advancing rapidly to destinies beyond the reach of mortal eye—when I contemplate these transcendent objects, and see the honour, the happiness, and the hopes of this beloved country committed to the issue, and the auspices of this day, I shrink from the contemplation & humble myself before the magnitude of the undertaking. Utterly, indeed, should I despair did not the presence of many whom I here see remind me that in the other high authorities provided by our constitution I shall find resources of wisdom, of virtue, and of zeal on which to rely under all difficulties. To you, then, gentlemen, who are charged with the sovereign functions of legislation, and to those associated with you, I look with encouragement for that guidance and support which may enable us to steer with safety the vessel in which we are all embarked amidst the conflicting elements of a troubled world.

During the contest of opinion through which we have passed, the animation of discussions and of exertions has sometimes worn an aspect which might impose on strangers unused to think freely & to speak & to write what they think, but this being now decided by the voice of the nation enounced according to the rules of the constitution all will of course arrange themselves under the will of the law & unite in common efforts for the common good. All too will bear in mind this sacred principle that though the will of the majority is in all cases to prevail that will, to be rightful, must be reasonable: that the minority possess their equal rights which equal laws must protect & to violate would be oppression. Let us then fellow-citizens unite with one heart & one mind; let us restore to social intercourse that harmony and affection without which Liberty, and even Life itself, are but dreary things. And let us reflect that having banished from our land that religious intolerance under which mankind so long bled & suffered, we have yet gained little if we countenance a political intolerance as despotic, as wicked and capable of as bitter & bloody persecutions. During the throes and convulsions of the ancient world, during the agonizing spasms of infuriated man, seeking through blood and slaughter his long-lost liberty, it was not wonderful that the agitation of the billows should reach even this distant and peaceful shore: that this should be more felt & feared by some & less by others, & should divide opinions as to measures of safety. But every difference of opinion is not a difference of principle. We have called by different names, brethren of the same principle. We are all republicans: we are all federalists. If there be any among us who would wish to dissolve this union or to change it's republican form, let them stand undisturbed, as monuments of the safety with which error of opinion may be tolerated where reason is left free to combat it. I know indeed that some honest men have feared that a republican government can not be strong, that this government is not strong enough; but would the honest patriot, in the full tide of successful experiment, abandon a government which has so far kept us free & firm on the theoretic and visionary fear that this government, the world's best hope, may by possibility want energy to preserve itself? I trust not. I believe this, on the contrary, the strongest government on earth. I believe it the only one where every man, at the call of the law, would fly to the standard of the law, and would meet invasions of public order, as his own personal concern. Sometimes it is said that man can not be trusted with the government of himself. Can he then be trusted with the government of others? Or have we found angels in the forms of kings to govern him? Let history answer this question.

Let us pursue with courage and confidence our own federal & republican principles, our attachment to Union and Representative government. Kindly separated by nature and a wide ocean from the exterminating havoc of one quarter of the globe, too high-minded to endure the degradations of the others; possessing a chosen country with room enough for our descendants to the 1000th and 1000th generation; entertaining a due sense of our equal right to the use of our own faculties, to the acquisitions of our own industry, to honor and confidence from our fellow-citizens resulting not from birth but from our actions and their sense of them; enlightened by a benign religion, professed indeed and practiced in various forms, yet all of them inculcating honesty, truth, temperance, gratitude & the love of man; acknowledging and adoring an overruling providence, which by all it's dispensations proves that it delights in the happiness of man here and his greater happiness hereafter—with all these blessings, what more is necessary to make us a happy and a prosperous people? Still one thing more, fellow citizens—a wise and frugal government, which shall restrain men from injuring one another, shall leave them otherwise free to regulate their own pursuits of industry and improvement, and shall not take from the mouth of labor, the bread it has earned.

This is the sum of good government, and this is necessary to close the circle of our felicities.

About to enter fellow citizens on the exercise of duties which comprehend everything dear & valuable to you, it is proper you should understand what I deem the essential principles of this government, and consequently those which ought to shape it's administration. I will compress them within the narrowest compass they will bear, stating the general principle, but not all it's limitations. Equal & exact justice to all men of whatever state or persuasion, religious or political: Peace, commerce & honest friendship with all nations, entangling alliances with none: the support of the State governments in all their rights, as the most competent administrations for our domestic concerns and the surest bulwarks against anti-republican tendencies: the preservation of the General government in its whole constitutional vigor, as the sheet anchor of our peace at home and safety abroad; a jealous care of the right of election by the people—a mild and safe corrective of abuses which are lopped by the sword of revolution where peaceable remedies are unprovided: absolute acquiescence in the decisions of the majority, the vital principle of republics, from which is no appeal but to force, the vital principle and immediate parent of despotism: a well disciplined militia, our best reliance in peace & for the first moments of war, till regulars may relieve them: the supremacy of the Civil over the Military authority: Economy in public expense, that labor may be lightly burthened: the honest paiment of our debts, and sacred preservation of the public faith: encouragement of Agriculture & of Commerce as it's handmaid: the diffusion of information and arraignment of all abuses at the bar of the public reason: freedom of Religion, freedom of the press & freedom of Person under the protection of the habeas corpus: and trial by Juries impartially selected. These Principles form the bright constellation which has gone before us & guided our steps through an age of Revolution and Reformation. The wisdom of our Sages & blood of our Heroes have been devoted to their attainment: They should be the Creed of our political faith, the Text of civic instruction, the Touchstone by which to try the services of those we trust; and should we wander from them in moments of error or alarm, let us hasten to retrace our steps and to regain the road which alone leads to Peace, Liberty & Safety.

I repair then fellow citizens, to the post you have assigned me. With experience enough in subordinate stations to know the difficulties of this the greatest of all, I have learnt to expect that it will rarely fall to the lot of imperfect man to retire from this station with the reputation & the favor which bring him into it. Without pretensions to that high confidence you reposed in our first & greatest revolutionary character, whose preeminent services had entitled him to the first place in his country's love, and had destined for him the fairest page in the volume of faithful history, I ask so much confidence only as may give firmness & effect to the legal administration of your affairs. I shall often go wrong through defect of judgment. When right, I shall often be thought wrong by those whose positions will not command a view of the whole ground. I ask your indulgence for my own errors, which will never be intentional: and your support against the errors of others, who may condemn what they would not if seen in all it's parts. The approbation implied by your suffrage is a great consolation to me for the past; and my future sollicitude will be to retain the good opinion of those who have bestowed it in advance, to conciliate that of others by doing them all the good in my power, and to be instrumental to the happiness & freedom of all.

Relying, then, on the patronage of your good will, I advance with obedience to the work, ready to retire from it whenever you become sensible how much better choice it is in your power to make. And may that infinite power which rules the destinies of the universe lead our councils to what is best, and give them a favorable issue for your peace & prosperity.

SECOND INAUGURAL ADDRESS

March 4, 1805

Proceeding, fellow-citizens, to that qualification which the Constitution requires before my entrance on the charge again conferred on me, it is my duty to express the deep sense I entertain of this new proof of confidence from my fellow-citizens at large, and the zeal with which it inspires me so to conduct myself as may best satisfy their just expectations.

On taking this station on a former occasion I declared the principles on which I believed it my duty to administer the affairs of our Commonwealth. My conscience tells me I have on every occasion acted up to that declaration according to its obvious import and to the understanding of every candid mind.

In the transaction of your foreign affairs we have endeavored to cultivate the friendship of all nations, and especially of those with which we have the most important relations. We have done them justice on all occasions, favored where favor was lawful, and cherished mutual interests and intercourse on fair and equal terms. We are firmly convinced, and we act on that conviction, that with nations as with individuals our interests soundly calculated will ever be found inseparable from our moral duties, and history bears witness to the fact that a just nation is trusted on its word when recourse is had to armaments and wars to bridle others.

At home, fellow-citizens, you best know whether we have done well or ill. The suppression of unnecessary offices, of useless establishments and expenses, enabled us to discontinue our internal taxes. These, covering our land with officers and opening our doors to their intrusions, had already begun that process of domiciliary vexation which once entered is scarcely to be restrained from reaching successively every article of property and produce. If among these taxes some minor ones fell which had not been inconvenient, it was because their amount would not have paid the officers who collected them, and because, if they had any merit, the State authorities might adopt them instead of others less approved.

The remaining revenue on the consumption of foreign articles is paid chiefly by those who can afford to add foreign luxuries to domestic comforts, being collected on our seaboard and frontiers only, and incorporated with the transactions of our mercantile citizens, it may be the pleasure and the pride of an American to ask, What farmer, what mechanic, what laborer ever sees a tax-gatherer of the United States? These contributions enable us to support the current expenses of the Government, to fulfill contracts with foreign nations, to extinguish the native right of soil within our limits, to extend those limits, and to apply such a surplus to our public debts as places at a short day their final redemption, and that redemption once effected the revenue thereby liberated may, by a just repartition of it among the States and a corresponding amendment of the Constitution, be applied *in time of peace* to rivers, canals, roads, arts, manufactures, education, and other great objects within each State. *In time of war*, if injustice by ourselves or others must sometimes produce war, increased as the same revenue will be by increased population and consumption, and aided by other resources reserved for that crisis, it may meet within the year all the expenses of the year without encroaching on the rights of future generations by burthening them with the debts of the past. War will then be but a suspension of useful works, and a return to a state of peace, a return to the progress of improvement.

I have said, fellow-citizens, that the income reserved had enabled us to extend our limits, but that extension may possibly pay for itself before we are called on, and in the meantime may keep down the accruing interest; in all events, it will replace the advances we shall have made. I know that the acquisition of Louisiana had been disapproved by some from a candid apprehension that the enlargement of our territory would endanger its union. But who can limit the extent to which the federative principle may operate effectively? The larger our association the less will it be shaken by local passions; and in any view is it not better that the opposite bank of the Mississippi should be settled by our own brethren and children than by strangers of another family? With which should we be most likely to live in harmony and friendly intercourse?

In matters of religion I have considered that its free exercise is placed by the Constitution independent of the powers of the General Government. I have therefore undertaken on no occasion to prescribe the religious exercises suited to it, but have left them, as the Constitution found them, under the direction and discipline of the church or State authorities acknowledged by the several religious societies.

The aboriginal inhabitants of these countries I have regarded with the commiseration their history inspires. Endowed with the faculties and the rights of men, breathing an ardent love of liberty and independence, and occupying a country which left them no desire but to be undisturbed, the stream of overflowing population from other regions directed itself on these shores; without power to divert or habits to contend against it, they have been overwhelmed by the current or driven before it; now reduced within limits too narrow for the hunter's state, humanity enjoins us to teach them agriculture and the domestic arts; to encourage them to that industry which alone can enable them to maintain their place in existence and to prepare them in time for that state of society which to bodily comforts adds the improvement of the mind and morals. We have therefore liberally furnished them with the implements of husbandry and household use; we have placed among them instructors in the arts of first necessity, and they are covered with the aegis of the law against aggressors from among ourselves.

But the endeavors to enlighten them on the fate which awaits their present course of life, to induce them to exercise their reason, follow its dictates, and change their pursuits with the change of circumstances have powerful obstacles to encounter; they are combated by the habits of their bodies, prejudices of their minds, ignorance, pride, and the influence of interested and crafty individuals among them who feel themselves something in the present order of things and fear to become nothing in any other. These persons inculcate a sanctimonious reverence for the customs of their ancestors; that whatsoever they did must be done through all time; that reason is a false guide, and to advance under its counsel in their physical, moral, or political condition is perilous innovation; that their duty is to remain as their Creator made them, ignorance being safety and knowledge full of danger; in short, my friends, among them also is seen the action and counteraction of good sense and of bigotry; they too have their antiphilosophists who find an interest in keeping things in their present state, who dread reformation, and exert all their faculties to maintain the ascendancy of habit over the duty of improving our reason and obeying its mandates.

In giving these outlines I do not mean, fellow-citizens, to arrogate to myself the merit of the measures. That is due, in the first place, to the reflecting character of our citizens at large, who, by the weight of public opinion, influence and strengthen the public measures. It is due to the sound discretion with which they select from among themselves those to whom they confide the legislative duties. It is due to the zeal and wisdom of the characters thus selected, who lay the foundations of public happiness in wholesome laws, the execution of which alone remains for others, and it is due to the able and faithful auxiliaries, whose patriotism has associated them with me in the executive functions.

During this course of administration, and in order to disturb it, the artillery of the press has been leveled against us, charged with whatsoever its licentiousness could devise or dare. These abuses of an institution so important to freedom and science are deeply to be regretted, inasmuch as they tend to lessen its usefulness and to sap its safety. They might, indeed, have been corrected by the wholesome punishments reserved to and provided by the laws of the several States against falsehood and defamation, but public duties more urgent press on the time of public servants, and the offenders have therefore been left to find their punishment in the public indignation.

Nor was it uninteresting to the world that an experiment should be fairly and fully made, whether freedom of discussion, unaided by power, is not sufficient for the propagation and protection of truth—whether a government conducting itself in the true spirit of its constitution, with zeal and purity, and doing no act which it would be unwilling the whole world should witness, can be written down by falsehood and defamation. The experiment has been tried; you have witnessed the scene; our fellow-citizens looked on, cool and collected; they saw the latent source from which these outrages proceeded; they gathered around their public functionaries, and when the Constitution called them to the decision by suffrage, they pronounced their verdict, honorable to those who had served them and consolatory to the friend of man who believes that he may be trusted with the control of his own affairs.

No inference is here intended that the laws provided by the States against false and defamatory publications should not be enforced; he who has time renders a service to public morals and public tranquillity in reforming these abuses by the salutary coercions of the law; but the experiment is noted to prove that, since truth and reason have maintained their ground against false opinions in league with false facts, the press, confined to truth, needs no other legal restraint; the public judgment will correct false reasoning and opinions on a full hearing of all parties; and no other definite line can be drawn between the inestimable liberty of the press and its demoralizing licentiousness. If there be still improprieties which this rule would not restrain, its supplement must be sought in the censorship of public opinion.

Contemplating the union of sentiment now manifested so generally as auguring harmony and happiness to our future course, I offer to our country sincere congratulations. With those, too, not yet rallied to the same point the disposition to do so is gaining strength; facts are piercing through the veil drawn over them, and our doubting brethren will at length see that the mass of their fellow-citizens with whom they can not yet resolve to act as to principles and measures, think as they think and desire what they desire; that our wish as well as theirs is that the public efforts may be directed honestly to the public good, that peace be cultivated, civil and religious liberty unassailed, law and order preserved, equality of rights maintained, and that state of property, equal or unequal, which results to every man from his own industry or that of his father's. When satisfied of these views it is not in human nature that they should not approve and support them. In the meantime let us cherish them with patient affection, let us do them justice, and more than justice, in all competitions of interest; and we need not doubt that truth, reason, and their own interests will at length prevail, will gather them into the fold of their country, and will complete that entire union of opinion which gives to a nation the blessing of harmony and the benefit of all its strength.

I shall now enter on the duties to which my fellow-citizens have again called me, and shall proceed in the spirit of those principles which they have approved. I fear not that any motives of interest may lead me astray; I am sensible of no passion which could seduce me knowingly from the path of justice, but the weaknesses of human nature and the limits of my own understanding will produce errors of judgment sometimes injurious to your interests. I shall need, therefore, all the indulgence which I have heretofore experienced from my constituents—the want of it will certainly not lessen with increasing years. I shall need, too, the favor of that Being in whose hands we are, who led our fathers, as Israel of old, from their native land and planted them in a country flowing with all the necessaries and comforts of life; who has covered our infancy with His providence and our riper years with His wisdom and power, and to whose goodness I ask you to join in supplications with me that He will so enlighten the minds of your servants, guide their councils, and prosper their measures that whatsoever they do shall result in your good, and shall secure to you the peace, friendship, and approbation of all nations.

SECRET LETTER TO CONGRESS REGARDING THE LEWIS & CLARK EXPEDITION

Gentlemen of the Senate, and of the House of Representatives:

As the continuance of the act for establishing trading houses with the Indian tribes will be under the consideration of the Legislature at its present session, I think it my duty to communicate the views which have guided me in the execution of that act, in order that you may decide on the policy of continuing it, in the present or any other form, or discontinue it altogether, if that shall, on the whole, seem most for the public good.

The Indian tribes residing within the limits of the United States, have, for a considerable time, been growing more and more uneasy at the constant diminution of the territory they occupy, although effected by their own voluntary sales: and the policy has long been gaining strength with them, of refusing absolutely all further sale, on any conditions; insomuch that, at this time, it hazards their friendship, and excites dangerous jealousies and perturbations in their minds to make any overture for the purchase of the smallest portions of their land. A very few tribes only are not yet obstinately in these dispositions. In order peaceably to counteract this policy of theirs, and to provide an extension of territory which the rapid increase of our numbers will call for, two measures are deemed expedient. First: to encourage them to abandon hunting, to apply to the raising stock, to agriculture and domestic manufacture, and thereby prove to themselves that less land and labor will maintain them in this, better than in their former mode of living. The extensive forests necessary in the hunting life, will then become useless, and they will see advantage in exchanging them for the means of improving their farms, and of increasing their domestic comforts. Secondly: to multiply trading houses among them, and place within their reach those things which will contribute more to their domestic comfort, than the possession of extensive, but uncultivated wilds. Experience and reflection will develop to them the wisdom of exchanging what they can spare and we want, for what we can spare and they want. In leading them to agriculture, to manufactures, and civilization; in bringing together their and our settlements, and in preparing them ultimately to participate in the benefits of our governments, I trust and believe we are acting for their greatest good. At these trading houses we have pursued the principles of the act of Congress, which directs that the commerce shall be carried on liberally, and requires only that the capital stock shall not be diminished. We consequently undersell private traders, foreign and domestic, drive them from the competition; and thus, with the good will of the Indians, rid ourselves of a description of men who are constantly endeavoring to excite in the Indian mind suspicions, fears, and irritations towards us. A letter now enclosed, shows the effect of our competition on the operations of the traders, while the Indians, perceiving the advantage of purchasing from us, are soliciting generally, our establishment of trading houses among them. In one quarter this is particularly interesting. The Legislature, reflecting on the late occurrences on the Mississippi, must be sensible how desirable it is to possess a respectable breadth of country on that river, from our Southern limit to the Illinois at least; so that we may present as firm a front on that as on our Eastern border. We possess what is below the Yazoo, and can probably acquire a certain breadth from the Illinois and Wabash to the Ohio; but between the Ohio and Yazoo, the country all belongs to the Chickasaws, friendly tribe within our limits, but the most decided against the alienation of lands. The portion of their country most important for us is exactly that which they do not inhabit. Their settlements are not on the Mississippi, but in the interior country. They have lately shown a desire to become agricultural; and this leads to the desire of buying implements and comforts. In the strengthening and gratifying of these wants, I see the only prospect of planting on the Mississippi itself, the means of its own safety. Duty has required me to submit these views to the judgment of the Legislature; but as their disclosure might embarrass and defeat their effect, they are committed to the special confidence of the two Houses.

While the extension of the public commerce among the Indian tribes, may deprive of that source of profit such of our citizens as are engaged in it, it might be worthy the attention of Congress, in their care of individual as well as of the general interest, to point, in another direction, the enterprise of these citizens, as profitably for themselves, and more usefully for the public. The river Missouri, and the Indians inhabiting it, are not as well known as is rendered desirable by their connexion with the Mississippi, and consequently with us. It is, however, understood, that the country on that river is inhabited by numerous tribes, who furnish great supplies of furs and peltry to the trade of another nation, carried on in a high latitude, through an infinite number of portages and lakes, shut up by ice through a long season. The commerce on that line could bear no competition with that of the Missouri, traversing a moderate climate, offering according to the best accounts, a continued navigation from its source, and possibly with a single portage, from the Western Ocean, and finding to the Atlantic a choice of channels through the Illinois or Wabash, the lakes and Hudson, through the Ohio and Susquehanna, or Potomac or James rivers, and through the Tennessee and Savannah, rivers. An intelligent officer, with ten or twelve chosen men, fit for the enterprise, and willing to undertake it, taken from our posts, where they may be spared without inconvenience, might explore the whole line, even to the Western Ocean, have conferences with the natives on the subject of commercial intercourse, get admission among them for our traders, as others are admitted, agree on convenient deposits for an interchange of articles, and return with the information acquired, in the course of two summers. Their arms and accoutrements, some instruments of observation, and light and cheap presents for the Indians, would be all the apparatus they could carry, and with an expectation of a soldier's portion of land on their return, would constitute the whole expense. Their pay would be going on, whether here or there. While other civilized nations have encountered great expense to enlarge the boundaries of knowledge by undertaking voyages of discovery, and for other literary purposes, in various parts and directions, our nation seems to owe to the same object, as well as to its own interests, to explore this, the only line of easy communication across the continent, and so directly traversing our own part of it. The interests of commerce place the principal object within the constitutional powers and care of Congress, and that it should incidentally advance the geographical knowledge of our own continent, cannot be but an additional gratification. The nation claiming the territory, regarding this as a literary pursuit, which is in the habit of permitting within its dominions, would not be disposed to view it with jealousy, even if the expiring state of its interests there did not render it a matter of indifference. The appropriation of two thousand five hundred dollars, "for the purpose of extending the external commerce of the United States," while understood and considered by the Executive as giving the legislative sanction, would cover the undertaking from notice, and prevent the obstructions which interested individuals might otherwise previously prepare in its way.

TH: JEFFERSON
Jan. 18. 1803

Abraham Lincoln

INTRODUCTION

The presidency of Abraham Lincoln saw the controversies that had figured so prominently during Thomas Jefferson's career—states' rights versus the power of the federal government, the challenges brought by expansion, and the question of slavery—come to a head in the cataclysm of the Civil War. No longer would leaders be able to compromise and kick the proverbial political can down the road. Lincoln's 1860 election on an antislavery platform triggered the secession of the seven Southern states that formed the Confederacy. It was Lincoln's genius that kept the nation together during this tribulation, defeated the rebellion, and ensured the continuity of the republic. The new nation that emerged from the firestorm would be one with a newly potent federal government, which, in turn, would enable the Progressive Era as exemplified by the presidency of Theodore Roosevelt.

THE LEAD-UP TO THE CIVIL WAR

The first party system, that is, the era of the Federalists and the Democratic-Republican Party, fell apart in the 1820s. However, many of the same arguments between those parties were embraced by the Democratic Party, which championed Jefferson's vision of an agrarian republic; and the Whig Party, which stood for limited, constitutional government but also economic modernization that would necessarily be driven by government policy. The Whigs' major weakness was their inability to reach a position on slavery, which ultimately led to their decline and the rise of the abolitionist Republican Party in the 1850s.

Slavery was, without a doubt, the single most divisive social and political question of the mid-nineteenth century. From Hartford and Birmingham to Boston and Baltimore, newspapers published invectives and editorials while preachers and abolitionists thundered from pulpits. But the heart of the matter played out in Congress: While slavery was firmly rooted in the old South, western expansion raised the question of whether new territories, including those taken from Mexico in the war of 1848, would be slave or free. Added to this were questions of how far slaveholders' property rights extended into free states—a question with no small bearing on the reach of the federal government. The question of slavery thus played out in every town and city in the United States.

The slavery issue was also emblematic of a larger divide. The United States was split into two different economic and social zones: The urban North, characterized by an industrial economy and high rates of immigration, and the South, which was agricultural and dominated by established, wealthy slave-owning families.

Because of its rapidly increasing population, the North had greater representation in Congress and the Electoral College. Thus, the South had a very real fear of their decreasing political power, while Northerners feared a "slave power" bloc in Congress that would work against their interests.

With the benefit of hindsight, the prehistory of the Civil War seems to be one of merely delaying the inevitable. The Missouri Compromise of 1820 admitted Maine as a free state to counterbalance Missouri as a slave state and forbade slavery north of the 36° 30' parallel in the Louisiana Purchase lands west of the Mississippi River. The Compromise of 1850 admitted California as a free state, permitted slavery in the New Mexico and Utah territories, and allowed each territory to vote on whether to be slave or free. However, it also passed the hated Fugitive Slave Act that compelled Northerners to aid in the recapture of escaped slaves and enabled bounty hunters to go into free states to arrest escaped African Americans—and sometimes free people. Antislavery forces found themselves agreeing with Jefferson's principles of local government and state nullification of federal overreach, as resistance and refusal to comply with the hated law were widespread.

The next looming controversy was over whether the unorganized territory usually referred to as "Nebraska" would be admitted as slave or free. The solution, the Kansas-Nebraska Act, drafted by the Democratic Senator Stephen A. Douglas of Illinois in 1854 with strong Southern support, repealed the Missouri Compromise. According to the new law, the people of the new Kansas and Nebraska territories could now vote on whether to be slave or free, which led to partisans from both sides flocking to the new territories to influence the ballot box. Two separate state legislatures, one proslavery and one antislavery, were elected in Kansas, with violence swiftly breaking out between the two sides.

Northern opposition to the Kansas-Nebraska Act, and to Douglas and the Democratic Party, led directly to the formation of the Republican Party. The Republican Party was the first to be based entirely in the North and the first to have opposition to slavery as one of the planks in its platform. It also supported the needs of the industrial and banking interests of the North over those of the agrarian South. In the 1890s, as we shall see in the chapter on Theodore Roosevelt, it also led the Progressive movement to modernize the United States. But in the period before, during, and after the Civil War, the Republican Party became virtually synonymous with the leadership of one man—Abraham Lincoln.

EARLY LIFE OF ABRAHAM LINCOLN

Abraham Lincoln was born on February 12, 1809, in a log cabin in Hodgenville, Kentucky, to Thomas and Nancy Lincoln. He came from a family of poor farmers; when he was seven, they moved to Indiana to seek a more secure livelihood. The family belonged to a Baptist denomination that opposed drinking, dancing, and slavery. When Abraham was nine, his mother died, leaving his eleven-year-old sister Sarah in charge of the household. His father remarried the following year; Lincoln became very close with his stepmother, Sarah "Sally" Bush Johnston.

Young Abraham Lincoln was bookish and disliked the hard work of a frontier farm. He was later remembered as always having had a book in his hand. Despite this, he had little formal schooling and was almost entirely self-educated. He was also remarkable for his physical stature—he reached six feet, four inches by young adulthood, though he never weighed more than 180 pounds. Despite his famed "scrawniness," Lincoln was well muscled and known as a proficient wrestler.

The Lincoln family moved to Illinois in 1830, when Abraham was twenty-one. Two years later, he and a partner opened a general store, but Lincoln eventually sold his share. He would also work as a carpenter, ferryman, and farm laborer. While working at the store, and at the urging of his friends, he entered politics in 1832 with a run for the Illinois General Assembly—interrupting his campaign to serve as a captain during the Black Hawk War, though he never saw combat—but, lacking education, influence, and money, he was defeated.

Lincoln's second run for the Assembly, in 1834, was successful. Advocating a "free soil" stance that opposed both the expansion of slavery and radical abolitionism, he also ran on positions typical of the Whig party to which he belonged, especially infrastructure expansion, such as building canals and railroads; modernizing banking; and supporting urbanization. He also advocated expanding the electorate to all white men, regardless of property ownership.

Lincoln was admitted to the Illinois Bar in 1836 and moved to Springfield, Illinois, to begin a law practice. He never formally studied law—as he himself said, "I studied with nobody"—but rather educated himself by "reading law," a method that disappeared in the late nineteenth century with the rise of professional law schools. As an attorney, he developed a reputation as a powerful orator who was to be feared when cross-examining witnesses and making closing statements.

MARRIAGE TO MARY TODD LINCOLN

Much has been written about Abraham Lincoln's sexuality, including his bed-sharing with close male friends—which was not uncommon in the days before central heating. He had two known romantic interests before becoming engaged to his wife, Mary Todd Lincoln, in 1840. In the 1830s, he was interested in a woman named Ann Rutledge, who died of scarlet fever in 1835; he also courted a woman named Mary Owens, but the two decided not to continue the relationship.

Mary Todd, whom Lincoln met in 1839, was a suitable match for the up-and-coming young attorney despite the fact that she came from a slave-owning (yet ostensibly antislavery) Kentucky family. Interestingly, she was also courted by Stephen A. Douglas, the Democratic politician who would later propose the Kansas-Nebraska Act and who would be Lincoln's great political rival. Lincoln displayed considerable ambivalence about the marriage, and even once broke off the engagement before the two reconciled and held a hastily arranged wedding. When someone asked the worried-seeming Lincoln where he was going on his wedding day, he responded "To hell, I suppose." Some have taken this as indicative of his sexuality, but it was equally likely he was referring to Mary's family's slave ownership. They had four sons, of whom only two survived their father; Robert, the eldest, lived to adulthood. The deaths of his children, as well as the earlier death of his mother and so many other people close to him, affected Lincoln profoundly.

FIRST TERM IN CONGRESS, LEGAL CAREER, AND PRESIDENCY

Lincoln ran for the House of Representatives in 1843 but was defeated by John J. Hardin. Hardin, however, retired after only one term, and Lincoln was elected in 1846. Like Hardin, Lincoln likewise pledged to serve only one term. He was also unpopular for being the only Whig from the Illinois delegation and for not supporting the 1848 war with Mexico that added Texas and the Southwest, including California, to the United States. After his term of office ended, Lincoln declined the new Whig President Zachary Taylor's offer of a governorship in the Oregon Territory and returned to his legal practice in Illinois, where he won a reputation as an honest and effective lawyer. The opening of the western frontier and industrialization created many new opportunities, and Lincoln had many chances to make his mark, especially in transportation law. (He also became the only president to hold a patent, for a flotation device to move boats in low water.)

It was the Kansas-Nebraska Act, and Senator Stephen A. Douglas's part in proposing the hated legislation, that catalyzed both Lincoln's later political career and the rise of the Republican Party. Like his Whig political hero, Henry Clay, Lincoln had always been in favor of gradual emancipation as a middle ground between radical abolition and the expansion of slavery. However, Douglas's compromise with southern slaveholders, that a popular vote should decide whether a territory should be slave or free, seemed like it would inevitably lead to new slave states coming into the Union and, with them, the increase of slaveholders' political power. In his 1854 "Peoria Speech," Lincoln said the Kansas-Nebraska Act had a "declared indifference, but… a covert's real zeal for the spread of slavery." Despite this, and perhaps because of the new party's ties with the anti-immigrant Know-Nothing movement, Lincoln resisted identifying as a Republican even as his beloved Whig party fell apart.

Lincoln was elected to the Illinois legislature in 1854, but rather than taking his seat, made a bid for the US Senate. Senators were at the time elected by state legislatures, and Lincoln, unable to gain a majority in a three-way race, threw his support to an antislavery Democrat. This, as well as his impassioned speechmaking, heralded his rise to prominence in the Illinois Republican Party. In the 1856 presidential election, he supported John C. Frémont (the same man whom Gutzon Borglum would later paint), but Democrat James Buchanan won in a three-way contest between Frémont, Buchanan, and the former Whig Millard Fillmore. Buchanan's presidency, which encompassed his support for the Kansas-Nebraska Act, a financial crisis, and the Dred Scott Decision in which the Supreme Court ruled that African Americans, whether enslaved or free, were not citizens, only further divided the nation, and Buchanan did not seek a second term.

THE LINCOLN-DOUGLAS DEBATES

Stephen A. Douglas was up for reelection to the Senate two years into Buchanan's term of office, and Illinois Republicans smelled blood. Accepting the nomination to run against him on the Republican ticket, and as a direct rebuke of Douglas, Lincoln gave his famous "House Divided" speech: "A house divided against itself cannot stand. I believe this government cannot endure permanently half slave and half free. I do not expect the Union to be dissolved—I do not expect the house to fall—but I do expect it will cease to be divided. It will become all one thing, or all the other." For the house to be one of bondage, of course, would be unendurable for Lincoln's party.

During the 1858 campaign, Lincoln and Douglas met in seven famous political debates, of which we have reproduced the first and the last. Such events were not just politics, but popular entertainment, widely reported in newspapers from coast to coast. Douglas was already known throughout the nation, and Lincoln's star was on the rise. Thousands of people attended to see two famous speakers give heartfelt orations on the central issue of the day. Whereas Douglas' position was essentially legal—Dred Scot was the law of the land—Lincoln's was based on slavery as a moral wrong.

The Lincoln-Douglas debates and an invitation by prominent eastern Republicans to speak at Cooper Union in New York City made Lincoln's national reputation, and he was soon spoken of as a presidential candidate for 1860. Running on his backwoods origins and with a masterful campaign organization, he soon won out over better established candidates and emerged as the Republican front-runner in a four-way race between himself, Douglas (representing northern Democrats), John C. Beckinridge (representing the Democrats from the slave states), and John Bell of Tennessee, who was backed by a coalition of Whigs and Know-Nothings. Meanwhile, the conflict over slavery was spilling over into factional fighting and even violence: In 1859, the Kansas antislavery partisan John Brown led a raid on Harpers' Ferry, Virginia, in an attempt to incite a slave revolt.

Lincoln won the Presidency with only 39.8 percent of the popular vote but 180 of the 303 electoral votes. He had received almost no support in the South. In response to his election, South Carolina, Florida, Mississippi, Alabama, Georgia, Louisiana, and Texas seceded from the Union, forming the Confederacy. Lincoln initially supported reconciliation measures, including a constitutional amendment to protect slavery where it existed, and his inaugural address reassured Southern slaveholders that he had "no purpose, directly or indirectly, to interfere with the institution of slavery in the States where it exists." Rather, the fight was over whether to expand slavery. His attempts were in vain: On April 12, 1861, a little over a month after Lincoln took office, Confederate forces fired on Fort Sumter in South Carolina. The Civil War had begun.

THE WAR YEARS AND EMANCIPATION

Lincoln was, understandably, horrified at the outbreak of a war he had tried so hard to avoid. However, the Confederates had taken the choice from him; he was compelled to become a war leader. In the name of preserving the Union, Lincoln would declare martial law, order the arrest of thousands of Confederate sympathizers without trial, appoint generals to defend Washington, D.C., and to defeat the Confederacy, work closely with his cabinet to manage the war effort, and negotiate delicate relations with Great Britain. He gave the beautifully eloquent, 272-word, three-minute Gettysburg Address, which has become one of the most famous and most-quoted speeches in the English language. He weathered the bruising midterm elections of 1862 and united various factions to easily defeat George McClellan and win reelection in 1864. However, the thing that he is best known for, and which would have the most lasting impact on the United States, was of course, his ending of slavery with the Emancipation Proclamation of 1862.

LINCOLN'S OPINIONS ON SLAVERY AND ABOLITION

Despite being known as the "Great Liberator," Lincoln's views on abolition, and on African Americans, were complex. In his early life, Lincoln was against both slavery and the immediate elimination of slavery. While the one was an inarguable evil, the question of how freed African Americans should be integrated into a society that would hold them apart also perplexed him, as it did other thinkers of the time. Sudden elimination of slavery would be a social and political disaster. It would be best, he held, if freed African Americans were settled in Liberia, and if slaveholders were compensated for their economic losses.

Even if the question of human bondage was the central question that had led to secession, Lincoln hesitated to make the Civil War about slavery. He countermanded emancipation efforts by Frémont and by General David Hunter, arguing that they were overreaching their power and would alienate slaveholders in loyal border states. He was also hesitant about the Confiscation Act, which allowed judges to free enslaved African Americans who were acting in support of the Confederacy. For him, the Civil War was, first, foremost, and only about preserving the Union. That was his official position: As a man, he was steadfastly for freedom. "I never, in my life, felt more certain that I was doing right, than I do in signing this paper," he said as he put his name to the executive order.

The Emancipation Proclamation, which went into effect on January 1, 1863, applied to three and a half million of the four million slaves then in the United States. (It applied only to "all persons held as slaves within any State or designated part of a State, the people whereof shall then be in rebellion against the United States," and therefore excluded Kentucky, Maryland, Delaware, Missouri, Tennessee, West Virginia, and occupied Louisiana.) It was at once a punitive measure, a means of recruiting African Americans into the Union Army, and a means of gaining sympathy in antislavery European countries. Some feared, rightly, that it would harden Southern resistance and end any chance of reconciliation, but Lincoln used it as a chance to extend an olive branch: In his Proclamation of Amnesty and Reconstruction, Lincoln gave rebel states lenient terms for readmission to the Union at the cost of accepting emancipation.

RECONSTRUCTION AND ASSASSINATION

Since some feared that the Emancipation would be seen as only a temporary war act, Lincoln pressed Congress for a constitutional amendment eliminating slavery—what would become ratified as the Thirteenth Amendment after his assassination. (Only about 15 percent of enslaved African Americans, those the Union had de facto control of, wound up being liberated because of the

Emancipation Proclamation.) Lincoln's plans for what should be done with freed African Americans were, however, ambiguous. He doubted, as he had in his early years, whether a truly integrated society could be achieved, and advocated voluntary emigration to freedmen's colonies. In an 1858 speech, he expressed doubts about intermarriage and African Americans serving as jurors. But by the standards of his time, Lincoln was a progressive indeed—and we must bear in mind that above all, Lincoln's goals were reuniting and reconciling the United States. To this end, he was a moderate and opposed radical plans to remake the South.

The great abolitionist activist Frederick Douglass recognized this in his "Oration in Memory of Abraham Lincoln," when he said, "He was preeminently the white man's President... He was willing to pursue, recapture, and send back the fugitive slave to his master, and to suppress a slave rising for liberty, though his guilty masters were already in arms against the Government." However, Douglass went on, "President Lincoln was a white man, and shared the prejudices common to his countrymen towards the colored race.... His great mission was to accomplish two things: first, to save his country from dismemberment and ruin; and, second, to free his country from the great crime of slavery.... Though Mr. Lincoln shared the prejudices of his white fellow-countrymen against the Negro, it is hardly necessary to say that in his heart of hearts he loathed and hated slavery." And, having met Lincoln several times, Douglass remarked, "in his company, I was never reminded of my humble origin, or of my unpopular color."

Abraham Lincoln was assassinated at Ford's Theater on April 14, 1865, by John Wilkes Booth, a Southern Confederate sympathizer who had become outraged three days earlier when he had heard Lincoln give a speech in favor of voting rights for African Americans. Mary Todd Lincoln, who would suffer what later generations might have called a nervous breakdown, was mocked for her excessive grieving even after the horrific experience of having her husband shot while sitting beside her and watching him die an excruciating death. The death of their son Tad in 1871 completed her mental decline, and she was institutionalized in her later years. Lincoln's death was a tragedy for the country, as well. He was succeeded by his vice president, Andrew Johnson, who did little to improve the lot of African Americans; likewise, without Lincoln's skilled hand on the wheel, the moderate, reconciliatory path plotted by the sixteenth president was doomed to fail. The wounds and divisions inflicted in this period pain America still.

LETTERS TO MARY TODD LINCOLN

Washington, April 16, 1848

Dear Mary:

In this troublesome world, we are never quite satisfied. When you were here, I thought you hindered me some in attending to business; but now, having nothing but business—no variety—it has grown exceedingly tasteless to me. I hate to sit down and direct documents, and I hate to stay in this old room by myself. You know I told you in last Sunday's letter, I was going to make a little speech during the week; but the week has passed away without my getting a chance to do so; and now my interest in the subject has passed away too. Your second and third letters have been received since I wrote before. Dear Eddy thinks father is "gone tapila." Has any further discovery been made as to the breaking into your grandmother's house? If I were she, I would not remain there alone. You mention that your uncle John Parker is likely to be at Lexington. Dont forget to present him my very kindest regards.

I went yesterday to hunt the little plaid stockings, as you wished; but found that McKnight has quit business, and Allen had not a single pair of the description you give, and only one plaid pair of any sort that I thought would fit "Eddy's dear little feet." I have a notion to make another trial tomorrow morning. If I could get them, I have an excellent chance of sending them. Mr. Warrick Tunstall, of St. Louis is here. He is to leave early this week, and to go by Lexington. He says he knows you, and will call to see you; and he voluntarily asked, if I had not some package to send to you.

I wish you to enjoy yourself in every possible way; but is there no danger of wounding the feelings of your good father, by being so openly intimate with the Wickliffe family?

Mrs. Broome has not removed yet; but she thinks of doing so tomorrow. All the house—or rather, all with whom you were on decided good terms—send their love to you. The others say nothing.

Very soon after you went away, I got what I think a very pretty set of shirt-bosom studs—modest little ones, jet, set in gold, only costing 50 cents a piece, or 1.50 for the whole.

Suppose you do not prefix the "Hon" to the address on your letters to me any more. I like the letters very much, but I would rather they should not have that upon them. It is not necessary, as I suppose you have thought, to have them to come free.

And you are entirely free from headache? That is good—good—considering it is the first spring you have been free from it since we were acquainted. I am afraid you will get so well, and fat, and young, as to be wanting to marry again. Tell Louisa I want her to watch you a little for me. Get weighed, and write me how much you weigh.

I did not get rid of the impression of that foolish dream about dear Bobby till I got your letter written the same day. What did he and Eddy think of the little letters father sent them? Dont let the blessed fellows forget father.

A day or two ago Mr. Strong, here in Congress, said to me that Matilda would visit here within two or three weeks. Suppose you write her a letter, and enclose it in one of mine; and if she comes I will deliver it to her, and if she does not, I will send it to her.

Most affectionately
A. Lincoln

Washington, June 12, 1848

My dear wife:

On my return from Philadelphia, yesterday, where, in my anxiety I had been led to attend the Whig convention I found your last letter. I was so tired and sleepy, having ridden all night, that I could not answer it till today; and now I have to do so in the H.R. The leading matter in your letter, is your wish to return to this side of the Mountains. Will you be a good girl in all things, if I consent? Then come along, and that as soon as possible. Having got the idea in my head, I shall be impatient till I see you. You will not have money enough to bring you; but I presume your uncle will supply you, and I will refund him here. By the way you do not mention whether you have received the fifty dollars I sent you. I do not much fear but that you got it; because the want of it would have induced you [to?] say something in relation to it. If your uncle is already at Lexington, you might induce him to start on earlier than the first of July; he could stay in Kentucky longer on his return, and so make up for lost time. Since I began this letter, the H.R. has passed a resolution for adjourning on the 17th. July, which probably will pass the Senate. I hope this letter will not be disagreeable to you; which, together with the circumstances under which I write, I hope will excuse me for not writing a longer one. Come on just as soon as you can. I want to see you, and our dear—dear boys very much. Everybody here wants to see our dear Bobby.

Affectionately
A. Lincoln

Washington, July 2, 1848

My dear wife:

Your letter of last Sunday came last night. On that day (Sunday) I wrote the principal part of a letter to you, but did not finish it, or send it till Tuesday, when I had provided a draft for $100 which I sent in it. It is now probable that on that day (Tuesday) you started to Shelbyville; so that when the money reaches Lexington, you will not be there. Before leaving, did you make any provision about letters that might come to Lexington for you? Write me whether you got the draft, if you shall not have already done so, when this reaches you. Give my kindest regards to your uncle John, and all the family. Thinking of them reminds me that I saw your acquaintance, Newton, of Arkansas, at the Philadelphia Convention. We had but a single interview, and that was so brief, and in so great a multitude of strange faces, that I am quite sure I should not recognize him, if I were to meet him again. He was a sort of Trinity, three in one, having the right, in his own person, to cast the three votes of Arkansas. Two or three days ago I sent your uncle John, and a few of our other friends, each a copy of the speech I mentioned in my last letter; but I did not send any to you, thinking you would be on the road here, before it would reach you. I send you one now. Last Wednesday, P. H. Hood & Co, dunned me for a little bill of $5.38 cents, and Walter Harper & Co, another for $8.50 cents, for goods which they say you bought. I hesitated to pay them, because my recollection is that you told me when you went away, there was nothing left unpaid. Mention in your next letter whether they are right.

Mrs. Richardson is still here; and what is more, has a baby—so Richardson says, and he ought to know. I believe Mary Hewett has left here and gone to Boston. I met her on the street about fifteen or twenty days ago, and she told me she was going soon. I have seen nothing of her since.

The music in the Capitol grounds on Saturdays, or, rather, the interest in it, is dwindling down to nothing. Yesterday evening the attendance was rather thin. Our two girls, whom you remember seeing first at Carusis, at the exhibition of the Ethiopian Serenaders, and whose peculiarities were the wearing of black fur bonnets, and never being seen in close company with other ladies, were at the music yesterday. One of them was attended by their brother, and the other had a member of Congress in tow. He went home with her; and if I were to guess, I would say, he went away a somewhat altered man—most likely in his pockets, and in some other particular. The fellow looked conscious of guilt, although I believe he was unconscious that everybody around knew who it was that had caught him.

I have had no letter from home, since I wrote you before, except short business letters, which have no interest for you.

By the way, you do not intend to do without a girl, because the one you had has left you? Get another as soon as you can to take charge of the dear codgers. Father expected to see you all sooner; but let it pass; stay as long as you please, and come when you please. Kiss and love the dear rascals.

Affectionately
A. Lincoln

EULOGY ON HENRY CLAY

July 6, 1852

Springfield, Illinois

On the fourth day of July, 1776, the people of a few feeble and oppressed colonies of Great Britain, inhabiting a portion of the Atlantic coast of North America, publicly declared their national independence, and made their appeal to the justice of their cause, and to the God of battles, for the maintainance of that declaration. That people were few in numbers, and without resources, save only their own wise heads and stout hearts. Within the first year of that declared independence, and while its maintainance was yet problematical—while the bloody struggle between those resolute rebels, and their haughty would-be-masters, was still waging, of undistinguished parents, and in an obscure district of one of those colonies, Henry Clay was born. The infant nation, and the infant child began the race of life together. For three quarters of a century they have travelled hand in hand. They have been companions ever. The nation has passed its perils, and is free, prosperous, and powerful. The child has reached his manhood, his middle age, his old age, and is dead. In all that has concerned the nation the man ever sympathised; and now the nation mourns for the man.

The day after his death, one of the public Journals, opposed to him politically, held the following pathetic and beautiful language, which I adopt, partly because such high and exclusive eulogy, originating with a political friend, might offend good taste, but chiefly, because I could not, in any language of my own, so well express my thoughts—

"Alas! who can realize that Henry Clay is dead! Who can realize that never again that majestic form shall rise in the council-chambers of his country to beat back the storms of anarchy which may threaten, or pour the oil of peace upon the troubled billows as they rage and menace around? Who can realize, that the workings of that mighty mind have ceased—that the throbbings of that gallant heart are stilled—that the mighty sweep of that graceful arm will be felt no more, and the magic of that eloquent tongue, which spake as spake no other tongue besides, is hushed—hushed forever! Who can realize that freedom's champion—the champion of a civilized world, and of all tongues and kindreds and people, has indeed fallen! Alas, in those dark hours, which, as they come in the history of all nations, must come in ours—those hours of peril and dread which our land has experienced, and which she may be called to experience again—to whom now may her people look up for that counsel and advice, which only wisdom and experience and patriotism can give, and which only the undoubting confidence of a nation will receive? Perchance, in the whole circle of the great and gifted of our land, there remains but one on whose shoulders the mighty mantle of the departed statesman may fall—one, while we now write, is doubtless pouring his tears over the bier of his brother and his friend—brother, friend ever, yet in political sentiment, as far apart as party could make them. Ah, it is at times like these, that the petty distinctions of mere party disappear. We see only the great, the grand, the noble features of the departed statesman; and we do not even beg permission to bow at his feet and mingle our tears with those who have ever been his political adherents—we do [not?] beg this permission—we claim it as a right, though we feel it as a privilege. Henry Clay belonged to his country—to the world, mere party cannot claim men like him. His career has been national—his fame has filled the earth—his memory will endure to 'the last syllable of recorded time.'

"Henry Clay is dead!—He breathed his last on yesterday at twenty minutes after eleven, in his chamber at Washington. To those who followed his lead in public affairs, it more appropriately belongs to pronounce his eulogy, and pay specific honors to the memory of the illustrious dead—but all Americans may show the grief which his death inspires, for, his character and fame are national property. As on a question of liberty, he knew no North, no South, no East, no West, but only the Union, which held them all in its sacred circle, so now his countrymen will know no grief, that is not as wide-spread as the bounds of the confederacy. The career of Henry Clay was a public career. From his youth he has been devoted to the public service, at a period too, in the world's history justly regarded as a remarkable era in human affairs. He witnessed in the beginning the throes of the French Revolution. He saw the rise and fall of Napoleon. He was called upon to legislate for America, and direct her policy when all Europe was the battle-field of contending dynasties, and when the struggle for supremacy imperilled the rights of all neutral nations. His voice, spoke war and peace in the contest with Great Britain.

"When Greece rose against the Turks and struck for liberty, his name was mingled with the battle-cry of freedom. When South America threw off the thraldom of Spain, his speeches were read at the head of her armies by Bolivar. His name has been, and will continue to be, hallowed in two hemispheres, for it is—

> 'One of the few the immortal names
> That were not born to die,'

"To the ardent patriot and profound statesman, he added a quality possessed by few of the gifted on earth. His eloquence has not been surpassed. In the effective power to move the heart of man, Clay was without an equal, and the heaven born endowment, in the spirit of its origin, has been most conspicuously exhibited against intestine feud. On at least three important occasions, he has quelled our civil commotions, by a power and influence, which belonged to no other statesman of his age and times. And in our last internal discord, when this Union trembled to its center—in old age, he left the shades of private life and gave the death blow to fraternal strife, with the vigor of his earlier years in a series of Senatorial efforts, which in themselves would bring immortality, by challenging comparison with the efforts of any statesman in any age. He exorcised the demon which possessed the body politic, and gave peace to a distracted land. Alas! the achievement cost him his life! He sank day by day to the tomb—his pale, but noble brow, bound with a triple wreath, put there by a grateful country. May his ashes rest in peace, while his spirit goes to take its station among the great and good men who preceded him!"

While it is customary, and proper, upon occasions like the present, to give a brief sketch of the life of the deceased, in the case of Mr. Clay, it is less necessary than most others; for his biography has been written and re-written, and read, and re-read, for the last twenty-five years; so that, with the exception of a few of the latest incidents of his life, all is as well known, as it can be. The short sketch which I give is, therefore merely to maintain the connection of this discourse.

Henry Clay was born on the 12th of April 1777, in Hanover County, Virginia. Of his father, who died in the fourth or fifth year of Henry's age, little seems to be known, except that he was a respectable man, and a preacher of the baptist persuasion. Mr. Clay's education, to the end of his life, was comparatively limited. I say "to the end of his life," because I have understood that, from time to time, he added something to his education during the greater part of his whole life. Mr. Clay's lack of a more perfect early education, however it may be regretted generally, teaches at least one profitable lesson; it teaches that in this country, one can scarcely be so poor, but that, if he will, he can acquire sufficient education to get through the world respectably. In his twenty-third year Mr. Clay was licenced to practice law, and emigrated to Lexington, Kentucky. Here he commenced and continued the practice till the year 1803, when he was first elected to the Kentucky Legislature. By successive elections he was continued in the Legislature till the latter part of 1806, when he was elected to fill a vacancy, of a single session, in the United States Senate. In 1807 he was again elected to the Kentucky House of Representatives, and by that body, chosen its Speaker. In 1808 he was re-elected to the same body. In 1809 he was again chosen to fill a vacancy of two years in the United States Senate. In 1811 he was elected to the United States House of Representatives, and on the first day of taking his seat in that body, he was chosen its speaker. In 1813 he was again elected Speaker. Early in 1814, being the period of our last British war, Mr. Clay was sent as commissioner, with others, to negotiate a treaty of peace, which treaty was concluded in the latter part of the same year. On his return from Europe he was again elected to the lower branch of Congress, and on taking his seat in December 1815 was called to his old post—the speaker's chair, a position in which he was retained by successive elections, with one brief intermission, till the inauguration of John Q. Adams in March 1825. He was then appointed Secretary of State, and occupied that important station till the inauguration of Gen. Jackson in March 1829. After this he returned to Kentucky, resumed the practice of the law, and continued it till the Autumn of 1831, when he was by the legislature of Kentucky, again placed in the United States Senate. By a re-election he continued in the Senate till he resigned his seat, and retired, in March 1848. In December 1849 he again took his seat in the Senate, which he again resigned only a few months before his death.

By the foregoing it is perceived that the period from the beginning of Mr. Clay's official life, in 1803, to the end of it in 1852, is but one year short of half a century; and that the sum of all the intervals in it, will not amount to ten years. But mere duration of time in office, constitutes the smallest part of Mr. Clay's history. Throughout that long period, he has constantly been the most loved, and most implicitly followed by friends, and the most dreaded by opponents, of all living American politicians. In all the great questions which have agitated the country, and particularly in those great and fearful crises, the Missouri question—the Nullification question, and the late slavery question, as connected with the newly acquired territory, involving and endangering the stability of the Union, his has been the leading and most conspicuous part. In 1824 he was first a candidate for the Presidency, and was defeated; and, although he was successively defeated for the same office in 1832 and in 1844, there has never been a moment since 1824 till after 1848 when a very large portion of the American people did not cling to him with an enthusiastic hope and purpose of still elevating him to the Presidency. With other men, to be defeated, was to be forgotten; but to him, defeat was but a trifling incident, neither changing him, or the world's estimate of him. Even those of both political parties who have been preferred to him for the highest office, have run far briefer courses than he, and left him, still shining high in the heavens of the political world. Jackson, Van Buren, Harrison, Polk, and Taylor, all rose after, and set long before him. The spell—the long enduring spell—with which the souls of men were bound to him, is a miracle. Who can compass it? It is probably true he owed his pre-eminence to no one quality, but to a fortunate combination of several. He was surpassingly eloquent; but many eloquent men fail utterly; and they are not, as a class, generally successful. His judgment was excellent; but many men of good judgment, live and die unnoticed. His will was indomitable; but this quality often secures to its owner nothing better than a character for useless obstinacy. These then were Mr. Clay's leading qualities. No one of them is very uncommon; but all taken together are rarely combined in a single individual; and this is probably the reason why such men as Henry Clay are so rare in the world.

Mr. Clay's eloquence did not consist, as many fine specimens of eloquence does [do], of types and figures—of antithesis, and elegant arrangement of words and sentences; but rather of that deeply earnest and impassioned tone, and manner, which can proceed only from great sincerity and a thorough conviction, in the speaker of the justice and importance of his cause. This it is, that truly touches the chords of sympathy; and those who heard Mr. Clay never failed to be moved by it, or ever afterwards, forgot the impression. All his efforts were made for practical effect. He never spoke merely to be heard. He never delivered a Fourth of July oration, or an eulogy on an occasion like this. As a politician or statesman, no one was so habitually careful to avoid all sectional ground. Whatever he did, he did for the whole country. In the construction of his measures he ever carefully surveyed every part of the field, and duly weighed every conflicting interest. Feeling, as he did, and as the truth surely is, that the world's best hope depended on the continued Union of these States, he was ever jealous of, and watchful for, whatever might have the slightest tendency to separate them.

Mr. Clay's predominant sentiment, from first to last, was a deep devotion to the cause of human liberty—a strong sympathy with the oppressed everywhere, and an ardent wish for their elevation. With him, this was a primary and all controlling passion. Subsidiary to this was the conduct of his whole life. He loved his country partly because it was his own country, but mostly because it was a free country; and he burned with a zeal for its advancement, prosperity and glory, because he saw in such, the advancement, prosperity and glory, of human liberty, human right and human nature. He desired the prosperity of his countrymen partly because they were his countrymen, but chiefly to show to the world that freemen could be prosperous.

That his views and measures were always the wisest, needs not to be affirmed; nor should it be, on this occasion, where so many, thinking differently, join in doing honor to his memory. A free people, in times of peace and quiet—when pressed by no common danger—naturally divide into parties. At such times the man who is of neither party, is not—cannot be, of any consequence. Mr. Clay, therefore, was of a party. Taking a prominent part, as he did, in all the great political questions of his country for the last half century, the wisdom of his course on many, is doubted and denied by a large portion of his countrymen;

and of such it is not now proper to speak particularly. But there are many others, about his course upon which, there is little or no disagreement amongst intelligent and patriotic Americans. Of these last are the War of 1812, the Missouri question, Nullification, and the now recent compromise measures. In 1812 Mr. Clay, though not unknown, was still a young man. Whether we should go to war with Great Britain, being the question of the day, a minority opposed the declaration of war by Congress, while the majority, though apparently inclining to war, had, for years, wavered, and hesitated to act decisively. Meanwhile British aggressions multiplied, and grew more daring and aggravated. By Mr. Clay, more than any other man, the struggle was brought to a decision in Congress. The question, being now fully before congress, came up, in a variety of ways, in rapid succession, on most of which occasions Mr. Clay spoke. Adding to all the logic, of which the subject was susceptible, that noble inspiration, which came to him as it came to no other, he aroused, and nerved, and inspired his friends, and confounded and bore-down all opposition. Several of his speeches, on these occasions, were reported, and are still extant; but the best of these all never was. During its delivery the reporters forgot their vocations, dropped their pens, and sat enchanted from near the beginning to quite the close. The speech now lives only in the memory of a few old men; and the enthusiasm with which they cherish their recollection of it is absolutely astonishing. The precise language of this speech we shall never know; but we do know—we cannot help knowing—that, with deep pathos, it pleaded the cause of the injured sailor—that it invoked the genius of the revolution—that it apostrophised the names of Otis, of Henry and of Washington—that it appealed to the interest, the pride, the honor and the glory of the nation—that it shamed and taunted the timidity of friends—that it scorned, and scouted, and withered the temerity of domestic foes—that it bearded and defied the British Lion—and rising, and swelling, and maddening in its course, it sounded the onset, till the charge, the shock, the steady struggle, and the glorious victory, all passed in vivid review before the entranced hearers.

Important and exciting as was the war question, of 1812, it never so alarmed the sagacious statesmen of the country for the safety of the republic, as afterwards did the Missouri question. This sprang from that unfortunate source of discord—negro slavery. When our Federal Constitution was adopted, we owned no territory beyond the limits or ownership of the States, except the territory North-West of the River Ohio, and east of the Mississippi. What has since been formed into the States of Maine, Kentucky, and Tennessee, was, I believe, within the limits of or owned by Massachusetts, Virginia, and North Carolina. As to the North Western Territory, provision had been made, even before the adoption of the Constitution, that slavery should never go there. On the admission of the States into the Union carved from the territory we owned before the constitution, no question—or at most, no considerable question—arose about slavery—those which were within the limits of or owned by the old states, following, respectively, the condition of the parent state, and those within the North West territory, following the previously made provision. But in 1803 we purchased Louisiana of the French; and it included with much more, what has since been formed into the State of Missouri. With regard to it, nothing had been done to forestall the question of slavery. When, therefore, in 1819, Missouri, having formed a State constitution, without excluding slavery, and with slavery already actually existing within its limits, knocked at the door of the Union for admission, almost the entire representation of the non-slave-holding states, objected. A fearful and angry struggle instantly followed. This alarmed thinking men, more than any previous question, because, unlike all the former, it divided the country by geographical lines. Other questions had their opposing partizans in all localities of the country and in almost every family; so that no division of the Union could follow such, without a separation of friends, to quite as great an extent, as that of opponents. Not so with the Missouri question. On this a geographical line could be traced which, in the main, would separate opponents only. This was the danger. Mr. Jefferson, then in retirement, wrote:

"I had for a long time ceased to read newspapers, or to pay any attention to public affairs, confident they were in good hands, and content to be a passenger in our bark to the shore from which I am not distant. But this momentous question, like a fire bell in the night, awakened, and filled me with terror. I considered it at once as the knell of the Union. It is hushed, indeed, for the moment. But this is a reprieve only, not a final sentence. A geographical line, co-inciding with a marked principle, moral and political, once conceived, and held up to the angry passions of men, will never be obliterated; and every irritation will mark it deeper and deeper. I can say, with conscious truth, that there is not a man on earth who would sacrifice more than I would to relieve us from this heavy reproach, in any practicable way. The cession of that kind of property, for so it is misnamed, is a bagatelle which would not cost me a second thought, if, in that way, a general emancipation, and expatriation could be effected; and, gradually, and with due sacrifices I think it might be. But as it is, we have the wolf by the ears and we can neither hold him, nor safely let him go. Justice is in one scale, and self-preservation in the other."

Mr. Clay was in congress, and, perceiving the danger, at once engaged his whole energies to avert it. It began, as I have said, in 1819; and it did not terminate till 1821. Missouri would not yield the point; and congress—that is, a majority in congress—by repeated votes, showed a determination to not admit the state unless it should yield. After several failures, and great labor on the part of Mr. Clay to so present the question that a majority could consent to the admission, it was, by a vote, rejected, and as all seemed to think, finally. A sullen gloom hung over the nation. All felt that the rejection of Missouri, was equivalent to a dissolution of the Union, because those states which already had, what Missouri was rejected for refusing to relinquish, would go with Missouri. All deprecated and deplored this, but none saw how to avert it. For the judgment of Members to be convinced of the necessity of yielding, was not the whole difficulty; each had a constituency to meet, and to answer to. Mr. Clay, though worn down, and exhausted, was appealed to by members, to renew his efforts at compromise. He did so, and by some judicious modifications of his plan, coupled with laborious efforts with individual members, and his own over-mastering eloquence upon the floor, he finally secured the admission of the State. Brightly, and captivating as it had previously shown, it was now perceived that his great eloquence, was a mere embellishment, or, at most, but a helping hand to his inventive genius, and his devotion to his country in the day of her extreme peril.

After the settlement of the Missouri question, although a portion of the American people have differed with Mr. Clay, and a majority even, appear generally to have been opposed to him on questions of ordinary administration, he seems constantly to have been regarded by all, as the man for a crisis. Accordingly, in the days of Nullification, and more recently in the re-appearance of the slavery question, connected with our territory newly acquired of Mexico, the task of devising a mode of adjustment, seems to have been cast upon Mr. Clay, by common consent—and his performance of the task, in each case, was little else than, a literal fulfilment of the public expectation.

Mr. Clay's efforts in behalf of the South Americans, and afterwards, in behalf of the Greeks, in the times of their respective struggles for civil liberty are among the finest on record, upon the noblest of all themes; and bear ample corroboration of what I have said was his ruling passion—a love of liberty and right, unselfishly, and for their own sakes.

Having been led to allude to domestic slavery so frequently already, I am unwilling to close without referring more particularly to Mr. Clay's views and conduct in regard to it. He ever was on principle and in feeling, opposed to slavery. The very earliest, and one of the latest public efforts of his life, separated by a period of more than fifty years, were both made in favor of gradual emancipation of the slaves in Kentucky. He did not perceive, that on a question of human right, the negroes were to be excepted from the human race. And yet Mr. Clay was the owner of slaves. Cast into life where slavery was already widely spread and deeply seated, he did not perceive, as I think no wise man has perceived, how it could be at once eradicated, without producing a greater evil, even to the cause of human liberty itself. His feeling and his judgment, therefore, ever led him to oppose both extremes of opinion on the subject. Those who would shiver into fragments the Union of these States; tear to tatters its now venerated constitution; and even burn the last copy of the Bible, rather than slavery should continue a single hour, together with all their more halting sympathisers, have received, and are receiving their just execration; and the name, and opinions, and influence of Mr. Clay, are fully, and, as I trust, effectually and enduringly, arrayed against them. But I would also, if I could, array his name, opinions, and influence against the opposite extreme—against a few, but an increasing number of men, who, for the sake of perpetuating slavery, are beginning to assail and to ridicule the white man's charter of freedom—the declaration that "all men are created free and equal." So far as I have learned, the first American, of any note, to do or attempt this, was the late John C. Calhoun; and if I mistake not, it soon after found its way into some of the messages of the Governors of South Carolina. We, however, look for, and are not much shocked by, political eccentricities and heresies in South Carolina. But, only last year, I saw with astonishment, what purported to be a letter of a very distinguished and influential clergyman of Virginia, copied, with apparent approbation, into a St. Louis newspaper, containing the following, to me, very extraordinary language—

"I am fully aware that there is a text in some Bibles that is not in mine. Professional abolitionists have made more use of it, than of any passage in the Bible. It came, however, as I trace it, from Saint Voltaire, and was baptized by Thomas Jefferson, and since almost universally regarded as canonical authority, 'All men are born free and equal.'

"This is a genuine coin in the political currency of our generation. I am sorry to say that I have never seen two men of whom it is true. But I must admit I never saw the Siamese twins, and therefore will not dogmatically say that no man ever saw a proof of this sage aphorism."

This sounds strangely in republican America. The like was not heard in the fresher days of the Republic. Let us contrast with it the language of that truly national man, whose life and death we now commemorate and lament. I quote from a speech of Mr. Clay delivered before the American Colonization Society in 1827.

"We are reproached with doing mischief by the agitation of this question. The society goes into no household to disturb its domestic tranquility; it addresses itself to no slaves to weaken their obligations of obedience. It seeks to affect no man's property. It neither has the power nor the will to affect the property of any one contrary to his consent. The execution of its scheme would augment instead of diminishing the value of the property left behind. The society, composed of free men, concerns itself only with the free. Collateral consequences we are not responsible for. It is not this society which has produced the great moral revolution which the age exhibits. What would they, who thus reproach us, have done? If they would repress all tendencies towards liberty, and ultimate emancipation, they must do more than put down the benevolent efforts of this society. They must go back to the era of our liberty and independence, and muzzle the cannon which thunders its annual joyous return. They must renew the slave trade with all its train of atrocities. They must suppress the workings of British philanthropy, seeking to meliorate the condition of the unfortunate West Indian slave. They must arrest the career of South American deliverance from thraldom. They must blow out the moral lights around us, and extinguish that greatest torch of all which America presents to a benighted world—pointing the way to their rights, their liberties, and their happiness. And when they have achieved all those purposes their work will be yet incomplete. They must penetrate the human soul, and eradicate the light of reason, and the love of liberty. Then, and not till then, when universal darkness and despair prevail, can you perpetuate slavery, and repress all sympathy, and all humane, and benevolent efforts among free men, in behalf of the unhappy portion of our race doomed to bondage."

The American Colonization Society was organized in 1816. Mr. Clay, though not its projector, was one of its earliest members; and he died, as for the many preceding years he had been, its President. It was one of the most cherished objects of his direct care and consideration; and the association of his name with it has probably been its very greatest collateral support. He considered it no demerit in the society, that it tended to relieve slave-holders from the troublesome presence of the free negroes; but this was far from being its whole merit in his estimation. In the same speech from which I have quoted he says: "There is a moral fitness in the idea of returning to Africa her children, whose ancestors have been torn from her by the ruthless hand of fraud and violence. Transplanted in a foreign land, they will carry back to their native soil the rich fruits of religion, civilization, law and liberty. May it not be one of the great designs of the Ruler of the universe, (whose ways are often inscrutable by short-sighted mortals,) thus to transform an original crime, into a signal blessing to that most unfortunate portion of the globe?" This suggestion of the possible ultimate redemption of the African race and African continent, was made twenty-five years ago. Every succeeding year has added strength to the hope of its realization. May it indeed be realized! Pharaoh's country was cursed with plagues, and his hosts were drowned in the Red Sea for striving to retain a captive people who had already served them more than four hundred years. May like disasters never befall us! If as the friends of colonization hope, the present and coming generations of our countrymen shall by any means, succeed in freeing our land from the dangerous presence of slavery; and, at the same time, in restoring a captive people to their long-lost father-land, with bright prospects for the future; and this too, so gradually, that neither races nor individuals shall have suffered by the change, it will indeed be a glorious consummation. And if, to such a consummation, the efforts of Mr. Clay shall have contributed, it will be what he most ardently wished, and none of his labors will have been more valuable to his country and his kind.

But Henry Clay is dead. His long and eventful life is closed. Our country is prosperous and powerful; but could it have been quite all it has been, and is, and is to be, without Henry Clay? Such a man the times have demanded, and such, in the providence of God was given us. But he is gone. Let us strive to deserve, as far as mortals may, the continued care of Divine Providence, trusting that, in future national emergencies, He will not fail to provide us the instruments of safety and security.

FIRST LECTURE ON DISCOVERIES AND INVENTIONS

April 6, 1858

All creation is a mine, and every man, a miner.

The whole earth, and all within it, upon it, and round about it, including himself, in his physical, moral, and intellectual nature, and his susceptabilities, are the infinitely various "leads" from which, man, from the first, was to dig out his destiny.

In the beginning, the mine was unopened, and the miner stood naked, and knowledgeless, upon it.

Fishes, birds, beasts, and creeping things, are not miners, but feeders and lodgers, merely. Beavers build houses; but they build them in nowise differently, or better now, than they did, five thousand years ago. Ants, and honeybees, provide food for winter; but just in the same way they did, when Solomon refered the sluggard to them as patterns of prudence.

Man is not the only animal who labors; but he is the only one who improves his workmanship. This improvement, he effects by Discoveries and Inventions. His first important discovery was the fact that he was naked; and his first invention was the fig-leaf-apron. This simple article—the apron—made of leaves, seems to have been the origin of clothing—the one thing for which nearly half of the toil and care of the human race has ever since been expended. The most important improvement ever made in connection with clothing, was the invention of spinning and weaving. The spinning jenny, and power loom, invented in modern times, though great improvements, do not, as inventions, rank with the ancient arts of spinning and weaving. Spinning and weaving brought into the department of clothing such abundance and variety of material. Wool, the hair of several species of animals, hemp, flax, cotten, silk, and perhaps other articles, were all suited to it, affording garments not only adapted to wet and dry, heat and cold, but also susceptable of high degrees of ornamental finish. Exactly when, or where, spinning and weaving originated is not known. At the first interview of the Almighty with Adam and Eve, after the fall, He made "coats of skins, and clothed them" Gen. 3–21.

The Bible makes no other alusion to clothing, before the flood. Soon after the deluge Noah's two sons covered him with a garment; but of what material the garment was made is not mentioned. Gen. 9–23.

Abraham mentions "thread" in such connection as to indicate that spinning and weaving were in use in his day—Gen. 14.23—and soon after, reference to the art is frequently made. "Linen breeches," are mentioned—Exod. 28.42—and it is said "all the women that were wise hearted, did spin with their hands" (Exod. 35–25) and, "all the women whose hearts stirred them up in wisdom, spun goat's hair" (Exod. 35–26). The work of the "weaver" is mentioned—(Exod. 35–35). In the book of Job, a very old book, date not exactly known, the "weavers shuttle" is mentioned.

The above mention of "thread" by Abraham is the oldest recorded allusion to spinning and weaving; and it was made about two thousand years after the creation of man, and now, near four thousand years ago. Profane authors think these arts originated in Egypt; and this is not contradicted, or made improbable, by any thing in the Bible; for the alusion of Abraham, mentioned, was not made until after he had sojourned in Egypt.

The discovery of the properties of iron, and the making of iron tools, must have been among the earliest of important discoveries and inventions. We can scarcely conceive the possibility of making much of anything else, without the use of iron tools. Indeed, an iron hammer must have been very much needed to make the first iron hammer with. A stone probably served as a substitute. How could the "gopher wood" for the Ark, have been gotten out without an axe? It seems to me an axe, or a miracle, was indispensable. Corresponding with the prime necessity for iron, we find at least one very early notice of it. Tubal-Cain was "an instructer of every artificer in brass and iron"—Gen. 4–22. Tubal-Cain was the seventh in decent from Adam; and his birth was about one thousand years before the flood. After the flood, frequent mention is made of iron, and instruments made of iron. Thus "instrument of iron" at Num: 35–16; "bedstead of iron" at Deut. 3–11—"the iron furnace" at 4–20—and "iron tool" at Deut. 27–5. At Deut. 19–5—very distinct mention of "the ax to cut down the tree" is made; and also at Deut. 8–9, the promised land is described as "a land whose stones are iron, and out of whose hills thou mayest dig brass." From the somewhat frequent mention of brass in connection with iron, it is not improbable that brass—perhaps what we now call copper—was used by the ancients for some of the same purposes as iron.

Transportation—the removal of person and goods from place to place—would be an early object, if not a necessity, with man. By his natural powers of locomotion, and without much assistance from discovery and invention, he could move himself about with considerable facility; and even, could carry small burthens with him. But very soon he would wish to lessen the labor, while he might, at the same time, extend, and expedite the business. For this object, wheel-carriages, and water-crafts—wagons and boats—are the most important inventions. The use of the wheel & axle, has been so long known, that it is difficult, without reflection, to estimate it at it's true value. The oldest recorded allusion to the wheel and axle is the mention of a "chariot" Gen. 41–43. This was in Egypt, upon the occasion of Joseph being made Governor by Pharaoh. It was about twenty-five hundred years after the creation of Adam. That the chariot then mentioned was a wheel-carriage drawn by animals, is sufficiently evidenced by the mention of chariot wheels, at Exod. 14–25, and the mention of chariots in connection with horses in the same chapter, verses 9 & 23. So much, at present, for land transportation.

Now, as to transportation by water, I have concluded, without sufficient authority perhaps, to use the term "boat" as a general name for all water-craft. The boat is indispensable to navigation. It is not probable that the philosophical principle upon which the use of the boat primarily depends—towit, the principle, that any thing will float, which can not sink without displacing more than it's own weight of water—was known, or even thought of, before the first boats were made. The sight of a crow standing on a piece of driftwood floating down the swollen current of a creek or river, might well enough suggest the specific idea to a savage, that he could himself get upon a log, or on two logs tied together, and somehow work his way to the opposite shore of the same stream. Such a suggestion, so taken, would be the birth of navigation; and such, not improbably, it really was. The leading idea was thus caught; and whatever came afterwards, were but improvements upon, and auxiliaries to, it.

As man is a land animal, it might be expected he would learn to travel by land somewhat earlier than he would by water. Still the crossing of streams, somewhat too deep for wading, would be an early necessity with him. If we pass by the Ark, which may be regarded as belonging rather to the miraculous than to human invention, the first notice we have of water-craft, is the mention of "ships" by Jacob—Gen. 49–13. It is not till we reach the book of Isaiah that we meet with the mention of "oars" and "sails."

As mans food—his first necessity—was to be derived from the vegetation of the earth, it was natural that his first care should be directed to the assistance of that vegetation. And accordingly we find that, even before the fall, the man was put into the garden of Eden "to dress it, and to keep it." And when afterwards, in consequence of the first transgression, labor was imposed on the race, as a penalty—a curse—we find the first born man—the first heir of the curse—was "a tiller of the ground." This was the beginning of agriculture; and although, both in point of time, and of importance, it stands at the head of all branches of human industry, it has derived less direct advantage from Discovery and Invention, than almost any other. The plow, of very early origin; and reaping, and threshing, machines, of modern invention are, at this day, the principle improvements in agriculture. And even the oldest of these, the plow, could not have been conceived of, until a precedent conception had been caught, and put into practice—I mean the conception, or idea, of substituting other forces in nature, for man's own muscular power. These other forces, as now used, are principally, the strength of animals, and the power of the wind, of running streams, and of steam.

Climbing upon the back of an animal, and making it carry us, might not, occur very readily. I think the back of the camel would never have suggested it. It was, however, a matter of vast importance. The earliest instance of it mentioned, is when "Abraham rose up early in the morning, and saddled his ass," Gen. 22–3 preparatory to sacrificing Isaac as a burnt-offering; but the allusion to the saddle indicates that riding had been in use some time; for it is quite probable they rode bare-backed awhile, at least, before they invented saddles.

The idea, being once conceived, of riding one species of animals, would soon be extended to others. Accordingly we find that when the servant of Abraham went in search of a wife for Isaac, he took ten camels with him; and, on his return trip, "Rebekah arose, and her damsels, and they rode upon the camels, and followed the man" Gen. 24–61.

The horse, too, as a riding animal, is mentioned early. The Red Sea being safely passed, Moses and the children of Israel sang to the Lord "the horse, and his rider hath he thrown into the sea." Exo. 15–1.

Seeing that animals could bear man upon their backs, it would soon occur that they could also bear other burthens. Accordingly we find that Joseph's bretheren, on their first visit to Egypt, "laded their asses with the corn, and departed thence" Gen. 42–26.

Also it would occur that animals could be made to draw burthens after them, as well as to bear them upon their backs; and hence plows and chariots came into use early enough to be often mentioned in the books of Moses—Deut. 22–10. Gen. 41–43. Gen. 46–29. Exo. 14–25.

Of all the forces of nature, I should think the wind contains the largest amount of motive power—that is, power to move things. Take any given space of the earth's surface—for instance, Illinois—and all the power exerted by all the men, and beasts, and running-water, and steam, over and upon it, shall not equal the one hundredth part of what is exerted by the blowing of the wind over and upon the same space. And yet it has not, so far in the world's history, become proportionably valuable as a motive power. It is applied extensively, and advantageously, to sail-vessels in navigation. Add to this a few windmills, and pumps, and you have about all. That, as yet, no very successful mode of controlling, and directing the wind, has been discovered; and that, naturally, it moves by fits and starts—now so gently as to scarcely stir a leaf, and now so roughly as to level a forest—doubtless have been the insurmountable difficulties. As yet, the wind is an untamed, and unharnessed force; and quite possibly one of the greatest discoveries hereafter to be made, will be the taming, and harnessing of the wind. That the difficulties of controlling this power are very great is quite evident by the fact that they have already been perceived, and struggled with more than three thousand years; for that power was applied to sail-vessels, at least as early as the time of the prophet Isaiah.

In speaking of running streams, as a motive power, I mean its application to mills and other machinery by means of the "water wheel"—a thing now well known, and extensively used; but, of which, no mention is made in the Bible, though it is thought to have been in use among the Romans—(Am. Ency.—Mill). The language of the Saviour "Two women shall be grinding at the mill, &c." indicates that, even in the populous city of Jerusalem, at that day, mills were operated by hand—having, as yet had no other than human power applied to them.

The advantageous use of Steam-power is, unquestionably, a modern discovery. And yet, as much as two thousand years ago the power of steam was not only observed, but an ingenius toy was actually made and put in motion by it, at Alexandria in Egypt. What appears strange is, that neither the inventor of the toy, nor any one else, for so long a time afterwards, should perceive that steam would move useful machinery as well as a toy.

SECOND LECTURE ON DISCOVERIES AND INVENTIONS

February 11, 1859

We have all heard of Young America. He is the most current youth of the age. Some think him conceited, and arrogant; but has he not reason to entertain a rather extensive opinion of himself? Is he not the inventor and owner of the present, and sole hope of the future? Men, and things, everywhere, are ministering unto him. Look at his apparel, and you shall see cotten fabrics from Manchester and Lowell; flax-linen from Ireland; wool-cloth from [Spain;] silk from France; furs from the Arctic regions, with a buffalo-robe from the Rocky Mountains, as a general out-sider. At his table, besides plain bread and meat made at home, are sugar from Louisiana; coffee and fruits from the tropics; salt from Turk's Island; fish from New-foundland; tea from China, and spices from the Indies. The whale of the Pacific furnishes his candle-light; he has a diamond-ring from Brazil; a gold-watch from California, and a spanish cigar from Havanna. He not only has a present supply of all these, and much more; but thousands of hands are engaged in producing fresh supplies, and other thousands, in bringing them to him. The iron horse is panting, and impatient, to carry him everywhere, in no time; and the lightening stands ready harnessed to take and bring his tidings in a trifle less than no time. He owns a large part of the world, by right of possessing it; and all the rest by right of wanting it, and intending to have it. As Plato had for the immortality of the soul, so Young America has "a pleasing hope—a fond desire—a longing after" teritory. He has a great passion—a perfect rage—for the "new"; particularly new men for office, and the new earth mentioned in the revelations, in which, being no more sea, there must be about three times as much land as in the present. He is a great friend of humanity; and his desire for land is not selfish, but merely an impulse to extend the area of freedom. He is very anxious to fight for the liberation of enslaved nations and colonies, provided, always, they have land, and have not any liking for his interference. As to those who have no land, and would be glad of help from any quarter, he considers they can afford to wait a few hundred years longer. In knowledge he is particularly rich. He knows all that can possibly be known; inclines to believe in spiritual rappings, and is the unquestioned inventor of "Manifest Destiny." His horror is for all that is old, particularly "Old Fogy"; and if there be any thing old which he can endure, it is only old whiskey and old tobacco.

If the said Young America really is, as he claims to be, the owner of all present, it must be admitted that he has considerable advantage of Old Fogy. Take, for instance, the first of all fogies, father Adam. There he stood, a very perfect physical man, as poets and painters inform us; but he must have been very ignorant, and simple in his habits. He had had no sufficient time to learn much by observation; and he had no near neighbors to teach him anything. No part of his breakfast had been brought from the other side of the world; and it is quite probable, he had no conception of the world having any other side. In all of these things, it is very plain, he was no equal of Young America; the most that can be said is, that according to his chance he may have been quite as much of a man as his very self-complaisant descendant. Little as was what he knew, let the Youngster discard all he has learned from others, and then show, if he can, any advantage on his side. In the way of land, and live stock, Adam was quite in the ascendant. He had dominion over all the earth, and all the living things upon, and round about it. The land has been sadly divided out since; but never fret, Young America will re-annex it.

The great difference between Young America and Old Fogy, is the result of Discoveries, Inventions, and Improvements. These, in turn, are the result of observation, reflection and experiment. For instance, it is quite certain that ever since water has been boiled in covered vessels, men have seen the lids of the vessels rise and fall a little, with a sort of fluttering motion, by force of the steam; but so long as this was not specially observed, and reflected and experimented upon, it came to nothing. At length however, after many thousand years, some man observes this long-known effect of hot water lifting a pot-lid, and begins a train of reflection upon it. He says "Why, to be sure, the force that lifts the pot-lid, will lift any thing else, which is no heavier than the pot-lid." "And, as man has much hard lifting to do, can not this hot-water power be made to help him?" He has become a little excited on the subject, and he fancies he hears a voice answering "Try me" He does try it; and the observation, reflection, and trial gives to the world the control of that tremendous, and now well known agent, called steam-power. This is not the actual history in detail, but the general principle.

But was this first inventor of the application of steam, wiser or more ingenious than those who had gone before him? Not at all. Had he not learned much of them, he never would have succeeded—probably, never would have thought of making the attempt. To be fruitful in invention, it is indispensable to have a habit of observation and reflection; and this habit, our steam friend acquired, no doubt, from those who, to him, were old fogies. But for the difference in habit of observation, why did yankees, almost instantly, discover gold in California, which had been trodden upon, and over-looked by indians and Mexican greasers, for centuries? Gold-mines are not the only mines overlooked in the same way. There are more mines above the Earth's surface than below it. All nature—the whole world, material, moral, and intellectual—is a mine; and, in Adam's day, it was a wholly unexplored mine. Now, it was the destined work of Adam's race to develope, by discoveries, inventions, and improvements, the hidden treasures of this mine. But Adam had nothing to turn his attention to the work. If he should do anything in the way of invention, he had first to invent the art of invention—the instance at least, if not the habit of observation and reflection. As might be expected he seems not to have been a very observing man at first; for it appears he went about naked a considerable length of time, before he even noticed that obvious fact. But when he did observe it, the observation was not lost upon him; for it immediately led to the first of all inventions, of which we have any direct account—the fig-leaf apron.

The inclination to exchange thoughts with one another is probably an original impulse of our nature. If I be in pain I wish to let you know it, and to ask your sympathy and assistance; and my pleasurable emotions also, I wish to communicate to, and share with you. But to carry on such communication, some instrumentality is indispensable. Accordingly speech—articulate sounds rattled off from the tongue—was used by our first parents, and even by Adam, before the creation of Eve. He gave names to the animals while she was still a bone in his side; and he broke out quite volubly when she first stood before him, the best present of his maker. From this it would appear that speech was not an invention of man, but rather the direct gift of his Creator. But whether Divine gift, or invention, it is still plain that if a mode of communication had been left to invention, speech must have been the first, from the superior adaptation to the end, of the organs of speech, over every other means within the whole range of nature. Of the organs of speech the tongue is the principal; and if we shall test it, we shall find the capacities of the tongue, in the utterance of articulate sounds, absolutely wonderful. You can count from one to one hundred, quite distinctly in about forty seconds. In doing this two hundred and eighty three distinct sounds or syllables are uttered, being seven to each second; and yet there shall be enough difference between every two, to be easily recognized by the ear of the hearer. What other signs to represent things could possibly be produced so rapidly? or, even, if ready made, could be arranged so rapidly to express the sense? Motions with the hands, are no adequate substitute. Marks for the recognition of the eye—writing—although a wonderful auxiliary for speech, is no worthy substitute for it. In addition to the more slow and laborious process of getting up a communication in writing, the materials—pen, ink, and paper—are not always at hand. But one always has his tongue with him, and the breath of his life is the ever-ready material with which it works. Speech, then, by enabling different individuals to interchange thoughts, and thereby to combine their powers of observation and reflection, greatly facilitates useful discoveries and inventions. What one observes, and would himself infer nothing from, he tells to another, and that other at once sees a valuable hint in it. A result is thus reached which neither alone would have arrived at.

And this reminds me of what I passed unnoticed before, that the very first invention was a joint operation, Eve having shared with Adam in the getting up of the apron. And, indeed, judging from the fact that sewing has come down to our times as "woman's work" it is very probable she took the leading part; he, perhaps, doing no more than to stand by and thread the needle. That proceeding may be reckoned as the mother of all "Sewing societies"; and the first and most perfect "world's fair" all inventions and all inventors then in the world, being on the spot.

But speech alone, valuable as it ever has been, and is, has not advanced the condition of the world much. This is abundantly evident when we look at the degraded condition of all those tribes of human creatures who have no considerable additional means of communicating thoughts. Writing—the art of communicating thoughts to the mind, through the eye—is the great invention of the world. Great in the astonishing range of analysis and combination which necessarily underlies the most crude and general conception of it—great, very great in enabling us to converse with the dead, the absent, and the unborn, at all distances of time and of space; and great, not only in its direct benefits, but greatest help, to all other inventions. Suppose the art, with all conception of it, were this day lost to the world, how long, think you, would it be, before even Young America could get up the letter A. with any adequate notion of using it to advantage? The precise period at which writing was invented, is not known; but it certainly was as early as the time of Moses; from which we may safely infer that it's inventors were very old fogies.

Webster, at the time of writing his Dictionary, speaks of the English Language as then consisting of seventy or eighty thousand words. If so, the language in which the five books of Moses were written must, at that time, now thirtythree or four hundred years ago, have consisted of at least one quarter as many, or, twenty thousand. When we remember that words are sounds merely, we shall conclude that the idea of representing those sounds by marks, so that whoever should at any time after see the marks, would understand what sounds they meant, was a bold and ingenius conception, not likely to occur to one man of a million, in the run of a thousand years. And, when it did occur, a distinct mark for each word, giving twenty thousand different marks first to be learned, and afterwards remembered, would follow as the second thought, and would present such a difficulty as would lead to the conclusion that the whole thing was impracticable. But the necessity still would exist; and we may readily suppose that the idea was conceived, and lost, and reproduced, and dropped, and taken up again and again, until at last, the thought of dividing sounds into parts, and making a mark, not to represent a whole sound, but only a part of one, and then of combining these marks, not very many in number, upon the principles of permutation, so as to represent any and all of the whole twenty thousand words, and even any additional number was somehow conceived and pushed into practice. This was the invention of phoenetic writing, as distinguished from the clumsy picture writing of some of the nations. That it was difficult of conception and execution, is apparant, as well by the foregoing reflections, as by the fact that so many tribes of men have come down from Adam's time to ours without ever having possessed it. It's utility may be conceived, by the reflection that, to it we owe everything which distinguishes us from savages. Take it from us, and the Bible, all history, all science, all government, all commerce, and nearly all social intercourse go with it.

The great activity of the tongue, in articulating sounds, has already been mentioned; and it may be of some passing interest to notice the wonderful powers of the eye, in conveying ideas to the mind from writing. Take the same example of the numbers from one to one hundred, written down, and you can run your eye over the list, and be assured that every number is in it, in about one half the time it would require to pronounce the words with the voice; and not only so, but you can, in the same short time, determine whether every word is spelled correctly, by which it is evident that every separate letter, amounting to eight hundred and sixty four, has been recognized, and reported to the mind, within the incredibly short space of twenty seconds, or one third of a minute.

I have already intimated my opinion that in the world's history, certain inventions and discoveries occurred, of peculiar value, on account of their great efficiency in facilitating all other inventions and discoveries. Of these were the arts of writing and of printing—the discovery of America, and the introduction of Patent-laws. The date of the first, as already stated, is unknown; but it certainly was as much as fifteen hundred years before the Christian era; the second—printing—came in 1436, or nearly three thousand years after the first. The others followed more rapidly—the discovery of America in 1492, and the first patent laws in 1624. Though not apposite to my present purpose, it is but justice to the fruitfulness of that period, to mention two other important events—the Lutheran Reformation in 1517, and, still earlier, the invention of negroes, or, of the present mode of using them, in 1434. But, to return to the consideration of printing, it is plain that it is but the other half—and in real utility, the better half—of writing; and that both together are but the assistants of speech in the communication of thoughts between man and man. When man was possessed of speech alone, the chances of invention, discovery, and improvement, were very limited; but by the introduction of each of these, they were greatly multiplied. When writing was invented, any important observation, likely to lead to a discovery, had at least a chance of being written down, and consequently, a better chance of never being forgotten; and of being seen, and reflected upon, by a much greater number of persons; and thereby the chances of a valuable hint being caught, proportionably augmented. By this means the observation of a single individual might lead to an important invention, years, and even centuries after he was dead. In one word, by means of writing, the seeds of invention were more permanently preserved, and more widely sown. And yet, for the three thousand years during which printing remained undiscovered after writing was in use, it was only a small portion of the people who could write, or read writing; and consequently the field of invention, though much extended, still continued very limited. At length printing came. It gave ten thousand copies of any written matter, quite as cheaply as ten were given before; and consequently a thousand minds were brought into the field where there was but one before. This was a great gain; and history shows a great changecorresponding to it, in point of time. I will venture to consider it, the true termination of that period called "the dark ages." Discoveries, inventions, and improvements followed rapidly, and have been increasing their rapidity ever since. The effects could not come, all at once. It required time to bring them out; and they are still coming. The capacity to read, could not be multiplied as fast as the means of reading. Spelling-books just began to go into the hands of the children; but the teachers were not very numerous, or very competent; so that it is safe to infer they did not advance so speedily as they do now-a-days. It is very probable—almost certain—that the great mass of men, at that time, were utterly unconscious, that their conditions, or their minds were capable of improvement. They not only looked upon the educated few as superior beings; but they supposed themselves to be naturally incapable of rising to equality. To immancipate the mind from this false and under estimate of itself, is the great task which printing came into the world to perform. It is difficult for us, now and here, to conceive how strong this slavery of the mind was; and how long it did, of necessity, take, to break it's shackles, and to get a habit of freedom of thought, established. It is, in this connection, a curious fact that a new country is most favorable—almost necessary—to the immancipation of thought, and the consequent advancement of civilization and the arts. The human family originated as is thought, somewhere in Asia, and have worked their way princip[al]ly Westward. Just now, in civilization, and the arts, the people of Asia are entirely behind those of Europe; those of the East of Europe behind those of the West of it; while we, here in America, think we discover, and invent, and improve, faster than any of them. They may think this is arrogance; but they can not deny that Russia has called on us to show her how to build steam-boats and railroads—while in the older parts of Asia, they scarcely know that such things as S.Bs & RR.s. exist. In anciently inhabited countries, the dust of ages—a real downright old-fogyism—seems to settle upon, and smother the intellects and energies of man. It is in this view that I have mentioned the discovery of America as an event greatly favoring and facilitating useful discoveries and inventions.

Next came the Patent laws. These began in England in 1624; and, in this country, with the adoption of our constitution. Before then [these?], any man might instantly use what another had invented; so that the inventor had no special advantage from his own invention. The patent system changed this; secured to the inventor, for a limited time, the exclusive use of his invention; and thereby added the fuel of interest to the fire of genius, in the discovery and production of new and useful things.

AUTOBIOGRAPHIES

Lincoln wrote three autobiographies within two years. The first was to satisfy a request for an entry in the Dictionary of Congress, *the second for a Republican friend who had it incorporated into an article published in a Pennsylvania newspaper, and the third, written from a third-person point of view, was at the request of a Chicago journalist who then used the information in a campaign biography for Lincoln.*

First Autobiography, June 1858

Born, February 12, 1809, in Hardin County, Kentucky.

Education defective.

Profession, a lawyer.

Have been a captain of volunteers in Black Hawk war.

Postmaster at a very small office.

Four times a member of the Illinois legislature, and was a member of the lower house of Congress.

Second Autobiography, December 1859

I was born Feb. 12, 1809, in Hardin County, Kentucky. My parents were both born in Virginia, of undistinguished families— second families, perhaps I should say. My mother, who died in my tenth year, was of a family of the name of Hanks, some of whom now reside in Adams and others in Macon Counties, Illinois. My paternal grandfather, Abraham Lincoln, emigrated from Rockingham County, Virginia, to Kentucky, about 1781 or 2, where, a year or two later, he was killed by indians, not in battle, but by stealth, when he was laboring to open a farm in the forest. His ancestors, who were Quakers, went to Virginia from Berks County, Pennsylvania. An effort to identify them with the New-England family of the same name ended in nothing more definite, than a similarity of Christian names in both families, such as Enoch, Levi, Mordecai, Solomon, Abraham, and the like.

My father, at the death of his father, was but six years of age; and he grew up, litterally [sic] without education. He removed from Kentucky to what is now Spencer County, Indiana, in my eighth year. We reached our new home about the time the State came into the Union. It was a wild region, with many bears and other wild animals, still in the woods. There I grew up. There were some schools, so called; but no qualification was ever required of a teacher beyond "readin, writin, and cipherin" to the Rule of Three. If a straggler supposed to understand latin happened to sojourn in the neighborhood, he was looked upon as a wizzard

[sic]. There was absolutely nothing to excite ambition for education. Of course when I came of age I did not know much. Still somehow, I could read, write, and cipher to the Rule of Three; but that was all. I have not been to school since. The little advance I now have upon this store of education, I have picked up from time to time under the pressure of necessity.

I was raised to farm work, which I continued till I was twenty-two. At twenty one I came to Illinois, and passed the first year in Macon County. Then I got to New-Salem (at that time in Sangamon, now in Menard County), where I remained a year as a sort of Clerk in a store. Then came the Black-Hawk war; and I was elected a Captain of Volunteers—a success which gave me more pleasure than any I have had since. I went the campaign, was elated, ran for the Legislature the same year (1832) and was beaten—the only time I ever have been beaten by the people. The next, and three succeeding biennial elections, I was elected to the Legislature. I was not a candidate afterwards. During this Legislative period I had studied law, and removed to Springfield to practise it. In 1846 I was once elected to the lower House of Congress. Was not a candidate for re-election. From 1849 to 1854, both inclusive, practiced law more assiduously than ever before. Always a whig in politics, and generally on the whig electoral tickets, making active canvasses—I was losing interest in politics, when the repeal of the Missouri Compromise aroused me again. What I have done since then is pretty well known.

If any personal description of me is thought desirable, it may be said, I am, in height, six feet, four inches, nearly; lean in flesh, weighing on an average one hundred and eighty pounds; dark complexion, with coarse black hair, and grey eyes—no other marks or brands recollected.

Third Autobiography, June 1860

Abraham Lincoln was born February 12, 1809, then in Hardin, now in the more recently formed county of La Rue, Kentucky. His father, Thomas, and grandfather, Abraham, were born in Rockingham County, Virginia, whither their ancestors had come from Berks County, Pennsylvania. His lineage has been traced no father back than this. The family were originally Quakers, though in later times they have fallen away from the peculiar habits of that people. The grandfather, Abraham, had four brothers—Isaac, Jacob, John, and Thomas. So far as known, the descendants of Jacob and John are still in Virginia. Isaac went to a place near where Virginia, North Carolina, and Tennessee join; and his descendants are in that region. Thomas came to Kentucky, and after many years died there, whence his descendants went to Missouri. Abraham, grandfather of the subject of this sketch, came to Kentucky, and was killed by Indians about the year 1784. He left a widow, three sons, and two daughters. The eldest son, Mordecai, remained in Kentucky till late in life, when he removed to Hancock County, Illinois, where soon after he died, and where several of his descendants still remain. The second son, Josiah, removed at an early day to a place on BlueRiver, now within Hancock County, Indiana, but no recent information of him or his family has been obtained. The eldest sister, Mary, married Ralph Crume, and some of her descendants are now known to be in Breckenridge County, Kentucky. The second sister, Nancy, married William Brumfield, and her family are not known to have left Kentucky, but there is no recent information from them. Thomas, the youngest son, and the father of the present subject, by the early death of his father, and very narrow circumstances of his mother, even in childhood was a wandering laboring-boy, and grew up literally without education. He never did more in the way of writing than to bunglingly write his own name. Before he was grown he passed one year as a hired hand with his uncle Isaac on Watauga, a branch of the Holston River. Getting back into Kentucky, and having reached his twenty-eighth year, he married Nancy Hanks—mother of the present subject—in the year 1806. She also was born in Virginia; and relatives of hers of the name of Hanks, and of other names, now reside in Coles, in Macon, and in Adams counties, Illinois, and also in Iowa. The present subject has no brother or sister of the whole or half blood. He had a sister, older than himself, who was grown and married, but died many years ago, leaving no child; also a brother, younger than himself, who died in infancy. Before leaving Kentucky, he and his sister were sent, for short periods, to A B C schools, the first kept by Zachariah Riney, and the second by Caleb Hazel.

At this time his father resided on Knob Creek, on the road from Bardstown, Kentucky, to Nashville, Tennessee, at a point three or three and a half miles south or southwest of Atherton's Ferry, on the Rolling Fork. From this place he removed to what is now Spencer County, Indiana, in the autumn of 1816, Abraham then being in his eighth year. This removal was partly on account of slavery, but chiefly on account of the difficulty in land titles in Kentucky. He settled in an unbroken forest, and the clearing away of surplus wood was the great task ahead. Abraham, though very young, was large of his age, and had an ax put into his hands at once; and from that till within his twenty-third year he was almost constantly handling that most useful instrument—less, of course, in plowing and harvesting seasons. At this place Abraham took an early start as a hunter, which was never much improved afterward. A few days before the completion of his eighth year, in the absence of his father, a flock of wild turkeys approached the new log cabin, and Abraham with a rifle-gun, standing inside, shot through a crack and killed one of them. He has never since pulled a trigger on any larger game. In the autumn of 1818 his mother died; and a year afterward his father married Mrs. Sally Johnston, at Elizabethtown, Kentucky, a widow with three children of her first marriage. She proved a good and kind mother to Abraham, and is still living in Coles County, Illinois. There were no children of this second marriage. His father's residence continued at the same place in Indiana till 1830. While here Abraham went to A B C schools by littles, kept successively by Andrew Crawford—Sweeney, and Azel W. Dorsey. He does not remember any other. The family of Mr. Dorsey now resides in Schuyler County, Illinois. Abraham now thinks that the aggregate of all his schooling did not amount to one year. He was never in a college or academy as a student, and never inside of a college or academy building till since he had a law license. What he has in the way of education he has picked up. After he was twenty-three and had separated from his father, he studied English grammar—imperfectly, of course, but so as to speak and write as well as he now does. He studied and nearly mastered the six books of Euclid since he was a member of Congress. He regrets his want of education, and does what he can to supply the want. In his tenth year he was kicked by a horse, and apparently killed for a time. When he was nineteen, still residing in Indiana, he made his first trip upon a flatboat to New Orleans. He was a hired hand merely, and he and a son of the owner, without other assistance, made the trip. The nature of part of the "cargo-load," as it was called, made it necessary for them to linger and trade along the sugar-coast; and one night they were attacked by seven negroes with intent to kill and rob them. They were hurt some in the mêlée, but succeeded in driving the negroes from the boat, and then "cut cable," "weighed anchor," and left.

March 1, 1830, Abraham having just completed his twenty-first year, his father and family, with the families of the two daughters and sons-in-law of his stepmother, left the old homestead in Indiana and came to Illinois. Their mode of conveyance was wagons drawn by ox-teams, and Abraham drove one of the teams. They reached the county of Macon, and stopped there some time within the same month of March. His father and family settled a new place on the north side of the Sangamon River, at the junction of the timberland and prairie, about ten miles westerly from Decatur. Here they built a log cabin, into which they removed, and made sufficient of rails to fence ten acres of ground, fenced and broke the ground, and raised a crop of sown corn upon it the same year. These are, or are supposed to be, the rails about which so much is being said just now, though these are far from being the first or only rails ever made by Abraham.

The sons-in-law were temporarily settled in other places in the county. In the autumn all hands were greatly afflicted with ague and fever, to which they had not been used, and by which they were greatly discouraged, so much so that they determined on leaving the county. They remained, however, through the succeeding winter, which was the winter of the very celebrated "deep snow" of Illinois. During that winter Abraham, together with his stepmother's son, John D. Johnston, and John Hanks, yet residing in Macon County, hired themselves to Denton Offutt to take a flatboat from Beardstown, Illinois, to New Orleans; and for that purpose were to join him—Offutt—at Springfield, Illinois, so soon as the snow should go off. When it did go off, which was about the first of March, 1831, the county was so flooded as to make traveling by land impracticable; to obviate which difficulty they purchased a large canoe, and came down the Sangamon River in it. This is the time and the manner of Abraham's first entrance into Sangamon County. They found Offutt at Springfield, but learned from him that he had failed in getting a boat at Beardstown. This led to their hiring themselves to him for twelve dollars per month each, and getting the timber out of the trees and building a boat at Old Sangamon town on the Sangamon River, seven miles northwest of Springfield, which boat they took to New Orleans, substantially upon the old contract.

During this boat-enterprise acquaintance with Offutt, who was previously an entire stranger, he conceived a liking for Abraham, and believing he could turn him to account, he contracted with him to act as clerk for him, on his return from New Orleans, in charge of a store and mill at New Salem, then in Sangamon, now in Menard County. Hanks had not gone to New Orleans, but having a family, and being likely to be detained from home longer than at first expected, had turned back from St. Louis. He is the same John Hanks who now engineers the "rail enterprise" at Decatur, and is a first cousin to Abraham's mother. Abraham's father, with his own family and others mentioned, had, in pursuance of their intention, removed from Macon to Coles County. John D. Johnston, the stepmother's son, went with them, and Abraham stopped indefinitely and for the first time, as it were, by himself at New Salem, before mentioned. This was in July, 1831. Here he rapidly made acquaintances and friends. In less than a year Offutt's business was failing—had almost failed—when the Black Hawk war of 1832 broke out. Abraham joined a volunteer company, and, to his own surprise, was elected captain of it. He says he has not since had any success in life which gave him so much satisfaction. He went to the campaign, served near three months, met the ordinary hardships of such an expedition, but was in no battle. He now owns, in Iowa, the land upon which his own warrants for the service were located. Returning from the campaign, and encouraged by his great popularity among his immediate neighbors, he the same year ran for the legislature, and was beaten—his own precinct, however, casting its votes 277 for and 7 against him—and that, too, while he was an avowed Clay man, and the precinct the autumn afterward giving a majority of 115 to General Jackson over Mr. Clay. This was the only time

Abraham was ever beaten on a direct vote of the people. He was now without means and out of business, but was anxious to remain with his friends who had treated him with so much generosity, especially as he had nothing elsewhere to go to. He studied what he should do—thought of learning the blacksmith trade—thought of trying to study law—rather thought he could not succeed at that without a better education. Before long, strangely enough, a man offered to sell, and did sell, to Abraham and another as poor as himself, an old stock of goods, upon credit. They opened as merchants; and he says that was the store. Of course they did nothing but get deeper and deeper in debt. He was appointed postmaster at New Salem—the office being too insignificant to make his politics an objection. The store winked out. The surveyor of Sangamon offered to depute to Abraham that portion of his work which was within his part of the county. He accepted, procured a compass and chain, studied Flint and Gibson a little, and went at it. This procured bread, and kept soul and body together. The election of 1834 came, and he was then elected to the legislature by the highest vote cast for any candidate. Major John T. Stuart, then in full practice of the law, was also elected. During the canvass, in a private conversation he encouraged Abraham [to] study law. After the election he borrowed books of Stuart, took them home with him, and went at it in good earnest. He studied with nobody. He still mixed in the surveying to pay board and clothing bills. When the legislature met, the lawbooks were dropped, but were taken up again at the end of the session. He was reelected in 1836, 1838, and 1840. In the autumn of 1836 he obtained a law license, and on April 15, 1837, removed to Springfield, and commenced the practice—his old friend Stuart taking him into partnership. March 3, 1837, by a protest entered upon the "Illinois House Journal" of that date, at pages 817 and 818, Abraham, with Dan Stone, another representative of Sangamon, briefly defined his position on the slavery question; and so far as it goes, it was then the same that it is now. The protest is as follows:

> "Resolutions upon the subject of domestic slavery having passed both branches of the General Assembly at its present session, the undersigned hereby protest against the passage of the same.
>
> "They believe that the institution of slavery is founded on both injustice and bad policy, but that the promulgation of Abolition doctrines tends rather to increase than abate its evils.
>
> "They believe that the Congress of the United States has no power under the Constitution to interfere with the institution of slavery in the different States.

"They believe that the Congress of the United States has the power, under the Constitution, to abolish slavery in the District of Columbia, but that the power ought not to be exercised unless at the request of the people of the District.

"The difference between these opinions and those contained in the above resolutions is their reason for entering this protest.

"Dan Stone,

"A Lincoln,

"Representatives from the County of Sangamon."

In 1838 and 1840, Mr. Lincoln's party voted for him as Speaker, but being in the minority he was not elected. After 1840 he declined a reelection to the legislature. He was on the Harrison electoral ticket in 1840, and on that of Clay in 1844, and spent much time and labor in both those canvasses. In November, 1842, he was married to Mary, daughter of Robert S. Todd, of Lexington, Kentucky. They have three living children, all sons, one born in 1843, one in 1850, and one in 1853. They lost one, who was born in 1846.

In 1846 he was elected to the lower House of Congress, and served one term only, commencing in December, 1847, and ending with the inauguration of General Taylor, in March 1849. All the battles of the Mexican war had been fought before Mr. Lincoln took his seat in Congress, but the American army was still in Mexico, and the treaty of peace was not fully and formally ratified till the June afterward. Much has been said of his course in Congress in regard to this war. A careful examination of the "Journal" and "Congressional Globe" shows that he voted for all the supply measures that came up, and for all the measures in any way favorable to the officers, soldiers, and their families, who conducted the war through: with the exception that some of these measures passed without yeas and nays, leaving no record as to how particular men voted. The "Journal" and "Globe" also show him voting that the war was unnecessarily and unconstitutionally begun by the President of the United States. This is the language of Mr. Ashmun's amendment, for which Mr. Lincoln and nearly or quite all other Whigs of the House of Representatives voted.

Mr. Lincoln's reasons for the opinion expressed by this vote were briefly that the President had sent General Taylor into an inhabited part of the country belonging to Mexico, and not to the United States, and thereby had provoked the first act of hostility, in fact the commencement of the war; that the place, being the country bordering on the east bank of the Rio Grande, was inhabited by native Mexicans, born there under the Mexican government, and had never submitted to, nor been conquered by, Texas or the United States, nor transferred to either by treaty; that although Texas claimed the Rio Grande as her boundary, Mexico had never recognized it, and neither Texas nor the United States had ever enforced it; that there was a broad desert between that and the country over which Texas had actual control; that the country where hostilities commenced, having once belonged to Mexico, must remain so until it was somehow legally transferred, which had never been done.

Mr. Lincoln thought the act of sending an armed force among the Mexicans was unnecessary, inasmuch as Mexico was in no way molesting or menacing the United States or the people thereof; and that it was unconstitutional, because the power of levying war is vested in Congress, and not in the President. He thought the principal motive for the act was to divert public attention from the surrender of "Fifty-four, forty, or fight" to Great Britain, on the Oregon boundary question.

Mr. Lincoln was not a candidate for reelection. This was determined upon and declared before he went to Washington, in accordance with an understanding among Whig friends, by which Colonel Hardin and Colonel Baker had each previously served a single term in this same district.

In 1848, during his term in Congress, he advocated General Taylor's nomination for the presidency, in opposition to all others, and also took an active part for his election after his nomination, speaking a few times in Maryland, near Washington, several times in Massachusetts, and canvassing quite fully his own district in Illinois, which was followed by a majority in the district of over 1500 for General Taylor.

Upon his return from Congress he went to the practice of the law with greater earnestness than ever before. In 1852 he was upon the Scott electoral ticket, and did something in the way of canvassing, but owing to the hopelessness of the cause in Illinois he did less than in previous presidential canvasses.

In 1854 his profession had almost superseded the thought of politics in his mind, when the repeal of the Missouri Compromise aroused him as he had never been before.

In the autumn of that year he took the stump with no broader practical aim or object than to secure, if possible, the reelection of Hon. Richard Yates to Congress. His speeches at once attracted a more marked attention than they had ever before done. As the canvass proceeded he was drawn to different parts of the State outside of Mr. Yates' district. He did not abandon the law, but gave his attention by turns to that and politics. The State agricultural fair was at Springfield that year, and Douglas was announced to speak there.

In the canvass of 1856 Mr. Lincoln made over fifty speeches, no one of which, so far as he remembers, was put in print. One of them was made at Galena, but Mr. Lincoln has no recollection of any part of it being printed; nor does he remember whether in that speech he said anything about a Supreme Court decision. He may have spoken upon that subject, and some of the newspapers may have reported him as saying what it now ascribed to him, but he thinks he could not have expressed himself as represented.

TEMPERANCE ADDRESS

Springfield, Illinois

February 22, 1842

Although the Temperance Cause has been in progress for near twenty years, it is apparent to all, that it is, just now, being crowned with a degree of success, hitherto unparalleled.

The list of its friends is daily swelled by the additions of fifties, of hundreds, and of thousands. The cause itself seems suddenly transformed from a cold abstract theory, to a living, breathing, active, and powerful chieftain, going forth "conquering and to conquer." The citadels of his great adversary are daily being stormed and dismantled; his temple and his altars, where the rites of his idolatrous worship have long been performed, and where human sacrifices have long been wont to be made, are daily desecrated and deserted. The trump of the conqueror's fame is sounding from hill to hill, from sea to sea, and from land to land, and calling millions to his standard at a blast.

For this new and splendid success, we heartily rejoice. That that success is so much greater now than heretofore, is doubtless owing to rational causes; and if we would have it continue, we shall do well to inquire what those causes are.

The warfare heretofore waged against the demon Intemperance, has, somehow or other, been erroneous. Either the champions engaged, or the tactics they adopted have not been the most proper. These champions for the most part have been preachers, lawyers, and hired agents. Between these and the mass of mankind, there is a want of *approachability*, if the term be admissible, partial, at least, fatal to their success. They are supposed to have no sympathy of feeling or interest, with those very persons whom it is their object to convince and persuade.

And again, it is so common and so easy to ascribe motives to men of these classes, other than those they profess to act upon. The preacher, it is said, advocates temperance because he is a fanatic, and desires a union of the Church and State; the lawyer, from his pride and vanity of hearing himself speak; and the hired agent, for his salary.

But when one, who has long been known as a victim of intemperance bursts the fetters that have bound him, and appears before his neighbors "clothed, and in his right mind," a redeemed specimen of long-lost humanity, and stands up with tears of joy trembling in his eyes, to tell of the miseries once endured, now to be endured no more forever; of his once naked and starving children, now clad and fed comfortably; of a wife long weighed down with woe, weeping, and a broken heart, now restored to health, happiness, and a renewed affection; and how easily it is all done, once it is resolved to be done; how simple his language, there is a logic, and an eloquence in it, that few, with human feelings, can resist. They cannot say that he desires a union of church and state, for he is not a church member; they cannot say he is vain of hearing himself speak, for his whole demeanor shows he would gladly avoid speaking at all; they cannot say he speaks for pay for he receives none, and asks for none. Nor can his sincerity in any way be doubted; or his sympathy for those he would persuade to imitate his example be denied.

In my judgment, it is to the battles of this new class of champions that our late success is greatly, perhaps chiefly, owing. But had the old school champions themselves been of the most wise selecting? Was their system of tactics, the most judicious? It seems to me, it was not. Too much denunciation against dram-sellers and dram-drinkers was indulged in. This, I think, was both impolitic and unjust. It was impolitic, because, it is not much in the nature of man to be driven to anything; still less to be driven about that which is exclusively his own business; and least of all, where such driving is to be submitted to, at the expense of pecuniary interest, or burning appetite. When the dram-seller and drinker, were incessantly told, not in accents of entreaty and persuasion, diffidently addressed by erring man to an erring brother; but in the thundering tones of anathema and denunciation, with which the lordly Judge often groups together all the crimes of the felon's life, and thrusts them in his face just ere he passes sentence of death upon him, that they were the authors of all the vice and misery and crime in the land; that they were the manufacturers and material of all the thieves and robbers and murderers that infested the earth; that their houses were the workshops of the devil; and that their persons should be shunned by all the good and virtuous, as moral pestilences—I say, when they were told all this, and in this way, it is not wonderful that they were slow, very slow, to acknowledge the truth of such denunciations, and to join the ranks of their denouncers in a hue and cry against themselves.

To have expected them to do otherwise than they did—to have expected them not to meet denunciation with denunciation, crimination with crimination, and anathema with anathema—was to expect a reversal of human nature, which is God's decree, and never can be reversed.

When the conduct of men is designed to be influenced, persuasion, kind, unassuming persuasion, should ever be adopted. It is an old and a true maxim, "that a drop of honey catches more flies than a gallon of gall." So with men. If you would win a man to your cause, first convince him that you are his sincere friend. Therein is a drop of honey that catches his heart, which, say what he will, is the great highroad to his reason, and which, when once gained, you will find but little trouble in convincing his judgment of the justice of your cause, if indeed that cause really be a just one. On the contrary, assume to dictate to his judgment, or to command his action, or to mark him as one to be shunned and despised, and he will retreat within himself, close all the avenues to his head and his heart; and though your cause be naked truth itself, transformed to the heaviest lance, harder than steel, and sharper than steel can be made, and though you throw it with more than Herculean force and precision, you shall be no more be able to pierce him, than to penetrate the hard shell of a tortoise with a rye straw. Such is man, and so must he be understood by those who would lead him, even to his own best interest.

On this point, the Washingtonians greatly excel the temperance advocates of former times. Those whom they desire to convince and persuade, are their old friends and companions. They know they are not demons, nor even the worst of men. They know that generally, they are kind, generous, and charitable, even beyond the example of their more staid and sober neighbors. They are practical philanthropists; and they glow with a generous and brotherly zeal, that mere theorizers are incapable of feeling. Benevolence and charity possess their hearts entirely; and out of the abundance of their hearts, their tongues give utterance, "Love through all their actions run, and all their words are mild." In this spirit they speak and act, and in the same, they are heard and regarded. And when such is the temper of the advocate, and such of the audience, no good cause can be unsuccessful. But I have said that denunciations against dram-sellers and dram-drinkers are unjust as well as impolitic. Let us see.

I have not enquired at what period of time the use of intoxicating drinks commenced; nor is it important to know. It is sufficient that to all of us who now inhabit the world, the practice of drinking them, is just as old as the world itself—that is, we have seen the one, just as long as we have seen the other. When all such of us, as have now reached the years of maturity, first opened our eyes upon the stage of existence, we found intoxicating liquor, recognized by everybody, used by every body, and repudiated by nobody. It commonly entered into the first draught of the infant, and the last draught of the dying man. From the sideboard of the parson, down to the ragged pocket of the houseless loafer, it was constantly found. Physicians prescribed it, in this, that, and the other disease; Government provided it for soldiers and sailors; and to have a rolling or raising, a husking or "hoe-down," any where about without it, was *positively insufferable*. So too, it was every where a respectable article of manufacture and merchandise. The making of it was regarded as an honorable livelihood, and he who could make most, was the most enterprising and respectable. Large and small manufactories of it were everywhere erected, in which all the earthly goods of their owners were invested. Wagons drew it from town to town; boats bore it from clime to clime, and the winds wafted it from nation to nation; and merchants bought and sold it, by wholesale and retail, with precisely the same feelings on the part of the seller, buyer, and bystander, as are felt at the selling and buying of flour, beef, bacon, or any other of the real necessaries of life. Universal public opinion not only tolerated, but recognized and adopted its use.

It is true, that even then it was known and acknowledged that many were greatly injured by it; but none seemed to think the injury arose from the use of a bad thing, but from the abuse of a very good thing. The victims of it were pitied and compassionated, just as are the heirs of consumption, and other hereditary diseases. Their failing was treated as a misfortune, and not as a crime, or even as a disgrace.

If, then, what I have been saying be true, is it wonderful, that some should think and act now as all thought and acted twenty years ago, and is it just to assail, condemn, or despise them for doing so? The universal sense of mankind, on any subject, is an argument, or at least an influence not easily overcome. The success of the argument in favor of the existence of an over-ruling Providence, mainly depends upon that sense; and men ought not, in justice, to be denounced for yielding to it in any case, or giving it up slowly, especially, where they are backed by interest, fixed habits, or burning appetites.

Another error, as it seems to me, into which the old reformers fell, was, the position that all habitual drunkards were utterly incorrigible, and therefore, must be turned adrift, and damned without remedy, in order that the grace of temperance might abound to the temperate then, and to all mankind some hundreds of years thereafter. There is in this something so repugnant to humanity, so uncharitable, so cold-blooded and feelingless, that it never did, nor ever can enlist the enthusiasm of a popular cause. We could not love the man who taught it—we could not hear him with patience. The heart could not throw open its portals to it, the generous man could not adopt it, it could not mix with his blood. It looked so fiendishly selfish, so like throwing fathers and brothers overboard, to lighten the boat for our security—that the noble-minded shrank from the manifest meanness of the thing. And besides this, the benefits of a reformation to be effected by such a system, were too remote in point of time, to warmly engage many in its behalf. Few can be induced to labor exclusively for posterity; and none will do it enthusiastically. Posterity has done nothing for us; and theorize on it as we may, practically we shall do very little for it, unless we are made to think, we are, at the same time, doing something for ourselves.

What an ignorance of human nature does it exhibit, to ask or expect a whole community to rise up and labor for the temporal happiness of others, after themselves shall be consigned to the dust, a majority of which community take no pains whatever to secure their own eternal welfare at a no greater distant day. Great distance, in either time or space, has wonderful power to lull and render quiescent the human mind. Pleasures to be enjoyed, or pains to be endured, after we shall be dead and gone, are but little regarded, even in our own cases, and much less in the cases of others.

Still, in addition to this, there is something so ludicrous in promises of good, or threats of evil, a great way off, as to render the whole subject with which they are connected, easily turned into ridicule. "Better lay down that spade you're stealing, Paddy—if you don't, you'll pay for it at the day of judgment." "Be the powers, if ye'll credit me so long I'll take another jist."

By the Washingtonians, this system of consigning the habitual drunkard to hopeless ruin, is repudiated. They adopt a more enlarged philanthropy. They go for present as well as future good. They labor for all now living, as well as all hereafter to live. They teach hope to all—despair to none. As applying to their cause, they deny the doctrine of unpardonable sin. As in Christianity it is taught, so in this they teach—

> "While the lamp holds out to burn,
> The vilest sinner may return."

And, what is a matter of more profound congratulation, they, by experiment upon experiment, and example upon example, prove the maxim to be no less true in the one case than in the other. On every hand we behold those, who but yesterday, were the chief of sinners, now the chief apostles of the cause. Drunken devils are cast out by ones, by sevens, and by legions; and their unfortunate victims, like the poor possessed, who was redeemed from his long and lonely wanderings in the tombs, are publishing to the ends of the earth how great things have been done for them.

To these new champions, and this new system of tactics, our late success is mainly owing; and to them we must mainly look for the final consummation. The ball is now rolling gloriously on, and none are so able as they to increase its speed, and its bulk—to add to its momentum and its magnitude—even though unlearned in letters, for this task none are so well educated. To fit them for this work, they have been taught in the true school. They have been in that gulf, from which they would teach others the means of escape. They have passed that prison wall, which others have long declared impassable; and who that has not shall dare to weigh opinions with them, as to the mode of passing?

But if it be true, as I have insisted, that those who have suffered by intemperance personally, and have reformed, are the most powerful and efficient instruments to push the reformation to ultimate success, it does not follow, that those who have not suffered, have no part left them to perform. Whether or not the world would be vastly benefitted by a total and final banishment from it of all intoxicating drinks, seems to me not now an open question. Three-fourths of mankind confess the affirmative with their tongues, and, I believe, all the rest acknowledge it in their hearts.

Ought any, then, to refuse their aid in doing what the good of the whole demands? Shall he who cannot do much, be, for that reason, excused if he do nothing? "But," says one, "what good can I do by signing the pledge? I never drink even without signing." This question has already been asked and answered more than millions of times. Let it be answered once more. For the man suddenly, or in any other way, to break off from the use of drams, who has indulged in them for a long course of years, and until his appetite for them has become ten or a hundred fold stronger, and more craving, than any natural appetite can be, requires a most powerful moral effort. In such an undertaking, he needs every moral support and influence, that can possibly be brought to his aid, and thrown around him. And not only so; but every moral prop, should be taken from whatever argument might rise in his mind to lure him to his backsliding. When he casts his eyes around him, he should be able to see, all that he respects, all that he admires, all that he loves, kindly and anxiously pointing him onward, and none beckoning him back to his former miserable "wallowing in the mire."

But it is said by some, that men will think and act for themselves; that none will disuse spirits or anything else because his neighbors do; and that moral influence is not that powerful engine contended for. Let us examine this. Let me ask the man who could maintain this position most stiffly, what compensation he will accept to go to church some Sunday and sit during the sermon with his wife's bonnet upon his head? Not a trifle, I'll venture. And why not? There would be nothing irreligious in it, nothing immoral, nothing uncomfortable. Then why not? Is it not because there would be something egregiously unfashionable in it? Then it is the influence of fashion; and what is the influence of fashion but the influence that other people's actions have on our own actions—the strong inclination each of us feels to do as we see all our neighbors do? Nor is the influence of fashion confined to any particular thing or class of things. It is just as strong on one subject as another. Let us make it as unfashionable to withhold our names from the temperance pledge, as for husbands to wear their wives' bonnets to church, and instances will be just as rare in the one case as the other.

"But," say some, "we are no drunkards, and we shall not acknowledge ourselves such, by joining a reformed drunkards' society, whatever our influence might be." Surely, no Christian will adhere to this objection.

If they believe, as they profess, that Omnipotence condescended to take on himself the form of sinful man, and, as such, to die an ignominious death for their sakes, surely they will not refuse submission to the infinitely lesser condescension, for the temporal, and perhaps eternal salvation, of a large, erring, and unfortunate class of their fellow-creatures. Nor is the condescension very great. In my judgment, such of us as have never fallen victims, have been spared more by the absence of appetite, than from any mental or moral superiority over those who have. Indeed, I believe, if we take habitual drunkards as a class, their heads and their hearts will bear an advantageous comparison with those of any other class. There seems ever to have been a proneness in the brilliant and warm-blooded to fall into this vice—the demon of intemperance ever seems to have delighted in sucking the blood of genius and of generosity. What one of us but can call to mind some dear relative, more promising in youth than all his fellows, who has fallen a sacrifice to his rapacity? He ever seems to have gone forth, like the Egyptian angel of death, commissioned to slay, if not the first, the fairest born of every family. Shall he now be arrested in his desolating career? In that arrest, all can give aid that will; and who shall be excused that can, and will not? Far around as human breath has ever blown, he keeps our fathers, our brothers, our sons, and our friends prostrate in the chains of moral death. To all the living, everywhere we cry, "Come sound the moral trump, that these may rise and stand up, an exceeding great army."—"Come from the four winds, O breath! and breathe upon these slain, that they may live." If the relative grandeur of revolutions shall be estimated by the great amount of human misery they alleviate, and the small amount they inflict, then, indeed, will this be the grandest the world shall ever have seen.

Of our political revolution of '76, we are all justly proud. It has given us a degree of political freedom, far exceeding that of any other nation of the earth. In it the world has found a solution of the long mooted problem, as to the capability of man to govern himself. In it was the germ which has vegetated, and still is to grow and expand into the universal liberty of mankind.

But with all these glorious results, past, present, and to come, it had its evils too. It breathed forth famine, swam in blood and rode in fire; and long, long after, the orphan's cry, and the widows' wail continued to break the sad silence that ensued. These were the price, the inevitable price, paid for the blessings it bought.

Turn now to the temperance revolution. In it we shall find a stronger bondage broken, a viler slavery, manumitted, a greater tyrant deposed—in it, more of want supplied, more disease healed, more sorrow assuaged. By it no orphans starving, no widows weeping. By it, none wounded in feeling, none injured in interest. Even the dram-maker and dram-seller will have glided into other occupations so gradually as never to have felt the change, and will stand ready to join all others in the universal song of gladness. And what a noble ally this, to the cause of political freedom. With such an aid, its march cannot fail to be on and on, till every son of earth shall drink in rich fruition the sorrow quenching draughts of perfect liberty. Happy day, when, all appetites controlled, all poisons subdued, all matter subjected, mind, all conquering mind, shall live and move the monarch of the world. Glorious consummation! Hail, fall of Fury! Reign of Reason, all hail!

And when the victory shall be complete—when there shall be neither a slave nor a drunkard on the earth—how proud the title of that *Land*, which may truly claim to be the birth-place and the cradle of both those revolutions that shall have ended in that victory. How nobly distinguished that People, who shall have planted, and nurtured to maturity, both the political and moral freedom of their species.

This is the one hundred and tenth anniversary of the birthday of Washington—we are met to celebrate this day. Washington is the mightiest name of earth—long since mightiest in the cause of civil liberty, still mightiest in moral reformation. On that name, an eulogy is expected. It cannot be. To add brightness to the sun, or glory to the name of Washington is alike impossible. Let none attempt it. In solemn awe pronounce the name, and in its naked, deathless splendor, leave it shining on.

PEORIA SPEECH

Peoria, Illinois

October 16, 1854

The repeal of the Missouri Compromise, and the propriety of its restoration, constitute the subject of what I am about to say.

As I desire to present my own connected view of this subject, my remarks will not be, specifically, an answer to Judge Douglas; yet, as I proceed, the main points he has presented will arise, and will receive such respectful attention as I may be able to give them.

I wish further to say, that I do not propose to question the patriotism, or to assail the motives of any man, or class of men; but rather to strictly confine myself to the naked merits of the question.

I also wish to be no less than National in all the positions I may take; and whenever I take ground which others have thought, or may think, narrow, sectional and dangerous to the Union, I hope to give a reason, which will appear sufficient, at least to some, why I think differently.

And, as this subject is no other, than part and parcel of the larger general question of domestic-slavery, I wish to *make* and to *keep* the distinction between the *existing* institution, and the *extension* of it, so broad, and so clear, that no honest man can misunderstand me, and no dishonest one, successfully misrepresent me.

In order to get a clear understanding of what the Missouri Compromise is, a short history of the preceding kindred subjects will perhaps be proper. When we established our independence, we did not own, or claim, the country to which this compromise applies. Indeed, strictly speaking, the confederacy then owned no country at all; the States respectively owned the country within their limits; and some of them owned territory beyond their strict State limits. Virginia thus owned the North-Western territory—the country out of which the principal part of Ohio, all Indiana, all Illinois, all Michigan and all Wisconsin, have since been formed. She also owned (perhaps within her then limits) what has since been formed into the State of Kentucky. North Carolina thus owned what is now the State of Tennessee; and South Carolina and Georgia, in separate parts, owned what are now Mississippi and Alabama. Connecticut, I think, owned the little remaining part of Ohio—being the same where they now send Giddings to Congress, and beat all creation at making cheese. These territories, together with the States themselves, constituted all the country over which the confederacy then claimed any sort of jurisdiction. We were then living under the Articles of Confederation, which were superceded by the Constitution several years afterwards. The question of ceding these territories to the general government was set on foot. Mr. Jefferson, the author of the Declaration of Independence, and otherwise a chief actor in the revolution; then a delegate in Congress; afterwards twice President; who was, is, and perhaps will continue to be, the most distinguished politician of our history; a Virginian by birth and continued residence, and withal, a slave-holder; conceived the idea of taking that occasion, to prevent slavery ever going into the north-western territory. He prevailed on the Virginia Legislature to adopt his views, and to cede the territory, making the prohibition of slavery therein, a condition of the deed. Congress accepted the cession, with the condition; and in the first Ordinance (which the acts of Congress were then called) for the government of the territory, provided that slavery should never be permitted therein. This is the famed ordinance of '87 so often spoken of. Thenceforward, for sixty-one years, and until in 1848, the last scrap of this territory came into the Union as the State of Wisconsin, all parties acted in quiet obedience to this ordinance. It is now what Jefferson foresaw and intended—the happy home of teeming millions of free, white, prosperous people, and no slave amongst them.

Thus, with the author of the Declaration of Independence, the policy of prohibiting slavery in new territory originated. Thus, away back of the constitution, in the pure fresh, free breath of the revolution, the State of Virginia, and the National congress put that policy in practice. Thus through sixty odd of the best years of the republic did that policy steadily work to its great and beneficent end. And thus, in those five states, and five millions of free, enterprising people, we have before us the rich fruits of this policy.

But now new light breaks upon us. Now congress declares this ought never to have been; and the like of it, must never be again. The sacred right of self government is grossly violated by it! We even find some men, who drew their first breath, and every other breath of their lives, under this very restriction, now live in dread of absolute suffocation, if they should be restricted in the "sacred right" of taking slaves to Nebraska. That perfect liberty they sigh for—the liberty of making slaves of other people—Jefferson never thought of; their own father never thought of; they never thought of themselves, a year ago. How fortunate for them, they did not sooner become sensible of their great misery! Oh, how difficult it is to treat with respect, such assaults upon all we have ever really held sacred.

But to return to history. In 1803 we purchased what was then called Louisiana, of France. It included the now states of Louisiana, Arkansas, Missouri, and Iowa; also the territory of Minnesota, and the present bone of contention, Kansas and Nebraska. Slavery already existed among the French at New Orleans; and, to some extent, at St. Louis. In 1812 Louisiana came into the Union as a slave state, without controversy. In 1818 or '19, Missouri showed signs of a wish to come in with slavery. This was resisted by northern members of Congress; and thus began the first great slavery agitation in the nation. This controversy lasted several months, and became very angry and exciting; the House of Representatives voting steadily for the prohibition of slavery in Missouri, and the Senate voting as steadily against it. Threats of breaking up the Union were freely made; and the ablest public men of the day became seriously alarmed. At length a compromise was made, in which, like all compromises, both sides yielded something. It was a law passed on the 6th day of March, 1820, providing that Missouri might come into the Union *with* slavery, but that in all the remaining part of the territory purchased of France, which lies north of 36 degrees and 30 minutes north latitude, slavery should never be permitted. This provision of law, *is the Missouri Compromise.* In excluding slavery North of the line, the same language is employed as in the Ordinance of '87. It directly applied to Iowa, Minnesota, and to the present bone of contention, Kansas and Nebraska. Whether there should or should not, be slavery south of that line, nothing was said in the law; but Arkansas constituted the principal remaining part, south of the line; and it has since been admitted as a slave state without serious controversy. More recently, Iowa, north of the line, came in as a free state without controversy. Still later, Minnesota, north of the line, had a territorial organization without controversy. Texas principally south of the line, and West of Arkansas; though originally within the purchase from France, had, in 1819, been traded off to Spain, in our treaty for the acquisition of Florida. It had thus become a part of Mexico. Mexico revolutionized and became independent of Spain. American citizens began settling rapidly, with their slaves in the southern part of Texas. Soon they revolutionized against Mexico, and established an independent government of their own, adopting a constitution, with slavery, strongly resembling the constitutions of our slave states. By still another rapid move, Texas, claiming a boundary much further West, than when we parted with her in 1819, was brought back to the United States, and admitted into the Union as a slave state. There then was little or no settlement in the northern part of Texas, a considerable portion of which lay north of the Missouri line; and in the resolutions admitting her into the Union, the Missouri restriction was expressly extended westward across her territory. This was in 1845, only nine years ago.

Thus originated the Missouri Compromise; and thus has it been respected down to 1845. And even four years later, in 1849, our distinguished Senator, in a public address, held the following language in relation to it:

"The Missouri Compromise had been in practical operation for about a quarter of a century, and had received the sanction and approbation of men of all parties in every section of the Union. It had allayed all sectional jealousies and irritations growing out of this vexed question, and harmonized and tranquilized the whole country. It had given to Henry Clay, as its prominent champion, the proud sobriquet of the '*Great Pacificator*' and by that title and for that service, his political friends had repeatedly appealed to the people to rally under his standard, as a presidential candidate, as the man who had exhibited the patriotism and the power to suppress, an unholy and treasonable agitation, and preserve the Union. He was not aware that any man or any party from any section of the Union, had ever urged as an objection to Mr. Clay, that he was the great champion of the Missouri Compromise. On the contrary, the effort was made by the opponents of Mr. Clay, to prove that he was not entitled to the exclusive merit of that great patriotic measure, and that the honor was equally due to others as well as to him, for securing its adoption—that it had its origin in the hearts of all patriotic men, who desired to preserve and perpetuate the blessings of our glorious Union—an origin akin that of the constitution of the United States, conceived in the same spirit of fraternal affection, and calculated to remove forever, the only danger, which seemed to threaten, at some distant day, to sever the social bond of union. All the evidences of public opinion at that day, seemed to indicate that this Compromise had been canonized in the hearts of the American people, as a sacred thing which no ruthless hand would ever be reckless enough to disturb."

I do not read this extract to involve Judge Douglas in an inconsistency. If he afterwards thought he had been wrong, it was right for him to change. I bring this forward merely to show the high estimate placed on the Missouri Compromise by all parties up to so late as the year 1849.

But, going back a little, in point of time, our war with Mexico broke out in 1846. When Congress was about adjourning that session, President Polk asked them to place two millions of dollars under his control, to be used by him in the recess, if found practicable and expedient, in negociating a treaty of peace with Mexico, and acquiring some part of her territory. A bill was duly got up, for the purpose, and was progressing swimmingly, in the House of Representatives, when a member by the name of David Wilmot, a democrat from Pennsylvania, moved as an amendment "Provided that in any territory thus acquired, there shall never be slavery."

This is the origin of the far-famed "Wilmot Proviso." It created a great flutter; but it stuck like wax, was voted into the bill, and the bill passed with it through the House. The Senate, however, adjourned without final action on it and so both appropriation and proviso were lost, for the time. The war continued, and at the next session, the president renewed his request for the appropriation, enlarging the amount, I think, to three million. Again came the proviso; and defeated the measure. Congress adjourned again, and the war went on. In Dec., 1847, the new congress assembled. I was in the lower House that term. The "Wilmot Proviso" or the principle of it, was constantly coming up in some shape or other, and I think I may venture to say I voted for it at least forty times; during the short term I was there. The Senate, however, held it in check, and it never became law. In the spring of 1848 a treaty of peace was made with Mexico; by which we obtained that portion of her country which now constitutes the territories of New Mexico and Utah, and the now state of California. By this treaty the Wilmot Proviso was defeated, as so far as it was intended to be, a condition of the acquisition of territory. Its friends however, were still determined to find some way to restrain slavery from getting into the new country. This new acquisition lay directly West of our old purchase from France, and extended west to the Pacific Ocean—and was so situated that if the Missouri line should be extended straight West, the new country would be divided by such extended line, leaving some North and some South of it. On Judge Douglas' motion a bill, or provision of a bill, passed the Senate to so extend the Missouri line. The Proviso men in the House, including myself, voted it down, because by implication, it gave up the Southern part to slavery, while we were bent on having it *all* free.

In the fall of 1848 the gold mines were discovered in California. This attracted people to it with unprecedented rapidity, so that on, or soon after, the meeting of the new congress in Dec., 1849, she already had a population of nearly a hundred thousand, had called a convention, formed a state constitution, excluding slavery, and was knocking for admission into the Union. The Proviso men, of course were for letting her in, but the Senate, always true to the other side would not consent to her admission. And there California stood, kept *out* of the Union, because she would not let slavery *into* her borders. Under all the circumstances perhaps this was not wrong. There were other points of dispute, connected with the general question of slavery, which equally needed adjustment. The South clamored for a more efficient fugitive slave law. The North clamored for the abolition of a peculiar species of slave trade in the District of Columbia, in connection with which, in view from the windows of the capitol, a sort of negro-livery stable, where droves of negroes were collected, temporarily kept, and finally taken to Southern markets, precisely like droves of horses, had been openly maintained for fifty years. Utah and New Mexico needed territorial governments; and whether slavery should or should not be prohibited within them, was another question. The indefinite Western boundary of Texas was to be settled. She was received a slave state; and consequently the farther West the slavery men could push her boundary, the more slave country they secured. And the farther East the slavery opponents could thrust the boundary back, the less slave ground was secured. Thus this was just as clearly a slavery question as any of the others.

These points all needed adjustment; and they were all held up, perhaps wisely to make them help to adjust one another. The Union, now, as in 1820, was thought to be in danger; and devotion to the Union rightfully inclined men to yield somewhat, in points where nothing else could have so inclined them. A compromise was finally effected. The south got their new fugitive-slave law; and the North got California, (the far best part of our acquisition from Mexico,) as a free State. The south got a provision that New Mexico and Utah, when admitted as States, may come in with or without slavery as they may then choose; and the north got the slave-trade abolished in the District of Columbia. The north got the western boundary of Texas, thence further back eastward than the south desired; but, in turn, they gave Texas ten millions of dollars, with which to pay her old debts. This is the Compromise of 1850.

Preceding the Presidential election of 1852, each of the great political parties, democrats and whigs, met in convention, and adopted resolutions endorsing the compromise of '50; as a "finality," a final settlement, so far as these parties could make it so, of all slavery agitation. Previous to this, in 1851, the Illinois Legislature had indorsed it.

During this long period of time Nebraska had remained, substantially an uninhabited country, but now emigration to, and settlement within it began to take place. It is about one third as large as the present United States, and its importance so long overlooked, begins to come into view. The restriction of slavery by the Missouri Compromise directly applies to it; in fact, was first made, and has since been maintained, expressly for it. In 1853, a bill to give it a territorial government passed the House of Representatives, and, in the hands of Judge Douglas, failed of passing the Senate only for want of time. This bill contained no repeal of the Missouri Compromise. Indeed, when it was assailed because it did not contain such repeal, Judge Douglas defended it in its existing form. On January 4th, 1854, Judge Douglas introduces a new bill to give Nebraska territorial government. He accompanies this bill with a report, in which last, he expressly recommends that the Missouri Compromise shall neither be affirmed nor repealed.

Before long the bill is so modified as to make two territories instead of one; calling the Southern one Kansas.

Also, about a month after the introduction of the bill, on the judge's own motion, it is so amended as to declare the Missouri Compromise inoperative and void; and, substantially, that the People who go and settle there may establish slavery, or exclude it, as they may see fit. In this shape the bill passed both branches of congress, and became a law.

This is the *repeal* of the Missouri Compromise. The foregoing history may not be precisely accurate in every particular; but I am sure it is sufficiently so, for all the uses I shall attempt to make of it, and in it, we have before us, the chief material enabling us to correctly judge whether the repeal of the Missouri Compromise is right or wrong.

I think, and shall try to show, that it is wrong; wrong in its direct effect, letting slavery into Kansas and Nebraska—and wrong in its prospective principle, allowing it to spread to every other part of the wide world, where men can be found inclined to take it.

This *declared* indifference, but as I must think, covert *real* zeal for the spread of slavery, I can not but hate. I hate it because of the monstrous injustice of slavery itself. I hate it because it deprives our republican example of its just influence in the world—enables the enemies of free institutions, with plausibility, to taunt us as hypocrites—causes the real friends of freedom to doubt our sincerity, and especially because it forces so many really good men amongst ourselves into an open war with the very fundamental principles of civil liberty—criticising the Declaration of Independence, and insisting that there is no right principle of action but *self-interest*.

Before proceeding, let me say I think I have no prejudice against the Southern people. They are just what we would be in their situation. If slavery did not now exist amongst them, they would not introduce it. If it did now exist amongst us, we should not instantly give it up. This I believe of the masses north and south. Doubtless there are individuals, on both sides, who would not hold slaves under any circumstances; and others who would gladly introduce slavery anew, if it were out of existence. We know that some southern men do free their slaves, go north, and become tip-top abolitionists; while some northern ones go south, and become most cruel slave-masters.

When southern people tell us they are no more responsible for the origin of slavery, than we; I acknowledge the fact. When it is said that the institution exists; and that it is very difficult to get rid of it, in any satisfactory way, I can understand and appreciate the saying. I surely will not blame them for not doing what I should not know how to do myself. If all earthly power were given me, I should not know what to do, as to the existing institution. My first impulse would be to free all the slaves, and send them to Liberia—to their own native land. But a moment's reflection would convince me, that whatever of high hope, (as I think there is) there may be in this, in the long run, its sudden execution is impossible. If they were all landed there in a day, they would all perish in the next ten days; and there are not surplus shipping and surplus money enough in the world to carry them there in many times ten days. What then? Free them all, and keep them among us as underlings? Is it quite certain that this betters their condition? I think I would not hold one in slavery, at any rate; yet the point is not clear enough for me to denounce people upon. What next? Free them, and make them politically and socially, our equals? My own feelings will not admit of this; and if mine would, we well know that those of the great mass of white people will not. Whether this feeling accords with justice and sound judgment, is not the sole question, if indeed, it is any part of it. A universal feeling, whether well or ill-founded, can not be safely disregarded. We can not, then, make them equals. It does seem to me that systems of gradual emancipation might be adopted; but for their tardiness in this, I will not undertake to judge our brethren of the south.

When they remind us of their constitutional rights, I acknowledge them, not grudgingly, but fully, and fairly; and I would give them any legislation for the reclaiming of their fugitives, which should not, in its stringency, be more likely to carry a free man into slavery, than our ordinary criminal laws are to hang an innocent one.

But all this; to my judgment, furnishes no more excuse for permitting slavery to go into our own free territory, than it would for reviving the African slave trade by law. The law which forbids the bringing of slaves *from* Africa; and that which has so long forbid the taking them *to* Nebraska, can hardly be distinguished on any moral principle; and the repeal of the former could find quite as plausible excuses as that of the latter.

The arguments by which the repeal of the Missouri Compromise is sought to be justified, are these:

First, that the Nebraska country needed a territorial government.

Second, that in various ways, the public had repudiated it, and demanded the repeal; and therefore should not now complain of it.

And lastly, that the repeal establishes a principle, which is intrinsically right.

I will attempt an answer to each of them in its turn. First, then, if that country was in need of a territorial organization, could it not have had it as well without as with the repeal? Iowa and Minnesota, to both of which the Missouri restriction applied, had, without its repeal, each in succession, territorial organizations. And even, the year before, a bill for Nebraska itself, was within an ace of passing, without the repealing clause; and this in the hands of the same men who are now the champions of repeal. Why no necessity then for the repeal? But still later, when this very bill was first brought in, it contained no repeal. But, say they, because the public had demanded, or rather commanded the repeal, the repeal was to accompany the organization, whenever that should occur.

Now I deny that the public ever demanded any such thing—ever repudiated the Missouri Compromise—ever commanded its repeal. I deny it, and call for the proof. It is not contended, I believe, that any such command has ever been given in express terms. It is only said that it was done in *principle*. The support of the Wilmot Proviso, is the first fact mentioned, to prove that the Missouri restriction was repudiated in principle, and the second is, the refusal to extend the Missouri line over the country acquired from Mexico. These are near enough alike to be treated together. The one was to exclude the chances of slavery from the whole new acquisition by the lump; and the other was to reject a division of it, by which one half was to be given up to those chances. Now whether this was a repudiation of the Missouri line, in principle, depends upon whether the Missouri law contained any principle requiring the line to be extended over the country acquired from Mexico. I contend it did not. I insist that it contained no general principle, but that it was, in every sense, specific. That its terms limit it to the country purchased from France, is undenied and undeniable. It could have no principle beyond the intention of those who made it. They did not intend to extend the line to country which they did not own. If they intended to extend it, in the event of acquiring additional territory, why did they not say so? It was just as easy to say, that "in all the country west of the Mississippi, which we now own, or may hereafter acquire there shall never be slavery," as to say, what they did say; and they would have said it if they had meant it. An intention to extend the law is not only not mentioned in the law, but is not mentioned in any contemporaneous history. Both the law itself, and the history of the times are a blank as to any principle of extension; and by neither the known rules for construing statutes and contracts, nor by common sense, can any such principle be inferred.

Another fact showing the specific character of the Missouri law—showing that it intended no more than it expressed—showing that the line was not intended as a universal dividing line between free and slave territory, present and prospective—north of which slavery could never go—is the fact that by that very law, Missouri came in as a slave state, north of the line. If that law contained any prospective principle, the whole law must be looked to in order to ascertain what the principle was. And by this rule, the south could fairly contend that inasmuch as they got one slave state north of the line at the inception of the law, they have the right to have another given them north of it occasionally—now and then in the indefinite westward extension of the line. This demonstrates the absurdity of attempting to deduce a prospective principle from the Missouri Compromise line.

When we voted for the Wilmot Proviso, we were voting to keep slavery out of the whole Mexican acquisition; and little did we think we were thereby voting, to let it into Nebraska, laying several hundred miles distant. When we voted against extending the Missouri line, little did we think we were voting to destroy the old line, then of near thirty years standing. To argue that we thus repudiated the

Missouri Compromise is no less absurd than it would be to argue that because we have, so far, forborne to acquire Cuba, we have thereby, *in principle*, repudiated our former acquisitions, and determined to throw them out of the Union! No less absurd than it would be to say that because I may have refused to build an addition to my house, I thereby have decided to destroy the existing house! And if I catch you setting fire to my house, you will turn upon me and say I *instructed* you to do it! The most conclusive argument, however, that, while voting for the Wilmot Proviso, and while voting against the *extension* of the Missouri line, we never thought of disturbing the original Missouri Compromise, is found in the facts, that there was then, and still is, an unorganized tract of fine country, nearly as large as the state of Missouri, lying immediately west of Arkansas, and south of the Missouri Compromise line; and that we never attempted to prohibit slavery as to it. I wish particular attention to this. It adjoins the original Missouri Compromise line, by its northern boundary; and consequently is part of the country, into which, by implication, slavery was permitted to go, by that compromise. There it has lain open ever since, and there it still lies. And yet no effort has been made at any time to wrest it from the south. In all our struggles to prohibit slavery within our Mexican acquisitions, we never so much as lifted a finger to prohibit it, as to this tract. Is not this entirely conclusive that at all times, we have held the Missouri Compromise as a sacred thing; even when against ourselves, as well as when for us?

Senator Douglas sometimes says the Missouri line itself was, *in principle*, only an extension of the line of the ordinance of '87—that is to say, an extension of the Ohio river. I think this is weak enough on its face. I will remark, however that, as a glance at the map will show, the Missouri line is a long way farther South than Page the Ohio; and that if our Senator, in proposing his extension, had stuck to the principle of jogging southward, perhaps it might not have been voted down so readily.

But next it is said that the compromises of '50 and the ratification of them by both political parties, in '52, established a *new principle*, which required the repeal of the Missouri Compromise. This again I deny. I deny it, and demand the proof. I have already stated fully what the compromises of '50 are. The particular part of those measures, for which the virtual repeal of the Missouri compromise is sought to be inferred (for it is admitted they contain nothing about it, in express terms) is the provision in the Utah and New Mexico laws, which permits them when they seek admission into the Union as States, to come in with or without slavery as they shall then see fit. Now I insist this provision was made for Utah and New Mexico, and for no other place whatever. It had no more direct reference to Nebraska than it had to the territories of the moon. But, say they, it had reference to Nebraska, in principle. Let us see. The North consented to this provision, not because they considered it right in itself; but because they were compensated—paid for it. They, at the same time, got California into the Union as a free State. This was far the best part of all they had struggled for by the Wilmot Proviso. They also got the area of slavery somewhat narrowed in the settlement of the boundary of Texas. Also, they got the slave trade abolished in the District of Columbia. For all these desirable objects the North could afford to yield something; and they did yield to the South the Utah and New Mexico provision. I do not mean that the whole North, or even a majority, yielded, when the law passed; but enough yielded, when added to the vote of the South, to carry the measure. Now can it be pretended that the principle of this arrangement requires us to permit the same provision to be applied to Nebraska, without any equivalent at all? Give us another free State; press the boundary of Texas still further back, give us another step toward the destruction of slavery in the District, and you present us a similar case. But ask us not to repeat, for nothing, what you paid for in the first instance. If you wish the thing again, pay again. That is the principle of the compromises of '50, if indeed they had any principles beyond their specific terms—it was the system of equivalents.

Again, if Congress, at that time, intended that all future territories should, when admitted as States, come in with or without slavery, at their own option, why did it not say so? With such an universal provision, all know the bills could not have passed. Did they, then—could they—establish a principle contrary to their own intention? Still further, if they intended to establish the principle that wherever Congress had control, it should be left to the people to do as they thought fit with slavery why did they not authorize the people of the District of Columbia at their adoption to abolish slavery within these limits? I personally know that this has not been left undone, because it was unthought of. It was frequently spoken of by members of Congress and by citizens of Washington six years ago; and I heard no one express a doubt that a system of gradual emancipation, with compensation to owners, would meet the approbation of a large majority of the white people of the District. But without the action of Congress they could say nothing; and Congress said "no." In the measures of 1850 Congress had the subject of slavery in the District expressly in hand. If they were then establishing the principle of allowing the people to do as they please with slavery, why did they not apply the principle to that people?

Again, it is claimed that by the Resolutions of the Illinois Legislature, passed in 1851, the repeal of the Missouri compromise was demanded. This I deny also. Whatever may be worked out by a criticism of the language of those resolutions, the people have never understood them as being any more than an endorsement of the compromises of 1850; and a release of our Senators from voting for the

Wilmot Proviso. The whole people are living witnesses, that this only, was their view. Finally, it is asked "If we did not mean to apply the Utah and New Mexico provision, to all future territories, what did we mean, when we, in 1852, endorsed the compromises of '50?"

For myself, I can answer this question most easily. I meant not to ask a repeal, or modification of the fugitive slave law. I meant not to ask for the abolition of slavery in the District of Columbia. I meant not to resist the admission of Utah and New Mexico, even should they ask to come in as slave States. I meant nothing about additional territories, because, as I understood, we then had no territory whose character as to slavery was not already settled. As to Nebraska, I regarded its character as being fixed, by the Missouri compromise, for thirty years—as unalterably fixed as that of my own home in Illinois. As to new acquisitions I said "sufficient unto the day is the evil thereof." When we make new acquisitions, we will, as heretofore, try to manage them some how. That is my answer. That is what I meant and said; and I appeal to the people to say, each for himself, whether that was not also the universal meaning of the free States.

And now, in turn, let me ask a few questions. If by any, or all these matters, the repeal of the Missouri Compromise was commanded, why was not the command sooner obeyed? Why was the repeal omitted in the Nebraska Bill of 1853? Why was it omitted in the original bill of 1854? Why, in the accompanying report, was such a repeal characterized as a departure from the course pursued in 1850? and its continued omission recommended?

I am aware Judge Douglas now argues that the subsequent express repeal is no substantial alteration of the bill. This argument seems wonderful to me. It is as if one should argue that white and black are not different. He admits, however, that there is a literal change in the bill; and that he made the change in deference to other Senators, who would not support the bill without. This proves that those other Senators thought the change a substantial one; and that the Judge thought their opinions worth deferring to. His own opinions, therefore, seem not to rest on a very firm basis even in his own mind—and I suppose the world believes, and will continue to believe, that precisely on the substance of that change this whole agitation has arisen.

I conclude then, that the public never demanded the repeal of the Missouri compromise.

I now come to consider whether the repeal, with its avowed principle, is intrinsically right. I insist that it is not. Take the particular case. A controversy had arisen between the advocates and opponents of slavery, in relation to its establishment within the country we had purchased of France. The southern, and then best part of the purchase, was already in as a slave state. The controversy was settled by also letting Missouri in as a slave State; but with the agreement that within all the remaining part of the purchase, North of a certain line, there should never be slavery. As to what was to be done with the remaining part south of the line, nothing was said; but perhaps the fair implication was, that it should come in with slavery if it should so choose. The southern part, except a portion heretofore mentioned, afterwards did come in with slavery, as the State of Arkansas. All these many years since 1820, the Northern part had remained a wilderness. At length settlements began in it also. In due course, Iowa, came in as a free State, and Minnesota was given a territorial government, without removing the slavery restriction. Finally the sole remaining part, North of the line, Kansas and Nebraska, was to be organized; and it is proposed, and carried, to blot out the old dividing line of thirty-four years standing, and to open the whole of that country to the introduction of slavery. Now, this, to my mind, is manifestly unjust. After an angry and dangerous controversy, the parties made friends by dividing the bone of contention. The one party first appropriates her own share, beyond all power to be disturbed in the possession of it; and then seizes the share of the other party. It is as if two starving men had divided their only loaf; the one had hastily swallowed his half, and then grabbed the other half just as he was putting it to his mouth!

Let me here drop the main argument, to notice what I consider rather an inferior matter. It is argued that slavery will not go to Kansas and Nebraska, in any event. This is a palliation—a lullaby. I have some hope that it will not; but let us not be too confident. As to climate, a glance at the map shows that there are five slave States—Delaware, Maryland, Virginia, Kentucky, and Missouri—and also the District of Columbia, all north of the Missouri compromise line. The census returns of 1850 show that, within these, there are 867,276 slaves—being more than one-fourth of all the slaves in the nation.

It is not climate, then, that will keep slavery out of these territories. Is there any thing in the peculiar nature of the country? Missouri adjoins these territories, by her entire western boundary, and slavery is already within every one of her western counties. I have even heard it said that there are more slaves, in proportion to whites, in the north western county of Missouri, than within any county of the State. Slavery pressed entirely up to the old western boundary of the State, and when, rather recently, a part of that boundary, at the north-west was moved out a little farther west, slavery followed on quite up to the new line. Now, when the restriction is removed, what is to prevent it from going still further? Climate will not. No peculiarity of the country will—nothing in nature will. Will the disposition of the people prevent it? Those nearest the scene, are all in favor of the extension. The yankees, who are opposed to it may be more numerous; but in military phrase, the battle-field is too far from their base of operations.

But it is said, there now is no law in Nebraska on the subject of slavery; and that, in such case, taking a slave there, operates his freedom. That is good book-law; but is not the rule of actual practice. Wherever slavery is, it has been first introduced without law. The oldest laws we find concerning it, are not laws introducing it; but regulating it, as an already existing thing. A white man takes his slave to Nebraska now; who will inform the negro that he is free? Who will take him before court to test the question of his freedom? In ignorance of his legal emancipation, he is kept chopping, splitting and plowing. Others are brought, and move on in the same track. At last, if ever the time for voting comes, on the question of slavery, the institution already in fact exists in the country, and cannot well be removed. The facts of its presence, and the difficulty of its removal will carry the vote in its favor. Keep it out until a vote is taken, and a vote in favor of it, can not be got in any population of forty thousand, on earth, who have been drawn together by the ordinary motives of emigration and settlement. To get slaves into the country simultaneously with the whites, in the incipient stages of settlement, is the precise stake played for, and won in this Nebraska measure.

The question is asked us, "If slaves will go in, notwithstanding the general principle of law liberates them, why would they not equally go in against positive statute law?—go in, even if the Missouri restriction were maintained?" I answer, because it takes a much bolder man to venture in, with his property, in the latter case, than in the former—because the positive congressional enactment is known to, and respected by all, or nearly all; whereas the negative principle that no law is free law, is not much known except among lawyers. We have some experience of this practical difference. In spite of the Ordinance of '87, a few negroes were brought into Illinois, and held in a state of quasi slavery; not enough, however to carry a vote of the people in favor of the institution when they came to form a constitution. But in the adjoining Missouri country, where there was no ordinance of '87—was no restriction—they were carried ten times, nay a hundred times, as fast, and actually made a slave State. This is fact—naked fact.

Another *lullaby* argument is, that taking slaves to new countries does not increase their number—does not make any one slave who otherwise would be free. There is some truth in this, and I am glad of it, but it is not *wholly* true. The African slave trade is not yet effectually suppressed; and if we make a reasonable deduction for the white people amongst us, who are foreigners, and the descendants of foreigners, arriving here since 1808, we shall find the increase of the black population out-running that of the white, to an extent unaccountable, except by supposing that some of them too, have been coming from Africa. If this be so, the opening of new countries to the institution, increases the demand for, and augments the price of slaves, and so does, in fact, make slaves of freemen by causing them to be brought from Africa, and sold into bondage.

But, however this may be, we know the opening of new countries to slavery, tends to the perpetuation of the institution, and so does *keep* men in slavery who otherwise would be free. This result we do not *feel* like favoring, and we are under no legal obligation to suppress our feelings in this respect.

Equal justice to the south, it is said, requires us to consent to the extending of slavery to new countries. That is to say, inasmuch as you do not object to my taking my hog to Nebraska, therefore I must not object to you taking your slave. Now, I admit this is perfectly logical, if there is no difference between hogs and negroes. But while you thus require me to deny the humanity of the negro, I wish to ask whether you of the south yourselves, have ever been willing to do as much? It is kindly provided that of all those who come into the world, only a small percentage are natural tyrants. That percentage is no larger in the slave States than in the free. The great majority, south as well as north, have human sympathies, of which they can no more divest themselves than they can of their sensibility to physical pain. These sympathies in the bosoms of the southern people, manifest in many ways, their sense of the wrong of slavery, and their consciousness that, after all, there is humanity in the negro. If they deny this, let me address them a few plain questions. In 1820 you joined the north, almost unanimously, in declaring the African slave trade piracy, and in annexing to it the punishment of death. Why did you do this? If you did not feel that it was wrong, why did you join in providing that men should be hung for it? The practice was no more than bringing wild negroes from Africa, to sell to such as would buy them. But you never thought of hanging men for catching and selling wild horses, wild buffaloes or wild bears.

Again, you have amongst you, a sneaking individual, of the class of native tyrants, known as the "*slave-dealer.*" He watches your necessities, and crawls up to buy your slave, at a speculating price. If you cannot help it, you sell to him; but if you can help it, you drive him from your door. You despise him utterly. You do not recognize him as a friend, or even as an honest man. Your children must not play with his; they may rollick freely with the little negroes, but not with the "slave-dealer's children". If you are obliged to deal with him, you try to get through the job without so much as touching him. It is common with you to join hands with the men you meet; but with the slave dealer you avoid the ceremony—instinctively shrinking from the snaky contact. If he grows rich and retires from business, you still remember him, and still keep up the ban of non-intercourse upon him and his family. Now why is this? You do not so treat the man who deals in corn, cattle or tobacco.

And yet again; there are in the United States and territories, including the District of Columbia, 433,643 free blacks. At $500 per head they are worth over two hundred millions of dollars. How comes this vast amount of property to be running about without owners? We do not see free horses or free cattle running at large. How is this? All these free blacks are the descendants of slaves, or have been slaves themselves, and they would be slaves now, but for *something* which has operated on their white owners, inducing them, at vast pecuniary sacrifices, to liberate them. What is that *something*? Is there any mistaking it? In all these cases it is your sense of justice, and human sympathy, continually telling you, that the poor negro has some natural right to himself—that those who deny it, and make mere merchandise of him, deserve kickings, contempt and death.

And now, why will you ask us to deny the humanity of the slave? and estimate him only as the equal of the hog? Why ask us to do what you will not do yourselves? Why ask us to do for nothing, what two hundred million of dollars could not induce you to do?

But one great argument in the support of the repeal of the Missouri Compromise, is still to come. That argument is "the sacred right of self government." It seems our distinguished Senator has found great difficulty in getting his antagonists, even in the Senate to meet him fairly on this argument—some poet has said

"Fools rush in where angels fear to tread."

At the hazzard of being thought one of the fools of this quotation, I meet that argument—I rush in, I take that bull by the horns.

I trust I understand, and truly estimate the right of self-government. My faith in the proposition that each man should do precisely as he pleases with all which is exclusively his own, lies at the foundation of the sense of justice there is in me. I extend the principles to communities of men, as well as to individuals. I so extend it, because it is politically wise, as well as naturally just; politically wise, in saving us from broils about matters which do not concern us. Here, or at Washington, I would not trouble myself with the oyster laws of Virginia, or the cranberry laws of Indiana.

The doctrine of self government is right—absolutely and eternally right—but it has no just application, as here attempted. Or perhaps I should rather say that whether it has such just application depends upon whether a negro is not or is a man. If he is not a man, why in that case, he who is a man may, as a matter of self-government, do just as he pleases with him. But if the negro is a man, is it not to that extent, a total destruction of self-government, to say that he too shall not govern himself? When the white man governs himself that is self-government;

but when he governs himself, and also governs another man, that is more than self-government—that is despotism. If the negro is a man, why then my ancient faith teaches me that "all men are created equal;" and that there can be no moral right in connection with one man's making a slave of another.

Judge Douglas frequently, with bitter irony and sarcasm, paraphrases our argument by saying "The white people of Nebraska are good enough to govern themselves, *but they are not good enough to govern a few miserable negroes*!!"

Well I doubt not that the people of Nebraska are, and will continue to be as good as the average of people elsewhere. I do not say the contrary. What I do say is, that no man is good enough to govern another man, *without that other's consent*. I say this is the leading principle—the sheet anchor of American republicanism. Our Declaration of Independence says:

"We hold these truths to be self evident: that all men are created equal; that they are endowed by their Creator with certain inalienable rights; that among these are life, liberty and the pursuit of happiness. That to secure these rights, governments are instituted among men, *deriving their just powers from the consent of the governed*."

I have quoted so much at this time merely to show that according to our ancient faith, the just powers of governments are derived from the consent of the governed. Now the relation of masters and slaves is, *pro tanto*, a total violation of this principle. The master not only governs the slave without his consent; but he governs him by a set of rules altogether different from those which he prescribes for himself. Allow *all* the governed an equal voice in the government, and that, and that only is self government.

Let it not be said I am contending for the establishment of political and social equality between the whites and blacks. I have already said the contrary. I am not now combating the argument of *necessity*, arising from the fact that the blacks are already amongst us; but I am combating what is set up as *moral* argument for allowing them to be taken where they have never yet been—arguing against the *extension* of a bad thing, which where it already exists, we must of necessity, manage as we best can.

In support of his application of the doctrine of self-government, Senator Douglas has sought to bring to his aid the opinions and examples of our revolutionary fathers. I am glad he has done this. I love the sentiments of those old-time men; and shall be most happy to abide by their opinions. He shows us that when it was in contemplation for the colonies to break off from Great Britain, and set up a new government for themselves, several of the states instructed their delegates to go for the measure *provided each state should be allowed to regulate its domestic concerns in its own way*. I do not quote; but this in substance. This was right. I see nothing objectionable in it. I also think it probable that it had some reference to the existence of slavery amongst them. I will not deny that it had. But had it, in any reference to the carrying of slavery into *new countries*? That is the question; and we will let the fathers themselves answer it.

This same generation of men, and mostly the same individuals of the generation, who declared this principle—who declared independence—who fought the war of the revolution through—who afterwards made the constitution under which we still live—these same men passed the ordinance of '87, declaring that slavery should never go to the north-west territory. I have no doubt Judge Douglas thinks they were very inconsistent in this. It is a question of discrimination between them and him. But there is not an inch of ground left for his claiming that their opinions—their example—their authority—are on his side in this controversy.

Again, is not Nebraska, while a territory, a part of us? Do we not own the country? And if we surrender the control of it, do we not surrender the right of self-government? It is part of ourselves. If you say we shall not control it because it is *only* part, the same is true of every other part; and when all the parts are gone, what has become of the whole? What is then left of us? What use for the general government, when there is nothing left for it to govern?

But you say this question should be left to the people of Nebraska, because they are more particularly interested. If this be the rule, you must leave it to each individual to say for himself whether he will have slaves. What better moral right have thirty-one citizens of Nebraska to say, that the thirty-second shall not hold slaves, than the people of the thirty-one States have to say that slavery shall not go into the thirty-second State at all?

But if it is a sacred right for the people of Nebraska to take and hold slaves there, it is equally their sacred right to buy them where they can buy them cheapest; and that undoubtedly will be on the coast of Africa; provided you will consent to not hang them for going there to buy them. You must remove this restriction too, from the sacred right of self-government. I am aware you say that taking slaves from the States of Nebraska, does not make slaves of freemen; but the African slave-trader can say just as much. He does not catch free negroes and bring them here. He finds them already slaves in the hands of their black captors, and he honestly buys them at the rate of about a red cotton handkerchief a head. This is very cheap, and it is a great abridgement of the sacred right of self-government to hang men for engaging in this profitable trade!

Another important objection to this application of the right of self-government, is that it enables the first *few*, to deprive the succeeding *many*, of a free exercise of the right of self-government. The first few may get slavery *in*, and the subsequent many cannot easily get it *out*. How common is the remark now in the slave

States—"If we were only clear of our slaves, how much better it would be for us." They are actually deprived of the privilege of governing themselves as they would, by the action of a very few, in the beginning. The same thing was true of the whole nation at the time our constitution was formed.

Whether slavery shall go into Nebraska, or other new territories, is not a matter of exclusive concern to the people who may go there. The whole nation is interested that the best use shall be made of these territories. We want them for the homes of free white people. This they cannot be, to any considerable extent, if slavery shall be planted within them. Slave States are places for poor white people to remove *from*; not to remove *to*. New free States are the places for poor people to go to and better their condition. For this use, the nation needs these territories.

Still further; there are constitutional relations between the slave and free States, which are degrading to the latter. We are under legal obligations to catch and return their runaway slaves to them—a sort of dirty, disagreeable job, which I believe, as a general rule the slave-holders will not perform for one another. Then again, in the control of the government—the management of the partnership affairs—they have greatly the advantage of us. By the constitution, each State has two Senators—each has a number of Representatives; in proportion to the number of its people—and each has a number of presidential electors, equal to the whole number of its Senators and Representatives together. But in ascertaining the number of the people, for this purpose, five slaves are counted as being equal to three whites. The slaves do not vote; they are only counted and so used, as to swell the influence of the white people's votes. The practical effect of this is more aptly shown by a comparison of the States of South Carolina and Maine. South Carolina has six representatives, and so has Maine; South Carolina has eight presidential electors, and so has Maine. This is precise equality so far; and, of course they are equal in Senators, each having two. Thus in the control of the government, the two States are equals precisely. But how are they in the number of their white people? Maine has 581,813—while South Carolina has 274,567. Maine has twice as many as South Carolina, and 32,679 over. Thus each white man in South Carolina is more than the double of any man in Maine. This is all because South Carolina, besides her free people, has 384,984 slaves. The South Carolinian has precisely the same advantage over the white man in every other free State, as well as in Maine. He is more than the double of any one of us in this crowd. The same advantage, but not to the same extent, is held by all the citizens of the slave States, over those of the free; and it is an absolute truth, without an exception, that there is no voter in any slave State, but who has more legal power in the government, than any voter in any free State. There is no instance of exact equality; and the disadvantage is against us the whole chapter through. This principle, in the aggregate, gives the slave States, in the present Congress, twenty additional representatives—being seven more than the whole majority by which they passed the Nebraska Bill.

Now all this is manifestly unfair; yet I do not mention it to complain of it, in so far as it is already settled. It is in the constitution; and I do not, for that cause, or any other cause, propose to destroy, or alter, or disregard the constitution. I stand to it, fairly, fully, and firmly.

But when I am told I must leave it altogether to *other people* to say whether new partners are to be bred up and brought into the firm, on the same degrading terms against me. I respectfully demur. I insist, that whether I shall be a whole man, or only, the half of one, in comparison with others, is a question in which I am somewhat concerned; and one which no other man can have a sacred right of deciding for me. If I am wrong in this—if it really be a sacred right of self-government, in the man who shall go to Nebraska, to decide whether he will be the *equal* of me or the *double* of me, then after he shall have exercised that right, and thereby shall have reduced me to a still smaller fraction of a man than I already am, I should like for some gentleman deeply skilled in the mysteries of sacred rights, to provide himself with a microscope, and peep about, and find out, if he can, what has become of my sacred rights! They will surely be too small for detection with the naked eye.

Finally, I insist, that if there is *any thing* which it is the duty of the *whole people* to never entrust to any hands but their own, that thing is the preservation and perpetuity, of their own liberties, and institutions. And if they shall think, as I do, that the extension of slavery endangers them, more than any, or all other causes, how recreant to themselves, if they submit the question, and with it, the fate of their country, to a mere hand-full of men, bent only on temporary self-interest. If this question of slavery extension were an insignificant one—one having no power to do harm—it might be shuffled aside in this way. But being, as it is, the great Behemoth of danger, shall the strong gripe of the nation be loosened upon him, to entrust him to the hands of such feeble keepers?

I have done with this mighty argument, of self-government. Go, sacred thing! Go in peace.

But Nebraska is urged as a great Union-saving measure. Well I too, go for saving the Union. Much as I hate slavery, I would consent to the extension of it rather than see the Union dissolved, just as I would consent to any *great* evil, to avoid a *greater* one. But when I go to Union saving, I must believe, at least, that the means I employ has some adaptation to the end. To my mind, Nebraska has no such adaptation.

"It hath no relish of salvation in it."

It is an aggravation, rather, of the only one thing which ever endangers the Union. When it came upon us, all was peace and quiet. The nation was looking to the forming of new bonds of Union; and a long course of peace and prosperity seemed to lie before us. In the whole range of possibility, there scarcely appears to me to have been any thing, out of which the slavery agitation could have been revived, except the very project of repealing the Missouri compromise. Every inch of territory we owned, already had a definite settlement of the slavery question, and by which, all parties were pledged to abide. Indeed, there was no uninhabited country on the continent, which we could acquire; if we except some extreme northern regions, which are wholly out of the question. In this state of case, the genius of Discord himself, could scarcely have invented a way of again getting us by the ears, but by turning back and destroying the peace measures of the past. The councils of that genius seem to have prevailed, the Missouri compromise was repealed; and here we are, in the midst of a new slavery agitation, such, I think, as we have never seen before.

Who is responsible for this? Is it those who resist the measure; or those who, causelessly, brought it forward, and pressed it through, having reason to know, and, in fact, knowing it must and would be so resisted? It could not but be expected by its author, that it would be looked upon as a measure for the extension of slavery, aggravated by a gross breach of faith. Argue as you will, and long as you will, this is the naked *front* and *aspect*, of the measure. And in this aspect, it could not but produce agitation. Slavery is founded in the selfishness of man's nature—opposition to it, is his love of justice. These principles are an eternal antagonism; and when brought into collision so fiercely, as slavery extension brings them, shocks, and throes, and convulsions must ceaselessly follow. Repeal the Missouri compromise—repeal all compromises—repeal the declaration of independence—repeal all past history, you still can not repeal human nature. It still will be the abundance of man's heart, that slavery extension is wrong; and out of the abundance of his heart, his mouth will continue to speak.

The structure, too, of the Nebraska Bill is very peculiar. The people are to decide the question of slavery for themselves; but *when* they are to decide; or *how* they are to decide; or whether, when the question is once decided, it is to remain so, or is it to be subject to an indefinite succession of new trials, the law does not say, Is it to be decided by the first dozen settlers who arrive there? or is it to await the arrival of a hundred? Is it to be decided by a vote of the people? or a vote of the legislature? or, indeed by a vote of any sort? To these questions, the law gives no answer. There is a mystery about this; for when a member proposed to give the legislature express authority to exclude slavery, it was hooted down by the friends of the bill. This fact is worth remembering. Some yankees, in the east, are sending emigrants to Nebraska, to exclude slavery from it; and, so far as I can judge, they expect the question to be decided by voting, in some way or other. But the Missourians are awake too. They are within a stone's throw of the contested ground. They hold meetings, and pass resolutions, in which not the slightest allusion to voting is made. They resolve that slavery already exists in the territory; that more shall go there; that they, remaining in Missouri will protect it; and that abolitionists shall be hung, or driven away. Through all this, bowie-knives and six-shooters are seen plainly enough; but never a glimpse of the ballot-box. And, really, what is to be the result of this? Each party *within*, having numerous and determined backers *without*, is it not probable that the contest will come to blows, and bloodshed? Could there be a more apt invention to bring about collision and violence, on the slavery question, than this Nebraska project is? I do not charge, or believe, that such was intended by Congress; but if they had literally formed a ring, and placed champions within it to fight out the controversy, the fight could be no more likely to come off, than it is. And if this fight should begin, is it likely to take a very peaceful, Union-saving turn? Will not the first drop of blood so shed, be the real knell of the Union?

The Missouri Compromise ought to be restored. For the sake of the Union, it ought to be restored. We ought to elect a House of Representatives which will vote its restoration. If by any means, we omit to do this, what follows? Slavery may or may not be established in Nebraska. But whether it be or not, we shall have repudiated—discarded from the councils of the Nation—the *spirit* of *compromise*; for who after this will ever trust in a national compromise? The spirit of mutual concession—that spirit which first gave us the constitution, and which has thrice saved the Union—we shall have strangled and cast from us forever. And what shall we have in lieu of it? The South flushed with triumph and tempted to excesses; the North, betrayed, as they believe, brooding on wrong and burning for revenge. One side will provoke; the other resent. The one will taunt, the other defy; one agrees, the other retaliates. Already a few in the North, defy all constitutional restraints, resist the execution of the fugitive slave law, and even menace the institution of slavery in the states where it exists.

Already a few in the South, claim the constitutional right to take to and hold slaves in the free states—demand the revival of the slave trade; and demand a treaty with Great Britain by which fugitive slaves may be reclaimed from Canada. As yet they are but few on either side. It is a grave question for the lovers of the Union, whether the final destruction of the Missouri Compromise, and with it the spirit of all compromise will or will not embolden and embitter each of these, and fatally increase the numbers of both.

But restore the compromise, and what then? We thereby restore the national faith, the national confidence, the national feeling of brotherhood. We thereby reinstate the spirit of concession and compromise—that spirit which has never failed us in past perils, and which may be safely trusted for all the future. The south ought to join in doing this. The peace of the nation is as dear to them as to us. In memories of the past and hopes of the future, they share as largely as we. It would be on their part, a great act—great in its spirit, and great in its effect. It would be worth to the nation a hundred years' purchase of peace and prosperity. And what of sacrifice would they make? They only surrender to us, what they gave us for a consideration long, long ago; what they have not now, asked for, struggled or cared for; what has been thrust upon them, not less to their own astonishment than to ours.

But it is said we cannot restore it; that though we elect every member of the lower house, the Senate is still against us. It is quite true, that of the Senators who passed the Nebraska Bill, a majority of the whole Senate will retain their seats in spite of the elections of this and the next year. But if at these elections, their several constituencies shall clearly express their will against Nebraska, will these senators disregard their will? Will they neither obey, nor make room for those who will?

But even if we fail to technically restore the compromise, it is still a great point to carry a popular vote in favor of the restoration. The moral weight of such a vote can not be estimated too highly. The authors of Nebraska are not at all satisfied with the destruction of the compromise—an endorsement of this *principle*, they proclaim to be the great object. With them, Nebraska alone is a small matter—to establish a principle, for *future use*, is what they particularly desire.

That future use is to be the planting of slavery wherever in the wide world, local and unorganized opposition can not prevent it. Now if you wish to give them this endorsement—if you wish to establish this principle—do so. I shall regret it; but it is your right. On the contrary if you are opposed to the principle—intend to give it no such endorsement—let no wheedling, no sophistry, divert you from throwing a direct vote against it.

Some men, mostly whigs, who condemn the repeal of the Missouri Compromise, nevertheless hesitate to go for its restoration, lest they be thrown in company with the abolitionist. Will they allow me as an old whig to tell them good humoredly, that I think this is very silly? Stand with anybody that stands *right*. Stand with him while he is right and *part* with him when he goes wrong. Stand *with* the abolitionist in restoring the Missouri Compromise; and stand *against* him when he attempts to repeal the fugitive slave law. In the latter case you stand with the southern disunionist. What of that? you are still right. In both cases you are right. In both cases you expose the dangerous extremes. In both you stand on middle ground and hold the ship level and steady. In both you are national and nothing less than national. This is good old whig ground. To desert such ground, because of any company, is to be less than a whig—less than a man—less than an American.

I particularly object to the *new* position which the avowed principle of this Nebraska law gives to slavery in the body politic. I object to it because it assumes that there *can* be *moral right* in the enslaving of one man by another. I object to it as a dangerous dalliance for a free people—a sad evidence that, feeling prosperity we forget right—that liberty, as a principle, we have ceased to revere. I object to it because the fathers of the republic eschewed, and rejected it. The argument of "Necessity" was the only argument they ever admitted in favor of slavery; and so far, and so far only as it carried them, did they ever go. They found the institution existing among us, which they could not help; and they cast blame upon the British King for having permitted its introduction. *Before* the constitution, they prohibited its introduction into the north-western Territory—the only country we owned, then free from it. At the framing and adoption of the constitution, they forbore to so much as mention the word "slave" or "slavery" in the whole instrument. In the provision for the recovery of fugitives, the slave is spoken of as a "*person held to service or labor*." In that prohibiting the abolition of the African slave trade for twenty years, that trade is spoken of as "The migration or importation of such persons as any of the States *now existing*, shall think proper to admit," &c. These are the only provisions alluding to slavery. Thus, the thing is hid away, in the constitution, just as an afflicted man hides away a wen or a cancer, which he dares not cut out at once, lest he bleed to death; with the promise, nevertheless, that the cutting may begin at the end of a given time. Less than this our fathers *could* not do; and *more* they *would* not do. Necessity drove them so far, and farther, they would not go. But this is not all. The earliest Congress, under the constitution, took the same view of slavery. They hedged and hemmed it in to the narrowest limits of necessity.

In 1794, they prohibited an out-going slave-trade—that is, the taking of slaves from the United States to sell.

In 1798, they prohibited the bringing of slaves from Africa, *into* the Mississippi Territory—this territory then comprising what are now the States of Mississippi and Alabama. This was *ten years* before they had the authority to do the same thing as to the States existing at the adoption of the constitution.

In 1800 they prohibited *american citizens* from trading in slaves between foreign countries—as, for instance, from Africa to Brazil.

In 1803 they passed a law in aid of one or two State laws, in restraint of the internal slave trade.

In 1807, in apparent hot haste, they passed the law, nearly a year in advance to take effect the first day of 1808—the very first day the constitution would permit—prohibiting the African slave trade by heavy pecuniary and corporal penalties.

In 1820, finding these provisions ineffectual, they declared the trade piracy, and annexed to it, the extreme penalty of death. While all this was passing in the general government, five or six of the original slave States had adopted systems of gradual emancipation; and by which the institution was rapidly becoming extinct within these limits.

Thus we see, the plain unmistakable spirit of that age, towards slavery, was hostility to the *principle*, and toleration, *only by necessity*.

But *now* it is to be transformed into a "sacred right." Nebraska brings it forth, places it on the high road to extension and perpetuity; and, with a pat on its back, says to it, "Go, and God speed you." Henceforth it is to be the chief jewel of the nation—the very figure-head of the ship of State. Little by little, but steadily as man's march to the grave, we have been giving up the *old* for the *new* faith. Near eighty years ago we began by declaring that all men are created equal; but now from that beginning we have run down to the other declaration, that for *some* men to enslave *others* is a "sacred right of self-government." These principles can not stand together. They are as opposite as God and mammon; and whoever holds to the one, must despise the other. When Pettit, in connection with his support of the Nebraska Bill, called the Declaration of Independence "a self-evident lie" he only did what consistency and candor require all other Nebraska men to do. Of the forty odd Nebraska Senators who sat present and heard him, no one rebuked him. Nor am I apprized that any Nebraska newspaper, or any Nebraska orator, in the whole nation, has ever yet rebuked him. If this had been said among Marion's men, Southerners though they were, what would have become of the man who said it? If this had been said to the men who captured Andre, the man who said it, would probably have been hung sooner than Andre was. If it had been said in old Independence Hall, seventy-eight years ago, the very door-keeper would have throttled the man, and thrust him into the street.

Let no one be deceived. The spirit of seventy-six and the spirit of Nebraska, are utter antagonisms; and the former is being rapidly displaced by the latter.

Fellow countrymen—Americans south, as well as north, shall we make no effort to arrest this? Already the liberal party throughout the world, express the apprehension "that the one retrograde institution in America, is undermining the principles of progress, and fatally violating the noblest political system the world ever saw." This is not the taunt of enemies, but the warning of friends. Is it quite safe to disregard it—to despise it? Is there no danger to liberty itself, in discarding the earliest practice, and first precept of our ancient faith? In our greedy chase to make profit of the negro, let us beware, lest we "cancel and tear to pieces" even the white man's charter of freedom.

Our republican robe is soiled, and trailed in the dust. Let us repurify it. Let us turn and wash it white, in the spirit, if not the blood, of the Revolution. Let us turn slavery from its claims of "moral right," back upon its existing legal rights, and its arguments of "necessity." Let us return it to the position our fathers gave it; and there let it rest in peace. Let us re-adopt the Declaration of Independence, and with it, the practices, and policy, which harmonize with it. Let north and south—let all Americans—let all lovers of liberty everywhere—join in the great and good work. If we do this, we shall not only have saved the Union; but we shall have so saved it, as to make, and to keep it, forever worthy of the saving. We shall have so saved it, that the succeeding millions of free happy people, the world over, shall rise up, and call us blessed, to the latest generations.

At Springfield, twelve days ago, where I had spoken substantially as I have here, Judge Douglas replied to me—and as he is to reply to me here, I shall attempt to anticipate him, by noticing some of the points he made there.

He commenced by stating I had assumed all the way through, that the principle of the Nebraska Bill, would have the effect of extending slavery. He denied that this was *intended*, or that this *effect* would follow.

I will not re-open the argument upon this point. That such was the intention, the world believed at the start, and will continue to believe. This was the *countenance* of the thing; and, both friends and enemies, instantly recognized it as such. That countenance can not now be changed by argument. You can as easily argue the color out of the negroes' skin. Like the "bloody hand" you may wash it, and wash it, the red witness of guilt still sticks, and stares horribly at you.

Next he says, congressional intervention never prevented slavery, any where—that it did not prevent it in the north west territory, nor in Illinois—that in fact, Illinois came into the Union as a slave State—that the principle of the Nebraska Bill expelled it from Illinois, from several old States, from every where.

Now this is mere quibbling all the way through. If the ordinance of '87 did not keep slavery out of the north-west territory, how happens it that the north-west shore of the Ohio River is entirely free from it; while the south east shore, less than a mile distant, along nearly the whole length of the river, is entirely covered with it?

If that ordinance did not keep it out of Illinois, what was it that made the difference between Illinois and Missouri? They lie side by side, the Mississippi river only dividing them; while their early settlements were within the same latitude. Between 1810 and 1820 the number of slaves in Missouri *increased* 7,211;

while in Illinois, in the same ten years, they *decreased* 51. This appears by the census returns. During nearly all of that ten years, both were territories—not States. During this time, the ordinance forbid slavery to go into Illinois; and *nothing* forbid it to go into Missouri. It *did* go into Missouri, and did *not* go into Illinois. That is the fact. Can any one doubt as to the reason of it?

But, he says, Illinois came into the Union as a slave State. Silence, perhaps, would be the best answer to this flat contradiction of the known history of the country. What are the facts upon which this bold assertion is based? When we first acquired the country, as far back as 1787, there were some slaves within it, held by the French inhabitants at Kaskaskia. The territorial legislation, admitted a few negroes, from the slave States, as indentured servants. One year after the adoption of the first State constitution the whole number of them was—what do you think? just 117—while the aggregate free population was 55,094—about 470 to one. Upon this state of facts, the people framed their constitution prohibiting the further introduction of slavery, with a sort of guaranty to the owners of the few indentured servants, giving freedom to their children to be born thereafter, and making no mention whatever, of any supposed slave for life. Out of this small matter, the Judge manufactures his argument that Illinois came into the Union as a slave State. Let the facts be the answer to the argument.

The principles of the Nebraska Bill, he says, expelled slavery from Illinois? The principle of that bill first planted it here—that is, it first came, because there was no law to prevent it—first came before we owned the country; and finding it here, and having the ordinance of '87 to prevent its increasing, our people struggled along, and finally got rid of it as best they could.

But the principle of the Nebraska Bill abolished slavery in several of the old States. Well, it is true that several of the old States, in the last quarter of the last century, did adopt systems of gradual emancipation, by which the institution has finally become extinct within their limits; but it *may* or *may not* be true that the principle of the Nebraska Bill was the cause that led to the adoption of these measures. It is now more than fifty years, since the last of these States adopted its system of emancipation. If Nebraska Bill is the real author of these benevolent works, it is rather deplorable, that he has, for so long a time, ceased working all together. Is there not some reason to suspect that it was the principle of the *revolution*, and not the principle of Nebraska Bill, that led to emancipation in these old States? Leave it to the people of those old emancipating States, and I am quite sure they will decide, that neither that, nor any other good thing, ever did, or ever will come of Nebraska Bill.

In the course of my main argument, Judge Douglas interrupted me to say, that the principle of the Nebraska Bill was very old; that it originated when God made man and placed good and evil before him, allowing him to choose for himself, being responsible for the choice he should make. At the time I thought this was merely playful; and I answered it accordingly. But in his reply to me he renewed it, as a serious argument. In seriousness then, the facts of this proposition are not true as stated. God did not place good and evil before man, telling him to make his choice. On the contrary, he did tell him there was one tree, of the fruit of which, he should not eat, upon pain of certain death. I should scarcely wish so strong a prohibition against slavery in Nebraska.

But this argument strikes me as not a little remarkable in another particular—in its strong resemblance to the old argument for the "Divine right of Kings." By the latter, the King is to do just as he pleases with his white subjects, being responsible to God alone. By the former the white man is to do just as he pleases with his black slaves, being responsible to God alone. The two things are precisely alike; and it is but natural that they should find similar arguments to sustain them.

I had argued, that the application of the principle of self-government, as contended for, would require the revival of the African slave trade—that no argument could be made in favor of a man's right to take slaves to Nebraska, which could not be equally well made in favor of his right to bring them from the coast of Africa. The Judge replied, that the constitution requires the suppression of the foreign slave trade; but does not require the prohibition of slavery in the territories. That is a mistake, in point of fact. The constitution does *not* require the action of Congress in either case; and it does *authorize* it in both. And so, there is still no difference between the cases.

In regard to what I had said, the advantage the slave States have over the free, in the matter of representation, the Judge replied that we, in the free States, count five free negroes as five white people, while in the slave States, they count five slaves as three whites only; and that the advantage, at last, was on the side of the free States.

Now, in the slave States, they count free negroes just as we do; and it so happens that besides their slaves, they have as many free negroes as we have, and thirty-three thousand over. Thus their free negroes more than balance ours; and their advantage over us, in consequence of their slaves, still remains as I stated it.

In reply to my argument, that the compromise measures of 1850, were a system of equivalents; and that the provisions of no one of them could fairly be carried to other subjects, without its corresponding equivalent being carried with it, the Judge denied out-right, that these measures had any connection with, or dependence upon, each other. This is mere desperation. If they have no connection, why are they always spoken of in connection? Why has he so spoken of them, a thousand times? Why has he constantly called them a *series* of measures? Why does everybody call them a compromise? Why was California kept out of the Union, six or seven months, if it was not because of its connection with the other measures? Webster's leading definition of the verb "to compromise" is "to adjust and settle a difference, by mutual agreement with concessions of claims by the parties." This conveys precisely the popular understanding of the word compromise. We knew, before the Judge told us, that these measures passed separately, and in distinct bills; and that no two of them were passed by the votes of precisely the same members. But we also know, and so does he know, that no one of them could have passed both branches of Congress but for the understanding that the others were to pass also. Upon this understanding each got votes, which it could have got in no other way. It is this fact, that gives to the measures their true character; and it is the universal knowledge of this fact, that has given them the name of compromise so expressive of that true character.

I had asked, "If in carrying the provisions of the Utah and New Mexico laws to Nebraska, you could clear away other objection, how can you leave Nebraska 'perfectly free' to introduce slavery *before* she forms a constitution—during her territorial government?—while the Utah and New Mexico laws only authorize it *when* they form constitutions, and are admitted into the Union?" To this Judge Douglas answered that the Utah and New Mexico laws, also authorized it *before*; and to prove this, he read from one of their laws, as follows: "That the legislative power of said territory shall extend to all rightful subjects of legislation consistent with the constitution of the United States and the provisions of this act."

Now it is perceived from the reading of this, that there is nothing express upon the subject; but that the authority is sought to be implied merely, for the general provision of "all rightful subjects of legislation." In reply to this, I insist, as a legal rule of construction, as well as the plain popular view of the matter, that the *express* provision for Utah and New Mexico coming in with slavery if they choose, when they shall form constitutions, is an *exclusion* of all implied authority on the same subject—that Congress, having the subject distinctly in their minds, when they made the express provision, they therein expressed their *whole* meaning on that subject.

The Judge rather insinuated that I had found it convenient to forget the Washington Territorial Law passed in 1853. This was a division of Oregon, organizing the northern part, as the territory of Washington. He asserted that, by this act, the ordinance of '87 theretofore existing in Oregon, was repealed; that nearly all the members of Congress voted for it, beginning in the H.R., with Charles Allen of Massachusetts, and ending with Richard Yates, of Illinois; and that he could not understand how those who now oppose the Nebraska Bill, so voted then, unless it was because it was then too soon after both the great political parties had ratified the compromises of 1850, and the ratification therefore too fresh, to be then repudiated.

Now I had seen the Washington act before; and I have carefully examined it since; and I aver that there is no repeal of the ordinance of '87, or of any prohibition of slavery, in it. In express terms, there is absolutely nothing in the whole law upon the subject—in fact, nothing to lead a reader to *think* of the subject. To my judgment, it is equally free from every thing from which such repeal can be legally implied; but however this may be, are men now to be entrapped by a legal implication, extracted from covert language, introduced perhaps, for the very purpose of entrapping them? I sincerely wish every man could read this law quite through, carefully watching every sentence, and every line, for a repeal of the ordinance of '87 or any thing equivalent to it.

Another point on the Washington act. If it was intended to be modelled after the Utah and New Mexico acts, as Judge Douglas, insists, why was it not inserted in it, as in them, that Washington was to come in with or without slavery as she may choose at the adoption of her constitution? It has no such provision in it; and I defy the ingenuity of man to give a reason for the omission, other than that it was not intended to follow the Utah and New Mexico laws in regard to the question of slavery.

The Washington act not only differs vitally from the Utah and New Mexico acts; but the Nebraska act differs vitally from both. By the latter act the people are left "perfectly free" to regulate their own domestic concerns, &c.; but in all the former, all their laws are to be submitted to Congress, and if disapproved are to be null. The Washington act goes even further; it absolutely prohibits the territorial legislature, by very strong and guarded language, from establishing banks, or borrowing money on the faith of the territory. Is this the sacred right of self-government we hear vaunted so much? No sir, the Nebraska Bill finds no model in the acts of '50 or the Washington act. It finds no model in any law from Adam till today. As Phillips says of Napoleon, the Nebraska act is grand, gloomy, and peculiar; wrapped in the solitude of its own originality; without a model, and without a shadow upon the earth.

In the course of his reply, Senator Douglas remarked, in substance, that he had always considered this government was made for the white people and not for the negroes. Why, in point of mere fact, I think so too. But in this remark of the Judge, there is a significance, which I think is the key to the great mistake (if there is any such mistake) which he has made in this Nebraska measure. It shows that the Judge has no very vivid impression that the negro is a human; and consequently has no idea that there can be any moral question in legislating about him. In his view, the question of whether a new country shall be slave or free, is a matter of as utter indifference, as it is whether his neighbor shall plant his farm with tobacco, or stock it with horned cattle. Now, whether this view is right or wrong, it is very certain that the great mass of mankind take a totally different view. They consider slavery a great moral wrong; and their feelings against it, is not evanescent, but eternal. It lies at the very foundation of their sense of justice; and it cannot be trifled with. It is a great and durable element of popular action, and, I think, no statesman can safely disregard it.

Our Senator also objects that those who oppose him in this measure do not entirely agree with one another. He reminds me that in my firm adherence to the constitutional rights of the slave States, I differ widely from others who are co-operating with me in opposing the Nebraska Bill; and he says it is not quite fair to oppose him in this variety of ways. He should remember that he took us by surprise—astounded us—by this measure. We were thunderstruck and stunned; and we reeled and fell in utter confusion. But we rose each fighting, grasping whatever he could first reach—a scythe—a pitchfork—a chopping axe, or a butcher's cleaver. We struck in the direction of the sound; and we are rapidly closing in upon him. He must not think to divert us from our purpose, by showing us that our drill, our dress, and our weapons, are not entirely perfect and uniform. When the storm shall be past, he shall find us still Americans; no less devoted to the continued Union and prosperity of the country than heretofore.

Finally, the Judge invokes against me, the memory of Clay and of Webster. They were great men; and men of great deeds. But where have I assailed them? For what is it, that their life-long enemy, shall now make profit, by assuming to defend them against me, their life-long friend? I go against the repeal of the Missouri compromise; did they ever go for it? They went for the compromise of 1850; did I ever go against them? They were greatly devoted to the Union; to the small measure of my ability, was I ever less so? Clay and Webster were dead before this question arose; by what authority shall our Senator say they would espouse his side of it, if alive? Mr. Clay was the leading spirit in making the Missouri compromise; is it very credible that if now alive, he would take the lead in the breaking of it? The truth is that some support from whigs is now a necessity with the Judge, and for thus it is, that the names of Clay and Webster are now invoked. His old friends have deserted him in such numbers as to leave too few to live by. He came to his own, and his own received him not, and Lo! he turns unto the Gentiles.

A word now as to the Judge's desperate assumption that the compromises of '50 had no connection with one another; that Illinois came into the Union as a slave state, and some other similar ones. This is no other than a bold denial of the history of the country. If we do not know that the Compromises of '50 were dependent on each other; if we do not know that Illinois came into the Union as a free state—we do not know any thing. If we do not know these things, we do not know that we ever had a revolutionary war, or such a chief as Washington. To deny these things is to deny our national axioms, or dogmas, at least; and it puts an end to all argument. If a man will stand up and assert, and repeat, and re-assert, that two and two do not make four, I know nothing in the power of argument that can stop him. I think I can answer the Judge so long as he sticks to the premises; but when he flies from them, I can not work an argument into the consistency of a maternal gag, and actually close his mouth with it. In such a case I can only commend him to the seventy thousand answers just in from Pennsylvania, Ohio and Indiana.

HOUSE DIVIDED SPEECH

Springfield, Illinois

June 16, 1858

Mr. President and Gentlemen of the Convention.

If we could first know where we are, and whither we are tending, we could then better judge what to do, and how to do it.

We are now far into the fifth year, since a policy was initiated, with the avowed object, and confident promise, of putting an end to slavery agitation.

Under the operation of that policy, that agitation has not only, not ceased, but has constantly augmented.

In my opinion, it will not cease, until a crisis shall have been reached, and passed.

"A house divided against itself cannot stand."

I believe this government cannot endure, permanently half slave and half free.

I do not expect the Union to be dissolved—I do not expect the house to fall—but I do expect it will cease to be divided.

It will become all one thing or all the other.

Either the opponents of slavery, will arrest the further spread of it, and place it where the public mind shall rest in the belief that it is in the course of ultimate extinction; or its advocates will push it forward, till it shall become alike lawful in all the States, old as well as new—North as well as South.

Have we no tendency to the latter condition?

Let any one who doubts, carefully contemplate that now almost complete legal combination—piece of machinery so to speak—compounded of the Nebraska doctrine, and the Dred Scott decision. Let him consider not only what work the machinery is adapted to do, and how well adapted; but also, let him study the history of its construction, and trace, if he can, or rather fail, if he can, to trace the evidence of design and concert of action, among its chief architects, from the beginning.

But, so far, Congress only, had acted; and an indorsement by the people, real or apparent, was indispensable, to save the point already gained, and give chance for more.

The new year of 1854 found slavery excluded from more than half the States by State Constitutions, and from most of the national territory by congressional prohibition.

Four days later, commenced the struggle, which ended in repealing that congressional prohibition.

This opened all the national territory to slavery, and was the first point gained.

This necessity had not been overlooked; but had been provided for, as well as might be, in the notable argument of "squatter sovereignty," otherwise called "sacred right of self government," which latter phrase, though expressive of the only rightful basis of any government, was so perverted in this attempted use of it as to amount to just this: That if any one man, choose to enslave another, no third man shall be allowed to object.

That argument was incorporated into the Nebraska Bill itself, in the language which follows: "It being the true intent and meaning of this act not to legislate slavery into any Territory or state, not to exclude it therefrom; but to leave the people thereof perfectly free to form and regulate their domestic institutions in their own way, subject only to the Constitution of the United States."

Then opened the roar of loose declamation in favor of "Squatter Sovereignty," and "Sacred right of self-government."

"But," said opposition members, "let us be more specific—let us amend the bill so as to expressly declare that the people of the territory may exclude slavery." "Not we," said the friends of the measure; and down they voted the amendment.

While the Nebraska Bill was passing through congress, a law case involving the question of a negroe's freedom, by reason of his owner having voluntarily taken him first into a free state and then a territory covered by the congressional prohibition, and held him as a slave, for a long time in each, was passing through the US Circuit Court for the District of Missouri; and both Nebraska Bill and law suit were brought to a decision in the same month of May, 1854. The negroe's name was "Dred Scott," which name now designates the decision finally made in the case.

Before the then next Presidential election, the law case came to, and was argued in, the Supreme Court of the United States; but the decision of it was deferred until after the election. Still, before the election, Senator Trumbull, on the floor of the Senate, requests the leading advocate of the Nebraska Bill to state his opinion whether the people of a territory can constitutionally exclude slavery from their limits; and the latter answers: "That is a question for the Supreme Court."

The election came. Mr. Buchanan was elected, and the indorsement, such as it was, secured. That was the second point gained. The indorsement, however, fell short of a clear popular majority by nearly four hundred thousand votes, and so, perhaps, was not overwhelmingly reliable and satisfactory.

The outgoing President, in his last annual message, as impressively as possible, echoed back upon the people the weight and authority of the indorsement.

The Supreme Court met again; did not announce their decision, but ordered a re-argument.

The Presidential inauguration came, and still no decision of the court; but the incoming President, in his inaugural address, fervently exhorted the people to abide by the forthcoming decision, whatever might be.

Then, in a few days, came the decision.

The reputed author of the Nebraska Bill finds an early occasion to make a speech at this capital indorsing the Dred Scott Decision, and vehemently denouncing all opposition to it.

The new President, too, seizes the early occasion of the Silliman letter to indorse and strongly construe that decision, and to express his astonishment that any different view had ever been entertained.

At length a squabble springs up between the President and the author of the Nebraska Bill, on the mere question of fact, whether the Lecompton Constitution was or was not, in any just sense, made by the people of Kansas; and in that squabble the latter declares that all he wants is a fair vote for the people, and that he cares not whether slavery be voted down or voted up. I do not understand his declaration that he cares not whether slavery be voted down or voted up, to be intended by him other than as an apt definition of the policy he would impress upon the public mind—the principle for which he declares he has suffered much, and is ready to suffer to the end.

And well may he cling to that principle. If he has any parental feeling, well may he cling to it. That principle, is the only shred left of his original Nebraska doctrine. Under the Dred Scott decision, "squatter sovereignty" squatted out of existence, tumbled down like temporary scaffolding—like the mould at the foundry served through one blast and fell back into loose sand—helped to carry an election, and then was kicked to the winds. His late joint struggle with the Republicans, against the Lecompton Constitution, involves nothing of the original Nebraska doctrine. That struggle was made on a point, the right of a people to make their own constitution, upon which he and the Republicans have never differed.

The several points of the Dred Scott decision, in connection with Senator Douglas' "care-not" policy, constitute the piece of machinery, in its present state of advancement. This was the third point gained.

The working points of that machinery are:

First, that no negro slave, imported as such from Africa, and no descendant of such slave can ever be a citizen of any State, in the sense of that term as used in the Constitution of the United States.

This point is made in order to deprive the negro, in every possible event, of the benefit of this provision of the United States Constitution, which declares that—

"The citizens of each State shall be entitled to all privileges and immunities of citizens in the several States."

Secondly, that "subject to the Constitution of the United States," neither Congress nor a Territorial Legislature can exclude slavery from any United States Territory.

This point is made in order that individual men may fill up the territories with slaves, without danger of losing them as property, and thus to enhance the chances of permanency to the institution through all the future.

Thirdly, that whether the holding a negro in actual slavery in a free State, makes him free, as against the holder, the United States courts will not decide, but will leave to be decided by the courts of any slave State the negro may be forced into by the master.

This point is made, not to be pressed immediately; but, if acquiesced in for a while, and apparently indorsed by the people at an election, then to sustain the logical conclusion that what Dred Scott's master might lawfully do with Dred Scott, in the free State of Illinois, every other master may lawfully do with any other one, or one thousand slaves, in Illinois, or in any other free State.

Auxiliary to all this, and working hand in hand with it, the Nebraska doctrine, or what is left of it, is to educate and mould public opinion, at least Northern public opinion, to not care whether slavery is voted down or voted up.

This shows exactly where we now are; and partially, also, whither we are tending.

It will throw additional light on the latter, to go back, and run the mind over the string of historical facts already stated. Several things will now appear less dark and mysterious than they did when they were transpiring. The people were to be left "perfectly free" "subject only to the Constitution." What the Constitution had to do with it, outsiders could not then see. Plainly enough now, it was an exactly fitted niche, for the Dred Scott decision to afterward come in, and declare the perfect freedom of the people, to be just no freedom at all.

Why was the amendment, expressly declaring the right of the people to exclude slavery, voted down? Plainly enough now, the adoption of it would have spoiled the niche for the Dred Scott decision.

Why was the court decision held up? Why even a Senator's individual opinion withheld, till after the presidential election? Plainly enough now, the speaking out then would have damaged the "perfectly free" argument upon which the election was to be carried.

Why the outgoing President's felicitation on the indorsement? Why the delay of a reargument? Why the incoming President's advance exhortation in favor of the decision?

These things look like the cautious patting and petting of a spirited horse, preparatory to mounting him, when it is dreaded that he may give the rider a fall.

And why the hasty after indorsements of the decision by the President and others?

We can not absolutely know that all these exact adaptations are the result of preconcert. But when we see a lot of framed timbers, different portions of which we know have been gotten out at different times and places and by different workmen—Stephen, Franklin, Roger, and James, for instance—and when we see these timbers joined together, and see they exactly make the frame of a house or a mill, all the tenons and mortices exactly fitting, and all the lengths and proportions of the different pieces exactly adapted to their respective places, and not a piece too many or too few—not omitting even scaffolding—or, if a single piece be lacking, we can see the place in the frame exactly fitted and prepared to yet bring such piece in—in such a case, we find it impossible not to believe that Stephen and Franklin and Roger and James all understood one another from the beginning, and all worked upon a common plan or draft drawn up before the first lick was struck.

It should not be overlooked that, by the Nebraska Bill, the people of a State, as well as Territory, were to be left "perfectly free" "subject only to the Constitution."

Why mention a State? They were legislating for territories, and not for or about States. Certainly the people of a State are and ought to be subject to the Constitution of the United States; but why is mention of this lugged into this merely territorial law? Why are the people of a territory and the people of a state therein lumped together, and their relation to the Constitution therein treated as being precisely the same?

While the opinion of the Court, by Chief Justice Taney, in the Dred Scott case, and the separate opinions of all the concurring Judges, expressly declare that the Constitution of the United States neither permits Congress nor a Territorial legislature to exclude slavery from any United States territory, they all omit to declare whether or not the same Constitution permits a state, or the people of a State, to exclude it.

Possibly, this is a mere omission; but who can be quite sure, if McLean or Curtis had sought to get into the opinion a declaration of unlimited power in the people of a state to exclude slavery from their limits, just as Chase and Macy sought to get such declaration, on behalf of the people of a territory, into the Nebraska Bill—I ask, who can be quite sure that it would not have been voted down, in the one case, as it had been in the other.

The nearest approach to the point of declaring the power of a State over slavery, is made by Judge Nelson. He approaches it more than once, using the precise idea, and almost the language too, of the Nebraska act. On one occasion his exact language is, "except in cases where the power is restrained by the Constitution of the United States, the law of the State is supreme over the subject of slavery within its jurisdiction."

In what cases the power of the states is so restrained by the US Constitution, is left an open question, precisely as the same question, as to the restraint on the power of the territories was left open in the Nebraska act. Put that and that together, and we have another nice little niche, which we may, ere long, see filled with another Supreme Court decision, declaring that the Constitution of the United States does not permit a state to exclude slavery from its limits.

And this may especially be expected if the doctrine of "care not whether slavery be voted down or voted up, shall gain upon the public mind sufficiently to give promise that such a decision can be maintained when made.

Such a decision is all that slavery now lacks of being alike lawful in all the States.

Welcome, or unwelcome, such decision is probably coming, and will soon be upon us, unless the power of the present political dynasty shall be met and overthrown.

We shall lie down pleasantly dreaming that the people of Missouri are on the verge of making their State free; and we shall awake to the reality, instead, that the Supreme Court has made Illinois a slave State.

To meet and overthrow the power of that dynasty, is the work now before all those who would prevent that consummation.

This is what we have to do.

But how can we best do it?

There are those who denounce us openly to their own friends, and yet whisper us softly, that Senator Douglas is the aptest instrument there is, with which to effect that object. They wish us to infer all, from the facts, that he now has a little quarrel with the present head of the dynasty; and that he has regularly voted with us, on a single point, upon which, he and we, have never differed.

They remind us that he is a great man, and that the largest of us are very small ones. Let this be granted. But "a living dog is better than a dead lion." Judge Douglas, if not a dead lion for this work, is at least a caged and toothless one. How can he oppose the advances of slavery? He don't care anything about it. His avowed mission is impressing the "public heart" to care nothing about it.

A leading Douglas Democratic newspaper thinks Douglas' superior talent will be needed to resist the revival of the African slave trade.

Does Douglas believe an effort to revive that trade is approaching? He has not said so. Does he really think so? But if it is, how can he resist it? For years he has labored to prove it a sacred right of white men to take negro slaves into the new territories. Can he possibly show that it is less a sacred right to buy them where they can be bought cheapest? And, unquestionably they can be bought cheaper in Africa than in Virginia.

He has done all in his power to reduce the whole question of slavery to one of a mere right of property; and as such, how can he oppose the foreign slave trade—how can he refuse that trade in that "property" shall be "perfectly free"—unless he does it as a protection to the home production? And as the home producers will probably not ask the protection, he will be wholly without a ground of opposition.

Senator Douglas holds, we know, that a man may rightfully be wiser to-day than he was yesterday—that he may rightfully change when he finds himself wrong.

But can we, for that reason, run ahead, and infer that he will make any particular change, of which he, himself, has given no intimation? Can we safely base our action upon any such vague inference?

Now, as ever, I wish not to misrepresent Judge Douglas' position, question his motives, or do ought that can be personally offensive to him.

Whenever, if ever, he and we can come together on principle so that our great cause may have assistance from his great ability, I hope to have interposed no adventitious obstacle.

But clearly, he is not now with us—he does not pretend to be—he does not promise to ever be.

Our cause, then, must be intrusted to, and conducted by its own undoubted friends—those whose hands are free, whose hearts are in the work—who do care for the result.

Two years ago the Republicans of the nation mustered over thirteen hundred thousand strong.

We did this under the single impulse of resistance to a common danger, with every external circumstance against us.

Of strange, discordant, and even, hostile elements, we gathered from the four winds, and formed and fought the battle through, under the constant hot fire of a disciplined, proud, and pampered enemy.

Did we brave all then to falter now? Now—when that same enemy is wavering, dissevered and belligerent?

The result is not doubtful. We shall not fail—if we stand firm, we shall not fail.

Wise councils may accelerate or mistakes delay it, but, sooner or later the victory is sure to come.

THE FIRST OF THE LINCOLN-DOUGLAS DEBATES

Ottowa, August 21, 1858

Mr. Douglas' Speech

Ladies and gentlemen: I appear before you today for the purpose of discussing the leading political topics which now agitate the public mind. By an arrangement between Mr. Lincoln and myself, we are present here today for the purpose of having a joint discussion, as the representatives of the two great political parties of the State and Union, upon the principles in issue between those parties and this vast concourse of people, shows the deep feeling which pervades the public mind in regard to the questions dividing us.

Prior to 1854 this country was divided into two great political parties, known as the Whig and Democratic parties. Both were national and patriotic, advocating principles that were universal in their application. An old line Whig could proclaim his principles in Louisiana and Massachusetts alike. Whig principles had no boundary sectional line, they were not limited by the Ohio river, nor by the Potomac, nor by the line of the free and slave States, but applied and were proclaimed wherever the Constitution ruled or the American flag waved over the American soil. ["Hear him," and three cheers.] So it was, and so it is with the great Democratic party, which, from the days of Jefferson until this period, has proven itself to be the historic party of this nation. While the Whig and Democratic parties differed in regard to a bank, the tariff, distribution, the specie circular and the sub-treasury, they agreed on the great slavery question which now agitates the Union. I say that the Whig party and the Democratic party agreed on this slavery question, while they differed on those matters of expediency to which I have referred. The Whig party and the Democratic party jointly adopted the Compromise measures of 1850 as the basis of a proper and just solution of this slavery question in all its forms. Clay was the great leader, with Webster on his right and Cass on his left, and sustained by the patriots in the Whig and Democratic ranks, who had devised and enacted the Compromise measures of 1850.

In 1851, the Whig party and the Democratic party united in Illinois in adopting resolutions indorsing and approving the principles of the Compromise measures of 1850, as the proper adjustment of that question. In 1852, when the Whig party assembled in Convention at Baltimore for the purpose of nominating a candidate for the Presidency, the first thing it did was to declare the Compromise measures of 1850, in substance and in principle, a suitable adjustment of that question.

[Here the speaker was interrupted by loud and long continued applause.] My friends, silence will be more acceptable to me in the discussion of these questions than applause. I desire to address myself to your judgment, your understanding, and your consciences, and not to your passions or your enthusiasm. When the Democratic Convention assembled in Baltimore in the same year, for the purpose of nominating a Democratic candidate for the Presidency, it also adopted the compromise measures of 1850 as the basis of Democratic action. Thus you see that up to 1853-54, the Whig party and the Democratic party both stood on the same platform with regard to the slavery question. That platform was the right of the people of each State and each Territory to decide their local and domestic institutions for themselves, subject only to the federal constitution.

During the session of Congress of 1853-54, I introduced into the Senate of the United States a bill to organize the Territories of Kansas and Nebraska on that principle which had been adopted in the compromise measures of 1850, approved by the Whig party and the Democratic party in Illinois in 1851, and endorsed by the Whig party and the Democratic party in national convention in 1852. In order that there might be no misunderstanding in relation to the principle involved in the Kansas and Nebraska Bill, I put forth the true intent and meaning of the act in these words: "It is the true intent and meaning of this act not to legislate slavery into any State or Territory, or to exclude it therefrom, but to leave the people thereof perfectly free to form and regulate their domestic institutions in their own way, subject only to the federal constitution." Thus, you see, that up to 1854, when the Kansas and Nebraska Bill was brought into Congress for the purpose of carrying out the principles which both parties had up to that time endorsed and approved, there had been no division in this country in regard to that principle except the opposition of the abolitionists. In the House of Representatives of the Illinois Legislature, upon a resolution asserting that principle, every Whig and every Democrat in the House voted in the affirmative, and only four men voted against it, and those four were old line Abolitionists. [Cheers.]

In 1854, Mr. Abraham Lincoln and Mr. Trumbull entered into an arrangement, one with the other, and each with his respective friends, to dissolve the old Whig party on the one hand, and to dissolve the old Democratic party on the other, and to connect the members of both into an Abolition party under the name and disguise of a Republican party. [Laughter and cheers, "hurrah for Douglas."] The terms of that arrangement between Mr. Lincoln and Mr. Trumbull have been published to the world by Mr. Lincoln's special friend, James H. Matheny, Esq., and they were, that Lincoln should have Shields's place in the U. S. Senate, which was then about to become vacant, and that Trumbull should have my seat when my term expired. [Great Laughter.] Lincoln went to work to abolitionize the Old Whig party all over the State, pretending that he was then as good a Whig as ever; [laughter] and Trumbull went to work in his part of the State preaching Abolitionism in its milder and lighter form, and trying to abolitionize the Democratic party, and bring old Democrats handcuffed and bound hand and foot into the Abolition camp. ["Good," "hurrah for Douglas," and cheers.] In pursuance of the arrangement, the parties met at Springfield in October, 1854, and proclaimed their new platform. Lincoln was to bring into the Abolition camp the old line Whigs, and transfer them over to Giddings, Chase, Fred Douglass, and Parson Lovejoy, who were ready to receive them and christen them in their new faith. [Laughter and cheers.] They laid down on that occasion a platform for their new Republican party, which was to be thus constructed. I have the resolutions of their State Convention then held, which was the first mass State Convention ever held in Illinois by the Black Republican party, and I now hold them in my hands and will read a part of them, and cause the others to be printed. Here are the most important and material resolutions of this Abolition platform:

1. *Resolved*, That we believe this truth to be self-evident, that when parties become subversive of the ends for which they are established, or incapable of restoring the government to the true principles of the constitution, it is the right and duty of the people to dissolve the political bands by which they may have been connected therewith, and to organize new parties upon such principles and with such views as the circumstances and exigencies of the nation may demand.

2. *Resolved*, That the times imperatively demand the reorganization of parties, and repudiating all previous party attachments, names and predilections, we unite ourselves together in defense of the liberty and constitution of the country, and will hereafter co-operate as the Republican party, pledged to the accomplishment of the following purposes: to bring the administration of the government back to the control of first principles; to restore Nebraska and Kansas to the position of free Territories; that, as the constitution of the United States, vests in the States, and not in Congress, the power to legislate for the extradition of fugitives from labor, to repeal and entirely abrogate the fugitive slave law; to restrict slavery to those States in which it exists; to prohibit the admission of any more slave States into the Union; to abolish slavery in the District of Columbia; to exclude slavery from all the territories over which the general government has exclusive jurisdiction; and to resist the acquirements of any more Territories unless the practice of slavery therein forever shall have been prohibited.

3. *Resolved*, That in furtherance of these principles we will use such constitutional and lawful means as shall seem best adapted to their accomplishment, and that we will support no man for office, under the general or State Government, who is not positively and fully committed to the support of these principles, and whose

personal character and conduct is not a guaranty that he is reliable, and who shall not have abjured old party allegiance and ties.

[The resolutions, as they were read, were cheered throughout.]

Now, gentlemen, your Black Republicans have cheered every one of those propositions, ["good and cheers,"] and yet I venture to say that you cannot get Mr. Lincoln to come out and say that he is now in favor of each one of them. [Laughter and applause. "Hit him again."] That these propositions, one and all, constitute the platform of the Black Republican party of this day, I have no doubt; ["good"] and when you were not aware for what purpose I was reading them, your Black Republicans cheered them as good Black Republican doctrines. ["That's it," etc.] My object in reading these resolutions, was to put the question to Abraham Lincoln this day, whether he now stands and will stand by each article in that creed and carry it out. ["Good." "Hit him again."] I desire to know whether Mr. Lincoln today stands as he did in 1854, in favor of the unconditional repeal of the fugitive slave law. I desire him to answer whether he stands pledged today, as he did in 1854, against the admission of any more slave States into the Union, even if the people want them. I want to know whether he stands pledged against the admission of a new State into the Union with such a Constitution as the people of that State may see fit to make. ["That's it;" "put it at him."] I want to know whether he stands today pledged to the abolition of slavery in the District of Columbia. I desire him to answer whether he stands pledged to the prohibition of the slave trade between the different States. ["He does."] I desire to know whether he stands pledged to prohibit slavery in all the territories of the United States, North as well as South of the Missouri Compromise line, ["Kansas too."] I desire him to answer whether he is opposed to the acquisition of any more territory unless slavery is prohibited therein. I want his answer to these questions. Your affirmative cheers in favor of this Abolition platform is not satisfactory. I ask Abraham Lincoln to answer these questions, in order that when I trot him down to lower Egypt, I may put the same questions to him. [Enthusiastic applause.] My principles are the same everywhere. [Cheers and "hark."] I can proclaim them alike in the North, the South, the East, and the West. My principles will apply wherever the Constitution prevails and the American flag waves. ["Good" and applause.] I desire to know whether Mr. Lincoln's principles will bear transplanting from Ottawa to Jonesboro? I put these questions to him today distinctly, and ask an answer. I have a right to an answer, for I quote from the platform of the Republican party, made by himself and others at the time that party was formed, and the bargain made by Lincoln to dissolve and kill the old Whig party, and transfer its members, bound hand and foot, to the Abolition party, under the direction of Giddings and Fred Douglass. [Cheers.] In the remarks

I have made on this platform, and the position of Mr. Lincoln upon it, I mean nothing personally disrespectful or unkind to that gentleman. I have known him for nearly twenty-five years. There were many points of sympathy between us when we first got acquainted. We were both comparatively boys, and both struggling with poverty in a strange land. I was a school-teacher in the town of Winchester, and he a flourishing grocery-keeper in the town of Salem. [Applause and laughter.] He was more successful in his occupation than I was in mine, and hence more fortunate in this world's goods. Lincoln is one of those peculiar men who perform with admirable skill everything which they undertake. I made as good a schoolteacher as I could, and when a cabinet maker I made a good bedstead and tables, although my old boss said I succeeded better with bureaus and secretaries than with anything else; [cheers,] but I believe that Lincoln was always more successful in business than I, for his business enabled him to get into the Legislature. I met him there, however, and had sympathy with him, because of the up-hill struggle we both had in life. He was then just as good at telling an anecdote as now. ["No doubt."] He could beat any of the boys wrestling, or running a foot-race, in pitching quoits or tossing a copper; could ruin more liquor than all the boys of the town together, [uproarious laughter,] and the dignity and impartiality with which he presided at a horse-race or fist-fight, excited the admiration and won the praise of everybody that was present and participated. [Renewed laughter.] I symphathised with him, because he was struggling with difficulties, and so was I. Mr. Lincoln served with me in the Legislature in 1836, when we both retired, and he subsided, or became submerged, and he was lost sight of as a public man for some years. In 1846, when Wilmot introduced his celebrated proviso, and the Abolition tornado swept over the country; Lincoln again turned up as a member of Congress from the Sangamon district. I was then in the Senate of the United States, and was glad to welcome my old friend and companion. Whilst in Congress, he distinguished himself by his opposition to the Mexican war, taking the side of the common enemy against his own country; ["that's true,"] and when he returned home he found that the indignation of the people followed him everywhere, and he was again submerged or obliged to retire into private life, forgotten by his former friends. ["And will be again."] He came up again in 1854, just in time to make this Abolition or Black Republican platform, in company with Giddings, Lovejoy, Chase and Fred Douglass, for the Republican party to sand upon. [Laughter, "Hit him again," &c.] Trumbull, too, was one of our own contemporaries. He was born and raised in old Connecticut, was bred a Federalist, but removing to Georgia, turned Nullifier, when nullification was popular, and as soon as he disposed of his clocks and wound up his business, migrated to Illinois, [laughter,] turned politician and lawyer here, and made his appearance in 1841, as a member of the Legislature. He became noted as the author of the scheme to repudiate a large portion of the State debt of Illinois, which, if successful, would have brought infamy and disgrace upon the fair escutcheon of our glorious State. The odium attached to that measure consigned him to oblivion for a time. I helped to do it. I walked into a public meeting in the hall of the House of Representatives, and replied to his repudiating speeches, and resolutions were carried over his head denouncing repudiation, and asserting the moral and legal obligation of Illinois to pay every dollar of the debt she owed and every bond that bore her seal. ["Good," and cheers.] Trumbull's malignity has followed me since I thus defeated his infamous scheme.

These two men having formed this combination to abolitionize the old Whig party and the old Democratic party, and put themselves into the Senate of the Untied States, in pursuance of their bargain, are now carrying out that arrangement. Matheny states that Trumbull broke faith; that the bargain was that Lincoln should be the Senator in Shields's place, and Trumbull was to wait for mine; [laughter and cheers,] and the story goes, that Trumbull cheated Lincoln, having control of four or five abolitionized Democrats who were holding over in the Senate; he would not let them vote for Lincoln, and which obliged the rest of the Abolitionists to support him in order to secure an Abolition Senator. There are a number of authorities for the truth of this besides Matheny, and I suppose that even Mr. Lincoln will not deny it. [Applause and laughter.]

Mr. Lincoln demands that he shall have the place intended for Trumbull, as Trumbull cheated him and got his, and Trumbull is stumping the State traducing me for the purpose of securing the position for Lincoln, in order to quiet him. ["Lincoln can never get it, &c."] It was in consequence of this arrangement that the Republican Convention was impanneled to instruct for Lincoln and nobody else, and it was on this account that they passed resolutions that he was their first, their last, and their only choice. Archy Williams was nowhere, Browning was nobody, Wentworth was not to be considered; they had no man in the Republican party for the place except Lincoln, for the reason that he demanded that they should carry out the arrangement. ["Hit him again."]

Having formed this new party for the benefit of deserters from Whiggery, and deserters from Democracy, and having laid down the Abolition platform which I have read, Lincoln now takes his stand and proclaims his Abolition doctrines. Let me read a part of them. In his speech at Springfield to the Convention, which nominated him for the Senate, he said:

"In my opinion it will not cease until a crisis shall have been reached and passed. 'A house divided against itself cannot stand.' I believe this government *cannot endure permanently half Slave and half Free*. I do not expect the Union to be dissolved—I do not expect the house to fall—*but I do expect it will cease to be divided.* It will become all one thing, or all the other. Either the opponents of slavery *will arrest the further spread of it*, and place it where the public mind shall rest in the belief *that it is in the course of ultimate extinction*: or its advocates *will push it forward till it shall became alike lawful in all the States*—old as well as new, North as well as South."

["Good, good," and cheers.]

I am delighted to hear you Black Republicans say "good." [Laughter and cheers.] I have no doubt that doctrine expresses your sentiments ["hit them again," "that's it,"] and I will prove to you now, if you will listen to me, that it is revolutionary and destructive of the existence of this Government. ["Hurrah for Douglas," "good," and cheers.] Mr. Lincoln, in the extract from which I have read, says that this Government cannot endure permanently in the same condition in which it was made by its framers—divided into free and slave States. He says that it has existed for about seventy years thus divided, and yet he tells you that it cannot endure permanently on the same principles and in the same relative condition in which our fathers made it. Why can it not exist divided into free and slave States? Washington, Jefferson, Franklin, Madison, Hamilton, Jay, and the great men of that day, made this Government divided into free States and slave States, and left each State perfectly free to do as it pleased on the subject of slavery. ["Right, right."] Why can it not exist on the same principles on which our fathers made it? ["It can."] They knew when they framed the Constitution that in a country as wide and broad as this, with such a variety of climate, production and interest, the people necessarily required different laws and institutions in different localities. They knew that the laws and regulations which would suit the granite hills of New Hampshire would be unsuited to the rice plantations of South Carolina, ["right, right,"] and they, therefore, provided that each State should retain its own Legislature and its own sovereignty, with the full and complete power to do as it pleased within its own limits, in all that was local and not national. [Applause.] One of the reserved rights of the States, was the right to regulate the relations between Master and Servant, on the slavery question. At the time the Constitution was framed, there were thirteen States in the Union, twelve of which were slaveholding States and one free State. Suppose this doctrine of uniformity preached by Mr. Lincoln, that the States should all be free or all be slave had prevailed, and what would have been the result? Of course, the twelve slaveholding States would have overruled the one free State, and slavery would have been fastened by a Constitutional provision on every inch of the American Republic, instead of being left as our fathers wisely left it, to each State to decide for itself. ["Good, good," and three cheers for Douglas.] Here I assert that uniformity in the local laws and institutions of the different States is neither possible or desirable. If uniformity had been adopted when the Government was established, it must inevitably have been the uniformity of slavery everywhere, or else the uniformity of negro citizenship and negro equality everywhere.

We are told by Lincoln that he is utterly opposed to the Dred Scott decision, and will not submit to it, for the reason that he says it deprives the negro of the rights and privileges of citizenship. [Laughter and applause.] That is the first and main reason which he assigns for his warfare on the Supreme Court of the United States and its decision. I ask you, are you in favor of conferring upon the negro the rights and privileges of citizenship? ["No, no."] Do you desire to strike out of our State Constitution that clause which keeps slaves and free negroes out of the State, and allow the free negroes to flow in, ["never,"] and cover your prairies with black settlements? Do you desire to turn this beautiful State into a free negro colony, ["no, no,"] in order that when Missouri abolishes slavery she can send one hundred thousand emancipated slaves into Illinois, to become citizens and voters, on an equality with yourselves? ["Never," "no."] If you desire negro citizenship, if you desire to allow them to come into the State and settle with the white man, if you desire them to vote on an equality with yourselves, and to make them eligible to office, to serve on juries, and to adjudge your rights, then support Mr. Lincoln and the Black Republican party, who are in favor of the citizenship of the negro. ["Never, never."] For one, I am opposed to negro citizenship in any and every form. [Cheers.] I believe this Government was made on the white basis. ["Good."] I believe it was made by white men for the benefit of white men and their posterity for ever, and I am in favor of confining citizenship to white men, men of European birth and descent, instead of conferring it upon negroes, Indians, and other inferior races. ["Good for you." "Douglas forever."]

Mr. Lincoln, following the example and lead of all the little Abolition orators, who go around and lecture in the basements of schools and churches, reads from the Declaration of Independence, that all men were created equal, and then asks, how can you deprive a negro of that equality which God and the Declaration of Independence awards to him? He and they maintain that negro equality is guarantied by the laws of God, and that it is asserted in the Declaration of Independence. If they think so, of course they have a right to say so, and so vote. I do not question Mr. Lincoln's conscientious belief that the negro was made his equal, and hence is his brother, [laughter,] but for my own part, I do not regard the negro as my equal, and positively deny that he is my brother or any kin to me whatever. ["Never." "Hit him again," and cheers.] Lincoln has evidently learned by heart Parson Lovejoy's catechism. [Laughter and applause.] He can repeat it as well as Farnsworth, and he is worthy of a medal from Father Giddings and Fred Douglass for his Abolitionism. [Laughter.] He holds that the negro was born his equal and yours, and that he was endowed with equality by the Almighty, and that no human law can deprive him of these rights which were guarantied to him by the Supreme ruler of the Universe. Now, I do not believe that the Almighty ever intended the negro to be the equal of the white man. ["Never, never."] If he did, he has been a long time demonstrating the fact. [Cheers.] For thousands of years the negro has been a race upon the earth, and during all that time, in all latitudes and climates, wherever he has wandered or been taken, he has been inferior to the race which he has there met. He belongs to an inferior race, and must always occupy an inferior position. ["Good," "that's so," &c.] I do not hold that because the negro is our inferior that therefore he ought to be a slave. By no means can such a conclusion be drawn from what I have said. On the contrary, I hold that humanity and Christianity both require that the negro shall have and enjoy every right, every privilege, and every immunity consistent with the safety of the society in which he lives. ["That's so."] On that point, I presume, there can be no diversity of opinion. You and I are bound to extend to our inferior and dependent beings every right, every privilege, every facility and immunity consistent with the public good. The question then arises, what rights and privileges are consistent with the public good? This is a question which each State and each Territory must decide for itself—Illinois has decided it for herself. We have provided that the negro shall not be a slave, and we have also provided that he shall not be a citizen, but protect him in his civil rights, in his life, his person and his property, only depriving him of all political rights whatsoever, and refusing to put him on an equality with the white man. ["Good."] That policy of Illinois is satisfactory to the Democratic party and to me, and if it were to the Republicans, there would then be no question upon the subject; but the Republicans say that he ought to be made a citizen, and when he becomes a citizen he becomes your equal, with all your rights and privileges. ["He never shall."] They assert the Dred Scott decision to be monstrous because it denies that the negro is or can be a citizen under the Constitution. Now, I hold that Illinois had a right to abolish and prohibit slavery as she did, and I hold that Kentucky has the same right to continue and protect slavery that Illinois had to abolish it. I hold that New York had as much right to abolish slavery as Virginia has to continue it, and that each and every State of this Union is a sovereign power, with the right to do as it pleases upon this question of slavery, and upon all its domestic institutions. Slavery is not the only question which comes up in this controversy. There is a far more important one to you, and that is, what shall be done with the free negro? We have settled the slavery question as far as we are concerned; we have prohibited it in Illinois forever, and in doing so, I think we have done wisely, and there is no man in the State who would be more strenuous in his opposition to the introduction of slavery than I would; [cheers] but when we settled it for ourselves, we exhausted all our power over that subject. We have done our whole duty, and can do no more. We must leave each and every other State to decide for itself the same question. In relation to the policy to be pursued toward the free negroes, we have said that they shall not vote; whilst Maine, on the other hand, has said that they shall vote. Maine is a sovereign State, and has the power to regulate the qualifications of voters within her limits. I would never consent to confer the right of voting and of citizenship upon a negro, but still I am not going to quarrel with Maine for differing from me in opinion. Let Maine take care of her own negroes and fix the qualifications of her own voters to suit herself, without interfering with Illinois, and Illinois will not interfere with Maine. So with the State of New York. She allows the negro to vote provided he owns two hundred and fifty dollars' worth of property, but not otherwise. While I would not make any distinction whatsoever between a negro who held property and one who did not; yet if the sovereign State of New York chooses to make that distinction it is her business and not mine, and I will not quarrel with her for it. She can do as she pleases on this question if she minds her own business, and we will do the same thing. Now, my friends, if we will only act conscientiously and rigidly upon this great principle of popular sovereignty, which guaranties to each State and Territory the right to do as it pleases on all things, local and domestic, instead of Congress interfering, we will continue at peace one with another. Why should Illinois be at war with Missouri, or Kentucky with Ohio, or Virginia with New York, merely because their institutions differ? Our fathers intended that our institutions should differ. They knew that the North and the South, having different climates, productions and interests, required different institutions. This doctrine of Mr. Lincoln, of uniformity among the institutions of the different States, is a new doctrine, never dreamed of by Washington, Madison, or the framers of this Government. Mr. Lincoln and the Republican party set themselves up as wiser than these men who made this Government, which has flourished for seventy years under the principle of popular sovereignty, recognizing the right of each State to do as it pleased. Under that principle, we have grown from a nation of three or four millions to a nation of about thirty millions of people; we have crossed the Allegheny mountains and filled up the whole North-west, turning the prairie into a garden, and building up churches and schools, thus spreading civilization and Christianity where before there was nothing but savage barbarism. Under that principle we have become, from a feeble nation, the most powerful on the face of the earth, and if we only adhere to that principle, we can go forward increasing in territory, in power, in strength and in glory until the Republic of America shall be the

North Star that shall guide the friends of freedom throughout the civilized world. ["Long may you live," and great applause.] And why can we not adhere to the great principle of self-government, upon which our institutions were originally based. ["We can."] I believe that this new doctrine preached by Mr. Lincoln and his party will dissolve the Union if it succeeds. They are trying to array all the Northern States in one body against the South, to excite a sectional war between the free States and the slave States, in order that the one or the other may be driven to the wall.

I am told that my time is out. Mr. Lincoln will now address you for an hour and a half, and I will then occupy an half hour in replying to him.

Mr. Lincoln's Speech

MY FELLOW-CITIZENS: When a man hears himself somewhat misrepresented, it provokes him-at least, I find it so with myself; but when misrepresentation becomes very gross and palpable, it is more apt to amuse him. The first thing I see fit to notice, is the fact that Judge Douglas alleges, after running through the history of the old Democratic and the old Whig parties, that Judge Trumbull and myself made an arrangement in 1854, by which I was to have the place of Gen. Shields in the United States Senate, and Judge Trumbull was to have the place of Judge Douglas. Now, all I have to say upon that subject is, that I think no man—not even Judge Douglas—can prove it, because it is not true. [Cheers.] I have no doubt he is "*conscientious*" in saying it. [Laughter.] As to those resolutions that he took such a length of time to read, as being the platform of the Republican party in 1854, I say I never had anything to do with them, and I think Trumbull never had. [Renewed laughter.] Judge Douglas cannot show that either of us ever did have anything to do with them. I believe *this* is true about those resolutions: There was a call for a Convention to form a Republican party at Springfield, and I think that my friend, Mr. Lovejoy, who is here upon this stand, had a hand in it. I think this is true, and I think if he will remember accurately, he will be able to recollect that he tried to get me into it, and I would not go in. [Cheers and laughter.] I believe it is also true that I went away from Springfield when the Convention was in session, to attend court in Tazewell County. It is true they did place my name, though without authority, upon the committee, and afterward wrote me to attend the meeting of the committee, but I refused to do so, and I never had anything to do with that organization. This is the plain truth about all that matter of the resolutions.

Now, about this story that Judge Douglas tells of Trumbull bargaining to sell out the old Democratic party, and Lincoln agreeing to sell out the old Whig party, I have the means of *knowing* about that; Judge Douglas cannot have; and I know there is no substance to it whatever. Yet I have no doubt he is "*conscientious*" about it. I know that after Mr. Lovejoy got into the Legislature that winter, he complained of me that I had told all the old Whigs of his district that the old Whig party was good enough for them, and some of them voted against him because I told them so. Now, I have no means of totally disproving such charges as this which the Judge makes. A man cannot prove a negative, but he has a right to claim that when a man makes an affirmative charge, he must offer some proof to show the truth of what he says. I certainly cannot introduce testimony to show the negative about things, but I have a right to claim that if a man says he *knows* a thing, then he must show *how* he knows it. I always have a right to claim this, and it is not satisfactory to me that he may be "conscientious" on the subject. [Cheers and Laughter.]

Now, gentlemen, I hate to waste my time on such things, but in regard to that general Abolition tilt that Judge Douglas makes, when he says that I was engaged at that time in selling out and abolitionizing the old Whig party-I hope you will permit me to read a part of a printed speech that I made then at Peoria, which will show altogether a different view of the position I took in that contest of 1854.

VOICE: "Put on your specs."

MR. LINCOLN: Yes, sir, I am obliged to do so. I am no longer a young man. [Laughter.]

"This is the *repeal* of the Missouri Compromise. The foregoing history may not be precisely accurate in every particular; but I am sure it is sufficiently so for all the uses I shall attempt to make of it, and in it we have before us, the chief materials enabling us to correctly judge whether the repeal of the Missouri Compromise is right or wrong.

"I think, and shall try to show, that it is wrong; wrong in its direct effect, letting slavery into Kansas and Nebraska—and wrong in its prospective principle, allowing it to spread to every other part of the wide world, where men can be found inclined to take it.

"This *declared* indifference, but, as I must think, covert real zeal for the spread of slavery, I cannot but hate. I hate it because of the monstrous injustice of slavery itself. I hate it because it deprives our republican example of its just influence in the world—enables the enemies of free institutions, with plausibility, to taunt us as hypocrites—causes the real friends of freedom to doubt our sincerity, and especially because it forces so many really good men amongst ourselves into an open war with the very fundamental principles of civil liberty—criticizing the Declaration of Independence, and insisting that there is no right principle of action but *self-interest*.

"Before proceeding, let me say I think I have no prejudice against the Southern people. They are just what we would be in their situation. If slavery did not now exist among them, they would not introduce it. If it did now exist amongst us, we should not instantly give it up. This I believe of the masses North and South. Doubtless there are individuals on both sides, who would not hold slaves under any circumstances; and others who would gladly introduce slavery anew, if it were out of existence. We know that some Southern men do free their slaves, go North, and become tiptop Abolitionists; while some Northern ones go South, and become most cruel slave-masters.

"When Southern people tell us they are no more responsible for the origin of slavery than we, I acknowledge the fact. When it is said that the institution exists, and that it is very difficult to get rid of it, in any satisfactory way, I can understand and appreciate the saying. I surely will not blame them for not doing what I should not know how to do myself. If all earthly power were given me, I should not know what to do, as to the existing institution. My first impulse would be to free all the slaves, and send them to Liberia—to their own native land. But a moment's reflection would convince me, that whatever of high hope, (as I think there is) there may be in this, in the long run, its sudden execution is impossible. If they were all landed there in a day, they would all perish in the next ten days; and there are not surplus shipping and surplus money enough in the world to carry them there in many times ten days. What then? Free them all, and keep them among us as underlings? Is it quite certain that this betters their condition? I think I would not hold one in slavery at any rate; yet the point is not clear enough to me to denounce people upon. What next? Free them, and make them politically and socially our equals? My own feelings will not admit of this; and if mine would, we well know that those of the great mass of white people will not. Whether this feeling accords with justice and sound judgment, is not the sole question, if, indeed, it is any part of it. A universal feeling, whether well or ill-founded, cannot be safely disregarded. We cannot, then, make them equals. It does seem to me that systems of gradual emancipation might be adopted; but for their tardiness in this, I will not undertake to judge our brethren of the South.

"When they remind us of their constitutional rights, I acknowledge them, not grudgingly, but fully and fairly; and I would give them any legislation for the reclaiming of their fugitives, which should not, in its stringency, be more likely to carry a free man into slavery, than our ordinary criminal laws are to hang an innocent one.

"But all this, to my judgment, furnishes no more excuse for permitting slavery to go into our own free territory, than it would for reviving the African slave-trade by law. The law which forbids the bringing of slaves *from* Africa, and that which has so long forbid the taking of them *to* Nebraska, can hardly be distinguished on any moral principle; and the repeal of the former could find quite as plausible excuses as that of the latter."

I have reason to know that Judge Douglas *knows* that I said this. I think he has the answer here to one of the questions he put to me. I do not mean to allow him to catechise me unless he pays back for it in kind. I will not answer questions one after another, unless he reciprocates; but as he has made this inquiry, and I have answered it before, he has got it without my getting anything in return. He has got my answer on the Fugitive Slave law.

Now, gentlemen, I don't want to read at any greater length, but this is the true complexion of all I have ever said in regard to the institution of slavery and the black race. This is the whole of it, and anything that argues me into his idea of perfect social and political equality with the negro, is but a specious and fantastic arrangement of words, by which a man can prove a horse-chestnut to be a chestnut horse. [Laughter.] I will say here, while upon this subject, that I have no purpose, directly or indirectly, to interfere with the institution of slavery in the States where it exists. I believe I have no lawful right to do so, and I have no inclination to do so. I have no purpose to introduce political and social equality between the white and the black races. There is a physical difference between the two, which, in my judgment, will probably forever forbid their living together upon the footing of perfect equality, and inasmuch as it becomes a necessity that there must be a difference, I, as well as Judge Douglas, am in favor of the race to which I belong having the superior position. I have never said anything to the contrary, but I hold that, notwithstanding all this, there is no reason in the world why the negro is not entitled to all the natural rights enumerated in the Declaration of Independence, the right to life, liberty, and the pursuit of happiness. [Loud cheers.] I hold that he is as much entitled to these as the white man. I agree with Judge Douglas he is not my equal in many respects—certainly not in color, perhaps not in moral or intellectual endowment. But in the right to eat the bread, without the leave of anybody else, which his own hand earns, *he is my equal and the equal of Judge Douglas, and the equal of every living man.* [Great applause.]

Now I pass on to consider one or two more of these little follies. The Judge is wofully at fault about his early friend Lincoln being a "grocery-keeper." [Laughter.] I don't know as it would be a great sin, if I had been; but he is mistaken. Lincoln never kept a grocery anywhere in the world. [Laughter.] It is true that Lincoln did work the latter part of one winter in a little still house, up at the head of a hollow. [Roars of laughter.] And so I think my friend, the Judge, is equally at fault when he charges me at the time when I was in Congress of having opposed our soldiers who were fighting in the Mexican war. The Judge did not make his charge very distinctly, but I can tell you what he can prove, by referring to the record. You remember I was an old Whig, and whenever the Democratic party tried to get me to vote that the war had been righteously begun by the President, I would not do it. But whenever they asked for any money, or land-warrants, or anything to pay the soldiers there, during all that time, I gave the same vote that Judge Douglas did. [Loud applause.] You can think as you please as to whether that was consistent. Such is the truth; and the Judge has the right to make all he can out of it. But when he, by a general charge, conveys the idea that I withheld supplies from the soldiers who were fighting in the Mexican war, or did anything else to hinder the soldiers, he is, to say the least, grossly and altogether mistaken, as a consultation of the records will prove to him.

As I have not used up so much of my time as I had supposed, I will dwell a little longer upon one or two of these minor topics upon which the Judge has spoken. He has read from my speech in Springfield, in which I say that "a house divided against itself cannot stand." Does the Judge say it *can* stand? [Laughter.] I don't know whether he does or not. The Judge does not seem to be attending to me just now, but I would like to know if it is his opinion that a house divided against itself *can stand*. If he does, then there is a question of veracity, not between him and me, but between the Judge and an authority of a somewhat higher character. [Laughter and applause.]

Now, my friends, I ask your attention to this matter for the purpose of saying something seriously. I know that the Judge may readily enough agree with me that the maxim which was put forth by the Saviour is true, but he may allege that I misapply it; and the Judge has a right to urge that, in my application, I do misapply it, and then I have a right to show that I do *not* misapply it. When he undertakes to say that because I think this nation, so far as the question of slavery is concerned, will all become one thing or all the other, I am in favor of bringing about a dead uniformity in the various States, in all their institutions, he argues erroneously. The great variety of the local institutions in the States, springing from differences in the soil, differences in the face of the country, and in the climate, are bonds of Union. They do not make "a house divided against itself," but they make a house united. If they produce in one section of the country what is called for by the wants of another section, and this other section can supply the wants of the first, they are not matters of discord but bonds of union, true bonds of union. But can this question of slavery be considered as among *these* varieties in the institutions of the country? I leave it to you to say whether, in the history of our Government, this institution of slavery has not always failed to be a bond of union, and, on the contrary, been an apple of discord, and an element of division in the house. [Cries of "Yes, yes," and applause.] I ask you to consider whether, so long as the moral constitution of men's minds shall continue to be the same, after this generation and assemblage shall sink into the grave, and another race shall arise, with the same moral and intellectual development we have—whether, if that institution is standing in the same irritating position in which it now is, it will not continue an element of division? [Cries of "Yes, yes."] If so, then I have a right to say that, in regard to this question, the Union is a house divided against itself; and when the Judge reminds me that I have often said to him that the institution of slavery has existed for eighty years in some States, and yet it does not exist in some others, I agree to the fact, and I account for it by looking at the position in which our fathers originally placed it—restricting it from the new Territories where it had not gone, and legislating to cut off its source by the abrogation of the slave-trade thus putting the seal of legislation *against its spread.* The public mind *did* rest in the belief that it was in the course of ultimate extinction. [Cries of "Yes, yes,"] But lately, I think—and in this I charge nothing on the Judge's motives—lately, I think, that he, and those acting with him, have placed that institution on a new basis, which looks to the *perpetuity and nationalization of slavery.* [Loud cheers.] And while it is placed upon this new basis, I say, and I have said, that I believe we shall not have peace upon the question until the opponents of slavery arrest the further spread of it, and place it where the public mind shall rest in the belief that it is in the course of ultimate extinction; or, on the other hand, that its advocates will push it forward until it shall become alike lawful in all the States, old as well as new, North as well as South. Now, I believe if we could arrest the spread, and place it where Washington, and Jefferson, and Madison placed it, it *would* be in the course of ultimate extinction, and the public mind *would*, as for eighty years past, believe that it was in the course of ultimate extinction. The crisis would be past and the institution might be let alone for a hundred years, if it should live so long, in the States where it exists, yet it would be going out of existence in the way best for both the black and the white races. [Great cheering.]

A VOICE: "Then do you repudiate Popular Sovereignty?"

MR. LINCOLN: Well, then, let us talk about Popular Sovereignty! [Laughter.] What is Popular Sovereignty? [Cries of "A humbug," "a humbug."] Is it the right of the people to have Slavery or not have it, as they see fit, in the territories? I will state—and I have an able man to watch me—my understanding is that Popular Sovereignty, as now applied to the question of slavery, does allow the people of a Territory to have slavery if they want to, but does not allow them *not* to have it if they *do not* want it. [Applause and laughter.] I do not mean that if this vast concourse of people were in a Territory of the United States, any one of them would be obliged to have a slave if he did not want one; but I do say that, as I understand the Dred Scott decision, if any one man wants slaves, all the rest have no way of keeping that one man from holding them.

When I made my speech at Springfield, of which the Judge complains, and from which he quotes, I really was not thinking of the things which he ascribes to me at all. I had no thought in the world that I was doing anything to bring about a war between the free and slave States. I had no thought in the world that I was doing anything to bring about a political and social equality of the black and white races. It never occurred to me that I was doing anything or favoring anything to reduce to a dead uniformity all the local institutions of the various States. But I must say, in all fairness to him, if he thinks I am doing something which leads to these bad results, it is none the better that I did not mean it. It is just as fatal to the country, if I have any influence in producing it, whether I intend it or not. But can it be true, that placing this institution upon the original basis—the basis upon which our fathers placed it—can have any tendency to set the Northern and the Southern States at war with one another, or that it can have any tendency to make the people of Vermont raise sugarcane, because they raise it in Louisiana, or that it can compel the people of Illinois to cut pine logs on the Grand Prairie, where they will not grow, because they cut pine logs in Maine, where they do grow? [Laughter.] The Judge says this is a new principle started in regard to this question. Does the Judge claim that he is working on the plan of the founders of Government? I think he says in some of his speeches—indeed, I have one here now—that he saw evidence of a policy to allow slavery to be south of a certain line, while north of it should be excluded, and he saw an indisposition on the part of the country to stand upon that policy, and therefore he set about studying the subject upon *original principles*, and upon *original principles* he got up the Nebraska Bill! I am fighting it upon these "original principles"—fighting it in the Jeffersonian, Washingtonian, and Madisonian fashion. [Laughter and applause.]

Now, my friends, I wish you to attend for a little while to one or two other things in that Springfield speech. My main object was to show, so far as my humble ability was capable of showing to the people of this country, what I believed was the truth—that there was a tendency, if not a conspiracy among those who have engineered this slavery question for the last four or five years, to make slavery perpetual and universal in this nation. Having made that speech principally for that object, after arranging the evidences that I thought tended to prove my proposition, I concluded with this bit of comment:

"We cannot absolutely know that these exact adaptations are the result of preconcert, but when we see a lot of framed timbers, different portions of which we know have been gotten out at different times and places, and by different workmen—Stephen, Franklin, Roger and James, for instance—and when we see these timbers joined together, and see they exactly make the frame of a house or a mill, all the tenons and mortices exactly fitting, and all the lengths and proportions of the different pieces exactly adapted to their respective places, and not a piece too many or too few—not omitting even the scaffolding—or if a single piece be lacking, we see the place in the frame exactly fitted and prepared yet to bring such piece in—in such a case we feel it impossible not to believe that Stephen and Franklin, and Roger and James, all understood one another from the beginning, and all worked upon a common plan or draft drawn before the first blow was struck." [Great cheers.]

When my friend, Judge Douglas, came to Chicago, on the 9th of July, this speech having been delivered on the 16th of June, he made an harangue there, in which he took hold of this speech of mine, showing that he had carefully read it; and while he paid no attention to *this* matter at all, but complimented me as being a "kind, amiable and intelligent gentleman," notwithstanding I had said this, he goes on and eliminates, or draws out, from my speech this tendency of mine to set the States at war with one another, to make all the institutions uniform, and set the niggers and white people to marrying together. [Laughter.] Then, as the Judge had complimented me with these pleasant titles (I must confess to my weakness), I was a little "taken," [laughter] for it came from a great man. I was not very much accustomed to flattery, and it came the sweeter to me. I was rather like the Hoosier, with the gingerbread, when he said he reckoned he loved it better than any other man, and got less of it. [Roars of laughter.] As the Judge had so flattered me, I could not make up my mind that he meant to deal unfairly with me; so I went to work to show him that he misunderstood the whole scope of my speech, and that I really never intended to set the people at war with one another. As an illustration, the next time I met him, which was at Springfield, I used this expression, that I claimed no right under the Constitution, nor had I any inclination, to enter into the Slave States and interfere with the institutions of slavery. He says upon that: Lincoln will not enter into the Slave States, but will go to the banks of the Ohio, on this side, and shoot over! [Laughter.] He runs on, step by step, in the horse-chestnut style of argument, until in the Springfield speech he says, "Unless he shall be successful in firing his batteries, until he shall have extinguished slavery in all the States, the Union shall be dissolved." Now I don't think that was exactly the way to treat "a kind, amiable, intelligent gentleman." I know if I had asked the Judge to show when or where it was I had said that, if I didn't succeed in firing into the slave States until slavery should be extinguished, the Union should be dissolved, he could not have shown it. I understand what he would do. He would say, "I don't mean to quote from you, but this was the *result* of what you say." But

I have the right to ask, and I do ask now: Did you not put it in such a form that an ordinary reader or listener would take it as an expression from me? [Laughter.]

In a speech at Springfield, on the night of the 17th, I thought I might as well attend to my own business a little, and I recalled his attention as well as I could to this charge of conspiracy to nationalize slavery. I called his attention to the fact that he had acknowledged, in my hearing twice, that he had carefully read the speech, and, in the language of the lawyers, as he had twice read the speech, and still had put in no plea or answer, I took a default on him. I insisted that I had a right then to renew that charge of conspiracy. Ten days afterward I met the Judge at Clinton—that is to say, I was on the ground, but not in the discussion—and heard him make a speech. Then he comes in with his plea to this charge, for the first time, and his plea when put in, as well as I can recollect it, amounted to this: that he never had any talk with Judge Taney or the President of the United States with regard to the Dred Scott decision before it was made. I (Lincoln) ought to know that the man who makes a charge without knowing it to be true, falsifies as much as he who knowingly tells a falsehood; and lastly, that he would pronounce the whole thing a falsehood; but he would make no personal application of the charge of falsehood, not because of any regard for the "kind, amiable, intelligent gentleman," but because of his own personal self-respect! [Roars of Laughter.] I have understood since then (but [turning to Judge Douglas] will not hold the Judge to it if he is not willing) that he has broken through the "self-respect," and has got to saying the thing *out*. The Judge nods to me that it is so. [Laughter.] It is fortunate for me that I can keep as good-humored as I do, when the Judge acknowledges that he has been trying to make a question of veracity with me. I know the Judge is a great man, while I am only a small man, but *I feel that I have got him*. [Tremendous cheering.] I demur to that plea. I waive all objections that it was not filed till after default was taken, and demur to it upon the merits. What if Judge Douglas never did talk with Chief Justice Taney and the President, before the Dred Scott decision was made, does it follow that he could not have had as perfect an understanding without talking as with it? I am not disposed to stand upon my legal advantage. I am disposed to take his denial as being like an answer in chancery, that he neither had any knowledge, information or belief in the existence of such a conspiracy. I am disposed to take his answer as being as broad as though he had put it in these words. And now, I ask, even if he had done so, have not I a right to *prove it on him*, and to offer the evidence of more than two witnesses, by whom to prove it; and if the evidence proves the existence of the conspiracy, does his broad answer denying all knowledge, information, or belief, disturb the fact? It can only show that he was *used* by conspirators, and was not a *leader* of them. [Vociferous cheering.]

Now, in regard to his reminding me of the moral rule that persons who tell what they do not know to be true, falsify as much as those who knowingly tell falsehoods. I remember the rule, and it must be borne in mind that in what I have read to you, I do not say that I *know* such a conspiracy to exist. To that I reply, *I believe it*. If the Judge says that I do *not* believe it, then *he* says what *he* does not know, and falls within his own rule, that he who asserts a thing which he does not know to be true, falsifies as much as he who knowingly tells a falsehood. I want to call your attention to a little discussion on that branch of the case, and the evidence which brought my mind to the conclusion which I expressed as *my belief*. If, in arraying that evidence, I had stated anything which was false or erroneous, it needed but that Judge Douglas should point it out, and I would have taken it back with all the kindness in the world. I do not deal in that way. If I have brought forward anything not a fact, if he will point it out, it will not even ruffle me to take it back. But if he will not point out anything erroneous in the evidence, is it not rather for him to show, by a comparison of the evidence, that I have *reasoned* falsely, than to call the "kind, amiable, intelligent gentleman" a liar? [Cheers and laughter.] If I have reasoned to a false conclusion, it is the vocation of an able debater to show by argument that I have wandered to an erroneous conclusion. I want to ask your attention to a portion of the Nebraska Bill, which Judge Douglas has quoted: "It being the true intent and meaning of this act, not to legislate slavery into any Territory or State, nor to exclude it therefrom, but to leave the people thereof perfectly free to form and regulate their domestic institutions in their own way, subject only to the Constitution of the United States." Thereupon Judge Douglas and others began to argue in favor of "Popular Sovereignty"—the right of the people to have slaves if they wanted them, and to exclude slavery if they did not want them. "But," said, in substance, a Senator from Ohio (Mr. Chase, I believe), "we more than suspect that you do not mean to allow the people to exclude slavery if they wish to, and if you do mean it, accept an amendment which I propose expressly authorizing the people to exclude slavery." I believe I have the amendment here before me, which was offered, and under which the people of the Territory, through their proper representatives, might, if they saw fit, prohibit the existence of slavery therein. And now I state it as a *fact*, to be taken back if there is any mistake about it, that Judge Douglas and those acting with him *voted that amendment down*. [Tremendous applause.] I now think that those men who voted it down, had a *real* reason for doing so. They know what that reason was. It looks to us, since we have seen the Dred Scott decision pronounced, holding that, "under the Constitution," the people cannot exclude slavery—I say it looks to outsiders, poor, simple, "amiable, intelligent gentlemen," as though the niche was left as a place to put that Dred Scott decision in [laughter and cheers] a niche which would have been spoiled by adopting the amendment. And now, I say again, if *this* was not the reason, it will avail the Judge much more to calmly and good-humoredly point out to these people what that *other* reason was for voting the amendment down, than, swelling himself up, to vociferate that he may be provoked to call somebody a liar. [Tremendous applause.]

Again: there is in that same quotation from the Nebraska Bill this clause—"It being the true intent and meaning of this bill not to legislate slavery into any Territory or *State*." I have always been puzzled to know what business the word "State" had in that connection, Judge Douglas knows. *He put it there*. He knows what he put it there for. We outsiders cannot say what he put it there for. The law they were passing was not about States, and was not making provisions for States. What was it placed there for? After seeing the Dred Scott decision, which holds that the people cannot exclude slavery from a *Territory*, if another Dred Scott decision shall come, holding that they cannot exclude it from a *State*, we shall discover that when the word was originally put there, it was in view of something which was to come in due time, we shall see that it was the *other half* of something. [Applause.] I now say again, if there is any different reason for putting it there, Judge Douglas, in a good-humored way, without calling anybody a liar, *can tell what the reason was*. [Renewed cheers.]

When the Judge spoke at Clinton, he came very near making a charge of falsehood against me. He used, as I found it printed in a newspaper, which, I remember, was very nearly like the real speech, the following language:

"I did not answer the charge [of conspiracy] before, for the reason that I did not suppose there was a man in America with a heart so corrupt as to believe such a charge could be true. I have too much respect for Mr. Lincoln to suppose he is serious in making the charge."

I confess this is rather a curious view, that out of respect for me he should consider I was making what I deemed rather a grave charge in fun. [Laughter.] I confess it strikes me rather strangely. But I let it pass. As the Judge did not for a moment believe that there was a man in America whose heart was so "corrupt" as to make such a charge, and as he places me among the "men in America" who have hearts base enough to make such a charge, I hope he will excuse me if I hunt out another charge very like this; and if it should turn out that in hunting I should find that other, and it should turn out to be Judge Douglas himself who made it, I hope he will reconsider this question of the deep corruption of heart he has thought fit to ascribe to me. [Great applause and laughter.] In Judge Douglas's speech of March 22d, 1858, which I hold in my hand, he says:

"In this connection there is another topic to which I desire to allude. I seldom refer to the course of newspapers, or notice the articles which they publish in regard to myself; but the course of the Washington *Union* has been so extraordinary, for the last two or three months, that I think it well enough to make some allusion to it. It has read me out of the Democratic party every other day, at least for two or three months, and keeps reading me out, [laughter] and, as if it had not succeeded, still continues to read me out, using such terms as "traitor," "renegade," "deserter," and other kind and polite epithets of that nature. Sir, I have no vindication to make of my Democracy against the Washington *Union*, or any other newspapers. I am willing to allow my history and action for the last twenty years to speak for themselves as to my political principles, and my fidelity to political obligations. The Washington *Union* has a personal grievance. When its editor was nominated for public printer I declined to vote for him, and stated that at some time I might give my reasons for doing so. Since I declined to give that vote, this scurrilous abuse, these vindictive and constant attacks have been repeated almost daily on me. Will my friend from Michigan read the article to which I allude?"

This is a part of the speech. You must excuse me from reading the entire article of the Washington *Union*, as Mr. Stuart read it for Mr. Douglas. The Judge goes on and sums up, as I think, correctly:

"Mr. President, you here find several distinct propositions advanced boldly by the Washington Union editorially, and apparently *authoritatively*, and any man who questions any of them is denounced as an Abolitionist, a Freesoiler, a fanatic. The propositions are, first, that the primary object of all government at its original institution is the protection of person and property; second, that the Constitution of the United States declares that the citizens of each State shall be entitled to all the privileges and immunities of citizens in the several States; and that, therefore, thirdly, all State laws, whether organic or otherwise, which prohibit the citizens of one State from settling in another with their slave property, and especially declaring it forfeited, are direct violations of the original intention of the Government and Constitution of the United States; and, fourth, that the emancipation of the slaves of the Northern States was a gross outrage on the rights of property, inasmuch as it was involuntarily done on the part of the owner.

"Remember that this article was published in the *Union* on the 17th of November, and on the 18th appeared the first article giving the adhesion of the *Union* to the Lecompton Constitution. It was in these words:

"'KANSAS AND HER CONSTITUTION—The vexed question is settled. The problem is solved. The dead point of danger is passed. All serious trouble to Kansas affairs is over and gone'—

"And a column, nearly, of the same sort. Then, when you come to look into the Lecompton Constitution, you find the same doctrine incorporated in it which was put forth editorially in the *Union*. What is it?

" 'Article 7, *Section 1.* The right of property is before and higher than any Constitutional sanction; and the right of the owner of a slave to such slave and its increase is the same and as inviolable as the right of the owner of any property whatever.'

"Then in the schedule is a provision that the Constitution may be amended after 1864 by a two-thirds vote.

" 'But no alteration shall be made to affect the right of property in the ownership of slaves.'

"It will be seen by these clauses in the Lecompton Constitution, that they are identical in spirit with the *authoritative* article in the Washington *Union* of the day previous to its indorsement of this Constitution."

I pass over some portions of the speech, and I hope that any one who feels interested in this matter will read the entire section of the speech, and see whether I do the Judge injustice. He proceeds: "When I saw that article in the *Union* of the 17th of November, followed by the glorification of the Lecompton Constitution on the 18th of November, and this clause in the Constitution asserting the doctrine that a State has no right to prohibit slavery within its limits, I saw that there was a *fatal blow* being struck at the sovereignty of the States of this Union."

I stop the quotation there, again requesting that it may all be read. I have read all of the portion I desire to comment upon. What is this charge that the Judge thinks I must have a very corrupt heart to make? It was a purpose on the part of certain high functionaries to make it impossible for the people of one State to prohibit the people of any other State from entering it with their "property," so called, and making it a slave State. In other words, it was a charge implying a design to make the institution of slavery national. And now I ask your attention to what Judge Douglas has himself done here. I know he made that part of the speech as a reason why he had refused to vote for a certain man for public printer, but when we get at it, the charge itself is the very one I made against him, that he thinks I am so corrupt for uttering. Now, whom does he make that charge against? Does he make it against that newspaper editor merely? No; he says it is identical in spirit with the Lecompton Constitution, and so the framers of that Constitution are brought in with the editor of the newspaper in that "fatal blow being struck." He did not call it a "conspiracy." In his language it is a "fatal blow being struck." And if the words carry the meaning better when changed from a "conspiracy" into a "fatal blow being struck," I will change my expression and call it "fatal blow being struck." We see the charge made not merely against the editor of the *Union*, but all the framers of the Lecompton Constitution; and not only so, but the article was an *authoritative* article. By whose authority? Is there any question but he means it was by the authority of the President and his Cabinet—the Administration?

Is there any sort of question but he means to make that charge? Then there are the editors of the *Union*, the framers of the Lecompton Constitution, the President of the United States and his Cabinet, and all the supporters of the Lecompton Constitution, in Congress and out of Congress, who are all involved in this "fatal blow being struck." I commend to Judge Douglas's consideration the question of *how corrupt a man's heart must be to make such a charge*! [Vociferous cheering.]

Now, my friends, I have but one branch of the subject, in the little time I have left, to which to call your attention, and as I shall come to a close at the end of that branch, it is probable that I shall not occupy quite all the time allotted to me. Although on these questions I would like to talk twice as long as I have, I could not enter upon another head and discuss it properly without running over my time. I ask the attention of the people here assembled and elsewhere, to the course that Judge Douglas is pursuing every day as bearing upon this question of making slavery national. Not going back to the records, but taking the speeches he makes, the speeches he made yesterday and day before, and makes constantly all over the country—I ask your attention to them. In the first place, what is necessary to make the institution national? Not war. There is no danger that the people of Kentucky will shoulder their muskets, and, with a young nigger stuck on every bayonet, march into Illinois and force them upon us. There is no danger of our going over there and making war upon them. Then what is necessary for the nationalization of slavery? It is simply the next Dred Scott decision. It is merely for the Supreme Court to decide that no *State* under the Constitution can exclude it, just as they have already decided that under the Constitution neither Congress nor the Territorial Legislature can do it. When that is decided and acquiesced in, the whole thing is done. This being true, and this being the way, as I think, that slavery is to be made national, let us consider what Judge Douglas is doing every day to that end. In the first place, let us see what influence he is exerting on public sentiment. In this and like communities, public sentiment is everything. With public sentiment, nothing can fail; without it nothing can succeed. Consequently he who moulds public sentiment, goes deeper than he who enacts statutes or pronounces decisions. He makes statutes and decisions possible or impossible to be executed. This must be borne in mind, as also the additional fact that Judge Douglas is a man of vast influence, so great that it is enough for many men to profess to believe anything, when they once find out that Judge Douglas professes to believe it. Consider also the attitude he occupies at the head of a large party—a party which he claims has a majority of all the voters in the country. This man sticks to a decision which forbids the people of a Territory from excluding slavery, and he does so not because he says it is right in itself—he does not give any opinion on that—but because it has been *decided by the court*, and being decided by court, he is, and you are bound to take it in your political action as law—not that he judges at all of its merits, but because a decision of the court is to him a "*Thus saith the Lord*." [Applause.] He places it on that ground alone, and you will bear in mind that, thus committing himself unreservedly to this decision, *commits him to the next one* just as firmly as to this. He did not commit himself on account of the merit or demerit of the decision, but it is a *Thus saith the Lord*. The next decision, as much as this, will be a *Thus saith the Lord*. There is nothing that can divert or turn him away from this decision. It is nothing that I point out to him that his great prototype, Gen. Jackson, did not believe in the binding force of decisions. It is nothing to him that Jefferson did not so believe. I have said that I have often heard him approve of Jackson's course in disregarding the decision of the Supreme Court pronouncing a National Bank constitutional. He says, I did not hear him say so. He denies the accuracy of my recollection. I say he ought to know better than I, but I will make no question about this thing, though it still seems to me that I heard him say it twenty times. [Applause and laughter.] I will tell him though, that he now claims to stand on the Cincinnati platform, which affirms that Congress *cannot* charter a National Bank, in the teeth of that old standing decision that Congress *can* charter a bank. [Loud applause.] And I remind him of another piece of history on the question of respect for judicial decisions, and it is a piece of Illinois history, belonging to a time when the large party to which Judge Douglas belonged, were displeased with a decision of the Supreme Court of Illinois, because they had decided that a Governor could not remove a Secretary of State. You will find the whole story in Ford's History of Illinois, and I know that Judge Douglas will not deny that he was then in favor of overslaughing that decision by the mode of adding five new Judges, so as to vote down the four old ones. Not only so, but it ended in *the Judge's sitting down on that very bench as one of the five new Judges to break down the four old ones*. [Cheers and laughter.] It was in this way precisely that he got his title of Judge. Now, when the Judge tells me that men appointed conditionally to sit as members of a court, will have to be catechised beforehand upon some subject, I say, "You know, Judge; you have tried it." [Laughter.] When he says a court of this kind will lose the confidence of all men, will be prostituted and disgraced by such a proceeding, I say, "You know best, Judge; you have been through the mill." But I cannot shake Judge Douglas's teeth loose from the Dred Scott decision. Like some obstinate animal (I mean no disrespect), that will hang on when he has once got his teeth fixed; you may cut off a leg, or you may tear away an arm, still he will not relax his hold. And so I may point out to the Judge, and say that he is bespattered all over, from the beginning of his political life to the present time, with attacks upon judicial decisions—I may cut off limb after limb of his public record, and strive to wrench him from a single dictum of the court—yet I cannot divert him from it. He hangs, to the last, to the Dred Scott decision. [Loud cheers.] These things show there is a purpose *strong as death and eternity* for which he adheres to this decision, and for which he will adhere to *all other decisions* of the same court. [Vociferous applause.]

A Hibernian: "Give us something besides Dred Scott."

Mr. Lincoln: Yes; no doubt you want to hear something that don't hurt. [Laughter and applause.] Now, having spoken of the Dred Scott decision, one more word and I am done. Henry Clay, my beau ideal of a statesman, the man for whom I fought all my humble life—Henry Clay once said of a class of men who would repress all tendencies to liberty and ultimate emancipation, that they must, if they would do this, go back to the era of our Independence, and muzzle the cannon which thunders its annual joyous return; they must blow out the moral lights around us; they must penetrate the human soul, and eradicate there the love of liberty; and then, and not till then, could they perpetuate slavery in this country! [Loud cheers.] To my thinking, Judge Douglas is, by his example and vast influence, doing that very thing in this community, [cheers,] when he says that the negro has nothing in the Declaration of Independence. Henry Clay plainly understood the contrary. Judge Douglas is going back to the era of our Revolution, and to the extent of his ability, muzzling the cannon which thunders its annual joyous return. When he invites any people, willing to have slavery, to establish it, he is blowing out the moral lights around us. [Cheers.] When he says he "cares not whether slavery is voted down or voted up"—that it is a sacred right of self-government—he is, in my judgment, penetrating the human soul and eradicating the light of reason and the love of liberty in this American people. [Enthusiastic and continued applause.] And now I will only say that when, by all these means and appliances, Judge Douglas shall succeed in bringing public sentiment to an exact accordance with his own views—when these vast assemblages shall echo back all these sentiments—when they shall come to repeat his views and to avow his principles, and to say all that he says on these mighty questions—then it needs only the formality of the second Dred Scott decision, which he indorses in advance, to make slavery alike lawful in all the States—old as well as new, North as well as South.

My friends, that ends the chapter. The Judge can take his half hour.

Mr. Douglas' Reply

Fellow citizens: I will now occupy the half hour allotted to me in replying to Mr. Lincoln. The first point to which I will call your attention is, as to what I said about the organization of the Republican party in 1854, and the platform that was formed on the 5th of October, of that year, and I will then put the question to Mr. Lincoln, whether or not, he approves of each article in that platform ["he answered that already"], and ask for a specific answer. ["He has answered." "You cannot make him answer," &c.] I did not charge him with being a member of the committee which reported that platform. ["Yes, you did."] I charged that that platform was the platform of the Republican party adopted by them. The fact that it was the platform of the Republican party is not denied, but Mr. Lincoln now says, that although his name was on the committee which reported it, that he does not think he was there, but thinks he was in Tazewell, holding court. ["He said he was there."] Gentlemen, I ask your silence, and no interruption. Now, I want to remind Mr. Lincoln that he was at Springfield when that Convention was held and those resolutions adopted. ["You can't do it." "He wasn't there," &c.]

Mr. Glover: chairman of the Republican committee—I hope no Republican will interrupt Mr. Douglas. The masses listened to Mr. Lincoln attentively, and as respectable men we ought now to hear Mr. Douglas, and without interruption. ["Good."]

Mr. Douglas: resuming—The point I am going to remind Mr. Lincoln of is this: that after I had made my speech in 1854, during the fair, he gave me notice that he was going to reply to me the next day. I was sick at the time, but I staid over in Springfield to hear his reply and to reply to him. On that day this very Convention, the resolutions adopted by which I have read, was to meet in the Senate chamber. He spoke in the hall of the House; and when he got through his speech—my recollection is distinct, and I shall never forget it—Mr. Codding walked in as I took the stand to reply, and gave notice that the Republican State Convention would meet instantly in the Senate chamber, and called upon the Republicans to retire there and go into this very Convention, instead of remaining and listening to me. ["Three cheers for Douglas."]

Mr. Lincoln: interrupting, excitedly and angrily—Judge, add that I went along with them. [This interruption was made in a pitiful, mean, sneaking way, as Lincoln floundered around the stand.]

Mr. Douglas: Gentlemen, Mr. Lincoln tells me to add that he went along with them to the Senate chamber. I will not add that, because I do not know whether he did or not.

Mr. Lincoln: again interrupting—I know he did not.

[Two of the Republican committee here seized Mr. Lincoln and by a sudden jerk caused him to disappear from the front of the stand, one of them saying quite audibly, "What are you making such a fuss for. Douglas didn't interrupt you, and can't you see that the people don't like it."]

Mr. Douglas: I do not know whether he knows it or not, that is not the point, and I will yet bring him on to the question.

In the first place—Mr. Lincoln was selected by the very men who made the Republican organization, on that day, to reply to me. He spoke for them and for that party, and he was the leader of the party; and on the very day he made his speech in reply to me, preaching up this same doctrine of negro equality, under the Declaration of Independence, this Republican party met in Convention. ["Three cheers for Douglas."] Another evidence that he was acting in concert with them is to be found in the fact that that Convention waited an hour after its time of meeting to hear Lincoln's speech, and Codding one of their leading men, marched in the moment Lincoln got through, and gave notice that they did not want to hear me, and would proceed with the business of the Convention. Still another fact. I have here a newspaper printed at Springfield, Mr. Lincoln's own town, in October, 1854, a few days afterward, publishing these resolutions, charging Mr. Lincoln with entertaining these sentiments, and trying to prove that they were also the sentiments of Mr. Yates, then candidate for Congress. This has been published on Mr. Lincoln over and over again, and never before has he denied it. ["Three cheers."]

But, my friends, this denial of his that he did not act on the committee, is a miserable quibble to avoid the main issue, [applause, "That's so"] which is, that this Republican platform declares in favor of the unconditional repeal of the Fugitive Slave law. Has Lincoln answered whether he indorsed that or not? ["No, no."] I called his attention to it when I first addressed you, and asked him for an answer, and I then predicted that he would not answer. ["Bravo, glourious," and cheers.] How does he answer. Why, that he was not on the committee that wrote the resolutions. [Laughter.] I then repeated the next proposition contained in the resolutions, which was to restrict slavery in those States in which it exists, and asked him whether he indorsed it. Does he answer yes, or no? He says in reply, "I was not on the committee at the time; I was up in Tazewell." The next question I put to him was, whether he was in favor of prohibiting the admission of any more slave States into the Union. I put the question to him distinctly, whether, if the people of the Territory, when they had sufficient population to make a State, should form their Constitution recognizing slavery, he would vote for or against its admission. ["That's it."] He is a candidate for the United States Senate, and it is possible, if he should be elected, that he would have to vote directly on that question. ["He never will."] I asked him to answer me and you, whether he would vote to admit a State into the Union, with slavery or without it, as its own people might choose. ["Hear him," "That's the doctrine," and applause.] He did not answer that question. ["He never will."] He dodges that question also, under the cover that he was not on the Committee at the time, that he was not present when the platform was made. I want to know if he should happen to be in the Senate when a State applied for admission, with a Constitution acceptable to her own people, he would vote to admit that State, if slavery was one of its institutions. ["That's the question."] He avoids the answer.

Mr. Lincoln: interrupting a third time excitedly, No, Judge—[Mr. Lincoln again disappeared suddenly aided by a pull from behind.]

Mr. Douglas: It is true he gives the Abolitionists to understand by a hint that he would not vote to admit such a State. And why? He goes on to say that the man who would talk about giving each State the right to have slavery, or not, as it pleased, was akin to the man who would muzzle the guns which thundered forth the annual joyous return of the day of our independence. [Great laughter.] He says that that kind of talk is casting a blight on the glory of this country. What is the meaning of that? That he is not in favor of each State to have the right of doing as it pleases on the slavery question? ["Stick it to him," "don't spare him," and applause.] I will put the question to him again and again, and I intend to force it out of him. [Immense applause.]

Then again, this platform which was made at Springfield by his own party, when he was its acknowledged head, provides that Republicans will insist on the abolition of slavery in the District of Columbia, and I asked Lincoln specifically whether he agreed with them in that? Did you get an answer? ["No, no."] He is afraid to answer it. ["We will not vote for him."] He knows I will trot him down to Egypt. [Laughter and cheers.] I intend to make him answer there, ["that's right,"] or I will show the people of Illinois that he does not intend to answer these questions. ["Keep him to the point," "give us more," etc.] The convention to which I have been alluding goes a little further, and pledges itself to exclude slavery from all the Territories over which the General Government has exclusive jurisdiction north of 36 deg. 30 min., as well as South. Now I want to know whether he approves that provision. ["He'll never answer," and cheers.] I want him to answer, and when he does, I want to know his opinion on another point, which is, whether he will redeem the pledge of this platform and resist the acquirement of any more territory unless slavery therein shall be forever prohibited. I want him to answer this last question. Each of the questions I have put to him are practical questions—questions based upon the fundamental principles of the Black Republican party, and I want to know whether he is the first, last, and only choice of a party with whom he does not agree in principle. ["Great applause," "Rake him down."] He does not deny but that that principle was unanimously adopted by the Republican party; he does not deny that the whole Republican party is pledged to it; he does not deny that a man who is not faithful to it is faithless to the Republican party; and now I want to know whether that party is unanimously in favor of a man who does not adopt that creed and agree with them in their principles: I want to know whether the man who does not agree with them, and who is afraid to avow his differences, and who dodges the issue, is the first, last, and only choice of the Republican party. [Cheers.]

A Voice: "How about this conspiracy?"

Mr. Douglas: Never mind, I will come to that soon enough. ["Bravo, Judge, hurrah, three cheers for Douglas."] But the platform which I have read to you not only lays down these principles, but it adds:

Resolved, That in furtherance of these principles we will use such constitutional and lawful means as shall seem best adapted to their accomplishment, and that we will support no man for office, under the general or state government, who is not positively and fully committed to the support of these principles, and whose personal character and conduct is not a guaranty that he is reliable, and who shall not have abjured old party allegiance and ties.

["Good," "you have him," &c.]

The Black Republican party stands pledged that they will never support Lincoln until he has pledged himself to that platform, [tremendous applause, men throwing up their hats, and shouting, "you've got him,"] but he cannot devise his answer; he has not made up his mind whether he will or not. [Great laughter.] He talked about everything else he could think of to occupy his hour and a half, and when he could not think of anything more to say, without an excuse for refusing to answer these questions, he sat down long before his time was out. [Cheers.]

In relation to Mr. Lincoln's charge of conspiracy against me, I have a word to say. In his speech today he quotes a playful part of his speech at Springfield, about Stephen, and James, and Franklin, and Roger, and says that I did not take exception to it. I did not answer it, and he repeats it again. I did not take exception to this figure of his. He has a right to be as playful as he pleases in throwing his arguments together, and I will not object; but I did take objection to his second Springfield speech, in which he stated that he intended his first speech as a charge of corruption or conspiracy against the Supreme Court of the United States, President Pierce, President Buchanan, and myself. That gave the offensive character to the charge. He then said that when he made it he did not know whether it was true or not [laughter], but inasmuch as Judge Douglas had not denied it, although he had replied to the other parts of his speech three times, he repeated it as a charge of conspiracy against me, thus charging me with moral turpitude. When he put it in that form I did say that inasmuch as he repeated the charge simply because I had not denied it, I would deprive him of the opportunity of ever repeating it again, by declaring that it was in all its bearings an infamous lie. ["Three cheers for Douglas."] He says he will repeat it until I answer his folly and nonsense, about Stephen, and Franklin, and Roger, and Bob, and James.

He studied that out, prepared that one sentence with the greatest care, committed it to memory, and put it in his first Springfield speech, and now he carries that speech around and reads that sentence to show how pretty it is. [Laughter.] His vanity is wounded because I will not go into that beautiful figure of his about the building of a house. [Renewed laughter.] All I have to say is, that I am not green enough to let him make a charge which he acknowledges he does not know to be true, and then take up my time in answering it, when I know it to be false and nobody else knows it to be true. [Cheers.]

I have not brought a charge of moral turpitude against him. When he, or any other man, brings one against me, instead of disproving it I will say that it is a lie, and let him prove it if he can. [Enthusiastic applause.]

I have lived twenty-five years in Illinois. I have served you with all the fidelity and ability which I possess, ["That's so," "good." and cheers,] and Mr. Lincoln is at liberty to attack my public action, my votes, and my conduct; but when he dares to attack my moral integrity, by a charge of conspiracy between myself, Chief Justice Taney and the Supreme Court, and two Presidents of the United States, I will repel it. ["Three cheers for Douglas."]

Mr. Lincoln has not character enough for integrity and truth, merely on his own *ipse dixit* to arraign President Buchanan, President Pierce, and nine judges of the Supreme Court, not one of whom would be complimented by being put on an equality with him. ["Hit him again, three cheers" &c.] There is an unpardonable presumption in a man putting himself up before thousands of people, and pretending that his *ipse dixit*, without proof, without fact and without truth, is enough to bring down and destroy the purest and best of living men. ["Hear him," "Three cheers."]

Fellow-citizens, my time is fast expiring; I must pass on. Mr. Lincoln wants to know why I voted against Mr. Chase's amendment to the Nebraska Bill. I will tell him. In the first place, the bill already conferred all the power which Congress had, by giving the people the whole power over the subject. Chase offered a proviso that they might abolish slavery, which by implication would convey the idea that they could prohibit by not introducing that institution. Gen. Cass asked him to modify his amendment, so as to provide that the people might either prohibit or introduce slavery, and thus make it fair and equal. Chase refused to so modify his proviso, and then Gen. Cass and all the rest of us, voted it down. [Immense cheering.] These facts appear on the journals and debates of Congress, where Mr. Lincoln found the charge, and if he had told the whole truth, there would have been no necessity for me to occupy your time in explaining the matter.

Mr. Lincoln wants to know why the word "state," as well as "territory," was put into the Nebraska Bill! I will tell him. It was put there to meet just such false arguments as he has been adducing. [Laughter.] That first, not only the people of the Territories should do as they pleased, but that when they come to be admitted as States, they should come into the Union with or without slavery, as the people determined. I meant to knock in the head this Abolition doctrine of Mr. Lincoln's, that there shall be no more slave States, even if the people want them. [Tremendous applause.] And it does not do for him to say, or for any other Black Republican to say, that there is nobody in favor of the doctrine of no more slave States, and that nobody wants to interfere with the right of the people to do as they please. What was the origin of the Missouri difficulty and the Missouri compromise? The people of Missouri formed a constitution as a slave State, and asked admission into the Union, but the Free Soil party of the North being in a majority, refused to admit her because she had slavery as one of her institutions. Hence this first slavery agitation arose upon a State and not upon a Territory, and yet Mr. Lincoln does not know why the word State was placed in the Kansas-Nebraska Bill. [Great laughter and applause.] The whole Abolition agitation arose on that doctrine of prohibiting a State from coming in with Slavery or not, as it pleased, and that same doctrine is here in this Republican platform of 1854; it has never been repealed; and every Black Republican stands pledged by that platform, never to vote for any man who is not in favor of it. Yet Mr. Lincoln does not know that there is a man in the world who is in favor of preventing a State from coming in as it pleases, notwithstanding. The Springfield platform says that they, the Republican party, will not allow a State to come in under such circumstances. He is an ignorant man. [Cheers.]

Now you see that upon these very points I am as far from bringing Mr. Lincoln up to the line as I ever was before. He does not want to avow his principles. I do want to avow mine, as clear as sunlight in mid-day. [Cheers and applause.] Democracy is founded upon the eternal principle of right. ["That is the talk."] The plainer these principles are avowed before the people, the stronger will be the support which they will receive. I only wish I had the power to make them so clear that they would shine in the heavens for every man, woman, and child to read. [Loud cheering.] The first of those principles that I would proclaim would be in opposition to Mr. Lincoln's doctrine of uniformity between the different States, and I would declare instead the sovereign right of each State to decide the slavery question as well as all other domestic questions for themselves, without interference from any other State or power whatsoever. ["Hurrah for Douglas."]

When that principle is recognized, you will have peace and harmony and fraternal feeling between all the States of this Union; until you do recognize that doctrine, there will be sectional warfare agitating and distracting the country. What does Mr. Lincoln propose? He says that the Union cannot exist divided into free and slave States. If it cannot endure thus divided, then he must strive to make them all free or all slave, which will inevitably bring about a dissolution of the Union. [Cries of "he can't do it."]

Gentlemen, I am told that my time is out, and I am obliged to stop. [Three times three cheers were here given for Senator Douglas.]

THE LAST OF THE LINCOLN-DOUGLAS DEBATES

Alton, October 15, 1858

MR. DOUGLAS' SPEECH

Long and loud bursts of applause greeted Senator Douglas when he appeared on the stand. As he was about to commence speaking, he was interrupted by Dr. Hope, one of the Danite faction.

DR. HOPE: Judge, before you commence speaking, allow me to ask you a question.

SENATOR DOUGLAS: If you will not occupy too much of my time.

DR. HOPE: Only an instant.

SENATOR DOUGLAS: What is your question?

MR. HOPE: Do you believe that the Territorial legislatures ought to pass laws to protect slavery in the territories?

SENATOR DOUGLAS: You will get an answer in the course of my remarks. [Applause.]

Ladies and Gentlemen: It is now nearly four months since the canvass between Mr. Lincoln and myself commenced. On the 16th of June the Republican Convention assembled at Springfield and nominated Mr. Lincoln as their candidate for the United States Senate, and he, on that occasion, delivered a speech in which he laid down what he understood to be the Republican creed and the platform on which he proposed to stand during the contest. The principal points in that speech of Mr. Lincoln's were: First, that this Government could not endure permanently divided into free and slave States, as our fathers made it; that they must all become free or all become slave; all become one thing or all become the other, otherwise this Union could not continue to exist. I give you his opinions almost in the identical language he used. His second proposition was a crusade against the Supreme Court of the United States because of the Dred Scott decision; urging as an especial reason for his opposition to that decision that it deprived the negroes of the rights and benefits of that clause in the Constitution of the United States which guaranties to the citizens of each State all the rights, privileges, and immunities of the citizens of the several States. On the 10th of July I returned home, and delivered a speech to the people of Chicago, in which I announced it to be my purpose to appeal to the people of Illinois to sustain the course I had pursued in Congress. In that speech I joined issue with Mr. Lincoln on the points which he had presented. Thus there was an issue clear and distinct made up between us on these two propositions laid down in the speech of Mr. Lincoln at Springfield, and controverted by me in my reply to him at Chicago. On the next day, the 11th of July, Mr. Lincoln replied to me at Chicago, explaining at some length, and reaffirming the positions which he had taken in his Springfield speech. In that Chicago speech he even went further than he had before, and uttered sentiments in regard to the negro being on an equality with the white man. ["That's so.] He adopted in support of this position the argument which Lovejoy and Codding, and other Abolition lecturers had made familiar in the northern and central portions of the State, to wit: that the Declaration of Independence having declared all men free and equal, by Divine law, also that negro equality was an inalienable right, of which they could not be deprived. He insisted, in that speech, that the Declaration of Independence included the negro in the clause, asserting that all men were created equal, and went so far as to say that if one man was allowed to take the position, that it did not include the negro, others might take the position that it did not include other men. He said that all these distinctions between this man and that man, this race and the other race, must be discarded, and we must all stand by the Declaration of Independence, declaring that all men were created equal.

The issue thus being made up between Mr. Lincoln and myself on three points, we went before the people of the State. During the following seven weeks, between the Chicago speeches and our first meeting at Ottawa, he and I addressed large assemblages of the people in many of the central counties. In my speeches I confined myself closely to those three positions which he had taken, controverting his proposition that this Union could not exist as our fathers made it, divided into free and slave States, controverting his proposition of a crusade against the Supreme Court because of the Dred Scott decision, and controverting his proposition that the Declaration of Independence included and meant the negroes as well as the white men, when it declared all men to be created equal. ["Cheers for Douglas."] I supposed at that time that these propositions constituted a distinct issue between us, and that the opposite positions we had taken upon them we would be willing to be held to in every part of the State, I never intended to waver one hair's breadth from that issue either in the north or the south, or wherever I should address the people of Illinois. I hold that when the time arrives that I cannot proclaim my political creed in the same terms not only in the northern but the southern part of Illinois, not only in the Northern but the Southern States, and wherever the American flag waves over American soil, that then there must be something wrong in that creed. ["Good, good," and cheers.] So long as we live under a common Constitution, so long as we live in a confederacy of sovereign and equal States, joined together as one for certain purposes, that any political creed is radically wrong which cannot be proclaimed in every State, and every section of that Union, alike. I took up Mr. Lincoln's three propositions in my several speeches, analyzed them, and pointed out what I believed to be the radical errors contained in them. First, in regard to his doctrine that this Government was in violation of the law of God, which says that a house divided against itself cannot stand, I repudiated it as a slander upon the immortal framers of our Constitution. I then said, I have often repeated, and now again assert, that in my opinion our Government can endure forever, divided into free and slave States as our fathers made it, each State having the right to prohibit, abolish or sustain slavery, just as it pleases. ["Good," "right," and cheers.] This Government was made upon the great basis of the sovereignty of the States, the right of each State to regulate its own domestic institutions to suit itself, and that right was conferred with the understanding and expectation that inasmuch as each locality had separate interests, each locality must have different and distinct local and domestic institutions, corresponding to its wants and interests. Our fathers knew when they made the Government, that the laws and institutions which were well adapted to the green mountains of Vermont, were unsuited to the rice plantations of South Carolina. They knew then, as well as we know now, that the laws and institutions which would be well adapted to the beautiful prairies of Illinois would not be suited to the mining regions of California. They knew that in a Republic as broad as this, having such a variety of soil, climate and interest, there must necessarily be a corresponding variety of local laws—the policy and institutions of each State adapted to its condition and wants. For this reason this Union was established on the right of each State to do as it pleased on the question of slavery, and every other question; and the various States were not allowed to complain of, much less interfere with the policy, of their neighbors. ["That's good doctrine," "that's the doctrine," and cheers.]

Suppose the doctrine advocated by Mr. Lincoln and the abolitionists of this day had prevailed when the Constitution was made, what would have been the result? Imagine for a moment that Mr. Lincoln had been a member of the Convention that framed the Constitution of the United States, and that when its members were about to sign that wonderful document, he had arisen in that Convention as he did at Springfield this summer, and addressing himself to the President, had said, "A house divided against itself cannot stand; [laughter] this government, divided into free and slave States, cannot endure, they must all be free or all be slave, they must all be one thing or all the other, otherwise, it is a violation of the law of God, and cannot continue to exist;"—suppose Mr. Lincoln had convinced that body of sages that that doctrine was sound, what would have been the result? Remember that the Union was then composed of thirteen States, twelve of which were slaveholding and one free. Do you think that the one free State would have outvoted the twelve slaveholding States, and thus have secured the abolition of slavery? ["No, no."] On the other hand, would not the twelve slaveholding States have outvoted the one free State, and thus have fastened slavery, by a Constitutional provision, on every foot of the American Republic forever? You see that if this abolition doctrine of Mr. Lincoln had prevailed when the Government was made, it would have established slavery as a permanent institution, in all the States, whether they wanted it or not, and the question for us to determine in Illinois now as one of the free States is, whether or not we are willing, having become the majority section, to enforce a doctrine on the minority, which we would have resisted with our heart's blood had it been attempted on us when we were in a minority. ["We never will," "good, good," and cheers.] How has the South lost her power as the majority section in this Union, and how have the free States gained it, except under the operation of that principle which declares the right of the people of each State and each Territory to form and regulate their domestic institutions in their own way. It was under that principle that slavery was abolished in New Hampshire, Rhode Island, Connecticut, New York, New Jersey, and Pennsylvania; it was under that principle that one half of the slaveholding States became free; it was under that principle that the number of free States increased until from being one out of twelve States, we have grown to be the majority of States of the whole Union, with the power to control the House of Representatives and Senate, and the power, consequently, to elect a President by Northern votes without the aid of a Southern State. Having obtained this power under the operation of that great principle, are you now prepared to abandon the principle and declare that merely because we have the power you will wage a war against the Southern States and their institutions until you force them to abolish slavery every where. ["No, never," and great applause.]

After having pressed these arguments home on Mr. Lincoln for seven weeks, publishing a number of my speeches, we met at Ottawa in joint discussion, and he then began to crawfish a little, and let himself down. [Immense applause.] I there propounded certain questions to him. Amongst others, I asked him whether he would vote for the admission of any more slave States in the event the people wanted them. He would not answer. [Applause and laughter.] I then told him that if he did not answer the question there I would renew it at Freeport, and would then trot him down into Egypt and again put it to him. [Cheers.] Well, at Freeport, knowing that the next joint discussion took place in Egypt, and being in dread of it, he did answer my question in regard to no more slave States in a mode which he hoped would be satisfactory to me, and accomplish the object he had in view.

I will show you what his answer was. After saying that he was not pledged to the Republican doctrine of "no more slave States," he declared:

I state to you freely, frankly, that I should be exceedingly sorry to ever be put in the position of having to pass upon that question. I should be exceedingly glad to know that there never would be another slave State admitted into this Union.

Here permit me to remark, that I do not think the people will ever force him into a position against his will. [Great laughter and applause.] He went on to say:

But I must add in regard to this, that if slavery shall be kept out of the Territory during the territorial existence of any one given Territory, and then the people should, having a fair chance and a clear field when they come to adopt a Constitution, if they should do the extraordinary thing of adopting a slave Constitution, uninfluenced by the actual presence of the institution among them, I see no alternative, if we own the country, but we must admit it into the Union.

That answer Mr. Lincoln supposed would satisfy the old line Whigs, composed of Kentuckians and Virginians, down in the southern part of the State. Now, what does it amount to? I desired to know whether he would vote to allow Kansas to come into the Union with slavery or not, as her people desired. He would not answer; but in a roundabout way said that if slavery should be kept out of a Territory during the whole of its territorial existence, and then the people, when they adopted a State Constitution, asked admission as a slave State, he supposed he would have to let the State come in. The case I put to him was an entirely different one. I desired to know whether he would vote to admit a State if Congress had not prohibited slavery in it during its territorial existence, as Congress never pretended to do under Clay's Compromise measures of 1850. He would not answer, and I have not yet been able to get an answer from him. [Laughter, "he'll answer this time," "he's afraid to answer," etc.] I have asked him whether he would vote to admit Nebraska if her people asked to come in as a State with a Constitution recognizing slavery, and he refused to answer. ["Put him through," "give it to him," and cheers.] I have put the question to him with reference to New Mexico, and he has not uttered a word in answer. I have enumerated the Territories, one after another, putting the same question to him with reference to each, and he has not said, and will not say, whether, if elected to Congress, he will vote to admit any Territory now in existence with such a Constitution as her people may adopt. He invents a case which does not exist, and cannot exist under this Government, and answers it; but he will not answer the question I put to him in connection with any of the Territories now in existence. ["Hurrah for Douglas," "three cheers for Douglas."] The contract we entered into with Texas when she entered the Union obliges us to allow four States to be formed out of the old State, and admitted with or without slavery as the respective inhabitants of each may determine. I have asked Mr. Lincoln three times in our joint discussions whether he would vote to redeem that pledge, and he has never yet answered. He is as silent as the grave on the subject. [Laughter, "Lincoln must answer," "he will," &c.] He would rather answer as to a state of the case which will never arise than commit himself by telling what he would do in a case which would come up for his action soon after his election to Congress. ["He'll never have to act on any question," and laughter.] Why can he not say whether he is willing to allow the people of each State to have slavery or not as they please, and to come into the Union when they have the requisite population as a slave or a free State as they decide? I have no trouble in answering the question. I have said everywhere, and now repeat it to you, that if the people of Kansas want a slave State they have a right, under the Constitution of the United States, to form such a State, and I will let them come into the Union with slavery or without, as they determine. ["That's right," "good," "hurrah for Douglas all the time," and cheers.] If the people of any other Territory desire slavery, let them have it. If they do not want it, let them prohibit it. It is their business, not mine. ["That's the doctrine."] It is none of our business in Illinois whether Kansas is a free State or a slave State. It is none of your business in Missouri whether Kansas shall adopt slavery or reject it. It is the business of her people and none of yours. The people of Kansas have as much right to decide that question for themselves as you have in Missouri to decide it for yourselves, or we in Illinois to decide it for ourselves. ["That's what we believe," "We stand by that," and cheers.]

And here I may repeat what I have said in every speech I have made in Illinois, that I fought the Lecompton Constitution to its death, not because of the slavery clause in it, but because it was not the act and deed of the people of Kansas. I said then in Congress, and I say now, that if the people of Kansas want a slave State, they have a right to have it. If they wanted the Lecompton Constitution, they had a right to have it. I was opposed to that Constitution because I did not believe that it was the act and deed of the people, but on the contrary, the act of a small, pitiful minority acting in the name of the majority. When at last it was determined to send that Constitution back to the people, and accordingly, in August last, the question of admission under it was submitted to a popular vote, the citizens rejected it by nearly ten to one, thus showing conclusively, that I was right when I said that the Lecompton Constitution was not the act and deed of the people of Kansas, and did not embody their will. [Cheers.]

I hold that there is no power on earth, under our system of Government, which has the right to force a Constitution upon an unwilling people. ["That's so."] Suppose that there had been a majority of ten to one in favor of slavery in Kansas, and suppose there had been an Abolition President, and an Abolition

Administration, and by some means the Abolitionists succeeded in forcing an Abolition Constitution on those slave-holding people, would the people of the South have submitted to that act for one instant? ["No, no."]Well, if you of the South would not have submitted to it a day, how can you, as fair, honorable and honest men, insist on putting a slave Constitution on a people who desire a free State? ["That's so," and cheers.] Your safety and ours depend upon both of us acting in good faith, and living up to that great principle which asserts the right of every people to form and regulate their domestic institutions to suit themselves, subject only to the Constitution of the United States. ["That's the doctrine," and immense applause.]

Most of the men who denounced my course on the Lecompton question, objected to it not because I was not right, but because they thought it expedient at that time, for the sake of keeping the party together, to do wrong. [Cheers.] I never knew the Democratic party to violate any one of its principles out of policy or expediency, that it did not pay the debt with sorrow. There is no safety or success for our party unless we always do right, and trust the consequences to God and the people. I chose not to depart from principle for the sake of expediency in the Lecompton question, and I never intend to do it on that or any other question. ["Good."]

But I am told that I would have been all right if I had only voted for the English bill after Lecompton was killed. [Laughter and cheers.] You know a general pardon was granted to all political offenders on the Lecompton question, provided they would only vote for the English bill. I did not accept the benefits of that pardon, for the reason that I had been right in the course I had pursued, and hence did not require any forgiveness. Let us see how the result has been worked out. English brought in his bill referring the Lecompton Constitution back to the people, with the provision that if it was rejected Kansas should be kept out of the Union until she had the full ratio of population required for a member of Congress, thus in effect declaring that if the people of Kansas would only consent to come into the Union under the Lecompton Constitution, and have a slave State when they did not want it, they should be admitted with a population of 35,000, but that if they were so obstinate as to insist upon having just such a Constitution as they thought best, and to desire admission as a free State, then they should be kept out until they had 93,420 inhabitants. I then said, and I now repeat to you, that whenever Kansas has people enough for a slave State she has people enough for a free State. I was and am willing to adopt the rule that no State shall ever come into the Union until she has the full ratio of population for a member of Congress, provided that rule is made uniform. I made that proposition in the Senate last winter, but a majority of the Senators would not agree to it; and I then said to them if you will not adopt the general rule I will not consent to make an exception of Kansas.

I hold that it is a violation of the fundamental principles of this Government to throw the weight of federal power into the scale, either in favor of the free or the slave States. Equality among all the States of this Union is a fundamental principle in our political system. We have no more right to throw the weight of the Federal Government into the scale in favor of the slaveholding than the free States, and last of all should our friends in the South consent for a moment that Congress should withhold its powers either way when they know that there is a majority against them in both Houses of Congress.

Fellow-citizens, how have the supporters of the English bill stood up to their pledges not to admit Kansas until she obtained a population of 93,420 in the event she rejected the Lecompton Constitution? How? The newspapers inform us that English himself, whilst conducting his canvass for re-election, and in order to secure it, pledged himself to his constituents that if returned he would disregard his own bill and vote to admit Kansas into the Union with such population as she might have when she made application. We are informed that every Democratic candidate for Congress in all the States where elections have recently been held, was pledged against the English bill, with perhaps one or two exceptions. Now, if I had only done as these anti-Lecompton men who voted for the English bill in Congress, pledging themselves to refuse to admit Kansas if she refused to become a slave State until she had a population of 93,420, and then returned to their people, forfeited their pledge, and made a new pledge to admit Kansas at any time she applied, without regard to population, I would have had no trouble. You saw the whole power and patronage of the Federal Government wielded in Indiana, Ohio, and Pennsylvania to re-elect anti-Lecompton men to Congress who voted against Lecompton, then voted for the English bill, and then denounced the English bill, and pledged themselves to their people to disregard it. My sin consists in not having given a pledge, and then in not having afterward forfeited it. For that reason, in this State, every postmaster, every route agent, every collector of the ports, and every federal office-holder, forfeits his head the moment he expresses a preference for the Democratic candidates against Lincoln and his Abolition associates. A Democratic Administration which we helped to bring into power, deems it consistent with its fidelity to principle and its regard to duty, to wield its power in this State in behalf of the Republican Abolition candidates in every county and every Congressional District against the Democratic party. All I have to say in reference to the matter is, that if that Administration have not regard enough for principle, if they are not sufficiently attached to the creed of the Democratic party to bury forever their personal hostilities in order to succeed in carrying out our glorious principles, I have. I have no personal difficulty with Mr. Buchanan or his cabinet. He chose to make certain recommendations to Congress, as he had a right to do, on the Lecompton question. I could not vote in favor of them. I had as much right to judge for myself how I should vote as he had how he should recommend. He undertook to say to me, if you do not vote as I tell you, I will take off the heads of your friends. I replied to him, "You did not elect me, I represent Illinois and I am accountable to Illinois, as my constituency, and to God, but not to the President or to any other power on earth."

And now this warfare is made on me because I would not surrender my connections of duty, because I would not abandon my constituency, and receive the orders of the executive authorities how I should vote in the Senate of the United States. I hold that an attempt to control the Senate on the part of the Executive is subversive of the principles of our Constitution. The Executive department is independent of the Senate, and the Senate is independent of the President. In matters of legislation the President has a veto on the action of the Senate, and in appointments and treaties the Senate has a veto on the President. He has no more right to tell me how I shall vote on his appointments than I have to tell him whether he shall veto or approve a bill that the Senate has passed. Whenever you recognize the right of the Executive to say to a Senator, "Do this, or I will take off the heads of your friends," you convert this Government from a republic into a despotism. Whenever you recognize the right of a President to say to a member of Congress, "Vote as I tell you, or I will bring a power to bear against you at home which will crush you," you destroy the independence of the representative, and convert him into a tool of Executive power. I resisted this invasion of the constitutional rights of a Senator, and I intend to resist it as long as I have a voice to speak, or a vote to give. Yet, Mr. Buchanan cannot provoke me to abandon one iota of Democratic principles out of revenge or hostility to his course. I stand by the platform of the Democratic party, and by its organization, and support its nominees. If there are any who choose to bolt, the fact only shows that they are not as good Democrats as I am.

My friends, there never was a time when it was as important for the Democratic party, for all national men, to rally and stand together as it is today. We find all sectional men giving up past differences and continuing the one question of slavery, and when we find sectional men thus uniting, we should unite to resist them and their treasonable designs. Such was the case in 1850, when Clay left the quiet and peace of his home, and again entered upon public life to quell agitation and restore peace to a distracted Union. Then we Democrats, with Cass at our head, welcomed Henry Clay, whom the whole nation regarded as having been preserved by God for the times. He became our leader in that great fight, and we rallied around him the same as the Whigs rallied around old Hickory in 1832, to put down nullification. Thus you see that whilst Whigs and Democrats fought fearlessly in old times about banks, the tariff, distribution, the specie circular, and the sub-treasury, all united as a band of brothers when the peace, harmony, or integrity of the Union was imperiled. It was so in 1850, when Abolitionism had even so far divided this country, North and South, as to endanger the peace of the Union; Whigs and Democrats united in establishing the Compromise measures of that year, and restoring tranquillity and good feeling. These measures passed on the joint action of the two parties. They rested on the great principle that the people of each State and each Territory should be left perfectly free to form and regulate their domestic institutions to suit themselves. You Whigs and we Democrats justified them in that principle. In 1854, when it became necessary to organize the Territories of Kansas and Nebraska, I brought forward the bill on the same principle. In the Kansas-Nebraska Bill you find it declared to be the true intent and meaning of the act not to legislate slavery into any State or Territory, nor to exclude it therefrom, but to leave the people thereof perfectly free to form and regulate their domestic institutions in their own way. ["That's so," and cheers.] I stand on that same platform in 1858 that I did in 1850, 1854, and 1856. The Washington *Union* pretending to be the organ of the Administration, in the number of the 5th of this month, devotes three columns and a half to establish these propositions: First, that Douglas, in his Freeport speech, held the same doctrine that he did in his Nebraska Bill in 1854; second, that in 1854 Douglas justified the Nebraska Bill upon the ground that it was based upon the same principle as Clay's Compromise measures of 1850. The Union thus proved that Douglas was the same in 1858 that he was in 1856, 1854, and 1850, and consequently argued that he was never a Democrat. Is it not funny that I was never a Democrat? There is no pretense that I have changed a hair's breadth. The *Union* proves by my speeches that I explained the Compromise measures of 1850 just as I do now, and that I explained the Kansas and Nebraska Bill in 1854 just as I did in my Freeport speech, and yet says that I am not a Democrat, and cannot be trusted, because I have not changed during the whole of that time. It has occured to me that in 1854 the author of the Kansas and Nebraska Bill was considered a pretty good Democrat. [Cheers] It has occurred to me that in 1856, when I was exerting every nerve and every energy for James Buchanan, standing on the same platform then that I do now, that I was a pretty good Democrat. [Renewed applause.] They now tell me that I am not a Democrat, because I assert that the people of a Territory, as well as those of a State, have the right to decide for themselves whether slavery can or cannot exist in such Territory. Let me read what James Buchanan said on that point when he accepted the Democratic nomination for the Presidency in 1856. In his letter of acceptance, he used the following language:

The recent legislation of Congress respecting domestic slavery, derived as it has been from the original and pure fountain of legitimate political power, the will of the majority, promises ere long to allay the dangerous excitement. This legislation is founded upon principles as ancient as free government itself, and in accordance with them has simply declared that the people of a Territory, like those of a State, shall decide for themselves whether slavery shall or shall not exist within their limits.

Dr. Hope will there find my answer to the question he propounded to me before I commenced speaking. [Vociferous shouts of applause.] Of course no man will consider it an answer, who is outside of the Democratic organization, bolts Democratic nominations, and indirectly aids to put Abolitionists into power over Democrats. But whether Dr. Hope considers it an answer or not, every fair-minded man will see that James Buchanan has answered the question, and has asserted that the people of a Territory, like those of a State, shall decide for themselves whether slavery shall or shall not exist within their limits. I answer specifically if you want a further answer, and say that while under the decision of the Supreme Court, as recorded in the opinion of Chief Justice Taney, slaves are property like all other property, and can be carried into any Territory of the United States the same as any other description of property, yet when you get them there they are subject to the local law of the Territory just like all other property. You will find in a recent speech delivered by that able and eloquent statesman, Hon. Jefferson Davis, at Bangor, Maine, that he took the same view of this subject that I did in my Freeport speech. He there said:

"If the inhabitants of any Territory should refuse to enact such laws and police regulations as would give security to their property or to his, it would be rendered more or less valueless in proportion to the difficulties of holding it without such protection. In the case of property in the labor of man, or what is usually called slave property, the insecurity would be so great that the owner could not ordinarily retain it. Therefore, though the right would remain, the remedy being withheld, it would follow that the owner would be practically debarred, by the circumstances of the case, from taking slave property into a Territory where the sense of the inhabitants was opposed to its introduction. So much for the oft-repeated fallacy of forcing slavery upon any community."

You will also find that the distinguished Speaker of the present House of Representatives, Hon. Jas. L. Orr, construed the Kansas and Nebraska Bill in this same way in 1856, and also that great intellect of the South, Alex. H. Stephens, put the same construction upon it in Congress that I did in my Freeport speech.

The whole South are rallying to the support of the doctrine that if the people of a Territory want slavery they have a right to have it, and if they do not want it that no power on earth can force it upon them. I hold that there is no principle on earth more sacred to all the friends of freedom than that which says that no institution, no law, no constitution, should be forced on an unwilling people contrary to their wishes; and I assert that the Kansas and Nebraska Bill contains that principle. It is the great principle contained in that bill. It is the principle on which James Buchanan was made President. Without that principle he never would have been made President of the United States. I will never violate or abandon that doctrine if I have to stand alone. ["Hurrah for Douglas."] I have resisted the blandishments and threats of power on the one side, and seduction on the other, and have stood immovably for that principle, fighting for it when assailed by Northern mobs, or threatened by Southern hostility. ["That's the truth," and cheers.] I have defended it against the North and the South, and I will defend it against whoever assails it, and I will follow it wherever its logical conclusions lead me. ["So will we all," "hurrah for Douglas."] I say to you that there is but one hope, one safety for this country, and that is to stand immovably by that principle which declares the right of each State and each Territory to decide these questions for themselves. ["Hear him, hear him."] This Government was founded on that principle, and must be administered in the same sense in which it was founded.

But the Abolition party really think that under the Declaration of Independence the negro is equal to the white man, and that negro equality is an inalienable right conferred by the Almighty, and hence that all human laws in violation of it are null and void. With such men it is no use for me to argue. I hold that the signers of the Declaration of Independence had no reference to negroes at all when they declared all men to be created equal. They did not mean negro, nor the savage Indians, nor the Fejee Islanders, nor any other barbarous race. They were speaking of white men. ["It's so, it's so," and cheers.] They alluded to men of European birth and European descent—to white men, and to none others, when they declared that doctrine. ["That's the truth."] I hold that this Government was established on the white basis. It was established by white men for the benefit of white men and their posterity forever, and should be administered by white men, and none others. But it does not follow, by any means, that merely because the negro is not a citizen, and merely because he is not our equal, that, therefore, he should be a slave. On the contrary, it does follow that we ought to extend to the negro race, and to all other dependent races all the rights, all the privileges, and all the immunities which they can exercise consistently with the safety of society. Humanity requires that we should give them all these privileges; Christianity commands that we should extend those privileges to them. The question then arises what are those privileges, and what is the nature and extent of them. My answer is that that is a question which each State must answer for itself. We in Illinois have decided it for ourselves. We tried slavery, kept it up for twelve years, and finding that it was not profitable, we abolished it for that reason, and became a free State. We adopted in its stead the policy that a negro in this State shall not be a slave and shall not be a citizen. We have a right to adopt that policy. For my part I think it is a wise and sound policy for us. You in Missouri must judge for yourselves whether it is a wise policy for you. If you choose to follow our example, very good; if you reject it, still well, it is your business, not ours. So with Kentucky. Let Kentucky adopt a policy to suit herself. If we do not like it we will keep away from it, and if she does not like ours let her stay at home, mind her own business and let us alone. If the people of all the States will act on that great principle, and each State mind its own business, attend to its own affairs, take care of its own negroes and not meddle with its neighbors, then there will be peace between the North and the South, the East and the West, throughout the whole Union. [Cheers.] Why can we not thus have peace? Why should we thus allow a sectional party to agitate this country, to array the North against the South, and convert us into enemies instead of friends, merely that a few ambitious men may ride into power on a sectional hobby? How long is it since these ambitious Northern men wished for a sectional organization? Did any one of them dream of a sectional party as long as the North was the weaker section and the South the stronger? Then all were opposed to sectional parties; but the moment the North obtained the majority in the House and Senate by the admission of California, and could elect a President without the aid of Southern votes, that moment ambitious Northern men formed a scheme to excite the North against the South, and make the people be governed in their votes by geographical lines, thinking that the North, being the stronger section, would outvote the South, and consequently they, the leaders, would ride into office on a sectional hobby. I am told that my hour is out. It was very short.

Mr. Lincoln's Speech

On being introduced to the audience, after the cheering had subsided Mr. Lincoln said:

Ladies and Gentlemen: I have been somewhat, in my own mind, complimented by a large portion of Judge Douglas's speech—I mean that portion which he devotes to the controversy between himself and the present Administration. This is the seventh time Judge Douglas and myself have met in these joint discussions, and he has been gradually improving in regard to his war with the Administration. [Laughter, "That's so."] At Quincy, day before yesterday, he was a little more severe upon the Administration than I had heard him upon any occasion, and I took pains to compliment him for it. I then told him to "give it to them with all the power he had"; and as some of them were present, I told them I would be very much obliged if they would *give it to him* in about the same way. [Uproarious laughter and cheers.] I take it he has now vastly improved upon the attack he made then upon the Administration. I flatter myself he has really taken my advice on this subject. All I can say now is to recommend to him and to them what I then commended—to prosecute the war against one another in the most vigorous manner. I say to them again, "Go it, husband! Go it, bear!" [Great laughter.]

There is one other thing I will mention before I leave this branch of the discussion—although I do not consider it much of my business, any way. I refer to that part of the Judge's remarks where he undertakes to involve Mr. Buchanan in an inconsistency. He reads something from Mr. Buchanan, from which he undertakes to involve him in an inconsistency; and he gets something of a cheer for having done so. I would only remind the Judge that while he is very valiantly fighting for the Nebraska Bill and the repeal of the Missouri Compromise, it has been but a little while since he was the *valiant advocate* of the Missouri Compromise. [Cheers.] I want to know if Buchanan has not as much right to be inconsistent as Douglas has? [Loud applause and laughter; "Good, good!" "Hurrah for Lincoln!"] Has Douglas the *exclusive right*, in this country, of being *on all sides of all questions*? Is nobody allowed that high privilege but himself? Is he to have an entire *monopoly* on that subject? [Great laughter.]

So far as Judge Douglas addressed his speech to me, or so far as it was about me, it is my business to pay some attention to it. I have heard the Judge state two or three times what he has stated today—that in a speech which I made at Springfield, Illinois, I had in a very especial manner complained that the Supreme Court in the Dred Scott case had decided that a negro could never be a citizen of the United States. I have omitted by some accident heretofore to analyze this statement, and it is required of me to notice it now. In point of fact it is *untrue*. I never have complained *especially* of the Dred Scott decision because it held that a negro could not be a citizen, and the Judge is always wrong when he says I ever did so complain of it. I have the speech here, and I will thank him or any of his friends to show where I said that a negro should be a citizen, and complained especially of the Dred Scott decision because it declared he could not be one. I have done no such thing, and Judge Douglas so persistently insisting that I have done so, has strongly impressed me with the belief of a predetermination on his part to misrepresent me. He could not get his foundation for insisting that I was in favor of this negro equality any where else as well he could by assuming that untrue proposition. Let me tell this audience what is true in regard to that matter; and the means by which they may correct me if I do not tell them truly is by a recurrence to the speech itself. I spoke of the Dred Scott decision in my Springfield speech, and I was then endeavoring to prove that the Dred Scott decision was a portion of a system or scheme to make slavery national in this country. I pointed out what things had been decided by the court. I mentioned as a fact that they had decided that a negro could not be a citizen—that they had done so, as I supposed, to deprive the negro, under all circumstances, of the remotest possibility of ever becoming a citizen and claiming the rights of a citizen of the United States under a certain clause of the Constitution. I stated that, without making any complaint of it at all. I then went on and stated the other points decided in the case, namely: that the bringing of a negro into the State of Illinois and holding him in slavery for two years here was a matter in regard to which they would not decide whether it would make him free or not; that they decided the further point that taking him into a United States Territory where slavery was prohibited by act of Congress, did not make him free, because that act of Congress, as they held, was unconstitutional. I mentioned these three things as making up the points decided in that case. I mentioned them in a lump taken in connection with the introduction of the Nebraska Bill, and the amendment of Chase, offered at the time, declaratory of the right of the people of the Territories to *exclude slavery*, which was voted down by the friends of the bill. I mentioned all these things together, as evidence tending to prove a combination and conspiracy to make the institution of slavery national. In that connection and in that way I mentioned the decision on the point that a negro could not be a citizen, and in no other connection.

Out of this, Judge Douglas builds up his beautiful fabrication—of my purpose to introduce a perfect, social, and political equality between the white and black races. His assertion that I made an "especial objection" (that is his exact language) to the decision on this account, is untrue in point of fact.

Now, while I am upon this subject, and as Henry Clay has been alluded to, I desire to place myself, in connection with Mr. Clay, as nearly right before this people as may be. I am quite aware what the Judge's object is here by all these allusions. He knows that we are before an audience, having strong sympathies southward by relationship, place of birth, and so on. He desires to place me in an extremely Abolition attitude. He read upon a former occasion, and alludes without reading today, to a portion of a speech which I delivered in Chicago. In his quotations from that speech, as he has made them upon former occasions, the extracts were taken in such a way as, I suppose, brings them within the definition of what is called *garbling*—taking portions of a speech which, when taken by themselves, do not present the entire sense of the speaker as expressed at the time. I propose, therefore, out of that same speech, to show how one portion of it which he skipped over (taking an extract before and an extract after) will give a different idea, and the true idea I intended to convey. It will take me some little time to read it, but I believe I will occupy the time that way.

You have heard him frequently allude to my controversy with him in regard to the Declaration of Independence. I confess that I have had a struggle with Judge Douglas on that matter, and I will try briefly to place myself right in regard to it on this occasion. I said—and it is between the extracts Judge Douglas has taken from this speech, and put in his published speeches:

"It may be argued that there are certain conditions that make necessities and impose them upon us, and to the extent that a necessity is imposed upon a man he must submit to it. I think that was the condition in which we found ourselves when we established this Government. We had slaves among us, we could not get our Constitution unless we permitted them to remain in slavery, we could not secure the good we did secure if we grasped for more; and having by necessity submitted to that much, it does not destroy the principle that is the charter of our liberties. Let the charter remain as our standard."

Now I have upon all occasions declared as strongly as Judge Douglas against the disposition to interfere with the existing institution of slavery. You hear me read it from the same speech from which he takes garbled extracts for the purpose of proving upon me a disposition to interfere with the institution of slavery, and establish a perfect social and political equality between negroes and white people.

Allow me while upon this subject briefly to present one other extract from a speech of mine, more than a year ago, at Springfield, in discussing this very same question, soon after Judge Douglas took his ground that negroes were not included in the Declaration of Independence:

"I think the authors of that notable instrument intended to include *all* men, but they did not mean to declare all men equal *in all respects*. They did not mean to say all men were equal in color, size, intellect, moral development or social capacity. They defined with tolerable distinctness in what they did consider all men created equal—equal in certain inalienable rights, among which are life, liberty, and the pursuit of happiness. This they said, and this they meant. They did not mean to assert the obvious untruth, that all were then actually enjoying that equality, or yet, that they were about to confer it immediately upon them. In fact they had no power to confer such a boon. They meant simply to declare the *right*, so that the *enforcement* of it might follow as fast as circumstances should permit.

"They meant to set up a standard maxim for free society which should be familiar to all: constantly looked to, constantly labored for, and even, though never perfectly attained, constantly approximated, and thereby constantly spreading and deepening its influence and augmenting the happiness and value of life to all people, of all colors, every where."

There again are the sentiments I have expressed in regard to the Declaration of Independence upon a former occasion—sentiments which have been put in print and read wherever any body cared to know what so humble an individual as myself chose to say in regard to it.

At Galesburgh the other day, I said in answer to Judge Douglas, that three years ago there never had been a man, so far as I knew or believed, in the whole world, who had said that the Declaration of Independence did not include negroes in the term "all men." I reassert it today. I assert that Judge Douglas and all his friends may search the whole records of the country, and it will be a matter of great astonishment to me if they shall be able to find that one human being three years ago had ever uttered the astounding sentiment that the term "all men" in the Declaration did not include the negro. Do not let me be misunderstood. I know that more than three years ago there were men who, finding this assertion constantly in the way of their schemes to bring about the ascendancy and perpetuation of slavery, *denied the truth of it*. I know that Mr. Calhoun and all the politicians of his school denied the truth of the Declaration. I know that it ran along in the mouth of some Southern men for a period of years, ending at last in that shameful though rather forcible declaration of Pettit of Indiana, upon the floor of the United States Senate, that the Declaration of Independence was in that respect "a self-evident lie," rather than a self-evident truth. But I say, with a perfect knowledge of all this hawking at the Declaration without directly attacking it, that three years ago there never had lived a man who had ventured to assail it in the sneaking way of pretending to believe it and then asserting it did not include the negro. I believe the first man who ever said it was Chief Justice Taney in the Dred Scott case, and the next to him was our friend, Stephen A. Douglas. And now it has become the catch-word of the entire party. I would like to call upon his friends every where to consider how they have come in so short a time to view this matter in a way so entirely different from their former belief? To ask whether they are not being borne along by an irresistible current—whither, they know not? [Great applause.]

In answer to my proposition at Galesburgh last week, I see that some man in Chicago has got up a letter addressed to the Chicago *Times*, to show, as he professes, that somebody *had* said so before; and he signs himself "An Old Line Whig," if I remember correctly. In the first place I would say he *was not* an old line Whig. I am somewhat acquainted with old line Whigs. I was with the old line Whigs from the origin to the end of that party; I became pretty well acquainted with them, and I know they always had some sense, whatever else you could ascribe to them. [Great Laughter.] I know there never was one who had not more sense than to try to show by the evidence he produces that some man had, prior to the time I named, said that negroes were not included in the term "all men" in the Declaration of Independence. What is the evidence he produces? I will bring forward *his* evidence and let you see what *he* offers by way of showing that somebody more than three years ago had said negroes were not included in the Declaration. He brings forward part of a speech from Henry Clay—the part of the speech of Henry Clay which I used to bring forward to prove precisely the contrary. [Laughter.] I guess we are surrounded to some extent today by the old friends of Mr. Clay, and they will be glad to hear anything from that authority. While he was in Indiana a man presented a petition to liberate his negroes, and he (Mr. Clay) made a speech in answer to it, which I suppose he carefully wrote out himself and caused to be published. I have before me an extract from that speech which constitutes the evidence this pretended "Old Line Whig" at Chicago brought forward to show that Mr. Clay didn't suppose the negro was included in the Declaration of Independence. Hear what Mr. Clay said:

"And what is the foundation of this appeal to me in Indiana, to liberate the slaves under my care in Kentucky? It is a general declaration in the act announcing to the world the independence of the thirteen American colonies, that all men are created equal. Now, as an abstract principle, *there is no doubt of the truth of that declaration*; and it is desirable, *in the original construction of society, and in organized societies*, to keep it in view as a great fundamental principle. But, then, I apprehend that in no society that ever did exist, or ever shall be formed, was or can the equality asserted among the members of the human race, be practically enforced and carried out. There are portions, large portions women, minors, insane, culprits, transient sojourners, that will always probably remain subject to the government of another portion of the community.

"That declaration, whatever may be the extent of its import, was made by the delegations of the thirteen States. In most of them slavery existed, and had long existed, and was established by law. It was introduced and forced upon the colonies by the paramount law of England. Do you believe, that in making that declaration the States that concurred in it intended that it should be tortured into a virtual emancipation of all the slaves within their respective limits? Would Virginia and other Southern States have ever united in a declaration which was to be interpreted into an abolition of slavery among them? Did any one of the thirteen colonies entertain such a design or expectation? To impute such a secret and unavowed purpose, would be to charge a political fraud upon the noblest band of patriots that ever assembled in council—a fraud upon the Confederacy of the Revolution—a fraud upon the union of those States whose Constitution not only recognized the lawfulness of slavery, but permitted the importation of slaves from Africa until the year 1808."

This is the entire quotation brought forward to prove that somebody previous to three years ago had said the negro was not included in the term "all men" in the Declaration. How does it do so? In what way has it a tendency to prove that? Mr. Clay says *it is true as an abstract principle* that all men are created equal, but that we cannot practically apply it in all cases. He illustrates this by bringing forward the cases of females, minors, and insane persons, with whom it cannot be enforced; but he says it is true as an abstract principle in the organization of society as well as in organized society, and it should be kept in view as a fundamental principle. Let me read a few words more before I add some comments of my own. Mr. Clay says a little further on:

"I desire no concealment of my opinions in regard to the institution of slavery. I look upon it as a great evil, and deeply lament that we have derived it from the parental Government, and from our ancestors. But here they are, and the question is, how can they be best dealt with? If a state of nature existed, and we were about to lay the foundations of society, *no man would be more strongly opposed than I should be, to incorporating the institution of slavery among its elements*."

Now, here in this same book—in this same speech—in this same extract brought forward to prove that Mr. Clay held that the negro was not included in the Declaration of Independence—no such statement on his part, but the declaration *that it is a great fundamental truth*, which should be constantly kept in view in the organization of society and in societies already organized. But if I say a word about it—if I attempt, as Mr. Clay said all good men ought to do, to keep it in view—if, in this "organized society," I ask to have the public eye turned upon it—if I ask, in relation to the organization of new Territories, that the public eye should be turned upon it—forthwith I am villified as you hear me today. What have I done, that I have not the license of Henry Clay's illustrious example here in doing? Have I done aught that I have not his authority for, while maintaining that in organizing new Territories and societies, this fundamental principle should be regarded, and in organized society holding it up to the public view and recognizing what he recognized as the great principle of free government? [Great applause, and cries of "Hurrah for Lincoln."]

And when this new principle—this new proposition that no human being ever thought of three years ago—is brought forward, I *combat* it as having an evil tendency, if not an evil design. I combat it as having a tendency to dehumanize the negro—to take away from him the right of ever striving to be a man. I combat it as being one of the thousand things constantly done in these days to prepare the public mind to make property, and nothing but property, of the *negro in all the*

States of this Union. [Tremendous applause. "Hurrah for Lincoln." "Hurrah for Trumbull."]

But there is a point that I wish, before leaving this part of the discussion, to ask attention to. I have read and I repeat the words of Henry Clay:

"I desire no concealment of my opinions in regard to the institution of slavery. I look upon it as a great evil, and deeply lament that we have derived it from the parental Government, and from our ancestors. I wish every slave in the United States was in the country of his ancestors. But here they are; the question is how they can best be dealt with? If a state of nature existed, and we were about to lay the foundations of society, no man would be more strongly opposed than I should be, to incorporate the institution of slavery among its elements."

The principle upon which I have insisted in this canvass, is in relation to laying the foundations of new societies. I have never sought to apply these principles to the old States for the purpose of abolishing slavery in those States. It is nothing but a miserable perversion of what I have said, to assume that I have declared Missouri, or any other slave State, shall emancipate her slaves. I have proposed no such thing. But when Mr. Clay says that in laying the foundations of societies in our Territories where it does not exist, he would be opposed to the introduction of slavery as an element, I insist that we have his warrant—his license for insisting upon the exclusion of that element which he declared in such strong and emphatic language *was most hateful to him.* [Loud applause.]

Judge Douglas has again referred to a Springfield speech in which I said "a house divided against itself cannot stand." The Judge has so often made the entire quotation from that speech that I can make it from memory. I used this language:

"We are now far into the fifth year, since a policy was initiated with the avowed object and confident promise of putting an end to the slavery agitation. Under the operation of this policy, that agitation has not only not ceased, but has constantly augmented. In my opinion it will not cease until a crisis shall have been reached and passed. 'A house divided against itself cannot stand.' I believe this Government cannot endure permanently half slave and half free. I do not expect the house to fall—but I do expect it will cease to be divided. It will become all one thing, or all the other. Either the opponents of slavery will arrest the further spread of it, and place it where the public mind shall rest in the belief that it is in the course of ultimate extinction, or its advocates will push it forward till it shall become alike lawful in all the States—old as well as new, North as well as South."

That extract and the sentiments expressed in it, have been extremely offensive to Judge Douglas. He has warred upon them as Satan wars upon the Bible. [Laughter.] His perversions upon it are endless. Here now are my views upon it in brief.

I said we were now far into the fifth year, since a policy was initiated with the avowed object and confident promise of putting an end to the slavery agitation. Is it not so? When that Nebraska Bill was brought forward four years ago last January, was it not for the "avowed object" of putting an end to the slavery agitation? We were to have no more agitation in Congress, it was all to be banished to the Territories. By the way, I will remark here that, as Judge Douglas is very fond of complimenting Mr. Crittenden in these days, Mr. Crittenden has said there was a falsehood in that whole business, for there was *no slavery agitation at that time to allay*. We were for a little while *quiet* on the troublesome thing, and that very allaying plaster of Judge Douglas's stirred it up again. [Applause and laughter.] But was it not understood or intimated with the "confident promise" of putting an end to the slavery agitation? Surely it was. In every speech you heard Judge Douglas make, until he got into this "imbroglio," as they call it, with the Administration about the Lecompton Constitution, every speech on that Nebraska Bill was full of his felicitations that we were *just at the end* of the slavery agitation. The last tip of the last joint of the old serpent's tail was just drawing out of view. But has it proved so? I have asserted that under that policy that agitation "has not only not ceased, but has constantly augmented." When was there ever a greater agitation in Congress than last winter? When was it as great in the country as today?

There was a collateral object in the introduction of that Nebraska policy which was to clothe the people of the Territories with a superior degree of self-government, beyond what they had ever had before. The first object and the main one of conferring upon the people a higher degree of "self -government," is a question of fact to be determined by you in answer to a single question. Have you ever heard or known of a people any where on earth who had as little to do, as, in the first instance of its use, the people of Kansas had with this same right of "self-government"? [Loud applause.] In its main policy and in its collateral object, *it has been nothing but a living, creeping lie from the time of its introduction till today*. [Loud cheers.]

I have intimated that I thought the agitation would not cease until a crisis should have been reached and passed. I have stated in what way I thought it would be reached and passed. I have said that it might go one way or the other. We might, by arresting the further spread of it, and placing it where the fathers originally placed it, put it where the public mind should rest in the belief that it was in the course of ultimate extinction. [Great applause.] Thus the agitation may cease. It may be pushed forward until it shall become alike lawful in all the States, old as well as new, North as well as South. I have said, and I repeat, my wish is that the further spread of it may be arrested, and that it may be placed where the public mind shall rest in the belief that it is in the course of ultimate extinction. I have expressed that as my wish. I entertain the opinion upon evidence sufficient to my mind, that the fathers of this Government placed that institution where the public mind did rest in the belief that it was in the course of ultimate extinction. Let me ask why they made provision that the source of slavery—the African slave-trade—should be cut off at the end of twenty years? Why did they make provision that in all the new territory we owned at that time, slavery should be forever inhibited? Why stop its spread in one direction and cut off its source in another, if they did not look to its being placed in the course of ultimate extinction?

Again; the institution of slavery is only mentioned in the Constitution of the United States two or three times, and in neither of these cases does the word "slavery" or "negro race" occur; but covert language is used each time, and for a purpose full of significance. What is the language in regard to the prohibition of the African slave-trade? It runs in about this way: "The migration or importation of such persons as any of the States now existing shall think proper to admit, shall not be prohibited by the Congress prior to the year one thousand eight hundred and eight."

The next allusion in the Constitution to the question of slavery and the black race, is on the subject of the basis of representation, and there the language used is, "Representatives and direct taxes shall be apportioned among the several States which may be included within this Union, according to their respective numbers, which shall be determined by adding to the whole number of free persons, including those bound to service for a term of years, and excluding Indians not taxed—three-fifths of all other persons."

It says "persons," not slaves, not negroes; but this "three-fifths" can be applied to no other class among us than the negroes.

Lastly, in the provision for the reclamation of fugitive slaves, it is said: "No person held to service or labor in one State, under the laws thereof, escaping into another, shall in consequence of any law or regulation therein, be discharged from such service or labor, but shall be delivered up, on claim of the party to whom such service or labor may be due." There again there is no mention of the word "negro" or of slavery. In all three of these places, being the only allusions to slavery in the instrument, covert language is used. Language is used not suggesting that slavery existed or that the black race were among us. And I understand the contemporaneous history of those times to be that covert language was used with a purpose, and that purpose was that in our Constitution, which it was hoped and is still hoped will endure forever—when it should be read by intelligent and patriotic men, after the institution of slavery had passed from among us—there should be nothing on the face of the great charter of liberty suggesting that such a thing as negro slavery had ever existed among us. [Enthusiastic applause.] This is part of the evidence that the fathers of the Government expected and intended the institution of slavery to come to an end. They expected and intended that it should be in the course of ultimate extinction. And when I say that I desire to see the further spread of it arrested, I only say I desire to see that done which the fathers have first done. When I say I desire to see it placed where the public mind will rest in the belief that it is in the course of ultimate extinction, I only say I desire to see it placed where they placed it. It is not true that our fathers, as Judge Douglas assumes, made this Government part slave and part free. Understand the sense in which he puts it. He assumes that slavery is a rightful thing within itself—was introduced by the framers of the Constitution. The exact truth is, that they found the institution existing among us, and they left it as they found it. But in making the Government they left this institution with many clear marks of disapprobation upon it. They found slavery among them, and they left it among them because of the difficulty—the absolute impossibility of its immediate removal. And when Judge Douglas asks me why we cannot let it remain part slave and part free, as the fathers of the Government made it, he asks a question based upon an assumption which is itself a falsehood; and I turn upon him and ask him the question, when the policy that the fathers of the Government had adopted in relation to this element among us was the best policy in the world—the only wise policy—the only policy that we can ever safely continue upon—that will ever give us peace unless this dangerous element masters us all and becomes a national institution—*I turn upon him and ask him why he could not let it alone*. [Great and prolonged cheering.] I turn and ask him why he was driven to the necessity of introducing a *new policy* in regard to it? He has himself said he introduced a new policy. He said so in his speech on the 22d of March of the present year, 1858. I ask him why he could not let it remain where our fathers placed it? I ask too of Judge Douglas and his friends why we shall not again place this institution upon the basis on which the fathers left it? I ask you, when he infers that I am in favor of setting the free and slave States at war, when the institution was placed in that attitude by those who made the constitution, *did they make any war*? ["No, no;" and cheers.] If we had no war out of it when thus placed, wherein is the ground of belief that we shall have war out of it if we return to that policy? Have we had any peace upon this matter springing from any other basis? ["No, no."] I maintain that we have not. I have proposed nothing more than a return to the policy of the fathers.

I confess, when I propose a certain measure of policy, it is not enough for me that I do not intend anything evil in the result, but it is incumbent on me to show that it has not a *tendency* to that result. I have met Judge Douglas in that point of view. I have not only made the declaration that I do not *mean* to produce a conflict between the States, but I have tried to show by fair reasoning, and I think I have shown to the minds of fair men, that I propose nothing but what has a most peaceful tendency. The quotation that I happened to make in that Springfield speech, that "a house divided against itself cannot stand," and which has proved so offensive to the Judge, was part and parcel of the same thing. He tries to show that variety in the domestic institutions of the different States is necessary and indispensable. I do not dispute it. I have no controversy with Judge Douglas about that. I shall very readily agree with him that it would be foolish for us to insist upon having a cranberry law here, in Illinois, where we have no cranberries, because they have a cranberry law in Indiana, where they have cranberries. [Laughter, "good, good."] I should insist that it would be exceedingly wrong in us to deny to Virginia the right to enact oyster laws where they have oysters, because we want no such laws here. [Renewed laughter.] I understand, I hope, quite as well as Judge Douglas or anybody else, that the variety in the soil and climate and face of the country, and consequent variety in the industrial pursuits and productions of a country, require systems of law conforming to this variety in the natural features of the country. I understand quite as well as Judge Douglas, that if we here raise a barrel of flour more than we want, and the Louisianians raise a barrel of sugar more than they want, it is of mutual advantage to exchange. That produces commerce, brings us together, and makes us better friends. We like one another the more for it. And I understand as well as Judge Douglas, or any body else, that these mutual accommodations are the cements which bind together the different parts of this Union—that instead of being a thing to "divide the house"— figuratively expressing the Union—they tend to sustain it; they are the props of the house tending always to hold it up.

But when I have admitted all this, I ask if there is any parallel between these things and this institution of slavery? I do not see that there is any parallel at all between them. Consider it. When have we had any difficulty or quarrel amongst ourselves about the cranberry laws of Indiana, or the oyster laws of Virginia, or the pine lumber laws of Maine, or the fact that Louisiana produces sugar, and Illinois flour? When have we had any quarrels over these things? When have we had perfect peace in regard to this thing which I say is an element of discord in this Union? We have sometimes had peace, but when was it? It was when the institution of slavery remained quiet where it was. We have had difficulty and turmoil whenever it has made a struggle to spread itself where it was not. I ask, then, if experience does not speak in thunder-tones, telling us that the policy which has given peace to the country heretofore, being returned to, gives the greatest promise of peace again. ["Yes, yes, yes."] You may say, and Judge Douglas has intimated the same thing, that all this difficulty in regard to the institution of slavery is the mere agitation of office seekers and ambitious Northern politicians. He thinks we want to get "his place," I suppose. [Cheers and laughter.] I agree that there are office seekers amongst us. The Bible says somewhere that we are desperately selfish. I think we would have discovered that fact without the Bible. I do not claim that I am any less so than the average of men, but I do claim that I am not more selfish than Judge Douglas. [Roars of laughter and applause.]

But is it true that all the difficulty and agitation we have in regard to this institution of slavery springs from office seeking—from the mere ambition of politicians? Is that the truth? How many times have we had danger from this question? Go back to the day of the Missouri Compromise. Go back to the Nullification question, at the bottom of which lay this same slavery question. Go back to the time of the Annexation of Texas. Go back to the troubles that led to the Compromise of 1850. You will find that every time, with the single exception of the Nullification question, they sprung from an endeavor to spread this institution. There never was a party in the history of this country, and there probably never will be, of sufficient strength to disturb the general peace of the country. Parties themselves may be divided and quarrel on minor questions, yet it extends not beyond the parties themselves. But does not this question make a disturbance outside of political circles? Does it not enter into the churches and rend them asunder? What divided the great Methodist Church into two parts, North and South? What has raised this constant disturbance in every Presbyterian General Assembly that meets? What disturbed the Unitarian Church in this very city two years ago? What has jarred and shaken the great American Tract Society recently, not yet splitting it, but sure to divide it in the end? Is it not this same mighty, deep-seated power that somehow operates on the minds of men, exciting and stirring them up in every avenue of society—in politics, in religion, in literature, in morals, in all the manifold relations of life? [Applause.] Is this the work of politicians? Is that irresistible power which for fifty years has shaken the Government and agitated the people to be stilled and subdued by pretending that it is an exceedingly simple thing, and we ought not to talk about it? [Great cheers and laughter.] If you will get every body else to stop talking about it, I assure you I will quit before they have half done so. [Renewed laughter.] But where is the philosophy or statesmanship which assumes that you can quiet that disturbing element in our society which has disturbed us for more than half a century, which has been the only serious danger that has threatened our institutions—I say, where is the philosophy or the statesmanship based on the assumption that we are to quit talking about it, [applause] and that the public mind is all at once to cease being agitated by it? Yet this is the policy here in the north that Douglas is advocating—

that we are to care nothing about it! I ask you if it is not a false philosophy? Is it not a false statesmanship that undertakes to build up a system of policy upon the basis of caring nothing about *the very thing that every body does care the most about?* ["Yes, yes," and applause] A thing which all experience has shown we care a very great deal about? [Laughter and applause.]

The Judge alludes very often in the course of his remarks to the exclusive right which the States have to decide the whole thing for themselves. I agree with him very readily that the different States have that right. He is but fighting a man of straw when he assumes that I am contending against the right of the States to do as they please about it. Our controversy with him is in regard to the new Territories. We agree that when the States come in as States they have the right and the power to do as they please. We have no power as citizens of the free States or in our federal capacity as members of the Federal Union through the General Government, to disturb slavery in the States where it exists. We profess constantly that we have no more inclination than belief in the power of the Government to disturb it; yet we are driven constantly to defend ourselves from the assumption that we are warring upon the rights of the *States*. What I insist upon is, that the new Territories shall be kept free from it while in the Territorial condition. Judge Douglas assumes that we have no interest in them—that we have no right whatever to interfere. I think we have some interest. I think that as white men we have. Do we not wish for an outlet for our surplus population, if I may so express myself? Do we not feel an interest in getting to that outlet with such institutions as we would like to have prevail there? If you go to the Territory opposed to slavery and another man comes upon the same ground with his slave, upon the assumption that the things are equal, it turns out that he has the equal right all his way and you have no part of it your way. If he goes in and makes it a slave Territory, and by consequence a slave State, is it not time that those who desire to have it a free State were on equal ground. Let me suggest it in a different way. How many Democrats are there about here ["A thousand"] who have left slave States and come into the free State of Illinois to get rid of the institution of slavery? [Another voice—"a thousand and one."] I reckon there are a thousand and one. [Laughter.] I will ask you, if the policy you are now advocating had prevailed when this country was in a Territorial condition, where would you have gone to get rid of it? [Applause.] Where would you have found your free State or Territory to go to? And when hereafter, for any cause, the people in this place shall desire to find new homes, if they wish to be rid of the institution, where will they find the place to go to? [Loud cheers.]

Now irrespective of the moral aspect of this question as to whether there is a right or wrong in enslaving a negro, I am still in favor of our new Territories being in such a condition that white men may find a home—may find some spot where they can better their condition—where they can settle upon new soil and better their condition in life. [Great and continued cheering.] I am in favor of this not merely, (I must say it here as I have elsewhere,) for our own people who are born amongst us, but as an outlet for *free white people every where*, the world over—in which Hans and Baptiste and Patrick, and all other men from all the world, may find new homes and better their conditions in life. [Loud and long continued applause.]

I have stated upon former occasions, and I may as well state again, what I understand to be the real issue in this controversy between Judge Douglas and myself. On the point of my wanting to make war between the free and the slave States, there has been no issue between us. So, too, when he assumes that I am in favor of introducing a perfect social and political equality between the white and black races. These are false issues, upon which Judge Douglas has tried to force the controversy. There is no foundation in truth for the charge that I maintain either of these propositions. The real issue in this controversy—the one pressing upon every mind—is the sentiment on the part of one class that looks upon the institution of slavery as a *wrong*, and of another class that *does not* look upon it as a wrong. The sentiment that contemplates the institution of slavery in this country as a wrong is the sentiment of the Republican party. It is the sentiment around which all their actions—all their arguments circle—from which all their propositions radiate. They look upon it as being a moral, social and political wrong; and while they contemplate it as such, they nevertheless have due regard for its actual existence among us, and the difficulties of getting rid of it in any satisfactory way and to all the constitutional obligations thrown about it. Yet having a due regard for these, they desire a policy in regard to it that looks to its not creating any more danger. They insist that it should as far as may be, *be treated* as a wrong, and one of the methods of treating it as a wrong is to *make provision that it shall grow no larger*. [Loud applause.] They also desire a policy that looks to a peaceful end of slavery at sometime, as being wrong. These are the views they entertain in regard to it as I understand them; and all their sentiments—all their arguments and propositions are brought within this range. I have said and I repeat it here, that if there be a man amongst us who does not think that the institution of slavery is wrong in any one of the aspects of which I have spoken, he is misplaced and ought not to be with us. And if there be a man amongst us who is so impatient of it as a wrong as to disregard its actual presence among us and the difficulty of getting rid of it suddenly in a satisfactory way, and to disregard the constitutional obligations thrown about it, that man is misplaced if he is on our platform. We disclaim sympathy with him in practical action. He is not placed properly with us.

On this subject of treating it as a wrong, and limiting its spread, let me say a word. Has any thing ever threatened the existence of this Union save and except this very institution of Slavery? What is it that we hold most dear amongst us? Our own liberty and prosperity. What has ever threatened our liberty and prosperity save and except this institution of Slavery? If this is true, how do you propose to improve the condition of things by enlarging Slavery—by spreading it out and making it bigger? You may have a wen or cancer upon your person and not be able to cut it out lest you bleed to death; but surely it is no way to cure it, to engraft it and spread it over your whole body. That is no proper way of treating what you regard a wrong. You see this peaceful way of dealing with it as a wrong—restricting the spread of it, and not allowing it to go into new countries where it has not already existed. That is the peaceful way, the old-fashioned way, the way in which the fathers themselves set us the example.

On the other hand, I have said there is a sentiment which treats it as not being wrong. That is the Democratic sentiment of this day. I do not mean to say that every man who stands within that range positively asserts that it is right. That class will include all who positively assert that it is right, and all who like Judge Douglas treat it as indifferent and do not say it is either right or wrong. These two classes of men fall within the general class of those who do not look upon it as a wrong. And if there be among you any body who supposes that he, as a Democrat can consider himself "as much opposed to slavery as anybody," I would like to reason with him. You never treat it as a wrong. What other thing that you consider as a wrong, do you deal with as you deal with that? Perhaps you *say* it is wrong, *but your leader never does, and you quarrel with any body who says it is wrong*. Although you pretend to say so yourself you can find no fit place to deal with it as a wrong. You must not say any thing about it in the free States, *because it is not here*. You must not say any thing about it in the slave States, *because it is there*. You must not say any thing about it in the pulpit, because that is religion and has nothing to do with it. You must not say any thing about it in politics, *because that will disturb the security of "my place."* There is no place to talk about it as being a wrong, although you say yourself it is a wrong. But finally you will screw yourself up to the belief that if the people of the slave States should adopt a system of gradual emancipation on the slavery question, you would be in favor of it. You would be in favor of it. You say that is getting it in the right place, and you would be glad to see it succeed. But you are deceiving yourself. You all know that Frank Blair and Gratz Brown, down there in St. Louis, undertook to introduce that system in Missouri. They fought as valiantly as they could for the system of gradual emancipation which you pretend you would be glad to see succeed. Now I will bring you to the test. After a hard fight they were beaten, and when the news came over here you threw up your hats and *hurrahed for Democracy*. More than that, take all the argument made in favor of the system you have proposed, and it carefully excludes the idea that there is any thing wrong in the institution of slavery. The arguments to sustain that policy carefully excluded it. Even here today you heard Judge Douglas quarrel with me because I uttered a wish that it might sometime come to an end. Although Henry Clay could say he wished every slave in the United States was in the country of his ancestors, I am denounced by those pretending to respect Henry Clay for uttering a wish that it might sometime, in some peaceful way, come to an end. The Democratic policy in regard to that institution will not tolerate the merest breath, the slightest hint, of the least degree of wrong about it. Try it by some of Judge Douglas's arguments. He says he "don't care whether it is voted up or voted down" in the Territories. I do not care myself in dealing with that expression, whether it is intended to be expressive of his individual sentiments on the subject, or only of the national policy he desires to have established. It is alike valuable for my purpose. Any man can say that who does not see any thing wrong in slavery, but no man can logically say it who does see a wrong in it; because no man can logically say he don't care whether a wrong is voted up or voted down. He may say he don't care whether an indifferent thing is voted up or down, but he must logically have a choice between a right thing and a wrong thing. He contends that whatever community wants slaves has a right to have them. So they have if it is not a wrong. But if it is a wrong, he cannot say people have a right to do wrong. He says that upon the score of equality, slaves should be allowed to go in a new Territory, like other property. This is strictly logical if there is no difference between it and other property. If it and other property are equal, his argument is entirely logical. But if you insist that one is wrong and the other right, there is no use to institute a comparison between right and wrong. You may turn over every thing in the Democratic policy from beginning to end, whether in the shape it takes on the statute book, in the shape it takes in the Dred Scott decision, in the shape it takes in conversation, or the shape it takes in short maxim—like arguments—it every where carefully excludes the idea that there is any thing wrong in it.

That is the real issue. That is the issue that will continue in this country when these poor tongues of Judge Douglas and myself shall be silent. It is the eternal struggle between these two principles—right and wrong—throughout the world. They are the two principles that have stood face to face from the beginning of time; and will ever continue to struggle. The one is the common right of humanity and the other the divine right of kings. It is the same principle in whatever shape it develops itself. It is the same spirit that says, "You work and toil and earn bread, and I'll eat it." No matter in what shape it comes, whether from the mouth of a king who seeks to bestride the people of his own nation and live by the fruit of their labor, or from one race of men as an apology for enslaving another race, it is the same tyrannical principle. I was glad to express my gratitude at Quincy, and I re-express it here to Judge Douglas—*that he looks to no end of the institution of slavery*. That will help the people to see where the struggle really is. It will hereafter place with us all men who really do wish the wrong may have an end. And whenever we can get rid of the fog which obscures the real question—when we can get Judge Douglas and his friends to avow a policy looking to its perpetuation—we can get out from among that class of men and bring them to the side of those who treat it as a wrong. Then there will soon be an end of it, and that end will be its "ultimate extinction." Whenever the issue can be distinctly made, and all extraneous matter thrown out so that men can fairly see the real difference between the parties, this controversy will soon be settled, and it will be done peaceably too. There will be no war, no violence. It will be placed again where the wisest and best men of the world placed it. Brooks of South Carolina once declared that when this Constitution was framed, its framers did not look to the institution existing until this day. When he said this, I think he stated a fact that is fully borne out by the history of the times. But he also said they were better and wiser men than the men of these days; yet the men of these days had experience which they had not, and by the invention of the cotton-gin it became a necessity in this country that slavery should be perpetual. I now say that, willingly or unwillingly, purposely or without purpose, Judge Douglas has been the most prominent instrument in changing the position of the institution of slavery which the fathers of the Government expected to come to an end ere this—and putting it upon Brooks's cotton-gin basis—placing it where he openly confesses he has no desire there shall ever be an end of it.

I understand I have ten minutes yet. I will employ it in saying something about this argument Judge Douglas uses, while he sustains the Dred Scott decision, that the people of the Territories can still somehow exclude slavery. The first thing I ask attention to is the fact that Judge Douglas constantly said, before the decision, that whether they could or not, *was a question for the Supreme Court*. But after the court has made the decision he virtually says it is *not* a question for the Supreme Court, but for the people. And how is it he tells us they can exclude it? He says it needs "police regulations," and that admits of "unfriendly legislation." Although it is a right established by the Constitution of the United States to take a slave into a Territory of the United States and hold him as property, yet unless the Territorial Legislature will give friendly legislation, and, more especially, if they adopt unfriendly legislation, they can practically exclude him. Now, without meeting this proposition as a matter of fact, I pass to consider the real Constitutional obligation. Let me take the gentleman who looks me in the face before me, and let us suppose that he is a member of the Territorial Legislature. The first thing he will do will be to swear that he will support the Constitution of the United States. His neighbor by his side in the Territory has slaves and needs Territorial legislation to enable him to enjoy that Constitutional right. Can he withhold the legislation which his neighbor needs for the enjoyment of a right which is fixed in his favor in the Constitution of the United States which he has sworn to support? Can he withhold it without violating his oath? And more especially, can he pass unfriendly legislation to violate his oath? Why, this is a *monstrous* sort of talk about the Constitution of the United States! *There has never been as outlandish or lawless a doctrine from the mouth of any respectable man on earth.* I do not believe it is a Constitutional right to hold slaves in a Territory of the United States. I believe the decision was improperly made and I go for reversing it. Judge Douglas is furious against those who go for reversing a decision. But he is for legislating it out of all force while the law itself stands. I repeat that there has never been so monstrous a doctrine uttered from the mouth of a respectable man.

I suppose most of us (I know it of myself) believe that the people of the Southern States are entitled to a Congressional Fugitive Slave law—that is a right fixed in the Constitution. But it cannot be made available to them without Congressional legislation. In the Judge's language, it is a "barren right" which needs legislation before it can become efficient and valuable to the persons to whom it is guarantied. And as the right is Constitutional I agree that the legislation shall be granted to it—and that not that we like the institution of slavery. We profess to have no taste for running and catching niggers—at least I profess no taste for that job at all. Why then do I yield support to a Fugitive Slave law? Because I do not understand that the Constitution, which guaranties that right, can be supported without it. And if I believed that the right to hold a slave in a Territory was equally fixed in the Constitution with the right to reclaim fugitives, I should be bound to give it the legislation necessary to support it. I say that no man can deny his obligation to give the necessary legislation to support slavery in a Territory, who believes it is a Constitutional right to have it there. No man can, who does not give the Abolitionists an argument to deny the obligation enjoined by the Constitution to enact a Fugitive Slave law. Try it now. It is the strongest Abolition argument ever made. I say if that Dred Scott decision is correct, then the right to hold slaves in a Territory is equally a Constitutional right with the right of a slaveholder to have his runaway returned. No one can show the distinction between them. The one is express, so that we cannot deny it. The other is construed to be in the Constitution, so that he who believes the decision to be correct believes in the right. And the man who argues that by unfriendly legislation, in spite of that Constitutional right, slavery may be driven from the Territories, cannot avoid furnishing an argument by which Abolitionists may deny the obligation to return fugitives, and claim the power to pass laws unfriendly to the right of the slaveholder to reclaim his fugitive. I do not know how such an argument may strike a popular assembly like this, but I defy anybody to go before a body of men whose minds are educated to estimating evidence and reasoning, and show that there is an iota of difference between the Constitutional right to reclaim a fugitive, and the Constitutional right to hold a slave, in a Territory, provided this Dred Scott decision is correct. I defy any man to make an argument that will justify unfriendly legislation to deprive a slaveholder of his right to hold his slave in a Territory, that will not equally, in all its length, breadth and thickness, furnish an argument for nullifying the Fugitive Slave law. Why, there is not such an Abolitionist in the nation as Douglas, after all. [Loud and enthusiastic applause.]

Mr. Douglas' Reply

Mr. Lincoln has concluded his remarks by saying that there is not such an Abolitionist as I am in all America. [Laughter.] If he could make the Abolitionists of Illinois believe that, he would not have much show for the Senate. [Great laughter and applause.] Let him make the Abolitionists believe the truth of that statement and his political back is broken. [Renewed laughter.]

His first criticism upon me is the expression of his hope that the war of the Administration will be prosecuted against me and the Democratic party of this State with vigor. He wants that war prosecuted with vigor; I have no doubt of it. His hopes of success, and the hopes of his party depend solely upon it. They have no chance of destroying the Democracy of this State except by the aid of federal patronage. ["That's a fact," "good," and cheers.] He has all the federal office-holders here as his allies, ["That's so,"] running separate tickets against the Democracy to divide the party, although the leaders all intend to vote directly the Abolition ticket, and only leave the greenhorns to vote this separate ticket who refuse to go into the Abolition camp. [Laughter and cheers.] There is something really refreshing in the thought that Mr. Lincoln is in favor of prosecuting one war vigorously. [Roars of laughter.] It is the first war I ever knew him to be in favor of prosecuting. [Renewed laughter.] It is the first war that I ever knew him to believe to be just or constitutional. [Laughter and cheers.] When the Mexican war [was] being waged, and the American army was surrounded by the enemy in Mexico, he thought that war was unconstitutional, unnecessary, and unjust. ["That's so," "you've got him," "he voted against it," &c.] He thought it was not commenced on the right *spot*. [Laughter.]

When I made an incidental allusion of that kind in the joint discussion over at Charleston some weeks ago, Lincoln, in replying, said that I, Douglas, had charged him with voting against supplies for the Mexican war, and then he reared up, full length, and swore that he never voted against the supplies—that it was a slander-and caught hold of Ficklin, who sat on the stand, and said, "Here, Ficklin, tell the people that it is a lie." [Laughter and cheers.] Well, Ficklin, who had served in Congress with him, stood up and told them all that he recollected about it. It was that when George Ashmun, of Massachusetts, brought forward a resolution declaring the war unconstitutional, unnecessary, and unjust, that Lincoln had voted for it. "Yes," said Lincoln, "I did." Thus he confessed that he voted that the war was wrong, that our country was in the wrong, and consequently that the Mexicans were in the right; but charged that I had slandered him by saying that he voted against the supplies. I never charged him with voting against the supplies in my life, because I knew that he was not in Congress when they were voted. [Tremendous shouts of laughter.] The war was commenced on the 13th day of May, 1846, and on that day we appropriated in Congress ten millions of dollars and fifty thousand men to prosecute it. During the same session we voted more men and more money, and at the next session we voted more men and more money, so that by the time Mr. Lincoln entered Congress we had enough men and enough money to carry on the war, and had no occasion to vote any more. [Laughter and cheers.] When he got into the House, being opposed to the war, and not being able to stop the supplies, because they had all gone forward, all he could do was to follow the lead of Corwin, and prove that the war was not begun on the right spot, and that it was unconstitutional, unnecessary, and wrong. Remember, too, that this he did after the war had been begun. It is one thing to be opposed to the declaration of a war, another and very different thing to take sides with the enemy against your own country after the war has been commenced. ["Good," and cheers.] Our army was in Mexico at the time, many battles had been fought; our citizens, who were defending the honor of their country's flag, were surrounded by the daggers, the guns and the poison of the enemy. Then it was that Corwin made his speech in which he declared that the American soldiers ought to be welcomed by the Mexicans with bloody hands and hospitable graves; then it was that Ashmun and Lincoln voted in the House of Representatives that the war was unconstitutional and unjust; and Ashmun's resolution, Corwin's speech, and Lincoln's vote, were sent to Mexico and read at the head of the Mexican army, to prove to them that there was a Mexican party in the Congress of the United States who were doing all in their power to aid them. ["That's the truth," "Lincoln's a traitor," etc.] That a man who takes sides with the common enemy against his own country in time of war should rejoice in a war being made on me now, is very natural. [Immense applause.] And in my opinion, no other kind of a man would rejoice in it. ["That's true," "hurrah for Douglas." and cheers.]

Mr. Lincoln has told you a great deal today about his being an old line Clay Whig. ["He never was."] Bear in mind that there are a great many old Clay Whigs down in this region. It is more agreeable, therefore, for him to talk about the old Clay Whig party than it is for him to talk Abolitionism. We did not hear much about the old Clay Whig party up in the Abolition districts. How much of an old line Henry Clay Whig was he? Have you read General Singleton's speech at Jacksonville? ["Yes, yes," and cheers.] You know that Gen. Singleton was, for twenty-five years, the confidential friend of Henry Clay in Illinois, and he testified that in 1847, when the Constitutional Convention of this State was in session, the Whig members were invited to a Whig caucus at the house of Mr. Lincoln's brother-in-law, where Mr. Lincoln proposed to throw Henry Clay overboard and take up Gen. Taylor in his place, giving, as his reason, that if the Whigs did not take up Gen. Taylor the Democrats would. [Cheers and laughter.] Singleton testifies that Lincoln, in that speech, urged, as another reason for throwing Henry Clay overboard, that the Whigs had fought long enough for principle and ought to begin to fight for success. Singleton also testifies that Lincoln's speech did have the effect of cutting Clay's throat, and that he (Singleton) and others withdrew from the caucus in indignation. He further states that when they got to Philadelphia to attend the National Convention of the Whig party, that Lincoln was there, the bitter and deadly enemy of Clay, and that he tried to keep him (Singleton) out of the Convention because he insisted on voting for Clay, and Lincoln was determined to have Taylor. [Laughter and applause.] Singleton says that Lincoln rejoiced with very great joy when he found the mangled remains of the murdered Whig statesman lying cold before him. Now, Mr. Lincoln tells you that he is an old line Clay Whig! [Laughter and cheers.] Gen. Singleton testifies to the facts I have narrated, in a public speech which has been printed and circulated broadcast over the State for weeks, yet not a lisp have we heard from Mr. Lincoln on the subject, except that he is an old Clay Whig.

What part of Henry Clay's policy did Lincoln ever advocate? He was in Congress in 1848-9, when the Wilmot proviso warfare disturbed the peace and harmony of the country, until it shook the foundation of the Republic from its center to its circumference. It was that agitation that brought Clay forth from his retirement at Ashland again to occupy his seat in the Senate of the United States, to see if he could not, by his great wisdom and experience, and the renown of his name, do something to restore peace and quiet to a disturbed country. Who got up that sectional strife that Clay had to be called upon to quell? I have heard Lincoln boast that he voted forty-two times for the Wilmot proviso, and that he would have voted as many times more if he could. [Laughter.] Lincoln is the man, in connection with Seward, Chase, Giddings, and other Abolitionists, who got up that strife that I helped Clay to put down. [Tremendous applause.] Henry Clay came back to the Senate in 1849, and saw that he must do something to restore peace to the country. The Union Whigs and the Union Democrats welcomed him the moment he arrived, as the man for the occasion. We believed that he, of all men on earth, had been preserved by Divine Providence to guide us out of our difficulties, and we Democrats rallied under Clay then, as you Whigs in nullification time rallied under the banner of old Jackson, forgetting party when the country was in danger, in order that we might have a country first, and parties afterwards. ["Three cheers for Douglas."]

And this reminds me that Mr. Lincoln told you that the slavery question was the only thing that ever disturbed the peace and harmony of the Union. Did not nullification once raise its head and disturb the peace of this Union in 1832? Was that the slavery question, Mr. Lincoln? Did not disunion raise its monster head during the last war with Great Britain? Was that the slavery question, Mr. Lincoln? The peace of this country has been disturbed three times, once during the war with Great Britain, once on the tariff question, and once on the slavery question. ["Three cheers for Douglas."] His argument, therefore, that slavery is the only question that has ever created dissension in the Union falls to the ground. It is true that agitators are enabled now to use this slavery question for the purpose of sectional strife. ["That's so."] He admits that in regard to all things else, the principle that I advocate, making each State and Territory free to decide for itself, ought to prevail. He instances the cranberry laws, and the oyster laws, and he might have gone through the whole list with the same effect. I say that all these laws are local and domestic, and that local and domestic concerns should be left to each State and each Territory to manage for itself. If agitators would acquiesce in that principle, there never would be any danger to the peace and harmony of the Union. ["That's so," and cheers.]

Mr. Lincoln tries to avoid the main issue by attacking the truth of my proposition, that our fathers made this Government divided into free and slave States, recognizing the right of each to decide all its local questions for itself. Did they not thus make it? It is true that they did not establish slavery in any of the States, or abolish it in any of them; but finding thirteen States, twelve of which were slave and one free, they agreed to form a government uniting them together, as they stood divided into free and slave States, and to guaranty forever to each State the right to do as it pleased on the slavery question. [Cheers.] Having thus made the government, and conferred this right upon each State forever, I assert that this Government can exist as they made it, divided into free and slave States, if any one State chooses to retain slavery. [Cheers.] He says that he looks forward to a time when slavery shall be abolished every where. I look forward to a time when each State shall be allowed to do as it pleases. If it chooses to keep slavery forever, it is not my business, but its own; if it chooses to abolish slavery, it is its own business—not mine. I care more for the great principle of self-government, the right of the people to rule, than I do for all the negroes in Christendom. [Cheers.] I would not endanger the perpetuity of this Union, I would not blot out the great inalienable rights of the white men for all the negroes that ever existed. [Renewed applause.] Hence, I say, let us maintain this Government on the principles that our fathers made it, recognizing the right of each State to keep slavery as long as its people determine, or to abolish it when they please. [Cheers.] But Mr. Lincoln says that when our fathers made this Government they did not look forward to the state of things now existing, and therefore he thinks the doctrine was wrong; and he quotes Brooks, of South Carolina, to prove that our fathers then thought that probably slavery would be abolished by each State acting for itself before this time. Suppose they did; suppose they did not foresee what has occurred—does that change the principles of our Government? They did not probably foresee the telegraph that transmits intelligence by lightning, nor did they foresee the railroads that now form the bonds of union between the different States, or the thousand mechanical inventions that have elevated mankind. But do these things change the principles of the Government? Our fathers, I say, made this Government on the principle of the right of each State to do as it pleases in its own domestic affairs, subject to the Constitution, and allowed the people of each to apply to every new change of circumstances such remedy as they may see fit to improve their condition. This right they have for all time to come. [Cheers.]

Mr. Lincoln went on to tell you that he does not at all desire to interfere with slavery in the States where it exists, nor does his party. I expected him to say that down here. [Laughter.] Let me ask him then how he expects to put slavery in the course of ultimate extinction every where, if he does not intend to interfere with it in the States where it exists? He says that he will prohibit it in all Territories, and the inference is, then, that unless they make free States out of them he will keep them out of the Union; for, mark you, he did not say whether or not he would vote to admit Kansas with slavery or not, as her people might apply (he forgot that as usual, etc.); he did not say whether or not he was in favor of bringing the Territories now in existence into the Union on the principle of Clay's Compromise measures on the slavery question. I told you that he would not. His idea is that he will prohibit slavery in all the Territories and thus force them all to become free States, surrounding the slave States with a cordon of free States and hemming them in, keeping the slaves confined to their present limits whilst they go on multiplying until the soil on which they live will no longer feed them, and he will thus be able to put slavery in a course of ultimate extinction by starvation. [Cheers.] He will extinguish slavery in the Southern States as the French general exterminated the Algerines when he smoked them out. He is going to extinguish slavery by surrounding the slave States, hemming in the slaves and starving them out of existence, as you smoke a fox out of his hole. He intends to do that in the name of humanity and Christianity, in order that we may get rid of the terrible crime and sin entailed upon our fathers of holding slaves. [Laughter and cheers.] Mr. Lincoln makes out that line of policy, and appeals to the moral sense of justice and to the Christian feeling of the community to sustain him. He says that any man who holds to the contrary doctrine is in the position of the king who claimed to govern by Divine right. Let us examine for a moment and see what principle it was that overthrew the Divine right of George the Third to govern us. Did not these colonies rebel because the British parliament had no right to pass laws concerning our property and domestic and private institutions without our consent? We demanded that the British Government should not pass such laws unless they gave us representation in the body passing them—and this the British government insisting on doing—we went to war, on the principle that the Home Government should not control and govern distant colonies without giving them a representation. Now, Mr. Lincoln proposes to govern the Territories without giving them a representation, and calls on Congress to pass laws controlling their property and domestic concerns without their consent and against their will. Thus, he asserts for his party the identical principle asserted by George III. and the Tories of the Revolution. [Cheers.]

I ask you to look into these things, and then tell me whether the Democracy or the Abolitionists are right. I hold that the people of a Territory, like those of a State (I use the language of Mr. Buchanan in his letter of acceptance,) have the right to decide for themselves whether slavery shall or shall not exist within their limits. ["That's the idea," "Hurrah for Douglas."] The point upon which Chief Justice Taney expresses his opinion is simply this, that slaves being property, stand on an equal footing with other property, and consequently that the owner has the same right to carry that property into a Territory that he has any other, subject to the same conditions. Suppose that one of your merchants was to take fifty or one hundred thousand dollars' worth of liquors to Kansas. He has a right to go there under that decision, but when he gets there he finds the Maine liquor law in force, and what can he do with his property after he gets it there? He cannot sell it, he cannot use it, it is subject to the local law, and that law is against him, and the best thing he can do with it is to bring it back into Missouri or Illinois and sell it. If you take negroes to Kansas, as Col. Jeff. Davis said in his

Bangor speech, from which I have quoted today, you must take them there subject to the local law. If the people want the institution of slavery they will protect and encourage it; but if they do not want it they will withhold that protection, and the absence of local legislation protecting slavery excludes it as completely as a positive prohibition. ["That's so," and cheers.] You slaveholders of Missouri might as well understand what you know practically, that you cannot carry slavery where the people do not want it. ["That's so."] All you have a right to ask is that the people shall do as they please; if they want slavery let them have it; if they do not want it, allow them to refuse to encourage it.

My friends, if, as I have said before, we will only live up to this great fundamental principle, there will be peace between the North and the South. Mr. Lincoln admits that under the Constitution on all domestic questions, except slavery, we ought not to interfere with the people of each State. What right have we to interfere with slavery any more than we have to interfere with any other question? He says that this slavery question is now the bone of contention. Why? Simply because agitators have combined in all the free States to make war upon it. Suppose the agitators in the States should combine in one-half of the Union to make war upon the railroad system of the other half? They would thus be driven to the same sectional strife. Suppose one section makes war upon any other peculiar institution of the opposite section, and the same strife is produced. The only remedy and safety is that we shall stand by the Constitution as our fathers made it, obey the laws as they are passed, while they stand the proper test and sustain the decisions of the Supreme Court and the constituted authorities.

COOPER INSTITUTE SPEECH

Delivered at Cooper Institute, New York

February 27, 1860

MR. PRESIDENT AND FELLOW-CITIZENS OF NEW YORK: The facts with which I shall deal this evening are mainly old and familiar; nor is there anything new in the general use I shall make of them. If there shall be any novelty, it will be in the mode of presenting the facts, and the inferences and observations following that presentation. In his speech last autumn at Columbus, Ohio, as reported in the New York Times, Senator Douglas said: "Our fathers, when they framed the government under which we live, understood this question just as well, and even better, than we do now."

I fully indorse this, and I adopt it as a text for this discourse. I so adopt it because it furnishes a precise and an agreed starting-point for a discussion between Republicans and that wing of the Democracy headed by Senator Douglas. It simply leaves the inquiry: What was the understanding those fathers had of the question mentioned?

What is the frame of government under which we live? The answer must be, "The Constitution of the United States." That Constitution consists of the original, framed in 1787, and under which the present government first went into operation, and twelve subsequently framed amendments, the first ten of which were framed in 1789.

Who were our fathers that framed the Constitution? I suppose the "thirty-nine" who signed the original instrument may be fairly called our fathers who framed that part of the present government. It is almost exactly true to say they framed it, and it is altogether true to say they fairly represented the opinion and sentiment of the whole nation at that time. Their names, being familiar to nearly all, and accessible to quite all, need not now be repeated.

I take these "thirty-nine," for the present, as being "our fathers who framed the government under which we live." What is the question which, according to the text, those fathers understood "just as well, and even better, than we do now"?

It is this: Does the proper division of local from Federal authority, or anything in the Constitution, forbid our Federal Government to control as to slavery in our Federal Territories?

Upon this, Senator Douglas holds the affirmative, and Republicans the negative. This affirmation and denial form an issue; and this issue—this question—is precisely what the text declares our fathers understood "better than we." Let us now inquire whether the "thirty-nine," or any of them, ever acted upon this question; and if they did, how they acted upon it—how they expressed that better understanding. In 1784, three years before the Constitution, the United States then owning the Northwestern Territory and no other, the Congress of the Confederation had before them the question of prohibiting slavery in that Territory; and four of the "thirty-nine" who afterward framed the Constitution were in that Congress, and voted on that question. Of these, Roger Sherman, Thomas Mifflin, and Hugh Williamson voted for the prohibition, thus showing that, in their understanding, no line dividing local from Federal authority, nor anything else, properly forbade the Federal Government to control as to slavery in Federal territory. The other of the four, James McHenry, voted against the prohibition, showing that for some cause he thought it improper to vote for it.

In 1787, still before the Constitution, but while the convention was in session framing it, and while the Northwestern Territory still was the only Territory owned by the United States, the same question of prohibiting slavery in the Territory again came before the Congress of the Confederation; and two more of the "thirty-nine" who afterward signed the Constitution were in that Congress, and voted on the question. They were William Blount and William Few; and they both voted for the prohibition—thus showing that in their understanding no line dividing local from Federal authority, nor anything else, properly forbade the Federal Government to control as to slavery in Federal territory. This time the prohibition became a law, being part of what is now well known as the ordinance of '87.

The question of Federal control of slavery in the Territories seems not to have been directly before the convention which framed the original Constitution; and hence it is not recorded that the "thirty-nine" or any of them, while engaged on that instrument, expressed any opinion on that precise question.

In 1789, by the first Congress which sat under the Constitution, an act was passed to enforce the ordinance of '87, including the prohibition of slavery in the Northwestern Territory. The bill for this act was reported by one of the "thirty-nine"—Thomas Fitzsimmons, then a member of the House of Representatives from Pennsylvania. It went through all its stages without a word of opposition, and finally passed both branches without ayes and nays, which is equivalent to a unanimous passage. In this Congress there were sixteen of the thirty-nine fathers who framed the original Constitution. They were John Langdon, Nicholas Gilman, William S. Johnson, Roger Sherman, Robert Morris, Thomas Fitzsimmons, William Few, Abraham Baldwin, Rufus King, William Paterson, George Clymer, Richard Bassett, George Read, Pierce Butler, Daniel Carroll, and James Madison.

This shows that, in their understanding, no line dividing local from Federal authority, nor anything in the Constitution, properly forbade Congress to prohibit slavery in the Federal territory; else both their fidelity to correct principle, and their oath to support the Constitution, would have constrained them to oppose the prohibition.

Again, George Washington, another of the "thirty-nine," was then President of the United States, and as such approved and signed the bill, thus completing its validity as a law, and thus showing that, in his understanding, no line dividing local from Federal authority, nor anything in the Constitution, forbade the Federal Government to control as to slavery in Federal territory.

No great while after the adoption of the original Constitution, North Carolina ceded to the Federal Government, the country now constituting the State of Tennessee; and a few years later Georgia ceded that which now constitutes the States of Mississippi and Alabama. In both deeds of cession it was made a condition by the ceding States that the Federal Government should not prohibit slavery in the ceded country. Besides this, slavery was then actually in the ceded country. Under these circumstances, Congress, on taking charge of these countries, did not absolutely prohibit slavery within them. But they did interfere with it—take control of it—even there, to a certain extent. In 1798, Congress organized the Territory of Mississippi. In the act of organization they prohibited the bringing of slaves into the Territory from any place without the United States, by fine, and giving freedom to slaves so brought. This act passed both branches of Congress without yeas and nays. In that Congress were three of the "thirty-nine" who framed the original Constitution. They were John Langdon, George Read, and Abraham Baldwin. They all probably voted for it. Certainly they would have placed their opposition to it upon record if, in their understanding, any line dividing local from Federal authority, or anything in the Constitution, properly forbade the Federal Government to control as to slavery in Federal territory.

In 1803 the Federal Government purchased the Louisiana country. Our former territorial acquisitions came from certain of our own States; but this Louisiana country was acquired from a foreign nation. In 1804 Congress gave a territorial organization to that part of it which now constitutes the State of Louisiana. New Orleans, lying within that part, was an old and comparatively large city. There were other considerable towns and settlements, and slavery was extensively and thoroughly intermingled with the people. Congress did not, in the Territorial Act, prohibit slavery; but they did interfere with it—take control of it—in a more marked and extensive way than they did in the case of Mississippi. The substance of the provision therein made in relation to slaves was:

1st. That no slave should be imported into the Territory from foreign parts.

2d. That no slave should be carried into it who had been imported into the United States since the first day of May, 1798.

3d. That no slave should be carried into it, except by the owner, and for his own use as a settler; the penalty in all the cases being a fine upon the violator of the law, and freedom to the slave.

This act also was passed without ayes or nays. In the Congress which passed it there were two of the "thirty-nine." They were Abraham Baldwin and Jonathan Dayton. As stated in the case of Mississippi, it is probable they both voted for it. They would not have allowed it to pass without recording their opposition to it if, in their understanding, it violated either the line properly dividing local from Federal authority, or any provision of the Constitution.

In 1819–20 came and passed the Missouri question. Many votes were taken, by yeas and nays, in both branches of Congress, upon the various phases of the general question. Two of the "thirty-nine"—Rufus King and Charles Pinckney—were members of that Congress. Mr. King steadily voted for slavery prohibition and against all compromises, while Mr. Pinckney as steadily voted against slavery prohibition and against all compromises. By this, Mr. King showed that, in his understanding, no line dividing local from Federal authority, nor anything in the Constitution, was violated by Congress prohibiting slavery in Federal territory; while Mr. Pinckney, by his votes, showed that, in his understanding, there was some sufficient reason for opposing such prohibition in that case.

The cases I have mentioned are the only acts of the "thirty-nine," or of any of them, upon the direct issue, which I have been able to discover.

To enumerate the persons who thus acted as being four in 1784, two in 1787, seventeen in 1789, three in 1798, two in 1804, and two in 1819–20, there would be thirty of them. But this would be counting John Langdon, Roger Sherman, William Few, Rufus King, and George Read each twice, and Abraham Baldwin three times. The true number of those of the "thirty-nine" whom I have shown to have acted upon the question which, by the text, they understood better than we, is twenty-three, leaving sixteen not shown to have acted upon it in any way.

Here, then, we have twenty-three out of our thirty-nine fathers "who framed the government under which we live," who have, upon their official responsibility and their corporal oaths, acted upon the very question which the text affirms they "understood just as well, and even better, than we do now"; and twenty-one of them—a clear majority of the whole "thirty-nine"—so acting upon it as to make them guilty of gross political impropriety and willful perjury if, in their understanding, any proper division between local and Federal authority, or anything in the Constitution they had made themselves, and sworn to support, forbade the Federal Government to control as to slavery in the Federal Territories. Thus the twenty-one acted; and, as actions speak louder than words, so actions under such responsibility speak still louder.

Two of the twenty-three voted against congressional prohibition of slavery in the Federal Territories, in the instances in which they acted upon the question. But for what reasons they so voted is not known. They may have done so because they thought a proper division of local from Federal authority, or some provision or principle of the Constitution, stood in the way; or they may, without any such question, have voted against the prohibition on what appeared to them to be sufficient grounds of expediency. No one who has sworn to support the Constitution can conscientiously vote for what he understands to be an unconstitutional measure, however expedient he may think it; but one may and ought to vote against a measure which he deems constitutional if, at the same time, he deems it inexpedient. It, therefore, would be unsafe to set down even the two who voted against the prohibition as having done so because, in their understanding, any proper division of local from Federal authority, or anything in the Constitution, forbade the Federal Government to control as to slavery in Federal territory.

The remaining sixteen of the "thirty-nine," so far as I have discovered, have left no record of their understanding upon the direct question of Federal control of slavery in the Federal Territories. But there is much reason to believe that their understanding upon that question would not have appeared different from that of their twenty-three compeers, had it been manifested at all.

For the purpose of adhering rigidly to the text, I have purposely omitted whatever understanding may have been manifested by any person, however distinguished, other than the thirty-nine fathers, who framed the original Constitution; and, for the same reason, I have also omitted whatever understanding may have been manifested by any of the "thirty-nine" even on any other phase of the general question of slavery. If we should look into their acts and declarations on those other phases, as the foreign slave-trade, and the morality and policy of slavery generally, it would appear to us that on the direct question of Federal control of slavery in Federal Territories, the sixteen, if they had acted at all, would probably have acted just as the twenty-three did. Among that sixteen were several of the most noted anti-slavery men of those times—as Dr. Franklin, Alexander Hamilton, and Gouverneur Morris—while there was not one now known to have been otherwise, unless it may be John Rutledge, of South Carolina.

The sum of the whole is, that of our thirty-nine fathers who framed the original Constitution, twenty-one—a clear majority of the whole—certainly understood that no proper division of local from Federal authority, nor any part of the Constitution, forbade the Federal Government to control slavery in the Federal Territories; while all the rest had probably the same understanding. Such, unquestionably, was the understanding of our fathers who framed the original Constitution; and the text affirms that they understood the question "better than we."

But, so far, I have been considering the understanding of the question manifested by the framers of the original Constitution. In and by the original instrument, a mode was provided for amending it; and, as I have already stated, the present frame of "the government under which we live" consists of that original, and twelve amendatory articles framed and adopted since. Those who now insist that Federal control of slavery in Federal Territories violates the Constitution, point us to the provisions which they suppose it thus violates; and, as I understand, they all fix upon provisions in these amendatory articles, and not in the original instrument. The Supreme Court, in the Dred Scott case, plant themselves upon the fifth amendment, which provides that no person shall be deprived of "life, liberty, or property without due process of law"; while Senator Douglas and his peculiar adherents plant themselves upon the tenth amendment, providing that "the powers not delegated to the United States by the Constitution are reserved to the States respectively, or to the people."

Now, it so happens that these amendments were framed by the first Congress which sat under the Constitution—the identical Congress which passed the act, already mentioned, enforcing the prohibition of slavery in the Northwestern Territory. Not only was it the same Congress, but they were the identical, same individual men who, at the same session, and at the same time within the session, had under consideration, and in progress toward maturity, these constitutional amendments, and this act prohibiting slavery in all the territory the nation then owned. The constitutional amendments were introduced before, and passed after, the act enforcing the ordinance of '87; so that, during the whole pendency of the act to enforce the ordinance, the constitutional amendments were also pending.

The seventy-six members of that Congress, including sixteen of the framers of the original Constitution, as before stated, were pre-eminently our fathers who framed that part of "the government under which we live" which is now claimed as forbidding the Federal Government to control slavery in the Federal Territories.

Is it not a little presumptuous in anyone at this day to affirm that the two things which that Congress deliberately framed and carried to maturity at the same time, are absolutely inconsistent with each other? And does not such affirmation become impudently absurd when coupled with the other affirmation from the same mouth, that those who did the two things alleged to be inconsistent, understood whether they really were inconsistent better than we—better than he who affirms that they are inconsistent?

It is surely safe to assume that the thirty-nine framers of the original Constitution, and the seventy-six members of the Congress which framed the amendments thereto, taken together, do certainly include those who may be fairly called "our fathers who framed the government under which we live." And so assuming, I defy any man to show that any one of them ever, in his whole life, declared that, in his understanding, any proper division of local from Federal authority, or any part of the Constitution, forbade the Federal Government to control as to slavery in the Federal Territories. I go a step further. I defy anyone to show that any living man in the whole world ever did, prior to the beginning of the present century (and I might almost say prior to the beginning of the last half of the present century), declare that, in his understanding, any proper division of local from Federal authority, or any part of the Constitution, forbade the Federal Government to control as to slavery in the Federal Territories. To those who now so declare I give not only "our fathers who framed the government under which we live," but with them all other living men within the century in which it was framed, among whom to search, and they shall not be able to find the evidence of a single man agreeing with them.

Now, and here, let me guard a little against being misunderstood. I do not mean to say we are bound to follow implicitly in whatever our fathers did. To do so would be to discard all the lights of current experience—to reject all progress, all improvement. What I do say is that, if we would supplant the opinions and policy of our fathers in any case, we should do so upon evidence so conclusive, and argument so clear, that even their great authority, fairly considered and weighed, cannot stand; and most surely not in a case whereof we ourselves declare they understood the question better than we.

If any man at this day sincerely believes that a proper division of local from Federal authority, or any part of the Constitution, forbids the Federal Government to control as to slavery in the Federal Territories, he is right to say so, and to enforce his position by all truthful evidence and fair argument which he can. But he has no right to mislead others, who have less access to history, and less leisure to study it, into the false belief that "our fathers who framed the government under which we live" were of the same opinion—thus substituting falsehood and deception for truthful evidence and fair argument. If any man at this day sincerely believes "our fathers who framed the government under which we live" used and applied principles, in other cases, which ought to have led them to understand that a proper division of local from Federal authority, or some part of the Constitution, forbids the Federal Government to control as to slavery in the Federal Territories, he is right to say so. But he should, at the same time, brave the responsibility of declaring that, in his opinion, he understands their principles better than they did themselves; and especially should he not shirk that responsibility by asserting that they "understood the question just as well, and even better, than we do now."

But enough! Let all who believe that "our fathers who framed the government under which we live understood this question just as well, and even better, than we do now," speak as they spoke, and act as they acted upon it. This is all Republicans ask—all Republicans desire—in relation to slavery. As those fathers marked it, so let it be again marked, as an evil not to be extended, but to be tolerated and protected only because of and so far as its actual presence among us makes that toleration and protection a necessity. Let all the guarantees those fathers gave it be not grudgingly, but fully and fairly, maintained. For this Republicans contend, and with this, so far as I know or believe, they will be content.

And now, if they would listen—as I suppose they will not—I would address a few words to the Southern people.

I would say to them: You consider yourselves a reasonable and a just people; and I consider that in the general qualities of reason and justice you are not inferior to any other people. Still, when you speak of us Republicans, you do so only to denounce us as reptiles, or, at the best, as no better than outlaws. You will grant a hearing to pirates or murderers, but nothing like it to "Black Republicans." In all your contentions with one another, each of you deems an unconditional condemnation of "Black Republicanism" as the first thing to be attended to. Indeed, such condemnation of us seems to be an indispensable prerequisite—license, so to speak—among you to be admitted or permitted to speak at all. Now can you or not be prevailed upon to pause and to consider whether this is quite just to us, or even to yourselves? Bring forward your charges and specifications, and then be patient long enough to hear us deny or justify.

You say we are sectional. We deny it. That makes an issue; and the burden of proof is upon you. You produce your proof; and what is it? Why, that our party has no existence in your section—gets no votes in your section. The fact is substantially true; but does it prove the issue? If it does, then in case we should, without change of principle, begin to get votes in your section, we should thereby cease to be sectional. You cannot escape this conclusion; and yet are you willing to abide by it? If you are, you will probably soon find that we have ceased to be sectional, for we shall get votes in your section this very year. You will then begin to discover, as the truth plainly is, that your proof does not touch the issue. The fact that we get no votes in your section is a fact of your making, and not of ours. And if there be fault in that fact, that fault is primarily yours, and remains so until you show that we repel you by some wrong principle or practice. If we do repel you by any wrong principle or practice, the fault is ours; but this brings you to where you ought to have started—to a discussion of the right or wrong of our principle. If our principle, put in practice, would wrong your section for the benefit of ours, or for any other object, then our principle, and we with it, are sectional, and are justly opposed and denounced as such. Meet us, then, on the question of whether our principle, put in practice, would wrong your section; and so meet us as if it were possible that something may be said on our side. Do you accept the challenge? No! Then you really believe that the principle which "our fathers who framed the government under which we live" thought so clearly right as to adopt it, and indorse it again and again, upon their official oaths, is in fact so clearly wrong as to demand your condemnation without a moment's consideration.

Some of you delight to flaunt in our faces the warning against sectional parties given by Washington in his Farewell Address. Less than eight years before Washington gave that warning, he had, as President of the United States, approved and signed an act of Congress enforcing the prohibition of slavery in the Northwestern Territory, which act embodied the policy of the government upon that subject up to and at the very moment he penned that warning; and about one year after he penned it, he wrote Lafayette that he considered that prohibition a wise measure, expressing in the same connection his hope that we should at some time have a confederacy of free States.

Bearing this in mind, and seeing that sectionalism has since arisen upon this same subject, is that warning a weapon in your hands against us, or in our hands against you? Could Washington himself speak, would he cast the blame of that sectionalism upon us, who sustain his policy, or upon you, who repudiate it? We respect that warning of Washington, and we commend it to you, together with his example pointing to the right application of it.

But you say you are conservative—eminently conservative—while we are revolutionary, destructive, or something of the sort. What is conservatism? Is it not adherence to the old and tried, against the new and untried? We stick to, contend for, the identical old policy on the point in controversy which was adopted by "our fathers who framed the government under which we live"; while you with one accord reject, and scout, and spit upon that old policy, and insist upon substituting something new. True, you disagree among yourselves as to what that substitute shall be. You are divided on new propositions and plans, but you are unanimous in rejecting and denouncing the old policy of the fathers. Some of you are for reviving the foreign slave-trade; some for a congressional slave code for the Territories; some for Congress forbidding the Territories to prohibit slavery within their limits; some for maintaining slavery in the Territories through the judiciary; some for the "gur-reat pur-rinciple" that "if one man would enslave another, no third man should object," fantastically called "popular sovereignty";

but never a man among you is in favor of Federal prohibition of slavery in Federal Territories, according to the practice of "our fathers who framed the government under which we live." Not one of all your various plans can show a precedent or an advocate in the century within which our government originated. Consider, then, whether your claim of conservatism for yourselves, and your charge of destructiveness against us, are based on the most clear and stable foundation.

Again, you say we have made the slavery question more prominent than it formerly was. We deny it. We admit that it is more prominent, but we deny that we made it so. It was not we, but you, who discarded the old policy of the fathers. We resisted, and still resist, your innovation; and thence comes the greater prominence of the question. Would you have that question reduced to its former proportions? Go back to that old policy. What has been will be again, under the same conditions. If you would have the peace of the old times, readopt the precepts and policy of the old times.

You charge that we stir up insurrections among your slaves. We deny it; and what is your proof? Harper's Ferry! John Brown! John Brown was no Republican; and you have failed to implicate a single Republican in his Harper's Ferry enterprise. If any member of our party is guilty in that matter you know it, or you do not know it. If you do know it, you are inexcusable for not designating the man and proving the fact. If you do not know it, you are inexcusable for asserting it, and especially for persisting in the assertion after you have tried and failed to make the proof. You need not be told that persisting in a charge which one does not know to be true, is simply malicious slander.

Some of you admit that no Republican designedly aided or encouraged the Harper's Ferry affair, but still insist that our doctrines and declarations necessarily lead to such results. We do not believe it. We know we hold no doctrine, and make no declaration, which were not held to and made by "our fathers who framed the government under which we live." You never dealt fairly by us in relation to this affair. When it occurred, some important State elections were near at hand, and you were in evident glee with the belief that, by charging the blame upon us, you could get an advantage of us in those elections. The elections came, and your expectations were not quite fulfilled. Every Republican man knew that, as to himself at least, your charge was a slander, and he was not much inclined by it to cast his vote in your favor. Republican doctrines and declarations are accompanied with a continual protest against any interference whatever with your slaves, or with you about your slaves. Surely this does not encourage them to revolt. True, we do, in common with "our fathers who framed the government under which we live," declare our belief that slavery is wrong; but the slaves do not hear us declare even this. For anything we say or do, the slaves would scarcely know there is a Republican party. I believe they would not, in fact, generally know it but for your misrepresentations of us in their hearing. In your political contests among yourselves, each faction charges the other with sympathy with Black Republicanism; and then, to give point to the charge, defines Black Republicanism to simply be insurrection, blood, and thunder among the slaves.

Slave insurrections are no more common now than they were before the Republican party was organized. What induced the Southampton insurrection, twenty-eight years ago, in which at least three times as many lives were lost as at Harper's Ferry? You can scarcely stretch your very elastic fancy to the conclusion that Southampton was "got up by Black Republicanism." In the present state of things in the United States, I do not think a general, or even a very extensive, slave insurrection is possible. The indispensable concert of action cannot be attained. The slaves have no means of rapid communication; nor can incendiary freemen, black or white, supply it. The explosive materials are everywhere in parcels; but there neither are, nor can be supplied, the indispensable connecting trains.

Much is said by Southern people about the affection of slaves for their masters and mistresses; and a part of it, at least, is true. A plot for an uprising could scarcely be devised and communicated to twenty individuals before some one of them, to save the life of a favorite master or mistress, would divulge it. This is the rule; and the slave revolution in Hayti was not an exception to it, but a case occurring under peculiar circumstances. The gunpowder plot of British history, though not connected with slaves, was more in point. In that case only about twenty were admitted to the secret; and yet one of them, in his anxiety to save a friend, betrayed the plot to that friend, and, by consequence, averted the calamity. Occasional poisonings from the kitchen and open or stealthy assassinations in the field, and local revolts extending to a score or so, will continue to occur as the natural results of slavery; but no general insurrections of slaves, as I think, can happen in this country for a long time. Whoever much fears, or much hopes, for such an event, will be alike disappointed.

In the language of Mr. Jefferson, uttered many years ago, "It is still in our power to direct the process of emancipation and deportation peaceably, and in such slow degrees, as that the evil will wear off insensibly; and their places be, *pari passu*, filled up by free white laborers. If, on the contrary, it is left to force itself on, human nature must shudder at the prospect held up."

Mr. Jefferson did not mean to say, nor do I, that the power of emancipation is in the Federal Government. He spoke of Virginia; and, as to the power of emancipation, I speak of the slaveholding States only. The Federal Government, however, as we insist, has the power of restraining the extension of the institution—the power to insure that a slave insurrection shall never occur on any American soil which is now free from slavery.

John Brown's effort was peculiar. It was not a slave insurrection. It was an attempt by white men to get up a revolt among slaves, in which the slaves refused to participate. In fact, it was so absurd that the slaves, with all their ignorance, saw plainly enough it could not succeed. That affair, in its philosophy, corresponds with the many attempts, related in history, at the assassination of kings and emperors. An enthusiast broods over the oppression of a people till he fancies himself commissioned by Heaven to liberate them. He ventures the attempt, which ends in little else than his own execution. Orsini's attempt on Louis Napoleon and John Brown's attempt at Harper's Ferry were, in their philosophy, precisely the same. The eagerness to cast blame on old England in the one case and on New England in the other, does not disprove the sameness of the two things.

And how much would it avail you, if you could, by the use of John Brown, Helper's Book, and the like, break up the Republican organization? Human action can be modified to some extent, but human nature cannot be changed. There is a judgment and a feeling against slavery in this nation which cast at least a million and a half of votes. You cannot destroy that judgment and feeling—that sentiment—by breaking up the political organization which rallies around it. You can scarcely scatter and disperse an army which has been formed into order in the face of your heaviest fire; but if you could, how much would you gain by forcing the sentiment which created it out of the peaceful channel of the ballot-box into some other channel? What would that other channel probably be? Would the number of John Browns be lessened or enlarged by the operation?

But you will break up the Union rather than submit to a denial of your constitutional rights.

That has a somewhat reckless sound; but it would be palliated, if not fully justified, were we proposing, by the mere force of numbers, to deprive you of some right plainly written down in the Constitution. But we are proposing no such thing.

When you make these declarations, you have a specific and well-understood allusion to an assumed constitutional right of yours to take slaves into the Federal Territories, and to hold them there as property. But no such right is specifically written in the Constitution. That instrument is literally silent about any such right. We, on the contrary, deny that such a right has any existence in the Constitution, even by implication.

Your purpose, then, plainly stated, is that you will destroy the government, unless you be allowed to construe and force the Constitution as you please, on all points in dispute between you and us. You will rule or ruin in all events.

This, plainly stated, is your language. Perhaps you will say the Supreme Court has decided the disputed constitutional question in your favor. Not quite so. But waiving the lawyer's distinction between dictum and decision, the court has decided the question for you in a sort of way. The court has substantially said, it is your constitutional right to take slaves into the Federal Territories, and to hold them there as property. When I say the decision was made in a sort of way, I mean it was made in a divided court, by a bare majority of the judges, and they not quite agreeing with one another in the reasons for making it; that it is so made that its avowed supporters disagree with one another about its meaning, and that it was mainly based upon a mistaken statement of fact—the statement in the opinion that "the right of property in a slave is distinctly and expressly affirmed in the Constitution."

An inspection of the Constitution will show that the right of property in a slave is not "distinctly and expressly affirmed" in it. Bear in mind, the judges do not pledge their judicial opinion that such right is impliedly affirmed in the Constitution; but they pledge their veracity that it is "distinctly and expressly" affirmed there—"distinctly," that is, not mingled with anything else—"expressly," that is, in words meaning just that, without the aid of any inference, and susceptible of no other meaning.

If they had only pledged their judicial opinion that such right is affirmed in the instrument by implication, it would be open to others to show that neither the word "slave" nor "slavery" is to be found in the Constitution, nor the word "property" even, in any connection with language alluding to the things slave, or slavery; and that wherever in that instrument the slave is alluded to, he is called a "person"; and wherever his master's legal right in relation to him is alluded to, it is spoken of as "service or labor which may be due"—as a debt payable in service or labor. Also it would be open to show, by contemporaneous history, that this mode of alluding to slaves and slavery, instead of speaking of them, was employed on purpose to exclude from the Constitution the idea that there could be property in man.

To show all this is easy and certain.

When this obvious mistake of the judges shall be brought to their notice, is it not reasonable to expect that they will withdraw the mistaken statement, and reconsider the conclusion based upon it?

And then it is to be remembered that "our fathers who framed the government under which we live"—the men who made the Constitution—decided this same constitutional question in our favor long ago: decided it without division among themselves when making the decision; without division among themselves about the meaning of it after it was made, and, so far as any evidence is left, without basing it upon any mistaken statement of facts.

Under all these circumstances, do you really feel yourselves justified to break up this government unless such a court decision as yours is shall be at once submitted to as a conclusive and final rule of political action? But you will not abide the election of a Republican president! In that supposed event, you say, you will destroy the Union; and then, you say, the great crime of having destroyed it will be upon us! That is cool. A highwayman holds a pistol to my ear, and mutters through his teeth, "Stand and deliver, or I shall kill you, and then you will be a murderer!"

To be sure, what the robber demanded of me—my money—was my own; and I had a clear right to keep it; but it was no more my own than my vote is my own; and the threat of death to me, to extort my money, and the threat of destruction to the Union, to extort my vote, can scarcely be distinguished in principle.

A few words now to Republicans. It is exceedingly desirable that all parts of this great Confederacy shall be at peace and in harmony one with another. Let us Republicans do our part to have it so. Even though much provoked, let us do nothing through passion and ill-temper. Even though the Southern people will not so much as listen to us, let us calmly consider their demands, and yield to them if, in our deliberate view of our duty, we possibly can. Judging by all they say and do, and by the subject and nature of their controversy with us, let us determine, if we can, what will satisfy them.

Will they be satisfied if the Territories be unconditionally surrendered to them? We know they will not. In all their present complaints against us, the Territories are scarcely mentioned. Invasions and insurrections are the rage now. Will it satisfy them if, in the future, we have nothing to do with invasions and insurrections? We know it will not. We so know, because we know we never had anything to do with invasions and insurrections; and yet this total abstaining does not exempt us from the charge and the denunciation.

The question recurs, What will satisfy them? Simply this: we must not only let them alone, but we must somehow convince them that we do let them alone. This, we know by experience, is no easy task. We have been so trying to convince them from the very beginning of our organization, but with no success. In all our platforms and speeches we have constantly protested our purpose to let them alone; but this has had no tendency to convince them. Alike unavailing to convince them is the fact that they have never detected a man of us in any attempt to disturb them.

These natural and apparently adequate means all failing, what will convince them? This, and this only: cease to call slavery wrong, and join them in calling it right. And this must be done thoroughly—done in acts as well as in words. Silence will not be tolerated—we must place ourselves avowedly with them. Senator Douglas's new sedition law must be enacted and enforced, suppressing all declarations that slavery is wrong, whether made in politics, in presses, in pulpits, or in private. We must arrest and return their fugitive slaves with greedy pleasure. We must pull down our free-State constitutions. The whole atmosphere must be disinfected from all taint of opposition to slavery, before they will cease to believe that all their troubles proceed from us.

I am quite aware they do not state their case precisely in this way. Most of them would probably say to us, "Let us alone; do nothing to us, and say what you please about slavery." But we do let them alone—have never disturbed them—so that, after all, it is what we say which dissatisfies them. They will continue to accuse us of doing, until we cease saying.

I am also aware they have not as yet in terms demanded the overthrow of our free-State constitutions. Yet those constitutions declare the wrong of slavery with more solemn emphasis than do all other sayings against it; and when all these other sayings shall have been silenced, the overthrow of these constitutions will be demanded, and nothing be left to resist the demand. It is nothing to the contrary that they do not demand the whole of this just now. Demanding what they do, and for the reason they do, they can voluntarily stop nowhere short of this consummation. Holding, as they do, that slavery is morally right and socially elevating, they cannot cease to demand a full national recognition of it as a legal right and a social blessing.

Nor can we justifiably withhold this on any ground save our conviction that slavery is wrong. If slavery is right, all words, acts, laws, and constitutions against it are themselves wrong, and should be silenced and swept away. If it is right, we cannot justly object to its nationality—its universality; if it is wrong, they cannot justly insist upon its extension—its enlargement. All they ask we could readily grant, if we thought slavery right; all we ask they could as readily grant, if they thought it wrong. Their thinking it right and our thinking it wrong is the precise fact upon which depends the whole controversy. Thinking it right, as they do, they are not to blame for desiring its full recognition as being right; but thinking it wrong, as we do, can we yield to them? Can we cast our votes with their view, and against our own? In view of our moral, social, and political responsibilities, can we do this?

Wrong as we think slavery is, we can yet afford to let it alone where it is, because that much is due to the necessity arising from its actual presence in the nation; but can we, while our votes will prevent it, allow it to spread into the national Territories, and to overrun us here in these free States? If our sense of duty forbids this, then let us stand by our duty fearlessly and effectively. Let us be diverted by none of those sophistical contrivances wherewith we are so industriously plied and belabored—contrivances such as groping for some middle ground between the right and the wrong: vain as the search for a man who should be neither a living man nor a dead man; such as a policy of "don't care" on a question about which all true men do care; such as Union appeals beseeching true Union men to yield to Disunionists, reversing the divine rule, and calling, not the sinners, but the righteous, to repentance; such as invocations to Washington, imploring men to unsay what Washington said and undo what Washington did.

Neither let us be slandered from our duty by false accusations against us, nor frightened from it by menaces of destruction to the government, nor of dungeons to ourselves. Let us have faith that right makes might, and in that faith let us to the end dare to do our duty as we understand it.

FAREWELL ADDRESS

Springfield, Illinois

February 11, 1861

My friends,

No one, not in my situation, can appreciate my feeling of sadness at this parting. To this place, and the kindness of these people, I owe everything. Here I have lived a quarter of a century, and have passed from a young to an old man. Here my children have been born, and one is buried. I now leave, not knowing when, or whether ever, I may return, with a task before me greater than that which rested upon Washington. Without the assistance of the Divine Being, who ever attended him, I cannot succeed. With that assistance I cannot fail. Trusting in Him, who can go with me, and remain with you, and be everywhere for good, let us confidently hope that all will yet be well. To His care commending you, as I hope in your prayers you will commend me, I bid you an affectionate farewell.

FIRST INAUGURAL ADDRESS

Washington, D.C.

March 4, 1861

Fellow-Citizens of the United States:

In compliance with a custom as old as the Government itself, I appear before you to address you briefly and to take in your presence the oath prescribed by the Constitution of the United States to be taken by the President "before he enters on the execution of this office."

I do not consider it necessary at present for me to discuss those matters of administration about which there is no special anxiety or excitement.

Apprehension seems to exist among the people of the Southern States that by the accession of a Republican Administration their property and their peace and personal security are to be endangered. There has never been any reasonable cause for such apprehension. Indeed, the most ample evidence to the contrary has all the while existed and been open to their inspection. It is found in nearly all the published speeches of him who now addresses you. I do but quote from one of those speeches when I declare that—

I have no purpose, directly or indirectly, to interfere with the institution of slavery in the States where it exists. I believe I have no lawful right to do so, and I have no inclination to do so.

Those who nominated and elected me did so with full knowledge that I had made this and many similar declarations and had never recanted them; and more than this, they placed in the platform for my acceptance, and as a law to themselves and to me, the clear and emphatic resolution which I now read:

Resolved, That the maintenance inviolate of the rights of the States, and especially the right of each State to order and control its own domestic institutions according to its own judgment exclusively, is essential to that balance of power on which the perfection and endurance of our political fabric depend; and we denounce the lawless invasion by armed force of the soil of any State or Territory, no matter what pretext, as among the gravest of crimes.

I now reiterate these sentiments, and in doing so I only press upon the public attention the most conclusive evidence of which the case is susceptible that the property, peace, and security of no section are to be in any wise endangered by the now incoming Administration. I add, too, that all the protection which, consistently with the Constitution and the laws, can be given will be cheerfully given to all the States when lawfully demanded, for whatever cause—as cheerfully to one section as to another.

There is much controversy about the delivering up of fugitives from service or labor. The clause I now read is as plainly written in the Constitution as any other of its provisions:

No person held to service or labor in one State, under the laws thereof, escaping into another, shall in consequence of any law or regulation therein be discharged from such service or labor, but shall be delivered up on claim of the party to whom such service or labor may be due.

It is scarcely questioned that this provision was intended by those who made it for the reclaiming of what we call fugitive slaves; and the intention of the lawgiver is the law. All members of Congress swear their support to the whole Constitution—to this provision as much as to any other. To the proposition, then, that slaves whose cases come within the terms of this clause "shall be delivered up" their oaths are unanimous. Now, if they would make the effort in good temper, could they not with nearly equal unanimity frame and pass a law by means of which to keep good that unanimous oath?

There is some difference of opinion whether this clause should be enforced by national or by State authority, but surely that difference is not a very material one. If the slave is to be surrendered, it can be of but little consequence to him or to others by which authority it is done. And should anyone in any case be content that his oath shall go unkept on a merely unsubstantial controversy as to *how* it shall be kept?

Again: In any law upon this subject ought not all the safeguards of liberty known in civilized and humane jurisprudence to be introduced, so that a free man be not in any case surrendered as a slave? And might it not be well at the same time to provide by law for the enforcement of that clause in the Constitution which guarantees that "the citizens of each State shall be entitled to all privileges and immunities of citizens in the several States"?

I take the official oath today with no mental reservations and with no purpose to construe the Constitution or laws by any hypercritical rules; and while I do not choose now to specify particular acts of Congress as proper to be enforced, I do suggest that it will be much safer for all, both in official and private stations, to conform to and abide by all those acts which stand unrepealed than to violate any of them trusting to find impunity in having them held to be unconstitutional.

It is seventy-two years since the first inauguration of a President under our National Constitution. During that period fifteen different and greatly distinguished citizens have in succession administered the executive branch of the Government. They have conducted it through many perils, and generally with great success. Yet, with all this scope of precedent, I now enter upon the same task for the brief constitutional term of four years under great and peculiar difficulty.

A disruption of the Federal Union, heretofore only menaced, is now formidably attempted.

I hold that in contemplation of universal law and of the Constitution the Union of these States is perpetual. Perpetuity is implied, if not expressed, in the fundamental law of all national governments. It is safe to assert that no government proper ever had a provision in its organic law for its own termination. Continue to execute all the express provisions of our National Constitution, and the Union will endure forever, it being impossible to destroy it except by some action not provided for in the instrument itself.

Again: If the United States be not a government proper, but an association of States in the nature of contract merely, can it, as a contract, be peaceably unmade by less than all the parties who made it? One party to a contract may violate it—break it, so to speak—but does it not require all to lawfully rescind it?

Descending from these general principles, we find the proposition that in legal contemplation the Union is perpetual confirmed by the history of the Union itself. The Union is much older than the Constitution. It was formed, in fact, by the Articles of Association in 1774. It was matured and continued by the Declaration of Independence in 1776. It was further matured, and the faith of all the then thirteen States expressly plighted and engaged that it should be perpetual, by the Articles of Confederation in 1778. And finally, in 1787, one of the declared objects for ordaining and establishing the Constitution was "*to form a more perfect Union.*"

But if destruction of the Union by one or by a part only of the States be lawfully possible, the Union is *less* perfect than before the Constitution, having lost the vital element of perpetuity.

It follows from these views that no State upon its own mere motion can lawfully get out of the Union; that *resolves* and *ordinances* to that effect are legally void, and that acts of violence within any State or States against the authority of the United States are insurrectionary or revolutionary, according to circumstances.

I therefore consider that in view of the Constitution and the laws the Union is unbroken, and to the extent of my ability, I shall take care, as the Constitution itself expressly enjoins upon me, that the laws of the Union be faithfully executed in all the States. Doing this I deem to be only a simple duty on my part, and I shall perform it so far as practicable unless my rightful masters, the American people, shall withhold the requisite means or in some authoritative manner direct the contrary. I trust this will not be regarded as a menace, but only as the declared purpose of the Union that it will constitutionally defend and maintain itself.

In doing this there needs to be no bloodshed or violence, and there shall be none unless it be forced upon the national authority. The power confided to me will be used to hold, occupy, and possess the property and places belonging to the Government and to collect the duties and imposts; but beyond what may be necessary for these objects, there will be no invasion, no using of force against or among the people anywhere. Where hostility to the United States in any interior locality shall be so great and universal as to prevent competent resident citizens from holding the Federal offices, there will be no attempt to force obnoxious strangers among the people for that object. While the strict legal right may exist in the Government to enforce the exercise of these offices, the attempt to do so would be so irritating and so nearly impracticable withal that I deem it better to forego for the time the uses of such offices.

The mails, unless repelled, will continue to be furnished in all parts of the Union. So far as possible the people everywhere shall have that sense of perfect security which is most favorable to calm thought and reflection. The course here indicated will be followed unless current events and experience shall show a modification or change to be proper, and in every case and exigency my best discretion will be exercised, according to circumstances actually existing and with a view and a hope of a peaceful solution of the national troubles and the restoration of fraternal sympathies and affections.

That there are persons in one section or another who seek to destroy the Union at all events and are glad of any pretext to do it I will neither affirm nor deny; but if there be such, I need address no word to them. To those, however, who really love the Union may I not speak?

Before entering upon so grave a matter as the destruction of our national fabric, with all its benefits, its memories, and its hopes, would it not be wise to ascertain precisely why we do it? Will you hazard so desperate a step while there is any possibility that any portion of the ills you fly from have no real existence? Will you, while the certain ills you fly to are greater than all the real ones you fly from, will you risk the commission of so fearful a mistake?

All profess to be content in the Union if all constitutional rights can be maintained. Is it true, then, that any right plainly written in the Constitution has been denied? I think not. Happily, the human mind is so constituted that no party can reach to the audacity of doing this. Think, if you can, of a single instance in which a plainly written provision of the Constitution has ever been denied. If by the mere force of numbers a majority should deprive a minority of any clearly written constitutional right, it might in a moral point of view justify revolution; certainly would if such right were a vital one. But such is not our case. All the vital rights of minorities and of individuals are so plainly assured to them by affirmations and negations, guaranties and prohibitions, in the Constitution that controversies never arise concerning them. But no organic law can ever be framed with a provision specifically applicable to every question which may occur in practical administration. No foresight can anticipate nor any document of reasonable length contain express provisions for all possible questions. Shall fugitives from labor be surrendered by national or by State authority? The Constitution does not expressly say. *May* Congress prohibit slavery in the Territories? The Constitution does not expressly say. *Must* Congress protect slavery in the Territories? The Constitution does not expressly say.

From questions of this class spring all our constitutional controversies, and we divide upon them into majorities and minorities. If the minority will not acquiesce, the majority must, or the Government must cease. There is no other alternative, for continuing the Government is acquiescence on one side or the other. If a minority in such case will secede rather than acquiesce, they make a precedent which in turn will divide and ruin them, for a minority of their own will secede from them whenever a majority refuses to be controlled by such minority. For instance, why may not any portion of a new confederacy a year or two hence arbitrarily secede again, precisely as portions of the present Union now claim to secede from it? All who cherish disunion sentiments are now being educated to the exact temper of doing this.

Is there such perfect identity of interests among the States to compose a new union as to produce harmony only and prevent renewed secession?

Plainly the central idea of secession is the essence of anarchy. A majority held in restraint by constitutional checks and limitations, and always changing easily with deliberate changes of popular opinions and sentiments, is the only true sovereign of a free people. Whoever rejects it does of necessity fly to anarchy or to despotism. Unanimity is impossible. The rule of a minority, as a permanent arrangement, is wholly inadmissible; so that, rejecting the majority principle, anarchy or despotism in some form is all that is left.

I do not forget the position assumed by some that constitutional questions are to be decided by the Supreme Court, nor do I deny that such decisions must be binding in any case upon the parties to a suit as to the object of that suit, while they are also entitled to very high respect and consideration in all parallel cases by all other departments of the Government. And while it is obviously possible that such decision may be erroneous in any given case, still the evil effect following it, being limited to that particular case, with the chance that it may be overruled and never become a precedent for other cases, can better be borne than could the evils of a different practice. At the same time, the candid citizen must confess that if the policy of the Government upon vital questions affecting the whole people is to be irrevocably fixed by decisions of the Supreme Court, the instant they are made in ordinary litigation between parties in personal actions the people will have ceased to be their own rulers, having to that extent practically resigned their Government into the hands of that eminent tribunal. Nor is there in this view any assault upon the court or the judges. It is a duty from which they may not shrink to decide cases properly brought before them, and it is no fault of theirs if others seek to turn their decisions to political purposes.

One section of our country believes slavery is right and ought to be extended, while the other believes it is wrong and ought not to be extended. This is the only substantial dispute. The fugitive-slave clause of the Constitution and the law for the suppression of the foreign slave trade are each as well enforced, perhaps, as any law can ever be in a community where the moral sense of the people imperfectly supports the law itself. The great body of the people abide by the dry legal obligation in both cases, and a few break over in each. This, I think, can not be perfectly cured, and it would be worse in both cases after the separation of the sections than before. The foreign slave trade, now imperfectly suppressed, would be ultimately revived without restriction in one section, while fugitive slaves, now only partially surrendered, would not be surrendered at all by the other.

Physically speaking, we can not separate. We can not remove our respective sections from each other nor build an impassable wall between them. A husband and wife may be divorced and go out of the presence and beyond the reach of each other, but the different parts of our country can not do this. They can not but remain face to face, and intercourse, either amicable or hostile, must continue between them. Is it possible, then, to make that intercourse more advantageous or more satisfactory after separation than before? Can aliens make treaties easier than friends can make laws? Can treaties be more faithfully enforced between aliens than laws can among friends? Suppose you go to war, you can not fight always; and when, after much loss on both sides and no gain on either, you cease fighting, the identical old questions, as to terms of intercourse, are again upon you.

This country, with its institutions, belongs to the people who inhabit it. Whenever they shall grow weary of the existing Government, they can exercise their constitutional right of amending it or their revolutionary right to dismember or overthrow it. I can not be ignorant of the fact that many worthy and patriotic citizens are desirous of having the National Constitution amended. While I make no recommendation of amendments, I fully recognize the rightful authority of the people over the whole subject, to be exercised in either of the modes prescribed in the instrument itself; and I should, under existing circumstances, favor rather than oppose a fair opportunity being afforded the people to act upon it. I will venture to add that to me the convention mode seems preferable, in that it allows amendments to originate with the people themselves, instead of only permitting them to take or reject propositions originated by others, not especially chosen for the purpose, and which might not be precisely such as they would wish to either accept or refuse. I understand a proposed amendment to the Constitution—which amendment, however, I have not seen—has passed Congress, to the effect that the Federal Government shall never interfere with the domestic institutions of the States, including that of persons held to service. To avoid misconstruction of what I have said, I depart from my purpose not to speak of particular amendments so far as to say that, holding such a provision to now be implied constitutional law, I have no objection to its being made express and irrevocable.

The Chief Magistrate derives all his authority from the people, and they have referred none upon him to fix terms for the separation of the States. The people themselves can do this if also they choose, but the Executive as such has nothing to do with it. His duty is to administer the present Government as it came to his hands and to transmit it unimpaired by him to his successor.

Why should there not be a patient confidence in the ultimate justice of the people? Is there any better or equal hope in the world? In our present differences, is either party without faith of being in the right? If the Almighty Ruler of Nations, with His eternal truth and justice, be on your side of the North, or on yours of the South, that truth and that justice will surely prevail by the judgment of this great tribunal of the American people.

By the frame of the Government under which we live this same people have wisely given their public servants but little power for mischief, and have with equal wisdom provided for the return of that little to their own hands at very short intervals. While the people retain their virtue and vigilance no Administration by any extreme of wickedness or folly can very seriously injure the Government in the short space of four years.

My countrymen, one and all, think calmly and well upon this whole subject. Nothing valuable can be lost by taking time. If there be an object to hurry any of you in hot haste to a step which you would never take deliberately, that object will be frustrated by taking time; but no good object can be frustrated by it. Such of you as are now dissatisfied still have the old Constitution unimpaired, and, on the sensitive point, the laws of your own framing under it; while the new Administration will have no immediate power, if it would, to change either. If it were admitted that you who are dissatisfied hold the right side in the dispute, there still is no single good reason for precipitate action. Intelligence, patriotism, Christianity, and a firm reliance on Him who has never yet forsaken this favored land are still competent to adjust in the best way all our present difficulty.

In your hands, my dissatisfied fellow-countrymen, and not in mine, is the momentous issue of civil war. The Government will not assail you. You can have no conflict without being yourselves the aggressors. You have no oath registered in heaven to destroy the Government, while I shall have the most solemn one to "preserve, protect, and defend it."

I am loath to close. We are not enemies, but friends. We must not be enemies. Though passion may have strained it must not break our bonds of affection. The mystic chords of memory, stretching from every battlefield and patriot grave to every living heart and hearthstone all over this broad land, will yet swell the chorus of the Union, when again touched, as surely they will be, by the better angels of our nature.

EMANCIPATION PROCLAMATION

Washington, D.C.
January 1, 1863

By the President of the United States of America:
A Proclamation.

Whereas, on the twenty-second day of September, in the year of our Lord one thousand eight hundred and sixty two, a proclamation was issued by the President of the United States, containing, among other things, the following, to wit:

"That on the first day of January, in the year of our Lord one thousand eight hundred and sixty-three, all persons held as slaves within any State or designated part of a State, the people whereof shall then be in rebellion against the United States, shall be then, thenceforward, and forever free; and the Executive Government of the United States, including the military and naval authority thereof, will recognize and maintain the freedom of such persons, and will do no act or acts to repress such persons, or any of them, in any efforts they may make for their actual freedom.

"That the Executive will, on the first day of January aforesaid, by proclamation, designate the States and parts of States, if any, in which the people thereof, respectively, shall then be in rebellion against the United States; and the fact that any State, or the people thereof, shall on that day be, in good faith, represented in the Congress of the United States by members chosen thereto at elections wherein a majority of the qualified voters of such State shall have participated, shall, in the absence of strong countervailing testimony, be deemed conclusive evidence that such State, and the people thereof, are not then in rebellion against the United States."

Now, therefore I, Abraham Lincoln, President of the United States, by virtue of the power in me vested as Commander-in-Chief, of the Army and Navy of the United States in time of actual armed rebellion against the authority and government of the United States, and as a fit and necessary war measure for suppressing said rebellion, do, on this first day of January, in the year of our Lord one thousand eight hundred and sixty three, and in accordance with my purpose so to do publicly proclaimed for the full period of one hundred days, from the day first above mentioned, order and designate as the States and parts of States wherein the people thereof respectively, are this day in rebellion against the United States, the following, to wit:

Arkansas, Texas, Louisiana, (except the Parishes of St. Bernard, Plaquemines, Jefferson, St. Johns, St. Charles, St. James Ascension, Assumption, Terrebonne,

Lafourche, St. Mary, St. Martin, and Orleans, including the City of New Orleans) Mississippi, Alabama, Florida, Georgia, South Carolina, North Carolina, and Virginia, (except the forty-eight counties designated as West Virginia, and also the counties of Berkley, Accomac, Northampton, Elizabeth City, York, Princess Ann, and Norfolk, including the cities of Norfolk and Portsmouth, and which excepted parts are, for the present, left precisely as if this proclamation were not issued.

And by virtue of the power, and for the purpose aforesaid, I do order and declare that all persons held as slaves within said designated States, and parts of States, are, and henceforward shall be free; and that the Executive government of the United States, including the military and naval authorities thereof, will recognize and maintain the freedom of said persons.

And I hereby enjoin upon the people so declared to be free to abstain from all violence, unless in necessary self-defence; and I recommend to them that, in all cases when allowed, they labor faithfully for reasonable wages.

And I further declare and make known, that such persons of suitable condition, will be received into the armed service of the United States to garrison forts, positions, stations, and other places, and to man vessels of all sorts in said service.

And upon this act, sincerely believed to be an act of justice, warranted by the Constitution, upon military necessity, I invoke the considerate judgment of mankind, and the gracious favor of Almighty God.

In witness whereof, I have hereunto set my hand and caused the seal of the United States to be affixed.

Done at the City of Washington, this first day of January, in the year of our Lord one thousand eight hundred and sixty three, and of the Independence of the United States of America the eighty-seventh.

By the President: Abraham Lincoln
William H. Seward, Secretary of State.

THE GETTYSBURG ADDRESS

Gettysburg, Pennsylvania

November 19, 1863

Four score and seven years ago our fathers brought forth on this continent, a new nation, conceived in Liberty, and dedicated to the proposition that all men are created equal.

Now we are engaged in a great civil war, testing whether that nation, or any nation so conceived and so dedicated, can long endure. We are met on a great battle-field of that war. We have come to dedicate a portion of that field, as a final resting place for those who here gave their lives that that nation might live. It is altogether fitting and proper that we should do this.

But, in a larger sense, we can not dedicate—we can not consecrate—we can not hallow—this ground. The brave men, living and dead, who struggled here, have consecrated it, far above our poor power to add or detract. The world will little note, nor long remember what we say here, but it can never forget what they did here. It is for us the living, rather, to be dedicated here to the unfinished work which they who fought here have thus far so nobly advanced. It is rather for us to be here dedicated to the great task remaining before us—that from these honored dead we take increased devotion to that cause for which they gave the last full measure of devotion—that we here highly resolve that these dead shall not have died in vain—that this nation, under God, shall have a new birth of freedom—and that government of the people, by the people, for the people, shall not perish from the earth.

SECOND INAUGURAL ADDRESS

Washington, D.C.

March 4, 1865

Fellow-Countrymen:

At this second appearing to take the oath of the Presidential office there is less occasion for an extended address than there was at the first. Then a statement somewhat in detail of a course to be pursued seemed fitting and proper. Now, at the expiration of four years, during which public declarations have been constantly called forth on every point and phase of the great contest which still absorbs the attention and engrosses the energies of the nation, little that is new could be presented. The progress of our arms, upon which all else chiefly depends, is as well known to the public as to myself, and it is, I trust, reasonably satisfactory and encouraging to all. With high hope for the future, no prediction in regard to it is ventured.

On the occasion corresponding to this four years ago all thoughts were anxiously directed to an impending civil war. All dreaded it, all sought to avert it. While the inaugural address was being delivered from this place, devoted altogether to saving the Union without war, urgent agents were in the city seeking to destroy it without war—seeking to dissolve the Union and divide effects by negotiation. Both parties deprecated war, but one of them would make war rather than let the nation survive, and the other would accept war rather than let it perish, and the war came.

One-eighth of the whole population were colored slaves, not distributed generally over the Union, but localized in the southern part of it. These slaves constituted a peculiar and powerful interest. All knew that this interest was somehow the cause of the war. To strengthen, perpetuate, and extend this interest was the object for which the insurgents would rend the Union even by war, while the Government claimed no right to do more than to restrict the territorial enlargement of it. Neither party expected for the war the magnitude or the duration which it has already attained. Neither anticipated that the cause of the conflict might cease with or even before the conflict itself should cease. Each looked for an easier triumph, and a result less fundamental and astounding. Both read the same Bible and pray to the same God, and each invokes His aid against the other. It may seem strange that any men should dare to ask a just God's assistance in wringing their bread from the sweat of other men's faces, but let us judge not, that we be not judged. The prayers of both could not be answered. That of neither has been answered fully. The Almighty has His own purposes. "Woe unto the world because of offenses; for it must needs be that offenses come, but woe to that man by whom the offense cometh." If we shall suppose that American slavery is one of those offenses which, in the providence of God, must needs come, but which, having continued through His appointed time, He now wills to remove, and that He gives to both North and South this terrible war as the woe due to those by whom the offense came, shall we discern therein any departure from those divine attributes which the believers in a living God always ascribe to Him? Fondly do we hope, fervently do we pray, that this mighty scourge of war may speedily pass away. Yet, if God wills that it continue until all the wealth piled by the bondsman's two hundred and fifty years of unrequited toil shall be sunk, and until every drop of blood drawn with the lash shall be paid by another drawn with the sword, as was said three thousand years ago, so still it must be said "the judgments of the Lord are true and righteous altogether." With malice toward none, with charity for all, with firmness in the right as God gives us to see the right, let us strive on to finish the work we are in, to bind up the nation's wounds, to care for him who shall have borne the battle and for his widow and his orphan, to do all which may achieve and cherish a just and lasting peace among ourselves and with all nations.

LAST PUBLIC ADDRESS

Washington, D.C.

April 11, 1865

We meet this evening, not in sorrow, but in gladness of heart. The evacuation of Petersburg and Richmond, and the surrender of the principal insurgent army, give hope of a righteous and speedy peace whose joyous expression can not be restrained. In the midst of this, however, He from whom all blessings flow, must not be forgotten. A call for a national thanksgiving is being prepared, and will be duly promulgated. Nor must those whose harder part gives us the cause of rejoicing, be overlooked. Their honors must not be parcelled out with others. I myself was near the front, and had the high pleasure of transmitting much of the good news to you; but no part of the honor, for plan or execution, is mine. To Gen. Grant, his skilful officers, and brave men, all belongs. The gallant Navy stood ready, but was not in reach to take active part.

By these recent successes the re-inauguration of the national authority—reconstruction—which has had a large share of thought from the first, is pressed much more closely upon our attention. It is fraught with great difficulty. Unlike a case of a war between independent nations, there is no authorized organ for us to treat with. No one man has authority to give up the rebellion for any other man. We simply must begin with, and mould from, disorganized and discordant elements. Nor is it a small additional embarrassment that we, the loyal people, differ among ourselves as to the mode, manner, and means of reconstruction.

As a general rule, I abstain from reading the reports of attacks upon myself, wishing not to be provoked by that to which I can not properly offer an answer. In spite of this precaution, however, it comes to my knowledge that I am much censured for some supposed agency in setting up, and seeking to sustain, the new State Government of Louisiana. In this I have done just so much as, and no more than, the public knows. In the Annual Message of Dec. 1863 and accompanying Proclamation, I presented a plan of re-construction (as the phrase goes) which, I promised, if adopted by any State, should be acceptable to, and sustained by, the Executive government of the nation. I distinctly stated that this was not the only plan which might possibly be acceptable; and I also distinctly protested that the Executive claimed no right to say when, or whether members should be admitted to seats in Congress from such States. This plan was, in advance, submitted to the then Cabinet, and distinctly approved by every member of it. One of them suggested that I should then, and in that connection, apply the Emancipation Proclamation to the theretofore excepted parts of Virginia and Louisiana; that

I should drop the suggestion about apprenticeship for freed-people, and that I should omit the protest against my own power, in regard to the admission of members to Congress; but even he approved every part and parcel of the plan which has since been employed or touched by the action of Louisiana. The new constitution of Louisiana, declaring emancipation for the whole State, practically applies the Proclamation to the part previously excepted. It does not adopt apprenticeship for freed-people; and it is silent, as it could not well be otherwise, about the admission of members to Congress. So that, as it applies to Louisiana, every member of the Cabinet fully approved the plan. The message went to Congress, and I received many commendations of the plan, written and verbal; and not a single objection to it, from any professed emancipationist, came to my knowledge, until after the news reached Washington that the people of Louisiana had begun to move in accordance with it. From about July 1862, I had corresponded with different persons, supposed to be interested, seeking a reconstruction of a State government for Louisiana. When the message of 1863, with the plan before mentioned, reached New-Orleans, Gen. Banks wrote me that he was confident the people, with his military co-operation, would reconstruct, substantially on that plan. I wrote him, and some of them to try it; they tried it, and the result is known. Such only has been my agency in getting up the Louisiana government. As to sustaining it, my promise is out, as before stated. But, as bad promises are better broken than kept, I shall treat this as a bad promise, and break it, whenever I shall be convinced that keeping it is adverse to the public interest. But I have not yet been so convinced.

I have been shown a letter on this subject, supposed to be an able one, in which the writer expresses regret that my mind has not seemed to be definitely fixed on the question whether the seceding States, so called, are in the Union or out of it. It would perhaps, add astonishment to his regret, were he to learn that since I have found professed Union men endeavoring to make that question, I have purposely forborne any public expression upon it. As appears to me that question has not been, nor yet is, a practically material one, and that any discussion of it, while it thus remains practically immaterial, could have no effect other than the mischievous one of dividing our friends. As yet, whatever it may hereafter become, that question is bad, as the basis of a controversy, and good for nothing at all—a merely pernicious abstraction.

We all agree that the seceded States, so called, are out of their proper relation with the Union; and that the sole object of the government, civil and military, in regard to those States is to again get them into that proper practical relation. I believe it is not only possible, but in fact, easier to do this, without deciding, or even considering, whether these States have ever been out of the Union, than with it. Finding themselves safely at home, it would be utterly immaterial whether they had ever been abroad. Let us all join in doing the acts necessary to restoring the proper practical relations between these States and the Union; and each forever after, innocently indulge his own opinion whether, in doing the acts, he brought the States from without, into the Union, or only gave them proper assistance, they never having been out of it.

The amount of constituency, so to speak, on which the new Louisiana government rests, would be more satisfactory to all, if it contained fifty, thirty, or even twenty thousand, instead of only about twelve thousand, as it does. It is also unsatisfactory to some that the elective franchise is not given to the colored man. I would myself prefer that it were now conferred on the very intelligent, and on those who serve our cause as soldiers. Still the question is not whether the Louisiana government, as it stands, is quite all that is desirable. The question is, "Will it be wiser to take it as it is, and help to improve it; or to reject, and disperse it?" "Can Louisiana be brought into proper practical relation with the Union sooner by sustaining, or by discarding her new State government?"

Some twelve thousand voters in the heretofore slave-state of Louisiana have sworn allegiance to the Union, assumed to be the rightful political power of the State, held elections, organized a State government, adopted a free-state constitution, giving the benefit of public schools equally to black and white, and empowering the Legislature to confer the elective franchise upon the colored man. Their Legislature has already voted to ratify the constitutional amendment recently passed by Congress, abolishing slavery throughout the nation. These twelve thousand persons are thus fully committed to the Union, and to perpetual freedom in the state—committed to the very things, and nearly all the things the nation wants—and they ask the nations recognition and it's assistance to make good their committal. Now, if we reject, and spurn them, we do our utmost to disorganize and disperse them. We in effect say to the white men "You are worthless, or worse—we will neither help you, nor be helped by you." To the blacks we say "This cup of liberty which these, your old masters, hold to your lips, we will dash from you, and leave you to the chances of gathering the spilled and scattered contents in some vague and undefined when, where, and how." If this course, discouraging and paralyzing both white and black, has any tendency to bring Louisiana into proper practical relations with the Union, I have, so far, been unable to perceive it. If, on the contrary, we recognize, and sustain the new government of Louisiana the converse of all this is made true. We encourage the hearts, and nerve the arms of the twelve thousand to adhere to their work, and argue for it, and proselyte for it, and fight for it, and feed it, and grow it, and ripen it to a complete success. The colored man too, in seeing all united for him, is inspired with vigilance, and energy, and daring, to the same end. Grant that he desires the elective franchise, will he not attain it sooner by saving the already advanced steps toward it, than by running backward over them? Concede that the new government of Louisiana is only to what it should be as the egg is to the fowl, we shall sooner have the fowl by hatching the egg than by smashing it? Again, if we reject Louisiana, we also reject one vote in favor of the proposed amendment to the national Constitution. To meet this proposition, it has been argued that no more than three fourths of those States which have not attempted secession are necessary to validly ratify the amendment. I do not commit myself against this, further than to say that such a ratification would be questionable, and sure to be persistently questioned; while a ratification by three-fourths of all the States would be unquestioned and unquestionable.

I repeat the question, "Can Louisiana be brought into proper practical relation with the Union sooner by sustaining or by discarding her new State Government?

What has been said of Louisiana will apply generally to other States. And yet so great peculiarities pertain to each state, and such important and sudden changes occur in the same state; and withal, so new and unprecedented is the whole case, that no exclusive, and inflexible plan can be safely prescribed as to details and colatterals [sic]. Such exclusive, and inflexible plan, would surely become a new entanglement. Important principles may, and must, be inflexible.

In the present "situation" as the phrase goes, it may be my duty to make some new announcement to the people of the South. I am considering, and shall not fail to act, when satisfied that action will be proper.

THEODORE ROOSEVELT

INTRODUCTION

Theodore Roosevelt differed from Gutzon Borglum's other subjects not only in that he was a contemporary of the sculptor—Roosevelt died in 1919, only seven years before the work began on Mt. Rushmore—but the two had actually met when Borglum's enormous granite bust of Lincoln was exhibited at the White House. Though Roosevelt was the last subject to be included in the plan, Borglum was enthusiastic about adding him. Not only would the late president's supporters bring a wealth of donations, but he had been an active participant in the United States' turn from conquering an inland empire to one abroad, and of making the "empire of democracy" a reality. In particular, Borglum saw Roosevelt's negotiation for and construction of the Panama Canal as the event that, more than any other, transformed the United States from a regional to a world power. To this contemporary estimation of Roosevelt, we can add how he is also remembered by modern historians: He was the embodiment of the Progressive movement, that is, of an activist government that recognized that in order to ensure freedom in an industrial society, principles of Jeffersonian democracy would have to be complicated, expanded—and sometimes transgressed. As it turned out, Roosevelt's "square deal" applied only to the United States. In his foreign policy, particularly with Latin America, he was not afraid to "speak softly and carry a big stick."

GROWTH OF AN AMERICAN EMPIRE

In 1893, the historian Frederick Jackson Turner declared in a speech to the American Historical Association that the "frontier" was closed. Up until the Oklahoma Land Rush of 1889, there had always been room to expand, places without established power structures, territory where a man could be free to forge his own destiny. (We should add that this man who was able to forge his own destiny was still a white man; this was the era of Jim Crow, when courts rolled back the freedoms won by African Americans in an effort at post-Civil War national reconciliation, when segregation became the law of the land.) This experience, Turner wrote, was essential to the creation of American national character: rough-hewn, dismissive of traditional hierarchies, and proudly individualistic.

We must qualify Turner's thesis, however: The Land Rush was only the closing of the domestic frontier. There were still new horizons elsewhere. Previously, US overseas possessions had been limited to small, uninhabited islands where guano was mined for fertilizer, though there were some tentative attempts at expansion, such as William Walker's brief takeover of Nicaragua in the 1850s and William H. Seward's purchase of Alaska from the Russian government in 1867. After the "closing of the frontier," this expansionistic attitude took on new force. The most significant development, encouraged by poets, politicians, and propagandists alike, was the ten-week Spanish-American War of 1898—in one swoop, the United States acquired Guam, Puerto Rico, and the Philippines, and became the preeminent power in the Caribbean and Central America. The war also provided a sort of national reconciliation as Americans—black and white, northerner and southerner—fought together for the ostensible purpose of freeing the former Spanish colonies from their tyrannical ruler.

The territorial acquisitions that followed the Spanish-American War were less justifiable in the name of democracy and freedom. In the same year as the war, the United States formally annexed Hawaii, which had been taken over by a group of American businessmen who had overthrown Queen Liliuokalani in 1893. The discovery of gold in the Yukon in 1896 triggered thousands of prospectors to rush to Alaska and necessitated its being organized as a territory. In 1900, the United States formally annexed American Samoa. In 1903, the United States encouraged Panama's independence from Colombia, which enabled the US to acquire the lease on what would become the Canal Zone. In the decades to come, the United States would participate in a series of "police actions" collectively known as the Banana Wars intended to protect the Canal Zone and American business interests in Central America. This was the theater in which Theodore Roosevelt lived his political career and in which he made the reputation that Borglum thought merited memorialization on Mt. Rushmore. Thomas Jefferson may have imagined an "empire of democracy," but the United States of the late nineteenth and early twentieth century showed what such an empire really meant.

EARLY LIFE OF THEODORE ROOSEVELT

Theodore Roosevelt, Jr. was born in 1858 to a wealthy New York City family. Though he suffered from asthma as a child, he was also bright, energetic, and able to take advantage of all the cultural and educational opportunities of the growing metropolis. On a family trip to Europe, he found that strenuous physical exercise helped his asthma, and he embarked on a self-improvement mission. As an adult, he enjoyed hunting, fishing, horseback riding, and combat sports such as shooting, boxing, wrestling, and fencing—he even brought Japanese jujitsu experts to the White House.

Roosevelt's father died in 1878 while young Theodore was attending Harvard College, and he came into considerable wealth. His new situation influenced his decision not to become a natural scientist and instead to attend law school and enter politics as a Republican. He was elected to the New York State Assembly and quickly made his name fighting corruption, particularly the influence of the new money of the Gilded Age.

Roosevelt married Alice Hathaway Lee on his twenty-second birthday. In 1884, Alice died four days after giving birth to their daughter and only eleven hours after Roosevelt's mother. Devastated and facing some political setbacks after backing a losing candidate, Roosevelt withdrew to a ranch he owned in the Dakota territory and essentially spent the next two years living in the saddle, hunting, working cattle, forming wilderness conservation organizations, beating an armed man senseless in a bar fight, and tracking down and arresting three men who stole his boat. Roosevelt's rugged "cowboy" persona was part of his appeal. In an era when the actual hard work of farm labor, such as Abraham Lincoln had done as a young man, was increasingly being replaced by factory jobs and white-collar labor, the idea of acting in a spectacularly "manly" way had broad appeal. The myth of the "Wild West" was created to fill this need in the national psyche, and Roosevelt embraced it wholeheartedly.

Roosevelt returned East in 1886, and, after a trip to England where he married his childhood friend Edith Kermit Carow, reentered politics. After he was defeated in a run for the mayor of New York City, he toyed for a while with pursuing a writing career. (Roosevelt was an extremely prolific author and published numerous books during his lifetime, mostly on history, but also on hunting, conservation, and self-help topics.) His opportunity to get back to politics came when he was appointed to the Civil Service Commission by presidents Benjamin Harrison and Grover Cleveland, where he continued his crusade against corruption. This led to his becoming president of the New York City Police Board in 1895 and then, two years later, assistant secretary of the Navy under President William McKinley (Roosevelt had earlier written a book on sea power in the War of 1812.)

He was spoiling for a fight: "I should welcome almost any war, for I think this country needs one," he wrote. Such a conflict would be a test of his generation's mettle as the Civil War had been for the previous. Since Secretary of the Navy John D. Long left most of the work up to Roosevelt, Roosevelt was able to make the necessary preparations for the Spanish-American War behind the backs of both Long and McKinley—and then resign his post and fight with the Rough Riders. He won glory leading his famous (and perhaps foolhardy) charge at the Battle of Kettle Hill, which he would later recall as his finest hour, and returned a hero.

The New York State Republican establishment soon asked Roosevelt to run for governor, and he was narrowly elected in 1898. His two years as governor gave him valuable experience, not the least in the ins and outs of implementing his "Square Deal" idea, in which the government was an impartial arbiter that ensured a level playing field for everyone. In his various political campaigns, Roosevelt would address "square deal" platforms to various constituencies—for instance, to African Americans, for the South, and for Mormons. But he would not be governor for long: McKinley's Vice President Garret Hobart died in office, and Roosevelt reluctantly accepted the nomination to be his replacement. When McKinley was assassinated in Buffalo, New York, six month later, Roosevelt, at the age of 42, became the youngest person to ever hold the office of president—a distinction he maintains to this day.

ROOSEVELT'S PRESIDENCY

While Lincoln's Republicans had supported business interests as a way to promote industrialization, by the late nineteenth century, powerful monopolies were exercising an inordinate amount of influence on the American economy and society. Roosevelt, often known as a "trust buster," set about remedying this in pursuit of "a square deal for every man." He broke up unfair practices in transportation and petroleum and negotiated on behalf of coal miners. Thanks to the Elkins Act, railroads were no longer allowed to charge less for favored customers, driving competitors out of business. He sought to ensure pure food and drugs; under unregulated capitalism, meat was often adulterated and produced in unsanitary conditions. The question of Native American sovereignty had been unfortunately settled by this time, with tribes segregated on reservations, but Roosevelt sought a "square deal" for them, too, by prosecuting corruption in the Indian Office. Roosevelt also famously set up the National Forest Service and set aside land for national parks and conservation. The frontier might be closed, Roosevelt held, but the wilderness had to be preserved for the good of the nation's soul.

Historians call this movement in which Roosevelt participated Progressivism: The belief that an activist, interventionist government is necessary to achieve social reform and give everyone a level playing field. Some criticized it as government overreach. Following the principles of Jeffersonian democracy, they argued that the government should be hands-off in regard to the economy (remember, Jefferson was even against a national bank) and that decisions about natural resources should be made at the state level. But Theodore Roosevelt lived in a very different world from that of the Founding Fathers. The breadth and power and scale of action brought by the Industrial Revolution would have been unimaginable. For liberty to continue, Roosevelt believed, a strong central government was essential to check the power of concentrated wealth and power.

In this sense, he was continuing Jefferson's legacy of ensuring the rights of the common person against those of the rich and powerful, even as he went against the Jeffersonian principle of small government.

Roosevelt's other accomplishments were many, including winning the Nobel Peace Prize for mediating the Russo-Japanese War, establishing a friendly relationship with Japan, and laying the foundations for the League of Nations. He easily won reelection in 1904, and, having promised to only serve two terms, left the presidency in 1909 to his handpicked successor William Howard Taft.

ROOSEVELT ON RACE

One important aspect of Roosevelt's progressivism was his attitude toward American race relations. To be sure, some of his record is nothing to be proud of. In 1906, he dishonorably discharged a regiment of African American soldiers for disobeying orders and conspiring to remain silent when a white man was shot to death and a police officer wounded in Brownsville, Texas. He not infrequently used racist language and had a patronizing attitude toward African Americans. His overall attitude, however, seems to have been what he told a crowd in Montana in 1903: "I fought beside colored troops at Santiago, and I hold that if a man is good enough to be put up and shot at then he is good enough for me to do what I can to get him a square deal."

One particular incident, Roosevelt's inviting the African American educator W.E.B. Du Bois for a White House dinner in 1901, created a furor among racist Southerners for whom dining together meant social equality. (The story was spun that the two had "actually" sent for a tray of sandwiches for a working lunch.) In 1905, following his reelection, he gave a speech to the New York City Republican Club in which he praised Lincoln and said, that while "the attitude of the North toward the negro is far from what it should be," the "peculiar circumstances of the South render the problem there far greater and far more acute." The role of his administration would be to "secure to each man, whatever his color, equality of opportunity, equality of treatment before the law." The path forward, was incremental, generational progress: "that the backward race [African Americans] be trained so that it may enter into the possession of true freedom while the forward race [that is, European Americans] is enabled to preserve unharmed the high civilization wrought out by its forefathers." This was not only the responsibility of African Americans, however: "it is quite as necessary to train the white man." This idea of "progress" was advocated by many, such as Du Bois, who saw the leadership of a "talented tenth" as necessary for the African American community to bootstrap itself up.

The idea of progress has a different meaning today. In the nineteenth century, it was used to justify the creation of colonial empires—"backwards" and "primitive" peoples in Asia, Africa, and the Middle East needed to be educated by the "civilized" and "advanced" Western nations. Roosevelt denied being an "imperialist"—such would be un-American—but he was a proud "expansionist." Take, for instance, his comment on Rudyard Kipling's poem "The White Man's Burden," written on the occasion of the US acquisition of the Philippines and offered up by the poet as a persuasion to empire:

> Take up the White Man's burden—
> Send forth the best ye breed—
> Go bind your sons to exile
> To serve your captives' need;
> To wait in heavy harness,
> On fluttered folk and wild—
> Your new-caught, sullen peoples,
> Half-devil and half-child.

The poem was, according to Roosevelt, "good sense from the expansion point of view." In this poem, Kipling depicts the task of governing colonies as an unavoidable responsibility in which Westerners are forced to drag their new "captives" kicking and screaming into the light of civilization. The line between "imperialism" and "expansionism" was often a fine distinction for those at the receiving end of American bullets: For instance, having aided the Philippine archipelago in breaking free from Spain, the US Army then brutally quashed Filipino resistance to American rule.

THE PANAMA CANAL

Nowhere were the rhetoric of progress, national pride, and blatant self-interest better displayed in Roosevelt's presidency than in his gaining the rights to build a canal across Central America. Some advocated purchasing rights to dig in Panama, where the French had been attempting to construct a canal since 1881, while others advocated for building a canal in Nicaragua. The US government backed the Panamanian option in 1902, and in 1903, Roosevelt's government signed the Hay–Herrán Treaty to lease the land in perpetuity. However, Panama was then part of Colombia, and the Colombian government refused to ratify the treaty. Roosevelt then turned to underhanded means: he backed rebels in Panama, which declared independence on November 3, 1903. The United States quickly recognized the new nation and leased the canal zone in perpetuity.

This action, the best example of Roosevelt's foreign policy principle of "speak softly and carry a big stick," was harshly criticized at home and abroad as "gunboat diplomacy" and an unjustified act of war on Colombia. Roosevelt, however, defended his choices to the end of his life and strongly disagreed with Woodrow Wilson's later admission that the United States had used unfair means to acquire the land (in the 1920s, the United States wound up paying Colombia reparations). In any case, the deed was done: What was left was to build the canal.

The construction of the Panama Canal from 1904 to 1914 was both a tremendous feat of engineering and a testimony to the Progressive Era's devotion to efficient, professional, and honest administration. It also mirrored the era's injustices: Some 5,600 workers out of 45,000—most of the manual laborers coming from Afro-Caribbean countries, such as Barbados and Jamaica—died from accidents and tropical diseases. But when it was complete, this monumental work of engineering left the United States a world economic power.

LIFE AFTER THE PRESIDENCY

Almost immediately after leaving office, Roosevelt embarked on an African safari (where he and his companions killed over 11,000 animals, including 512 "big game" animals) and a European tour. But he was bored and still relatively young, and—despite the custom established by George Washington of serving only two terms, later codified as the 22nd Amendment in 1947—turned against Taft and ran for President again in 1912. This caused a split in the Republican party; when Taft won the nomination anyway, Roosevelt campaigned as a candidate for a new third ticket, the Progressive Party—often called the "Bull Moose" party since Roosevelt said he felt "as fit as a bull moose." While campaigning in Milwaukee in 1912, Roosevelt was shot in the chest with a .38 caliber revolver by John Flammang Schrank. The bullet, slowed by a steel eyeglass case and a 50-page speech, lodged in his pectoral muscle. Perceiving he was not badly hurt, he continued to give his speech and carried the bullet in his chest for the rest of his life.

Roosevelt had a stronger showing than Taft, but Governor Woodrow Wilson of New Jersey, a Progressive-minded Democrat, won both the popular vote and the lion's share of the Electoral College. Nonetheless, Roosevelt still fared better than any third-party candidate before or since. Though defeated, he was soon back in the newspapers: In 1913–14, he undertook a scientific expedition to the Amazon, but an infection in his leg combined with previous injuries from the assassination attempt and a carriage accident left him so debilitated that he begged to be left behind to commit suicide with an overdose of morphine. He survived, albeit weakened, and returned to a United States that was trying to remain neutral in the face of the outbreak of war in Europe. What World War I would have been like had Roosevelt been elected president is a fascinating historical might-have-been question. Most probably, the United States would have become involved much earlier, as Roosevelt was staunchly pro-Allies and against German submarine warfare. He organized a volunteer force in 1917, but it never saw action—a slight for which he never forgave Wilson. The war also brought a personal loss to Roosevelt: His youngest son Quentin, a pilot, was shot down over German lines in 1918.

Theodore Roosevelt died unexpectedly on January 5, 1919, at the age of 60. The cause was a pulmonary embolism; a blood clot, likely from his infected leg, had traveled to his lungs. In the end, Roosevelt's famous toughness and willingness to weather adversity had done him more harm than good. His son, Archibald, telegraphed his surviving siblings—Alice, Theodore Roosevelt III, Kermit, and Ethel—"the Old Lion is dead." Vice President Thomas R. Marshall remarked that, "Death had to take Roosevelt sleeping, for if he had been awake, there would have been a fight."

BOYHOOD AND YOUTH

Excerpt from Roosevelt's Autobiography

Naturally grandfather on my father's side was of almost purely Dutch blood. When he was young he still spoke some Dutch, and Dutch was last used in the services of the Dutch Reformed Church in New York while he was a small boy.

About 1644 his ancestor Klaes Martensen van Roosevelt came to New Amsterdam as a "settler"—the euphemistic name for an immigrant who came over in the steerage of a sailing ship in the seventeenth century instead of the steerage of a steamer in the nineteenth century. From that time for the next seven generations from father to son every one of us was born on Manhattan Island.

My father's paternal ancestors were of Holland stock; except that there was one named Waldron, a wheelwright, who was one of the Pilgrims who remained in Holland when the others came over to found Massachusetts, and who then accompanied the Dutch adventurers to New Amsterdam. My father's mother was a Pennsylvanian. Her forbears had come to Pennsylvania with William Penn, some in the same ship with him; they were of the usual type of the immigration of that particular place and time. They included Welsh and English Quakers, an Irishman—with a Celtic name, and apparently not a Quaker—and peace-loving Germans, who were among the founders of Germantown, having been driven from their Rhineland homes when the armies of Louis the Fourteenth ravaged the Palatinate; and, in addition, representatives of a by-no-means altogether peaceful people, the Scotch-Irish, who came to Pennsylvania a little later, early in the eighteenth century. My grandmother was a woman of singular sweetness and strength, the keystone of the arch in her relations with her husband and sons. Although she was not herself Dutch, it was she who taught me the only Dutch I ever knew, a baby song of which the first line ran, "Trippe troppa tronjes." I always remembered this, and when I was in East Africa it proved a bond of union between me and the Boer settlers, not a few of whom knew it, although at first they always had difficulty in understanding my pronunciation—at which I do not wonder. It was interesting to meet these men whose ancestors had gone to the Cape about the time that mine went to America two centuries and a half previously, and to find that the descendants of the two streams of emigrants still crooned to their children some at least of the same nursery songs.

Of my great-grandfather Roosevelt and his family life a century and over ago I know little beyond what is implied in some of his books that have come down to me—the Letters of Junius, a biography of John Paul Jones, Chief Justice Marshall's

Life of Washington. They seem to indicate that his library was less interesting than that of my wife's great-grandfather at the same time, which certainly included such volumes as the original *Edinburgh Review*, for we have then now on our own book-shelves. Of my grandfather Roosevelt my most vivid childish reminiscence is not something I saw, but a tale that was told me concerning him. In his boyhood Sunday was as dismal a day for small Calvinistic children of Dutch descent as if they had been of Puritan or Scotch Covenanting or French Huguenot descent—and I speak as one proud of his Holland, Huguenot, and Covenanting ancestors, and proud that the blood of that stark Puritan divine Jonathan Edwards flows in the veins of his children. One summer afternoon, after listening to an unusually long Dutch Reformed sermon for the second time that day, my grandfather, a small boy, running home before the congregation had dispersed, ran into a party of pigs, which then wandered free in New York's streets. He promptly mounted a big boar, which no less promptly bolted and carried him at full speed through the midst of the outraged congregation.

By the way, one of the Roosevelt documents which came down to me illustrates the change that has come over certain aspects of public life since the time which pessimists term "the earlier and better days of the Republic." Old Isaac Roosevelt was a member of an Auditing Committee which shortly after the close of the Revolution approved the following bill:

The State of New York, to John Cape Dr.

To a Dinner Given by His Excellency the Governor and Council to their Excellencies the Minnister of France and General Washington & Co.

1783

December

To 120 dinners at	48: 0:0
To 135 Bottles Madira	54: 0:0
" 36 ditto Port	10:16:0
" 60 ditto English Beer	9: 0:0
" 30 Bouls Punch	9: 0:0
" 8 dinners for Musick	1:12:0
" 10 ditto for Sarvts	2: 0:0
" 60 Wine Glasses Broken	4:10:0
" 8 Cutt decanters Broken	3: 0:0
" Coffee for 8 Gentlemen	1:12:0
" Music fees &ca	8: 0:0

" Fruit & Nuts	5: 0:0
	£156:10:0
By Cash	100:16:0
	55:14:0

We a Committee of Council having examined the above account do certify it (amounting to one hundred and fifty-six Pounds ten Shillings) to be just.

December 17th 1783.

Isaac Roosevelt
Jas. Duane
Egbt. Benson
Fred. Jay

Received the above Contents in full
New York 17th December 1783

John Cape

Think of the Governor of New York now submitting such a bill for such an entertainment of the French Ambassador and the President of the United States! Falstaff's views of the proper proportion between sack and bread are borne out by the proportion between the number of bowls of punch and bottles of port, Madeira, and beer consumed, and the "coffee for eight gentlemen"—apparently the only ones who lasted through to that stage of the dinner. Especially admirable is the nonchalant manner in which, obviously as a result of the drinking of said bottles of wine and bowls of punch, it is recorded that eight cut-glass decanters and sixty wine-glasses were broken.

During the Revolution some of my forefathers, North and South, served respectably, but without distinction, in the army, and others rendered similar service in the Continental Congress or in various local legislatures. By that time those who dwelt in the North were for the most part merchants, and those who dwelt in the South, planters.

My mother's people were predominantly of Scotch, but also of Huguenot and English, descent. She was a Georgian, her people having come to Georgia from South Carolina before the Revolution. The original Bulloch was a lad from near Glasgow, who came hither a couple of centuries ago, just as hundreds of thousands of needy, enterprising Scotchmen have gone to the four quarters of the globe in the intervening two hundred years. My mother's great-grandfather, Archibald Bulloch, was the first Revolutionary "President" of Georgia. My grandfather, her father, spent the winters in Savannah and the summers at Roswell, in the Georgia uplands near Atlanta, finally making Roswell his permanent home. He used to travel thither with his family and their belongings in his own carriage, followed by a baggage wagon. I never saw Roswell until I was President, but my mother told me so much about the place that when I did see it I felt as if I already knew every nook and corner of it, and as if it were haunted by the ghosts of all the men and women who had lived there. I do not mean merely my own family, I mean the slaves. My mother and her sister, my aunt, used to tell us children all kinds of stories about the slaves. One of the most fascinating referred to a very old darky called Bear Bob, because in the early days of settlement he had been partially scalped by a black bear. Then there was Mom' Grace, who was for a time my mother's nurse, and whom I had supposed to be dead, but who greeted me when I did come to Roswell, very respectable, and apparently with years of life before her. The two chief personages of the drama that used to be repeated to us were Daddy Luke, the Negro overseer, and his wife, Mom' Charlotte. I never saw either Daddy Luke or Mom' Charlotte, but I inherited the care of them when my mother died. After the close of the war they resolutely refused to be emancipated or leave the place. The only demand they made upon us was enough money annually to get a new "critter," that is, a mule. With a certain lack of ingenuity the mule was reported each Christmas as having passed away, or at least as having become so infirm as to necessitate a successor—a solemn fiction which neither deceived nor was intended to deceive, but which furnished a gauge for the size of the Christmas gift.

My maternal grandfather's house was on the line of Sherman's march to the sea, and pretty much everything in it that was portable was taken by the boys in blue, including most of the books in the library. When I was President the facts about my ancestry were published, and a former soldier in Sherman's army sent me back one of the books with my grandfather's name in it. It was a little copy of the poems of "Mr. Gray"—an eighteenth-century edition printed in Glasgow.

On October 27, 1858, I was born at No. 28 East Twentieth Street, New York City, in the house in which we lived during the time that my two sisters and my brother and I were small children. It was furnished in the canonical taste of the New York which George William Curtis described in the *Potiphar Papers*. The black haircloth furniture in the dining-room scratched the bare legs of the children when they sat on it. The middle room was a library, with tables, chairs, and bookcases of gloomy respectability. It was without windows, and so was available only at night. The front room, the parlor, seemed to us children to be a room of much splendor, but was open for general use only on Sunday evening or on rare occasions when there were parties. The Sunday evening family gathering was the redeeming feature in a day which otherwise we children did not enjoy—chiefly because we were all of us made to wear clean clothes and keep neat. The ornaments of that parlor I remember now, including the gas chandelier decorated with a great quantity of cut-glass prisms. These prisms struck me as possessing peculiar magnificence. One of them fell off one day, and I hastily grabbed it and stowed it away, passing several days of furtive delight in the treasure, a delight always alloyed with fear that I would be found out and convicted of larceny. There was a Swiss wood-carving representing a very big hunter on one side of an exceedingly small mountain, and a herd of chamois, disproportionately small for the hunter and large for the mountain, just across the ridge. This always fascinated us; but there was a small chamois kid for which we felt agonies lest the hunter might come on it and kill it. There was also a Russian moujik drawing a gilt sledge on a piece of malachite. Some one mentioned in my hearing that malachite was a valuable marble. This fixed in my mind that is was valuable exactly as diamonds are valuable. I accepted that moujik as a priceless work of art, and it was not until I was well in middle age that it occurred to me that I was mistaken.

Now and then we children were taken round to our grandfather's house; a big house for the New York of those days, on the corner of Fourteenth Street and Broadway, fronting Union Square. Inside there was a large hall running up to the roof; there was a tessellated black-and-white marble floor, and a circular staircase round the sides of the hall, from the top floor down. We children much admired both the tessellated floor and the circular staircase. I think we were right about the latter, but I am not so sure as to the tessellated floor.

The summers we spent in the country, now at one place, now at another. We children, of course, loved the country beyond anything. We disliked the city. We were always wildly eager to get to the country when spring came, and very sad when in the late fall the family moved back to town. In the country we of course had all kinds of pets—cats, dogs, rabbits, a coon, and a sorrel Shetland pony named General Grant. When my younger sister first heard of the real General Grant, by the way, she was much struck by the coincidence that some one should have given him the same name as the pony. (Thirty years later my own children had *their* pony Grant.) In the country we children ran barefoot much of the time, and the seasons went by in a round of uninterrupted and enthralling pleasures—supervising the haying and harvesting, picking apples, hunting frogs successfully and woodchucks unsuccessfully, gathering hickory-nuts and chestnuts for sale to patient parents, building wigwams in the woods, and sometimes playing Indians in too realistic manner by staining ourselves (and incidentally our clothes) in liberal fashion with poke-cherry juice. Thanksgiving was an appreciated festival, but it in no way came up to Christmas. Christmas was an occasion of literally delirious joy. In the evening we hung up our stockings—or rather the biggest stockings we could borrow from the grown-ups—and before dawn we trooped in to open them while sitting on father's and mother's bed; and the bigger presents were arranged, those for each child on its own table, in the drawing-room, the doors to which were thrown open after breakfast. I never knew any one else have what seemed to me such attractive Christmases, and in the next generation I tried to reproduce them exactly for my own children.

My father, Theodore Roosevelt, was the best man I ever knew. He combined strength and courage with gentleness, tenderness, and great unselfishness. He would not tolerate in us children selfishness or cruelty, idleness, cowardice, or untruthfulness. As we grew older he made us understand that the same standard of clean living was demanded for the boys as for the girls; that what was wrong in a woman could not be right in a man. With great love and patience, and the most understanding sympathy and consideration, he combined insistence on discipline. He never physically punished me but once, but he was the only man of whom I was ever really afraid. I do not mean that it was a wrong fear, for he was entirely just, and we children adored him. We used to wait in the library in the evening until we could hear his key rattling in the latch of the front hall, and then rush out to greet him; and we would troop into his room while he was dressing, to stay there as long as we were permitted, eagerly examining anything which came out of his pockets which could be regarded as an attractive novelty. Every child has fixed in his memory various details which strike it as of grave importance. The trinkets he used to keep in a little box on his dressing-table we children always used to speak of as "treasures." The word, and some of the trinkets themselves, passed on to the next generation. My own children, when small, used to troop into my room while I was dressing, and the gradually accumulating trinkets in the "ditty-box"—the gift of an enlisted man in the navy—always excited rapturous joy. On occasions of solemn festivity each child would receive a trinket for his or her "very own." My children, by the way, enjoyed one pleasure I do not remember enjoying myself. When I came back from riding, the child who brought the bootjack would itself promptly get into the boots, and clump up and down the room with a delightful feeling of kinship with Jack of the seven-league strides.

The punishing incident I have referred to happened when I was four years old. I bit my elder sister's arm. I do not remember biting her arm, but I do remember running down to the yard, perfectly conscious that I had committed a crime. From the yard I went into the kitchen, got some dough from the cook, and crawled under the kitchen table. In a minute or two my father entered from the yard and asked where I was. The warm-hearted Irish cook had a characteristic contempt for "informers," but although she said nothing she compromised between informing and her conscience by casting a look under the table. My father immediately dropped on all fours and darted for me. I feebly heaved the dough at him, and, having the advantage of him because I could stand up under the table, got a fair start for the stairs, but was caught halfway up them. The punishment that ensued fitted the crime, and I hope—and believe—that it did me good.

I never knew any one who got greater joy out of living than did my father, or any one who more whole-heartedly performed every duty; and no one whom I have ever met approached his combination of enjoyment of life and performance of duty. He and my mother were given to a hospitality that at that time was associated more commonly with southern than northern households; and, especially in their later years when they had moved up town, in the neighborhood of Central Park, they kept a charming, open house.

My father worked hard at his business, for he died when he was forty-six, too early to have retired. He was interested in every social reform movement, and he did an immense amount of practical charitable work himself. He was a big, powerful man, with a leonine face, and his heart filled with gentleness for those who needed help or protection, and with the possibility of much wrath against a bully or an oppressor. He was very fond of riding both on the road and across the country, and was also a great whip. He usually drove four-in-hand, or else a spike team, that is, a pair with a third horse in the lead. I do not suppose that such a team exists now. The trap that he drove we always called the high phaëton. The wheels turned under in front. I have it yet. He drove long-tailed horses, harnessed loose in light American harness, so that the whole rig had no possible resemblance to anything that would be seen now. My father always excelled in improving every spare half-hour or three-quarters of an hour, whether for work or enjoyment. Much of his four-in-hand driving was done in the summer afternoons when he would come out on the trait from his business in New York. My mother and one or perhaps two of us children might meet him at the station. I can see him now getting out of the car in his linen duster, jumping into the wagon, and instantly driving off at a rattling pace, the duster sometimes bagging like a balloon. The four-in-hand, as can be gathered from the above description, did not in any way in his eyes represent possible pageantry. He drove it because he liked it. He was always preaching caution to his boys, but in this respect he did not practice his preaching overmuch himself; and, being an excellent whip, he liked to take chances. Generally they came out all right. Occasionally they did not; but he was even better at getting out of a scrape than into it. Once when we were driving into New York late at night the leaders stopped. He flicked them, and the next moment we could dimly make out that they had jumped. I then appeared that the street was closed and that a board had been placed across it, resting on two barrels, but without a lantern. Over this board the leaders had jumped, and there was considerable excitement before we got the board taken off the barrels and resumed our way. When in the city on Thanksgiving or Christmas, my father was very apt to drive my mother and a couple of friends up to the racing park to take lunch. But he was always back in time to go to the dinner at the Newsboys' Lodging-House, and not infrequently also to Miss Sattery's Night School for little Italians. At a very early age we children were taken with him and were required to help. He was a staunch friend of Charles Loring Brace, and was particularly interested in the Newsboys' Lodging-House and in the night schools and in getting the children off the streets and out on farms in the West. When I was President, the Governor of Alaska under me, Governor Brady, was one of these ex-newsboys who had been sent from New York out West by Mr. Brace and my father. My father was greatly interested in the societies to prevent cruelty to children and cruelty to animals. On Sundays he had a mission class. On his way to it he used to drop us children at our Sunday-school in Dr. Adams's Presbyterian Church on Madison Square; I remember hearing my aunt, my mother's sister, saying that when he walked along with us children he always reminded her of Greatheart in Bunyan. Under the spur of his example I taught a mission class myself for three years before going to college and for all four years that I was in college. I do not think I made much of a success of it. But the other day on getting out of a taxi in New York the chauffeur spoke to me and told me that he was one of my old Sunday-school pupils. I remembered him well, and was much pleased to find that he was an ardent Bull Mooser!

My mother, Martha Bulloch, was a sweet, gracious, beautiful Southern woman, a delightful companion and beloved by everybody. She was entirely "unreconstructed" to the day of her death. Her mother, my grandmother, one of the dearest of old ladies, lived with us, and was distinctly overindulgent to us children, being quite unable to harden her heart towards us even when the occasion demanded it. Towards the close of the Civil War, although a very small boy, I grew to have a partial but alert understanding of the fact that the family were not one in their views about that conflict, my father being a strong Lincoln Republican; and once, when I felt that I had been wronged by maternal discipline during the day, I attempted a partial vengeance by praying with loud fervor for the success of the Union arms, when we all came to say our prayers before my mother in the evening. She was not only a most devoted mother, but was also blessed with a strong sense of humor, and she was too much amused to punish me; but I was warned not to repeat the offense, under penalty of my father's being informed—he being the dispenser of serious punishment. Morning prayers were with my father. We used to stand at the foot of the stairs, and when father came down we called out, "I speak for you and the cubby-hole too!" There were three of us young children, and we used to sit with father on the sofa while he conducted morning prayers. The place between father and the arm of the sofa we called the "cubby-hole." The child who got that place we regarded as especially favored both in comfort and somehow or other in rank and title. The two who were left to sit on the much wider expanse of sofa on the other side of father were outsiders for the time being.

My aunt Anna, my mother's sister, lived with us. She was as devoted to us children as was my mother herself, and we were equally devoted to her in return. She taught us our lessons while we were little. She and my mother used to entertain us by the hour with tales of life on the Georgia plantations; of hunting fox, deer, and wildcat; of the long-tailed driving horses, Boone and Crockett, and of the riding horses, one of which was named Buena Vista in a fit of patriotic exaltation during the Mexican War; and of the queer goings-on in the Negro quarters. She knew all the "Br'er Rabbit" stories, and I was brought up on them. One of my uncles, Robert Roosevelt, was much struck with them, and took them down from her dictation, publishing them in *Harper's*, where they fell flat. This was a good many years before a genius arose who in "Uncle Remus" made the stories immortal.

My mother's two brothers, James Dunwoodie Bulloch and Irvine Bulloch, came to visit us shortly after the close of the war. Both came under assumed names, as they were among the Confederates who were at that time exempted from the amnesty. "Uncle Jimmy" Bulloch was a dear old retired sea-captain, utterly unable to "get on" in the worldly sense of that phrase, as valiant and simple and upright a soul as ever lived, a veritable Colonel Newcome. He was an Admiral in the Confederate navy, and was the builder of the famous Confederate war vessel *Alabama*. My uncle Irvine Bulloch was a midshipman on the *Alabama*, and fired the last gun discharged from her batteries in the fight with the *Kearsarge*. Both of these uncles lived in Liverpool after the war.

My uncle Jimmy Bulloch was forgiving and just in reference to the Union forces, and could discuss all phases of the Civil War with entire fairness and generosity. But in English politics he promptly became a Tory of the most ultra-conservative school. Lincoln and Grant he could admire, but he would not listen to anything in favor of Mr. Gladstone. The only occasions on which I ever shook his faith in me were when I would venture meekly to suggest that some of the manifestly preposterous falsehoods about Mr. Gladstone could not be true. My uncle was one of the best men I have ever known, and when I have sometimes been tempted to wonder how good people can believe of me the unjust and impossible things they do believe, I have consoled myself by thinking of Uncle Jimmy Bulloch's perfectly sincere conviction that Gladstone was a man of quite exceptional and nameless infamy in both public and private life.

I was a sickly, delicate boy, suffered much from asthma, and frequently had to be taken away on trips to find a place where I could breathe. One of my memories is of my father walking up and down the room with me in his arms at night when I was a very small person, and of sitting up in bed gasping, with my father and mother trying to help me. I went very little to school. I never went to the public schools, as my own children later did, both at the "Cove School" at Oyster Bay and at the "Ford School" in Washington. For a few months I attended Professor McMullen's school in Twentieth Street near the house where I was born, but most of the time I had tutors. As I have already said, my aunt taught me when I was small. At one time we had a French governess, a loved and valued "mam'selle," in the household.

When I was ten years old I made my first journey to Europe. My birthday was spent in Cologne, and in order to give me a thoroughly "party" feeling I remember that my mother put on full dress for my birthday dinner. I do not think I gained anything from this particular trip abroad. I cordially hated it, as did my younger brother and sister. Practically all the enjoyment we had was in exploring any ruins or mountains when we could get away from our elders, and in playing in the different hotels. Our one desire was to get back to America, and we regarded Europe with the most ignorant chauvinism and contempt. Four years later, however, I made another journey to Europe, and was old enough to enjoy it thoroughly and profit by it.

While still a small boy I began to take an interest in natural history. I remember distinctly the first day that I started on my career as zoölogist. I was walking up Broadway, and as I passed the market to which I used sometimes to be sent before breakfast to get strawberries I suddenly saw a dead seal laid out on a slab of wood. That seal filled me with every possible feeling of romance and adventure. I asked where it was killed, and was informed in the harbor. I had already begun to read some of Mayne Reid's books and other boys' books of adventure, and I felt that this seal brought all these adventures in realistic fashion before me. As long as that seal remained there I haunted the neighborhood of the market day after day. I measured it, and I recall that, not having a tape measure, I had to do my best to get its girth with a folding pocket foot-rule, a difficult undertaking. I carefully made a record of the utterly useless measurements, and at once began to write a natural history of my own, on the strength of that seal. This, and subsequent natural histories, were written down in blank books in simplified spelling, wholly unpremeditated and unscientific. I had vague aspirations of in some way or another owning and preserving that seal, but they never got beyond the purely formless stage. I think, however, I did get the seal's skull, and with two of my cousins promptly started what we ambitiously called the "Roosevelt Museum of Natural

History." The collections were at first kept in my room, until a rebellion on the part of the chambermaid received the approval of the higher authorities of the household and the collection was moved up to a kind of bookcase in the back hall upstairs. It was the ordinary small boy's collection of curios, quite incongruous and entirely valueless except from the standpoint of the boy himself. My father and mother encouraged me warmly in this, as they always did in anything that could give me wholesome pleasure or help to develop me.

The adventure of the seal and the novels of Mayne Reid together strengthened my instinctive interest in natural history. I was too young to understand much of Mayne Reid, excepting the adventure part and the natural history part—these enthralled me. But of course my reading was not wholly confined to natural history. There was very little effort made to compel me to read books, my father and mother having the good sense not to try to get me to read anything I did not like, unless it was in the way of study. I was given the chance to read books that they thought I ought to read, but if I did not like them I was then given some other good book that I did like. There were certain books that were *taboo*. For instance, I was not allowed to read dime novels. I obtained some surreptitiously and did read them, but I do not think that the enjoyment compensated for the feeling of guilt. I was also forbidden to read the only one of Ouida's books which I wished to read—*Under Two Flags*. I did read it, nevertheless, with greedy and fierce hope of coming on something unhealthy; but as a matter of fact all the parts that might have seemed unhealthy to an older person made no impression on me whatever. I simply enjoyed in a rather confused way the general adventures.

I think there ought to be children's books. I think that the child will like grown-up books also, and I do not believe a child's book is really good unless grown-ups get something out of it. For instance, there is a book I did not have when I was a child because it was not written. It is Laura E. Richard's "Nursery Rhymes." My own children loved them dearly, and their mother and I loved them almost equally; the delightfully light-hearted "Man from New Mexico who Lost his Grandmother out in the Snow," the adventures of "The Owl, the Eel, and the Warming-Pan," and the extraordinary genealogy of the kangaroo whose "father was a whale with a feather in his tail who lived in the Greenland sea," while "his mother was a shark who kept very dark in the Gulf of Caribee."

As a small boy I had *Our Young Folks*, which I then firmly believed to be the very best magazine in the world—a belief, I may add, which I have kept to this day unchanged, for I seriously doubt if any magazine for old or young has ever surpassed it. Both my wife and I have the bound volumes of *Our Young Folks* which we preserved from our youth. I have tried to read again the Mayne Reid books which I so dearly loved as a boy, only to find, alas! that it is impossible. But

I really believe that I enjoy going over *Our Young Folks* now nearly as much as ever. *Cast Away in the Cold*, *Grandfather's Struggle for a Homestead*, *The William Henry Letters*, and a dozen others like them were first-class, good healthy stories, interesting in the first place, and in the next place teaching manliness, decency, and good conduct. At the cost of being deemed effeminate, I will add that I greatly liked the girls' stories—*Pussy Willow* and *A Summer in Leslie Goldthwaite's Life*, just as I worshiped *Little Men* and *Little Women* and *An Old-Fashioned Girl*.

This enjoyment of the gentler side of life did not prevent my reveling in such tales of adventure as Ballantyne's stories, or Marryat's *Midshipman Easy*. I suppose everybody has kinks in him, and even as a child there were books which I ought to have liked and did not. For instance, I never cared at all for the first part of *Robinson Crusoe* (and although it is unquestionably the best part, I do not care for it now); whereas the second part, containing the adventures of Robinson Crusoe, with the wolves in the Pyrenees, and out in the Far East, simply fascinated me. What I did like in the first part were the adventures before Crusoe finally reached his island, the fight with the Sallee Rover, and the allusion to the strange beasts at night taking their improbable bath in the ocean. Thanks to being already an embryo zoölogist, I dislike the *Swiss Family Robinson* because of the wholly impossible collection of animals met by that worthy family as they ambled inland from the wreck. Even in poetry it was the relation of adventures that most appealed to me as a boy. At a pretty early age I began to read certain books of poetry, notably Longfellow's poem, *The Saga of King Olaf*, which absorbed me. This introduced me to Scandinavian literature; and I have never lost my interest in and affection for it.

Among my first books was a volume of a hopelessly unscientific kind by Mayne Reid, about mammals, illustrated with pictures no more artistic than but quite as thrilling as those in the typical school geography. When my father found how deeply interested I was in this not very accurate volume, he gave me a little book by J. G. Wood, the English writer of popular books on natural history, and then a larger one of his called *Homes Without Hands*. Both of these were cherished possessions. They were studied eagerly; and they finally descended to my children. The *Homes Without Hands*, by the way, grew to have an added association in connection with a pedagogical failure on my part. In accordance with what I believed was some kind of modern theory of making education interesting and not letting it become a task, I endeavored to teach my eldest small boy one or two of his letters from the title-page. As the letter "H" appeared in the title an unusual number of times, I selected that to begin on, my effort being to keep the small boy interested, not to let him realize that he was learning a lesson, and to convince him that he was merely having a good time. Whether it was the theory or my method of applying it that was defective I do not know, but I certainly absolutely eradicated from his brain any ability to learn what "H" was; and long after he had learned all the other letters of the alphabet in the old-fashioned way, he proved wholly unable to remember "H" under any circumstances.

Quite unknown to myself, I was, while a boy, under a hopeless disadvantage in studying nature. I was very near-sighted, so that the only things I could study were those I ran against or stumbled over. When I was about thirteen I was allowed to take lessons in taxidermy from a Mr. Bell, a tall, clean-shaven, white-haired old gentleman, as straight as an Indian, who had been a companion of Audubon's. He had a musty little shop, somewhat on the order of Mr. Venus's shop in *Our Mutual Friend*, a little shop in which he had done very valuable work for science. This "vocational study," as I suppose it would be called by modern educators, spurred and directed my interest in collecting specimens for mounting and preservation. It was this summer that I got my first gun, and it puzzled me to find that my companions seemed to see things to shoot at which I could not see at all. One day they read aloud an advertisement in huge letters on a distant billboard, and I then realized that something was the matter, for not only was I unable to read the sign but I could not even see the letters. I spoke of this to my father, and soon afterwards got my first pair of spectacles, which literally opened an entirely new world to me. I had no idea how beautiful the world was until I got those spectacles. I had been a clumsy and awkward little boy, and while much of my clumsiness and awkwardness was doubtless due to general characteristics, a good deal of it was due to the fact that I could not see and yet was wholly ignorant that I was not seeing. The recollection of this experience gives me a keen sympathy with those who are trying in our public schools and elsewhere to remove the physical causes of deficiency in children, who are often unjustly blamed for being obstinate or unambitious, or mentally stupid.

This same summer, too, I obtained various new books on mammals and birds, including the publications of Spencer Baird, for instance, and made an industrious book-study of the subject. I did not accomplish much in outdoor study because I did not get spectacles until late in the fall, a short time before I started with the rest of the family for a second trip to Europe. We were living at Dobbs Ferry, on the Hudson. My gun was a breech-loading, pin-fire double-barrel, of French manufacture. It was an excellent gun for a clumsy and often absent-minded boy. There was no spring to open it, and if the mechanism became rusty it could be opened with a brick without serious damage. When the cartridges stuck they could be removed in the same fashion. If they were loaded, however, the result was not always happy, and I tattooed myself with partially unburned grains of powder more than once.

When I was fourteen years old, in the winter of '72 and '73, I visited Europe for the second time, and this trip formed a really useful part of my education. We went to Egypt, journeyed up the Nile, traveled through the Holy Land and part of Syria, visited Greece and Constantinople; and then we children spent the summer in a German family in Dresden. My first real collecting as a student of natural history was done in Egypt during this journey. By this time I had a good working knowledge of American bird life from the superficially scientific standpoint. I had no knowledge of the ornithology of Egypt, but I picked up in Cairo a book by an English clergyman, whose name I have now forgotten, who described a trip up the Nile, and in an appendix to his volume gave an account of his bird collection. I wish I could remember the name of the author now, for I owe that book very much. Without it I should have been collecting entirely in the dark, whereas with its aid I could generally find out what the birds were. My first knowledge of Latin was obtained by learning the scientific names of the birds and mammals which I collected and classified by the aid of such books as this one.

The birds I obtained up the Nile and in Palestine represented merely the usual boy's collection. Some years afterward I gave them, together with the other ornithological specimens I had gathered, to the Smithsonian Institution in Washington, and I think some of them also to the American Museum of Natural History in New York. I am told that the skins are to be found yet in both places and in other public collections. I doubt whether they have my original labels on them. With great pride the directors of the "Roosevelt Museum," consisting of myself and the two cousins aforesaid, had printed a set of Roosevelt Museum labels in pink ink preliminary to what was regarded as my adventurous trip to Egypt. This bird-collecting gave what was really the chief zest to my Nile journey. I was old enough and had read enough to enjoy the temples and the desert scenery and the general feeling of romance; but this in time would have palled if I had not also had the serious work of collecting and preparing my specimens. Doubtless the family had their moments of suffering—especially on one occasion when a well-meaning maid extracted from my taxidermist's outfit the old tooth-brush with which I put on the skins the arsenical soap necessary for their preservation, partially washed it, and left it with the rest of my wash kit for my own personal use. I suppose that all growing boys tend to be grubby; but the ornithological small boy, or indeed the boy with the taste for natural history of any kind, is generally the very grubbiest of all. An added element in my case was the fact that while in Egypt I suddenly started to grow. As there were no tailors up the Nile, when I got back to Cairo I needed a new outfit. But there was one suit of clothes too good to throw away, which we kept for a "change," and which was known as my "Smike suit," because it left my wrists and ankles as bare as those of poor Smike himself.

When we reached Dresden we younger children were left to spend the summer in the house of Herr Minckwitz, a member of either the Municipal or the Saxon Government—I have forgotten which. It was hoped that in this way we would acquire some knowledge of the German language and literature. They were the very kindest family imaginable. I shall never forget the unwearied patience of the two daughters. The father and mother, and a shy, thin, student cousin who was living in the flat, were no less kind. Whenever I could get out into the country I collected specimens industriously and enlivened the household with hedge-hogs and other small beasts and reptiles which persisted in escaping from partially closed bureau drawers. The two sons were fascinating students from the University of Leipsic, both of them belonging to dueling corps, and much scarred in consequence. One, a famous swordsman, was called *Der Rothe Herzog* (the Red Duke), and the other was nicknamed *Herr Nasehorn* (Sir Rhinoceros) because the tip of his nose had been cut off in a duel and sewn on again. I learned a good deal of German here, in spite of myself, and above all I became fascinated with the *Nibelungenlied.* German prose never became really easy to me in the sense that French prose did, but for German poetry I cared as much as for English poetry. Above all, I gained an impression of the German people which I never got over. From that time to this it would have been quite impossible to make me feel that the Germans were really foreigners. The affection, the *Gemüthlichkeit* (a quality which cannot be exactly expressed by any single English word), the capacity for hard work, the sense of duty, the delight in studying literature and science, the pride in the new Germany, the more than kind and friendly interest in three strange children—all these manifestations of the German character and of German family life made a subconscious impression upon me which I did not in the least define at the time, but which is very vivid still forty years later.

When I got back to America, at the age of fifteen, I began serious study to enter Harvard under Mr. Arthur Cutler, who later founded the Cutler School in New York. I could not go to school because I knew so much less than most boys of my age in some subjects and so much more in others. In science and history and geography and in unexpected parts of German and French I was strong, but lamentably weak in Latin and Greek and mathematics. My grandfather had made his summer home in Oyster Bay a number of years before, and my father now made Oyster Bay the summer home of his family also. Along with my college preparatory studies I carried on the work of a practical student of natural history. I worked with greater industry than either intelligence or success, and made very few additions to the sum of human knowledge; but to this day certain obscure ornithological publications may be found in which are recorded such items as, for instance, that on one occasion a fish-crow, and on another an Ipswich sparrow, were obtained by one Theodore Roosevelt, Jr., at Oyster Bay, on the shore of Long Island Sound.

In the fall of 1876 I entered Harvard, graduating in 1880. I thoroughly enjoyed Harvard, and I am sure it did me good, but only in the general effect, for there was very little in my actual studies which helped me in after life. More than one of my own sons have already profited by their friendship with certain of their masters in school or college. I certainly profited by my friendship with one of my tutors, Mr. Cutler; and in Harvard I owed much to the professor of English, Mr. A. S. Hill. Doubtless through my own fault, I saw almost nothing of President Eliot and very little of the professors. I ought to have gained much more than I did gain from writing the themes and forensics. My failure to do so may have been partly due to my taking no interest in the subjects. Before I left Harvard I was already writing one or two chapters of a book I afterwards published on the Naval War of 1812. Those chapters were so dry that they would have made a dictionary seem light reading by comparison. Still, they represented purpose and serious interest on my part, not the perfunctory effort to do well enough to get a certain mark; and corrections of them by a skilled older man would have impressed me and have commanded my respectful attention. But I was not sufficiently developed to make myself take an intelligent interest in some of the subjects assigned me—the character of the Gracchi, for instance. A very clever and studious lad would no doubt have done so, but I personally did not grow up to this particular subject until a good many years later. The frigate and sloop actions between the American and British sea-tigers of 1812 were much more within my grasp. I worked drearily at the Gracchi because I had to; my conscientious and much-to-be-pitied professor dragging me through the theme by main strength, with my feet firmly planted in dull and totally idea-proof resistance.

I had at the time no idea of going into public life, and I never studied elocution or practiced debating. This was a loss to me in one way. In another way it was not. Personally I have not the slightest sympathy with debating contests in which each side is arbitrarily assigned a given proposition and told to maintain it without the least reference to whether those maintaining it believe in it or not. I know that under our system this is necessary for lawyers, but I emphatically disbelieve in it as regards general discussion of political, social, and industrial matters. What we need is to turn out of our colleges young men with ardent convictions on the side of the right; not young men who can make a good argument for either right or wrong as their interest bids them. The present method of carrying on debates on such subjects as "Our Colonial Policy," or "The Need of a Navy," or "The Proper Position of the Courts in Constitutional Questions," encourages precisely the wrong attitude among those who take part in them. There is no effort to instill sincerity and intensity of conviction. On the contrary, the net result is to make the contestants feel that their convictions have nothing to do with their arguments. I am sorry I did not study elocution in college; but I am exceedingly glad that I did not take part in the type of debate in which stress is laid, not upon getting a speaker to think rightly, but on getting him to talk glibly on the side to which he is assigned, without regard either to what his convictions are or to what they ought to be.

I was a reasonably good student in college, standing just within the first tenth of my class, if I remember rightly; although I am not sure whether this means the tenth of the whole number that entered or of those that graduated. I was given a Phi Beta Kappa "key." My chief interests were scientific. When I entered college, I was devoted to out-of-doors natural history, and my ambition was to be a scientific man of the Audubon, or Wilson, or Baird, or Coues type—a man like Hart Merriam, or Frank Chapman, or Hornaday, to-day. My father had from the earliest days instilled into me the knowledge that I was to work and to make my own way in the world, and I had always supposed that this meant that I must enter business. But in my freshman year (he died when I was a sophomore) he told me that if I wished to become a scientific man I could do so. He explained that I must be sure that I really intensely desired to do scientific work, because if I went into it I must make it a serious career; that he had made enough money to enable me to take up such a career and do non-remunerative work of value *if I intended to do the very best work there was in me*; but that I must not dream of taking it up as a dilettante. He also gave me a piece of advice that I have always remembered, namely, that, if I was not going to earn money, I must even things up by not spending it. As he expressed it, I had to keep the fraction constant, and if I was not able to increase the numerator, then I must reduce the denominator. In other words, if I went into a scientific career, I must definitely abandon all thought of the enjoyment that could accompany a money-making career, and must find my pleasures elsewhere.

After this conversation I fully intended to make science my life-work. I did not, for the simple reason that at that time Harvard, and I suppose our other colleges, utterly ignored the possibilities of the faunal naturalist, the outdoor naturalist and observer of nature. They treated biology as purely a science of the laboratory and the microscope, a science whose adherents were to spend their time in the study of minute forms of marine life, or else in section-cutting and the study of the tissues of the higher organisms under the microscope. This attitude was, no doubt, in part due to the fact that in most colleges then there was a not always intelligent copying of what was done in the great German universities. The sound revolt against superficiality of study had been carried to an extreme; thoroughness in minutiæ as the only end of study had been erected into a fetish. There was a total failure to understand the great variety of kinds of work that could be done by naturalists, including what could be done by outdoor naturalists—the kind of work which Hart Merriam and his assistants in the Biological Survey have carried to such a high degree of perfection as regards North American mammals. In the entirely proper desire to be thorough and to avoid slipshod methods, the tendency was to treat as not serious, as unscientific, any kind of work that was not carried on with laborious minuteness in the laboratory. My taste was specialized in a totally different direction, and I had no more desire or ability to be a microscopist and section-cutter than to be a mathematician. Accordingly I abandoned all thought of becoming a scientist. Doubtless this meant that I really did not have the intense devotion to science which I thought I had; for, if I had possessed such devotion, I would have carved out a career for myself somehow without regard to discouragements.

As regards political economy, I was of course while in college taught the *laissez-faire* doctrines—one of them being free trade—then accepted as canonical. Most American boys of my age were taught both by their surroundings and by their studies certain principles which were very valuable from the standpoint of National interest, and certain others which were very much the reverse. The political economists were not especially to blame for this; it was the general attitude of the writers who wrote for us of that generation. Take my beloved *Our Young Folks*, the magazine of which I have already spoken, and which taught me much more than any of my text-books. Everything in this magazine instilled the individual virtues, and the necessity of character as the chief factor in any man's success—a teaching in which I now believe as sincerely as ever, for all the laws that the wit of man can devise will never make a man a worthy citizen unless he has within himself the right stuff, unless he has self-reliance, energy, courage, the power of insisting on his own rights and the sympathy that makes him regardful of the rights of others. All this individual morality I was taught by the books I read at home and the books I studied at Harvard. But there was almost no teaching of the need for collective action, and of the fact that in addition to, not as a substitute for, individual responsibility, there is a collective responsibility. Books such as Herbert Croly's *Promise of American Life* and Walter E. Weyl's *New Democracy* would generally at that time have been treated either as unintelligible or else as pure heresy.

The teaching which I received was genuinely democratic in one way. It was not so democratic in another. I grew into manhood thoroughly imbued with the feeling that a man must be respected for what he made of himself. But I had also, consciously or unconsciously, been taught that socially and industrially pretty much the whole duty of the man lay in thus making the best of himself; that he should be honest in his dealings with others and charitable in the old-fashioned way to the unfortunate; but that it was no part of his business to join with others in trying to make things better for the many by curbing the abnormal and excessive development of individualism in a few. Now I do not mean that this training was by any means all bad. On the contrary, the insistence upon individual responsibility was, and is, and always will be, a prime necessity. Teaching of the kind I absorbed from both my text-books and my surroundings is a healthy anti-scorbutic to the sentimentality which by complacently excusing the individual for all his shortcomings would finally hopelessly weaken the spring of moral purpose. It also keeps alive that virile vigor for the lack of which in the average individual no possible perfection of law or of community action can ever atone. But such teaching, if not corrected by other teaching, means acquiescence in a riot of lawless business individualism which would be quite as destructive to real civilization as the lawless military individualism of the Dark Ages. I left college and entered the big world owing more than I can express to the training I had received, especially in my own home; but with much else also to learn if I were to become really fitted to do my part in the work that lay ahead for the generation of Americans to which I belonged.

THE VIGOR OF LIFE

Excerpt from Roosevelt's Autobiography

Looking back, a man really has a more objective feeling about himself as a child than he has about his father or mother. He feels as if that child were not the present he, individually, but an ancestor; just as much an ancestor as either of his parents. The saying that the child is the father to the man may be taken in a sense almost the reverse of that usually given to it. The child is father to the man in the sense that his individuality is separate from the individuality of the grown-up into which he turns. This is perhaps one reason why a man can speak of his childhood and early youth with a sense of detachment.

Having been a sickly boy, with no natural bodily prowess, and having lived much at home, I was at first quite unable to hold my own when thrown into contact with other boys of rougher antecedents. I was nervous and timid. Yet from reading of the people I admired—ranging from the soldiers of Valley Forge, and Morgan's riflemen, to the heroes of my favorite stories—and from hearing of the feats performed by my Southern forefathers and kinsfolk, and from knowing my father, I felt a great admiration for men who were fearless and who could hold their own in the world, and I had a great desire to be like them. Until I was nearly fourteen I let this desire take no more definite shape than day-dreams. Then an incident happened that did me real good. Having an attack of asthma, I was sent off by myself to Moosehead Lake. On the stage-coach ride thither I encountered a couple of other boys who were about my own age, but very much more competent and also much more mischievous. I have no doubt they were good-hearted boys, but they were boys! They found that I was a foreordained and predestined victim, and industriously proceeded to make life miserable for me. The worst feature was that when I finally tried to fight them I discovered that either one singly could not only handle me with easy contempt, but handle me so as not to hurt me much and yet to prevent my doing any damage whatever in return.

The experience taught me what probably no amount of good advice could have taught me. I made up my mind that I must try to learn so that I would not again be put in such a helpless position; and having become quickly and bitterly conscious that I did not have the natural prowess to hold my own, I decided that I would try to supply its place by training. Accordingly, with my father's hearty approval, I started to learn to box. I was a painfully slow and awkward pupil, and certainly worked two or three years before I made any perceptible improvement whatever. My first boxing-master was John Long, an ex-prize-fighter. I can see his rooms now, with colored pictures of the fights between Tom Hyer and Yankee Sullivan, and Heenan and Sayers, and other great events in the annals of the squared circle. On one occasion, to excite interest among his patrons, he held a series of "championship" matches for the different weights, the prizes being, at least in my own class, pewter mugs of a value, I should suppose, approximating fifty cents. Neither he nor I had any idea that I could do anything, but I was entered in the lightweight contest, in which it happened that I was pitted in succession against a couple of reedy striplings who were even worse than I was. Equally to their surprise and to my own, and to John Long's, I won, and the pewter mug became one of my most prized possessions. I kept it, and alluded to it, and I fear bragged about it, for a number of years, and I only wish I knew where it was now. Years later I read an account of a little man who once in a fifth-rate handicap race won a worthless pewter medal and joyed in it ever after. Well, as soon as I read that story I felt that that little man and I were brothers.

This was, as far as I remember, the only one of my exceedingly rare athletic triumphs which would be worth relating. I did a good deal of boxing and wrestling in Harvard, but never attained to the first rank in either, even at my own weight. Once, in the big contests in the Gym, I got either into the finals or semi-finals, I forgot which; but aside from this the chief part I played was to act as trial horse for some friend or classmate who did have a chance of distinguishing himself in the championship contests.

I was fond of horseback-riding, but I took to it slowly and with difficulty, exactly as with boxing. It was a long time before I became even a respectable rider, and I never got much higher. I mean by this that I never became a first-flight man in the hunting field, and never even approached the bronco-busting class in the West. Any man, if he chooses, can gradually school himself to the requisite nerve, and gradually learn the requisite seat and hands, that will enable him to do respectably across country, or to perform the average work on a ranch. Of my ranch experiences I shall speak later. At intervals after leaving college I hunted on Long Island with the Meadowbrook hounds. Almost the only experience I ever had in this connection that was of any interest was on one occasion when I broke my arm. My purse did not permit me to own expensive horses. On this occasion I was riding an animal, a buggy horse originally, which its owner sold because now and then it insisted on thoughtfully lying down when in harness. It never did this under the saddle; and when he turned it out to grass it would solemnly hop over the fence and get somewhere where it did not belong. The last trait was what converted it into a hunter. It was a natural jumper, although without any speed. On the hunt in question I got along very well until the pace winded my ex-buggy horse, and it turned a somersault over a fence. When I got on it after the fall I found I could not use my left arm. I supposed it was merely a strain. The buggy horse was a sedate animal which I rode with a snaffle. So we pounded along at the tail of the hunt, and I did not appreciate that my arm was broken for three or four fences. Then we came to a big drop, and the jar made the bones slip past one another so as to throw the hand out of position. It did not hurt me at all, and as the horse was as easy to sit as a rocking-chair, I got in at the death.

I think August Belmont was master of the hunt when the above incident occurred. I know he was master on another occasion on which I met with a mild adventure. On one of the hunts when I was out a man was thrown, dragged by one stirrup, and killed. In consequence I bought a pair of safety stirrups, which I used the next time I went out. Within five minutes after the run began I found that the stirrups were so very "safe" that they would not stay in at all. First one went off at one jump, and then the other at another jump—with a fall for me on each occasion. I hated to give up the fun so early, and accordingly finished the run without any stirrups. My horse never went as fast as on that run. Doubtless a first-class horseman can ride as well without stirrups as with them. But I was not a first-class horseman. When anything unexpected happened, I was apt to clasp the solemn buggy horse firmly with my spurred heels, and the result was that he laid himself out to do his best in the way of galloping. He speedily found that, thanks to the snaffle bit, I could not pull him in, so when we came to a down grade he would usually put on steam. Then if there was a fence at the bottom and he checked at all, I was apt to shoot forward, and in such event we went over the fence in a way that reminded me of Leech's picture, in *Punch*, of Mr. Tom Noddy and his mare jumping a fence in the following order: Mr. Tom Noddy, I; his mare, II. However, I got in at the death this time also.

I was fond of walking and climbing. As a lad I used to go to the north woods, in Maine, both in fall and winter. There I made life friends of two men, Will Dow and Bill Sewall: I canoed with them, and tramped through the woods with them, visiting the winter logging camps on snow-shoes. Afterward they were with me in the West. Will Dow is dead. Bill Sewall was collector of customs under me, on the Aroostook border. Except when hunting I never did any mountaineering save for a couple of conventional trips up the Matterhorn and the Jungfrau on one occasion when I was in Switzerland.

I never did much with the shotgun, but I practiced a good deal with the rifle. I had a rifle-range at Sagamore Hill, where I often took friends to shoot. Once or twice when I was visited by parties of released Boer prisoners, after the close of the South African War, they and I held shooting matches together. The best man with both pistol and rifle who ever shot there was Stewart Edward White. Among the many other good men was a stanch friend, Baron Speck von Sternberg, afterwards German Ambassador at Washington during my Presidency. He was a capital shot, rider, and walker, a devoted and most efficient servant of Germany, who had fought with distinction in the Franco-German War when barely more than a boy; he was the hero of the story of "the pig dog" in Archibald Forbes's volume of reminiscences. It was he who first talked over with me the raising of a regiment of horse riflemen from among the ranchmen and cowboys of the plains. When Ambassador, the poor, gallant, tender-hearted fellow was dying of a slow and painful disease, so that he could not play with the rest of us, but the agony of his mortal illness never in the slightest degree interfered with his work. Among the other men who shot and rode and walked with me was Cecil Spring-Rice, who has just been appointed British Ambassador to the United States. He was my groomsman, my best man, when I was married—at St. George's, Hanover Square, which made me feel as if I were living in one of Thackeray's novels.

My own experience as regards marksmanship was much the same as my experience as regards horsemanship. There are men whose eye and hand are so quick and so sure that they achieve a perfection of marksmanship to which no practice will enable ordinary men to attain. There are other men who cannot learn to shoot with any accuracy at all. In between come the mass of men of ordinary abilities who, if they choose resolutely to practice, can by sheer industry and judgment make themselves fair rifle shots. The men who show this requisite industry and judgment can without special difficulty raise themselves to the second class of respectable rifle shots; and it is to this class that I belong. But to have reached this point of marksmanship with the rifle at a target by no means implies ability to hit game in the field, especially dangerous game. All kinds of other qualities, moral and physical, enter into being a good hunter, and especially a good hunter after dangerous game, just as all kinds of other qualities in addition to skill with the rifle enter into being a good soldier. With dangerous game, after a fair degree of efficiency with the rifle has been attained, the prime requisites are cool judgment and that kind of nerve which consists in avoiding being rattled. Any beginner is apt to have "buck fever," and therefore no beginner should go at dangerous game.

Buck fever means a state of intense nervous excitement which may be entirely divorced from timidity. It may affect a man the first time he has to speak to a large audience just as it affects him the first time he sees a buck or goes into battle. What such a man needs is not courage but nerve control, cool-headedness. This he can get only by actual practice. He must, by custom and repeated exercise of self-mastery, get his nerves thoroughly under control. This is largely a matter of habit, in the sense of repeated effort and repeated exercise of will power. If the man has the right stuff in him, his will grows stronger and stronger with each exercise of it—and if he has not the right stuff in him he had better keep clear of dangerous game hunting, or indeed of any other form of sport or work in which there is bodily peril.

After he has achieved the ability to exercise wariness and judgment and the control over his nerves *which will make him shoot as well at the game as at a target*, he can begin his essays at dangerous game hunting, and he will then find that it does not demand such abnormal prowess as the outsider is apt to imagine. A man who can hit a soda-water bottle at the distance of a few yards can brain a lion or a bear or an elephant at that distance, and if he cannot brain it when it charges he can at least bring it to a standstill. All he has to do is to shoot as accurately as he would at a soda-water bottle; and to do this requires nerve, at least as much as it does physical address. Having reached this point, the hunter must not imagine that he is warranted in taking desperate chances. There are degrees in proficiency; and what is a warrantable and legitimate risk for a man to take when he has reached a certain grade of efficiency may be a foolish risk for him to take before he has reached that grade. A man who has reached the degree of proficiency indicated above is quite warranted in walking in at a lion at bay, in an open plain, to, say, within a hundred yards. If the lion has not charged, the man ought at that distance to knock him over and prevent his charging; and if the lion is already charging, the man ought at that distance to be able to stop him. But the amount of prowess which warrants a man in relying on his ability to perform this feat does not by any means justify him in thinking that, for instance, he can crawl after a wounded lion into thick cover. I have known men of indifferent prowess to perform this latter feat successfully, but at least as often they have been unsuccessful, and in these cases the result has been unpleasant. The man who habitually follows wounded lions into thick cover must be a hunter of the highest skill, or he can count with certainty on an ultimate mauling.

The first two or three bucks I ever saw gave me buck fever badly, but after I had gained experience with ordinary game I never had buck fever at all with dangerous game. In my case the overcoming of buck fever was the result of conscious effort and a deliberate determination to overcome it. More happily constituted men never have to make this determined effort at all—which may perhaps show that the average man can profit more from my experiences than he can from those of the exceptional man.

I have shot only five kinds of animals which can fairly be called dangerous game—that is, the lion, elephant, rhinoceros, and buffalo in Africa, and the big grizzly bear a quarter of a century ago in the Rockies. Taking into account not only my own personal experience, but the experiences of many veteran hunters, I regard all the four African animals, but especially the lion, elephant, and buffalo, as much more dangerous than the grizzly. As it happened, however, the only narrow escape I personally ever had was from a grizzly, and in Africa the animal killed closest to me as it was charging was a rhinoceros—all of which goes to show that a man must not generalize too broadly from his own personal experiences. On the whole, I think the lion the most dangerous of all these five animals; that is, I think that, if fairly hunted, there is a larger percentage of hunters killed or mauled for a given number of lions killed than for a given number of any one of the other animals. Yet I personally had no difficulties with lions. I twice killed lions which were at bay and just starting to charge, and I killed a heavy-maned male while it was in full charge. But in each instance I had plenty of leeway, the animal being so far off that even if my bullet had not been fatal I should have had time for a couple more shots. The African buffalo is undoubtedly a dangerous beast, but it happened that the few that I shot did not charge. A bull elephant, a vicious "rogue," which had been killing people in the native villages, did charge before being shot at. My son Kermit and I stopped it at forty yards. Another bull elephant, also unwounded, which charged, nearly got me, as I had just fired both cartridges from my heavy double-barreled rifle in killing the bull I was after—the first wild elephant I had ever seen. The second bull came through the thick brush to my left like a steam plow through a light snowdrift, everything snapping before his rush, and was so near that he could have hit me with his trunk. I slipped past him behind a tree. People have asked me how I felt on this occasion. My answer has always been that I suppose I felt as most men of like experience feel on such occasions. At such a moment a hunter is so very busy that he has no time to get frightened. He wants to get in his cartridges and try another shot.

Rhinoceros are truculent, blustering beasts, much the most stupid of all the dangerous game I know. Generally their attitude is one of mere stupidity and bluff. But on occasions they do charge wickedly, both when wounded and when entirely unprovoked. The first I ever shot I mortally wounded at a few rods' distance, and it charged with the utmost determination, whereat I and my companion both fired, and more by good luck than anything else brought it to the ground just thirteen paces from where we stood. Another rhinoceros may or may not have been meaning to charge me; I have never been certain which. It heard us and came at us through rather thick brush, snorting and tossing its head. I am by no means sure that it had fixedly hostile intentions, and indeed with my present experience I think it likely that if I had not fired it would have flinched at the last moment and either retreated or gone by me. But I am not a rhinoceros mind reader, and its actions were such as to warrant my regarding it as a suspicious character. I stopped it with a couple of bullets, and then followed it up and killed it. The skins of all these animals which I thus killed are in the National Museum at Washington.

But, as I said above, the only narrow escape I met with was not from one of these dangerous African animals, but from a grizzly bear. It was about twenty-four years ago. I had wounded the bear just at sunset, in a wood of lodge-pole pines, and, following him, I wounded him again, as he stood on the other side of a thicket. He then charged through the brush, coming with such speed and with such an irregular gait that, try as I would, I was not able to get the sight of my rifle on the brain-pan, though I hit him very hard with both the remaining barrels of my magazine Winchester. It was in the days of black powder, and the smoke hung. After my last shot, the first thing I saw was the bear's left paw as he struck at me, so close that I made a quick movement to one side. He was, however, practically already dead, and after another jump, and while in the very act of trying to turn to come at me, he collapsed like a shot rabbit.

By the way, I had a most exasperating time trying to bring in his skin. I was alone, traveling on foot with one very docile little mountain mare for a pack pony. The little mare cared nothing for bears or anything else, so there was no difficulty in packing her. But the man without experience can hardly realize the work it was to get that bearskin off the carcass and then to pack it, wet, slippery, and heavy, so that it would ride evenly on the pony. I was at the time fairly well versed in packing with a "diamond hitch," the standby of Rocky Mountain packers in my day; but the diamond hitch is a two-man job; and even working with a "squaw hitch," I got into endless trouble with that wet and slippery bearskin. With infinite labor I would get the skin on the pony and run the ropes over it until to all seeming it was fastened properly. Then off we would start, and after going about a hundred yards I would notice the hide beginning to bulge through between two ropes. I would shift one of them, and then the hide would bulge somewhere else. I would shift the rope again; and still the hide would flow slowly out as if it was lava. The first thing I knew it would come down on one side, and the little mare, with her feet planted resolutely, would wait for me to perform my part by getting that bearskin back in its proper place on the McClellan saddle which I was using as a makeshift pack saddle. The feat of killing the bear the previous day sank into nothing compared with the feat of making the bearskin ride properly as a pack on the following three days.

The reason why I was alone in the mountains on this occasion was because, for the only time in all my experience, I had a difficulty with my guide. He was a crippled old mountain man, with a profound contempt for "tenderfeet," a contempt that in my case was accentuated by the fact that I wore spectacles—which at that day and in that region were usually held to indicate a defective moral character in the wearer. He had never previously acted as guide, or, as he expressed it, "trundled a tenderfoot," and though a good hunter, who showed me much game, our experience together was not happy. He was very rheumatic and liked to lie abed late, so that I usually had to get breakfast, and, in fact, do most of the work around camp. Finally one day he declined to go out with me, saying that he had a pain. When, that afternoon, I got back to camp, I speedily found what the "pain" was. We were traveling very light indeed, I having practically nothing but my buffalo sleeping-bag, my wash kit, and a pair of socks. I had also taken a flask of whisky for emergencies—although, as I found that the emergencies never arose and that tea was better than whisky when a man was cold or done out, I abandoned the practice of taking whisky on hunting trips twenty years ago. When I got back to camp the old fellow was sitting on a tree-trunk, very erect, with his rifle across his knees, and in response to my nod of greeting he merely leered at me. I leaned my rifle against a tree, walked over to where my bed was lying, and, happening to rummage in it for something, I found the whisky flask was empty. I turned on him at once and accused him of having drunk it, to which he merely responded by asking what I was going to do about it. There did not seem much to do, so I said that we would part company—we were only four or five days from a settlement—and I would go in alone, taking one of the horses. He responded by cocking his rifle and saying that I could go alone and be damned to me, but I could not take any horse. I answered "all right," that if I could not I could not, and began to move around to get some flour and salt pork. He was misled by my quietness and by the fact that I had not in any way resented either his actions or his language during the days we had been together, and did not watch me as closely as he ought to have done. He was sitting with the cocked rifle across his knees, the muzzle to the left. My rifle was leaning against a tree near the cooking things to his right. Managing to get near it, I whipped it up and threw the bead on him, calling, "Hands up!" He of course put up his hands, and then said, "Oh, come, I was only joking"; to which I answered, "Well, I am not. Now straighten your legs and let your rifle go to the ground." He remonstrated, saying the rifle would go off, and I told him to let it go off. However, he straightened his legs in such fashion that it came to the ground without a jar. I then made him move back, and picked up the rifle. By this time he was quite sober, and really did not seem angry, looking at me quizzically. He told me that if I would give him back his rifle, he would call it quits and we could go on together. I did not think it best to trust him, so I told him that our hunt was pretty well through, anyway, and that I would go home. There was a blasted pine on the trail, in plain view of the camp, about a mile off, and I told him that I would leave his rifle at that blasted pine if I could see him in camp, but that he must not come after me, for if he did I should assume that it was with hostile intent and would shoot. He said he had no intention of coming after me; and as he was very much crippled with rheumatism, I did not believe he would do so.

Accordingly I took the little mare, with nothing but some flour, bacon, and tea, and my bed-roll, and started off. At the blasted pine I looked round, and as I could see him in camp, I left his rifle there. I then traveled till dark, and that night, for the only time in my experience, I used in camping a trick of the old-time trappers in the Indian days. I did not believe I would be followed, but still it was not possible to be sure, so, after getting supper, while my pony fed round, I left the fire burning, repacked the mare and pushed ahead until it literally became so dark that I could not see. Then I picketed the mare, slept where I was without a fire until the first streak of dawn, and then pushed on for a couple of hours before halting to take breakfast and to let the little mare have a good feed. No plainsman needs to be told that a man should not lie near a fire if there is danger of an enemy creeping up on him, and that above all a man should not put himself in a position where he can be ambushed at dawn. On this second day I lost the trail, and toward nightfall gave up the effort to find it, camped where I was, and went out to shoot a grouse for supper. It was while hunting in vain for a grouse that I came on the bear and killed it as above described.

When I reached the settlement and went into the store, the storekeeper identified me by remarking: "You're the tenderfoot that old Hank was trundling, ain't you?" I admitted that I was. A good many years later, after I had been elected Vice-President, I went on a cougar hunt in northwestern Colorado with Johnny Goff, a famous hunter and mountain man. It was midwinter. I was rather proud of my achievements, and pictured myself as being known to the few settlers in the neighborhood as a successful mountain-lion hunter. I could not help grinning when I found out that they did not even allude to me as the Vice-President-elect, let alone as a hunter, but merely as "Johnny Goff's tourist."

Of course during the years when I was most busy at serious work I could do no hunting, and even my riding was of a decorous kind. But a man whose business is sedentary should get some kind of exercise if he wishes to keep himself in as good physical trim as his brethren who do manual labor. When I worked on a ranch, I needed no form of exercise except my work, but when I worked in an office the case was different. A couple of summers I played polo with some of my neighbors. I shall always believe we played polo in just the right way for middle-aged men with stables of the general utility order. Of course it was polo which was chiefly of interest to ourselves, the only onlookers being the members of our faithful families. My two ponies were the only occupants of my stable except a cart-horse. My wife and I rode and drove them, and they were used for household errands and for the children, and for two afternoons a week they served me as polo ponies. Polo is a good game, infinitely better for vigorous men than tennis or golf or anything of that kind. There is all the fun of football, with the horse thrown in; and if only people would be willing to play it in simple fashion it would be almost as much within their reach as golf. But at Oyster Bay our great and permanent amusements were rowing and sailing; I do not care for the latter, and am fond of the former. I suppose it sounds archaic, but I cannot help thinking that the people with motor boats miss a great deal. If they would only keep to rowboats or canoes, and use oar or paddle themselves, they would get infinitely more benefit than by having their work done for them by gasoline. But I rarely took exercise merely as exercise. Primarily I took it because I liked it. Play should never be allowed to interfere with work; and a life devoted merely to play is, of all forms of existence, the most dismal. But the joy of life is a very good thing, and while work is the essential in it, play also has its place.

When obliged to live in cities, I for a long time found that boxing and wrestling enabled me to get a good deal of exercise in condensed and attractive form. I was reluctantly obliged to abandon both as I grew older. I dropped the wrestling earliest. When I became Governor, the champion middleweight wrestler of America happened to be in Albany, and I got him to come round three or four afternoons a week. Incidentally I may mention that his presence caused me a difficulty with the Comptroller, who refused to audit a bill I put in for a wrestling-mat, explaining that I could have a billiard-table, billiards being recognized as a proper Gubernatorial amusement, but that a wrestling-mat symbolized something unusual and unheard of and could not be permitted. The middleweight champion was of course so much better than I was that he could not only take care of himself but of me too and see that I was not hurt—for wrestling is a much more violent amusement than boxing. But after a couple of months he had to go away, and he left as a substitute a good-humored, stalwart professional oarsman. The oarsman turned out to know very little about wrestling. He could not even take care of himself, not to speak of me. By the end of our second afternoon one of his long ribs had been caved in and two of my short ribs badly damaged, and my left shoulder-blade so nearly shoved out of place that it creaked. He was nearly as pleased as I was when I told him I thought we would "vote the war a failure" and abandon wrestling. After that I took up boxing again. While President I used to box with some of the aides, as well as play single-stick with General Wood. After a few years I had to abandon boxing as well as wrestling, for in one bout a young captain of artillery cross-countered me on the eye, and the blow smashed the little blood-vessels. Fortunately it was my left eye, but the sight has been dim ever since, and if it had been the right eye I should have been entirely unable to shoot.

Accordingly I thought it better to acknowledge that I had become an elderly man and would have to stop boxing. I then took up jiujitsu for a year or two.

When I was in the Legislature and was working very hard, with little chance of getting out of doors, all the exercise I got was boxing and wrestling. A young fellow turned up who was a second-rate prize-fighter, the son of one of my old boxing teachers. For several weeks I had him come round to my rooms in the morning to put on the gloves with me for half an hour. Then he suddenly stopped, and some days later I received a letter of woe from him from the jail. I found that he was by profession a burglar, and merely followed boxing as the amusement of his lighter moments, or when business was slack.

Naturally, being fond of boxing, I grew to know a good many prize-fighters, and to most of those I knew I grew genuinely attached. I have never been able to sympathize with the outcry against prize-fighters. The only objection I have to the prize ring is the crookedness that has attended its commercial development. Outside of this I regard boxing, whether professional or amateur, as a first-class sport, and I do not regard it as brutalizing. Of course matches can be conducted under conditions that make them brutalizing. But this is true of football games and of most other rough and vigorous sports. Most certainly prize-fighting is not half as brutalizing or demoralizing as many forms of big business and of the legal work carried on in connection with big business. Powerful, vigorous men of strong animal development must have some way in which their animal spirits can find vent. When I was Police Commissioner I found (and Jacob Riis will back me up in this) that the establishment of a boxing club in a tough neighborhood always tended to do away with knifing and gun-fighting among the young fellows who would otherwise have been in murderous gangs. Many of these young fellows were not naturally criminals at all, but they had to have some outlet for their activities. In the same way I have always regarded boxing as a first-class sport to encourage in the Young Men's Christian Association. I do not like to see young Christians with shoulders that slope like a champagne bottle. Of course boxing should be encouraged in the army and navy. I was first drawn to two naval chaplains, Fathers Chidwick and Rainey, by finding that each of them had bought half a dozen sets of boxing-gloves and encouraged their crews in boxing.

When I was Police Commissioner, I heartily approved the effort to get boxing clubs started in New York on a clean basis. Later I was reluctantly obliged to come to the conclusion that the prize ring had become hopelessly debased and demoralized, and as Governor I aided in the passage of and signed the bill putting a stop to professional boxing for money. This was because some of the prize-fighters themselves were crooked, while the crowd of hangers-on who attended and made up and profited by the matches had placed the whole business on a basis of commercialism and brutality that was intolerable. I shall always maintain that boxing contests themselves make good, healthy sport. It is idle to compare them with bull-fighting; the torture and death of the wretched horses in bull-fighting is enough of itself to blast the sport, no matter how great the skill and prowess shown by the bull-fighters. Any sport in which the death and torture of animals is made to furnish pleasure to the spectators is debasing. There should always be the opportunity provided in a glove fight or bare-fist fight to stop it when one competitor is hopelessly outclassed or too badly hammered. But the men who take part in these fights are hard as nails, and it is not worth while to feel sentimental about their receiving punishment which as a matter of fact they do not mind. Of course the men who look on ought to be able to stand up with the gloves, or without them, themselves; I have scant use for the type of sportsmanship which consists merely in looking on at the feats of some one else.

Some as good citizens as I know are or were prize-fighters. Take Mike Donovan, of New York. He and his family represent a type of American citizenship of which we have a right to be proud. Mike is a devoted temperance man, and can be relied upon for every movement in the interest of good citizenship. I was first intimately thrown with him when I was Police Commissioner. One evening he and I—both in dress suits—attended a temperance meeting of Catholic societies. It culminated in a lively set-to between myself and a Tammany Senator who was a very good fellow, but whose ideas of temperance differed radically from mine, and, as the event proved, from those of the majority of the meeting. Mike evidently regarded himself as my backer—he was sitting on the platform beside me—and I think felt as pleased and interested as if the set-to had been physical instead of merely verbal. Afterward I grew to know him well both while I was Governor and while I was President, and many a time he came on and boxed with me.

Battling Nelson was another stanch friend, and he and I think alike on most questions of political and industrial life; although he once expressed to me some commiseration because, as President, I did not get anything like the money return for my services that he aggregated during the same term of years in the ring. Bob Fitzsimmons was another good friend of mine. He has never forgotten his early skill as a blacksmith, and among the things that I value and always keep in use is a penholder made by Bob out of a horseshoe, with an inscription saying that it is "Made for and presented to President Theodore Roosevelt by his friend and admirer, Robert Fitzsimmons." I have for a long time had the friendship of John L. Sullivan, than whom in his prime no better man ever stepped into the ring. He is now a Massachusetts farmer. John used occasionally to visit me at the White House, his advent always causing a distinct flutter among the waiting Senators and Congressmen. When I went to Africa he presented me with a gold-mounted rabbit's foot for luck. I carried it through my African trip; and I certainly had good luck.

On one occasion one of my prize-fighting friends called on me at the White House on business. He explained that he wished to see me alone, sat down opposite me, and put a very expensive cigar on the desk, saying, "Have a cigar." I thanked him and said I did not smoke, to which he responded, "Put it in your pocket." He then added, "Take another; put both in your pocket." This I accordingly did. Having thus shown at the outset the necessary formal courtesy, my visitor, an old and valued friend, proceeded to explain that a nephew of his had enlisted in the Marine Corps, but had been absent without leave, and was threatened with dishonorable discharge on the ground of desertion. My visitor, a good citizen and a patriotic American, was stung to the quick at the thought of such an incident occurring in his family, and he explained to me that it must not occur, that there must not be the disgrace to the family, although he would be delighted to have the offender "handled rough" to teach him a needed lesson; he added that he wished I would take him and handle him myself, for he knew that I would see that he "got all that was coming to him." Then a look of pathos came into his eyes, and he explained: "That boy I just cannot understand. He was my sister's favorite son, and I always took a special interest in him myself. I did my best to bring him up the way he ought to go. But there was just nothing to be done with him. His tastes were naturally low. He took to music!" What form this debasing taste for music assumed I did not inquire; and I was able to grant my friend's wish.

While in the White House I always tried to get a couple of hours' exercise in the afternoons—sometimes tennis, more often riding, or else a rough cross-country walk, perhaps down Rock Creek, which was then as wild as a stream in the White Mountains, or on the Virginia side along the Potomac. My companions at tennis or on these rides and walks we gradually grew to style the Tennis Cabinet; and then we extended the term to take in many of my old-time Western friends such as Ben Daniels, Seth Bullock, Luther Kelly, and others who had taken part with me in more serious outdoor adventures than walking and riding for pleasure. Most of the men who were oftenest with me on these trips—men like Major-General Leonard Wood; or Major-General Thomas Henry Barry; or Presley Marion Rixey, Surgeon-General of the Navy; or Robert Bacon, who was afterwards Secretary of State; or James Garfield, who was Secretary of the Interior; or Gifford Pinchot, who was chief of the Forest Service—were better men physically than I was; but I could ride and walk well enough for us all thoroughly to enjoy it. Often, especially in the winters and early springs, we would arrange for a point to point walk, not turning aside for anything—for instance, swimming Rock Creek or even the Potomac if it came in our way. Of course under such circumstances we had to arrange that our return to Washington should be when it was dark, so that our appearance might scandalize no one. On several occasions we thus swam Rock Creek in the early spring when the ice was floating thick upon it. If we swam the Potomac, we usually took off our clothes. I remember one such occasion when the French Ambassador, Jusserand, who was a member of the Tennis Cabinet, was along, and, just as we were about to get in to swim, somebody said, "Mr. Ambassador, Mr. Ambassador, you haven't taken off your gloves," to which he promptly responded, "I think I will leave them on; we might meet ladies!"

We liked Rock Creek for these walks because we could do so much scrambling and climbing along the cliffs; there was almost as much climbing when we walked down the Potomac to Washington from the Virginia end of the Chain Bridge. I would occasionally take some big-game friend from abroad, Selous or St. George Littledale or Captain Radclyffe or Paul Niedicke, on these walks. Once I invited an entire class of officers who were attending lectures at the War College to come on one of these walks; I chose a route which gave us the hardest climbing along the rocks and the deepest crossings of the creek; and my army friends enjoyed it hugely—being the right sort, to a man.

On March 1, 1909, three days before leaving the Presidency, various members of the Tennis Cabinet lunched with me at the White House. "Tennis Cabinet" was an elastic term, and of course many who ought to have been at the lunch were, for one reason or another, away from Washington; but, to make up for this, a goodly number of out-of-town honorary members, so to speak, were present—for instance, Seth Bullock; Luther Kelly, better known as Yellowstone Kelly in the days when he was an army scout against the Sioux; and Abernathy, the wolf-hunter. At the end of the lunch Seth Bullock suddenly reached forward, swept aside a mass of flowers which made a centerpiece on the table, and revealed a bronze cougar by Proctor, which was a parting gift to me. The lunch party and the cougar were then photographed on the lawn.

Some of the younger officers who were my constant companions on these walks and rides pointed out to me the condition of utter physical worthlessness into which certain of the elder ones had permitted themselves to lapse, and the very bad effect this would certainly have if ever the army were called into service. I then looked into the matter for myself, and was really shocked at what I found. Many of the older officers were so unfit physically that their condition would have excited laughter, had it not been so serious, to think that they belonged to the military arm of the Government. A cavalry colonel proved unable to keep his horse at a smart trot for even half a mile, when I visited his post; a Major-General proved afraid even to let his horse canter, when he went on a ride with us; and certain otherwise good men proved as unable to walk as if they had been sedentary brokers. I consulted with men like Major-Generals Wood and Bell, who were themselves of fine physique, with bodies fit to meet any demand. It was late in my administration; and we deemed it best only to make a beginning—experience teaches the most inveterate reformer how hard it is to get a totally non-military nation to accept seriously any military improvement. Accordingly, I merely issued directions that each officer should prove his ability to walk fifty miles, or ride one hundred, in three days.

This is, of course, a test which many a healthy middle-aged woman would be able to meet. But a large portion of the press adopted the view that it was a bit of capricious tyranny on my part; and a considerable number of elderly officers, with desk rather than field experience, intrigued with their friends in Congress to have the order annulled. So one day I took a ride of a little over one hundred miles myself, in company with Surgeon-General Rixey and two other officers. The Virginia roads were frozen and in ruts, and in the afternoon and evening there was a storm of snow and sleet; and when it had been thus experimentally shown, under unfavorable conditions, how easy it was to do in one day the task for which the army officers were allowed three days, all open objection ceased. But some bureau chiefs still did as much underhanded work against the order as they dared, and it was often difficult to reach them. In the Marine Corps Captain Leonard, who had lost an arm at Tientsin, with two of his lieutenants did the fifty miles in one day; for they were vigorous young men, who laughed at the idea of treating a fifty-mile walk as over-fatiguing. Well, the Navy Department officials rebuked them, and made them take the walk over again in three days, on the ground that taking it in one day did not comply with the regulations! This seems unbelievable; but Leonard assures me it is true. He did not inform me at the time, being afraid to "get in wrong" with his permanent superiors. If I had known of the order, short work would have been made of the bureaucrat who issued it.*

* One of our best naval officers sent me the following letter, after the above had appeared:

"I note in your Autobiography now being published in the Outlook that you refer to the reasons which led you to establish a physical test for the Army, and to the action you took (your 100-mile ride) to prevent the test being abolished. Doubtless you did not know the following facts:

"1. The first annual navy test of 50 miles in three days was subsequently reduced to 25 miles in two days in each quarter.

"2. This was further reduced to 10 miles each month, which is the present 'test,' and there is danger lest even this utterly insufficient test be abolished.

"I enclose a copy of a recent letter to the Surgeon General which will show our present deplorable condition and the worse condition into which we are slipping back.

"The original test of 50 miles in three days did a very great deal of good. It decreased by thousands of dollars the money expended on street car fare, and by a much greater sum the amount expended over the bar. It eliminated a number of the wholly unfit; it taught officers to walk; it forced them to learn the care of their feet and that of their men; and it improved their general health and was rapidly forming a taste for physical exercise."

In no country with an army worth calling such is there a chance for a man

The enclosed letter ran in part as follows:

"I am returning under separate cover 'The Soldiers' Foot and the Military Shoe.'

"The book contains knowledge of a practical character that is valuable for the men who HAVE TO MARCH, WHO HAVE SUFFERED FROM FOOT TROUBLES, AND WHO MUST AVOID THEM IN ORDER TO ATTAIN EFFICIENCY.

"The words in capitals express, according to my idea, the gist of the whole matter as regards military men.

"The army officer whose men break down on test gets a black eye. The one whose men show efficiency in this respect gets a bouquet.

"To such men the book is invaluable. There is no danger that they will neglect it. They will actually learn it, for exactly the same reasons that our fellows learn the gunnery instructions—or did learn them before they were withdrawn and burned.

"BUT, I have not been able to interest a single naval officer in this fine book. They will look at the pictures and say it is a good book, but they won't read it. The marine officers, on the contrary, are very much interested, because they have to teach their men to care for their feet and they must know how to care for their own. But the naval officers feel no such necessity, simply because their men do not have to demonstrate their efficiency by practice marches, and they themselves do not have to do a stunt that will show up their own ignorance and inefficiency in the matter.

"For example, some time ago I was talking with some chaps about shoes—the necessity of having them long enough and wide enough, etc., and one of them said: 'I have no use for such shoes, as I never walk except when I have to, and any old shoes do for the 10-mile-a-month stunt,' so there you are!

"When the first test was ordered, Edmonston (Washington shoe man) told me that he sold more real walking shoes to naval officers in three months than he had in the three preceding years. I know three officers who lost both big-toe nails after the first test, and another who walked nine miles in practice with a pair of heavy walking shoes that were too small and was laid up for three days—could not come to the office. I know plenty of men who after the first test had to borrow shoes from larger men until their feet 'went down' to their normal size.

"This test may have been a bit too strenuous for old hearts (of men who had never taken any exercise), but it was excellent as a matter of instruction and training of handling feet—and in an emergency (such as we soon may have in Mexico) sound hearts are not much good if the feet won't stand.

"However, the 25-mile test in two days each quarter answered the same purpose, for the reason that 12.5 miles will produce sore feet with bad shoes, and sore feet and lame muscles even with good shoes, if there has been no practice marching.

"It was the necessity of doing 12.5 MORE MILES ON THE SECOND DAY WITH SORE FEET AND LAME MUSCLES that made 'em sit up and take notice—made 'em practice walking, made 'em avoid street cars, buy proper shoes, show some curiosity about sox and the care of the feet in general.

"All this passed out with the introduction of the last test of 10 miles a month. As one fellow said: 'I can do that in sneakers'—but he couldn't if the second day involved a tramp on the sore feet.

"The point is that whereas formerly officers had to practice walking a bit and give some attention to proper footgear, now they don't have to, and the natural consequence is that they don't do it.

"There are plenty of officers who do not walk any more than is necessary to reach a street car that will carry them from their residences to their offices. Some who have motors do not do so much. They take no exercise. They take cocktails instead and are getting beefy and 'ponchy,' and something should be done to remedy this state of affairs.

"It would not be necessary if service opinion required officers so to order their lives that it would be common knowledge that they were 'hard,' in order to avoid the danger of being selected out.

physically unfit to stay in the service. Our countrymen should understand that every army officer—and every marine officer—ought to be summarily removed from the service unless he is able to undergo far severer tests than those which, as a beginning, I imposed. To follow any other course is to put a premium on slothful incapacity, and to do the gravest wrong to the Nation.

I have mentioned all these experiences, and I could mention scores of others, because out of them grew my philosophy—perhaps they were in part caused by my philosophy—of bodily vigor as a method of getting that vigor of soul without which vigor of the body counts for nothing. The dweller in cities has less chance than the dweller in the country to keep his body sound and vigorous. But he can do so, if only he will take the trouble. Any young lawyer, shopkeeper, or clerk, or shop-assistant can keep himself in good condition if he tries. Some of the best men who have ever served under me in the National Guard and in my regiment were former clerks or floor-walkers. Why, Johnny Hayes, the Marathon victor, and at one time world champion, one of my valued friends and supporters, was a floor-walker in Bloomingdale's big department store. Surely with Johnny Hayes as an example, any young man in a city can hope to make his body all that a vigorous man's body should be.

I once made a speech to which I gave the title *The Strenuous Life*. Afterwards I published a volume of essays with this for a title. There were two translations of it which always especially pleased me. One was by a Japanese officer who knew English well, and who had carried the essay all through the Manchurian campaign, and later translated it for the benefit of his countrymen. The other was by an Italian lady, whose brother, an officer in the Italian army who had died on duty in a foreign land, had also greatly liked the article and carried it round with him. In translating the title the lady rendered it in Italian as *Vigor di Vita*. I thought this

---

"We have no such service opinion, and it is not in process of formation. On the contrary, it is known that the 'Principal Dignitaries' unanimously advised the Secretary to abandon all physical tests. He, a civilian, was wise enough not to take the advice.

"I would like to see a test established that would oblige officers to take sufficient exercise to pass it without inconvenience. For the reasons given above, 20 miles in two days every other month would do the business, while 10 miles each month does not touch it, simply because nobody has to walk on 'next day' feet. As for the proposed test of so many hours 'exercise' a week, the flat foots of the pendulous belly muscles are delighted. They are looking into the question of pedometers, and will hang one of these on their wheezy chests and let it count every shuffling step they take out of doors.

"If we had an adequate test throughout 20 years, there would at the end of that time be few if any sacks of blubber at the upper end of the list; and service opinion against that sort of thing would be established."

These tests were kept during my administration. They were afterwards abandoned; not through perversity or viciousness; but through weakness, and inability to understand the need of preparedness in advance, if the emergencies of war are to be properly met, when, or if, they arrive.

translation a great improvement on the original, and have always wished that I had myself used "The Vigor of Life" as a heading to indicate what I was trying to preach, instead of the heading I actually did use.

There are two kinds of success, or rather two kinds of ability displayed in the achievement of success. There is, first, the success either in big things or small things which comes to the man who has in him the natural power to do what no one else can do, and what no amount of training, no perseverance or will power, will enable any ordinary man to do. This success, of course, like every other kind of success, may be on a very big scale or on a small scale. The quality which the man possesses may be that which enables him to run a hundred yards in nine and three-fifths seconds, or to play ten separate games of chess at the same time blindfolded, or to add five columns of figures at once without effort, or to write the *Ode to a Grecian Urn*, or to deliver the Gettysburg speech, or to show the ability of Frederick at Leuthen or Nelson at Trafalgar. No amount of training of body or mind would enable any good ordinary man to perform any one of these feats. Of course the proper performance of each implies much previous study or training, but in no one of them is success to be attained save by the altogether exceptional man who has in him the something additional which the ordinary man does not have.

This is the most striking kind of success, and it can be attained only by the man who has in him the quality which separates him in kind no less than in degree from his fellows. But much the commoner type of success in every walk of life and in every species of effort is that which comes to the man who differs from his fellows not by the kind of quality which he possesses but by the degree of development which he has given that quality. This kind of success is open to a large number of persons, if only they seriously determine to achieve it. It is the kind of success which is open to the average man of sound body and fair mind, who has no remarkable mental or physical attributes, but who gets just as much as possible in the way of work out of the aptitudes that he does possess. It is the only kind of success that is open to most of us. Yet some of the greatest successes in history have been those of this second class—when I call it second class I am not running it down in the least, I am merely pointing out that it differs in kind from the first class. To the average man it is probably more useful to study this second type of success than to study the first. From the study of the first he can learn inspiration, he can get uplift and lofty enthusiasm. From the study of the second he can, if he chooses, find out how to win a similar success himself.

I need hardly say that all the successes I have ever won have been of the second type. I never won anything without hard labor and the exercise of my best judgment and careful planning and working long in advance. Having been a rather sickly and awkward boy, I was as a young man at first both nervous and distrustful of my own prowess. I had to train myself painfully and laboriously not merely as regards my body but as regards my soul and spirit.

When a boy I read a passage in one of Marryat's books which always impressed me. In this passage the captain of some small British man-of-war is explaining to the hero how to acquire the quality of fearlessness. He says that at the outset almost every man is frightened when he goes into action, but that the course to follow is for the man to keep such a grip on himself that he can act just as if he was not frightened. After this is kept up long enough it changes from pretense to reality, and the man does in very fact become fearless by sheer dint of practicing fearlessness when he does not feel it. (I am using my own language, not Marryat's.) This was the theory upon which I went. There were all kinds of things of which I was afraid at first, ranging from grizzly bears to "mean" horses and gun-fighters; but by acting as if I was not afraid I gradually ceased to be afraid. Most men can have the same experience if they choose. They will first learn to bear themselves well in trials which they anticipate and which they school themselves in advance to meet. After a while the habit will grow on them, and they will behave well in sudden and unexpected emergencies which come upon them unawares.

It is of course much pleasanter if one is naturally fearless, and I envy and respect the men who are naturally fearless. But it is a good thing to remember that the man who does not enjoy this advantage can nevertheless stand beside the man who does, and can do his duty with the like efficiency, *if he chooses to*. Of course he must not let his desire take the form merely of a day-dream. Let him dream about being a fearless man, and the more he dreams the better he will be, always provided he does his best to realize the dream in practice. He can do his part honorably and well provided only he sets fearlessness before himself as an ideal, schools himself to think of danger merely as something to be faced and overcome, and regards life itself as he should regard it, not as something to be thrown away, but as a pawn to be promptly hazarded whenever the hazard is warranted by the larger interests of the great game in which we are all engaged.

PROFESSIONALISM IN SPORTS

Article published in the North American Review
August, 1890

It is hardly necessary at the present day to enter a plea for athletic exercise and manly outdoor sports. During the last twenty-five years there has been a wonderful growth of interest in and appreciation of healthy muscular amusements; and this growth can best be promoted by stimulating, within proper bounds, the spirit of rivalry on which all our games are based. The effect upon the physique of the sedentary classes, especially in the towns and cities, has already been very marked. We are much less liable than we were to reproaches on the score of our national ill health, of the bad constitutions of our men, and of the fragility and early decay of our women.

There are still plenty of people who look down on, as of little moment, the proper development of the body; but the men of good sense sympathize as little with these as they do with the even more noxious extremists who regard physical development as an end instead of a means. As a nation, we have many tremendous problems to work out, and we need to bring every ounce of vital power possible to their solution. No people has ever yet done great and lasting work if its physical type was infirm and weak. Goodness and strength must go hand in hand if the Republic is to be preserved. The good man who is ready and able to strike a blow for the right, and to put down evil with the strong arm, is the citizen who deserves our most hearty respect. There is a certain tendency in the civilization of our time to underestimate or overlook the need of the virile, masterful qualities of the heart and mind which have built up and alone can maintain and defend this very civilization, and which generally go hand in hand with good health and the capacity to get the utmost possible use out of the body. There is no better way of counteracting this tendency than by encouraging bodily exercise, and especially the sports which develop such qualities as courage, resolution, and endurance.

The best of all sports for this purpose are those which follow the Macedonian rather than the Greek model: big-game hunting, mountaineering, the chase with horse and hound, all wilderness life with all its keen, hardy pleasures. The hunter and mountaineer lead healthier lives—in time of need they would make better soldiers—than the trained athlete. Nor need these pleasures be confined to the rich. The trouble with our men of small means is quite as often that they do not know how to enjoy pleasures lying at their doors as that they cannot afford them. From New York to Minneapolis, from Boston to San Francisco, there is no large city from which it is impossible to reach a tract of perfectly wild, wooded or mountainous land within forty-eight hours; and any two young men who can get a months' holiday in August or September cannot use it to better advantage than by tramping on foot, pack on back, over such a tract. Let them go alone; a season or two will teach them much woodcraft, and will enormously increase their stock of health, hardihood, and self-reliance. If one carries a light rifle or fowling-piece, and the other a fishing rod, they will soon learn to help fill out their own bill of fare. Of course they must expect to find the life pretty hard, and filled with disappointments at first; but the cost will be very trifling, and if they have courage, their reward is sure to come.

However, most of our people, whether from lack of means, time, or inclination, do not take to feats of this kind, and must get their fun and exercise in athletics proper. The years of late boyhood and early manhood—say from twelve or fourteen to twenty-eight or thirty, and often until much later—are those in which athletic sports prove not only most attractive, but also most beneficial to the individual and the race. In college—and in most of the schools which are preparatory for college—rowing, foot-ball, base-ball, running, jumping, sparring, and the like have assumed a constantly increasing prominence. Nor is this in any way a matter for regret. Of course any good is accompanied by some evil; and a small number of college boys, who would probably turn out badly anyhow, neglect everything for their sports, and so become of little use to themselves or anyone else. But as a whole college life has been greatly the gainer by the change. Only a small proportion of college boys are going to become real students and do original work in literature, science, or art; and these are certain to study their best in any event. The others are going into business or law or some kindred occupation; and these, of course, can study but little that will be directly of use to them in after-life. The college education of such men should be largely devoted to making them good citizens, and able to hold their own in the world; and character is far more important than intellect in making a man a good citizen or successful in his calling meaning by character not only such qualities as honesty and truthfulness, but courage, perseverance, and self-reliance.

Now, athletic sports, if followed properly, and not elevated into a fetish, are admirable for developing character, besides bestowing on the participants an invaluable fund of health and strength. In each of the larger colleges there are from fifty to a hundred men who, on the various class and college crews and ball teams, or in the track and gymnasium games, compete for the different championships; and for every one such man who actually competes there are five or ten who take part in the practice games, train more or less, and get a great deal of benefit from the work. The careful system of measurements which have been taken at Harvard shows a marked improvement in the physique of the men even during the last ten years; and—what is more important—this shows that this improvement is, if anything, more marked in the case of the average man than in that of the picked champions.

The colleges contain but a small proportion of the men interested in amateur athletics, as can be seen by the immense number of ball clubs, rowing clubs, polo clubs, hunt clubs, bicycle clubs, snow-shoe clubs, lacrosse clubs, and athletic clubs proper which are to be found scattered among our cities and towns. Almost any man of sedentary life who wishes to get exercise enough to keep him in vigorous health can readily do so at one of these clubs; and an increasing proportion of our young men are finding this out and acting accordingly. More than one of our most famous athletes originally took to athletics for his health; and, on the other hand, be it remembered always that the sports which prove most beneficial bodily to a man are those which interest and amuse him. If he belongs to a rowing club or baseball nine, the eagerness and excitement of a contest with a rival association spur him on to keep his body in good condition; and, as with the college athletes, there are scores of outsiders, whom these championship contests attract, and whose love for athletics is increased thereby, for every individual contestant who directly participates in them. It is needless to say that under the head of manly sports I do not include pigeon-shooting; and still less rabbit-coursing, or any other game where the man does nothing but look on.

Already this awakening of interest in manly sports, this proper care of the body, have had a good effect upon our young men; but there are, of course, accompanying dangers in any such movement. With very few exceptions the man who makes some athletic pursuit his main business, instead of turning to it as a health-giving pastime, ceases to be a particularly useful citizen. Of course I do not refer to the men who act as trainers and instructors at the different colleges and clubs; these perform a most useful and honorable function, and among them several could be named who have rendered as high service as any men in the community.

But the amateur athlete who thinks of nothing but athletics, and makes it the serious business of his life, becomes a bore, if nothing worse. A young man who has broken a running or jumping record, who has stroked a winning club crew, or played on his college nine or eleven, has a distinct claim to our respect; but if, when middle-aged, he has still done nothing more in the world, he forfeits even this claim which he originally had.

It is so in an even more marked degree with the "professional" athlete. In America, the difference between amateurs and professionals is in one way almost the reverse of what it is in England, and accords better with the ways of life of our democratic community. In England, the average professional is a man who works for his living, and the average amateur is one who does not; whereas with us the amateur usually is, and always ought to be, a man who, like other American citizens, works hard at some regular calling—it matters not what, so long as it is respectable—while the professional is very apt to be a gentleman of more or less elegant leisure, aside from his special pursuit.

The mere statement of the difference is enough to show that the amateur, and not the professional, is the desirable citizen, the man who should be encouraged. Our object is to get as many of our people as possible to take part in manly, healthy, vigorous pastimes, which will benefit the whole nation; it is not to produce a limited class of athletes who shall make it the business of their lives to do battle with one another for the popular amusement. Most masterful nations have shown a strong taste for manly sports. In the old days, when we ourselves were still a people of backwoodsmen, at every merrymaking there were sure to be trials of skill and strength, at running, wrestling, and rifle shooting, among the young men. We should encourage by every method the spirit which makes such trials popular; it is a very excellent revival of old-time American ways. But the existence of a caste of gladiators in the midst of a population which does not itself participate in any manly sports is usually, as it was at Rome, a symptom of national decadence.

The Romans who, when the stern and simple strength of Rome was departing, flocked to the gladiatorial shows, were influenced only by a ferocious craving for bloody excitement; not by any sympathy with men of stout heart and tough sinew. So it is, to a lesser extent, today. In baseball alone, the professional teams, from a number of causes, have preserved a fairly close connection with non-professional players, and have done good work in popularizing a most admirable and characteristic American game; but even here the outlook is now less favorable, and, aside from this one pastime, professionalism is the curse of many an athletic sport, and the chief obstacle to its healthy development. Professional rowing is under a dark cloud of suspicion because of the crooked practices which have disgraced it. Horse-racing is certainly not in an ideal condition. A prize fight is simply brutal and degrading. The people who attend it, and make a hero of the prize fighter, are—excepting boys who go for fun and don't know any better—to a very great extent, men who hover on the border-line of criminality; and those who are not are speedily brutalized, and are never rendered more manly. They form as ignoble a body as do the kindred frequenters of rat-pit and cock-pit. The prize fighter and his fellow professional athletes of the same ilk are, together with their patrons in every rank of life, the very worst foes with whom the cause of general athletic development has to contend.

THE STRENUOUS LIFE

Speech given before the Hamilton Club, Chicago, Illinois
April 10, 1899

Gentlemen: In speaking to you, men of the greatest city of the West, men of the State which gave to the country Lincoln and Grant, men who pre-eminently and distinctly embody all that is most American in the American character, I wish to preach, not the doctrine of ignoble ease, but the doctrine of the strenuous life, the life of toil and effort, of labor and strife; to preach that highest form of success which comes, not to the man who desires mere easy peace, but to the man who does not shrink from danger, from hardship, or from bitter toil, and who out of these wins the splendid ultimate triumph.

A life of slothful ease, a life of that peace which springs merely from lack either of desire or of power to strive after great things, is as little worthy of a nation as of an individual. I ask only that what every self-respecting American demands from himself and from his sons shall be demanded of the American nation as a whole. Who among you would teach your boys that ease, that peace, is to be the first consideration in their eyes—to be the ultimate goal after which they strive? You men of Chicago have made this city great, you men of Illinois have done your share, and more than your share, in making America great, because you neither preach nor practice such a doctrine. You work yourselves, and you bring up your sons to work. If you are rich and worth your salt, you will teach your sons that though they may have leisure, it is not to be spent in idleness; for wisely used leisure merely means that those who possess it, being free from the necessity of working for their livelihood, are all bound to carry on some kind of non-remunerative work in science, in letters, in art, in exploration, in historical research—work of this type we most need in this country, the successful carrying out of which reflects most honor upon the nation. We do not admire the man of timid peace. We admire the man who embodies victorious effort; the man who never wrongs his neighbor, who is prompt to help a friend, but who has those virile qualities necessary to win in the stern strife of actual life. It is hard to fail, but it is worse to never have tried to succeed. In this life we get nothing save by effort. Freedom from effort in the present merely means that there has been some stored up effort in the past. A man can be freed from the necessity of work only by the fact that he or his fathers before him have worked to good purpose. If the freedom thus purchased is used aright, and the man still does actual work, though of a different kind, whether as a writer or as a general, whether in the field of politics or in the field of exploration and adventure, he shows he deserves his good fortune. But if he treats this period of freedom from the need of actual labor as a period , not of preparation, but of mere enjoyment, even though perhaps not of the vicious enjoyment, he shows that he is simply a cumberer of the earth's surface, and he surely unfits himself to hold his own with his fellows if the need to do so should again arise. A mere life of ease is not in the end a very satisfactory life, and, above all, it is a life which ultimately unfits those who follow it for serious work in the world.

In the last analysis a healthy state can exist only when the men and women who make it up can lead clean, vigorous, healthy lives; when the children are so trained that they shall endeavor, not to shirk difficulties, but to overcome them; not to seek ease, but to know how to rest triumph from toil and risk. The man must be glad to do a man's work, to dare and endure and to labor; to keep himself, and those dependent on him. The woman must be the housewife, the helpmeet of the homemaker, the wise and fearless mother of many healthy children. In one of Daudet's powerful and melancholy books he speaks of "the fear of maternity, the haunting terror of the young wife of the present day." When such words can be truthfully written of a nation, that nation is rotten to the heart's core. When men fear work or fear of righteous war, when women fear motherhood, they tremble on the brink of doom; and well it is they should vanish from the earth, where they are fit subjects for the scorn of all men and women who are themselves strong and brave and high-minded.

As it is with the individual, so it is with the nation. It is a base untruth to say that happy is the nation that has no history. Thrice happy is the nation that has a glorious history. Far better it is to dare mighty things, to win glorious triumphs, even though checkered by failure, than to take rank with those poor spirits who neither enjoy much nor suffer much, because they live in the gray twilight that knows not victory nor defeat. If, in 1861, the men who loved the Union had believed that peace was the end of all things, and war and strife the worst of all things, and had acted upon their belief, we would have saved hundreds of thousands of lives, we would have saved hundreds of millions of dollars. Moreover, besides saving all the blood and treasure we then lavished, we would have prevented the heartbreak of many women, the dissolution of many homes, and we would have spared the country those months of doom and shame when it seemed as if our armies marched only to defeat. We could have avoided all this suffering simply by shrinking from strife. And if we had thus avoided it, we would have shown that we were weaklings, and that we were unfit to stand among the great nations of the earth. Thank God for the iron in the blood of our fathers, the men who upheld the wisdom of Lincoln, and bore the sword or rifle in the armies of Grant! Let us, the children of the men who proved themselves equal to the mighty days, let us, the children of the men who carried the great Civil War to a triumphant conclusion, praise the God of our fathers that the ignoble counsels of peace were rejected; that the suffering and loss, the blackness of sorrow and despair, were unflinchingly faced, and the years of strife endured; for in the end the slave was freed, the Union restored, and the mighty American republic placed once more as a helmeted queen among nations.

We of this generation do not have to face a task such as that our fathers faced, but we have our tasks, and woe to us if we fail to perform them! We cannot, if we would, play the part of China, and be content to rot by inches in ignoble ease within our borders, taking no interest in what goes on beyond them, sunk in scrambling commercialism; heedless of higher life, the life of aspiration, of toil and risk, busying ourselves only with the wants of our bodies for the day, until suddenly we should find, beyond a shadow of question, what China has already found, that in this world the nation that has trained itself into a career of unwarlike and isolated ease is bound, in the end, to go down before other nations which have not lost the manly and adventurous qualities. If we are to be a really great people, we must strive in good faith to play a great part in the world. We cannot avoid meeting great issues. All that we can determine for ourselves is whether we shall meet them well or ill. In 1898 we could not help being brought face to face with the problem of war with Spain. All we could decide was whether we should shrink like cowards from the contest, or enter into it as beseemed a brave and high-spirited people; and, once in, whether failure or success shall crown our banners. So it is now.

We cannot avoid the responsibilities that confront us in Hawaii, Cuba, Porto Rico, and the Phillippines. All we can decide is whether we shall meet them in a way that will redound to the national credit, of whether we shall make of our dealings with these new problems a dark and shameful page in our history. To refuse to deal with them at all merely amounts to dealing with them badly. We have a given problem to solve. If we undertake the solution, there is, of course, always danger that we may not solve it aright; but to refuse to undertake the solution simply renders it certain that we cannot possibly solve it aright. The timid man, the lazy man, the man who distrusts his country, the over-civilized man, who has lost the great fighting, the masterful values, the ignorant man, and the man of dull mind, whose soul is incapable of feeling the mighty lift that thrills "stern men with empires in their brains"—all these, of course, shrink from seeing the nation undertake its new duties; shrink from seeing us build a navy and an army adequate to our needs; shrink from seeing us do our share of the world's work, by bringing order out of the chaos in the great, fair tropic islands from which the valor of our soldiers and sailors has driven the Spanish flag. These are the men who fear the strenuous life, who fear the only national life which is really worth leading. They believe in that cloistered life which saps the hearty virtues in a nation, as it saps them in the individual; or else they are wedded to that base spirit of grain and greed which recognizes commercialism the be-all and end-all of national life, instead of realizing that, though an indispensable element, it is, after all, but one of the many elements that go to make up true national greatness. No country can long endure if its foundations are not laid deep in the material prosperity which comes from thrift, from business energy and enterprise, from hard, unsparing efforts in the fields of industrial activity; but neither was any nation ever yet truly great if it relied upon material prosperity alone. All honor must be paid to the architects of our material prosperity, to the great captains of industry who have built our factories and our railroads, to the strong men who toil for wealth with brain or hand; for great is the debt of the nation to these and their kind. But our debt is yet greater to the men whose highest type is to be found in a statesman like Lincoln, a soldier like Grant. They showed by their lives that they recognized the law of work, the law of strife; they toiled to win a competence for themselves and those dependent upon them; but they recognized that there were yet other and even loftier duties—duties to the nation and duties to the race.

We cannot sit huddled within our own borders and avow ourselves merely an assemblage of well-to-do hucksters who care nothing for what happens beyond. Such a policy would defeat even its own end; for as the nations grow to have ever wider and wider interests, and are brought into closer and closer contact, if we are to hold our own in the struggle for naval and commercial supremacy, we must build up our power without our own borders. We must build the Isthmian Canal, and we must grasp the points of vantage which will enable us to have our say in deciding the destiny of the oceans of the East and the West.

So much for the commercial side. From the standpoint of international honor the argument is even stronger. The guns that thundered off Manila and Santiago left us echoes of glory, but they also left us a legacy of duty. If we drove out a medieval tyranny only to make room for savage anarchy, we had better not begun the task at all. It is worse than idle to say that we have no duty to perform, and can leave to their fates the islands we have conquered. Such a course would be a course of infamy. It would be followed at once by utter chaos in the wretched islands themselves. Some stronger, manlier power would have to step in and do the work, and we would have shown ourselves weaklings, unable to carry to successful completion the labors that great and high-spirited nations are eager to undertake.

The work must be done; we cannot escape our responsibility; and if we are worth our salt, we shall be glad of the chance to do the work—glad of the chance to show ourselves equal to one of the great tasks set modern civilization. But let us not deceive ourselves as to the importance of the task. Let us not be mislead by the vainglory into underestimating the strain it will put on our powers. Above all, let us, as we value our own self-respect, face the responsibilities with proper seriousness, courage and high resolve. We must demand the highest order of integrity and ability in our public men who are to grapple with these new problems. We must hold to a rigid accountability those public servants who show unfaithfulness to the interests of the nation or the inability to rise to the high level of the new demands upon our strength and our resources.

Of course we must remember not to judge any public servant by any one act, and especially should we beware of attacking the men who are merely the occasions and not the causes of disaster. Let me illustrate what I mean by the army and the navy. If twenty years ago we had gone to war, we should have the navy as absolutely unprepared as the army. At that time our ships could not have encountered with success the fleets of Spain any more than nowadays we can put untrained soldiers, no matter how brave, who are armed with archaic black-powder weapons, against well-drilled regulars armed with the highest type of modern repeating rifle. But in the early eighties the attention of the nation became directed to our naval deeds. Congress most wisely made a series of appropriations to build up a new navy, and under a succession of able and patriotic secretaries, of both political parties, the navy was gradually built up, until its material became equal to its splendid personnel, with the result that in the summer of 1898 it leaped to its proper place as one of the most brilliant and formidable fighting navies in the entire world. We rightly pay all honor to the men controlling the navy at the time it won these great deeds, honor to Secretary Long and Admiral Dewey, to the captains who handled the ships in action, to the daring lieutenants who braved death in the smaller craft, and to the heads of the bureaus at Washington who saw that the ships were so commanded, so armed, so equipped, so well engined, as to insure the best results. But let us also keep ever in mind that all of this would not have availed if it had not been for the wisdom of the men who during the preceding fifteen years had built up the navy. Keep in mind the secretaries of the navy during those years; keep in mind the senators and congressmen who by their votes gave the money necessary to build and to armor the ships, to construct the great guns, and to train the crews; remember also those who actually did build the ships, the armor, and the guns; and remember the admirals and captains who handled battle-ship, cruiser, and torpedo-boat on the high seas, alone and in squadrons, developing the seamanship, the gunnery, and the power of acting together, which their successors utilized so gloriously at Manila and off Santiago. And, gentleman, remember the converse, too. Remember that justice has two sides. Be just to those who built up the navy, and, for the sake of the future of the country, keep in mind those who opposed its building up. Read the *Congressional Record*. Find out the senators and congressmen who opposed the grants for building the new ships; who opposed the purchase of armor, without which the ships were worthless; who opposed any adequate maintenance for the Navy Department, and strove to cut down the number of men necessary to man our fleets. The men who did these things were one and all working to bring disaster on the country. They have no share in the glory of Manila, in the honor of Santiago. They have no cause to feel proud of the valor of our sea-captains, of the renown of our flag. Their motives may or may not have been good, but their acts were heavily fraught with evil. They did ill for the national honor, and we won in spite of their sinister opposition.

Now, apply all this to our public men of to-day. Our army never has been built up as it should be built up. I shall not discuss with an audience this puerile suggestion that a nation of seventy millions of freemen is in danger of losing its liberties from the existence of an army of one hundred thousand men, three fourths of whom will be employed in foreign islands, in certain coast fortresses, and on Indian reservations. No man of good sense and stout heart can such a proposition seriously. If we are such weaklings as the proposition implies, then we are unworthy of freedom in any event. To no body of men in the United States is the country so much indebted as to the splendid officers and enlisted men of the regular army and navy. There is no body from which the country has less to fear, and none of which it should be prouder, none which it should be more anxious to upbuild.

Our army needs complete reorganization—not merely enlarging—and the reorganization can only come as a result of legislation. A proper general staff should be established, and the positions of ordnance, commissary, and quartermaster officers should be filled by detail from the line. Above all, the army must be given the chance to exercise in large bodies. Never again should we see, as we saw in the Spanish War, major-generals in command of divisions who had never before commanded three companies together in the field. Yet, incredible to relate, Congress has shown a queer inability to learn some of the lessons of war. There were large bodies of men in both branches who opposed the declaration of war, who opposed the ratification of peace, who opposed the upbuilding of the army, and who even opposed the purchase of the armor at a reasonable price for the battle-ships and cruisers, thereby putting an absolute stop to the building of any new fighting ships for the navy. If, during the years to come, any disaster should befall our arms, afloat or ashore, and thereby should shame the United States, remember the blame will lie upon the men whose names appear on the roll-calls of Congress on the wrong side of these great questions. On them will lie the burden of the loss of our soldiers and sailors, of any dishonor to the flag; and upon you and the people of this country will lie the blame if you do not repudiate, in no unmistakable way, what these men have done. The blame will not rest upon the untrained commander of the untried troops, upon the civil officers of a department the organization of which has been left utterly inadequate, or upon the admiral with an insufficient number of ships; but upon the public men who have so lamentably failed in forethought as to refuse to remedy these evils long in advance, and upon the nation that stands behind those public men.

So, at the present hour, no small share of the responsibility for the blood shed in the Philippines, the blood of our brothers, and the blood of their wild and ignorant foes, lies at the thresholds of those who so long delayed the adoption of the treaty of peace, and of those who by their worse than foolish words deliberately invited a savage people to plunge into a war fraught with sure disaster for them—a war, too, in which our own brave men who follow the flag must pay with their blood for the silly, mock humanitarianism of the prattlers who sit at home in peace.

The army and the navy are the sword and the shield which this nation must carry if she is to do her duty among the nations of the earth—if she is not to stand merely as the China of the Western Hemisphere. Our proper conduct towards the tropic islands we have wrested from Spain is merely the form of which our duty has taken at the moment. Of course we are bound to handle the affairs of our own household well. We must see that there is civic honesty, civic cleanliness, civic good sense in our home administration of the city, State, and nation. We must strive for honesty in office, for honesty towards the creditors of the nation and of the individual; for the widest freedom of the individual initiative where possible, and for the wisest control of individual initiative where it is hostile to the welfare of the many. But because we set our own household in order we are not thereby excused from playing our part in the great affairs of the world. A man's first duty is to his own home, but he is not thereby excused from doing his duty to the State; for if he fails in this second duty it is under the penalty of ceasing to be a freeman. In the same way, while a nations first duty in within its own borders, it is not thereby absolved from facing its duties in the world as a whole; and if it refuses to do so, it merely forfeits its right to struggle for a place among the peoples that shape the destiny of mankind.

In the West Indies and the Philippines alike was are confronted by most difficult problems. It is cowardly to shrink from solving them in the proper way; for solved they must be, if not by us, then by some stronger and more manful race. If we are too weak, too selfish, or too foolish to solve them, some bolder and abler people must undertake the solution. Personally, I am far too firm a believer in the greatness of my country and the power of my countrymen to admit for one moment that we shall ever be driven to the ignoble alternative.

The problems are different for the different islands. Porto Rico is not large enough to stand alone. We must govern it wisely and well, primarily in the interest of its own people. Cuba is, in my judgement, entitled ultimately to settle for itself whether it shall be an independent State or an integral portion of the mightiest of Republics. But until order and stable liberty are secured, we must remain in the island to insure them, and infinite tact, judgement, moderation, and courage must be shown by our military and civil representatives in keeping the island pacified, in relentlessly stamping out brigandage, in protecting all alike, and yet in showing proper recognition to the men who have fought for Cuban liberty. The Philippines offer a yet graver problem. Their population includes half-caste and native Christians, warlike Moslems, and wild pagans. Many of their people are utterly unfit for self-government and show no signs of becoming fit. Others may in time become fit but at the present can only take part in self-government under a wise supervision, at once firm and beneficent. We have driven Spanish tyranny from the islands. If we now let it be replaced by savage anarchy, our work has been for harm and not for good. I have scant patience with those who fear to undertake the task of governing the Philippines, and who openly avow that they do fear to undertake it, or that they shrink from it because of the expense and trouble; but I have even scanter patience with those who make a pretense of humanitarianism to hide and cover their timidity, and who cant about "liberty" and the "consent of the governed," in order to excuse themselves for their unwillingness to play the part of men. Their doctrines, if carried out, would make it incumbent upon us to leave the Apaches of Arizona to work out their own salvation, and to decline to interfere in a single Indian reservation. Their doctrines condemn your forefathers and mine for ever having settled in these United States.

England's rule in India and Egypt has been of great benefit to England, for it has trained up generations of men accustomed to look at the larger and loftier side of public life. It has been of even greater benefit to India and Egypt. And finally, and most of all, it has advanced the cause of civilization. So, if we do our duty aright in the Philippines, we will add to that national renown which is the highest and finest part of national life, will greatly benefit the people of the Philippine Islands, and, above all, we will play our part well in the great work of uplifting mankind. But to do this work, keep ever in mind that we must show in a very high degree the qualities of courage, of honesty, and of good judgement. Resistance must be stamped out. The first and all-important work to be done is to establish the supremacy of our flag. We must put down armed resistance before we can accomplish anything else, and there should be no parleying, no faltering, in dealing with our foe. As for those in our own country who encourage the foe, we can afford contemptuously to disregard them; but it must be remembered that their utterances are not saved from being treasonable merely by the fact that they are despicable.

When once we have put down armed resistance, when once our rule is acknowledged, than an even more difficult task will begin, for then we must see to it that the islands are administered with absolute honesty and with good judgement. If we let the public service of the islands be turned into prey of the spoils of politician, we shall have begun to tread the path which Spain trod to her own destruction. We must send out there only good and able men, chosen for their fitness, and not because of their partizan service, and these men must not only administer impartial justice to the natives and serve their own government with honesty and fidelity, but show the utmost tact and firmness, remembering that, with such people as those with whom we are to deal, weakness is the greatest of crimes, and next to weakness comes lack of consideration for their principles and prejudices.

I preach to you, then, my countrymen, that our country calls not for the life of ease but for the life of strenuous endeavor. The twentieth century looms before us big with the fate of many nations. If we stand idly by, if we seek merely swollen, slothful ease and ignoble peace, if we shrink from the hard contests where men must win at the hazard of their lives and at the risk of all they hold dear, then the bolder and stronger peoples will pass us by, and will win for themselves the domination of the world. Let us therefore boldly face the life of strife, resolute to do our duty well and manfully; resolute to be both honest and brave, to serve high ideals, yet to use practical methods. Above all, let us shrink from no strife, through hard and dangerous endeavor, that we shall ultimately win the goal of true national greatness.

APPLIED IDEALISM

Excerpt from Roosevelt's Autobiography

IN the spring of 1899 I was appointed by President Harrison Civil Service Commissioner. For nearly five years I had not been very active in political life; although I had done some routine work in the organization and had made campaign speeches, and in 1886 had run for Mayor of New York against Abram S. Hewitt, Democrat, and Henry George, Independent, and had been defeated.

I served six years as Civil Service Commissioner—four years under President Harrison and then two years under President Cleveland. I was treated by both Presidents with the utmost consideration. Among my fellow-Commissioners there was at one time ex-Governor Hugh Thompson, of South Carolina, and at another time John R. Proctor, of Kentucky. They were Democrats and ex-Confederate soldiers. I became deeply attached to both, and we stood shoulder to shoulder in every contest in which the Commission was forced to take part.

Civil Service Reform had two sides. There was, first, the effort to secure a more efficient administration of the public service, and, second, the even more important effort to withdraw the administrative offices of the Government from the domain of spoils politics, and thereby cut out of American political life a fruitful source of corruption and degradation. The spoils theory of politics is that public office is so much plunder which the victorious political party is entitled to appropriate to the use of its adherents. Under this system the work of the Government was often done well even in those days, when Civil Service Reform was only an experiment, because the man running an office if himself an able and far-sighted man, knew that inefficiency in administration would be visited on his head in the long run, and therefore insisted upon most of his subordinates doing good work; and, moreover, the men appointed under the spoils system were necessarily men of a certain initiative and power, because those who lacked these qualities were not able to shoulder themselves to the front. Yet there were many flagrant instances of inefficiency, where a powerful chief quartered friend, adherent, or kinsman upon the Government. Moreover, the necessarily haphazard nature of the employment, the need of obtaining and holding the office by service wholly unconnected with official duty, inevitably tended to lower the standard of public morality, alike among the office-holders and among the politicians who rendered party service with the hope of reward in office. Indeed, the doctrine that "To the victor belong the spoils," the cynical battle-cry of the spoils politician in America for the sixty years preceding my own entrance into public life, is so nakedly vicious that few right-thinking men of trained mind defend it. To appoint, promote, reduce, and expel from the public service, letter-carriers, stenographers, women typewriters, clerks, because of the politics of themselves or their friends, without regard to their own service, is, from the standpoint of the people at large, as foolish and degrading as it is wicked.

Such being the case, it would seem at first sight extraordinary that it should be so difficult to uproot the system. Unfortunately, it was permitted to become habitual and traditional in American life, so that the conception of public office as something to be used primarily for the good of the dominant political party became ingrained in the mind of the average American, and he grew so accustomed to the whole process that it seemed part of the order of nature. Not merely the politicians but the bulk of the people accepted this in a matter-of-course way as the only proper attitude. There were plenty of communities where the citizens themselves did not think it natural, or indeed proper, that the Post-Office should be held by a man belonging to the defeated party. Moreover, unless both sides were forbidden to use the offices for purposes of political reward, the side that did use them possessed such an advantage over the other that in the long run it was out of the question for the other not to follow the bad example that had been set. Each party profited by the offices when in power, and when in opposition each party insincerely denounced its opponents for doing exactly what it itself had done and intended again to do.

It was necessary, in order to remedy the evil, both gradually to change the average citizen's mental attitude toward the question, and also to secure proper laws and proper administration of the laws. The work is far from finished even yet. There are still masses of office-holders who can be used by an unscrupulous Administration to debauch political conventions and fraudulently overcome public sentiment, especially in the "rotten borough" districts—those where the party is not strong, and where the office-holders in consequence have a disproportionate influence. This was done by the Republican Administration in 1912, to the ruin of the Republican party. Moreover, there are numbers of States and municipalities where very little has as yet been done to do away with the spoils system. But in the National Government scores of thousands of offices have been put under the merit system, chiefly through the action of the National Civil Service Commission.

The use of Government offices as patronage is a handicap difficult to overestimate from the standpoint of those who strive to get good government. Any effort for reform of any sort, National, State, or municipal, results in the reformers immediately finding themselves face to face with an organized band of drilled mercenaries who are paid out of the public chest to train themselves with such skill that ordinary good citizens when they meet them at the polls are in much the position of militia matched against regular troops. Yet these citizens themselves support and pay their opponents in such a way that they are drilled to overthrow the very men who support them. Civil Service Reform is designed primarily to give the average American citizen a fair chance in politics, to give to this citizen the same weight in politics that the "ward heeler" has.

Patronage does not really help a party. It helps the bosses to get control of the machinery of the party—as in 1912 was true of the Republican party—but it does not help the party. On the average, the most sweeping party victories in our history have been won when the patronage was against the victors. All that the patronage does is to help the worst element in the party retain control of the party organization. Two of the evil elements in our Government against which good citizens have to contend are, 1, the lack of continuous activity on the part of these good citizens themselves, and, 2, the ever-present activity of those who have only an evil self-interest in political life. It is difficult to interest the average citizen in any particular movement to the degree of getting him to take an efficient part in it. He wishes the movement well, but he will not, or often cannot, take the time and the trouble to serve it efficiently; and this whether he happens to be a mechanic or a banker, a telegraph operator or a storekeeper. He has his own interests, his own business, and it is difficult for him to spare the time to go around to the primaries, to see to the organization, to see to getting out the vote—in short, to attend to all the thousand details of political management.

On the other hand, the spoils system breeds a class of men whose financial interest it is to take this necessary time and trouble. They are paid for so doing, and they are paid out of the public chest. Under the spoils system a man is appointed to an ordinary clerical or ministerial position in the municipal, Federal, or State government, not primarily because he is expected to be a good servant, but because he has rendered help to some big boss or to the henchman of some big boss. His stay in office depends not upon how he performs service, but upon how he retains his influence in the party. This necessarily means that his attention to the interests of the public at large, even though real, is secondary to his devotion to his organization, or to the interest of the ward leader who put him in his place. So he and his fellows attend to politics, not once a year, not two or three times a year, like the average citizen, but every day in the year. It is the one thing that they talk of, for it is their bread and butter. They plan about it and they scheme about it. They do it because it is their business. I do not blame them in the least. I blame us, the people, for we ought to make it clear as a bell that the business of serving the people in one of the ordinary ministerial Government positions, which have nothing to do with deciding the policy of the Government, should have no necessary connection with the management of primaries, of caucuses, and of nominating conventions. As a result of our wrong thinking and supineness, we

American citizens tend to breed a mass of men whose interests in governmental matters are often adverse to ours, who are thoroughly drilled, thoroughly organized, who make their livelihood out of politics, and who frequently make their livelihood out of bad politics. They know every little twist and turn, no matter how intricate, in the politics of their several wards, and when election day comes the ordinary citizen who has merely the interest that all good men, all decent citizens, should have in political life, finds himself as helpless before these men as if he were a solitary volunteer in the presence of a band of drilled mercenaries on a field of battle. There are a couple of hundred thousand Federal offices, not to speak of State and municipal offices. The men who fill these offices, and the men who wish to fill them, within and without the dominant party for the time being, make a regular army, whose interest it is that the system of bread-and-butter politics shall continue. Against their concrete interest we have merely the generally unorganized sentiment of the community in favor of putting things on a decent basis. The large number of men who believe vaguely in good are pitted against the smaller but still larger number of men whose interest it often becomes to act very concretely and actively for evil; and it is small wonder that the struggle is doubtful.

During my six years' service as Commissioner the field of the merit system was extended at the expense of the spoils system so as to include several times the number of offices that had originally been included. Generally this was done by the introduction of competitive entrance examinations; sometimes, as in the Navy-Yards, by a system of registration. This of itself was good work.

Even better work was making the law efficient and genuine where it applied. As was inevitable in the introduction of such a system, there was at first only partial success in its application. For instance, it applied to the ordinary employees in the big custom-houses and post-offices, but not to the heads of these offices. A number of the heads of the offices were slippery politicians of a low moral grade, themselves appointed under the spoils system, and anxious, directly or indirectly, to break down the merit system and to pay their own political debts by appointing their henchmen and supporters to the positions under them. Occasionally these men acted with open and naked brutality. Ordinarily they sought by cunning to evade the law. The Civil Service Reformers, on the other hand, were in most cases not much used to practical politics, and were often well-nigh helpless when pitted against veteran professional politicians. In consequence I found at the beginning of my experiences that there were many offices in which the execution of the law was a sham. This was very damaging, because it encouraged the politicians to assault the law everywhere, and, on the other hand, made good people feel that the law was not worth while defending.

The first effort of myself and my colleagues was to secure the genuine enforcement of the law. In this we succeeded after a number of lively fights. But of course in these fights we were obliged to strike a large number of influential politicians, some of them in Congress, some of them the supporters and backers of men who were in Congress. Accordingly we soon found ourselves engaged in a series of contests with prominent Senators and Congressmen. There were a number of Senators and Congressmen—men like Congressman (afterwards Senator) H. C. Lodge, of Massachusetts; Senator Cushman K. Davis, of Minnesota; Senator Orville H. Platt, of Connecticut; Senator Cockrell, of Missouri; Congressman (afterwards President) McKinley, of Ohio, and Congressman Dargan, of South Carolina—who abhorred the business of the spoilsman, who efficiently and resolutely championed the reform at every turn, and without whom the whole reform would certainly have failed. But there were plenty of other Senators and Congressmen who hated the whole reform and everything concerned with it and everybody who championed it; and sometimes, to use a legal phrase, their hatred was for cause, and sometimes it was peremptory—that is, sometimes the Commission interfered with their most efficient, and incidentally most corrupt and unscrupulous, supporters, and at other times, where there was no such interference, a man nevertheless had an innate dislike of anything that tended to decency in government. These men were always waging war against us, and they usually had the more or less open support of a certain number of Government officials, from Cabinet officers down. The Senators and Congressmen in question opposed us in many different ways. Sometimes, for instance, they had committees appointed to investigate us—during my public career without and within office I grew accustomed to accept appearances before investigating committees as part of the natural order of things. Sometimes they tried to cut off the appropriation for the Commission.

Occasionally we would bring to terms these Senators or Congressmen who fought the Commission by the simple expedient of not holding examinations in their districts. This always brought frantic appeals from their constituents, and we would explain that unfortunately the appropriations had been cut, so that we could not hold examinations in every district, and that obviously we could not neglect the districts of those Congressmen who believed in the reform and therefore in the examinations. The constituents then turned their attention to the Congressman, and the result was that in the long run we obtained sufficient money to enable us to do our work. On the whole, the most prominent leaders favored us. Any man who is the head of a big department, if he has any fitness at all, wishes to see that department run well; and a very little practical experience shows him that it cannot be run well if he must make his appointments to please spoilsmongering politicians. As with almost every reform that I have ever undertaken, most of the opposition took the guise of shrewd slander. Our opponents relied chiefly on downright misrepresentation of what it was that we were trying to accomplish, and of our methods, acts, and personalities. I had more than one lively encounter with the authors and sponsors of these misrepresentations, which at the time were full of interest to me. But it would be a dreary thing now to go over the record of exploded mendacity, or to expose the meanness and malice shown by some men of high official position. A favorite argument was to call the reform Chinese, because the Chinese had constructed a governmental system based in part on the theory of written competitive examinations. The argument was simple. There had been written examinations in China; it was proposed to establish written examinations in the United States; therefore the proposed system was Chinese. The argument might have been applied still further. For instance, the Chinese had used gunpowder for centuries; gunpowder is used in Springfield rifles; therefore Springfield rifles were Chinese. One argument is quite as logical as the other. It was impossible to answer every falsehood about the system. But it was possible to answer certain falsehoods, especially when uttered by some Senator or Congressman of note. Usually these false statements took the form of assertions that we had asked preposterous questions of applicants. At times they also included the assertion that we credited people to districts where they did not live; this simply meaning that these persons were not known to the active ward politicians of those districts.

One opponent with whom we had a rather lively tilt was a Republican Congressman from Ohio, Mr. Grosvenor, one of the floor leaders. Mr. Grosvenor made his attack in the House, and enumerated our sins in picturesque rather than accurate fashion. There was a Congressional committee investigating us at the time, and on my next appearance before them I asked that Mr. Grosvenor be requested to meet me before the committee. Mr. Grosvenor did not take up the challenge for several weeks, until it was announced that I was leaving for my ranch in Dakota; whereupon, deeming it safe, he wrote me a letter expressing his ardent wish that I should appear before the committee to meet him. I promptly canceled my ticket, waited, and met him. He proved to be a person of happily treacherous memory, so that the simple expedient of arranging his statements in pairs was sufficient to reduce him to confusion. For instance, he had been trapped into making the unwary remark, "I do not want to repeal the Civil Service Law, and I never said so." I produced the following extract from one of his speeches: "I will vote not only to strike out this provision, but I will vote to repeal the whole law." To this he merely replied that there was "no inconsistency between those two statements." He asserted that "Rufus P. Putnam, fraudulently credited to

Washington County, Ohio, never lived in Washington County, Ohio, or in my Congressional district, or in Ohio as far as I know." We produced a letter which, thanks to a beneficent Providence, he had himself written about Mr. Rufus P. Putnam, in which he said: "Mr. Rufus P. Putnam is a legal resident of my district and has relatives living there now." He explained, first, that he had not written the letter; second, that he had forgotten he had written the letter; and, third, that he was grossly deceived when he wrote it. He said: "I have not been informed of one applicant who has found a place in the classified service from my district." We confronted him with the names of eight. He looked them over and said, "Yes, the eight men are living in my district as now constituted," but added that his district had been gerrymandered so that he could no longer tell who did and who didn't live in it. When I started further to question him, he accused me of a lack of humor in not appreciating that his statements were made "in a jesting way," and then announced that "a Congressman making a speech on the floor of the House of Representatives was perhaps in a little different position from a witness on the witness stand"—a frank admission that he did not consider exactitude of statement necessary when he was speaking as a Congressman. Finally he rose with great dignity and said that it was his "constitutional right" not to be questioned elsewhere as to what he said on the floor of the House of Representatives; and accordingly he left the delighted committee to pursue its investigations without further aid from him.

A more important opponent was the then Democratic leader of the Senate, Mr. Gorman. In a speech attacking the Commission Mr. Gorman described with moving pathos how a friend of his, "a bright young man from Baltimore," a Sunday-school scholar, well recommended by his pastor, wished to be a letter-carrier; and how he went before us to be examined. The first question we asked him, said Mr. Gorman, was the shortest route from Baltimore to China, to which the "bright young man" responded that he didn't want to go to China, and had never studied up that route. Thereupon, said Mr. Gorman, we asked him all about the steamship lines from the United States to Europe, then branched him off into geology, tried him in chemistry, and finally turned him down.

Apparently Mr. Gorman did not know that we kept full records of our examinations. I at once wrote to him stating that I had carefully looked through all our examination papers and had not been able to find one question even remotely resembling any of these questions which he alleged had been asked, and that I would be greatly obliged if he would give me the name of the "bright young man" who had deceived him.

However, that "bright young man" remained permanently without a name. I also asked Mr. Gorman, if he did not wish to give us the name of his informant, to give us the date of the examination in which he was supposed to have taken part; and I offered, if he would send down a representative to look through our files, to give him all the aid we could in his effort to discover any such questions. But Mr. Gorman, not hitherto known as a sensitive soul, expressed himself as so shocked at the thought that the veracity of the "bright young man" should be doubted that he could not bring himself to answer my letter. So I made a public statement to the effect that no such questions had ever been asked. Mr. Gorman brooded over this; and during the next session of Congress he rose and complained that he had received a very "impudent" letter from me (my letter was a respectful note calling attention to the fact that, if he wished, he could by personal examination satisfy himself that his statements had no foundation in fact). He further stated that he had been "cruelly" called to account by me because he had been endeavoring to right a "great wrong" that the Civil Service Commission had committed; but he never, then or afterwards, furnished any clue to the identity of that child of his fondest fancy, the bright young man without a name.*

The incident is of note chiefly as shedding light on the mental make-up of the man who at the time was one of the two or three most influential leaders of the Democratic party. Mr. Gorman had been Mr. Cleveland's party manager in the Presidential campaign, and was the Democratic leader in Congress. It seemed extraordinary that he should be so reckless as to make statements with no foundation in fact, which he might have known that I would not permit to pass unchallenged. Then, as now, the ordinary newspaper, in New York and elsewhere, was quite as reckless in its misstatements of fact about public men and measures; but for a man in Mr. Gorman's position of responsible leadership such action seemed hardly worth while. However, it is at least to be said for Mr. Gorman that he was not trying by falsehood to take away any man's character. It would be well for writers and speakers to bear in mind the remark of Pudd'nhead Wilson to the effect that while there are nine hundred and ninety-nine kinds of falsehood, the only kind specifically condemned in Scripture, just as murder, theft, and adultery are condemned, is bearing false witness against one's neighbor.

One of the worst features of the old spoils system was the ruthless cruelty and brutality it so often bred in the treatment of faithful public servants without political influence. Life is hard enough and cruel enough at best, and this is as true of public service as of private service. Under no system will it be possible to do away with all favoritism and brutality and meanness and malice. But at least we

* This is a condensation of a speech I at the time made to the St. Louis Civil Service Reform Association. Senator Gorman was then the Senate leader of the party that had just been victorious in the Congressional elections.

can try to minimize the exhibition of these qualities. I once came across a case in Washington which very keenly excited my sympathy. Under an Administration prior to the one with which I was connected a lady had been ousted from a Government position. She came to me to see if she could be reinstated. (This was not possible, but by active work I did get her put back in a somewhat lower position, and this only by an appeal to the sympathy of a certain official.) She was so pallid and so careworn that she excited my sympathy and I made inquiries about her. She was a poor woman with two children, a widow. She and her two children were in actual want. She could barely keep the two children decently clad, and she could not give them the food growing children need. Three years before she had been employed in a bureau in a department of Washington, doing her work faithfully, at a salary of about $800. It was enough to keep her and her two children in clothing, food, and shelter. One day the chief of the bureau called her up and told her he was very sorry that he had to dismiss her. In great distress she asked him why; she thought that she had been doing her work satisfactorily. He answered her that she had been doing well, and that he wished very much that he could keep her, that he would do so if he possibly could, but that he could not; for a certain Senator, giving his name, a very influential member of the Senate, had demanded her place for a friend of his who had influence. The woman told the bureau chief that it meant turning her out to starve. She had been thirteen or fourteen years in the public service; she had lost all touch with her friends in her native State; dismissal meant absolute want for her and her children. On this the chief, who was a kind man, said he would not have her turned out, and sent her back to her work.

But three weeks afterwards he called her up again and told her he could not say how sorry he was, but the thing had to be done. The Senator had been around in person to know why the change had not been made, and had told the chief that he would be himself removed if the place were not given him. The Senator was an extremely influential man. His wants had to be attended to, and the woman had to go. And go she did, and turned out she was, to suffer with her children and to starve outright, or to live in semi-starvation, just as might befall. I do not blame the bureau chief, who hated to do what he did, although he lacked the courage to refuse; I do not even very much blame the Senator, who did not know the hardship that he was causing, and who had been calloused by long training in the spoils system; but this system, a system which permits and encourages such deeds, is a system of brutal iniquity.

Any man accustomed to dealing with practical politics can with difficulty keep a straight face when he reads or listens to some of the arguments advanced against Civil Service Reform. One of these arguments, a favorite with machine politicians, takes the form of an appeal to "party loyalty" in filling minor offices. Why, again and again these very same machine politicians take just as good care of henchmen of the opposite party as of those of their own party. In the underworld of politics the closest ties are sometimes those which knit together the active professional workers of opposite political parties. A friend of mine in the New York Legislature—the hero of the alpha and omega incident—once remarked to me: "When you have been in public life a little longer, Mr. Roosevelt, you will understand that there are no politics in politics." In the politics to which he was referring this remark could be taken literally.

Another illustration of this truth was incidentally given me, at about the same time, by an acquaintance, a Tammany man named Costigan, a good fellow according to his lights. I had been speaking to him of a fight in one of the New York downtown districts, a Democratic district in which the Republican party was in a hopeless minority, and, moreover, was split into the Half-Breed and Stalwart factions. It had been an interesting fight in more than one way. For instance, the Republican party, at the general election, polled something like five hundred and fifty votes, and yet at the primary the two factions polled seven hundred and twenty-five all told. The sum of the parts was thus considerably greater than the whole. There had been other little details that made the contest worthy of note. The hall in which the primary was held had been hired by the Stalwarts from a conscientious gentleman. To him the Half-Breeds applied to know whether they could not hire the hall away from their opponents, and offered him a substantial money advance. The conscientious gentleman replied that his word was as good as his bond, that he had hired the hall to the Stalwarts, and that it must be theirs. But he added that he was willing to hire the doorway to the Half-Breeds if they paid him the additional sum of money they had mentioned. The bargain was struck, and the meeting of the hostile hosts was spirited, when the men who had rented the doorway sought to bar the path of the men who had rented the hall. I was asking my friend Costigan about the details of the struggle, as he seemed thoroughly acquainted with them, and he smiled good-naturedly over my surprise at there having been more votes cast than there were members of the party in the whole district. Said I, "Mr. Costigan, you seem to have a great deal of knowledge about this; how did it happen?" To which he replied, "Come now, Mr. Roosevelt, you know it's the same gang that votes in *all* the primaries."

So much for most of the opposition to the reform. There was, however, some honest and at least partially justifiable opposition both to certain of the methods advocated by Civil Service Reformers and to certain of the Civil Service Reformers themselves. The pet shibboleths of the opponents of the reform were that the system we proposed to introduce would give rise to mere red-tape bureaucracy, and that the reformers were pharisees. Neither statement was true. Each statement contained some truth.

If men are not to be appointed by favoritism, wise or unwise, honest or dishonest, they must be appointed in some automatic way, which generally means by competitive examination. The easiest kind of competitive examination is an examination in writing. This is entirely appropriate for certain classes of work, for lawyers, stenographers, typewriters, clerks, mathematicians, and assistants in an astronomical observatory, for instance. It is utterly inappropriate for carpenters, detectives, and mounted cattle inspectors along the Rio Grande—to instance three types of employment as to which I had to do battle to prevent well-meaning bureaucrats from insisting on written competitive entrance examinations. It would be quite possible to hold a very good competitive examination for mounted cattle inspectors by means of practical tests in brand reading and shooting with rifle and revolver, in riding "mean" horses and in roping and throwing steers. I did my best to have examinations of this kind instituted, but my proposal was of precisely the type which most shocks the routine official mind, and I was never able to get it put into practical effect.

The important point, and the point most often forgotten by zealous Civil Service Reformers, was to remember that the routine competitive examination was merely a means to an end. It did not always produce ideal results. But it was normally better than a system of appointments for spoils purposes; it sometimes worked out very well indeed; and in most big governmental offices it not only gave satisfactory results, but was the only system under which good results could be obtained. For instance, when I was Police Commissioner we appointed some two thousand policemen at one time. It was utterly impossible for the Commissioners each to examine personally the six or eight thousand applicants. Therefore they had to be appointed either on the recommendation of outsiders or else by written competitive examination. The latter method—the one we adopted—was infinitely preferable. We held a rigid physical and moral pass examination, and then, among those who passed, we held a written competitive examination, requiring only the knowledge that any good primary common school education would meet—that is, a test of ordinary intelligence and simple mental training. Occasionally a man who would have been a good officer failed, and occasionally a man who turned out to be a bad officer passed; but, as a rule, the men with intelligence sufficient to enable them to answer the questions were of a type very distinctly above that of those who failed.

The answers returned to some of the questions gave an illuminating idea of the intelligence of those answering them. For instance, one of our questions in a given examination was a request to name five of the New England States. One competitor, obviously of foreign birth, answered: "England, Ireland, Scotland, Wales, and Cork." His neighbor, who had probably looked over his shoulder but who had North of Ireland prejudices, made the same answer except that he substituted Belfast for Cork. A request for a statement as to the life of Abraham Lincoln elicited, among other less startling pieces of information, the fact that many of the applicants thought that he was a general in the Civil War; several thought that he was President of the Confederate States; three thought he had been assassinated by Jefferson Davis, one by Thomas Jefferson, one by Garfield, several by Guiteau, and one by Ballington Booth—the last representing a memory of the fact that he had been shot by a man named Booth, to whose surname the writer added the name with which he was most familiar in connection therewith. A request to name five of the States that seceded in 1861 received answers that included almost every State in the Union. It happened to be at the time of the silver agitation in the West, and the Rocky Mountain States accordingly figured in a large percentage of the answers. Some of the men thought that Chicago was on the Pacific Ocean. Others, in answer to a query as to who was the head of the United States Government, wavered between myself and Recorder Goff; one brilliant genius, for inscrutable reasons, placed the leadership in the New York Fire Department. Now of course some of the men who answered these questions wrong were nevertheless quite capable of making good policemen; but it is fair to assume that on the average the candidate who has a rudimentary knowledge of the government, geography, and history of his country is a little better fitted, in point of intelligence, to be a policeman than the one who has not.

Therefore I felt convinced, after full experience, that as regards very large classes of public servants by far the best way to choose the men for appointment was by means of written competitive examination. But I absolutely split off from the bulk of my professional Civil Service Reform friends when they advocated written competitive examinations for promotion. In the Police Department I found these examinations a serious handicap in the way of getting the best men promoted, and never in any office did I find that the written competitive promotion examination did any good. The reason for a written competitive entrance examination is that it is impossible for the head of the office, or the candidate's prospective immediate superior, himself to know the average candidate or to test his ability. But when once in office the best way to test any man's ability is by long experience in seeing him actually at work. His promotion should depend upon the judgment formed of him by his superiors.

So much for the objections to the examinations. Now for the objections to the men who advocated the reform. As a rule these men were high-minded and disinterested. Certain of them, men like the leaders in the Maryland and Indiana Reform Associations, for instances, Messrs. Bonaparte and Rose, Foulke and Swift, added common sense, broad sympathy, and practical efficiency to their high-mindedness. But in New York, Philadelphia, and Boston there really was a certain mental and moral thinness among very many of the leaders in the Civil Service Reform movement. It was this quality which made them so profoundly antipathetic to vigorous and intensely human people of the stamp of my friend Joe Murray—who, as I have said, always felt that my Civil Service Reform affiliations formed the one blot on an otherwise excellent public record. The Civil Service Reform movement was one from above downwards, and the men who took the lead in it were not men who as a rule possessed a very profound sympathy with or understanding of the ways of thought and life of their average fellow-citizen. They were not men who themselves desired to be letter-carriers or clerks or policemen, or to have their friends appointed to these positions. Having no temptation themselves in this direction, they were eagerly anxious to prevent other people getting such appointments as a reward for political services. In this they were quite right. It would be impossible to run any big public office to advantage save along the lines of the strictest application of Civil Service Reform principles; and the system should be extended throughout our governmental service far more widely than is now the case.

But there are other and more vital reforms than this. Too many Civil Service Reformers, when the trial came, proved tepidly indifferent or actively hostile to reforms that were of profound and far-reaching social and industrial consequence. Many of them were at best lukewarm about movements for the improvement of the conditions of toil and life among men and women who labor under hard surroundings, and were positively hostile to movements which curbed the power of the great corporation magnates and directed into useful instead of pernicious channels the activities of the great corporation lawyers who advised them.

Most of the newspapers which regarded themselves as the especial champions of Civil Service Reform and as the highest exponents of civic virtue, and which distrusted the average citizen and shuddered over the "coarseness" of the professional politicians, were, nevertheless, given to vices even more contemptible than, although not so gross as, those they denounced and derided. Their editors were refined men of cultivated tastes, whose pet temptations were backbiting, mean slander, and the snobbish worship of anything clothed in wealth and the outward appearances of conventional respectability. They were not robust or powerful men; they felt ill at ease in the company of rough, strong men; often they had in them a vein of physical timidity. They avenged themselves to themselves for an uneasy subconsciousness of their own shortcomings by sitting in cloistered—or, rather, pleasantly upholstered—seclusion, and sneering at and lying about men who made them feel uncomfortable. Sometimes these were bad men, who made them feel uncomfortable by the exhibition of coarse and repellent vice; and sometimes they were men of high character, who held ideals of courage and of service to others, and who looked down and warred against the shortcomings of swollen wealth, and the effortless, easy lives of those whose horizon is bounded by a sheltered and timid respectability. These newspapers, owned and edited by these men, although free from the repulsive vulgarity of the yellow press, were susceptible to influence by the privileged interests, and were almost or quite as hostile to manliness as they were to unrefined vice—and were much more hostile to it than to the typical shortcomings of wealth and refinement. They favored Civil Service Reform; they favored copyright laws, and the removal of the tariff on works of art; they favored all the proper (and even more strongly all the improper) movements for international peace and arbitration; in short, they favored all good, and many goody-goody, measures so long as they did not cut deep into social wrong or make demands on National and individual virility. They opposed, or were lukewarm about, efforts to build up the army and the navy, for they were not sensitive concerning National honor; and, above all, they opposed every non-milk-and-water effort, however sane, to change our social and economic system in such a fashion as to substitute the ideal of justice towards all for the ideal of kindly charity from the favored few to the possibly grateful many.

Some of the men foremost in the struggle for Civil Service Reform have taken a position of honorable leadership in the battle for those other and more vital reforms. But many of them promptly abandoned the field of effort for decency when the battle took the form, not of a fight against the petty grafting of small bosses and small politicians—a vitally necessary battle, be it remembered—but of a fight against the great intrenched powers of privilege, a fight to secure justice through the law for ordinary men and women, instead of leaving them to suffer cruel injustice either because the law failed to protect them or because it was twisted from its legitimate purposes into a means for oppressing them.

One of the reasons why the boss so often keeps his hold, especially in municipal matters, is, or at least has been in the past, because so many of the men who claim to be reformers have been blind to the need of working in human fashion for social and industrial betterment. Such words as "boss" and "machine" now imply evil, but both the implication the words carry and the definition of the words themselves are somewhat vague. A leader is necessary; but his opponents always call him a boss. An organization is necessary; but the men in opposition always call it a machine. Nevertheless, there is a real and deep distinction between the leader and the boss, between organizations and machines. A political leader who fights openly for principles, and who keeps his position of leadership by stirring the consciences and convincing the intellects of his followers, so that they have confidence in him and will follow him because they can achieve greater results under him than under any one else, is doing work which is indispensable in a democracy. The boss, on the other hand, is a man who does not gain his power by open means, but by secret means, and usually by corrupt means. Some of the worst and most powerful bosses in our political history either held no public office or else some unimportant public office. They made no appeal either to intellect or conscience. Their work was done behind closed doors, and consisted chiefly in the use of that greed which gives in order that in return it may get. A boss of this kind can pull wires in conventions, can manipulate members of the Legislature, can control the giving or withholding of office, and serves as the intermediary for bringing together the powers of corrupt politics and corrupt business. If he is at one end of the social scale, he may through his agents traffic in the most brutal forms of vice and give protection to the purveyors of shame and sin in return for money bribes. If at the other end of the scale, he may be the means of securing favors from high public officials, legislative or executive, to great industrial interests; the transaction being sometimes a naked matter of bargain and sale, and sometimes being carried on in such manner that both parties thereto can more or less successfully disguise it to their consciences as in the public interest. The machine is simply another name for the kind of organization which is certain to grow up in a party or section of a party controlled by such bosses as these and by their henchmen, whereas, of course, an effective organization of decent men is essential in order to secure decent politics.

If these bosses were responsible for nothing but pure wickedness, they would probably last but a short time in any community. And, in any event, if the men who are horrified by their wickedness were themselves as practical and as thoroughly in touch with human nature, the bosses would have a short shrift. The trouble is that the boss does understand human nature, and that he fills a place which the reformer cannot fill unless he likewise understands human nature. Sometimes the boss is a man who cares for political power purely for its own sake, as he might care for any other hobby; more often he has in view some definitely selfish object such as political or financial advancement. He can rarely accomplish much unless he has another side to him. A successful boss is very apt to be a man who, in addition to committing wickedness in his own interest, also does look after the interests of others, even if not from good motives. There are some communities so fortunate that there are very few men who have private interests to be served, and in these the power of the boss is at a minimum. There are many country communities of this type. But in communities where there is poverty and ignorance, the conditions are ripe for the growth of a boss. Moreover, wherever big business interests are liable either to be improperly favored or improperly discriminated against and blackmailed by public officials—and the result is just as vicious in one case as in the other—the boss is almost certain to develop. The best way of getting at this type of boss is by keeping the public conscience aroused and alert, so that it will tolerate neither improper attack upon, nor improper favoritism towards, these corporations, and will quickly punish any public servant guilty of either.

There is often much good in the type of boss, especially common in big cities, who fulfills towards the people of his district in rough and ready fashion the position of friend and protector. He uses his influence to get jobs for young men who need them. He goes into court for a wild young fellow who has gotten into trouble. He helps out with cash or credit the widow who is in straits, or the breadwinner who is crippled or for some other cause temporarily out of work. He organizes clambakes and chowder parties and picnics, and is consulted by the local labor leaders when a cut in wages is threatened. For some of his constituents he does proper favors, and for others wholly improper favors; but he preserves human relations with all. He may be a very bad and very corrupt man, a man whose action in blackmailing and protecting vice is of far-reaching damage to his constituents. But these constituents are for the most part men and women who struggle hard against poverty and with whom the problem of living is very real and very close. They would prefer clean and honest government, if this clean and honest government is accompanied by human sympathy, human understanding. But an appeal made to them for virtue in the abstract, an appeal made by good men who do not really understand their needs, will often pass quite unheeded, if on the other side stands the boss, the friend and benefactor, who may have been guilty of much wrong-doing in things that they are hardly aware concern them, but who appeals to them, not only for the sake of favors to come, but in the name of gratitude and loyalty, and above all of understanding and fellow-feeling. They have a feeling of clan-loyalty to him; his and their relations may be substantially those which are right and proper among primitive people still in the clan stage of moral development. The successful fight against this type of vicious boss, and the type of vicious politics which produces it, can be made only by men who have a genuine fellow-feeling for and understanding of the people for and with whom they are to work, and who in practical fashion seek their social and industrial benefit.

There are communities of poor men, whose lives are hard, in which the boss, though he would be out of place in a more advanced community, if fundamentally an honest man, meets a real need which would otherwise not be met. Because of his limitations in other than purely local matters it may be our duty to fight such a boss; but it may also be our duty to recognize, within his limitations, both his sincerity and his usefulness.

Yet again even the boss who really is evil, like the business man who really is evil, may on certain points be sound, and be doing good work. It may be the highest duty of the patriotic public servant to work with the big boss or the big business man on these points, while refusing to work with him on others. In the same way there are many self-styled reformers whose conduct is such as to warrant Tom Reed's bitter remark, that when Dr. Johnson defined patriotism as the last refuge of a scoundrel he was ignorant of the infinite possibilities contained in the word reform. Yet, none the less, it is our duty to work for the reforms these men champion, without regard to the misconduct of the men themselves on other points. I have known in my life many big business men and many big political bosses who often or even generally did evil, but who on some occasions and on certain issues were right. I never hesitated to do battle against these men when they were wrong; and, on the other hand, as long as they were going my way I was glad to have them do so. To have repudiated their aid when they were right and were striving for a right end, and for what was of benefit to the people—no matter what their motives may have been—would have been childish, and moreover would have itself been misconduct against the people.

My duty was to stand with every one while he was right, and to stand against him when he went wrong; and this I have tried to do as regards individuals and as regards groups of individuals. When a business man or labor leader, politician or reformer, is right, I support him; when he goes wrong, I leave him. When Mr. Lorimer upheld the war for the liberation of Cuba, I supported him; when he became United States Senator by improper methods, I opposed him. The principles or methods which the Socialists advocate and which I believe to be in the interest of the people I support, and those which I believe to be against the interest of the people I oppose. Moreover, when a man has done evil, but changes, and works for decency and righteousness, and when, as far as I can see, the change is real and the man's conduct sincere, then I welcome him and work heartily with him, as an equal with an equal. For thirty years after the Civil War the creed of mere materialism was rampant in both American politics and American business, and many, many strong men, in accordance with the prevailing commercial and political morality, did things for which they deserve blame and condemnation; but if they now sincerely change, and strive for better things, it is unwise and unjust to bar them from fellowship. So long as they work for evil, smite them with the sword of the Lord and of Gideon! When they change and show their faith by their works, remember the words of Ezekiel: "If the wicked will turn from all the sins he has committed, and keep all my statutes, and do that which is lawful and right, he shall surely live, he shall not die. All his transgressions that he hath committed, they shall not be mentioned unto him: in his righteousness that he hath done he shall live. Have I any pleasure at all that the wicked should die? saith the Lord God; and not that he should return from his ways and live?"

Every man who has been in practical politics grows to realize that politicians, big and little, are no more all of them bad than they are all of them good. Many of these men are very bad men indeed, but there are others among them—and some among those held up to special obloquy, too—who, even although they may have done much that is evil, also show traits of sterling worth which many of their critics wholly lack. There are few men for whom I have ever felt a more cordial and contemptuous dislike than for some of the bosses and big professional politicians with whom I have been brought into contact. On the other hand, in the case of some political leaders who were most bitterly attacked as bosses, I grew to know certain sides of their characters which inspired in me a very genuine regard and respect.

To read much of the assault on Senator Hanna, one would have thought that he was a man incapable of patriotism or of far-sighted devotion to the country's good. I was brought into intimate contact with him only during the two and a half years immediately preceding his death. I was then President, and perforce watched all his actions at close range. During that time he showed himself to be a man of rugged sincerity of purpose, of great courage and loyalty, and of unswerving devotion to the interests of the Nation and the people as he saw those interests. He was as sincerely desirous of helping laboring men as of helping capitalists. His ideals were in many ways not my ideals, and there were points where both by temperament and by conviction we were far apart. Before this time he had always been unfriendly to me; and I do not think he ever grew to like me, at any rate not until the very end of his life. Moreover, I came to the Presidency under circumstances which, if he had been a smaller man, would inevitably have thrown him into violent antagonism to me. He was the close and intimate friend of President McKinley. He was McKinley's devoted ally and follower, and his trusted adviser, who was in complete sympathy with him. Partly because of this friendship, his position in the Senate and in the country was unique.

With McKinley's sudden death, Senator Hanna found himself bereft of his dearest friend, while I, who had just come to the Presidency, was in his view an untried man, whose trustworthiness on many public questions was at least doubtful. Ordinarily, as has been shown, not only in our history, but in the history of all other countries, in countless instances, over and over again, this situation would have meant suspicion, ill will, and, at the last, open and violent antagonism.

Such was not the result, in this case, primarily because Senator Hanna had in him the quality that enabled him to meet a serious crisis with dignity, with power, and with disinterested desire to work for the common good. Within a few days of my accession he called on me, and with entire friendliness and obvious sincerity, but also with entire self-respect, explained that he mourned McKinley as probably no other man did; that he had not been especially my friend, but that he wished me to understand that thenceforward, on every question where he could conscientiously support me, I could count upon his giving me as loyal aid as it was in his power to render. He added that this must not be understood as committing him to favor me for nomination and election, because that matter must be left to take care of itself as events should decide; but that, aside from this, what he said was to be taken literally; in other words, he would do his best to make my Administration a success by supporting me heartily on every point on which he conscientiously could, and that this I could count upon. He kept his word absolutely. He never became especially favorable to my nomination; and most of his close friends became bitterly opposed to me and used every effort to persuade him to try to bring about my downfall. Most men in his position would have been tempted to try to make capital at my expense by antagonizing me and discrediting me so as to make my policies fail, just for the sake of making them fail. Senator Hanna, on the contrary, did everything possible to make them succeed. He kept his word in the letter and the spirit, and on every point on which he felt conscientiously able to support me he gave me the heartiest and most effective support, and did all in his power to make my Administration a success; and this with no hope of any reward for himself, of any gratitude from me, or of any appreciation by the public at large, but solely because he deemed such action necessary for the well-being of the country as a whole.

My experience with Senator Quay was similar. I had no personal relations with him before I was President, and knew nothing of him save by hearsay. Soon after I became President, Senator Quay called upon me, told me he had known me very slightly, that he thought most men who claimed to be reformers were hypocrites, but that he deemed me sincere, that he thought conditions had become such that aggressive courage and honesty were necessary in order to remedy them, that he believed I intended to be a good and efficient President, and that to the best of his ability he would support me in it making my Administration a success. He kept his word with absolute good faith. He had been in the Civil War, and was a medal of honor man; and I think my having been in the Spanish War gave him at the outset a kindly feeling toward me. He was also a very well-read man—I owe to him, for instance, my acquaintance with the writings of the Finnish novelist Topelius. Not only did he support me on almost every public question in which I was most interested—including, I am convinced, every one on which he felt he conscientiously could do so—but he also at the time of his death gave a striking proof of his disinterested desire to render a service to certain poor people, and this under conditions in which not only would he never know if the service were rendered but in which he had no reason to expect that his part in it would ever be made known to any other man.

Quay was descended from a French voyageur who had some Indian blood in him. He was proud of this Indian blood, took an especial interest in Indians, and whenever Indians came to Washington they always called on him. Once during my Administration a delegation of Iroquois came over from Canada to call on me at the White House. Their visit had in it something that was pathetic as well as amusing. They represented the descendants of the Six Nations, who fled to Canada after Sullivan harried their towns in the Revolutionary War. Now, a century and a quarter later, their people thought that they would like to come back into the United States; and these representatives had called upon me with the dim hope that perhaps I could give their tribes land on which they could settle. As soon as they reached Washington they asked Quay to bring them to call on me, which he did, telling me that of course their errand was hopeless and that he had explained as much to them, but that they would like me to extend the courtesy of an interview. At the close of the interview, which had been conducted with all the solemnities of calumet and wampum, the Indians filed out. Quay, before following them, turned to me with his usual emotionless face and said, "Good-by, Mr. President; this reminds one of the Flight of a Tartar Tribe, doesn't it?" I answered, "So you're fond of De Quincey, Senator?" to which Quay responded, "Yes; always liked De Quincey; good-by." And away he went with the tribesmen, who seemed to have walked out of a remote past.

Quay had become particularly concerned about the Delawares in the Indian Territory. He felt that the Interior Department did not do them justice. He also felt that his colleagues of the Senate took no interest in them. When in the spring of 1904 he lay in his house mortally sick, he sent me word that he had something important to say to me, and would have himself carried round to see me. I sent back word not to think of doing so, and that on my way back from church next Sunday I would stop in and call on him. This I accordingly did. He was lying in his bed, death written on his face. He thanked me for coming, and then explained that, as he was on the point of death and knew he would never return to Washington—it was late spring and he was about to leave—he wished to see me to get my personal promise that, after he died, I would myself look after the interests of the Delaware Indians. He added that he did not trust the Interior Department—although he knew that I did not share his views on this point—and that still less did he believe that any of his colleagues in the Senate would exert themselves in the interests of the Delawares, and that therefore he wished my personal assurance that I would personally see that no injustice was done them. I told him I would do so, and then added, in rather perfunctory fashion, that he must not take such a gloomy view of himself, that when he got away for the summer I hoped he would recover and be back all right when Congress opened. A gleam came into the old fighter's eyes and he answered: "No, I am dying, and you know it. I don't mind dying; but I do wish it were possible for me to get off into the great north woods and crawl out on a rock in the sun and die like a wolf!"

I never saw him again. When he died I sent a telegram of sympathy to his wife. A paper which constantly preached reform, and which kept up its circulation by the no less constant practice of slander, a paper which in theory condemned all public men who violated the eighth commandment, and in practice subsisted by incessant violation of the ninth, assailed me for sending my message to the dead man's wife. I knew the editors of this paper, and the editor who was their predecessor. They had led lives of bodily ease and the avoidance of bodily risk; they earned their livelihood by the practice of mendacity for profit; and they delivered malignant judgment on a dead man who, whatever his faults, had in his youth freely risked his life for a great ideal, and who when death was already clutching his breast had spent almost his last breath on behalf of humble and friendless people whom he had served with disinterested loyalty.

There is no greater duty than to war on the corrupt and unprincipled boss, and on the corrupt and unprincipled business man; and for the matter of that, on the corrupt and unprincipled labor leader also, and on the corrupt and unprincipled editor, and on any one else who is corrupt and unprincipled. But where the conditions are such, whether in politics or in business, that the great majority of men have behaved in a way which is gradually seen to be improper, but which at one time did not conflict with the generally accepted morality, then the warfare on the system should not include warfare on the men themselves, unless they decline to amend their ways and to dissociate themselves from the system. There are many good, unimaginative citizens who in politics or in business act in accordance with accepted standards, in a matter-of-course way, without questioning these standards; until something happens which sharply arouses them to the situation, whereupon they try to work for better things. The proper course in such event is to let bygones be bygones, and if the men prove by their actions the sincerity of their conversion, heartily to work with them for the betterment of business and political conditions.

By the time that I was ending my career as Civil Service Commissioner I was already growing to understand that mere improvement in political conditions by itself was not enough. I dimly realized that an even greater fight must be waged to improve economic conditions, and to secure social and industrial justice, justice as between individuals and justice as between classes. I began to see that political effort was largely valuable as it found expression and resulted in such social and industrial betterment. I was gradually puzzling out, or trying to puzzle out, the answers to various questions—some as yet unsolvable to any of us, but for the solution of which it is the bounden duty of all of us to work. I had grown to realize very keenly that the duty of the Government to protect women and children must be extended to include the protection of all the crushable elements of labor. I saw that it was the affair of all our people to see that justice obtained between the big corporation and its employees, and between the big corporation and its smaller rivals, as well as its customers and the general public. I saw that it was the affair of all of us, and not only of the employer, if dividends went up and wages went down; that it was to the interest of all of us that a full share of the benefit of improved machinery should go to the workman who used the machinery; and also that it was to the interest of all of us that each man, whether brain worker or hand worker, should do the best work of which he was capable, and that there should be some correspondence between the value of the work and the value of the reward. It is these and many similar questions which in their sum make up the great social and industrial problems of to-day, the most interesting and important of the problems with which our public life must deal.

In handling these problems I believe that much can be done by the Government. Furthermore, I believe that, after all that the Government can do has been done, there will remain as the most vital of all factors the individual character of the average man and the average woman. No governmental action can do more than supplement individual action. Moreover, there must be collective action of kinds distinct from governmental action. A body of public opinion must be formed, must make itself felt, and in the end transform, and be transformed by, the gradual raising of individual standards of conduct.

It is curious to see how difficult it is to make some men understand that insistence upon one factor does not and must not mean failure fully to recognize other factors. The selfish individual needs to be taught that we must now shackle cunning by law exactly as a few centuries back we shackled force by law. Unrestricted individualism spells ruin to the individual himself. But so does the elimination of individualism, whether by law or custom. It is a capital error to fail to recognize the vital need of good laws. It is also a capital error to believe that good laws will accomplish anything unless the average man has the right stuff in him. The toiler, the manual laborer, has received less than justice, and he must be protected, both by law, by custom, and by the exercise of his right to increase his wage; and yet to decrease the quantity and quality of his work will work only evil. There must be a far greater meed of respect and reward for the hand worker than we now give him, if our society is to be put on a sound basis; and this respect and reward cannot be given him unless he is as ambitious to do the best possible work as is the highest type of brain worker, whether doctor or writer or artist. There must be a raising of standards, and not a leveling down to the standard of the poorest and most inefficient. There is urgent need of intelligent governmental action to assist in making the life of the man who tills the soil all that it should be, and to see that the manual worker gets his full share of the reward for what he helps produce; but if either farmer, mechanic, or day laborer is shiftless or lazy, if he shirks downright hard work, if he is stupid or self-indulgent, then no law can save him, and he must give way to a better type.

I suppose that some good people will misunderstand what I say, and will insist on taking only half of it as representing the whole. Let me repeat. When I say, that, even after we have all the good laws necessary, the chief factor in any given man's success or failure must be that man's own character, it must not be inferred that I am in the least minimizing the importance of these laws, the real and vital need for them. The struggle for individual advancement and development can be brought to naught, or indefinitely retarded, by the absence of law or by bad law. It can be immeasurably aided by organized effort on the part of the State. Collective action and individual action, public law and private character, are both necessary. It is only by a slow and patient inward transformation such as these laws aid in bringing about that men are really helped upward in their struggle for a higher and a fuller life. Recognition of individual character as the most important of all factors does not mean failure fully to recognize that we must have good laws, and that we must have our best men in office to enforce these laws. The Nation collectively will in this way be able to be of real and genuine service to each of us individually; and, on the other hand, the wisdom of the collective action will mainly depend on the high individual average of citizenship.

The relationship of man and woman is the fundamental relationship that stands at the base of the whole social structure. Much can be done by law towards putting women on a footing of complete and entire equal rights with man—including the right to vote, the right to hold and use property, and the right to enter any profession she desires on the same terms as a man. Yet when this has been done it will amount to little unless on the one hand the man himself realizes his duty to the woman, and unless on the other hand the woman realizes that she has no claim to rights unless she performs the duties that go with those rights and that alone justify her in appealing to them. A cruel, selfish, or licentious man is an abhorrent member of the community; but, after all, his actions are no worse in the long run than those of the woman who is content to be a parasite on others, who is cold, selfish, caring for nothing but frivolous pleasure and ignoble ease. The law of worthy effort, the law of service for a worthy end, without regard to whether it brings pleasure or pain, is the only right law of life, whether for man or for woman. The man must not be selfish; nor, if the woman is wise, will she let the man grow selfish, and this not only for her own sake but for his. One of the prime needs is to remember that almost every duty is composed of two seemingly conflicting elements, and that overinsistence on one, to the exclusion of the other, may defeat its own end. Any man who studies the statistics of the birth-rate among the native Americans of New England, or among the native French of France, needs not to be told that when prudence and forethought are carried to the point of cold selfishness and self-indulgence, the race is bound to disappear. Taking into account the women who for good reasons do not marry, or who when married are childless or are able to have but one or two children, it is evident that the married woman able to have children must on an average have four or the race will not perpetuate itself. This is the mere statement of a self-evident truth. Yet foolish and self-indulgent people often resent this statement as if it were in some way possible by denunciation to reverse the facts of nature; and, on the other hand, improvident and shiftless people, inconsiderate and brutal people, treat the statement as if it justified heads of families in having enormous numbers of badly nourished, badly brought up, and badly cared for children for whom they make no effort to provide. A man must think well before he marries. He must be a tender and considerate husband and realize that there is no other human being to whom he owes so much of love and regard and consideration as he does to the woman who with pain bears and with labor rears the children that are his. No words can paint the scorn and contempt which must be felt by all right-thinking men, not only for the brutal husband, but for the husband who fails to show full loyalty and consideration to his wife. Moreover, he must work, he must do his part in the world. On the other hand, the woman must realize that she has no more right to shirk the business of wifehood and motherhood than the man has to shirk his business as breadwinner for the household. Women should have free access to every field of labor which they care to enter, and when their work is as valuable as that of a man it should be paid as highly. Yet normally for the man and the woman whose welfare is more important than the welfare of any other human beings, the woman must remain the housemother, the homekeeper, and the man must remain the breadwinner, the provider for the wife who bears his children and for the children she brings into the world. No other work is as valuable or as exacting for either man or woman; it must always, in every healthy society, be for both man and woman the prime work, the most important work; normally all other work is of secondary importance, and must come as an addition to, not a substitute for, this primary work. The partnership should be one of equal rights, one of love, of self-respect, and unselfishness, above all a partnership for the performance of the most vitally important of all duties. The performance of duty, and not an indulgence in vapid ease and vapid pleasure, is all that makes life worth while.

Suffrage for women should be looked on from this standpoint. Personally I feel that it is exactly as much a "right" of women as of men to vote. But the important point with both men and women is to treat the exercise of the suffrage as a duty, which, in the long run, must be well performed to be of the slightest value. I always favored woman's suffrage, but only tepidly, until my association with women like Jane Addams and Frances Kellor, who desired it as one means of enabling them to render better and more efficient service, changed me into a zealous instead of a lukewarm adherent of the cause—in spite of the fact that a few of the best women of the same type, women like Mary Antin, did not favor the movement. A vote is like a rifle: its usefulness depends upon the character of the user. The mere possession of the vote will no more benefit men and women not sufficiently developed to use it than the possession of rifles will turn untrained Egyptian fellaheen into soldiers. This is as true of woman as of man—and no more true. Universal suffrage in Hayti has not made the Haytians able to govern themselves in any true sense; and woman suffrage in Utah in no shape or way affected the problem of polygamy. I believe in suffrage for women in America, because I think they are fit for it. I believe for women, as for men, more in the duty of fitting one's self to do well and wisely with the ballot than in the naked right to cast the ballot.

I wish that people would read books like the novels and stories, at once strong and charming, of Henry Bordeaux, books like Kathleen Norris's "Mother," and Cornelia Comer's "Preliminaries," and would use these, and other such books, as tracts, now and then! Perhaps the following correspondence will give a better idea than I can otherwise give of the problems that in everyday life come before men and women, and of the need that the man shall show himself unselfish and considerate, and do his full share of the joint duty:

January 3, 1913.

Colonel Theodore Roosevelt:

Dear Sir—I suppose you are willing to stand sponsor for the assertion that the women of the country are not doing their duty unless they have large families. I wonder if you know the real reason, after all. Society and clubs are held largely to blame, but society really takes in so few people, after all. I thought, when I got married at twenty, that it was the proper thing to have a family, and, as we had very little of this world's goods, also thought it the thing to do all the necessary work for them. I have had nine children, did all my own work, including washing, ironing, house-cleaning, and the care of the little ones as they came along, which was about every two years; also sewed everything they wore, including trousers for the boys and caps and jackets for the girls while little. I also helped them all in their school work, and started them in music, etc. But as they grew older I got behind the times. I never belonged to a club or a society or lodge, nor went to any one's house scarcely; there wasn't time. In consequence, I knew nothing that was going on in the town, much less the events of the country, and at the same time my husband kept growing in wisdom and knowledge, from mixing with men and hearing topics of the times discussed. At the beginning of our married life I had just as quick a mind to grasp things as he did, and had more school education, having graduated from a three years' high school. My husband more and more declined to discuss things with me; as he said, "I didn't know anything about it." When I'd ask he'd say, "Oh, you wouldn't understand if I'd tell you." So here I am, at forty-five years, hopelessly dull and uninteresting, while he can mix with the brightest minds in the country as an equal. He's a strong Progressive man, took very active part in the late campaign, etc. I am also Progressive, and tried my best, after so many years of shut-in life, to grasp the ideas you stood for, and read everything I could find during the summer and fall. But I've been out of touch with people too long now, and my husband would much rather go and talk to some woman who hasn't had any children, because *she knows things* (I am not specifying any particular woman). I simply bore him to death because I'm not interesting. Now, tell me, how was it my fault? I was only doing what I thought was my duty. No woman can keep up with things who never talks with any one but young children. As soon as my children grew up they took the same attitude as their father, and frequently say, "Oh, mother doesn't know." They look up to and admire their father because he's a man of the world and knows how to act when he goes out. How can I urge my daughters now to go and raise large families? It means by the time you have lost your figure and charm for them they are all ashamed of you. Now, as a believer in woman's rights, do a little talking to the men as to their duties to their wives, or else refrain from urging us women to have children. I am only one of thousands of middle-class respectable women who give their lives to raise a nice family, and then who become bitter from the injustice done us. Don't let this go into the waste-basket, but think it over.

Yours respectfully, ——— ———.

New York, January 11, 1913.

My Dear Mrs. ———:

Most certainly your letter will not go into the waste-paper basket. I shall think it over and show it to Mrs. Roosevelt. Will you let me say, in the first place, that a woman who can write such a letter is certainly not "hopelessly dull and uninteresting"! If the facts are as you state, then I do not wonder that you feel bitterly and that you feel that the gravest kind of injustice has been done you. I have always tried to insist to men that they should do their duty to the women even more than the women to them. Now I hardly like to write specifically about your husband, because you might not like it yourself. It seems to me almost incredible that any man who is the husband of a woman who has borne him nine children should not feel that they and he are lastingly her debtors. You say that you have had nine children, that you did all your own work, including washing, ironing, house-cleaning, and the care of the little ones as they came along; that you sewed everything they wore, including trousers for the boys and caps and jackets for the girls while little; that you helped them all in their school work and started them in music; but that as they grew older you got behind the times, that you never belonged to a club or society or lodge, nor went to any one's house, as you hardly had time to do so; and that in consequence your husband outgrew you, and that your children look up to him and not to you and feel that they have outgrown you. If these facts are so, you have done a great and wonderful work, and the only explanation I can possibly give of the attitude you describe on the part of your husband and children is that they do not understand what it is that you have done. I emphatically believe in unselfishness, but I also believe that it is a mistake to let other people grow selfish, even when the other people are husband and children.

Now, I suggest that you take your letter to me, of which I send you back a copy, and this letter, and then select out of your family the one with whom you feel most sympathy, whether it is your husband or one of your children. Show the two letters to him or her, and then have a frank talk about the matter. If any man, as you say, becomes ashamed of his wife because she has lost her figure in bearing his children, then that man is a hound and has every cause to be ashamed of himself. I am sending you a little book called *Mother*, by Kathleen Norris, which will give you my views on the matter. Of course there are base and selfish men, just as there are, although I believe in smaller number, base and selfish women. Man and woman alike should profit by the teachings in such a story as this of *Mother*.

Sincerely yours,
THEODORE ROOSEVELT.

January 21, 1913.

Colonel Theodore Roosevelt:

My dear Sir—Your letter came as a surprise, for I wasn't expecting an answer. The next day the book came, and I thank you for your ready sympathy and understanding. I feel as though you and Mrs. Roosevelt would think I was hardly loyal to my husband and children; but knowing of no other way to bring the idea which was so strong in my mind to your notice, I told my personal story. If it will, in a small measure, be the means of helping some one else by moulding public opinion, through you, I shall be content. You have helped me more than you know. Just having you interested is as good as a tonic, and braces me up till I feel as though I shall refuse to be "laid on the shelf." ... To think that you'd bother to send me a book. I shall always treasure it both for the text of the book and the sender. I read it with absorbing interest. The mother was so splendid. She was ideal. The situations are so startlingly real, just like what happens here every day with variations. ——— ———.

A narrative of facts is often more convincing than a homily; and these two letters of my correspondent carry their own lesson.

Parenthetically, let me remark that whenever a man thinks that he has outgrown the woman who is his mate, he will do well carefully to consider whether his growth has not been downward instead of upward, whether the facts are not merely that he has fallen away from his wife's standard of refinement and of duty.

THE BIG STICK AND THE SQUARE DEAL

Excerpt from Roosevelt's Autobiography

ONE of the vital questions with which as President I had to deal was the attitude of the Nation toward the great corporations. Men who understand and practice the deep underlying philosophy of the Lincoln school of American political thought are necessarily Hamiltonian in their belief in a strong and efficient National Government and Jeffersonian in their belief in the people as the ultimate authority, and in the welfare of the people as the end of Government. The men who first applied the extreme Democratic theory in American life were, like Jefferson, ultra individualists, for at that time what was demanded by our people was the largest liberty for the individual. During the century that had elapsed since Jefferson became President the need had been exactly reversed. There had been in our country a riot of individualistic materialism, under which complete freedom for the individual—that ancient license which President Wilson a century after the term was excusable has called the "New" Freedom—turned out in practice to mean perfect freedom for the strong to wrong the weak. The total absence of governmental control had led to a portentous growth in the financial and industrial world both of natural individuals and of artificial individuals—that is, corporations. In no other country in the world had such enormous fortunes been gained. In no other country in the world was such power held by the men who had gained these fortunes; and these men almost always worked through, and by means of, the giant corporations which they controlled. The power of the mighty industrial overlords of the country had increased with giant strides, while the methods of controlling them, or checking abuses by them, on the part of the people, through the Government, remained archaic and therefore practically impotent. The courts, not unnaturally, but most regrettably, and to the grave detriment of the people and of their own standing, had for a quarter of a century been on the whole the agents of reaction, and by conflicting decisions which, however, in their sum were hostile to the interests of the people, had left both the nation and the several States well-nigh impotent to deal with the great business combinations. Sometimes they forbade the Nation to interfere, because such interference trespassed on the rights of the States; sometimes they forbade the States to interfere (and often they were wise in this), because to do so would trespass on the rights of the Nation; but always, or well-nigh always, their action was negative action against the interests of the people, ingeniously devised to limit their power against wrong, instead of affirmative action giving to the people power to right wrong. They had rendered these decisions sometimes as upholders of property rights against human rights, being especially zealous in securing the rights of the very men who were most competent to take care of themselves; and sometimes in the name of liberty, in the name of the so-called "new freedom," in reality the old, old "freedom," which secured to the powerful the freedom to prey on the poor and the helpless.

One of the main troubles was the fact that the men who saw the evils and who tried to remedy them attempted to work in two wholly different ways, and the great majority of them in a way that offered little promise of real betterment. They tried (by the Sherman law method) to bolster up an individualism already proved to be both futile and mischievous; to remedy by more individualism the concentration that was the inevitable result of the already existing individualism. They saw the evil done by the big combinations, and sought to remedy it by destroying them and restoring the country to the economic conditions of the middle of the nineteenth century. This was a hopeless effort, and those who went into it, although they regarded themselves as radical progressives, really represented a form of sincere rural toryism. They confounded monopolies with big business combinations, and in the effort to prohibit both alike, instead of where possible prohibiting one and drastically controlling the other, they succeeded merely in preventing any effective control of either.

On the other hand, a few men recognized that corporations and combinations had become indispensable in the business world, that it was folly to try to prohibit them, but that it was also folly to leave them without thoroughgoing control. These men realized that the doctrines of the old *laissez faire* economists, of the believers in unlimited competition, unlimited individualism, were in the actual state of affairs false and mischievous. They realized that the Government must now interfere to protect labor, to subordinate the big corporation to the public welfare, and to shackle cunning and fraud exactly as centuries before it had interfered to shackle the physical force which does wrong by violence.

The big reactionaries of the business world and their allies and instruments among politicians and newspaper editors took advantage of this division of opinion, and especially of the fact that most of their opponents were on the wrong path; and fought to keep matters absolutely unchanged. These men demanded for themselves an immunity from governmental control which, if granted, would have been as wicked and as foolish as immunity to the barons of the twelfth century. Many of them were evil men. Many others were just as good men as were some of these same barons; but they were as utterly unable as any medieval castle-owner to understand what the public interest really was. There have been aristocracies which have played a great and beneficent part at stages in the growth of mankind; but we had come to the stage where for our people what was needed was a real democracy; and of all forms of tyranny the least attractive and the most vulgar is the tyranny of mere wealth, the tyranny of a plutocracy.

When I became President, the question as to the *method* by which the United States Government was to control the corporations was not yet important. The absolutely vital question was whether the Government had power to control them at all. This question had not yet been decided in favor of the United States Government. It was useless to discuss methods of controlling big business by the National Government until it was definitely settled that the National Government had the power to control it. A decision of the Supreme Court had, with seeming definiteness, settled that the National Government had not the power.

This decision I caused to be annulled by the court that had rendered it; and the present power of the National Government to deal effectively with the trusts is due solely to the success of the Administration in securing this reversal of its former decision by the Supreme Court.

The Constitution was formed very largely because it had become imperative to give to some central authority the power to regulate and control interstate commerce. At that time when corporations were in their infancy and big combinations unknown, there was no difficulty in exercising the power granted. In theory, the right of the Nation to exercise this power continued unquestioned. But changing conditions obscured the matter in the sight of the people as a whole; and the conscious and the unconscious advocates of an unlimited and uncontrollable capitalism gradually secured the whittling away of the National power to exercise this theoretical right of control until it practically vanished. After the Civil War, with the portentous growth of industrial combinations in this country, came a period of reactionary decisions by the courts which, as regards corporations, culminated in what is known as the Knight case.

The Sherman Anti-Trust Law was enacted in 1890 because the formation of the Tobacco Trust and the Sugar Trust, the only two great trusts then in the country (aside from the Standard Oil Trust, which was a gradual growth), had awakened a popular demand for legislation to destroy monopoly and curb industrial combinations. This demand the Anti-Trust Law was intended to satisfy. The Administrations of Mr. Harrison and Mr. Cleveland evidently construed this law as prohibiting such combinations in the future, not as condemning those which had been formed prior to its enactment. In 1895, however, the Sugar Trust, whose output originally was about fifty-five per cent of all sugar produced in the United States, obtained control of three other companies in Philadelphia by exchanging its stock for theirs, and thus increased its business until it controlled ninety-eight per cent of the entire product. Under Cleveland, the Government brought proceedings against the Sugar Trust, invoking the Anti-Trust Law, to set aside the acquisition of these corporations. The test case was on the absorption of the Knight Company.* The Supreme Court of the United States, with but one dissenting vote, held adversely to the Government. They took the ground that the power conferred by the Constitution to regulate and control interstate commerce did not extend to the production or manufacture of commodities within a State, and that nothing in the Sherman Anti-Trust Law prohibited a corporation from acquiring all the stock of other corporations through exchange of its stock for theirs, such exchange not being "commerce" in the opinion of the Court, even though by such acquisition the corporation was enabled to control the entire production of a commodity that was a necessary of life. The effect of this decision was not merely the absolute nullification of the Anti-Trust Law, so far as industrial corporations were concerned, but was also in effect a declaration that, under the Constitution, the National Government could pass no law really effective for the destruction or control of such combinations.

This decision left the National Government, that is, the people of the Nation, practically helpless to deal with the large combinations of modern business. The courts in other cases asserted the power of the Federal Government to enforce the Anti-Trust Law so far as transportation rates by railways engaged in interstate commerce were concerned. But so long as the trusts were free to control the production of commodities without interference from the General Government, they were well content to let the transportation of commodities take care of itself—especially as the law against rebates was at that time a dead letter; and the Court by its decision in the Knight case had interdicted any interference by the President or by Congress with the production of commodities. It was on the authority of this case that practically all the big trusts in the United States, excepting those already mentioned, were formed. Usually they were organized as "holding" companies, each one acquiring control of its constituent corporations by exchanging its stock for theirs, an operation which the Supreme Court had thus decided could not be prohibited, controlled, regulated, or even questioned by the Federal Government.

Such was the condition of our laws when I acceded to the Presidency. Just before my accession, a small group of financiers, desiring to profit by the governmental impotence to which we had been reduced by the Knight decision, had arranged to take control of practically the entire railway system in the Northwest—possibly as the first step toward controlling the entire railway system of the country. This control of the Northwestern railway systems was to be effected by organizing a new "holding" company, and exchanging its stock against the stock of the various corporations engaged in railway transportation throughout that vast territory, exactly as the Sugar Trust had acquired control of the Knight company and other

* The case is known in the law books as U. S. vs. E. C. Knight, 156 U. S., Sept., p. 1.

concerns. This company was called the Northern Securities Company. Not long after I became President, on the advice of the Attorney-General, Mr. Knox, and through him, I ordered proceedings to be instituted for the dissolution of the company. As far as could be told by their utterances at the time, among all the great lawyers in the United States Mr. Knox was the only one who believed that this action could be sustained. The defense was based expressly on the ground that the Supreme Court in the Knight case had explicitly sanctioned the formation of such a company as the Northern Securities Company. The representatives of privilege intimated, and sometimes asserted outright, that in directing the action to be brought I had shown a lack of respect for the Supreme Court, which had already decided the question at issue by a vote of eight to one. Mr. Justice White, then on the Court and now Chief Justice, set forth the position that the two cases were in principle identical with incontrovertible logic. In giving the views of the dissenting minority on the action I had brought, he said:

"The parallel between the two cases [the Knight case and the Northern Securities case] is complete. The one corporation acquired the stock of other and competing corporations in exchange for its own. It was conceded for the purposes of the case, that in doing so monopoly had been brought about in the refining of sugar, that the sugar to be produced was likely to become the subject of interstate commerce, and indeed that part of it would certainly become so. But the power of Congress was decided not to extend to the subject, because the ownership of the stock in the corporations was not itself commerce."*

Mr. Justice White was entirely correct in this statement. The cases were parallel. It was necessary to reverse the Knight case in the interests of the people against monopoly and privilege just as it had been necessary to reverse the Dred Scott case in the interest of the people against slavery and privilege; just as later it became necessary to reverse the New York Bakeshop case in the interest of the people against that form of monopolistic privilege which put human rights below property rights where wage workers were concerned.

By a vote of five to four the Supreme Court reversed its decision in the Knight case, and in the Northern Securities case sustained the Government. The power to deal with industrial monopoly and suppress it and to control and regulate combinations, of which the Knight case had deprived the Federal Government, was thus restored to it by the Northern Securities case. After this later decision was rendered, suits were brought by my direction against the American Tobacco Company and the Standard Oil Company. Both were adjudged criminal conspiracies, and their dissolution ordered. The Knight case was finally overthrown. The vicious doctrine it embodied no longer remains as an obstacle to

* Northern Securities Company et al. vs. U. S., 156 U. S., Sept., pp. 391-2.

obstruct the pathway of justice when it assails monopoly. Messrs. Knox, Moody, and Bonaparte, who successively occupied the position of Attorney-General under me, were profound lawyers and fearless and able men; and they completely established the newer and more wholesome doctrine under which the Federal Government may now deal with monopolistic combinations and conspiracies.

The decisions rendered in these various cases brought under my direction constitute the entire authority upon which any action must rest that seeks through the exercise of national power to curb monopolistic control. The men who organized and directed the Northern Securities Company were also the controlling forces in the Steel Corporation, which has since been prosecuted under the act. The proceedings against the Sugar Trust for corruption in connection with the New York Custom House are sufficiently interesting to be considered separately.

From the standpoint of giving complete control to the National Government over big corporations engaged in inter-State business, it would be impossible to over-estimate the importance of the Northern Securities decision and of the decisions afterwards rendered in line with it in connection with the other trusts whose dissolution was ordered. The success of the Northern Securities case definitely established the power of the Government to deal with all great corporations. Without this success the National Government must have remained in the impotence to which it had been reduced by the Knight decision as regards the most important of its internal functions. But our success in establishing the power of the National Government to curb monopolies did not establish the right method of exercising that power. We had gained the power. We had not devised the proper method of exercising it.

Monopolies can, although in rather cumbrous fashion, be broken up by law suits. Great business combinations, however, cannot possibly be made useful instead of noxious industrial agencies merely by law suits, and especially by law suits supposed to be carried on for their destruction and not for their control and regulation. I at once began to urge upon Congress the need of laws supplementing the Anti-Trust Law—for this law struck at all big business, good and bad, alike, and as the event proved was very inefficient in checking bad big business, and yet was a constant threat against decent business men. I strongly urged the inauguration of a system of thoroughgoing and drastic Governmental regulation and control over all big business combinations engaged in inter-State industry.

Here I was able to accomplish only a small part of what I desired to accomplish. I was opposed both by the foolish radicals who desired to break up all big business, with the impossible ideal of returning to mid-nineteenth century industrial conditions; and also by the great privileged interests themselves, who used these ordinarily—but sometimes not entirely—well-meaning "stool pigeon progressives" to further their own cause. The worst representatives of big business encouraged the outcry for the total abolition of big business, because they knew that they could not be hurt in this way, and that such an outcry distracted the attention of the public from the really efficient method of controlling and supervising them, in just but masterly fashion, which was advocated by the sane representatives of reform. However, we succeeded in making a good beginning by securing the passage of a law creating the Department of Commerce and Labor, and with it the erection of the Bureau of Corporations. The first head of the Department of Commerce and Labor was Mr. Cortelyou, later Secretary of the Treasury. He was succeeded by Mr. Oscar Straus. The first head of the Bureau of Corporations was Mr. Garfield, who was succeeded by Mr. Herbert Knox Smith. No four better public servants from the standpoint of the people as a whole could have been found.

The Standard Oil Company took the lead in opposing all this legislation. This was natural, for it had been the worst offender in the amassing of enormous fortunes by improper methods of all kinds, at the expense of business rivals and of the public, including the corruption of public servants. If any man thinks this condemnation extreme, I refer him to the language officially used by the Supreme Court of the nation in its decision against the Standard Oil Company. Through their counsel, and by direct telegrams and letters to Senators and Congressmen from various heads of the Standard Oil organization, they did their best to kill the bill providing for the Bureau of Corporations. I got hold of one or two of these telegrams and letters, however, and promptly published them; and, as generally happens in such a case, the men who were all-powerful as long as they could work in secret and behind closed doors became powerless as soon as they were forced into the open. The bill went through without further difficulty.

The true way of dealing with monopoly is to prevent it by administrative action before it grows so powerful that even when courts condemn it they shrink from destroying it. The Supreme Court in the Tobacco and Standard Oil cases, for instance, used very vigorous language in condemning these trusts; but the net result of the decision was of positive advantage to the wrongdoers, and this has tended to bring the whole body of our law into disrepute in quarters where it is of the very highest importance that the law be held in respect and even in reverence. My effort was to secure the creation of a Federal Commission which should neither excuse nor tolerate monopoly, but prevent it when possible and unroot it when discovered; and which should in addition effectively control and regulate all big combinations, and should give honest business certainty as to what the law was and security as long as the law was obeyed. Such a Commission would furnish a steady expert control, a control adapted to the problem; and dissolution is neither control nor regulation, but is purely negative; and negative remedies are of little permanent avail. Such a Commission would have complete power to examine into every big corporation engaged or proposing to engage in business between the States. It would have the power to discriminate sharply between corporations that are doing well and those that are doing ill; and the distinction between those who do well and those who do ill would be defined in terms so clear and unmistakable that no one could misapprehend them. Where a company is found seeking its profits through serving the community by stimulating production, lowering prices, or improving service, while scrupulously respecting the rights of others (including its rivals, its employees, its customers, and the general public), and strictly obeying the law, then no matter how large its capital, or how great the volume of its business it would be encouraged to still more abundant production, or better service, by the fullest protection that the Government could afford it. On the other hand, if a corporation were found seeking profit through injury or oppression of the community, by restricting production through trick or device, by plot or conspiracy against competitors, or by oppression of wage-workers, and then extorting high prices for the commodity it had made artificially scarce, it would be prevented from organizing if its nefarious purpose could be discovered in time, or pursued and suppressed by all the power of Government whenever found in actual operation. Such a commission, with the power I advocate, would put a stop to abuses of big corporations and small corporations alike; it would draw the line on conduct and not on size; it would destroy monopoly, and make the biggest business man in the country conform squarely to the principles laid down by the American people, while at the same time giving fair play to the little man and certainty of knowledge as to what was wrong and what was right both to big man and little man.

Although under the decision of the courts the National Government had power over the railways, I found, when I became President, that this power was either not exercised at all or exercised with utter inefficiency. The law against rebates was a dead letter. All the unscrupulous railway men had been allowed to violate it with impunity; and because of this, as was inevitable, the scrupulous and decent railway men had been forced to violate it themselves, under penalty of being beaten by their less scrupulous rivals. It was not the fault of these decent railway men. It was the fault of the Government.

Thanks to a first-class railway man, Paul Morton of the Santa Fé, son of Mr. Cleveland's Secretary of Agriculture, I was able completely to stop the practice. Mr. Morton volunteered to aid the Government in abolishing rebates. He frankly stated that he, like every one else, had been guilty in the matter; but he insisted that he uttered the sentiments of the decent railway men of the country when he said that he hoped the practice would be stopped, and that if I would really stop it, and not merely make believe to stop it, he would give the testimony which would put into the hands of the Government the power to put a complete check to the practice. Accordingly he testified, and on the information which he gave us we were able to take such action through the Inter-State Commerce Commission and the Department of Justice, supplemented by the necessary additional legislation, that the evil was absolutely eradicated. He thus rendered, of his own accord, at his own personal risk, and from purely disinterested motives, an invaluable service to the people, a service which no other man who was able to render was willing to render. As an immediate sequel, the world-old alliance between Blifil and Black George was immediately revived against Paul Morton. In giving rebates he had done only what every honest railway man in the country had been obliged to do because of the failure of the Government to enforce the prohibition as regards dishonest railway men. But unlike his fellows he had then shown the courage and sense of obligation to the public which made him come forward and without evasion or concealment state what he had done, in order that we might successfully put an end to the practice; and put an end to the practice we did, and we did it because of the courage and patriotism he had shown. The unscrupulous railway men, whose dishonest practices were thereby put a stop to, and the unscrupulous demagogues who were either under the influence of these men or desirous of gaining credit with thoughtless and ignorant people no matter who was hurt, joined in vindictive clamor against Mr. Morton. They actually wished me to prosecute him, although such prosecution would have been a piece of unpardonable ingratitude and treachery on the part of the public toward him—for I was merely acting as the steward of the public in this matter. I need hardly say that I stood by him; and later he served under me as Secretary of the Navy, and a capital Secretary he made too.

We not only secured the stopping of rebates, but in the Hepburn Rate Bill we were able to put through a measure which gave the Inter-State Commerce Commission for the first time real control over the railways. There were two or three amusing features in the contest over this bill. All of the great business interests which objected to Governmental control banded to fight it, and they were helped by the honest men of ultra-conservative type who always dread change, whether good or bad. We finally forced it through the House. In the Senate it was referred to a committee in which the Republican majority was under the control of Senator Aldrich, who took the lead in opposing the bill. There was one Republican on the committee, however, whom Senator Aldrich could not control—Senator Dolliver, of Iowa. The leading Democrat on the committee was Senator Tillman, of South Carolina, with whom I was not on good terms, because I had been obliged to cancel an invitation to him to dine at the White House on account of his having made a personal assault in the Senate Chamber on his colleague from South Carolina; and later I had to take action against him on account of his conduct in connection with certain land matters. Senator Tillman favored the bill. The Republican majority in the committee under Senator Aldrich, when they acted adversely on the bill, turned it over to Senator Tillman, thereby making him its sponsor. The object was to create what it was hoped would be an impossible situation in view of the relations between Senator Tillman and myself. I regarded the action as simply childish. It was a curious instance of how able and astute men sometimes commit blunders because of sheer inability to understand intensity of disinterested motive in others. I did not care a rap about Mr. Tillman's getting credit for the bill, or having charge of it. I was delighted to go with him or with any one else just so long as he was traveling in my way—and no longer.

There was another amusing incident in connection with the passage of the bill. All the wise friends of the effort to secure Governmental control of corporations know that this Government control must be exercised through administrative and not judicial officers if it is to be effective. Everything possible should be done to minimize the chance of appealing from the decisions of the administrative officer to the courts. But it is not possible Constitutionally, and probably would not be desirable anyhow, completely to abolish the appeal. Unwise zealots wished to make the effort totally to abolish the appeal in connection with the Hepburn Bill. Representatives of the special interests wished to extend the appeal to include what it ought not to include. Between stood a number of men whose votes would mean the passage of, or the failure to pass, the bill, and who were not inclined towards either side. Three or four substantially identical amendments were proposed, and we then suddenly found ourselves face to face with an absurd situation. The good men who were willing to go with us but had conservative misgivings about the ultra-radicals would not accept a good amendment if one of the latter proposed it; and the radicals would not accept their own amendment if one of the conservatives proposed it. Each side got so wrought up as to be utterly unable to get matters into proper perspective; each prepared to stand on unimportant trifles; each announced with hysterical emphasis—the reformers just as hysterically as the reactionaries—that the decision as regards each unimportant trifle determined the worth or worthlessness of the measure. Gradually we secured a measurable return to sane appreciation of the essentials. Finally both sides reluctantly agreed to accept the so-called Allison amendment which did not, as a matter of fact, work any change in the bill at all. The amendment was drawn by Attorney-General Moody after consultation with the Inter-State Commerce Commission, and was forwarded by me to Senator Dolliver; it was accepted, and the bill became law.

Thanks to this law and to the way in which the Inter-State Commerce Commission was backed by the Administration, the Commission, under men like Prouty, Lane, and Clark, became a most powerful force for good. Some of the good that we had accomplished was undone after the close of my Administration by the unfortunate law creating a Commerce Court; but the major part of the immense advance we had made remained. There was one point on which I insisted, and upon which it is necessary always to insist. The Commission cannot do permanent good unless it does justice to the corporations precisely as it exacts justice from them. The public, the shippers, the stock and bondholders, and the employees, all have their rights, and none should be allowed unfair privileges at the expense of the others. Stock watering and swindling of any kind should of course not only be stopped but punished. When, however, a road is managed fairly and honestly, and when it renders a real and needed service, then the Government must see that it is not so burdened as to make it impossible to run it at a profit. There is much wise legislation necessary for the safety of the public, or—like workmen's compensation—necessary to the well-being of the employee, which nevertheless imposes such a burden on the road that the burden must be distributed between the general public and the corporation, or there will be no dividends. In such a case it may be the highest duty of the commission to raise rates; and the commission, when satisfied that the necessity exists, in order to do justice to the owners of the road, should no more hesitate to raise rates, than under other circumstances to lower them.

So much for the "big stick" in dealing with the corporations when they went wrong. Now for a sample of the square deal.

In the fall of 1907 there were severe business disturbances and financial stringency, culminating in a panic which arose in New York and spread over the country. The damage actually done was great, and the damage threatened was incalculable. Thanks largely to the action of the Government, the panic was stopped before, instead of being merely a serious business check, it became a frightful and Nation-wide calamity, a disaster fraught with untold misery and woe to all our people. For several days the Nation trembled on the brink of such a calamity, of such a disaster.

During these days both the Secretary of the Treasury and I personally were in hourly communication with New York, following every change in the situation, and trying to anticipate every development. It was the obvious duty of the Administration to take every step possible to prevent appalling disaster by checking the spread of the panic before it grew so that nothing could check it. And events moved with such speed that it was necessary to decide and to act on the instant, as each successive crisis arose, if the decision and action were to accomplish anything. The Secretary of the Treasury took various actions, some on his own initiative, some by my direction. Late one evening I was informed that two representatives of the Steel Corporation wished to see me early the following morning, the precise object not being named. Next morning, while at breakfast, I was informed that Messrs. Frick and Gary were waiting at the office. I at once went over, and, as the Attorney-General, Mr. Bonaparte, had not yet arrived from Baltimore, where he had been passing the night, I sent a message asking the Secretary of State, Mr. Root, who was also a lawyer, to join us, which he did. Before the close of the interview and in the presence of the three gentlemen named, I dictated a note to Mr. Bonaparte, setting forth exactly what Messrs. Frick and Gary had proposed, and exactly what I had answered—so that there might be no possibility of misunderstanding. This note was published in a Senate Document while I was still President. It runs as follows:

THE WHITE HOUSE, Washington,
November 4, 1907.

My dear Mr. Attorney-General:

Judge E. H. Gary and Mr. H. C. Frick, on behalf of the Steel Corporation, have just called upon me. They state that there is a certain business firm (the name of which I have not been told, but which is of real importance in New York business circles), which will undoubtedly fail this week if help is not given. Among its assets are a majority of the securities of the Tennessee Coal Company. Application has been urgently made to the Steel Corporation to purchase this stock as the only means of avoiding a failure. Judge Gary and Mr. Frick informed me that as a mere business transaction they do not care to purchase the stock; that under ordinary circumstances they would not consider purchasing the stock, because but little benefit will come to the Steel Corporation from the purchase; that they are aware that the purchase will be used as a handle for attack upon them on the ground that they are striving to secure a monopoly of the business and prevent competition—not that this would represent what could honestly be said, but what might recklessly and untruthfully be said.

They further informed me that, as a matter of fact, the policy of the company has been to decline to acquire more than sixty per cent of the steel properties, and that this purpose has been persevered in for several years past, with the object of preventing these accusations, and, as a matter of fact, their proportion of steel properties has slightly decreased, so that it is below this sixty per cent, and the acquisition of the property in question will not raise it above sixty per cent. But they feel that it is immensely to their interest, as to the interest of every responsible business man, to try to prevent a panic and general industrial smash-up at this time, and that they are willing to go into this transaction, which they would not otherwise go into, because it seems the opinion of those best fitted to express judgment in New York that it will be an important factor in preventing a break that might be ruinous; and that this has been urged upon them by the combination of the most responsible bankers in New York who are now thus engaged in endeavoring to save the situation. But they asserted that they did not wish to do this if I stated that it ought not to be done. I answered that, while of course I could not advise them to take the action proposed, I felt it no public duty of mine to interpose any objections.

Sincerely yours,

(Signed) THEODORE ROOSEVELT.

HON. CHARLES J. BONAPARTE,
Attorney-General.

Mr. Bonaparte received this note in about an hour, and that same morning he came over, acknowledged its receipt, and said that my answer was the only proper answer that could have been made, having regard both to the law and to the needs of the situation. He stated that the legal situation had been in no way changed, and that no sufficient ground existed for prosecution of the Steel Corporation. But I acted purely on my own initiative, and the responsibility for the act was solely mine.

I was intimately acquainted with the situation in New York. The word "panic" means fear, unreasoning fear; to stop a panic it is necessary to restore confidence; and at the moment the so-called Morgan interests were the only interests which retained a full hold on the confidence of the people of New York—not only the business people, but the immense mass of men and women who owned small investments or had small savings in the banks and trust companies. Mr. Morgan and his associates were of course fighting hard to prevent the loss of confidence and the panic distrust from increasing to such a degree as to bring any other big financial institutions down; for this would probably have been followed by a general, and very likely a worldwide, crash. The Knickerbocker Trust Company had already failed, and runs had begun on, or were threatened as regards, two other big trust companies. These companies were now on the fighting line, and it was to the interest of everybody to strengthen them, in order that the situation might be saved. It was a matter of general knowledge and belief that they, or the individuals prominent in them, held the securities of the Tennessee Coal and Iron Company, which securities had no market value, and were useless as a source of strength in the emergency. The Steel Corporation securities, on the contrary, were immediately marketable, their great value being known and admitted all over the world—as the event showed. The proposal of Messrs. Frick and Gary was that the Steel Corporation should at once acquire the Tennessee Coal and Iron Company, and thereby substitute, among the assets of the threatened institutions (which, by the way, they did not name to me), securities of great and immediate value for securities which at the moment were of no value. It was necessary for me to decide on the instant, before the Stock Exchange opened, for the situation in New York was such that any hour might be vital, and failure to act for even an hour might make all subsequent effort to act utterly useless. From the best information at my disposal, I believed (what was actually the fact) that the addition of the Tennessee Coal and Iron property would only increase the proportion of the Steel Company's holdings by about four per cent, making them about sixty-two per cent instead of about fifty-eight per cent of the total value in the country; an addition which, by itself, in my judgment (concurred in, not only by the Attorney-General but by every competent lawyer), worked no change in the legal status of the Steel corporation. The diminution in the percentage of holdings, and production, has gone on steadily, and the percentage is now about ten per cent less than it was ten years ago.

The action was emphatically for the general good. It offered the only chance for arresting the panic, and it did arrest the panic. I answered Messrs. Frick and Gary, as set forth in the letter quoted above, to the effect that I did not deem it my duty to interfere, that is, to forbid the action which more than anything else in actual fact saved the situation. The result justified my judgment. The panic was stopped, public confidence in the solvency of the threatened institution being at once restored.

Business was vitally helped by what I did. The benefit was not only for the moment. It was permanent. Particularly was this the case in the South. Three or four years afterwards I visited Birmingham. Every man I met, without exception, who was competent to testify, informed me voluntarily that the results of the action taken had been of the utmost benefit to Birmingham, and therefore to Alabama, the industry having profited to an extraordinary degree, not only from the standpoint of the business, but from the standpoint of the community at large and of the wage-workers, by the change in ownership. The results of the action I took were beneficial from every standpoint, and the action itself, at the time when it was taken, was vitally necessary to the welfare of the people of the United States.

I would have been derelict in my duty, I would have shown myself a timid and unworthy public servant, if in that extraordinary crisis I had not acted precisely as I did act. In every such crisis the temptation to indecision, to non-action, is great, for excuses can always be found for non-action, and action means risk and the certainty of blame to the man who acts. But if the man is worth his salt he will do his duty, he will give the people the benefit of the doubt, and act in any way which their interests demand and which is not affirmatively prohibited by law, unheeding the likelihood that he himself, when the crisis is over and the danger past, will be assailed for what he has done.

Every step I took in this matter was open as the day, and was known in detail at the moment to all people. The press contained full accounts of the visit to me of Messrs. Frick and Gary, and heralded widely and with acclamation the results of that visit. At the time the relief and rejoicing over what had been done were well-nigh universal. The danger was too imminent and too appalling for me to be willing to condemn those who were successful in saving them from it. But I fully understood and expected that when there was no longer danger, when the fear had been forgotten, attack would be made upon me; and as a matter of fact after a year had elapsed the attack was begun, and has continued at intervals ever since; my ordinary assailant being some politician of rather cheap type.

If I were on a sail-boat, I should not ordinarily meddle with any of the gear; but if a sudden squall struck us, and the main sheet jammed, so that the boat threatened to capsize, I would unhesitatingly cut the main sheet, even though I were sure that the owner, no matter how grateful to me at the moment for having saved his life, would a few weeks later, when he had forgotten his danger and his fear, decide to sue me for the value of the cut rope. But I would feel a hearty contempt for the owner who so acted.

There were many other things that we did in connection with corporations. One of the most important was the passage of the meat inspection law because of scandalous abuses shown to exist in the great packing-houses in Chicago and elsewhere. There was a curious result of this law, similar to what occurred in connection with the law providing for effective railway regulation. The big beef men bitterly opposed the law; just as the big railway men opposed the Hepburn Act. Yet three or four years after these laws had been put on the statute books every honest man both in the beef business and the railway business came to the conclusion that they worked good and not harm to the decent business concerns. They hurt only those who were not acting as they should have acted. The law providing for the inspection of packing-houses, and the Pure Food and Drugs Act, were also extremely important; and the way in which they were administered was even more important. It would be hard to overstate the value of the service rendered in all these cases by such cabinet officers as Moody and Bonaparte, and their outside assistants of the stamp of Frank Kellogg.

It would be useless to enumerate all the suits we brought. Some of them I have already touched upon. Others, such as the suits against the Harriman railway corporations, which were successful, and which had been rendered absolutely necessary by the grossly improper action of the corporations concerned, offered no special points of interest. The Sugar Trust proceedings, however, may be mentioned as showing just the kind of thing that was done and the kind of obstacle encountered and overcome in prosecutions of this character.

It was on the advice of my secretary, William Loeb, Jr., afterward head of the New York Custom-House, that the action was taken which started the uncovering of the frauds perpetrated by the Sugar Trust and other companies in connection with the importing of sugar. Loeb had from time to time told me that he was sure that there was fraud in connection with the importations by the Sugar Trust through the New York Custom-House. Finally, some time toward the end of 1904, he informed me that Richard Parr, a sampler at the New York Appraisers' Stores (whose duties took him almost continually on the docks in connection with the sampling of merchandise), had called on him, and had stated that in his belief the sugar companies were defrauding the Government in the matter of weights, and had stated that if he could be made an investigating officer of the Treasury Department, he was confident that he could show there was wrongdoing. Parr had been a former school fellow of Loeb in Albany, and Loeb believed him to be loyal, honest, and efficient. He thereupon laid the matter before me, and advised the appointment of Parr as a special employee of the Treasury Department, for the specific purpose of investigating the alleged sugar frauds. I instructed the Treasury Department accordingly, and was informed that there was no vacancy in the force of special employees, but that Parr would be given the first place that opened up. Early in the spring of 1905 Parr came to Loeb again, and said that he had received additional information about the sugar frauds, and was anxious to begin the investigation. Loeb again discussed the matter with me; and I notified the Treasury Department to appoint Parr immediately. On June 1, 1905, he received his appointment, and was assigned to the port of Boston for the purpose of gaining some experience as an investigating officer. During the month he was transferred to the Maine District, with headquarters at Portland, where he remained until March, 1907. During his service in Maine he uncovered extensive wool smuggling frauds. At the conclusion of the wool case, he appealed to Loeb to have him transferred to New York, so that he might undertake the investigation of the sugar underweighing frauds. I now called the attention of Secretary Cortelyou personally to the matter, so that he would be able to keep a check over any subordinates who might try to interfere with Parr, for the conspiracy was evidently widespread, the wealth of the offenders great, and the corruption in the service far-reaching—while moreover as always happens with "respectable" offenders, there were many good men who sincerely disbelieved in the possibility of corruption on the part of men of such high financial standing. Parr was assigned to New York early in March, 1907, and at once began an active investigation of the conditions existing on the sugar docks. This terminated in the discovery of a steel spring in one of the scales of the Havemeyer & Elder docks in Brooklyn, November 20, 1907, which enabled us to uncover what were probably the most colossal frauds ever perpetrated in the Customs Service. From the beginning of his active work in the investigation of the sugar frauds in March, 1907, to March 4, 1909, Parr, from time to time, personally reported to Loeb, at the White House, the progress of his investigations, and Loeb in his turn kept me personally advised. On one occasion there was an attempt made to shunt Parr off the investigation and substitute another agent of the Treasury, who was suspected of having some relations with the sugar companies under investigation; but Parr reported the facts to Loeb, I sent for Secretary Cortelyou, and Secretary Cortelyou promptly took charge of the matter himself, putting Parr back on the investigation.

During the investigation Parr was subjected to all sorts of harassments, including an attempt to bribe him by Spitzer, the dock superintendent of the Havemeyer & Elder Refinery, for which Spitzer was convicted and served a term in prison. Brzezinski, a special agent, who was assisting Parr, was convicted of perjury and also served a term in prison, he having changed his testimony, in the trial of Spitzer for the attempted bribery of Parr, from that which he gave before the Grand Jury. For his extraordinary services in connection with this investigation Parr was granted an award of $100,000 by the Treasury Department.

District-Attorney Stimson, of New York, assisted by Denison, Frankfurter, Wise, and other employees of the Department of Justice, took charge of the case, and carried on both civil and criminal proceedings. The trial in the action against the Sugar Trust, for the recovery of duties on the cargo of sugar, which was being sent over the scales at the time of the discovery of the steel spring by Parr, was begun in 1908; judgment was rendered against the defendants on March 5, 1909, the day after I left office. Over four million dollars were recovered and paid back into the United States Treasury by the sugar companies which had perpetrated the various forms of fraud. These frauds were unearthed by Parr, Loeb, Stimson, Frankfurter, and the other men mentioned and their associates, and it was to them that the people owed the refunding of the huge sum of money mentioned. We had already secured heavy fines from the Sugar Trust, and from various big railways, and private individuals, such as Edwin Earle, for unlawful rebates. In the case of the chief offender, the American Sugar Refining Company (the Sugar Trust), criminal prosecutions were carried on against every living man whose position was such that he would naturally know about the fraud. All of them were indicted, and the biggest and most responsible ones were convicted. The evidence showed that the president of the company, Henry O. Havemeyer, virtually ran the entire company, and was responsible for all the details of the management. He died two weeks after the fraud was discovered, just as proceedings were being begun. Next to him in importance was the secretary and treasurer, Charles R. Heike, who was convicted. Various other officials and employees of the Trust, and various Government employees, were indicted, and most of them convicted. Ernest W. Gerbracht, the superintendent of one of the refineries, was convicted, but his sentence was commuted to a short jail imprisonment, because he became a Government witness and greatly assisted the Government in the suits.

Heike's sentence was commuted so as to excuse him from going to the penitentiary; just as the penitentiary sentence of Morse, the big New York banker, who was convicted of gross fraud and misapplication of funds, was commuted. Both commutations were granted long after I left office. In each case the commutation was granted because, as was stated, of the prisoner's age and state of health. In Morse's case the President originally refused the request, saying that Morse had exhibited "fraudulent and criminal disregard of the trust imposed upon him," that "he was entirely unscrupulous as to the methods he adopted," and "that he seemed at times to be absolutely heartless with regard to the consequences to others, and he showed great shrewdness in obtaining large sums of money from the bank without adequate security and without making himself personally liable therefor." The two cases may be considered in connection with the announcement in the public press that on May 17, 1913, the President commuted the sentence of Lewis A. Banks, who was serving a very long term penitentiary sentence for an attack on a girl in the Indian Territory; "the reason for the commutation which is set forth in the press being that 'Banks is in poor health.'"

It is no easy matter to balance the claims of justice and mercy in such cases. In these three cases, of all of which I had personal cognizance, I disagreed radically with the views my successors took, and with the views which many respectable men took who in these and similar cases, both while I was in office and afterward, urged me to show, or to ask others to show, clemency. It then seemed to me, and it now seems to me, that such clemency is from the larger standpoint a gross wrong to the men and women of the country.

One of the former special assistants of the district-attorney, Mr. W. Cleveland Runyon, in commenting bitterly on the release of Heike and Morse on account of their health, pointed out that their health apparently became good when once they themselves became free men, and added:

"The commutation of these sentences amounts to a direct interference with the administration of justice by the courts. Heike got a $25,000 salary and has escaped his imprisonment, but what about the six $18 a week checkers, who were sent to jail, one of them a man of more than sixty? It is cases like this that create discontent and anarchy. They make it seem plain that there is one law for the rich and another for the poor man, and I for one will protest."

In dealing with Heike the individual (or Morse or any other individual), it is necessary to emphasize the social aspects of his case. The moral of the Heike case, as has been well said, is "how easy it is for a man in modern corporate organization to drift into wrongdoing." The moral restraints are loosened in the case of a man like Heike by the insulation of himself from the sordid details of crime, through industrially coerced intervening agents. Professor Ross has made the penetrating observation that "distance disinfects dividends"; it also weakens individual responsibility, particularly on the part of the very managers of large business, who should feel it most acutely. One of the officers of the Department of Justice who conducted the suit, and who inclined to the side of mercy in the matter, nevertheless writes: "Heike is a beautiful illustration of mental and moral obscuration in the business life of an otherwise valuable member of society. Heike had an ample share in the guidance of the affairs of the American Sugar Company, and we are apt to have a foreshortened picture of his responsibility, because he operated from the easy coign of vantage of executive remoteness. It is difficult to say to what extent he did, directly or indirectly, profit by the sordid practices of his company. But the social damage of an individual in his position may be just as deep, whether merely the zest of the game or hard cash be his dominant motive."

I have coupled the cases of the big banker and the Sugar Trust official and the case of the man convicted of a criminal assault on a woman. All of the criminals were released from penitentiary sentences on grounds of ill health. The offenses were typical of the worst crimes committed at the two ends of the social scale. One offense was a crime of brutal violence; the other offenses were crimes of astute corruption. All of them were offenses which in my judgment were of such a character that clemency towards the offender worked grave injustice to the community as a whole, injustice so grave that its effects might be far-reaching in their damage.

Every time that rape or criminal assault on a woman is pardoned, and anything less than the full penalty of the law exacted, a premium is put on the practice of lynching such offenders. Every time a big monied offender, who naturally excites interest and sympathy, and who has many friends, is excused from serving a sentence which a man of less prominence and fewer friends would have to serve, justice is discredited in the eyes of plain people—and to undermine faith in justice is to strike at the foundation of the Republic. As for ill health, it must be remembered that few people are as healthy in prison as they would be outside; and there should be no discrimination among criminals on this score; either all criminals who grow unhealthy should be let out, or none. Pardons must sometimes be given in order that the cause of justice may be served; but in cases such as these I am considering, while I know that many amiable people differ from me, I am obliged to say that in my judgment the pardons work far-reaching harm to the cause of justice.

Among the big corporations themselves, even where they did wrong, there was a wide difference in the moral obliquity indicated by the wrongdoer. There was a wide distinction between the offenses committed in the case of the Northern Securities Company, and the offenses because of which the Sugar Trust, the Tobacco Trust, and the Standard Oil Trust were successfully prosecuted under my Administration. It was vital to destroy the Northern Securities Company; but the men creating it had done so in open and above-board fashion, acting under what they, and most of the members of the bar, thought to be the law established by the Supreme Court in the Knight sugar case. But the Supreme Court in its decree dissolving the Standard Oil and Tobacco Trusts, condemned them in the severest language for moral turpitude; and an even severer need of condemnation should be visited on the Sugar Trust.

However, all the trusts and big corporations against which we proceeded—which included in their directorates practically all the biggest financiers in the country—joined in making the bitterest assaults on me and on my Administration. Of their actions I wrote as follows to Attorney-General Bonaparte, who had been a peculiarly close friend and adviser through the period covered by my public life in high office and who, together with Attorney-General Moody, possessed the same understanding sympathy with my social and industrial program that was possessed by such officials as Straus, Garfield, H. K. Smith, and Pinchot. The letter runs:

> January 2, 1908.
>
> My dear Bonaparte:
>
> I must congratulate you on your admirable speech at Chicago. You said the very things it was good to say at this time. What you said bore especial weight because it represented what you had done. You have shown by what you have actually accomplished that the law is enforced against the wealthiest corporation, and the richest and most powerful manager or manipulator of that corporation, just as resolutely and fearlessly as against the humblest citizen. The Department of Justice is now in very fact the Department of Justice, and justice is meted out with an even hand to great and small, rich and poor, weak and strong. Those who have denounced you and the action of the Department of Justice are either misled, or else are the very wrongdoers, and the agents of the very wrongdoers, who have for so many years gone scot-free and flouted the laws with impunity. Above all, you are to be congratulated upon the bitterness felt and expressed towards you by the representatives and agents of the great law-defying corporations of immense wealth, who, until within the last half-dozen years, have treated themselves and have expected others to treat them as being beyond and above all possible check from law.
>
> It was time to say something, for the representatives of predatory wealth, of wealth accumulated on a giant scale by iniquity, by wrongdoing in many forms, by plain swindling, by oppressing wage-workers, by manipulating securities, by unfair and unwholesome competition and by stock-jobbing—in short, by conduct abhorrent to every man of ordinarily decent conscience, have during the last few months made it evident that they are banded together to work

for a reaction, to endeavor to overthrow and discredit all who honestly administer the law, and to secure a return to the days when every unscrupulous wrongdoer could do what he wished unchecked, provided he had enough money. They attack you because they know your honesty and fearlessness, and dread them. The enormous sums of money these men have at their control enable them to carry on an effective campaign. They find their tools in a portion of the public press, including especially certain of the great New York newspapers. They find their agents in some men in public life—now and then occupying, or having occupied, positions as high as Senator or Governor—in some men in the pulpit, and most melancholy of all, in a few men on the bench. By gifts to colleges and universities they are occasionally able to subsidize in their own interest some head of an educational body, who, save only a judge, should of all men be most careful to keep his skirts clear from the taint of such corruption. There are ample material rewards for those who serve with fidelity the Mammon of unrighteousness, but they are dearly paid for by that institution of learning whose head, by example and precept, teaches the scholars who sit under him that there is one law for the rich and another for the poor. The amount of money the representatives of the great monied interests are willing to spend can be gauged by their recent publication broadcast throughout the papers of this country from the Atlantic to the Pacific of huge advertisements, attacking with envenomed bitterness the Administration's policy of warring against successful dishonesty, advertisements that must have cost enormous sums of money. This advertisement, as also a pamphlet called *The Roosevelt Panic*, and one or two similar books and pamphlets, are written especially in the interest of the Standard Oil and Harriman combinations, but also defend all the individuals and corporations of great wealth that have been guilty of wrongdoing. From the railroad rate law to the pure food law, every measure for honesty in business that has been pressed during the last six years, has been opposed by these men, on its passage and in its administration, with every resource that bitter and unscrupulous craft could suggest, and the command of almost unlimited money secure. These men do not themselves speak or write; they hire others to do their bidding. Their spirit and purpose are made clear alike by the editorials of the papers owned in, or whose policy is dictated by, Wall Street, and by the speeches of public men who, as Senators, Governors, or Mayors, have served these their masters to the cost of the plain people. At one time one of their writers or speakers attacks the rate law as the cause of the panic; he is, whether in public life or not, usually a clever corporation lawyer, and he is not so foolish a being as to believe in the truth of what he says; he has too closely represented the railroads not to know well that the Hepburn Rate Bill has helped every honest railroad, and has hurt only the railroads that regarded themselves as above the law. At another time, one of them assails the Administration for not imprisoning people under the Sherman Anti-Trust Law; for declining to make what he well knows, in view of the actual attitude of juries (as shown in the Tobacco Trust cases and in San Francisco in one or two of the cases brought against corrupt business men) would have been the futile endeavor to imprison defendants whom we are actually able to fine. He raises the usual clamor, raised by all who object to the enforcement of the law, that we are fining corporations instead of putting the heads of the corporations in jail; and he states that this does not really harm the chief offenders. Were this statement true, he himself would not be found attacking us. The extraordinary violence of the assault upon our policy contained in speeches like these, in the articles in the subsidized press, in such huge advertisements and pamphlets as those above referred to, and the enormous sums of money spent in these various ways, give a fairly accurate measure of the anger and terror which our actions have caused the corrupt men of vast wealth to feel in the very marrow of their being.

The man thus attacking us is usually, like so many of his fellows, either a great lawyer, or a paid editor who takes his commands from the financiers and his arguments from their attorneys. If the former, he has defended many malefactors, and he knows well that, thanks to the advice of lawyers like himself, a certain kind of modern corporation has been turned into an admirable instrument by which to render it well nigh impossible to get at the really guilty man, so that in most cases the only way of punishing the wrong is by fining the corporation or by proceeding personally against some of the minor agents. These lawyers and their employers are the men mainly responsible for this state of things, and their responsibility is shared with the legislators who ingeniously oppose the passing of just and effective laws, and with those judges whose one aim seems to be to construe such laws so that they cannot be executed. Nothing is sillier than this outcry on behalf of the "innocent stockholders" in the corporations. We are besought to pity the Standard Oil Company for a fine relatively far less great than the fines every day inflicted in the police courts upon multitudes of push cart peddlers and other petty offenders, whose woes never extort one word from the men whose withers are wrung by the woes of the mighty. The stockholders have the control of the corporation in their own hands. The corporation officials are elected by those holding the majority of the stock and can keep office only by having behind them the good-will of these majority stockholders. They are not entitled to the slightest pity if they deliberately choose to resign into the hands of great wrongdoers the control of the corporations in which they own the stock. Of course innocent people have become involved in these big corporations and suffer because of the misdeeds of their criminal associates. Let these innocent people be careful not to invest in corporations where those in control are not men of probity, men who respect the laws; above all let them avoid the men who make it their one effort to evade or defy the laws. But if these honest innocent people are in the majority in any corporation they can immediately resume control and throw out of the directory the men who misrepresent them. Does any man for a moment suppose that the majority stockholders of the Standard Oil are others than Mr. Rockefeller and his associates themselves and the beneficiaries of their wrongdoing? When the stock is watered so that the innocent investors suffer, a grave wrong is indeed done to these innocent investors as well as to the public; but the public men, lawyers and editors, to whom I refer, do not under these circumstances express sympathy for the innocent; on the contrary they are the first to protest with frantic vehemence against our efforts by law to put a stop to over-capitalization and stock-watering. The apologists of successful dishonesty always declaim against any effort to punish or prevent it on the ground that such effort will "unsettle business." It is they who by their acts have unsettled business; and the very men raising this cry spend hundreds of thousands of dollars in securing, by speech, editorial, book or pamphlet, the defense by misstatement of what they have done; and yet when we correct their misstatements by telling the truth, they declaim against us for breaking silence, lest "values be unsettled!" They have hurt honest business men, honest working men, honest farmers; and now they clamor against the truth being told.

The keynote of all these attacks upon the effort to secure honesty in business and in politics, is expressed in a recent speech, in which the speaker stated that prosperity had been checked by the effort for the "moral regeneration of the business world," an effort which he denounced as "unnatural, unwarranted, and injurious" and for which he stated the panic was the penalty. The morality of such a plea is precisely as great as if made on behalf of the men caught in a gambling establishment when that gambling establishment is raided by the police. If such words mean anything they mean that those whose sentiments they represent stand against the effort to bring about a moral regeneration of business which will prevent a repetition of the insurance, banking, and street railroad scandals in New York; a repetition of the Chicago and Alton deal; a repetition of the combination between certain professional politicians, certain professional labor leaders and certain big financiers from the disgrace of which San Francisco has just been rescued; a repetition of the successful efforts by the Standard Oil people to crush out every competitor, to overawe the common carriers, and to establish a monopoly which treats the public with the contempt which the public deserves so long as it permits men like the public men of whom I speak to represent it in politics, men like the heads of colleges to whom I refer to educate its youth. The outcry against stopping dishonest practices among the very wealthy is precisely similar to the outcry raised against every effort for cleanliness and decency in city government because, forsooth, it will "hurt business." The same outcry is made against the Department of Justice for prosecuting the heads of colossal corporations that is made against the men who in San Francisco are prosecuting with impartial severity the wrongdoers among business men, public officials, and labor leaders alike. The principle is the same in the two cases. Just as the blackmailer and the bribe giver stand on the same evil eminence of infamy, so the man who makes an enormous fortune by corrupting Legislatures and municipalities and fleecing his stockholders and the public stands on a level with the creature who fattens on the blood money of the gambling house, the saloon and the brothel. Moreover, both kinds of corruption in the last analysis are far more intimately connected than would at first sight appear; the wrong-doing is at bottom the same. Corrupt business and corrupt politics act and react, with ever increasing debasement, one on the other; the rebate-taker, the franchise-trafficker, the manipulator of securities, the purveyor and protector of vice, the black-mailing ward boss, the ballot box stuffer, the demagogue, the mob leader, the hired bully and mankiller, all alike work at the same web of corruption, and all alike should be abhorred by honest men.

The "business" which is hurt by the movement for honesty is the kind of business which, in the long run, it pays the country to have hurt. It is the kind of business which has tended to make the very name "high finance" a term of scandal to which all honest American men of business should join in putting an end. One of the special pleaders for business dishonesty, in a recent speech, in denouncing the Administration for enforcing the law against the huge and corrupt corporations which have defied the law, also denounced it for endeavoring to secure a far-reaching law making employers liable for injuries to their employees. It is meet and fit that the apologists for corrupt wealth should oppose every effort to relieve weak and helpless people from crushing misfortune brought upon them by injury in the business from which they gain a bare livelihood and their employers fortunes. It is hypocritical baseness to speak of a girl who works in a factory where the dangerous machinery is unprotected as having the "right" freely to contract to expose herself to dangers to life and limb. She has no alternative but to suffer want or else to expose herself to such dangers, and when she loses a hand or is otherwise maimed or disfigured for life it is a moral wrong that the burden of the risk necessarily incidental to the business should be placed with crushing weight upon her weak shoulders and the man who has profited by her work escape scot-free. This is what our opponents advocate, and it is proper that they should advocate it, for it rounds out their advocacy of those most dangerous members of the criminal class, the criminals of vast wealth, the men who can afford best to pay for such championship in the press and on the stump.

It is difficult to speak about the judges, for it behooves us all to treat with the utmost respect the high office of judge; and our judges as a whole are brave and upright men. But there is need that those who go wrong should not be allowed to feel that there is no condemnation of their wrongdoing. A judge who on the bench either truckles to the mob or bows down before a corporation; or who, having left the bench to become a corporation lawyer, seeks to aid his clients by denouncing as enemies of property all those who seek to stop the abuses of the criminal rich; such a man performs an even worse service to the body politic than the Legislator or Executive who goes wrong. In no way can respect for the courts be so quickly undermined as by teaching the public through the action of a judge himself that there is reason for the loss of such respect. The judge who by word or deed makes it plain that the corrupt corporation, the law-defying corporation, the law-defying rich man, has in him a sure and trustworthy ally, the judge who by misuse of the process of injunction makes it plain that in him the wage-worker has a determined and unscrupulous enemy, the judge who when he decides in an employers' liability or a tenement house factory case shows that he has neither sympathy for nor understanding of those fellow citizens of his who most need his sympathy and understanding; these judges work as much evil as if they pandered to the mob, as if they shrank from sternly repressing violence and disorder. The judge who does his full duty well stands higher, and renders a better service to the people, than any other public servant; he is entitled to greater respect; and if he is a true servant of the people, if he is upright, wise and fearless, he will unhesitatingly disregard even the wishes of the people if they conflict with the eternal principles of right as against wrong. He must serve the people; but he must serve his conscience first. All honor to such a judge; and all honor cannot be rendered him if it is rendered equally to his brethren who fall immeasurably below the high ideals for which he stands. There should be a sharp discrimination against such judges. They claim immunity from criticism, and the claim is heatedly advanced by men and newspapers like those of whom I speak. Most certainly they can claim immunity from untruthful criticism; and their champions, the newspapers and the public men I have mentioned, exquisitely illustrate by their own actions mendacious criticism in its most flagrant and iniquitous form.

But no servant of the people has a right to expect to be free from just and honest criticism. It is the newspapers, and the public men whose thoughts and deeds show them to be most alien to honesty and truth who themselves loudly object to truthful and honest criticism of their fellow-servants of the great monied interests.

We have no quarrel with the individuals, whether public men, lawyers or editors, to whom I refer. These men derive their sole power from the great, sinister offenders who stand behind them. They are but puppets who move as the strings are pulled by those who control the enormous masses of corporate wealth which if itself left uncontrolled threatens dire evil to the Republic. It is not the puppets, but the strong, cunning men and the mighty forces working for evil behind, and to a certain extent through, the puppets, with whom we have to deal. We seek to control law-defying wealth, in the first place to prevent its doing evil, and in the next place to avoid the vindictive and dreadful radicalism which if left uncontrolled it is certain in the end to arouse. Sweeping attacks upon all property, upon all men of means, without regard to whether they do well or ill, would sound the death knell of the Republic; and such attacks become inevitable if decent citizens permit rich men whose lives are corrupt and evil to domineer in swollen pride, unchecked and unhindered, over the destinies of this country. We act in no vindictive spirit, and we are no respecters of persons. If a labor union does what is wrong, we oppose it as fearlessly as we oppose a corporation that does wrong; and we stand with equal stoutness for the rights of the man of wealth and for the rights of the wage-workers; just as much so for one as for the other. We seek to stop wrongdoing; and we desire to punish the wrongdoer only so far as is necessary in order to achieve this end. We are the stanch upholders of every honest man, whether business man or wage-worker.

I do not for a moment believe that our actions have brought on business distress; so far as this is due to local and not world-wide causes, and to the actions of any particular individuals, it is due to the speculative folly and flagrant dishonesty of a few men of great wealth, who now seek to shield themselves from the effects of their own wrongdoings by ascribing its results to the actions of those who have sought to put a stop to the wrongdoing. But if it were true that to cut out rottenness from the body politic meant a momentary check to an unhealthy seeming prosperity, I should not for one moment hesitate to put the knife to the cancer. On behalf of all our people, on behalf no less of the honest man of means than of the honest man who earns each day's livelihood by that day's sweat of his brow, it is necessary to insist upon honesty in business and politics alike, in all walks of life, in big things and in little things; upon just and fair dealing as between man and man. We are striving for the right in the spirit of Abraham Lincoln when he said:

"Fondly do we hope—fervently do we pray—that this mighty scourge may speedily pass away. Yet, if God wills that it continue until all the wealth piled by the bondsmen's two hundred and fifty years of unrequited toil shall be sunk, and until every drop of blood drawn with the lash shall be paid by another drawn with the sword, as was said three thousand years ago, so still it must be said, 'The judgments of the Lord are true and righteous altogether.'

"With malice toward none; with charity for all; with firmness in the right, as God gives us to see the right, let us strive on to finish the work we are in."

Sincerely yours,
(Signed) THEODORE ROOSEVELT.

HON. CHARLES J. BONAPARTE,
Attorney-General.

THE SQUARE DEAL

Speech given at the State Fair in Syracuse, New York
September 7, 1903

Governor Higgins, my fellow citizens:

In speaking on Labor Day at the annual fair of the New York State Agricultural Association, it is natural to keep especially in mind the two bodies who compose the majority of our people and upon whose welfare depends the welfare of the entire State. If circumstances are such that thrift, energy, industry, and forethought enable the farmer, the tiller of the soil, on the one hand, and the wage-worker on the other, to keep themselves, their wives, and their children in reasonable comfort, then the State is well off, and we can be assured that the other classes in the community will likewise prosper. On the other hand, if there is in the long run a lack of prosperity among the two classes named, then all other prosperity is sure to be more seeming than real.

It has been our profound good fortune as a nation that hitherto, disregarding exceptional periods of depression and the normal and inevitable fluctuations, there has been on the whole from the beginning of our government to the present day a progressive betterment alike in the condition of the tiller of the soil and in the condition of the man who, by his manual skill and labor, supports himself and his family, and endeavors to bring up his children so that they may be at least as well off as, and, if possible, better off than, he himself has been. There are, of course, exceptions, but as a whole the standard of living among the farmers of our country has risen from generation to generation, and the wealth represented on the farms has steadily increased, while the wages of labor have likewise risen, both as regards the actual money paid and as regards the purchasing power which that money represents.

Side by side with this increase in the prosperity of the wage-worker and the tiller of the soil has gone on a great increase in prosperity among the business men and among certain classes of professional men; and the prosperity of these men has been partly the cause and partly the consequence of the prosperity of farmer and wage-worker. It cannot be too often repeated that in this country, in the long run, we all of us tend to go up or go down together. If the average of well-being is high, it means that the average wage-worker, the average farmer, and the average business man are all alike well-off. If the average shrinks, there is not one of these classes which will not feel the shrinkage. Of course, there are always some men who are not affected by good times, just as there are some men who are not affected by bad times. But speaking broadly, it is true that if prosperity comes, all of us tend to share more or less therein, and that if adversity comes each of us, to a greater or less extent, feels the tension.

Unfortunately, in this world the innocent frequently find themselves obliged to pay some of the penalty for the misdeeds of the guilty; and so if hard times come, whether they be due to our own fault or to our misfortune, whether they be due to some burst of speculative frenzy that has caused a portion of the business world to lose its head—a loss which no legislation can possibly supply—or whether they be due to any lack of wisdom in a portion of the world of labor—in each case, the trouble once started is felt more or less in every walk of life.

It is all-essential to the continuance of our healthy national life that we should recognize this community of interest among our people. The welfare of each of us is dependent fundamentally upon the welfare of all of us, and therefore in public life that man is the best representative of each of us who seeks to do good to each by doing good to all; in other words, whose endeavor it is not to represent any special class and promote merely that class's selfish interests, but to represent all true and honest men of all sections and all classes and to work for their interests by working for our common country.

We can keep our government on a sane and healthy basis, we can make and keep our social system what it should be, only on condition of judging each man, not as a member of a class, but on his worth as a man. It is an infamous thing in our American life, and fundamentally treacherous to our institutions, to apply to any man any test save that of his personal worth, or to draw between two sets of men any distinction save the distinction of conduct, the distinction that marks off those who do well and wisely from those who do ill and foolishly. There are good citizens and bad citizens in every class as in every locality, and the attitude of decent people toward great public and social questions should be determined, not by the accidental questions of employment or locality, but by those deep-set principles which represent the innermost souls of men.

The failure in public and in private life thus to treat each man on his own merits, the recognition of this government as being either for the poor as such or for the rich as such, would prove fatal to our Republic, as such failure and such recognition have always proved fatal in the past to other republics. A healthy republican government must rest upon individuals, not upon classes or sections. As soon as it becomes government by a class or by a section, it departs from the old American ideal.

Many qualities are needed by a people which would preserve the power of self- government in fact as well as in name. Among these qualities are forethought, shrewdness, self-restraint, the courage which refuses to abandon one's own rights, and the disinterested and kindly good sense which enables one to do justice to the rights of others. Lack of strength and lack of courage and unfit men for self-government on the one hand; and on the other, brutal arrogance, envy—in short, any manifestation of the spirit of selfish disregard, whether of one's own duties or of the rights of others, are equally fatal.

In the history of mankind many republics have risen, have flourished for a less or greater time, and then have fallen because their citizens lost the power of governing themselves and thereby of governing their state; and in no way has this loss of power been so often and so clearly shown as in the tendency to turn the government into a government primarily for the benefit of one class instead of a government for the benefit of the people as a whole. Again and again in the republics of ancient Greece, in those of medieval Italy and medieval Flanders, this tendency was shown, and wherever the tendency became a habit it invariably and inevitably proved fatal to the state. In the final result, it mattered not one whit whether the movement was in favor of one class or of another.

The outcome was equally fatal, whether the country fell into the hands of a wealthy oligarchy which exploited the poor or whether it fell under the domination of a turbulent mob which plundered the rich. In both cases there resulted violent alternations between tyranny and disorder, and a final complete loss of liberty to all citizens—destruction in the end overtaking the class which had for the moment been victorious as well as that which had momentarily been defeated. The death-knell of the Republic had rung as soon as the active power became lodged in the hands of those who sought, not to do justice to all citizens, rich and poor alike, but to stand for one special class and for its interests as opposed to the interests of others.

The reason why our future is assured lies in the fact that our people are genuinely skilled in and fitted for self-government and therefore will spurn the leadership of those who seek to excite this ferocious and foolish class antagonism. The average American knows not only that he himself intends to do what is right, but that his average fellow countryman has the same intention and the same power to make his intention effective. He knows, whether he be business man, professional man, farmer, mechanic, employer, or wage-worker, that the welfare of each of these men is bound up with the welfare of all the others; that each is neighbor to the other, is actuated by the same hopes and fears, has fundamentally the same ideals, and that all alike have much the same virtues and the same faults. Our average fellow citizen is a sane and healthy man who believes in decency and has a wholesome mind. He therefore feels an equal scorn alike for the man of wealth guilty of the mean and base spirit of arrogance toward those who are less well off, and for the man of small means who in his turn either feels, or seeks to excite in others the feeling of mean and base envy for those who are better off. The two feelings, envy and arrogance, are but opposite sides of the same shield, but different developments of the same spirit....

The line of cleavage between good citizenship and bad citizenship separates the rich man who does well from the rich man who does ill, the poor man of good conduct from the poor man of bad conduct. This line of cleavage lies at right angles to any such arbitrary line of division as that separating one class from another, one locality from another, or men with a certain degree of property from those of a less degree of property.

The good citizen is the man who, whatever his wealth or his poverty, strives manfully to do his duty to himself, to his family, to his neighbor, to the States; who is incapable of the baseness which manifests itself either in arrogance or in envy, but who while demanding justice for himself is no less scrupulous to do justice to others. It is because the average American citizen, rich or poor, is of just this type that we have cause for our profound faith in the future of the Republic.

There is no worse enemy of the wage-worker than the man who condones mob violence in any shape or who preaches class hatred; and surely the slightest acquaintance with our industrial history should teach even the most short-sighted that the times of most suffering for our people as a whole, the times when business is stagnant, and capital suffers from shrinkage and gets no return from its investments, are exactly the times of hardship, and want, and grim disaster among the poor. If all the existing instrumentalities of wealth could be abolished, the first and severest suffering would come among those of us who are least well-off at present. The wage-worker is well off only when the rest of the country is well-off; and he can best contribute to this general well-being by showing sanity and a firm purpose to do justice to others.

In his turn, the capitalist who is really a conservative, the man who has forethought as well as patriotism, should heartily welcome every effort, legislative or otherwise, which has for its object to secure fair dealing by capital, corporate or individual, toward the public and toward the employee. Such laws as the franchise-tax law in this State, which the Court of Appeals recently unanimously decided constitutional—such a law as that passed in Congress last year for the purpose of establishing a Department of Commerce and Labor, under which there should be a bureau to oversee and secure publicity from the great corporations which do an interstate business—such a law as that passed at the same time for the regulation of the great highways of commerce so as to keep these roads clear on fair terms to all producers in getting their goods to market—these laws are in the interest not merely of the people as a whole, but of the propertied classes. For in no way is the stability of property better assured than by making it patent to our people that property bears its proper share of the burdens of the State; that property is handled not only in the interest of the owner, but in the interest of the whole community.

Among ourselves we differ in many qualities of body, head, and heart; we are unequally developed, mentally as well as physically. But each of us has the right to ask that he shall be protected from wrongdoing as he does his work and carries his burden through life. No man needs sympathy because he has to work, because he has a burden to carry. Far and away the best prize that life offers is the chance to work hard at work worth doing; and this is a prize open to every man, for there can be no better worth doing than that done to keep in health and comfort and with reasonable advantages those immediately dependent upon the husband, the father, or the son. There is no room in our healthy American life for the mere idler, for the man or the woman whose object it is throughout life to shirk the duties which life ought to bring. Life can mean nothing worth meaning, unless its prime aim is the doing of duty, the achievement of results worth achieving. A recent writer has finely said: "After all, the saddest thing that can happen to a man is to carry no burdens. To be bent under too great a load is bad; to be crushed by it is lamentable; but even in that there are possibilities that are glorious. But to carry no load at all—there is nothing in that. No one seems to arrive at any goal really worth reaching in this world who does not come to it heavy laden."

Surely from our own experience each one of us knows that this is true. From the greatest to the smallest, happiness and usefulness are largely found in the same soul, and the joy of life is won in its deepest and truest sense only by those who have not shirked life's burdens. The men whom we most delight to honor in all this land are those who, in the iron years from '61 to '65, bore on their shoulders the burden of saving the Union. They did not choose the easy task. They did not shirk the difficult duty. Deliberately and of their own free will they strove for an ideal, upward and onward across the stony slopes of greatness. They did the hardest work that was then to be done; they bore the heaviest burden that any generation of Americans ever had to bear; and because they did this they have won such proud joy as it has fallen to the lot of no other men to win, and have written their names forevermore on the golden honor-roll of the nation. As it is with the soldier, so it is with the civilian. To win success in the business world, to become a first-class mechanic, a successful farmer, an able lawyer or doctor, means that the man has devoted his best energy and power through long years to the achievement of his ends. So it is in the life of the family, upon which in the last analysis the whole welfare of the nation rests. The man or woman who, as bread-winner and home-maker, or as wife and mother, has done all that he or she can do, patiently and uncomplainingly, is to be honored; and is to be envied by all those who have never had the good fortune to feel the need and duty of doing such work. The woman who has borne, and who has reared as they should be reared, a family of children, has in the most emphatic manner deserved well of the Republic. Her burden has been heavy, and she has been able to bear it worthily only by the possession of resolution, of good sense, of conscience, and of unselfishness. But if she has borne it well, then to her shall come the supreme blessing, for in the words of the oldest and greatest of books, "Her children shall rise up and call her blessed;" and among the benefactors of the land, her place must be with those who have done the best and the hardest work, whether as lawgivers or as soldiers, whether in public or private life.

This is not a soft and easy creed to preach. It is a creed willingly learned only by men and women who, together with the softer virtues, possess also the stronger; who can do, and dare, and die at need, but who while life lasts will never flinch from their allotted task. You farmers, and wage-workers, and business men of this great State, of this mighty and wonderful nation, are gathered together today, proud of your State and still prouder of your nation, because your forefathers and predecessors have lived up to just this creed. You have received from their hands a great inheritance, and you will leave an even greater inheritance to your children, and your children's children, provided only that you practice alike in your private and your public lives the strong virtues that have given us as a people greatness in the past. It is not enough to be well-meaning and kindly, but weak; neither is it enough to be strong, unless morality and decency go hand in hand with strength. We must possess the qualities which make us do our duty in our homes and among our neighbors, and in addition we must possess the qualities which are indispensable to the make-up of every great and masterful nation—the qualities of courage and hardihood, of individual initiative and yet of power to combine for a common end, and above all, the resolute determination to permit no man and no set of men to sunder us one from the other by lines of caste or creed or section. We must act upon the motto of all for each and each for all. There must be ever present in our minds the fundamental truth that in a republic such as ours the only safety is to stand neither for nor against any man because he is rich or because he is poor, because he is engaged in one occupation or another, because he works with his brains or because he works with his hands. We must treat each man on his worth and merits as a man. We must see that each is given a square deal, because he is entitled to no more and should receive no less.

Finally, we must keep ever in mind that a republic such as ours can exist only by virtue of the orderly liberty which comes through the equal domination of the law over all men alike, and through its administration in such resolute and fearless fashion as shall teach all that no man is above it and no man below it.

INAUGURAL ADDRESS

Saturday, March 4, 1905

Roosevelt acceded to the presidency on September 14, 1901, following the assassination of William McKinley. This inaugural address was made after he was elected to his second term.

My fellow citizens, no people on earth have more cause to be thankful than ours, and this is said reverently, in no spirit of boastfulness in our own strength, but with gratitude to the Giver of Good who has blessed us with the conditions which have enabled us to achieve so large a measure of well-being and of happiness. To us as a people it has been granted to lay the foundations of our national life in a new continent. We are the heirs of the ages, and yet we have had to pay few of the penalties which in old countries are exacted by the dead hand of a bygone civilization. We have not been obliged to fight for our existence against any alien race; and yet our life has called for the vigor and effort without which the manlier and hardier virtues wither away. Under such conditions it would be our own fault if we failed; and the success which we have had in the past, the success which we confidently believe the future will bring, should cause in us no feeling of vainglory, but rather a deep and abiding realization of all which life has offered us; a full acknowledgment of the responsibility which is ours; and a fixed determination to show that under a free government a mighty people can thrive best, alike as regards the things of the body and the things of the soul.

Much has been given us, and much will rightfully be expected from us. We have duties to others and duties to ourselves; and we can shirk neither. We have become a great nation, forced by the fact of its greatness into relations with the other nations of the earth, and we must behave as beseems a people with such responsibilities. Toward all other nations, large and small, our attitude must be one of cordial and sincere friendship. We must show not only in our words, but in our deeds, that we are earnestly desirous of securing their good will by acting toward them in a spirit of just and generous recognition of all their rights. But justice and generosity in a nation, as in an individual, count most when shown not by the weak but by the strong. While ever careful to refrain from wrongdoing others, we must be no less insistent that we are not wronged ourselves. We wish peace, but we wish the peace of justice, the peace of righteousness. We wish it because we think it is right and not because we are afraid. No weak nation that acts manfully and justly should ever have cause to fear us, and no strong power should ever be able to single us out as a subject for insolent aggression.

Our relations with the other powers of the world are important; but still more important are our relations among ourselves. Such growth in wealth, in population, and in power as this nation has seen during the century and a quarter of its national life is inevitably accompanied by a like growth in the problems which are ever before every nation that rises to greatness. Power invariably means both responsibility and danger. Our forefathers faced certain perils which we have outgrown. We now face other perils, the very existence of which it was impossible that they should foresee. Modern life is both complex and intense, and the tremendous changes wrought by the extraordinary industrial development of the last half century are felt in every fiber of our social and political being. Never before have men tried so vast and formidable an experiment as that of administering the affairs of a continent under the forms of a Democratic republic. The conditions which have told for our marvelous material well-being, which have developed to a very high degree our energy, self-reliance, and individual initiative, have also brought the care and anxiety inseparable from the accumulation of great wealth in industrial centers. Upon the success of our experiment much depends, not only as regards our own welfare, but as regards the welfare of mankind. If we fail, the cause of free self-government throughout the world will rock to its foundations, and therefore our responsibility is heavy, to ourselves, to the world as it is to-day, and to the generations yet unborn. There is no good reason why we should fear the future, but there is every reason why we should face it seriously, neither hiding from ourselves the gravity of the problems before us nor fearing to approach these problems with the unbending, unflinching purpose to solve them aright.

Yet, after all, though the problems are new, though the tasks set before us differ from the tasks set before our fathers who founded and preserved this Republic, the spirit in which these tasks must be undertaken and these problems faced, if our duty is to be well done, remains essentially unchanged. We know that self-government is difficult. We know that no people needs such high traits of character as that people which seeks to govern its affairs aright through the freely expressed will of the freemen who compose it. But we have faith that we shall not prove false to the memories of the men of the mighty past. They did their work, they left us the splendid heritage we now enjoy. We in our turn have an assured confidence that we shall be able to leave this heritage unwasted and enlarged to our children and our children's children. To do so we must show, not merely in great crises, but in the everyday affairs of life, the qualities of practical intelligence, of courage, of hardihood, and endurance, and above all the power of devotion to a lofty ideal, which made great the men who founded this Republic in the days of Washington, which made great the men who preserved this Republic in the days of Abraham Lincoln.

CITIZENSHIP IN A REPUBLIC (THE MAN IN THE ARENA)

Speech given at the Sorbonne, Paris

April 23, 1910

Strange and impressive associations rise in the mind of a man from the New World who speaks before this august body in this ancient institution of learning. Before his eyes pass the shadows of mighty kings and war-like nobles, of great masters of law and theology; through the shining dust of the dead centuries he sees crowded figures that tell of the power and learning and splendor of times gone by; and he sees also the innumerable host of humble students to whom clerkship meant emancipation, to whom it was well-nigh the only outlet from the dark thralldom of the Middle Ages.

This was the most famous university of medieval Europe at a time when no one dreamed that there was a New World to discover. Its services to the cause of human knowledge already stretched far back into the remote past at a time when my forefathers, three centuries ago, were among the sparse bands of traders, ploughmen, wood-choppers, and fisher folk who, in hard struggle with the iron unfriendliness of the Indian-haunted land, were laying the foundations of what has now become the giant republic of the West. To conquer a continent, to tame the shaggy roughness of wild nature, means grim warfare; and the generations engaged in it cannot keep, still less add to, the stores of garnered wisdom which where once theirs, and which are still in the hands of their brethren who dwell in the old land. To conquer the wilderness means to wrest victory from the same hostile forces with which mankind struggled on the immemorial infancy of our race. The primeval conditions must be met by the primeval qualities which are incompatible with the retention of much that has been painfully acquired by humanity as through the ages it has striven upward toward civilization. In conditions so primitive there can be but a primitive culture. At first only the rudest school can be established, for no others would meet the needs of the hard-driven, sinewy folk who thrust forward the frontier in the teeth of savage men and savage nature; and many years elapse before any of these schools can develop into seats of higher learning and broader culture.

The pioneer days pass; the stump-dotted clearings expand into vast stretches of fertile farm land; the stockade clusters of log cabins change into towns; the hunters of game, the fellers of trees, the rude frontier traders and tillers of the soil, the men who wander all their lives long through the wilderness as the heralds and harbingers of an oncoming civilization, themselves vanish before the civilization for which they have prepared the way. The children of their successors and supplanters, and then their children and their children and children's children, change and develop with extraordinary rapidity. The conditions accentuate vices and virtues, energy and ruthlessness, all the good qualities and all the defects of an intense individualism, self-reliant, self-centered, far more conscious of its rights than of its duties, and blind to its own shortcomings. To the hard materialism of the frontier days succeeds the hard materialism of an industrialism even more intense and absorbing than that of the older nations; although these themselves have likewise already entered on the age of a complex and predominantly industrial civilization.

As the country grows, its people, who have won success in so many lines, turn back to try to recover the possessions of the mind and the spirit, which perforce their fathers threw aside in order better to wage the first rough battles for the continent their children inherit. The leaders of thought and of action grope their way forward to a new life, realizing, sometimes dimly, sometimes clear-sightedly, that the life of material gain, whether for a nation or an individual, is of value only as a foundation, only as there is added to it the uplift that comes from devotion to loftier ideals. The new life thus sought can in part be developed afresh from what is roundabout in the New World; but it can be developed in full only be freely drawing upon the treasure-houses of the Old World, upon the treasures stored in the ancient adobes of wisdom and learning, such as this is where I speak to-day. It is a mistake for any nation to merely copy another; but it is even a greater mistake, it is a proof of weakness in any nation, not to be anxious to learn from one another and willing and able to adapt that learning to the new national conditions and make it fruitful and productive therein. It is for us of the New World to sit at the feet of Gamaliel of the Old; then, if we have the right stuff in us, we can show that Paul in his turn can become a teacher as well as a scholar.

Today I shall speak to you on the subject of individual citizenship, the one subject of vital importance to you, my hearers, and to me and my countrymen, because you and we a great citizens of great democratic republics. A democratic republic such as ours—an effort to realize its full sense government by, of, and for the people—represents the most gigantic of all possible social experiments, the one fraught with great responsibilities alike for good and evil. The success of republics like yours and like ours means the glory, and our failure of despair, of mankind; and for you and for us the question of the quality of the individual citizen is supreme. Under other forms of government, under the rule of one man or very few men, the quality of the leaders is all-important. If, under such governments, the quality of the rulers is high enough, then the nations for generations lead a brilliant career, and add substantially to the sum of world achievement, no matter how low the quality of average citizen; because the average citizen is an almost negligible quantity in working out the final results of that type of national greatness. But with you and us the case is different. With you here, and with us in my own home, in the long run, success or failure will be conditioned upon the way in which the average man, the average women, does his or her duty, first in the ordinary, every-day affairs of life, and next in those great occasional cries which call for heroic virtues. The average citizen must be a good citizen if our republics are to succeed. The stream will not permanently rise higher than the main source; and the main source of national power and national greatness is found in the average citizenship of the nation. Therefore it behooves us to do our best to see that the standard of the average citizen is kept high; and the average cannot be kept high unless the standard of the leaders is very much higher.

It is well if a large proportion of the leaders in any republic, in any democracy, are, as a matter of course, drawn from the classes represented in this audience to-day; but only provided that those classes possess the gifts of sympathy with plain people and of devotion to great ideals. You and those like you have received special advantages; you have all of you had the opportunity for mental training; many of you have had leisure; most of you have had a chance for enjoyment of life far greater than comes to the majority of your fellows. To you and your kind much has been given, and from you much should be expected. Yet there are certain failings against which it is especially incumbent that both men of trained and cultivated intellect, and men of inherited wealth and position should especially guard themselves, because to these failings they are especially liable; and if yielded to, their-your- chances of useful service are at an end. Let the man of learning, the man of lettered leisure, beware of that queer and cheap temptation to pose to himself and to others as a cynic, as the man who has outgrown emotions and beliefs, the man to whom good and evil are as one. The poorest way to face life is to face it with a sneer. There are many men who feel a kind of twisted pride in cynicism; there are many who confine themselves to criticism of the way others do what they themselves dare not even attempt. There is no more unhealthy being, no man less worthy of respect, than he who either really holds, or feigns to hold, an attitude of sneering disbelief toward all that is great and lofty, whether in achievement or in that noble effort which, even if it fails, comes to second achievement. A cynical habit of thought and speech, a readiness to criticize work which the critic himself never tries to perform, an intellectual aloofness which will not accept contact with life's realities—all these are marks, not as the possessor would fain to think, of superiority but of weakness. They mark the men unfit to bear their part painfully in the stern strife of living, who seek, in the affection of contempt for the achievement of others, to hide from others and from themselves in their own weakness. The role is easy; there is none easier, save only the role of the man who sneers alike at both criticism and performance.

It is not the critic who counts; not the man who points out how the strong man stumbles or where the doer of deeds could have done them better. The credit belongs to the man who is actually in the arena, whose face is marred by dust and sweat and blood; who strives valiantly; who errs, who comes short again and again, because there is no effort without error and shortcoming; but who does actually strive to do the deeds; who knows great enthusiasms, the great devotions; who spends himself in a worthy cause; who at the best knows in the end the triumph of high achievement, and who at the worst, if he fails, at least fails while daring greatly, so that his place shall never be with those cold and timid souls who neither know victory nor defeat. Shame on the man of cultivated taste who permits refinement to develop into fastidiousness that unfits him for doing the rough work of a workaday world. Among the free peoples who govern themselves there is but a small field of usefulness open for the men of cloistered life who shrink from contact with their fellows. Still less room is there for those who deride the slight of what is done by those who actually bear the brunt of the day; nor yet for others who always profess that they would like to take action, if only the conditions of life were not exactly what they actually are. The man who does nothing cuts the same sordid figure in the pages of history, whether he be a cynic, or fop, or voluptuary. There is little use for the being whose tepid soul knows nothing of great and generous emotion, of the high pride, the stern belief, the lofty enthusiasm, of the men who quell the storm and ride the thunder. Well for these men if they succeed; well also, though not so well, if they fail, given only that they have nobly ventured, and have put forth all their heath and strength. It is war-worn Hotspur, spent with hard fighting, he of the many errors and valiant end, over whose memory we love to linger, not over the memory of the young lord who "but for the vile guns would have been a valiant soldier."

France has taught many lessons to other nations: surely one of the most important lessons is the lesson her whole history teaches, and that a high artistic and literary development is compatible with notable leadership in arms and statecraft. The brilliant gallantry of the French soldier has for many centuries been proverbial; and during these same centuries at every court in Europe the "freemasons of fashion" have treated the French tongue as their common speech; while every artist and man of letters, and every man of science able to appreciate that marvelous instrument of precision, French prose, had turned toward France for aid and inspiration. How long the leadership in arms and letters has lasted is curiously illustrated by the fact that the earliest masterpiece in a modern tongue is the splendid French epic which tells of Roland's doom and the vengeance of Charlemagne when the lords of the Frankish hosts where stricken at Roncesvalles. Let those who have, keep, let those who have not, strive to attain, a high standard of cultivation and scholarship. Yet let us remember that these stand second to certain other things. There is need of a sound body, and even more of a sound mind. But above mind and above body stands character—the sum of those qualities which we mean when we speak of a man's force and courage, of his good faith and sense of honor. I believe in exercise for the body, always provided that we keep in mind that physical development is a means and not an end. I believe, of course, in giving to all the people a good education. But the education must contain much besides book-learning in order to be really good. We must ever remember that no keenness and subtleness of intellect, no polish, no cleverness, in any way make up for the lack of the great solid qualities. Self restraint, self mastery, common sense, the power of accepting individual responsibility and yet of acting in conjunction with others, courage and resolution—these are the qualities which mark a masterful people. Without them no people can control itself, or save itself from being controlled from the outside. I speak to brilliant assemblage; I speak in a great university which represents the flower of the highest intellectual development; I pay all homage to intellect and to elaborate and specialized training of the intellect; and yet I know I shall have the assent of all of you present when I add that more important still are the commonplace, every-day qualities and virtues.

Such ordinary, every-day qualities include the will and the power to work, to fight at need, and to have plenty of healthy children. The need that the average man shall work is so obvious as hardly to warrant insistence. There are a few people in every country so born that they can lead lives of leisure. These fill a useful function if they make it evident that leisure does not mean idleness; for some of the most valuable work needed by civilization is essentially non-remunerative in its character, and of course the people who do this work should in large part be drawn from those to whom remuneration is an object of indifference. But the average man must earn his own livelihood. He should be trained to do so, and should be trained to feel that he occupies a contemptible position if he does not do so; that he is not an object of envy if he is idle, at whoever end of the social scale he stands, but an object of contempt an object of derision. In the next place, the good man should be both a strong and a brave man; that is, he should be able to fight, he should be able to serve his country as a soldier, if the need arises. There are well-meaning philosophers who declaim against the unrighteousness of war. They are right only if they lay all their emphasis upon the unrighteousness. War is a dreadful thing, and unjust war is a crime against humanity. But it is such a crime because it is unjust, not because it is a war. The choice must ever be in favor of righteousness, and this is whether the alternative be peace or whether the alternative be war. The question must not be merely, is there to be peace or war? The question must be, is it right to prevail? Are the great laws or righteousness once more to be fulfilled? And the answer from a strong and virile person must be "Yes," whatever the cost. Every honorable effort should always be made to avoid war, just as every honorable effort should always be made the individual in private life to keep out of a brawl, to keep out of trouble; but no self-respecting individual, no self-respecting nation, can or ought to submit to wrong.

Finally, even more important than ability to work, even more important than ability to fight at need, is it to remember that chief of blessings for any nations is that it shall leave its seed to inherit the land. It was the crown of blessings in Biblical times and it is the crown of blessings now. The greatest of all curses is in the curse of sterility, and the severest of all condemnations should be that visited upon willful sterility. The first essential in any civilization is that the man and woman shall be father and mother of healthy children, so that the race shall increase and not decrease. If that is not so, if through no fault of the society there is failure to increase, it is a great misfortune. If the failure is due to the deliberate and willful fault, then it is not merely a misfortune, it is one of those crimes of ease and self-indulges, of shrinking for pain and effort and risk, which in the long run Nature punishes more heavily than any other. If we of the great republics, if we, the free people who claim to have emancipated ourselves from the thralldom of wrong and error, bring down on our heads the curse that comes upon the willfully barren, then it will be an idle waste of breath to prattle of our achievements, to boast of all that we have done. No refinement of life, no delicacy of taste, no material progress, no sordid heaping up riches, no sensuous development of art and literature, can in any way compensate for the loss of the great fundamental virtues; and of these great fundamental virtues the greatest is the race's power to perpetuate the race. Character must show itself in the man's performance both of the duty he owes himself and of the duty he owes the state. The man's foremost duty is owed to himself and his family; and he can do this duty only by earning money, by providing what is essential to material well-being; it is only after this has been done that he can hope to build a higher superstructure on the solid material foundation; it is only after this has been done that he can help in his movements for the general well-being. He must pull his own weight first, and only after this can his surplus strength be of use to the general public. It is not good to excite that bitter laughter which expresses contempt; and contempt is what we feel for the being whose enthusiasm to benefit mankind is such that he is a burden to those nearest him; who wishes to do great things for humanity in the abstract, but who cannot keep his wife in comfort or educate his children.

Nevertheless, while laying all stress on this point, while not merely acknowledging but insisting upon the fact that there must be a basis of material well-being for the individual as for the nation, let us with equal emphasis insist that this material well-being represents nothing but the foundation, and the foundation, though indispensable, is worthless unless upon it is raised the superstructure of a higher life. That is why I decline to recognize the mere multimillionaire, the man of mere wealth, as an asset of value to any country; and especially as not an asset to my own country. If he has earned or uses his wealth in a way that makes him a real benefit, of real use—and such is often the case—why, then he does become an asset of real worth. But it is the way in which it has been earned or used, and not the mere fact of wealth, that entitles him to the credit. There is need in business, as in most other forms of human activity, of the great guiding intelligences. Their places cannot be supplied by any number of lesser intelligences. It is a good thing that they should have ample recognition, ample reward. But we must not transfer our admiration to the reward instead of the deed rewarded; and if what should be the reward exists without the service having been rendered, then admiration will only come from those who are men of soul. The truth is that, after a certain measure of tangible material success or ward has been achieve, the question of increasing it becomes of constantly less importance compared to the other things that can be done in life. It is a bad thing for a nation to raise and to admire a false standard of success; and there can be no falser standard than that set by the deification of material well-being in and for itself. But the man, having far surpassed the limits of providing for the wants; both of the body and mind, of himself and of those depending upon him, then piles up a great fortune, for the acquisition of retention of which he returns no corresponding benefit to the nation as a whole, should himself be made to feel that, so far from being desirable, he is an unworthy, citizen of the community: that is to be neither admired nor envied; that his right-thinking fellow countrymen put him low in the scale of citizenship, and leave him to be consoled by the admiration of those whose level of purpose is even lower than his own.

My position as regards the moneyed interests can be put in a few words. In every civilized society property rights must be carefully safeguarded; ordinarily, and in the great majority of cases, human rights and property rights are fundamentally and in the long run identical; but when it clearly appears that there is a real conflict between them, human rights must have the upper hand, for property belongs to man and not man to property. In fact, it is essential to good citizenship clearly to understand that there are certain qualities which we in a democracy are prone to admire in and of themselves, which ought by rights to be judged admirable or the reverse solely from the standpoint of the use made of them. Foremost among these I should include two very distinct gifts—the gift of money-making and the gift of oratory. Money-making, the money touch I have spoken of above. It is a quality which in a moderate degree is essential. It may be useful when developed to a very great degree, but only if accompanied and controlled by other qualities; and without such control the possessor tends to develop into one of the least attractive types produced by a modern industrial democracy. So it is with the orator. It is highly desirable that a leader of opinion in democracy should be able to state his views clearly and convincingly. But all that the oratory can do of value to the community is enable the man thus to explain himself; if it enables the orator to put false values on things, it merely makes him power for mischief. Some excellent public servants have not that gift at all, and must merely rely on their deeds to speak for them; and unless oratory does represent genuine conviction based on good common sense and able to be translated into efficient performance, then the better the oratory the greater the damage to the public it deceives. Indeed, it is a sign of marked political weakness in any commonwealth if the people tend to be carried away by mere oratory, if they tend to value words in and for themselves, as divorced from the deeds for which they are supposed to stand. The phrase-maker, the phrase-monger, the ready talker, however great his power, whose speech does not make for courage, sobriety, and right understanding, is simply a noxious element in the body politic, and it speaks ill for the public if he has influence over them. To admire the gift of oratory without regard to the moral quality behind the gift is to wrong to the republic.

Of course all that I say of the orator applies with even greater force to the orator's latter day and more influential brother, the journalist. The power of the journalist is great, but he is entitled neither to respect nor admiration because of that power unless it is used aright. He can do, and often does, great good. He can do, and he often does, infinite mischief. All journalists, all writers, for the very reason that they appreciate the vast possibilities of their profession, should bear testimony against those who deeply discredit it. Offenses against taste and morals, which are bad enough in a private citizen, are infinitely worse if made into instruments for debauching the community through a newspaper. Mendacity, slander, sensationalism, inanity, vapid triviality, all are potent factors for the debauchery of the public mind and conscience. The excuse advanced for vicious writing that the public demands it and that demand must be supplied, can no more be admitted than if it were advanced by purveyors of food who sell poisonous adulterations. In short, the good citizen in a republic must realize that they ought to possess two sets of qualities, and that neither avails without the other. He must have those qualities which make for efficiency; and that he also must have those qualities which direct the efficiency into channels for the public good. He is useless if he is inefficient. There is nothing to be done with that type of citizen of whom all that can be said is that he is harmless. Virtue which is dependent upon a sluggish circulation is not impressive. There is little place in active life for the timid good man. The man who is saved by weakness from robust wickedness is likewise rendered immune from robuster virtues. The good citizen in a republic must first of all be able to hold his own. He is no good citizen unless he has the ability which will make him work hard and which at need will make him fight hard. The good citizen is not a good citizen unless he is an efficient citizen.

But if a man's efficiency is not guided and regulated by a moral sense, then the more efficient he is the worse he is, the more dangerous to the body politic. Courage, intellect, all the masterful qualities, serve but to make a man more evil if they are merely used for that man's own advancement, with brutal indifference to the rights of others. It speaks ill for the community if the community worships those qualities and treats their possessors as heroes regardless of whether the qualities are used rightly or wrongly. It makes no difference as to the precise way in which this sinister efficiency is shown. It makes no difference whether such a man's force and ability betray themselves in a career of money-maker or politician, soldier or orator, journalist or popular leader. If the man works for evil, then the more successful he is the more they should be despised and condemned by all upright and far-seeing men. To judge a man merely by success is an abhorrent wrong; and if the people at large habitually so judge men, if they grow to condone wickedness because the wicked man triumphs, they show their inability to understand that in the last analysis free institutions rest upon the character of citizenship, and that by such admiration of evil they prove themselves unfit for liberty. The homely virtues of the household, the ordinary workaday virtues which make the woman a good housewife and housemother, which make the man a hard worker, a good husband and father, a good soldier at need, stand at the bottom of character. But of course many other must be added thereto if a state is to be not only free but great. Good citizenship is not good citizenship if only exhibited in the home. There remains the duties of the individual in relate to the State, and these duties are none too easy under the conditions which exist where the effort is made to carry on the free government in a complex industrial civilization. Perhaps the most important thing the ordinary citizen, and, above all, the leader of ordinary citizens, has to remember in political life is that he must not be a sheer doctrinaire. The closer philosopher, the refined and cultured individual who from his library tells how men ought to be governed under ideal conditions, is of no use in actual governmental work; and the one-sided fanatic, and still more the mob-leader, and the insincere man who to achieve power promises what by no possibility can be performed, are not merely useless but noxious.

The citizen must have high ideals, and yet he must be able to achieve them in practical fashion. No permanent good comes from aspirations so lofty that they have grown fantastic and have become impossible and indeed undesirable to realize. The impractical visionary is far less often the guide and precursor than he is the embittered foe of the real reformer, of the man who, with stumblings and shortcomings, yet does in some shape, in practical fashion, given effect to the hopes and desires of those who strive for better things. Woe to the empty phrase-maker, to the empty idealist, who, instead of making ready the ground for the man of action, turns against him when he appears and hampers him when he does work! Moreover, the preacher of ideals must remember how sorry and contemptible is the figure which he will cut, how great the damage he will do, if he does not himself, in his own life, strive measurably to realize the ideals that he preaches for others. Let him remember also that the worth of the ideal must be largely determined by the success with which it can in practice be realized. We should abhor the so-called "practical" men whose practicality assumes the shape of that peculiar baseness which finds its expression in disbelief in morality and decency, in disregard of high standards of living and conduct. Such a creature is the worst enemy of the body of politic. But only less desirable as a citizen is his nominal opponent and real ally, the man of fantastic vision who makes the impossible better forever the enemy of the possible good.

We can just as little afford to follow the doctrinaires of an extreme individualism as the doctrinaires of an extreme socialism. Individual initiative, so far from being discouraged, should be stimulated; and yet we should remember that, as society develops and grows more complex, we continually find that things which once it was desirable to leave to individual initiative can, under changed conditions, be performed with better results by common effort. It is quite impossible, and equally undesirable, to draw in theory a hard-and-fast line which shall always divide the two sets of cases. Thus everyone who is not cursed with the pride of the closet philosopher will see, if he will only take the trouble to think about of our closet phenomena. For instance, when people lived on isolated farms or in little hamlets, each house can be left to attend to its own drainage and water-supply; but the mere multiplication of families in a given area produces new problems which, because they differ in size, are found to differ not only in degree, but in kind from the old; and the questions of drainage and water-supply have to be considered from the common standpoint. It is not a matter for abstract dogmatizing to decide when this point is reached; it is a matter to be tested by practical experiment. Much of the discussion about socialism and individualism is entirely pointless, because of the failure to agree on terminology. It is not good to be a slave of names. I am a strong individualist by personal habit, inheritance, and conviction; but it is a mere matter of common sense to recognize that the State, the community, the citizens acting together, can do a number of things better than if they were left to individual action. The individualism which finds its expression in the abuse of physical force is checked very early in the growth of civilization, and we of to-day should in our turn strive to shackle or destroy that individualism which triumphs by greed and cunning, which exploits the weak by craft instead of ruling them by brutality. We ought to go with any man in the effort to bring about justice and the equality of opportunity, to turn the tool-user more and more into the tool-owner, to shift burdens so that they can be more equitably borne. The deadening effect on any race of the adoption of a logical and extreme socialistic system could not be overstated; it would spell sheer destruction; it would produce grosser wrong and outrage, fouler immortality, than any existing system. But this does not mean that we not with great advantage adopt certain of the principles professed by some given set of men who happen to call themselves Socialists; to be afraid to do so would be to make a mark of weakness on our part.

But we should not take part in acting a lie any more than in telling a lie. We should not say that men are equal when they are not equal, nor proceed upon the assumption that there is an equality where it does not exist; but we should strive to bring about a measurable equality, at least to the extent of preventing the inequality which is due to force or fraud. Abraham Lincoln, a man of the plain people, blood of their blood, and bone of their bone, who all his life toiled and wrought and suffered for them, at the end died for them, who always strove to represent them, who would never tell an untruth to or for them, spoke of the doctrine of equality with his usual mixture of idealism and sound common sense. He said (I omit what was merely local significance):

> "I think the authors of the Declaration of Independence intended to include all men, but they did not mean to declare all men equal in

all respects. They did not mean to say all men were equal in color, size, intellect, moral development or social capacity. They defined with tolerable distinctness in what they did consider all men created equal-equal in certain inalienable rights, among which are life, liberty and pursuit of happiness. This they said, and this they meant. They did not mean to assert the obvious untruth that all were actually enjoying that equality, or yet that they were about to confer it immediately upon them. They meant to set up a standard maxim for free society which should be familiar to all—constantly looked to, constantly labored for, and, even though never perfectly attained, constantly approximated, and thereby constantly spreading and deepening its influence, and augmenting the happiness and value of life to all people, everywhere."

We are bound in honor to refuse to listen to those men who would make us desist from the effort to do away with the inequality which means injustice; the inequality of right, opportunity, of privilege. We are bound in honor to strive to bring even nearer the day when, as far is humanly possible, we shall be able to realize the ideal that each man shall have an equal opportunity to show the stuff that is in him by the way in which he renders service. There should, so far as possible, be equal of opportunity to render service; but just so long as there inequality of service there should and must be inequality of reward. We may be sorry for the general, the painter, the artists, the worker in any profession or of any kind, whose misfortune rather than whose fault is that he does his work ill. But the reward must go to the man who does his work well; for any other course is to create a new kind of privilege, the privilege of folly and weakness; and special privilege is injustice, whatever form it takes.

To say that the thriftless, the lazy, the vicious, the incapable, ought to have reward given to those who are far-sighted, capable, and upright, is to say what is not true and cannot be true. Let us try to level up, but let us beware of the evil of leveling down. If a man stumbles, it is a good thing to help him to his feet. Every one of us needs a helping hand now and then. But if a man lies down, it is a waste of time to try and carry him; and it is a very bad thing for every one if we make mane feel that the same reward will come to those who shirk their work and those who do it. Let us, then, take into account the actual facts of life and not be misled into following any proposal for achieving the millennium, for recreating the golden age, until we have subjected it to hardheaded examination. On the other hand, it is foolish to reject a proposal merely because it is advanced by visionaries. If a given scheme is proposed, look at it on its merits, and, in considering it, disregard formulas. It does not matter in the least who proses it, or why. It seems good, try it. If it proves good, accept it; otherwise reject it. There are plenty of good men calling themselves Socialists with whom, up to a certain point, it is quite possible to work. If the next step is one which both we and they wish to take, why of course take it, without any regard to the fact that our views as to the tenth step may differ. But, on the other hand, keep clearly in mind that, though it has been worthwhile to take one step, this does not in the least mean that it may not be highly disadvantageous to take the next. It is just as foolish to refuse all progress because people demanding it desire at some points to go to absurd extremes, as it would be to go to these absurd extremes simply because some of the measure advocated by the extremists were wise.

The good citizen will demand liberty for himself, and as a matter of pride he will see to it that others receive liberty which he thus claims as his own. Probably the best test of true love of liberty in any country is the way in which minorities are treated in that country. Not only should there be complete liberty in matters of religion and opinion, but complete liberty for each man to lead his life as he desires, provided only that in so he does not wrong his neighbor. Persecution is bad because it is persecution, and without reference to which side happens at the most to be the persecuted and which the persecuted. Class hatred is bad in just the same way, and without regard to the individual who, at a given time, substitutes loyalty to a class for loyalty to a nation, of substitutes hatred of men because they happen to come in a certain social category, for judgment awarded them according to their conduct. Remember always that the same measure of condemnation should be extended to the arrogance which would look down upon or crush any man because he is poor and to envy and hatred which would destroy a man because he is wealthier. The overbearing brutality of the man of wealthier or power, and the envious and hateful malice directed against the wealth or power, are really at root merely different manifestations of the same quality, merely two sides of the same shield. The man who, if born to wealth and power, exploits and ruins his less fortunate brethren is at heart the same as the greedy and violent demagogue who excites those who have not property to plunder those who have. The gravest wrong upon his country is inflicted by that man, whatever his station, who seeks to make his countrymen divide primarily in the line that separated class from class, occupation from occupation, men of more wealth from men of less wealth, instead of remembering that the only safe standard is that which judges each man on his worth as a man, whether he be rich or whether he be poor, without regard to his profession or to his station in life. Such is the only true democratic test, the only test that can with propriety be applied in a republic. There have been many republics in the past, both in what we call antiquity and in what we call the Middle Ages. They fell, and the prime factor in their fall was the fact that the parties tended to divide along the wealth from poverty. It made no difference which side was successful; it made no difference whether the republic fell under the rule of and oligarchy or the rule of a mob. In either case, when once loyalty to a class had been substituted for loyalty to the republic, the end of the republic was at hand. There is no greater need to-day than the need to keep ever in mind the fact that the cleavage between right and wrong, between good citizenship and bad citizenship, runs at right angles to, and not parallel with, the lines of cleavage between class and class, between occupation and occupation. Ruin looks us in the face if we judge a man by his position instead of judging him by his conduct in that position.

In a republic, to be successful we must learn to combine intensity of conviction with a broad tolerance of difference of conviction. Wide differences of opinion in matters of religious, political, and social belief must exist if conscience and intellect alike are not to be stunted, if there is to be room for healthy growth. Bitter internecine hatreds, based on such differences, are signs, not of earnestness of belief, but of that fanaticism which, whether religious or antireligious, democratic or antidemocratic, it itself but a manifestation of the gloomy bigotry which has been the chief factor in the downfall of so many, many nations.

Of one man in especial, beyond any one else, the citizens of a republic should beware, and that is of the man who appeals to them to support him on the ground that he is hostile to other citizens of the republic, that he will secure for those who elect him, in one shape or another, profit at the expense of other citizens of the republic. It makes no difference whether he appeals to class hatred or class interest, to religious or antireligious prejudice. The man who makes such an appeal should always be presumed to make it for the sake of furthering his own interest. The very last thing an intelligent and self-respecting member of a democratic community should do is to reward any public man because that public man says that he will get the private citizen something to which this private citizen is not entitled, or will gratify some emotion or animosity which this private citizen ought not to possess. Let me illustrate this by one anecdote from my own experience. A number of years ago I was engaged in cattle-ranching on the great plains of the western United States. There were no fences. The cattle wandered free, the ownership of each one was determined by the brand; the calves were branded with the brand of the cows they followed. If on a round-up an animal was passed by, the following year it would appear as an unbranded yearling, and was then called a maverick. By the custom of the country these mavericks were branded with the brand of the man on whose range they were found. One day I was riding the range with a newly hired cowboy, and we came upon a maverick. We roped and threw it; then we built a fire, took out a cinch-ring, heated it in the fire; and then the cowboy started to put on the brand. I said to him, "It's so-and-so's brand," naming the man on whose range we happened to be. He answered: "That's all right, boss; I know my business." In another moment I said to him: "Hold on, you are putting on my brand!" To which he answered: "That's all right; I always put on the boss's brand." I answered: "Oh, very well. Now you go straight back to the ranch and get whatever is owing to you; I don't need you any longer." He jumped up and said: "Why, what's the matter? I was putting on your brand." And I answered: "Yes, my friend, and if you will steal for me then you will steal from me."

Now, the same principle which applies in private life applies also in public life. If a public man tried to get your vote by saying that he will do something wrong in your interest, you can be absolutely certain that if ever it becomes worth his while he will do something wrong against your interest. So much for the citizenship to the individual in his relations to his family, to his neighbor, to the State. There remains duties of citizenship with the Sates, the aggregation of all the individuals, owes in connection with other States, with other nations. Let me say at once that I am no advocate for a foolish cosmopolitanism. I believe that a man must be a good patriot before he can be, and as the only possible way of being, a good citizen of the world. Experience teaches us that the average man who protests that his international feeling swamps his national feeling, that he does not care for his country because he cares so much for mankind, in actual practice proves himself the foe of mankind; that the man who says that he does not care to be a citizen of any one country, because he is the citizen of the world he happens at the moment to be in. In the dim future all moral needs and moral standards may change; but at present, if a man can view his own country and all other countries from the same level with tepid indifference, it is wise to distrust him, just as it is wise to distrust the man who can take the same dispassionate view of his wife and mother. However broad and deep a man's sympathies, however intense his activities, he need have no fear that they will be cramped by love of his native land.

Now, this does not mean in the least that a man should not wish to do good outside of his native land. On the contrary, just as I think that the man who loves his family is more apt to be a good neighbor than the man who does not, so I think that the most useful member of the family of nations is normally a strongly patriotic nation. So far from patriotism being inconsistent with a proper regard for the rights of other nations, I hold that the true patriot, who is as jealous of national honor as a gentleman of his own honor, will be careful to see that the nations neither inflect nor suffer wrong, just as a gentleman scorns equally to wrong others or to suffer others to wrong him. I do not for one moment admit that a man should act deceitfully as a public servant in his dealing with other nations, any more than he should act deceitfully in his dealings as a private citizen with other private citizens. I do not for one moment admit that a nation should treat other nations in a different spirit from that in which an honorable man would treat other men.

In practically applying this principle to the two sets of cases there is, of course, a great practical difference to be taken into account. We speak of international law; but international law is something wholly different from private or municipal law, and the capital difference is that there is a sanction for the one and no sanction for the other; that there is an outside force which compels individuals to obey the one, while there is no such outside force to compel obedience as regards to the other. International law will, I believe, as the generations pass, grow stronger and stronger until in some way or other there develops the power to make it respected. But as yet it only in the first formative period. As yet, as a rule, each nation is of necessity to judge for itself in matters of vital importance between it and its neighbors, and actions must be of necessity, where this is the case, be different from what they are where, as among private citizens, there is an outside force whose action is all-powerful and must be invoked in any crisis of importance. It is the duty of wise statesman, gifted with the power of looking ahead, to try to encourage and build up every movement which will substitute or tend to substitute some other agency for force in the settlement of international disputes. It is the duty of every honest statesman to try to guide the nation so that it shall not wrong any other nation. But as yet the great civilized peoples, if they are to be true to themselves and to the cause of humanity and civilization, must keep in mind that in the last resort they must possess both the will and the power to resent wrong-doings from others. The men who sanely believe in a lofty morality preach righteousness; but do not preach weakness, whether among private citizens or among nations. We believe that our ideals should be so high, but not so high as to make it impossible measurably to realize them. We sincerely and earnestly believe in peace; but if peace and justice conflict, we scorn the man who would not stand for justice though the whole world came in arms against him.

And now, my hosts, a word in parting. You and I belong to the only two republics among the great powers of the world. The ancient friendship between France and the United States has been, on the whole, a sincere and disinterested friendship. A calamity to you would be a sorrow to us. But it would be more than that. In the seething turmoil of the history of humanity certain nations stand out as possessing a peculiar power or charm, some special gift of beauty or wisdom or strength, which puts them among the immortals, which makes them rank forever with the leaders of mankind. France is one of these nations. For her to sink would be a loss to all the world. There are certain lessons of brilliance and of generous gallantry that she can teach better than any of her sister nations. When the French peasantry sang of Malbrook, it was to tell how the soul of this warrior-foe took flight upward through the laurels he had won. Nearly seven centuries ago, Froisart, writing of the time of dire disaster, said that the realm of France was never so stricken that there were not left men who would valiantly fight for it. You have had a great past. I believe you will have a great future. Long may you carry yourselves proudly as citizens of a nation which bears a leading part in the teaching and uplifting of mankind.

THE NEW NATIONALISM

Speech given at Osawatomie, Kansas

August 31, 1910

We come here to-day to commemorate one of the epoch-making events of the long struggle for the rights of man—the long struggle for the uplift of humanity. Our country—this great Republic—means nothing unless it means the triumph of a real democracy, the triumph of popular government, and, in the long run, of an economic system under which each man shall be guaranteed the opportunity to show the best that there is in him. That is why the history of America is now the central feature of the history of the world; for the world has set its face hopefully toward our democracy; and, O my fellow citizens, each one of you carries on your shoulders not only the burden of doing well for the sake of your own country, but the burden of doing well and of seeing that this nation does well for the sake of mankind.

There have been two great crises in our country's history: first, when it was formed, and then, again, when it was perpetuated; and, in the second of these great crises—in the time of stress and strain which culminated in the Civil War, on the outcome of which depended the justification of what had been done earlier, you men of the Grand Army, you men who fought through the Civil War, not only did you justify your generation, not only did you render life worth living for our generation, but you justified the wisdom of Washington and Washington's colleagues. If this Republic had been founded by them only to be split asunder into fragments when the strain came, then the judgment of the world would have been that Washington's work was not worth doing. It was you who crowned Washington's work, as you carried to achievement the high purpose of Abraham Lincoln.

Now, with this second period of our history the name of John Brown will be forever associated; and Kansas was the theater upon which the first act of the second of our great national life dramas was played. It was the result of the struggle in Kansas which determined that our country should be in deed as well as in name devoted to both union and freedom; that the great experiment of democratic government on a national scale should succeed and not fail. In name we had the Declaration of Independence in 1776; but we gave the lie by our acts to the words of the Declaration of Independence until 1865; and words count for nothing except in so far as they represent acts. This is true everywhere; but, O my friends, it should be truest of all in political life. A broken promise is bad enough in private life. It is worse in the field of politics. No man is worth his salt in public life who makes on the stump a pledge which he does not keep after election; and, if he makes such a pledge and does not keep it, hunt him out of public life. I care for the great deeds of the past chiefly as spurs to drive us onward in the present. I speak of the men of the past partly that they may be honored by our praise of them, but more that they may serve as examples for the future.

It was a heroic struggle; and, as is inevitable with all such struggles, it had also a dark and terrible side. Very much was done of good, and much also of evil; and, as was inevitable in such a period of revolution, often the same man did both good and evil. For our great good fortune as a nation, we, the people of the United States as a whole, can now afford to forget the evil, or, at least, to remember it without bitterness, and to fix our eyes with pride only on the good that was accomplished. Even in ordinary times there are very few of us who do not see the problems of life as through a glass, darkly; and when the glass is clouded by the murk of furious popular passion, the vision of the best and the bravest is dimmed. Looking back, we are all of us now able to do justice to the valor and the disinterestedness and the love of the right, as to each it was given to see the right, shown both by the men of the North and the men of the South in that contest which was finally decided by the attitude of the West. We can admire the heroic valor, the sincerity, the self-devotion shown alike by the men who wore the blue and the men who wore the gray; and our sadness that such men should have had to fight one another is tempered by the glad knowledge that ever hereafter their descendants shall be found fighting side by side, struggling in peace as well as in war for the uplift of their common country. all alike resolute to raise to the highest pitch of honor and usefulness the nation to which they all belong. As for the veterans of the Grand Army of the Republic, they deserve honor and recognition such as is paid to no other citizens of the Republic; for to them the republic owes its all; for to them it owes its very existence. It is because of what you and your comrades did in the dark years that we of to-day walk, each of us, head erect, and proud that we belong, not to one of a dozen little squabbling contemptible commonwealths, but to the mightiest nation upon which the sun shines.

I do not speak of this struggle of the past merely from the historic standpoint. Our interest is primarily in the application to-day of the lessons taught by the contest of half a century ago. It is of little use for us to pay lip-loyalty to the mighty men of the past unless we sincerely endeavor to apply to the problems of the present precisely the qualities which in other crises enable the men of that day to meet those crises. It is half melancholy and half amusing to see the way in which well-meaning people gather to do honor to the man who, in company with

John Brown, and under the lead of Abraham Lincoln, faced and solved the great problems of the nineteenth century, while, at the same time, these same good people nervously shrink from, or frantically denounce, those who are trying to meet the problems of the twentieth century in the spirit which was accountable for the successful solution of the problems of Lincoln's time.

Of that generation of men to whom we owe so much, the man to whom we owe most is, of course, Lincoln. Part of our debt to him is because he forecast our present struggle and saw the way out. He said:

> "I hold that while man exists it is his duty to improve not only his own condition, but to assist in ameliorating mankind."

And again:

> "Labor is prior to, and independent of, capital. Capital is only the fruit of labor, and could never have existed if labor had not first existed. Labor is the superior of capital, and deserves much the higher consideration."

If that remark was original with me, I should be even more strongly denounced as a Communist agitator than I shall be anyhow. It is Lincoln's. I am only quoting it; and that is one side; that is the side the capitalist should hear. Now, let the working man hear his side.

> "Capital has its rights, which are as worthy of protection as any other rights.... Nor should this lead to a war upon the owners of property. Property is the fruit of labor. Property is desirable; is a positive good in the world."

And then comes a thoroughly Lincoln-like sentence:

> "Let not him who is houseless pull down the house of another, but let him work diligently and build one for himself, thus by example assuring that his own shall be safe from violence when built."

It seems to me that, in these words, Lincoln took substantially the attitude that we ought to take; he showed the proper sense of proportion in his relative estimates of capital and labor, of human rights and property rights. Above all, in this speech, as in many others, he taught a lesson in wise kindliness and charity; an indispensable lesson to us of today. But this wise kindliness and charity never weakened his arm or numbed his heart. We cannot afford weakly to blind ourselves to the actual conflict which faces us to-day. The issue is joined, and we must fight or fail.

In every wise struggle for human betterment one of the main objects, and often the only object, has been to achieve in large measure equality of opportunity. In the struggle for this great end, nations rise from barbarism to civilization, and through it people press forward from one stage of enlightenment to the next. One of the chief factors in progress is the destruction of special privilege. The essence of any struggle for healthy liberty has always been, and must always be, to take from some one man or class of men the right to enjoy power, or wealth, or position, or immunity, which has not been earned by service to his or their fellows. That is what you fought for in the Civil War, and that is what we strive for now.

At many stages in the advance of humanity, this conflict between the men who possess more than they have earned and the men who have earned more than they possess is the central condition of progress. In our day it appears as the struggle of freemen to gain and hold the right of self-government as against the special interests, who twist the methods of free government into machinery for defeating the popular will. At every stage, and under all circumstances, the essence of the struggle is to equalize opportunity, destroy privilege, and give to the life and citizenship of every individual the highest possible value both to himself and to the commonwealth. That is nothing new. All I ask in civil life is what you fought for in the Civil War. I ask that civil life be carried on according to the spirit in which the army was carried on. You never get perfect justice, but the effort in handling the army was to bring to the front the men who could do the job. Nobody grudged promotion to Grant, or Sherman, or Thomas, or Sheridan, because they earned it. The only complaint was when a man got promotion which he did not earn.

Practical equality of opportunity for all citizens, when we achieve it, will have two great results. First, every man will have a fair chance to make of himself all that in him lies; to reach the highest point to which his capacities, unassisted by special privilege of his own and unhampered by the special privilege of others, can carry him, and to get for himself and his family substantially what he has earned. Second, equality of opportunity means that the commonwealth will get from every citizen the highest service of which he is capable. No man who carries the burden of the special privileges of another can give to the commonwealth that service to which it is fairly entitled.

I stand for the square deal. But when I say that I am for the square deal, I mean not merely that I stand for fair play under the present rules of the games, but that I stand for having those rules changed so as to work for a more substantial equality of opportunity and of reward for equally good service. One word of warning, which, I think, is hardly necessary in Kansas. When I say I want a square deal for the poor man, I do not mean that I want a square deal for the man who remains poor because he has not got the energy to work for himself. If a man who has had a chance will not make good, then he has got to quit. And you men of the Grand Army, you want justice for the brave man who fought, and punishment for the coward who shirked his work. Is not that so?

Now, this means that our government, National and State, must be freed from the sinister influence or control of special interests. Exactly as the special interests of cotton and slavery threatened our political integrity before the Civil War, so now the great special business interests too often control and corrupt the men and methods of government for their own profit. We must drive the special interests out of politics. That is one of our tasks to-day. Every special interest is entitled to justice—full, fair, and complete—and, now, mind you, if there were any attempt by mob-violence to plunder and work harm to the special interest, whatever it may be, and I most dislike and the wealthy man, whomsoever he may be, for whom I have the greatest contempt, I would fight for him, and you would if you were worth your salt. He should have justice. For every special interest is entitled to justice, but not one is entitled to a vote in Congress, to a voice on the bench, or to representation in any public office. The Constitution guarantees protections to property, and we must make that promise good. But it does not give the right of suffrage to any corporation.

The true friend of property, the true conservative, is he who insists that property shall be the servant and not the master of the commonwealth; who insists that the creature of man's making shall be the servant and not the master of the man who made it. The citizens of the United States must effectively control the mighty commercial forces which they have themselves called into being.

There can be no effective control of corporations while their political activity remains. To put an end to it will be neither a short nor an easy task, but it can be done.

We must have complete and effective publicity of corporate affairs, so that people may know beyond peradventure whether the corporations obey the law and whether their management entitles them to the confidence of the public. It is necessary that laws should be passed to prohibit the use of corporate funds directly or indirectly for political purposes; it is still more necessary that such laws should be thoroughly enforced. Corporate expenditures for political purposes, and especially such expenditures by public-service corporations, have supplied one of the principal sources of corruption in our political affairs.

It has become entirely clear that we must have government supervision of the capitalization, not only of public-service corporations, including, particularly, railways, but of all corporations doing an interstate business. I do not wish to see the nation forced into the ownership of the railways if it can possibly be avoided, and the only alternative is thoroughgoing and effective legislation, which shall be based on a full knowledge of all the facts, including a physical valuation of property. This physical valuation is not needed, or, at least, is very rarely needed, for fixing rates; but it is needed as the basis of honest capitalization.

We have come to recognize that franchises should never be granted except for a limited time, and never without proper provision for compensation to the public. It is my personal belief that the same kind and degree of control and supervision which should be exercised over public-service corporations should be extended also to combinations which control necessaries of life, such as meat, oil, and coal, or which deal in them on an important scale. I have no doubt that the ordinary man who has control of them is much like ourselves. I have no doubt he would like to do well, but I want to have enough supervision to help him realize that desire to do well.

I believe that the officers, and, especially, the directors, of corporations should be held personally responsible when any corporation breaks the law.

Combinations in industry are the result of an imperative economic law which cannot be repealed by political legislation. The effort at prohibiting all combination has substantially failed. The way out lies, not in attempting to prevent such combinations, but in completely controlling them in the interest of the public welfare. For that purpose the Federal Bureau of Corporations is an agency of first importance. Its powers, and, therefore, its efficiency, as well as that of the Interstate Commerce Commission, should be largely increased. We have a right to expect from the Bureau of Corporations and from the Interstate Commerce Commission a very high grade of public service. We should be as sure of the proper conduct of the interstate railways and the proper management of interstate business as we are now sure of the conduct and management of the national banks, and we should have as effective supervision in one case as in the other. The Hepburn Act, and the amendment to the act in the shape in which it finally passed Congress at the last session, represent a long step in advance, and we must go yet further.

There is a wide-spread belief among our people that under the methods of making tariffs, which have hitherto obtained, the special interests are too influential. Probably this is true of both the big special interests and the little special interests. These methods have put a premium on selfishness, and, naturally, the selfish big interests have gotten more than their smaller, though equally selfish brothers. The duty of Congress is to provide a method by which the interest of the whole people shall be all that receives consideration. To this end there must be an expert tariff commission, wholly removed from the possibility of political pressure or of improper business influence. Such a commission can find the real difference between cost of production, which is mainly the difference of labor cost here and abroad. As fast as its recommendations are made, I believe in revising one schedule at a time. A general revision of the tariff almost inevitably leads to logrolling and the subordination of the general public interest to local and special interests.

The absence of effective State, and, especially, national, restraint upon unfair money-getting has tended to create a small class of enormously wealthy and economically powerful men, whose chief object is to hold and increase their power. The prime need is to change the conditions which enable these men to accumulate power which is not for the general welfare that they should hold or exercise. We grudge no man a fortune which represents his own power and sagacity, when exercised with entire regard to the welfare of his fellows. Again, comrades over there, take the lesson from your own experience. Not only did you not grudge, but you gloried in the promotion of the great generals who gained their promotion by leading the army to victory. So it is with us. We grudge no man a fortune in civil life if it is honorably obtained and well used. It is not even enough that it should have gained without doing damage to the community. We should permit it to be gained only so long as the gaining represents benefit to the community. This, I know, implies a policy of a far more active governmental interference with social and economic conditions in this country than we have yet had, but I think we have got to face the fact that such an increase in governmental control is now necessary.

No man should receive a dollar unless that dollar has been fairly earned. Every dollar received should represent a dollar's worth of service rendered—not gambling in stocks, but service rendered. The really big fortune, the swollen fortune, by the mere fact of its size acquires qualities which differentiate it in kind as well as in degree from what is possessed by men of relatively small means. Therefore, I believe in a graduated income tax on big fortunes, and in another tax which is far more easily collected and far more effective—a graduated inheritance tax on big fortunes, properly safeguarded against evasion and increasing rapidly in amount with the size of the estate.

The people of the United States suffer from periodical financial panics to a degree substantially unknown among the other nations which approach us in financial strength. There is no reason why we should suffer what they escape. It is of profound importance that our financial system should be promptly investigated, and so thoroughly and effectively revised as to make it certain that hereafter our currency will no longer fail at critical times to meet our needs.

It is hardly necessary for me to repeat that I believe in an efficient army and a navy large enough to secure for us abroad that respect which is the surest guaranty of peace. A word of special warning to my fellow citizens who are as progressive as I hope I am. I want them to keep up their interest in our internal affairs; and I want them also continually to remember Uncle Sam's interest abroad. Justice and fair dealing among nations rest upon principles identical with those which control justice and fair dealing among the individuals of which nations are composed, with the vital exception that each nation must do its own part in international police work. If you get into trouble here, you can call for the police; but if Uncle Sam gets into trouble, he has got to be his own policeman, and I want to see him strong enough to encourage the peaceful aspirations of other peoples in connection with us. I believe in national friendships and heartiest good-will to all nations; but national friendships, like those between men, must be founded on respect as well as on liking, on forbearance as well as upon trust. I should be heartily ashamed of any American who did not try to make the American Government act as justly toward the other nations in international relations as he himself would act toward any individual in private relations. I should be heartily ashamed to see us wrong a weaker power, and I should hang my head forever if we tamely suffered wrong from a stronger power.

Of conservation I shall speak more at length elsewhere. Conservation means development as much as it does protection. I recognize the right and duty of this generation to develop and use the natural resources of our land; but I do not recognize the right to waste them, or to rob, by wasteful use, the generations that come after us. I ask nothing of the nation except that it so behave as each farmer here behaves with reference to his own children. That farmer is a poor creature who skins the land and leaves it worthless to his children. The farmer is a good farmer who, having enabled the land to support himself and to provide for the education of his children leaves it to them a little better than he found it himself. I believe the same thing of a nation.

Moreover, I believe that the natural resources must be used for the benefit of all our people, and not monopolized for the benefit of the few, and here again is another case in which I am accused of taking a revolutionary attitude. People forget now that one hundred years ago there were public men of good character who advocated the nation selling its public lands in great quantities, so that the nation could get the most money out of it, and giving it to the men who could cultivate it for their own uses. We took the proper democratic ground that the land should be granted in small sections to the men who were actually to till it and live on it. Now, with the water-power with the forests, with the mines, we are brought face to face with the fact that there are many people who will go with us in conserving the resources only if they are to be allowed to exploit them for their benefit. That is one of the fundamental reasons why the special interest should be driven out of politics. Of all the questions which can come before this nation, short of the actual preservation of its existence in a great war, there is none which compares in importance with the great central task of leaving this land even a better land for our descendants than it is for us, and training them into a better race to inhabit the land and pass it on. Conservation is a great moral issue for it involves the patriotic duty of insuring the safety and continuance of the nation. Let me add that the health and vitality of our people are at least as well worth conserving as their forests, waters, lands, and minerals, and in this great work the national government must bear a most important part.

I have spoken elsewhere also of the great task which lies before the farmers of the country to get for themselves and their wives and children not only the benefits of better farming, but also those of better business methods and better conditions of life on the farm. The burden of this great task will fall, as it should, mainly upon the great organizations of the farmers themselves. I am glad it will, for I believe they are all able to handle it. In particular, there are strong reasons why the Departments of Agriculture of the various States, and the United States Department of Agriculture, and the agricultural colleges and experiment stations should extend their work to cover all phases of farm life, instead of limiting themselves, as they have far too often limited themselves in the past, solely to the question of the production of crops. And now a special word to the farmer. I want to see him make the farm as fine a farm as it can be made; and let him remember to see that the improvement goes on indoors as well as out; let him remember that the farmer's wife should have her share of thought and attention just as much as the farmer himself.

Nothing is more true than that excess of every kind is followed by reaction; a fact which should be pondered by reformer and reactionary alike. We are face to face with new conceptions of the relations of property to human welfare, chiefly because certain advocates of the rights of property as against the rights of men have been pushing their claims too far. The man who wrongly holds that every human right is secondary to his profit must now give way to the advocate of human welfare, who rightly maintains that every man holds his property subject to the general right of the community to regulate its use to whatever degree the public welfare may require it.

But I think we may go still further. The right to regulate the use of wealth in the public interest is universally admitted. Let us admit also the right to regulate the terms and conditions of labor, which is the chief element of wealth, directly in the interest of the common good. The fundamental thing to do for every man is to give him a chance to reach a place in which he will make the greatest possible contribution to the public welfare. Understand what I say there. Give him a chance, not push him up if he will not be pushed. Help any man who stumbles; if he lies down, it is a poor job to try to carry him; but if he is a worthy man, try your best to see that he gets a chance to show the worth that is in him. No man can be a good citizen unless he has a wage more than sufficient to cover the bare cost of living, and hours of labor short enough so that after his day's work is done he will have time and energy to bear his share in the management of the community, to help in carrying the general load. We keep countless men from being good citizens by the conditions of life with which we surround them. We need comprehensive workmen's compensation acts, both State and national laws to regulate child labor and work for women, and, especially, we need in our common schools not merely education in book learning, but also practical training for daily life and work. We need to enforce better sanitary conditions for our workers and to extend the use of safety appliances for our workers in industry and commerce, both within and between the States. Also, friends, in the interest of the working man himself, we need to set our faces like flint against mob-violence just as against corporate greed; against violence and injustice and lawlessness by wage-workers just as much as against lawless cunning and greed and selfish arrogance of employers. If I could ask but one thing of my fellow countrymen, my request would be that, whenever they go in for reform, they remember the two sides, and that they always exact justice from one side as much as from the other. I have small use for the public servant who can always see and denounce the corruption of the capitalist, but who cannot persuade himself, especially before elections, to say a word about lawless mob-violence. And I have equally small use for the man, be he a judge on the bench, or editor of a great paper, or wealthy and influential private citizen, who can see clearly enough and denounce the lawlessness of mob-violence, but whose eyes are closed so that he is blind when the question is one of corruption in business on a gigantic scale. Also remember what I said about excess in reformer and reactionary alike. If the reactionary man, who thinks of nothing but the rights of property, could have his way, he would bring about a revolution; and one of my chief fears in connection with progress comes because I do not want to see our people, for lack of proper leadership, compelled to follow men whose intentions are excellent, but whose eyes are a little too wild to make it really safe to trust them. Here in Kansas there is one paper which habitually denounces me as the tool of Wall Street, and at the same time frantically repudiates the statement that I am a Socialist on the ground that is an unwarranted slander of the Socialists.

National efficiency has many factors. It is a necessary result of the principle of conservation widely applied. In the end it will determine our failure or success as a nation. National efficiency has to do, not only with natural resources and with men, but is equally concerned with institutions. The State must be made efficient for the work which concerns only the people of the State; and the nation for that which concerns all the people. There must remain no neutral ground to serve as a refuge for lawbreakers, and especially for lawbreakers of great wealth, who can hire the vulpine legal cunning which will teach them how to avoid both jurisdictions. It is a misfortune when the national legislature fails to do its duty in providing a national remedy, so that the only national activity is the purely negative activity of the judiciary in forbidding the State to exercise power in the premises.

I do not ask for over centralization; but I do ask that we work in a spirit of broad and far-reaching nationalism when we work for what concerns our people as a whole. We are all Americans. Our common interests are as broad as the continent. I speak to you here in Kansas exactly as I would speak in New York or Georgia, for the most vital problems are those which affect us all alike. The National Government belongs to the whole American people, and where the whole American people are interested, that interest can be guarded effectively only by the National Government. The betterment which we seek must be accomplished, I believe, mainly through the National Government.

The American people are right in demanding that New Nationalism, without which we cannot hope to deal with new problems. The New Nationalism puts the national need before sectional or personal advantage. It is impatient of the utter confusion that results from local legislatures attempting to treat national issues as local issues. It is still more impatient of the impotence which springs from over division of governmental powers, the impotence which makes it possible for local selfishness or for legal cunning, hired by wealthy special interests, to bring national activities to a deadlock. This New Nationalism regards the executive power as the steward of the public welfare. It demands of the judiciary that it shall be interested primarily in human welfare rather than in property, just as it demands that the representative body shall represent all the people rather than any one class or section of the people.

I believe in shaping the ends of government to protect property as well as human welfare. Normally, and in the long run, the ends are the same; but whenever the alternative must be faced, I am for men and not for property, as you were in the Civil War. I am far from underestimating the importance of dividends; but I rank dividends below human character. Again, I do not have any sympathy with the reformer who says he does not care for dividends. Of course, economic welfare is necessary, for a man must pull his own weight and be able to support his family. I know well that the reformers must not bring upon the people economic ruin, or the reforms themselves will go down in the ruin. But we must be ready to face temporary disaster, whether or not brought on by those who will war against us to the knife. Those who oppose all reform will do well to remember that ruin in its worst form is inevitable if our national life brings us nothing better than swollen fortunes for the few and the triumph in both politics and business of a sordid and selfish materialism.

If our political institutions were perfect, they would absolutely prevent the political domination of money in any part of our affairs. We need to make our political representatives more quickly and sensitively responsive to the people whose servants they are. More direct action by the people in their own affairs under proper safeguards is vitally necessary. The direct primary is a step in this direction, if it is associated with a corrupt-services act effective to prevent the advantage of the man willing recklessly and unscrupulously to spend money over his more honest competitor. It is particularly important that all moneys received or expended for campaign purposes should be publicly accounted for, not only after election, but before election as well. Political action must be made simpler, easier, and freer from confusion for every citizen. I believe that the prompt removal of unfaithful or incompetent public servants should be made easy and sure in whatever way experience shall show to be most expedient in any given class of cases.

One of the fundamental necessities in a representative government such as ours is to make certain that the men to whom the people delegate their power shall serve the people by whom they are elected, and not the special interests. I believe that every national officer, elected or appointed, should be forbidden to perform any service or receive any compensation, directly or indirectly, from interstate corporations; and a similar provision could not fail to be useful within the States.

The object of government is the welfare of the people. The material progress and prosperity of a nation are desirable chiefly so far as they lead to the moral and material welfare of all good citizens. Just in proportion as the average man and woman are honest, capable of sound judgment and high ideals, active in public affairs—but, first of all, sound in their home life, and the father and mother of healthy children whom they bring up well—just so far, and no farther, we may count our civilization a success. We must have—I believe we have already—a genuine and permanent moral awakening, without which no wisdom of legislation or administration really means anything; and, on the other hand, we must try to secure the social and economic legislation without which any improvement due to purely moral agitation is necessarily evanescent. Let me again illustrate by a reference to the Grand Army. You could not have won simply as a disorderly and disorganized mob. You needed generals; you needed careful administration of the most advanced type; and a good commissary—the cracker line. You well remember that success was necessary in many different lines in order to bring about general success. You had to have the administration at Washington good, just as you had to have the administration in the field; and you had to have the work of the generals good. You could not have triumphed without that administration and leadership; but it would all have been worthless if the average soldier had not had the right stuff in him. He had to have the right stuff in him, or you could not get it out of him. In the last analysis, therefore, vitally necessary though it was to have the right kind of organization and the right kind of generalship, it was even more vitally necessary that the average soldier should have the fighting edge, the right character. So it is in our civil life. No matter how honest and decent we are in our private lives, if we do not have the right kind of law and the right kind of administration of the law, we cannot go forward as a nation. That is imperative; but it must be an addition to, and not a substitution for, the qualities that make us good citizens. In the last analysis, the most important elements in any man's career must be the sum of those qualities which, in the aggregate, we speak of as character. If he has not got it, then no law that the wit of man can devise, no administration of the law by the boldest and strongest executive, will avail to help him. We must have the right kind of character—character that makes a man, first of all, a good man in the home, a good father, a good husband—that makes a man a good neighbor. You must have that, and, then, in addition, you must have the kind of law and the kind of administration of the law which will give to those qualities in the private citizen the best possible chance for development. The prime problem of our nation is to get the right type of good citizenship, and, to get it, we must have progress, and our public men must be genuinely progressive.

IT TAKES MORE THAN THAT TO KILL A BULL MOOSE: THE LEADER AND THE CAUSE

Speech given in Milwaukee, Wisconsin, directly after an assassination attempt

October 14, 1912

Friends, I shall ask you to be as quiet as possible. I don't know whether you fully understand that I have just been shot; but it takes more than that to kill a Bull Moose. But fortunately I had my manuscript, so you see I was going to make a long speech, and there is a bullet—there is where the bullet went through—and it probably saved me from it going into my heart. The bullet is in me now, so that I cannot make a very long speech, but I will try my best.

And now, friends, I want to take advantage of this incident to say a word of solemn warning to my fellow countrymen.

First of all, I want to say this about myself: I have altogether too important things to think of to feel any concern over my own death; and now I cannot speak to you insincerely within five minutes of being shot. I am telling you the literal truth when I say that my concern is for many other things. It is not in the least for my own life. I want you to understand that I am ahead of the game, anyway. No man has had a happier life than I have led; a happier life in every way. I have been able to do certain things that I greatly wished to do, and I am interested in doing other things. I can tell you with absolute truthfulness that I am very much uninterested in whether I am shot or not. It was just as when I was colonel of my regiment. I always felt that a private was to be excused for feeling at times some pangs of anxiety about his personal safety, but I cannot understand a man fit to be a colonel who can pay any heed to his personal safety when he is occupied as he ought to be with the absorbing desire to do his duty.

I am in this cause with my whole heart and soul. I believe that the Progressive movement is making life a little easier for all our people; a movement to try to take the burdens off the men and especially the women and children of this country. I am absorbed in the success of that movement.

Friends, I ask you now this evening to accept what I am saying as absolutely true, when I tell you I am not thinking of my own success. I am not thinking of my life or of anything connected with me personally. I am thinking of the movement. I say this by way of introduction, because I want to say something very serious to our people and especially to the newspapers. I don't know anything about who the man was who shot me to-night. He was seized at once by one of the stenographers in my party, Mr. Martin, and I suppose is now in the hands of the police. He shot to kill. He shot—the shot, the bullet went in here—I will show you.

I am going to ask you to be as quiet as possible for I am not able to give to challenge of the bull moose quite as loudly. Now, I do not know who he was or what he represented. He was a coward. He stood in the darkness in the crowd around the automobile and when they cheered me, and I got up to bow, he stepped forward and shot me in the darkness.

Now, friends, of course, I do not know, as I say, anything about him; but it is a very natural thing that weak and vicious minds should be inflamed to acts of violence by the kind of awful mendacity and abuse that have been heaped upon me for the last three months by the papers in the interest of not only Mr. Debs but of Mr. Wilson and Mr. Taft.

Friends, I will disown and repudiate any man of my party who attacks with such foul slander and abuse any opponent of any other party; and now I wish to say seriously to all the daily newspapers, to the Republicans, the Democrat, and Socialist parties, that they cannot, month in and month out and year in and year out, make the kind of untruthful, of bitter assault that they have made and not expect that brutal, violent natures, or brutal and violent characters, especially when the brutality is accompanied by a not very strong mind; they cannot expect that such natures will be unaffected by it.

Now, friends, I am not speaking for myself at all, I give you my word, I do not care a rap about being shot; not a rap. I have had a good many experiences in my time and this is one of them. What I care for is my country. I wish I were able to impress upon my people—our people, the duty to feel strongly but to speak the truth of their opponents. I say now, I have never said one word one the stump against any opponent that I cannot defend. I have said nothing that I could not substantiate and nothing that I ought not to have said—nothing that I—nothing that, looking back at, I would not say again.

Now, friends, it ought not to be too much to ask that our opponents—[*speaking to someone on the stage*]—I am not sick at all. I am all right. I cannot tell you of what infinitesimal importance I regard this incident as compared with the great issues at stake in this campaign, and I ask it not for my sake, not the least in the world, but for the sake of common country, that they make up their minds to speak only the truth, and not use that kind of slander and mendacity which if taken seriously must incite weak and violent natures to crimes of violence. Don't you make any mistake. Don't you pity me. I am all right. I am all right and you cannot escape listening to the speech either.

And now, friends, this incident that has just occurred—this effort to assassinate me—emphasizes to a peculiar degree the need of the Progressive movement. Friends, every good citizen ought to do everything in his or her power to prevent the coming of the day when we shall see in this country two recognized creeds fighting one another, when we shall see the creed of the "Havenots" arraigned against the creed of the "Haves." When that day comes then such incidents as this to-night will be commonplace in our history. When you make poor men—when you permit the conditions to grow such that the poor man as such will be swayed by his sense of injury against the men who try to hold what they improperly have won, when that day comes, the most awful passions will be let loose and it will be an ill day for our country.

Now, friends, what we who are in this movement are endeavoring to do is forestall any such movement for justice now—a movement in which we ask all just men of generous hearts to join with the men who feel in their souls that lift upward which bids them refuse to be satisfied themselves while their countrymen and countrywomen suffer from avoidable misery. Now, friends, what we Progressives are trying to do is to enroll rich or poor, whatever their social or industrial position, to stand together for the most elementary rights of good citizenship, those elementary rights which are the foundation of good citizenship in this great Republic of ours.

[*At this point a renewed effort was made to persuade Mr. Roosevelt to conclude his speech.*]

My friends are a little more nervous than I am. Don't you waste any sympathy on me. I have had an A-1 time in life and I am having it now. I never in my life was in any movement in which I was able to serve with such whole-hearted devotion as in this; in which I was able to feel as I do in this that common weal. I have fought for the good of our common country.

And now, friends, I shall have to cut short much of that speech that I meant to give you, but I want to touch on just two or three points. In the first place, speaking to you here in Milwaukee, I wish to say that the Progressive party is making its appeals to all our fellow citizens without any regard to their creed or to their birthplace. We do not regard as essential the way in which a man worships his God or as being affected by where he was born. We regard it as a matter of spirit and purpose. In New York, while I was police commissioner, the two men from whom I got the most assistance were Jacob Riis, who was born in Denmark, and Arthur von Briesen, who was born in Germany—both of them as fine examples of the best and highest American citizenship as you could find in any part of this country.

I have just been introduced by one of your own men here—Henry Cochems. His grandfather, his father, and that father's seven brothers, all served in the United States army, and they entered it four years after they had come to this country from Germany. Two of them left their lives, spent their lives, on the field of battle. I am all right—I am a little sore. Anybody has a right to be sore with a bullet in him. You would find that if I was in battle now I would be leading my men just the same. Just the same way I am going to make this speech.

At one time I promoted five men for gallantry on the field of battle. Afterward in making some inquiries about them I found that two of them were Protestants, two Catholic, and one a Jew. One Protestant came from Germany and one was born in Ireland. I did not promote them because of their religion. It just happened that way. If all five of them had been Jews I would have promoted them, or if all five of them had been Protestants I would have promoted them; or if they had been Catholics. In that regiment I had a man born in Italy who distinguished himself by gallantry; there was another young fellow, a son of Polish parents, and another who came here when he was a child from Bohemia, who likewise distinguished themselves; and friends, I assure you, that I was incapable of considering any question whatever, but the worth of each individual as a fighting man. If he was a good fighting man, then I saw that Uncle Sam got the benefit of it. That is all.

I make the same appeal to our citizenship. I ask in our civic life that we in the same way pay heed only to the man's quality of citizenship, to repudiate as the worst enemy that we can have whoever tries to get us to discriminate for or against any man because of his creed or birthplace.

Now, friends, in the same way I want out people to stand by one another without regard to differences or class or occupation. I have always stood by labor-unions. I am going to make one omission to-night. I have prepared my speech because Mr. Wilson had seen fit to attack me by showing up his record in comparison with mine. But I am not going to do that to-night. I am going to simply speak of what I myself have done and what I think ought to be done in this country of ours.

It is essential that here should be organizations of labor. This is an era of organization. Capital organizes and therefore labor must organize. My appeal for organized labor is two-fold; to the outsider and the capitalist I make my appeal to treat the laborer fairly, to recognize the fact that he must organize that there must be such organization, that the laboring man must organize for his own protection, and that it is the duty of the rest of is to help him and not hinder him in organizing. That is one-half of the appeal that I make.

Now, the other half is to the labor man himself. My appeal to him is to remember that as he wants justice, so he must do justice. I want every labor man, every labor leader, every organized union man, to take the lead in denouncing crime or violence. I want them to take the lead in denouncing disorder and in denouncing the inciting of riot; that in this country we shall proceed under the protection of our laws and with all respect to the laws, and I want the labor men to feel in their turn that exactly as justice must be done them so they must do justice. They must bear their duty as citizens, their duty to this great country of ours, and that they must not rest content unless they do that duty to the fullest degree.

I know these doctors, when they get hold of me, will never let me go back, and there are just a few more things that I want to say to you. And here I have got to make one comparison between Mr. Wilson and myself, simply because he has invited it and I cannot shrink from it. Mr. Wilson has seen fit to attack me, to say that I did not do much against the trusts when I was President. I have got two answers to make to that. In the first place what I did, and then I want to compare what I did when I was President with what Mr. Wilson did not do when he was governor.

When I took the office the antitrust law was practically a dead letter and the interstate commerce law in as poor a condition. I had to revive both laws. I did. I enforced both. It will be easy enough to do now what I did then, but the reason that it is easy now is because I did it when it was hard.

Nobody was doing anything. I found speedily that the interstate commerce law by being made perfect could be made a most useful instrument for helping solve some of our industrial problems. So with the antitrust law. I speedily found out that almost the only positive good achieved by such a successful lawsuit as the Northern Securities suit, for instance, was in establishing the principle that the government was supreme over the big corporation, but by itself that the law did not accomplish any of the things that we ought to have accomplished; and so I began to fight for the amendment of the law along the lines of the interstate commerce law, and now we propose, we Progressives, to establish an interstate commission having the same power over industrial concerns that the Interstate Commerce Commission has over railroads, so that whenever there is in the future a decision rendered in such important matters as the recent suits against the Standard Oil, the Sugar—no, not that—Tobacco—Tobacco Trust—we will have a commission which will see that the decree of the court is really made effective; that it is not made a merely nominal decree. Our opponents have said that we intend to legalize monopoly. Nonsense. They have legalized monopoly. At this moment the Standard Oil and Tobacco Trust monopolies are legalized; they are being carried on under the decree of the Supreme Court. Our proposal is really to break up monopoly. Our proposal is to lay down certain requirements, and then to require the commerce commission—the industrial commission—to see that the trusts live up to those requirements. Our opponents have spoken as if we were going to let the commission declare what those requirements should be. Not at all. We are going to put the requirements in the law and then see that the commission requires them to obey that law.

And now, friends, as Mr. Wilson has invited the comparison, I only want to say this: Mr. Wilson has said that the States are the proper authorities to deal with the trusts. Well, about eighty percent of the trusts are organized in New Jersey. The Standard Oil, the Tobacco, the Sugar, the Beef, all those trusts are organized in the state of New Jersey and the laws of New Jersey say that their charters can at any time be amended or repealed if they misbehave themselves and give the government ample power to act about those laws, and Mr. Wilson has been governor a year and nine months and he has not opened his lips. The chapter describing what Mr. Wilson has done about trusts in New Jersey would read precisely like a chapter describing snakes in Ireland, which ran: "There are no snakes in Ireland." Mr. Wilson has done precisely and exactly nothing about the trusts.

I tell you, and I told you at the beginning, I do not say anything on the stump that I do not believe. I do not say anything I do not know. Let any of Mr. Wilson's friends on Tuesday point out one thing or let Mr. Wilson point out one thing that he has done about the trusts as governor of New Jersey.

And now, friends, there is one thing I want to say especially to you people here in Wisconsin. All that I have said so far is what I would say in any part of the Union. I have a peculiar right to ask that in this great contest you men and women of Wisconsin shall stand with us. You have taken the lead in progressive movements here in Wisconsin. You have taught the rest of us to look to you for inspiration and leadership. Now, friends, you have made that movement here locally. You will being doing a dreadful injustice to yourselves; you will be doing a dreadful injustice to the rest of us throughout the Union, if you fail to stand with us now that we are making this national movement. What I am about to say now I want you to understand. If I speak of Mr. Wilson I speak with no mind of bitterness. I merely want to discuss the difference of policy between the Progressive and the Democratic party and to ask you to think for yourselves which party you will follow. I will say that, friends, because the Republican party is beaten. Nobody needs to have any idea that anything can be done with the Republican party.

When the Republican party—not the Republican party—when the bosses in control of the Republican party, the Barneses and Penroses, last June stole the nomination and wrecked the Republican party for good and all—I want to point out to you that nominally they stole that nomination from me, but it was really from you. They did not like me, and the longer they live the less cause they will have to like me. But while they don't like me, they dread you. You are the people that they dread. They dread the people themselves, and those bosses and the big special interests behind them made up their mind that they would rather see the Republican party wrecked than see it come under the control of the people themselves. So I am not dealing with the Republican party. There are only two ways you can vote this year. You can be progressive or reactionary. Whether you vote Republican or Democratic it does not make a difference, you are voting reactionary.

Now, the Democratic party in its platform and through the utterances of Mr. Wilson has distinctly committed itself to the old flintlock, muzzle-loaded doctrine of States' rights, and I have said distinctly we are for people's rights. We are for the rights of the people. If they can be obtained best through National Government, then we are for national rights. We are for people's rights however it is necessary to secure them.

Mr. Wilson has made a long essay against Senator Beveridge's bill to abolish child labor. It is the same kind of argument that would be made against our bill to prohibit women from working more than eight hours a day in industry. It is the same kind of argument that would have to be made; if it is true, it would apply equally against our proposal to insist that in continuous industries there shall be by law one day's rest in seven and three-shift eight-hour day. You have labor laws here in Wisconsin, and chamber of commerce will tell you that because of that fact there are industries that will not come to Wisconsin. They prefer to stay outside where they can work children of tender years, where they can work women fourteen and sixteen hours a day, where if it is a continuous industry, they can work men twelve hours a day and seven days a week.

Now, friends, I know that you of Wisconsin would never repeal those laws even if they are at your commercial hurt, just as I am trying to get New York to adopt such laws even though it will be to the New York's commercial hurt. But if possible I want to arrange it so that we can have justice without commercial hurt, and you can only get that if you have justice enforced nationally. You won't be burdened in Wisconsin with industries not coming to the State if the same good laws are extended all over the other States. Do you see what I mean? The States all compete in a common market; and it is not justice to the employers of a State that has enforced just and proper laws to have them exposed to the competition of another State where no such laws are enforced. Now, the Democratic platform, and their speakers declare we shall not have such laws. Mr. Wilson has distinctly declared that we shall not have a national law to prohibit the labor of children, to prohibit child labor. He has distinctly declared that we shall not have a law to establish a minimum wage for women.

I ask you to look at our declaration and hear and read our platform about social and industrial justice and then, friends, vote for the Progressive ticket without regard to me, without regard to my personality, for only by voting for that platform can you be true to the cause of progress throughout this Union.

A MANLY LETTER

Excerpt from Roosevelt's Autobiography

There was a sequel to the "round robin" incident which caused a little stir at the moment; Secretary Alger had asked me to write him freely from time to time. Accordingly, after the surrender of Santiago, I wrote him begging that the cavalry division might be put into the Porto Rican fighting, preparatory to what we supposed would be the big campaign against Havana in the fall. In the letter I extolled the merits of the Rough Riders and of the Regulars, announcing with much complacency that each of our regiments was worth "three of the National Guard regiments, armed with their archaic black powder rifles."* Secretary Alger believed, mistakenly, that I had made public the round robin, and was naturally irritated, and I suddenly received from him a published telegram, not alluding to the round robin incident, but quoting my reference to the comparative merits of the cavalry regiments and the National Guard regiments and rebuking me for it. The publication of the extract from my letter was not calculated to help me secure the votes of the National Guard if I ever became a candidate for office. However, I did not mind the matter much, for I had at the time no idea of being a candidate for anything—while in the campaign I ate and drank and thought and dreamed regiment and nothing but regiment, until I got the brigade, and then I devoted all my thoughts to handling the brigade. Anyhow, there was nothing I could do about the matter.

When our transport reached Montauk Point, an army officer came aboard and before doing anything else handed me a sealed letter from the Secretary of War which ran as follows:

War Department,
Washington,
August 10, 1898.

Dear Col. Roosevelt:

You have been a most gallant officer and in the battle before Santiago showed superb soldierly qualities. I would rather add to, than detract from, the honors you have so fairly won, and I wish you all good things. In a moment of aggravation under great stress of feeling, first because I thought you spoke in a disparaging manner of the volunteers (probably without intent, but because of your great enthusiasm for your own men) and second that I believed your published letter would

* I quote this sentence from memory; it is substantially correct.

embarrass the Department I sent you a telegram which with an extract from a private letter of yours I gave to the press. I would gladly recall both if I could, but unable to do that I write you this letter which I hope you will receive in the same friendly spirit in which I send it. Come and see me at a very early day. No one will welcome you more heartily than I.

Yours very truly,
(Signed) R. A. ALGER.

I thought this a manly letter, and paid no more heed to the incident; and when I was President, and General Alger was Senator from Michigan, he was my stanch friend and on most matters my supporter.